S0-CIE-285

HOME AND AUTO do-it-yourself ENCYCLOPEDIA

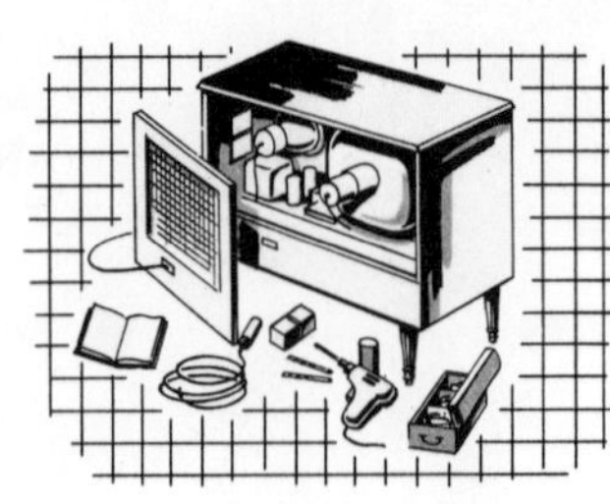

do-it

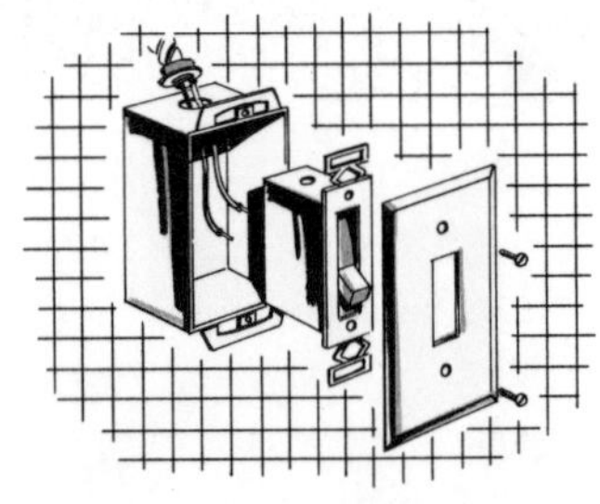

HOME AND AUTO yourself ENCYCLOPEDIA

A MANUAL OF HOME, AUTO AND APPLIANCE PROJECTS
FOR CONSTRUCTION, REPAIR AND SERVICING

from the 21 volume

COMPLETE DO-IT-YOURSELF HANDYMAN ENCYCLOPEDIA

by the editors of

Science & Mechanics

H. S. STUTTMAN CO., INC. *Publishers* • New York, N.Y. 10016

ISBN 0-87475-790-8
Library of Congress Catalog Card No. 74-21375

All instructions and diagrams have been checked for accuracy. However, success and safety in working with tools depend on individual accuracy, care, caution and skill. For this reason, the authors and publishers cannot guarantee the result of any project, nor assume responsibility for damage to property or injury to persons. In using any tools, building any projects, or carrying out any procedures, persons do so entirely at their own risk.

PRINTED IN THE UNITED STATES OF AMERICA

1P-2601-15

INTRODUCTION

OUR HOMES, OUR AUTOMOBILES, ALL OUR APPLIANCES are the end result of applied science and technology and we take it for granted that these products will always function properly. Therefore, we are invariably annoyed when a malfunction deprives us of their use and enjoyment. This annoyance becomes more aggravated when even minor repairs and adjustments are difficult to obtain and result in constantly increasing costs. The words "do-it-yourself" have, therefore, become of utmost importance.

THE HOME AND AUTO "DO-IT-YOURSELF" ENCYCLOPEDIA represents the combined efforts of the writers, editors and technical consultants of Science & Mechanics magazine. With this authoritative background, this volume can provide the "how-to" answers to questions pertaining to mechanical techniques and procedures dealing with care, maintenance and repair of the home, auto and electrical appliances.

In this new edition, the authors have demonstrated that a reader can be motivated with the desire and equipped with the knowledge to "do-it-yourself." With just a few basic tools (skilled craftsmen even show how to use them), the reader acquires confidence to plan and complete a wide range and diversity of projects. This is amply demonstrated in the accompanying Table of Contents. This skillful combination of practical projects with instructions in the craft techniques for completing these projects motivates the reader to gradually develop basic skills. As he becomes familiar with the craft techniques that help execute each project, he grows in confidence and quickly discovers countless opportunities for eliminating unnecessary labor costs.

Simplified, yet authoritative and jargon-free, instructions are combined with informative step-by-step self-teaching illustrations that encourage the reader to acquire new skills and improve on those he already has. Because the reader is exposed to this wide diversity of *attainable* projects, he is motivated to refine and improve on his methods for creating, building and repairing. The fun and enjoyment in each project is heightened in the knowledge of the substantial savings that have been effected.

The reader's attention is called to legal and safety aspects of many of the licensed crafts which prompt the editors to include a warning note. Some community local laws and regulations prohibit anyone but licensed professionals from doing certain jobs. In such cases, a practical knowledge of the craft enables the reader to better evaluate both the cost and quality of work performed.

To make this edition more useful to the reader, and to encourage browsing and using this volume as a source of ideas, cross reference aids are provided. The alphabetic headings at the top of each page cover broad classifications of projects. The caption underneath each heading is the title of the project, craft or technique that may logically fall within this alphabetic heading. At the end of most articles *"See also"* references direct the reader to other articles dealing with the same general subject under another alphabetic entry. A complete alphabetic Index is contained in the back section and will provide aid in quickly locating information within any topic.

In producing this work, the authors were fortunate in having the advice and guidance of Mr. Joel Davis, President and Publisher of SCIENCE & MECHANICS PUBLICATIONS, INC. The publishers wish to express their gratitude for his assistance and admiration for his dedication to the task of showing readers how to "do-it-yourself."

H. S. STUTTMAN CO., INC.
PUBLISHERS

EDITORIAL BOARD

CONTRIBUTORS

Initials at end of articles identify the author

F. C.	Frank Cogan	**E. M. L.**	Edwin M. Love
P. A. C.	Paul Corey	**G. M.**	George Meyerink
G. D.	George Daniels	**B. M.**	Burt Murphy
H. L. D.	Homer L. Davidson	**N. R.**	N. Raskhodoff
M. E. F.	Mark E. Fineman	**R. T.**	Ralph Treves
H. F.	Herbert Friedman	**D. W.**	David Weems
J. H.	Jorma Hyypia	**P. W.**	Paul Weissler

CONTENTS

CREDITS

In striving to make this publication as complete, accurate and up to date as possible, a great deal of assistance and technical information was obtained from manufacturers' trade associations. The editors are deeply grateful to all of them for their help and wish to thank the following for the illustrations they have made available:

Allied International Films Ltd.
American Plywood Association
The Company Rohm and Haas
Dupont Paint Company
Fluidmaster
General Electric Company
Hartline Products Co., Inc.
In-Sink-Erator Division,
Emerson Electric Company
George Meyerink
MRL Inc.
Pittsburgh Paint Company
Portland Cement Association
Red Devil, Inc.
Reynolds Aluminum
Set Products
Sunbeam Appliance Company
3M Company
Tile Council of America
True Temper Corporation
United States Gypsum
Wallcovering Industry Bureau, Inc.
Western Wood Products
Association

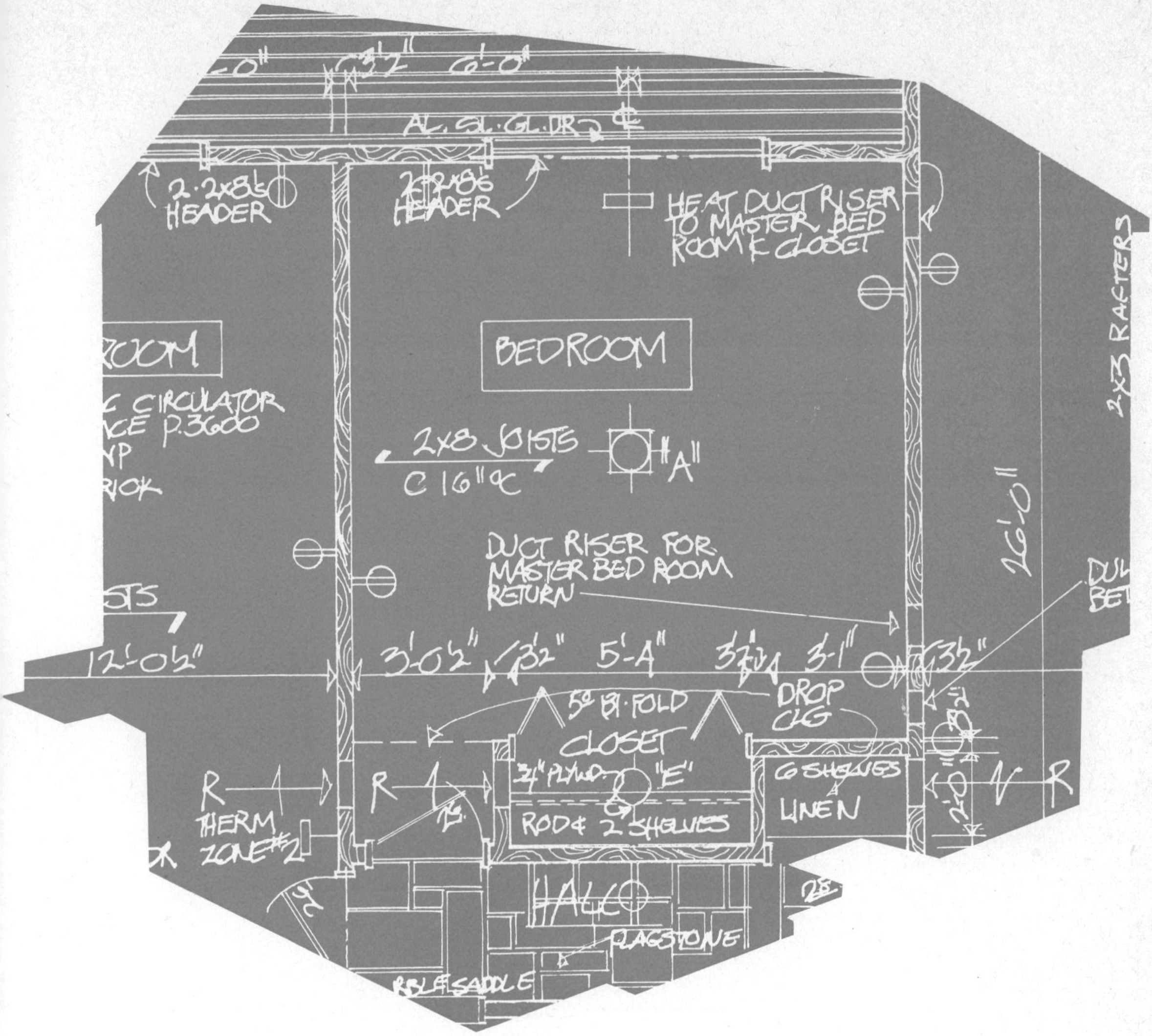

AL. SL. GL. DR.
2·2x8½ HEADER
2·2x8½ HEADER
HEAT DUCT RISER TO MASTER BED ROOM & CLOSET
ROOM
BEDROOM
2x8 JOISTS @ 16" o.c.
"A"
DUCT RISER FOR MASTER BED ROOM RETURN
2x3 RAFTERS
26'-0"
12'-0½"
3'-0½"
3½"
5'-4"
3½"
3'-1"
3½"
5° BI-FOLD
CLOSET
DROP CLG
3/4" PLYWD.
"E"
ROD & 2 SHELVES
6 SHELVES
LINEN
THERM ZONE #2
HALL
FLAGSTONE
SADDLE

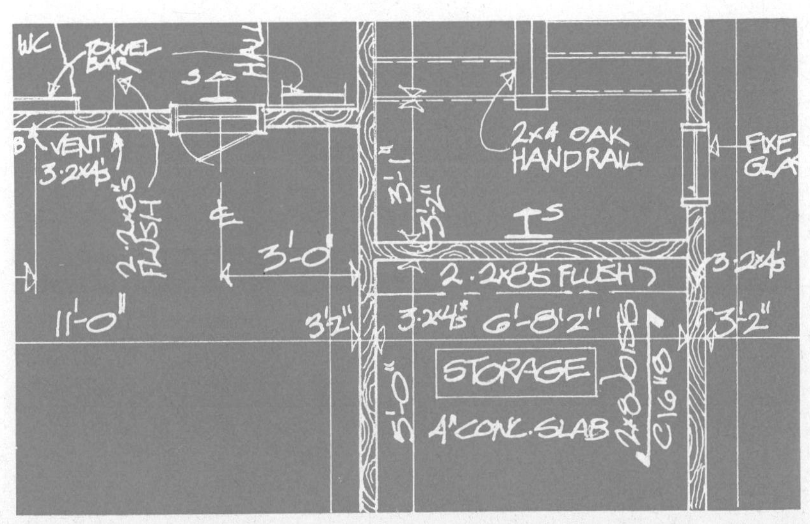

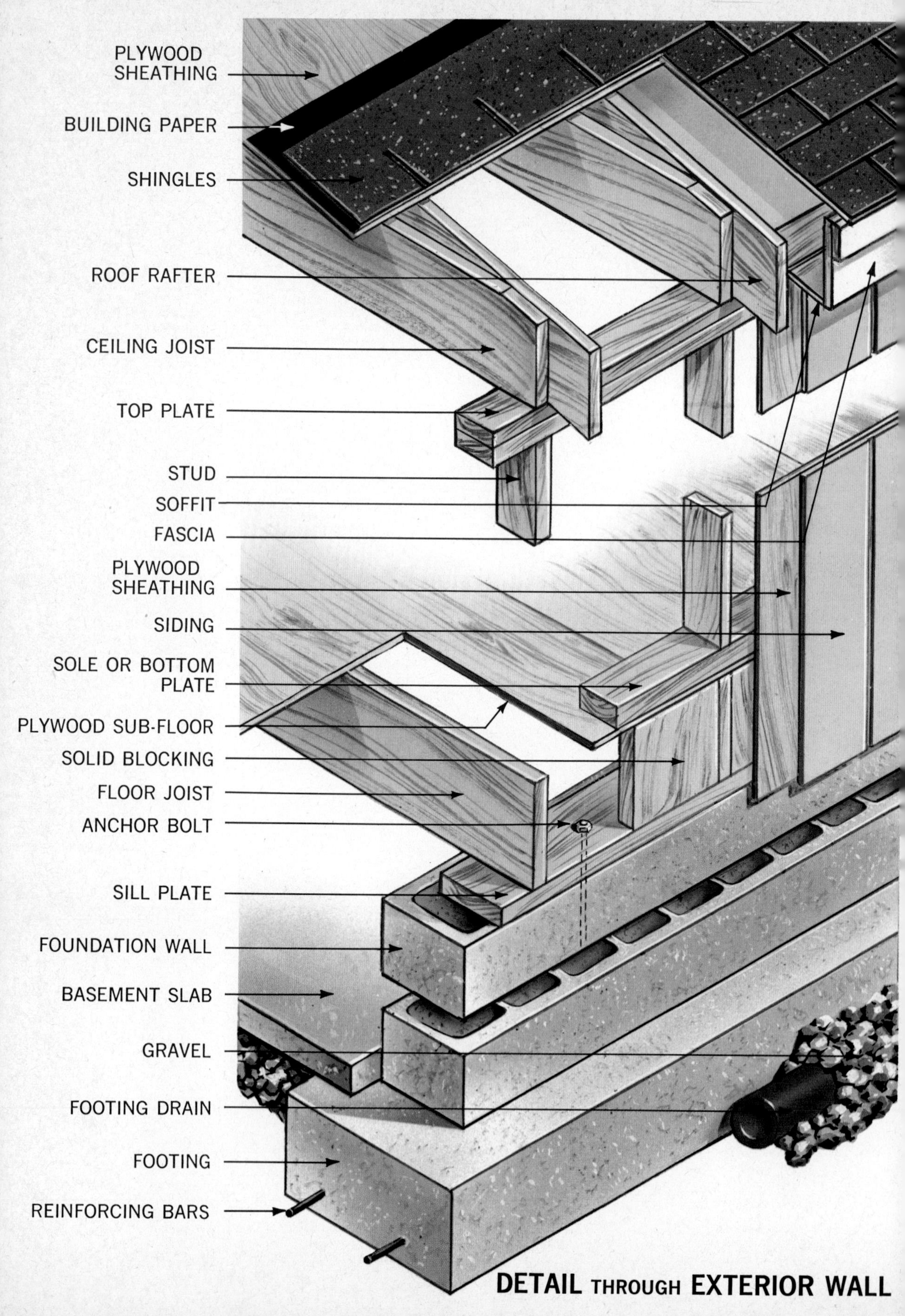
PLYWOOD SHEATHING
BUILDING PAPER
SHINGLES
ROOF RAFTER
CEILING JOIST
TOP PLATE
STUD
SOFFIT
FASCIA
PLYWOOD SHEATHING
SIDING
SOLE OR BOTTOM PLATE
PLYWOOD SUB-FLOOR
SOLID BLOCKING
FLOOR JOIST
ANCHOR BOLT
SILL PLATE
FOUNDATION WALL
BASEMENT SLAB
GRAVEL
FOOTING DRAIN
FOOTING
REINFORCING BARS

DETAIL THROUGH EXTERIOR WALL

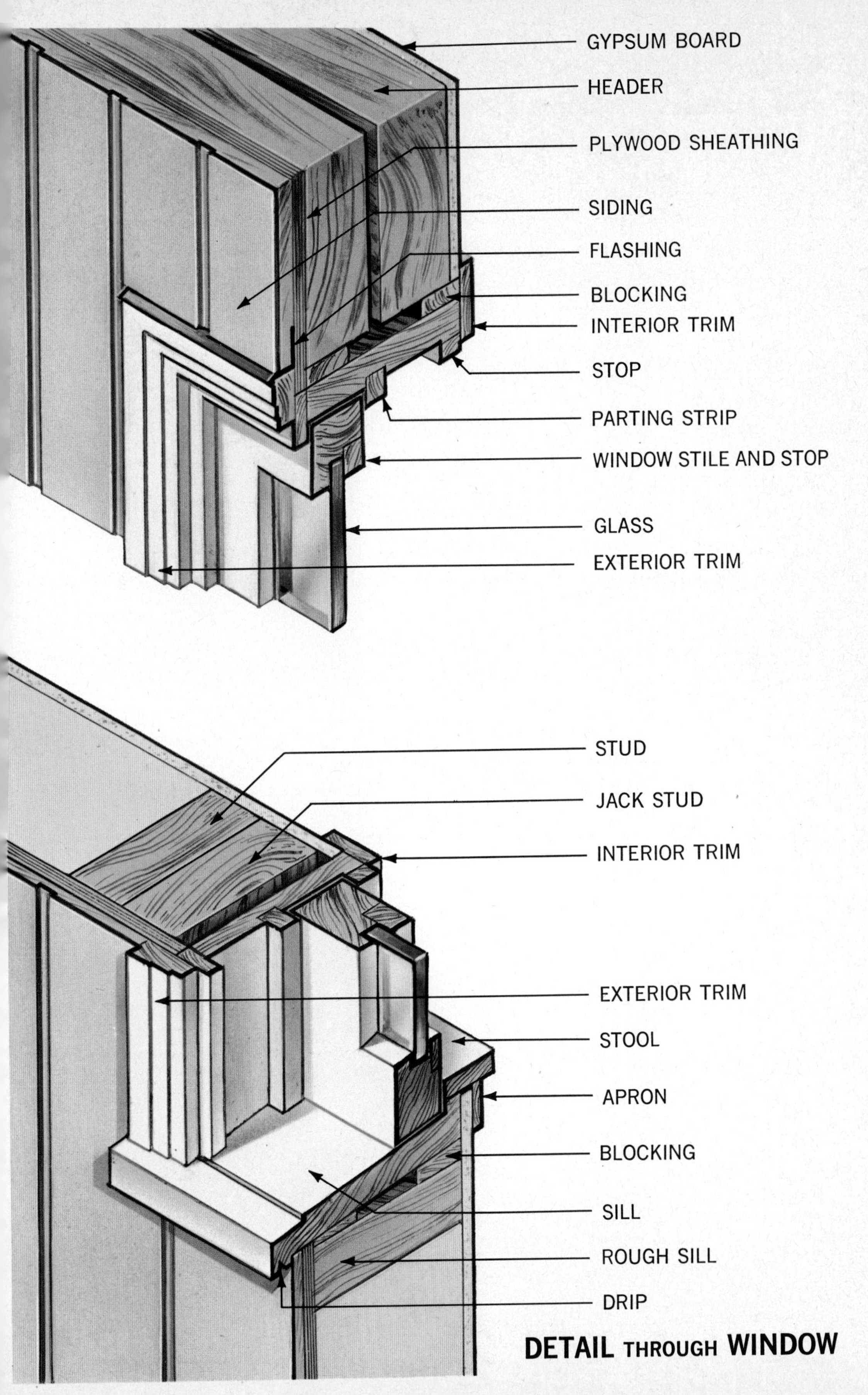
GYPSUM BOARD
HEADER
PLYWOOD SHEATHING
SIDING
FLASHING
BLOCKING
INTERIOR TRIM
STOP
PARTING STRIP
WINDOW STILE AND STOP
GLASS
EXTERIOR TRIM
STUD
JACK STUD
INTERIOR TRIM
EXTERIOR TRIM
STOOL
APRON
BLOCKING
SILL
ROUGH SILL
DRIP

DETAIL THROUGH WINDOW

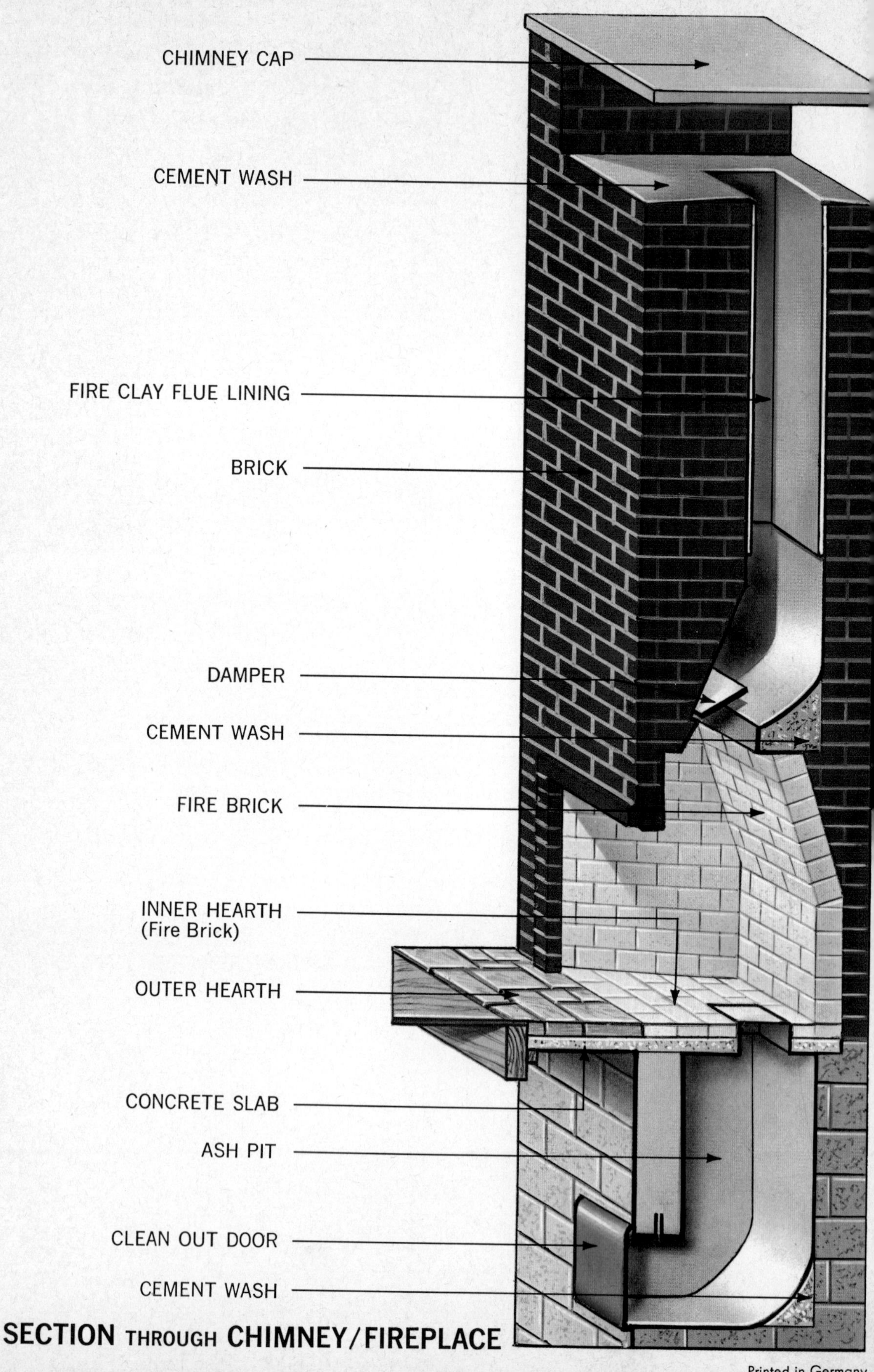

SECTION THROUGH CHIMNEY/FIREPLACE

Printed in Germany

How to Plan Your Home Additions

Refinish your basement, attic, garage or breezeway to add space, increase equity

One place to look for additional space in your home is at the top. Here, an attic has been refinished inexpensively into a cheerful bedroom for two children.

YOUR HOME may be your castle, but are there also times when it does not live up to your expectations? Then perhaps it is time to provide the extra room you need for recreation, sleeping, craftwork, or to house a live-in relative.

The cost of converting an unfinished basement or attic, or even a breezeway or garage into extra living space need not be prohibitive. You can cut the total conversion cost to a third or even a quarter of a contracted job by doing much or all of the work yourself because, in most instances, labor costs far exceed the cost of materials.

Do-it-yourself home improvement is now easier than ever thanks to the availability of materials that eliminate much of the hard work that you would have had to do for a similar conversion only a decade ago. Examples of easy-to-use construction materials include self-stick floor tile, beautifully prefinished wall paneling of several varieties and almost endless designs, colors and textures, and attractive ceiling coverings that can be installed in a professional manner by anyone. So, it doesn't make much sense for the average homeowner to spend, say, from fifteen hundred to two thousand dollars on a home improvement job that he can do in his spare time for perhaps five hundred dollars.

The secret of success really comes down to one thing: careful planning. Plan all major design features of the new room in detail before buying materials or starting work; shop thoroughly for the best construction materials for your purpose (should walls be of plywood, hardboard or gypsum board, for example); compare prices of competitive materials, but do not sacrifice quality for cheapness; buy lumber in standard sizes and in lengths that minimize waste; seek reliable information concerning proper installation of construction materials that are unfamiliar to you.

Evaluate the relative merits of finishing an attic or basement, or perhaps adding an extension onto your home. Each home, and the space requirements of the family that lives in it are to some degree unique; the type of space expansion that was ideal for your neighbor may be a poor choice for you. So study in detail the pros and cons of converting all possible areas in your home. You might be surprised to conclude that the area that initially seems least attractive is in fact the best place in the home for improvement.

Basement. To this day you can find people—including some architects—who turn thumbs down on basement improvements on the grounds that below-grade rooms are damp, dingy and especially depressing if there are no windows. This may have been true in the past, but a basement room that is properly finished, properly illuminated, and equipped with dehumidifying equipment if necessary can be as pleasant as any other room in the home. Also, it is one of the best places for relatively noisy activities—within reasonable limits of course. For example, you wouldn't want to work in a woodworking shop under a bedroom when someone is sleeping. On the other hand, if you are trying to sleep, would you prefer that your teenagers dance above or below you?

A typical basement does not exhibit the cold and hot seasonal temperature extremes that are normal for attic areas. Thus cooling and heating is easier and less expensive, and there is no need to buy insulating materals for a roof.

The very first dollars spent on basement improvement can make the area more usable. For example, just by laying an inexpensive vinyl asbestos floor on the concrete sub-base you have an area that is much better for use as a play area. If money is on the short side, just paint concrete or block walls to add visual appeal at lowest possible cost.

Before starting more extensive improvements, take a critical look at your basement stairs. If they are too steep or flimsy, or if there is inadequate headroom (perhaps because of heating ducts), rebuild the stairway first. By adding a landing, and making the stairs turn a right angle, you may be able to provide extra headroom. Is there now a basement door leading to the yard? If not, consider adding one for convenience and safety. This outside entrance is especially important if you intend to put a woodworking shop in the basement. How else would you get large pieces of lumber into the shop? In fact, it may be impossible to get the 4-by-8 foot wall paneling for your recreation room into the basement until you add that outside entrance.

Wall paneling can be supported by a framework made of 2-by-3 or 2-by-4 studding, or you can save on lumber costs by using 1-by-2 or preferably 1-by-3 furring attached to the masonry wall. But what about electrical outlets? Clearly, these could not be set into walls where the space between the foundation and paneling is only one inch. This is a good example of the kind of oversight in initial planning that could lead to grief and be costly later on.

Basic electrical wiring is not difficult for any reasonably adept do-it-yourselfer who takes the trouble to consult readily available reference material. Just be sure that you understand local wiring regulations and that you have your work inspected by a town official before you bury it under paneling. By following the sensible rules established for your protection, you will have a safe place in which to live and play, and you can avoid unnecessary alterations. For example, if you install the ungrounded kind of outlet you have in your living room, in the basement, the electrical inspector will surely insist that you replace them with grounding type receptacles.

Analyze your basement area carefully during the initial planning stage to make sure that every cubic foot of usable space will be utilized to best advantage. For example, you probably have large sewer pipes running a couple of feet above the basement floor, along one or more walls. These should be hidden behind the new paneling, of course, but why run the paneling straight to the ceiling and thereby waste some excellent storage space? Instead, plan for cupboards or built-in bookcases above the pipes. Also, remember to use removable panel sections wherever there are clean-out plugs in the sewer piping.

Are you hard-pressed to find a good place to add that sauna you would like to have? Take a tip from one imaginative Finn who put his steam bath under a porch just off the kitchen by excavating and building a small room under the porch and adding a connecting door through the basement wall. A curtained-off corner of the basement recreation room served as a dressing room. Another advantage of placing the steam bath *outside* of the main house area is that it can be aired out easily to keep excessive moisture out of the house.

No basement improvements should be attempted if there is any problem whatever with excessive moisture or actual water leakage into the basement. Correct such faults before the remodeling begins and, to make sure all is well, wait until after a prolonged rainy spell before starting on major basement improvements. It can be heartbreaking to see water seeping under the new paneling you have so carefully installed. If complete waterproofing of the basement just isn't feasible at reasonable cost, you might be wiser to look for extra room in some other part of the house.

Attic. Finishing an attic is no more difficult than improving the basement unless dormers must be added to obtain more light, ventilation and/or headroom. But even the construction of a new dormer can be handled by a reasonably competent do-it-yourselfer. Small gable ("doghouse") dormers are useful mainly to provide light and ventilation; a larger shed dormer is

Not a window in sight, but refinished basement is still attractive. Note space-saving spiral staircase at right. One caution: don't decide to finish your basement until you are sure it is not incurably damp.

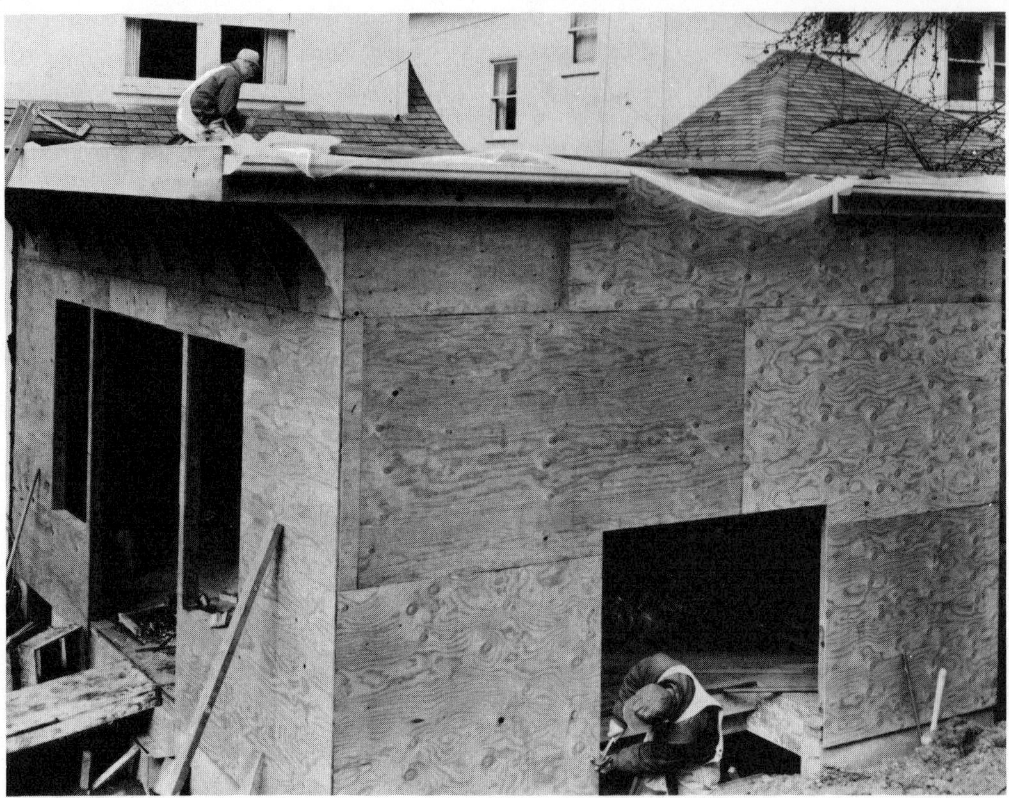

used where extra headroom is required. You will also probably find that it is cheaper to build a shed dormer than to construct two or three doghouse dormers. Often, the original roof can be kept in place until the dormer is largely completed. Another possibility is raising a portion of the original roof to form the roof of a shed dormer; this is not as difficult or costly as one might think, but it is not the kind of job a do-it-yourselfer should attempt single handed.

It is especially important to provide sufficient headroom at the top of the attic stairs. If headroom cannot be achieved by adding a dormer, it may be possible to relocate the stairway, or to install a stairway that emerges where there is more headroom. For example, a prefabricated metal spiral stairway may be the ideal solution. And don't overlook the possibility of building a new stairway *outside* of the existing house structure. This could be especially convenient if the lower end of the stairway can lead to an outside door as well as to the lower floor of the house.

▲ Building an actual extension is the most costly way of increasing usable space. Improving existing space—attic, basement, garage or breezeway—is cheaper.

If the attic area is to be used for relatively noisy activities during evening hours, consider adding sound insulation to the floor. At least plan on using a thick carpet with a resilient pad underneath. If such wall-to-wall carpeting is to be used, do not waste money installing a fine hardwood floor that will never be seen.

A bathroom in the attic area is desirable, especially if the area is to be used for sleeping or for accommodating overnight guests. Try to locate the bathroom over an existing bathroom on the lower level to keep plumbing costs down.

Do not stint on insulation in the attic ceiling and walls. Use the best and heaviest insulation you can. You will then be more comfortable, and spend less on heating and air-conditioning expenses.

If the attic ceiling slants, try to make the knee walls at least four feet high to permit easy furniture placement. Don't overlook the possibility of adding storage drawers that slide through the walls into the unused portions of the attic, near the eaves. But, box in the drawer areas and insulate thoroughly. Other left-over areas of the attic, even if only high enough to be crawl spaces, should be made accessible for storage of items that are not used frequently.

Provide plenty of electrical outlets to power TV sets, radios, electric toys, and perhaps even space heaters in lieu of conventional hot water or hot air systems.

Garage conversion. If you don't mind leaving the car out in the open, or if you can provide a carport or other shelter elsewhere on your property, the existing garage can probably be converted into a very useful living area. The conversion may be quite easy, and cost less than you might think, because you already have a roof and three walls (the garage doors must be replaced by a fourth wall). The garage floor probably slopes toward the front, or toward a central water drain, and this will have to be leveled before you can add a tile floor. If headroom in the garage permits, it may be preferable to install a wooden floor at a somewhat higher level to bring the floor of the converted garage to the same level as the floors in the rest of the house. But be sure to scrub out all grease and oil from the original garage floor before covering it with a new floor, to eliminate all possibility of unwanted odors seeping into the room.

You may want to keep the garage ceiling where it is, or raise it higher, perhaps even form a cathedral ceiling. But do not start pulling out existing joists indiscriminately until you have found some other way to hold the garage structure together. If there is good storage space above the garage ceiling, make it available by adding a spiral staircase, or perhaps a fold-down

BASEMENT FINISHING COSTS

Item	Unit Cost	Quantity Needed	Cost
Vinyl asbestos floor tile	33¢/sq. ft.	320 sq. ft.	$106
Prefinished plywood panels	$8 each	18	144
2-by-4 for wall framing	18¢/foot	576 ft.	104
Acoustic ceiling tile	30¢/sq. ft.	320 sq. ft.	96
1-by-2 furring for ceiling	5¢/ft.	340 ft.	17
			$467 +tax

The basic cost of finishing a 16 by 20 foot basement area was around $500 in terms of early 1973 prices for medium quality floor tile, wall paneling and ceiling tile. To the estimated $467 add the cost of such incidentals as nails, adhesive to apply wall paneling, staples for ceiling tile, and purchase of rental of stapler. Also add expenditures for electrical wiring, fixtures, possibly professional service to connect the new wiring to the main circuit breaker system. If you hire professional contractors to do the whole job, expect a total cost that is three to four times as much as the materials cost.

An attached garage is often good prospect for refinishing t add living space to a house. Here refinishing is under way, with new subflooring in place over the ol garage floor.

Use of prefinished wood panel ing is one way to cut costs of home improvement. Here paneling is be ing installed in a new addition to house.

staircase. The attic, even if small, is an ideal place in which to store sporting equipment, games, or lumber if you make the garage into a shop.

If the garage door leading into the interior of the house now connects with the kitchen, it might be preferable to relocate it so that traffic can flow into and through a family room, living room or hallway. But before you start tearing out walls to create doorways, make certain that the walls do not contain water or heating system pipes that would be hard to relocate.

Plan new electrical wiring to suit the power requirements of the kind of room you are planning. Conventional wiring is adequate for a recreation room or den. But you should install heavier wiring, and several separate branch circuits, if the area is to be used for a shop containing such power tools as circular or radial arm saws, sanding machines, drill press.

The kind of paneling you use on the walls depends on how the room is to be

used. A rumpus room where the kids will bang around should have plastic coated walls that are resistant to impact and easy to clean. Less rugged paneling can be used in a sitting room, or where no violent play is anticipated. For a shop or studio, consider using perforated hardboard which will make the hanging of tools or paintings a joy.

If the garage wall is of conventional wood construction, new paneling can be installed on the existing studding quickly and easily. If you have concrete walls, you will first have to add furring. Remember that thin, 1-by-3 furring can save you money but you would have to run new electrical wiring on top of the new paneling.

Porches and breezeways. If the garage you are converting to new uses is connected to the house by means of a breezeway, you should close in the breezeway as well so that getting to the new room will not entail dashing across a cold, windswept no-man's land.

Even if you leave the garage untouched, conversion of the breezeway into an all-seasons living area may be desirable. How useful this area would be for your needs depends on the size of the breezeway as is, or after expansion. Small or large, be sure that it is made just as weatherproof as the remainder of the house. Do not stint on insulation, and use double-glazed windows and sliding glass doors. Don't overlook the probable need of a radiator or two. If extending the conventional house heating system to this area is too complicated or costly, consider installing electrical heating units into the breezeway walls.

An open porch can also be converted into a closed-in room for year-around use provided it is at least nine feet in its shorter dimension, and if it has—or can be made to have—direct access to the kitchen, dining room, family room or hallway. If your main reason for doubting the wisdom of closing in the porch is that you would miss the cooling breezes during the summertime, just plan your renovation to include large screenable windows.

New wing. Suppose your basement is too wet for finishing or you have no basement, the attic has insufficient headroom, there is no porch or breezeway, and you can't bear the thought of evicting the family bus—then what? Your only recourse is to add a new extension to the house. This is bound to be the most costly way to solve your space problem because you must pay for new exterior as well as interior walls, insulation, and a supporting foundation. But if you do all or most of the work yourself, the cost may not be at all prohibitive.

You face at least two new planning problems if you decide to add an extension to your home. First, you must be sure that you have enough space on your lot, so that the addition does not violate set-back-requirements, and you must obtain approval of your building plan from the local building department. Secondly, unlike home improvements made inside your existing building, the new addition will be visible to neighbors. Be sure that the addition blends well with the existing structure and that it does not convert your home into an eye-sore that your neighbors will resent. If you have doubts about the visual aspects of the planned addition, consult an architect, or at least an experienced builder. And it wouldn't hurt to show your plans to your nearest neighbors to get their reaction, provided you can take honest criticism without feeling offended. Remember, you won't enjoy your new living space to the fullest extent if you see neighbors scowling across the backyard fence.

J.H.

See also: BASEMENTS; CONCRETE; ELECTRICAL, HOME; FENCES; HOME IMPROVEMENT; PAINTING, HOUSE; STONEWORK; TILE, CERAMIC; WALLBOARD; WALL COVERINGS.

How to Repair Your Room Air Conditioner

You can keep your machine working and save on repair bills by replacing some broken parts yourself

THE ROOM AIR CONDITIONER is a refrigeration unit plus some fans and filters. The filters remove the major dust particles from the air. The fans, usually mounted on each end of a single motor, move the air. One *recirculates* the room air over the evaporator (cooling coil) and the other blows the outside air over the condenser to cool it. Each is separated from the other by a wall to keep the room air and the outside air from mixing. A special door in this partition can be opened to allow some fresh air to mix with the room air.

Before condemning the air conditioner for not doing its job you must be certain that you are not expecting to cool a larger room than it was designed to do. And don't compare the operation of your machine with that of a friend, since the conditions of location and use will be different.

Air conditioners should be connected to a separate electrical circuit having large enough wire and fusing to handle its load. An approximate relation between B.T.U. capacity, wattage and wire size is shown in the accompanying chart.

B.T.U. Capacity	Volts	Watts	Wire Size	Fuse Size
10,000	115	1400	14	15
16,000	220	2650	14	15
20,000	220	3350	12	20

In many machines, removing the grill and inner enclosure will expose the controls and associated wiring. More extensive service to get at the fan and compressor will require removal of the outer enclosure assembly. Usually these parts are fastened with #6 or #8 hex-head slotted screws. Decorative trim is usually fastened with Phillips-head screws.

Basically, a medium sized standard screw driver, a Phillips-head screw driver, a set of nut drivers and a pair of channel-lock pliers should be all you need to remove the serviceable parts and clean the unit.

When cleaning the unit, remove the excess rust and paint over the rusty spots with a rust-inhibiting primer. This will do much to extend the unit's life.

Though you can see most of the parts when you remove the cover of your air conditioner (see drawing) it's best to disconnect any part from its wiring before checking it for electrical continuity. When you do, make a pencil sketch to remind you where the wires are connected. Wiring connections for this unit are shown in the accompanying wiring diagram.

To check the switch with your continuity tester, there should be no contin-

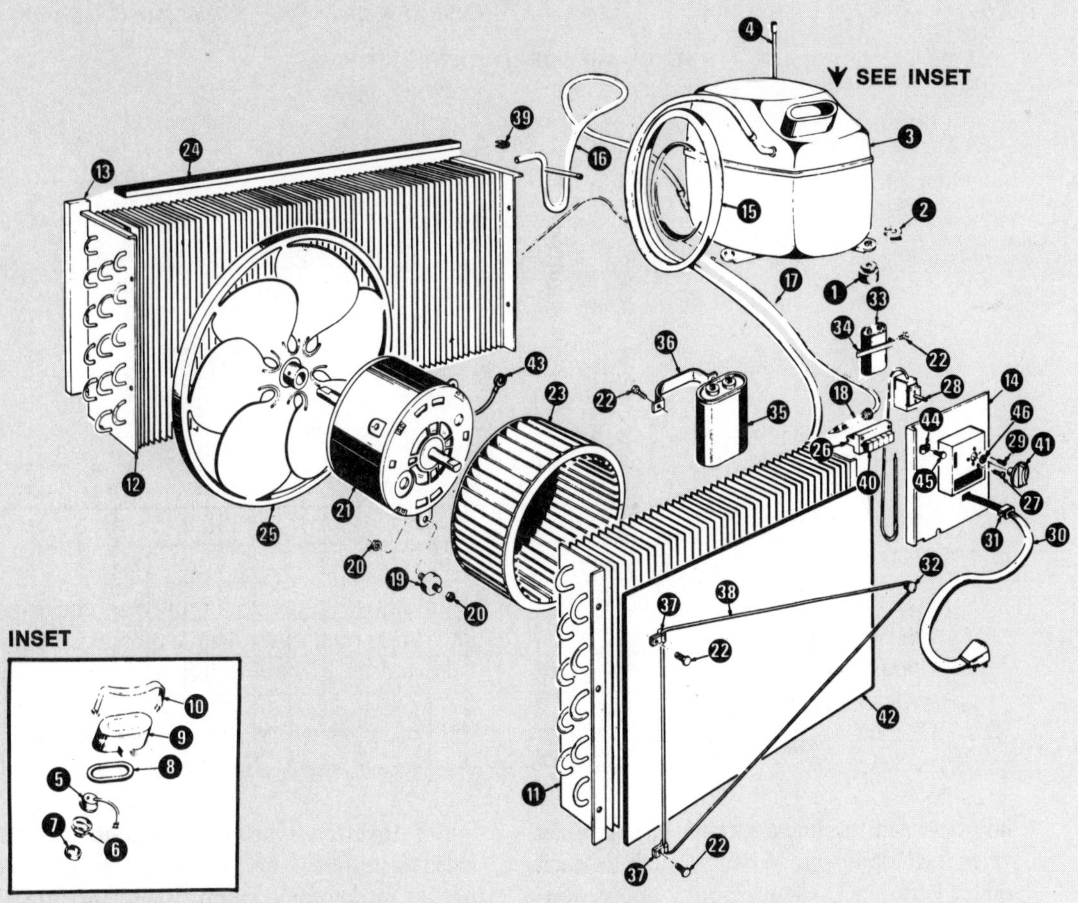

REF. NO.	PART NAME	QTY.	REF. NO.	PART NAME	QTY.
1	Compressor Isolator	3	25	Condenser Fan	1
2	Retainer Spring	3	26	Pushbutton Switch	1
3	Compressor	1	27	No. 8—32x3/8″ Round Head Phillips Machine Screw	2
4	Compressor Charging Tube	1	28	Thermostat	1
5	Motor Protector	1	29	No. 6—32x3/16″ Round Head Phillips Machine Screw	2
6	Protector Spring	1	30	Power Cord	1
7	Adaptor Protector	1	31	Strain Relief	1
8	Cover Seal	1	32	Ratchet Rivet	2
9	Terminal Cover	1	33	Capacitor	1
10	Cover Strap	1	34	Capacitor Strap	1
11	Evaporator Coil	1	35	Fan Capacitor	1
12	Condenser Coil	1	36	Capacitor Strap	1
13	Condenser Side Seal	1	37	Clamp	3
14	Panel Assembly	1	38	Filter Retainer	1
15	Suction Tube	1	39	"U" Type Clip	2
16	Discharge Tube Assembly	1	40	Pushbutton	5
17	Restrictor Tube Assembly	1	41	Thermostat Knob	1
18	Strainer .250 I.D.	1	42	Unit Filter	1
19	Motor Isolator	3	43	Motor Ground Wire	1
20	1/4—20 Hex Nut Keps	6	44	Thermostat Bulb Clamp	1
21	Fan Motor—115 V.	1	45	No. 8x1/2″ Hex Head Sheet Metal Screw	2
22	No. 8—15x3/8″ Hex Washer Head Tapping Screw	As Required	46	Thermostat Knob Seal	1
23	Evaporator Blower Wheel	1			
24	Condenser Top Seal	1			

WINDOW AIR CONDITIONER CHECKLIST

PROBLEM / POSSIBLE CAUSE	LOW LINE VOLTAGE	IMPROPERLY FUSED	WIRE OR PART SHORTED	DEFECTIVE STARTING RELAY	DEFECTIVE MOTOR—COMPRESSOR	THERMOSTAT SET TOO WARM	THERMOSTAT SET TOO COLD	FAN SPEED SET TOO SLOW	DEFECTIVE DEFROST THERMOSTAT	CLOGGED AIR FILTER	LOW OUTSIDE TEMPERATURE	LOOSE PARTS	FAN HITTING	SHIPPING BOLTS STILL TIGHT	NOT ENOUGH SLOPE TO OUTSIDE	DRAIN PLUGGED	ABNORMALLY HIGH HUMIDITY	INADEQUATE SEAL
BLOWS FUSES	√	√	√	√	√													
COMPRESSOR SHORT CYCLES	√			√	√			√	√	√								
NOISY OPERATION					√							√	√	√				
EVAPORATOR FROSTS UP							√	√			√							
UNIT RUNS TOO MUCH						√				√							√	
MOISTURE DRIPS INTO ROOM															√	√	√	√
WON'T START	√		√	√	√													

uity between the line and any other contact when switch is *off*. When turned to each other position, switch should show continuity.

The motor starting relay must show continuity when it is disconnected from the circuit. Contacts will open when motor reaches normal speed, as indicated by your test light. Motor relay must be mounted in correct position or it will not operate properly.

To test the motor starting capacitor, use an ohmmeter. But first disconnect capacitor leads and short its terminals to discharge it; otherwise you can get a strong shock.

With ohmmeter at its highest scale and connected to capacitor terminals, a low resistance reading will indicate a leak or short. On a good capacitor, the needle will swing to zero, then within a few seconds slowly change to a resistance reading of over 100,000 ohms. Check running capacitor the same way.

The overload protector should show continuity under normal conditions. Check the fan motor for continuity and for lubrication. The fan should spin freely when the blades are turned by hand.

The defrost thermostat normally opens at 30° F. to stop the compressor. Below this, for test, it must show no continuity. Above 60°, continuity should be shown. Between 30° and 60°, the stat will not show continuity when warming up, but will when cooling down.

The control thermostat will show continuity as the knob is turned, depending on room temperature. Failure to get a continuity change at some point near room temperature is cause to suspect this unit. Make sure that thermostat feeler bulb temperature is within the thermostat's operating range. Anything between 65° and 75° will do.

Unless you have special tools and some experience, don't get involved with the

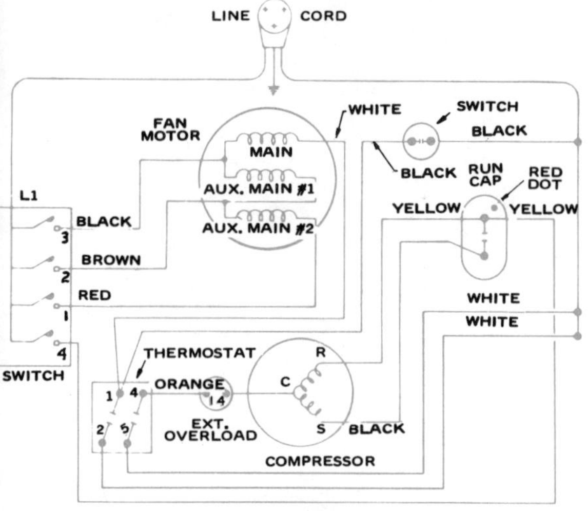

◀ *Electrical wiring for an air conditioner diagramed schematically and pictorially.* ▼

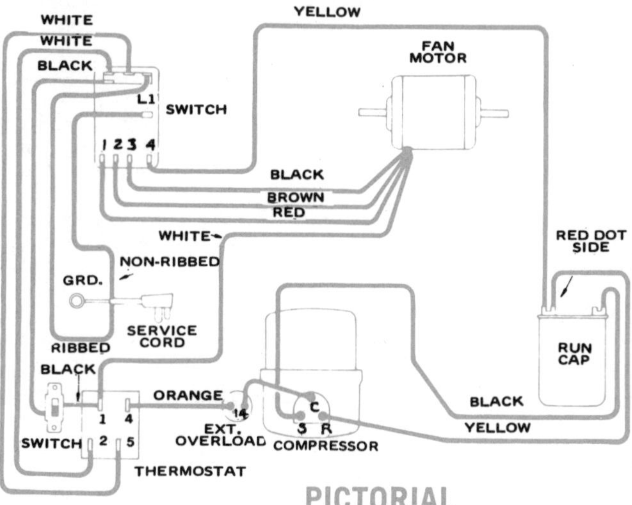

SCHEMATIC

REFRIGERATION SYSTEM

▼ **Simple Refrigerant Circuit**

A. Dual capillary used with 4-row evaporators

B. Expansion valve used on $2^1/_4$ h.p. models only

C. All other models have single capillary

Fan switch is master switch; supplies current through thermostat to compressor on "Hi Fan" and "Lo-Fan" settings only. Thermostat controls compressor

Thermostat sensing bulb is located in room-air intake

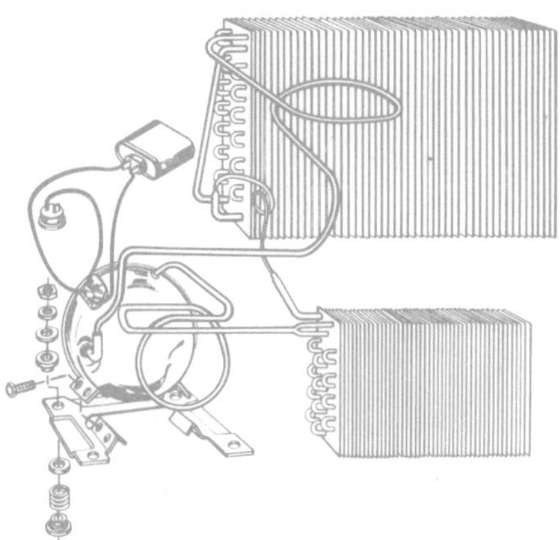

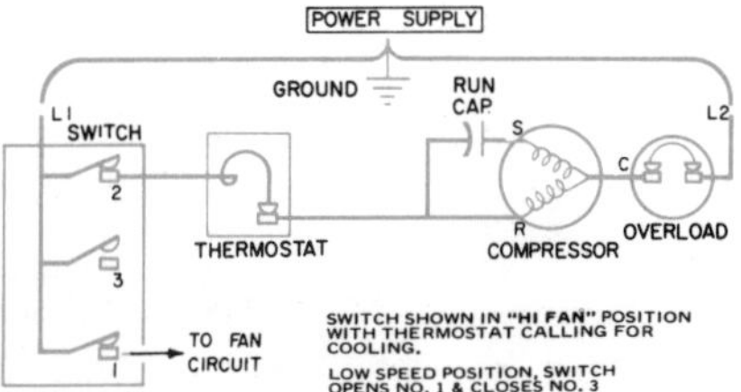

CONDENSATE FLOW SYSTEM

▲ *Evaporator condensate drains into insulated plastic pan beneath evaporator coil*

Evaporator pan drains through tubes to plastic pan beneath condenser coil

Condenser fan blade slinger ring sprays water (from plastic pan beneath condenser) onto condenser coil

Overflow from condenser pan goes into unit base (unusual condition, caused by very high indoor humidity)

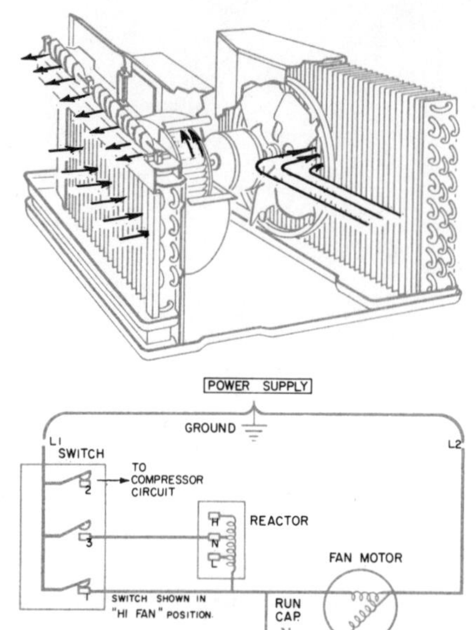

AIR FLOW SYSTEM

Filtered room air is pulled through evaporator coil
Cooled air discharged into room at high velocity by squirrel-cage blower wheel
Adjustable wafer-discs direct cooled air to left side, straight ahead or to right side of room
Condenser fan blade pushes air through full-width, full-height condenser coil
Condenser air pulled in through vents in sides of cabinet
Fan switch provides "Hi" or "Lo" fan speeds
Setting thermostat on "OFF THERM" (or "Fan only" on some models) allows operation of fan only at either high or low speed
Adjustable-tap reactor allows correcting high or low voltage fan speed variations

compressor, evaporator or condenser. Together, they form the sealed refrigerating system.

Should any of the parts prove to be defective, they will have to be removed and replaced. The best source of replacement parts for your air conditioner is from the manufacturer of the machine or the dealer who sold it. Usually the Yellow Pages listing under air conditioning equipment will include local dealers and suppliers of parts. G.M.

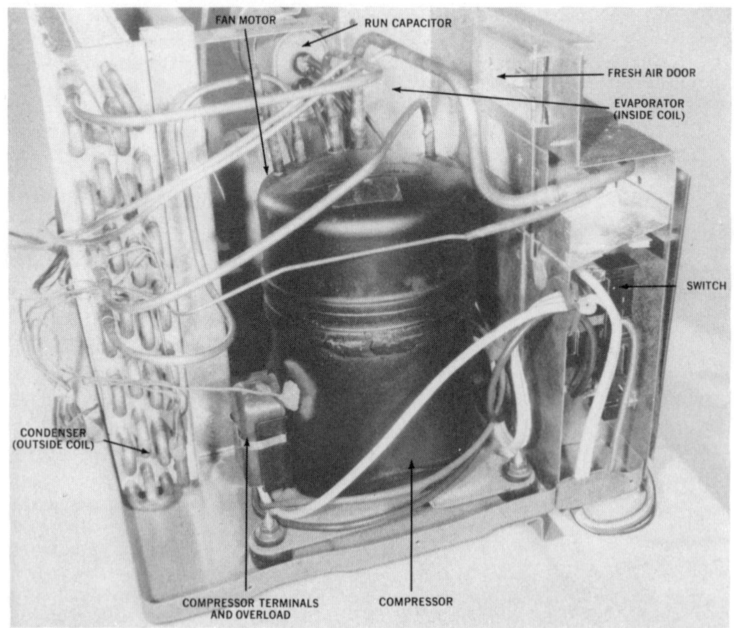

Principal components of a typical air conditioning unit.

Seasonal Maintenance for Your Air Conditioner

Get this job done in the spring for dependable summer-long operation

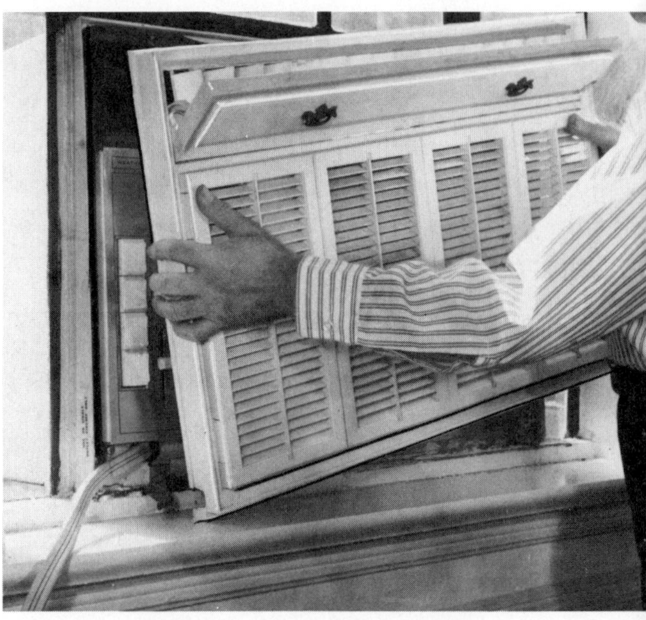

▲ Room air conditioners need seasonal check-up to keep them trouble-free. A little attention beforehand will avoid costly breakdowns. First step is to lift off the front cover, held by spring clips.

TAKE A LOOK at your air conditioner before the hot weather strikes. Just a few maintenance details may be all it needs to get it into shape for dependable performance all season.

Two routine chores, often overlooked, are quickly gotten out of the way. One is washing or replacing the filter, depending on the type. The other is cleaning the evaporator and condenser coils.

To get at the mechanism, remove the front cover panel. Every make of air conditioner has a panel that is held with clips and can be lifted off, though some have catches or retainer screws that must be loosened first.

With the front cover off, clean the deflecting louvers with a dry cloth or brush. To reach the condenser coils and fins, pull the machine forward from the housing in which it rests on small wheels or runners.

If the conditioner is installed in the window so that most of the housing extends on the outside, and the metal case is securely fastened, it is all right to pull the machine forward as it will remain balanced. However, if the machine is only partly mounted into the wall and most of the case projects into the room take the precaution of placing a wooden box or other support under the case before drawing out the chassis, which is quite heavy.

Use a vacuum cleaner with the brush attachment to remove accumulated lint and dust, making sure the ventilator fins are clear for air passage.

If necessary, reverse the vacuum hose to blow dust out of the fins. Wipe the coils and meter housing with a clean damp cloth. Check the fan meter to see if it has any lubricating cups and if so, add oil. Even the "permanent" type of motor bearings should be given a few drops of #20 motor oil.

The filter is located directly behind the front louvers, extending all the way across so it can be lifted out from the top. The woven plastic or metal type is renewed by flushing under a faucet. Wash in detergent if the filter is greasy. The fiberglass type should be replaced with a new one at the start of each season, and again each month to insure maximum cooling benefits.

Check the wiring to see that the terminals are tight and the cord insulation undamaged. Then slide the mechanism back and replace the cover.

Now think back to last summer to recall any breakdowns or annoyances with that particular unit. Did the fuses blow every so often? Was there a tinny rattle or excessive vibration? Some of these conditions can be corrected or at least alleviated.

Best cure for an overloaded circuit is to bring in a separate line for the air conditioner. This is not necessarily an extensive job, as a separate circuit line can be carried directly to the room concealed inside the walls, or through a conduit attached outside along the house wall. But if your house has inadequate wiring, installation of a larger electrical service may be required, and is worthwhile for efficient use of modern appliances.

Noise problems may be inherent in the operation of the machine, but sometimes they result from a loose hinge or missing gasket on the exhaust door. The source can be tracked down by operating the machine with the cover off.

Vibration in the walls results when an installation is not adequately braced. If the matter is sufficiently bothersome, fit a brace under the machine and insulate with rubber or felt padding. In any event, the opening should be tightly caulked both inside and on the outside.

Conditioners installed in double-hung windows should be thoroughly checked to make sure that the supports are adequate and that the sash is tight so that it doesn't rattle when the machine is running.

A frequent cause of service calls is a worn electric receptacle which results in the uncertain contact with the plug prongs. Replace the receptacle with a new one, or get the locking type of plug that twists into the receptacle and can't be dislodged by vibration. R.T.

▲ Lift out filter located behind the condenser coils. Woven plastic type is cleaned under faucet. Other types should be replaced with new ones.

◀ Clean the air deflectors and casing with a brush or vacuum cleaner. Check the wire insulation and connections.

With machine cover off, clean compressor coils, housing, etc., thoroughly with vacuum hose and damp cloth.

Where necessary, reverse vacuum hose to blow out lint from evaporator fins, and inside the case. Wipe fan meter with cloth, apply a few drops of oil to bearings.

Check electric cord and wall receptacle, which are common causes of conditioner failure.

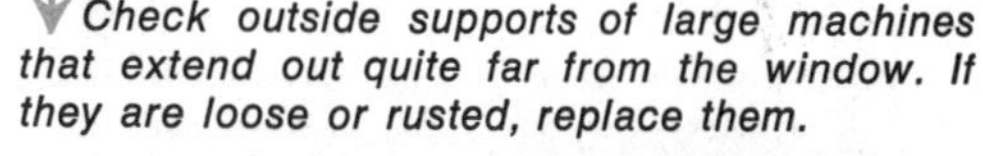

Check outside supports of large machines that extend out quite far from the window. If they are loose or rusted, replace them.

Install a Burglar Alarm

Here's how to select an alarm, and instructions for a complete alarm system

YOUR TELEPHONE RINGS, but goes unanswered because you are in the shower or away from home. Ten minutes later a stranger rings your doorbell. If you answer, he pretends to be looking for a friend in the neighborhood. If you do not answer the door, he will soon be inside, calmly taking his pick of your valuables.

Let's face facts. Lights left burning in an unoccupied house may discourage a wandering amateur housebreaker, but only the din of a burglar alarm upsets the pro.

The chance of your home being burglarized increases every year. Why be one of the victims when a good burglar alarm costs so little and is so easy to install.

What type of alarm? Many different kinds of burglar alarm systems are available. Each type has advantages and disadvantages. So investigate all available systems carefully before deciding which is best for your particular needs.

Those simple little alarms that fasten directly to doors deserve only passing mention here since they offer minimal protection at best. They may be adequate for apartments, or in other homes where there are few avenues of entry.

More reliable systems include photo-electric devices, ultrasonic alarms, switch and break-wire systems, and those that automatically telephone the police or anyone else of your choosing. A telephone system is the most expensive, but it may be the only wise choice for an isolated rural home where ordinary alarms would not be heard by neighbors or passersby.

A typical photo-electric unit costing $100 or more can protect only a limited area because triggering of the alarm depends on the breaking of a light beam by the intruder. Perhaps this is all the protection you need. However, bear these points in mind. First, give preference to a system that utilizes an invisible infra-red beam and place the two units (light box and receiver) where the prowler cannot see them readily. If he spots the boxes, he can determine exactly where the light beam is whether it is invisible or not; he can then either crawl under or step over it. Secondly, consider only a unit having a *modulated* light source because only this type will work in lighted as well as dark areas, and because it cannot be frustrated by the light from a burglar's flashlight.

▼ Below: Alert DC-6 alarm with blinker lens removed to show prewired, mounted electronic assembly. Right: A circuit tester helps you check switches. Tape a flashlight bulb socket to a dry cell. Solder stiff wires to socket; one serves as probe, the other contacts cell bottom. Touch probe and cell terminal to switch leads. Bulb lights if the switch is properly closed. ➤

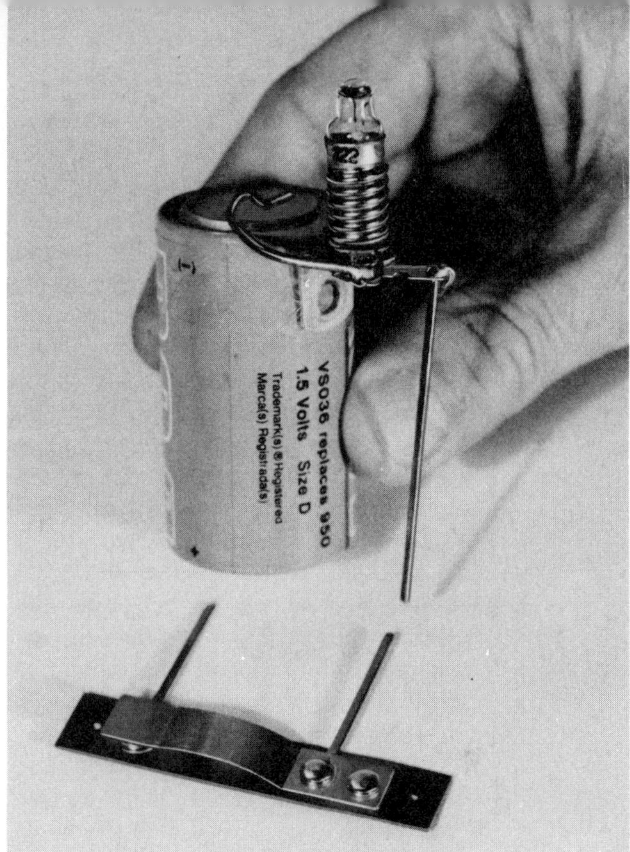

Finally, remember that the light beam must be where pet dogs and cats cannot intercept it.

One of the newest types of alarms utilizes ultrasonic sound to trigger the alarm. Such a unit consists of a single box placed in a strategic position from which it sends out a sound "pattern" that is inaudible to the human ear. The same unit also serves as a receiver. When an intruder steps into the sound area (about 100 square feet), he disturbs the pattern and sets off the alarm. These are good provided there is no air turbulence in the sound area. Cats and dogs will activate the alarm, as will air currents created by heating or air-conditioning systems. Incidentally, dogs and cats *can* hear the sound even though you cannot, and they may not enjoy it.

If you have no wandering pets, and all you wish to do is protect one room and perhaps a staircase to the second floor, either the photo-electric or ultrasonic system may be a good choice. Both are quiet, efficient, and least troublesome to install and maintain.

Perhaps the best choice for an average private home is a switch and break-wire system. Such a system can guard every possible avenue of entry into the house, even protect the henhouse and mailbox if you wish. Some models can also protect against smoke, fire, flooding and freezing. Finally, these systems are relatively inexpensive—only $20 to $40 for a typical basic unit.

The major disadvantage of a switch and break-wire system is that it cannot simply be plugged in for instant operation. You must run wire around the house to the various door and window switches. Also, you should check the switches periodically to make sure they are clean and that they make good contact. These are minor disadvantages considering the degree of protection these systems provide.

Compare the relative merits of switch and break-wire alarms made by different manufacturers. They are not all alike. Some give only an audible alarm, others simultaneously turn on a red light visible from the street. Some are primarily intruder alarms, others can utilize special sensors to detect other home hazards of the types already mentioned.

Plan for security. Careful advance planning will ensure the installation of an uncomplicated, foolproof alarm system. Start by making a rough drawing of your floor plan; on it indicate all windows and doors that need protection. Cross out those windows that require no protection—for example, upper story windows that cannot be reached from fire escapes, trees or porch roofs (provided that you do not keep long ladders lying about). If you do not store valuable tools in the garage, this area may be left unprotected provided that you *do* protect any door leading from the garage into the house.

Next, decide where you should locate the master control unit containing the alarm horn. If the system you select makes only an audible sound, it can be placed wherever it is best heard by neighbors, and where you can conveniently reach it to turn it on and off. If the system also turns on a signal light, place the box in the corner of a window, facing the street, so that the light will be visible to passersby.

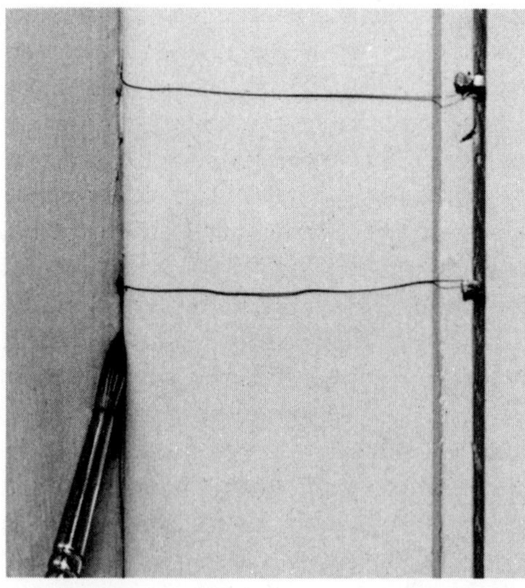

▲As can be seen here, switch installed on a door jamb is virtually invisible. Wire has been pushed into crevice between the door jamb and a cupboard wall, then held in place with small dabs of clear cement. Hair wires can be hidden with trim paint.

If placing the entire master control box in a window is inconvenient, remove the front panel from the master box and mount it alone in a window, then lead the wires from the flasher bulb back to the master control. A good way to make a connection in the control box is to make a plug from the base of an extra bulb that fits the original bulb socket. Break off the glass part of the bulb, remove the filaments, and drill through the base contact with a 1/16 inch drill. Poke a wire through this hole and solder the end to the base terminal. Solder another lead wire to the outside of the bulb base. Attach your flasher leads to these wires, and simply plug into the original bulb socket.

Use of the front panel, with the flasher light, as a separate, remote unit has another advantage besides eliminating a bulky box in the window. You can hide the master control box wherever you wish, making it harder for an intruder to find it and tamper with it.

Using the floor plan as a guide, trace the best wiring route while you study the house itself for problem areas. The wire should not be run across or along electric power cables. Remember that you must route a singlewire loop to and from the control box so that it makes a *series* circuit through all the switches.

The fine "hair" wire (only 0.003 inches in diameter) is virtually invisible when properly installed. It is fairly delicate, so handle it carefully. In extensive wiring jobs, especially if you have to lead the wire from one floor level to another, your wiring job will be much easier if you substitute a heavier insulated wire for those stretches where concealment is no problem. Use telephone or other low-voltage wire readily available from any electronics supply shop.

The wire may be run through the attic or basement wherever convenient. In rooms, run it along baseboards, mouldings, window and door frames—wherever it is least visible. Planning the best wire route should be done with deliberation and care to avoid unnecessary back-tracking. To fasten the wire in place, just drive a small brad in part way, give the wire a twist around it, and tap the nail in all the way. Be careful with the hair wire; nailing down too hard may break it. In some places you may find it easier to glue the wire in place with small dabs of transparent glue; hold the wire in position with pieces of paper masking tape until the glue dries.

The accompanying illustrations show how the wire is attached to switches mounted in ordinary doors and sliding glass doors. Similar placements work with windows. Just cut the wire where it passes a switch, sandpaper the enamel coating from the hair wire, wrap around the switch terminals. For a really trouble-free job, add a touch of solder to each connection.

You need switches only on doors and windows that are opened and closed frequently. If some windows are rarely or never opened, you can protect them *without* using switches. Simply run the wire over the window and across the frame so that it will be broken if an intruder opens the window or breaks the glass. If you have inside screens, the wire can be threaded through the screen mesh where it will be virtually invisible. When the wire breaks, the alarm will sound.

Horn location. Alarms of this kind have the noise-making horn mounted inside the master control box. This is not really the best place for it in many applications. If the control box is hidden in a closet or cupboard, the sound will be muffled. In any case, the sound will be not as loud *outside* the house as it should be.

There is a simple solution. Remove the horn from the box and place it where it can be heard best, running a double-wire lead from the master control box to the horn.

Power in the *Alert* system is supplied by two six-volt batteries housed inside the control box. Other makes of alarms use ordinary flashlight cells. There really isn't much difference in operation except that the bigger batteries will keep the horn blaring for up to eight hours instead of half an hour. Only you can shut off the sound, by use of a key switch on the side of the master control box. The intruder cannot stop the alarm by simply closing a window or door he has opened. Once it is started, only the key will turn it off.

By-pass switch. But how are you going to get into the house without setting off the alarm? You can't unless you install a by-pass switch lock that inactivates the switch on your main entry. This tumbler-type lock is mounted on the door, or in a wall near the door, and is connected to the door switch terminals. This is an extra-cost item, but hardly expendable. When you turn the key in the lock, that door's alarm switch is inactivated permitting you to enter. You need not use this by-pass when leaving your home because the alarm system has a built-in delay (about 45 seconds) that lets you get out of the house before it becomes operative.

Think like a burglar. After you have installed and tested your alarm system, go outside and study the house as a burglar might. Is there any way that you could frustrate the alarm system—for example, by breaking a small pane of glass and reaching in to bridge the window switch with a length of wire? Have you missed protecting any avenue of entry, such as a basement window? Can the warning light be seen from the street? Can the horn be heard by your neighbors? Did you place the warning stickers where would-be intruders will see them?

About those stickers. Most burglars will leave a house alone if they are warned that an alarm system is in use. However, in some cases you should not use such warnings. If you live in a remote area and must rely on a warning system that automatically telephones the police, you should never advertise your security system. In this case you want the burglar to stick around until the police have time to respond to your call for help.

When your system is "go," tell your neighbors what the noise and signal light mean. You may wish to leave a duplicate cut-off key with a trusted neighbor so that the alarm can be turned off in your absence. Finally, let your police department know what kind of intruder protection you have.

Other applications. As mentioned before, some switch and break-wire alarm systems can also be fitted with special sensors to detect smoke, fire, basement flooding and freezing conditions.

Note that a typical switch and break-wire system can be used in other ways, and in other places, without the use of special sensors. With it you can guard your boat, camping trailer, car, henhouse, or even use it as a safety device around the swimming pool. In the latter case, make a "fence" around the pool area with the wire; anyone running toward the pool will break the wire and sound the alarm.

You may want to add a double-pole double-throw switch near the control box so that you can use the alarm system conveniently as a swimming pool safety system when you are at home, and as an intruder alarm when you are absent.

The system is also a good vandal detector. For example, the demolition of roadside mailboxes by juvenile marauders plague many a suburban community. A switch and break-wire alarm can be used to detect night time vandals. Just disconnect the house alarm wiring from the alarm box terminals and substitute a hair wire loop running to the mailbox. Wrap the wire around the flag, and run it through the holes in the mailbox latch. Anyone who twists the flag or attempts to open the box will break the wire and set off the alarm. If you do not want to tip off the vandals with an audible alarm, disconnect one wire leading to the

▲*Break-wire, shown above, is best for sliding doors which are infrequently opened. A small nail stuck into door handle holds a wire loop that will break and sound the alarm when door is opened. Avoid slack in the wire which would defeat this purpose.*

▲*For sliding doors used more often, cement a switch near the top of vertical channel so that it is closed by door edge. To prevent shorting, use clear adhesive tape to insulate hair wire leads from door frame.*

horn. Place the alarm box where you will see the light go on—perhaps the best place is near the TV set.

It is just as easy to detect fourfooted vandals. A break-wire fence around your garden will alert you to marauding deer. A simple switch system at the henhouse may tell you when that pesky skunk is on the prowl for eggs.

We are all properly concerned about the rising incidence of "crime in the streets." Yet, statistically, the largest number of crimes are committed *off* the streets, as burglaries of home and places of business. In this area, we can create some alarming situations for uninvited guests. J.H.

By-pass switch can be weatherproofed with cover designed for outside sockets. A cover also camouflages switch, and can be padlocked for added security during extended absence from home.

WHERE TO FIND IT

Burglar alarm kits are available from electronic supply houses, such as Lafayette or Allied, and from some local burglar alarm installation companies. Check the Yellow Pages.

The unit described here is Lafayette's moderate-cost Alert DC-6. It includes 12 contact switches and 750 feet of wire, but a by-pass switch lock (recommended) is extra. The switch allows you to enter the house without triggering the alarm. Write to Lafayette Radio Electronics, P.O. Box 10, Syosset, Long Island, New York 11791. A fire sensor for the DC-6 is available from the equipment's manufacturer, MRL, Inc., 7227 Lee Highway, Falls Church, Va. 22046.

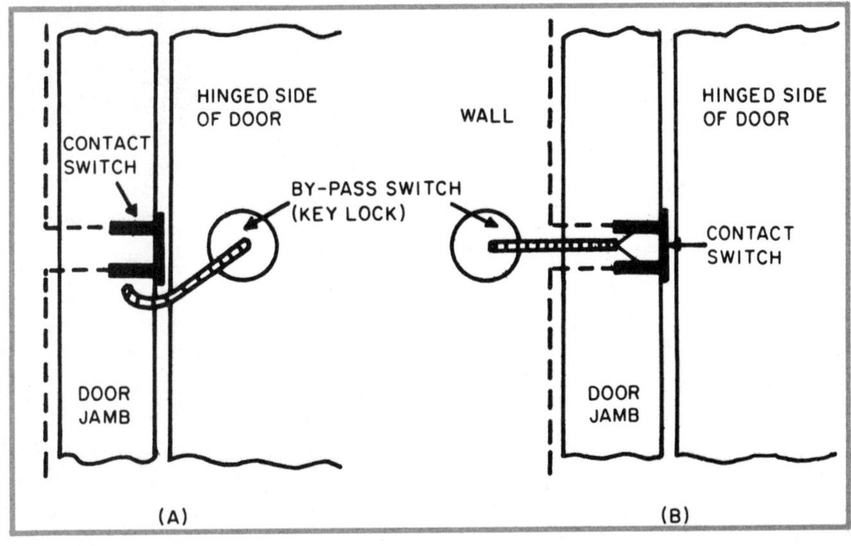

Place the by-pass itch that enables you enter house without ggering alarm near or your most used door. tallation is simplest on or (A); the contact itch is shorted by concting cable. Switch unted on wall (B) inves more work but minates a dangling ble and jutting wires.

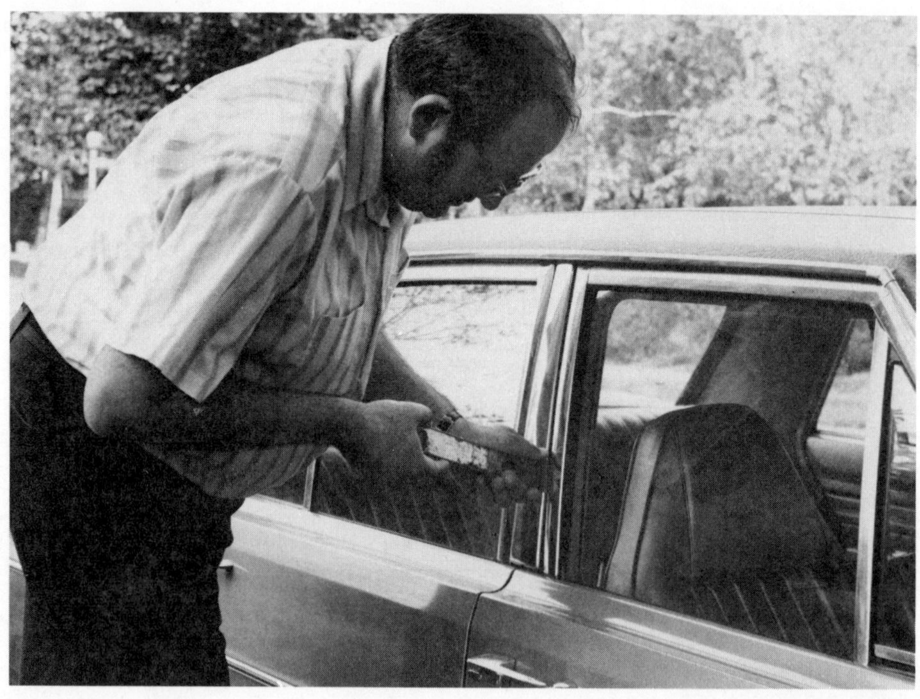

Install a Burglar Alarm in Your Car

Shrill alarm sounds whenever trunk, hood or doors are tampered with

TWO HOURS of work and a modest investment can put a theft alarm in your car that will sound whenever anyone tampers with the doors, trunk or hood. It will keep on sounding until you turn it off with a key.

In addition, the switch key on the fender next to the driver's door tells a would-be thief: "Careful. This car is wired for sound. Try something easier."

Unike some other alarms, this one cannot be silenced by a piece of tape holding down a trip switch or by the reclosing of an opened door. Turning it off requires either a key, or a hard yank on the right wires. And, if the wires are concealed, no thief will want to take the time to find them while the siren is churning out its loud, shrill warning.

How it works. The schematic diagram shows how the siren and locking circuits work (also, see "Electronics"). M1, an electronic siren module, in conjunction with speaker SPKR, comprise the *siren.* The positive voltage input is fed through S1, a key-lock switch, to the module. R1 is simply a dropping resistor for the module which works best with a 6- to 10-volt input.

The negative battery connection to the

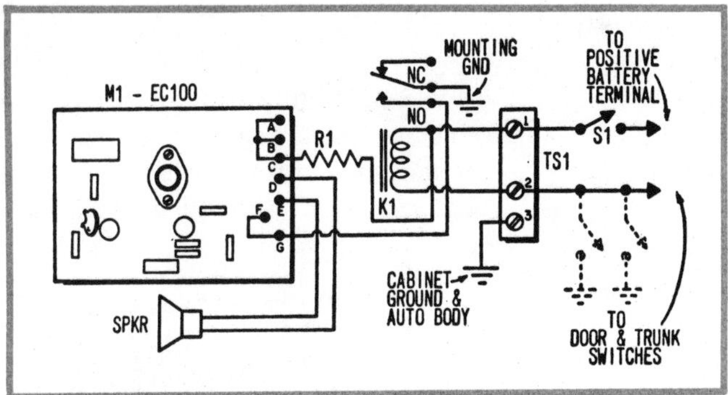

Noisemaker of the Auto Siren Sentry is the Eico EC 100 module (M1) that drives the speaker. Relay K1 keeps siren sounding even if car door is reclosed.

siren module is made through normally closed pushbutton switches, like those used to turn on courtesy lights when a door is opened (these switches are indicated by the dotted lines in the schematic).

Trace the circuit through. Note that when a door is opened, the associated switch connects terminal 2 of terminal strip TS1 to ground—completing the power connection to the module and the siren "sounds off." Also note that when terminal 2 is grounded relay K1 is energized, pulling down K1's armature or wiper contact. When the moving contact touches this normally open terminal (#2) it parallels the door and trunk switches and "permanently" grounds the relay and the module's ground connection —the siren keeps sounding even if the door is closed (opening the switch). The only way K1 can be released—to turn off the *Auto Siren Sentry*—is by interrupting the positive battery connection by opening key switch S1.

Protecting the user. Since key-switch S1 is mounted on the fender—and you want it there for all to see—it protects the user against the embarrassment which might be caused by the siren going off as he attempts to leave the car (which will happen if the alarm switch is mounted inside the car). After the user leaves the car, the alarm is set by turning S1 to *on.* Before getting into the car, the driver then turns S1 to *off.* Naturally, if S1 is mounted inside the car the alarm will sound whenever the driver enters the car. Mount the key switch out on the fender for your own peace of mind.

Construction. Actually there isn't much involved in building the *Auto Siren Sentry.* The siren module is an Eicocraft Siren Module Kit—type EC100, which can be assembled in a matter of minutes. There is but a handful of components which are mounted on a pre-punched and "component position marked" printed circuit board. However, assemble only the board itself, do not make the external connections given in the instructions; the *Auto Siren Sentry* uses a simpler external wiring than that given with the module.

After the module is completed, connect a 10-inch length of black wire to terminal *G,* loop the wire under the board and solder the end to *F.* Connect a one-inch length of bare wire to *C.* Connect a bare-wire jumper from point *A* to point *B.* Then connect two wires of the same color to *D* and *E,* the speaker terminals. Note that the board shows the battery conncetion to *A* and *B;* ignore these instructions. In the *Auto Siren Sentry* the positive battery connection is the short bare wire at *C* while the negative battery connection is the black wire going to *F* and *G.*

After all cabinet holes are cut in the main section of a 3 x 5 x 7-inch aluminum cabinet, mount the siren module as shown in the photographs, with the bottom as close as possible to one side; use stand-offs between the board and the cabinet to avoid shorting the printed-circuit wiring. The stand-offs as well as the necessary mounting hardware are supplied with the module.

The speaker is a three-inch waterproof type. The speaker specified in the Parts List is supplied in a metal cabinet having an integral gimbal bracket. If the speaker is installed as shown, in an aluminum cabinet, place a piece of perforated phenolic board in front of the speaker, to prevent possible damage to the cone. (If desired, the speaker can be used in the cabinet supplied.) Mount the speaker cabinet near the radiator, facing outwards, and connect the speaker leads from the module to the terminals on the speaker cabinet.

The wiper contact on K1 is *automatically grounded* when the relay is mounted in the cabinet—the wiper contact is connected directly to the frame of K1.

While only a three-lug terminal strip is required if the speaker is mounted in the aluminum cabinet, we show a five terminal type in the photographs to illustrate the arrangement when an external speaker is used. The speaker would connect to the two terminals shown unused. To reduce the possibility of wiring errors, place the battery connections on opposite ends of TS1, as shown, with at least the switch terminal in between.

Install the *Auto Siren Sentry* on any convenient surface under the hood. Just make certain the alarm doesn't project above hood line or you won't be able to close it.

Installing the switches. Any existing door switch automatically becomes part of the *Auto Siren Sentry* when the wire from terminal 2 of TS1 is connected to the courtesy light circuit. These switches are the self-grounding type, always switching the ground lead of the courtesy lights: therefore, when you look at these switches you will see only *one* connecting wire. All other switches which may be added should be of the same type, self-grounding, with their leads connected to the wiring of any of the original door switches. Additional switches for the hood, trunk or rear doors can be purchased from your car dealer at nominal cost.

The key switch should be installed so some smart "cooky" can't jump the terminals. If the switch is installed in the part of the fender that faces the tire anyone can reach under the car and jump the terminals, making the alarm inoperative. Install the switch on part of the *double fender.* Part of each fender, near the door, is shielded by the sides of the firewall, and access to the space between the fender and firewall is only through a small area which is exposed when the door is open. Place the switch so that its terminals are in the concealed space.

Positive grounds. The circuit shown is for cars with the more common *negative* ground battery. If your car uses a positive ground battery simply reverse the connections to siren module terminals C and G.

Six-volt systems. If your car uses six-volts, eliminate R1—use a direct connection from terminal 1 of TS1 and use the alternate six-volt relay specified in the parts list.

H.F.

PARTS LIST — Construction Time: 2 hours

K1	S.p.d.t. relay (Potter and Brumfield RS5D—12VDC, Allied 41D5504—P&B RS5D-6VDC—Allied 41D5896 or equivalent)
M1	Siren Module EC 100 or equivalent
R1	10-ohm, 5 watt resistor
Spkr	Weatherproof speaker (Lafayette 44C-5201 or equivalent)
TS1	Terminal Strip
	3 x 5 x 7 inch aluminum chassis box
Misc.	Wire, solder, mounting hardware, solder jugs, etc.

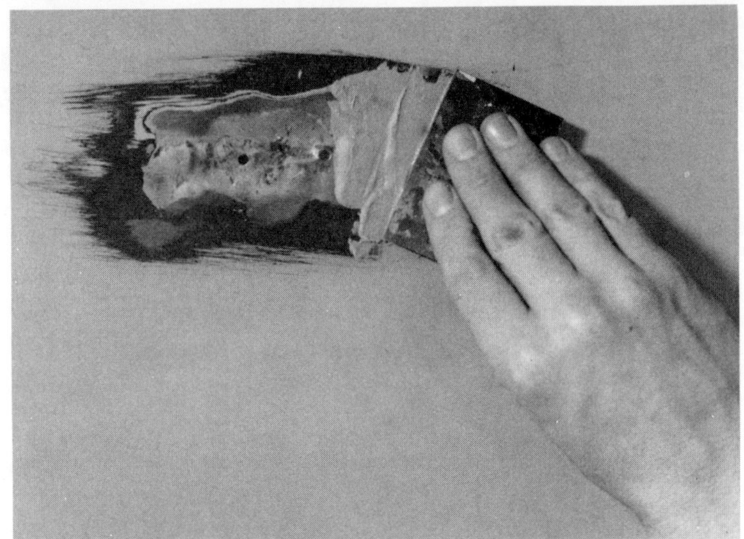

➤ *Use an epoxy patching putty to repair dent in auto body. Before putty is applied, dents are hammered or pulled out as much as possible, then sanded down to the bare metal. Two holes are where sheet metal screws were driven part way in to pull metal out.*

How to Repair Dents and Rust-outs

You can use a kit to fill minor dents and rusted-out spots in your car's body

YOU DON'T NEED a professional auto body shop to repair small dents, rust-outs and deep scratches. Body repair products designed for easy use by car owners are available, and with just a bit of care, you can do a job with which you'll be thoroughly satisfied.

If you tried body patching years ago with the fiberglass kits and gave up because they were difficult to use, make another try with today's epoxy products.

No special tools are necessary, and everything you need should cost only a few dollars. In some cases, you may find complete kits in the automotive departments of discount houses.

The items required are: four grades of sandpaper (40, 80, 240 and 400 grit), filler putty, putty hardener (sold with the putty in all cases), metallic tape, a sanding block and a putty applicator (doctor's tongue depressor or equivalent).

If the problem is a small dent, hammer it out if possible; the less putty you have to use to fill a dent, the more durable the repair. Dents in fenders often can be knocked out with a hammer in back, and a block of wood held against the front.

Dents that cannot be hammered from the back (because of lack of access, such as in doors, or inadequate swing room for the hammer) can be pulled out by drilling small holes across the dent, inserting sheet metal screws and then pulling on the screws with a claw hammer. A piece of hardwood should be used to brace the back of the hammer.

After pulling out the dent to as close to the original surface line as possible, clean the area with a wax and grease remover, and sand the surface with coarse paper (40 grit) down to bare metal. It is now ready for filling with putty, which is described later.

If the problem is a rust-out begin by cleaning the body around it with a wax and grease remover, then remove metal particles from the rust-out, breaking off any pieces of metal that have been rust-weakened. Sand a two-inch border around the rustout with 40 grit paper, down to bare metal.

At this point, you have two choices for bridging the gap of the rust-out: 1) you can use wire mesh (as fine a screen as you can get) coiled up inside the space behind the rust-out. The mesh, which has a certain amount of springiness, should be much larger than the rust-out opening. Coil it, slip it in and it will unwind and cover the hole from the inside. Note: this type of repair is recommended for rocker panels only, but inasmuch as they are the most common rust-out problems, the method is useful. 2) you can use a metallic tape patch. To do this, crimp the edges of the rust-out inward with a screwdriver (this will create a depression in the border area). Cut a patch larger than the rust-out but smaller than the depression created by the crimping. Apply the patch, trimming if necessary with a razor blade. With 40 grit paper, feather the edges of the patch to the sheet metal.

Most body putties come in tubes and must be mixed with a hardening fluid just before application. Follow the instructions for proportions of putty to hardener very carefully. One popular body kit specifies that you squeeze out two beads of putty side by side and just touching, and run a thin stream of hardener in the valley they form.

Mix the putty and hardener very thoroughly with a stick and apply over the dent or rust-out. Apply enough putty and just shape it approximately with the stick. Once the putty dries and hardens, you can sand it down. Remember, it's a lot easier to sand down than to mix more putty and apply it to depressions.

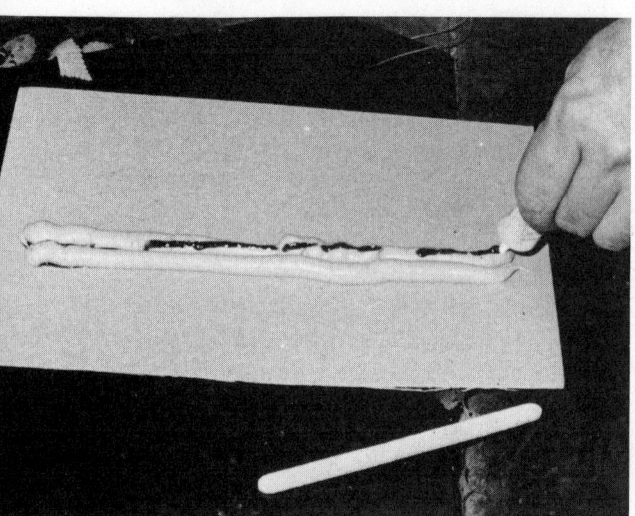

▲ *In one patching kit, two beads of putty are squeezed out side by side and touching. The valley between them is filled with hardener from a separate tube.*

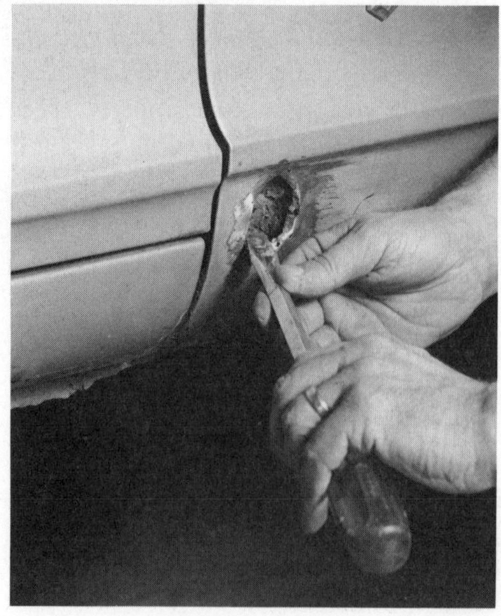

➤ *To use a tape patch on a rusted out spot, first remove all rusted metal. Then sand a two-inch border around the hole down to the bare metal. When this is done, use a screw driver, as shown, to crimp the edge of the hole inward.*

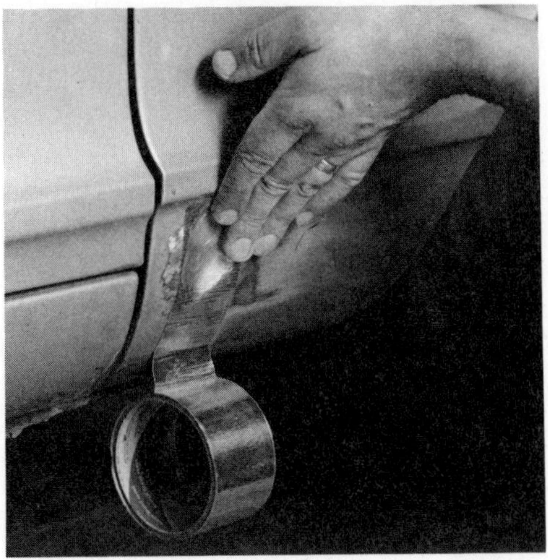

▲ Apply metallic patching tape to the prepared hole, trimming it so the patch is larger than the hole, but smaller than the depression around the hole that was formed by crimping.

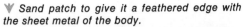

▼ Sand patch to give it a feathered edge with the sheet metal of the body.

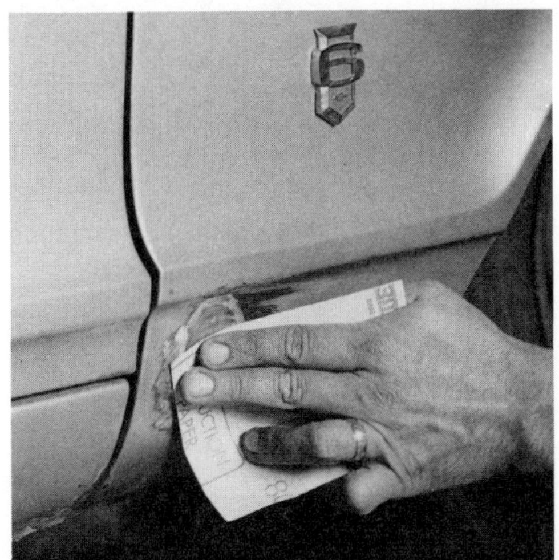

▼ Apply patching putty to damaged area, making sure you use enough. It is easier to sand off excess than it is to apply additional putty later on. Applicator here is a piece of plastic, but anything convenient will do.

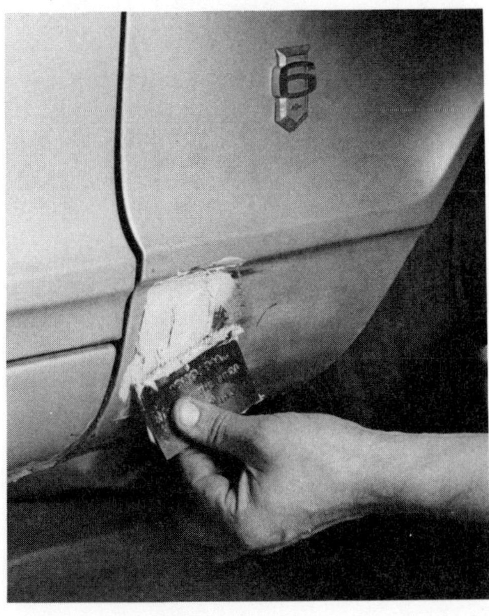

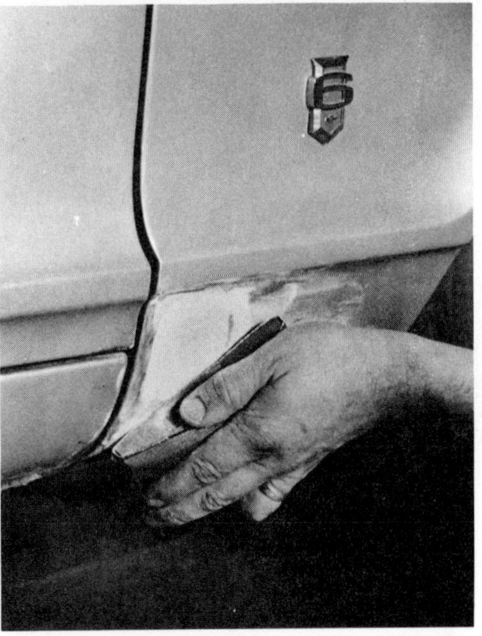

▲ Once patch has hardened, use sandpaper on block to shape it and bring it flush with the surrounding metal. Initial sanding can be with coarse grit, but use 80 grit for final work before painting with primer.

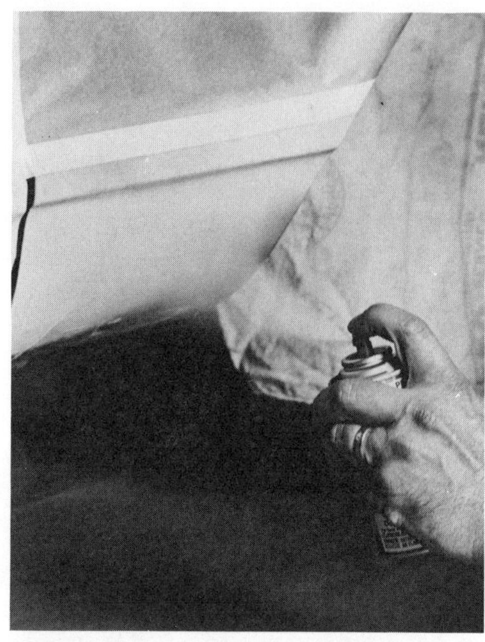

▲ Use an aerosol retouching paint, and hold can about eight inches away to get an even coat.

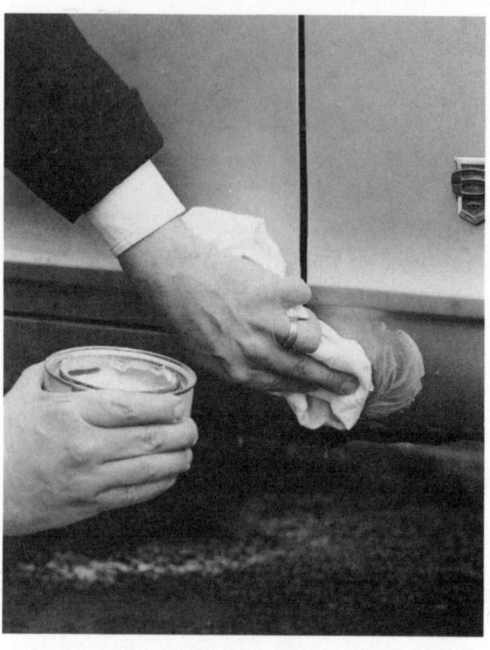

▲ After the repaired area has received a final coat of touch-up paint, wait a week and polish it.

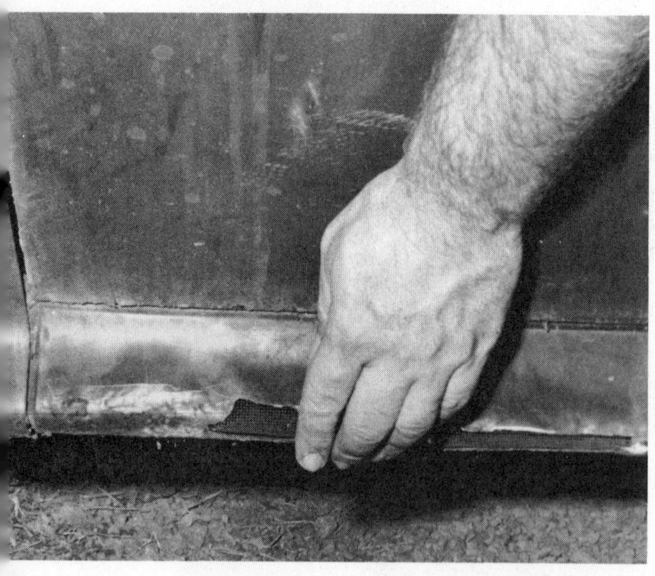

▲ Use wire mesh to provide support for putty when patching a rusted out rocker panel. Use a lot of mesh. Roll up tight and insert in rusted out area. It has some springiness and will uncoil slightly to press itself against rust-out.

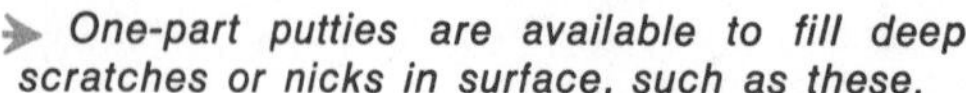

➤ One-part putties are available to fill deep scratches or nicks in surface, such as these.

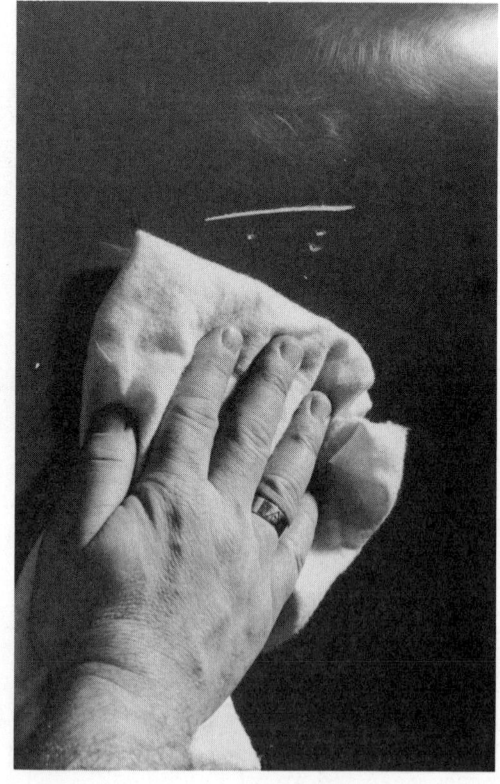

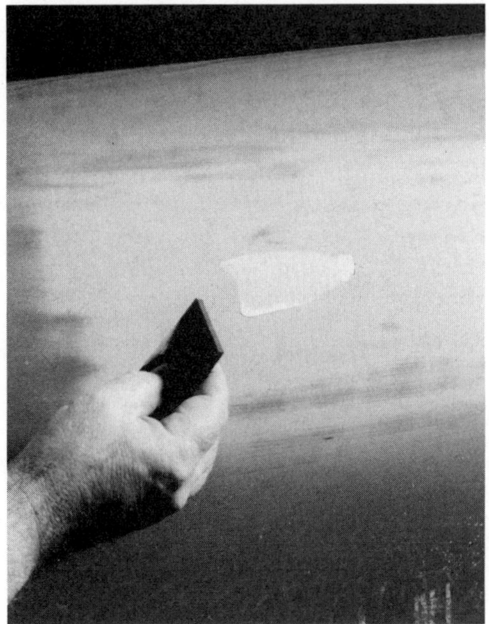

◀Patching putty has been applied to dent. Dent and the area around it has been sanded.

▼Patched dent is sanded to desired shape with a block. Then apply a coat of primer.

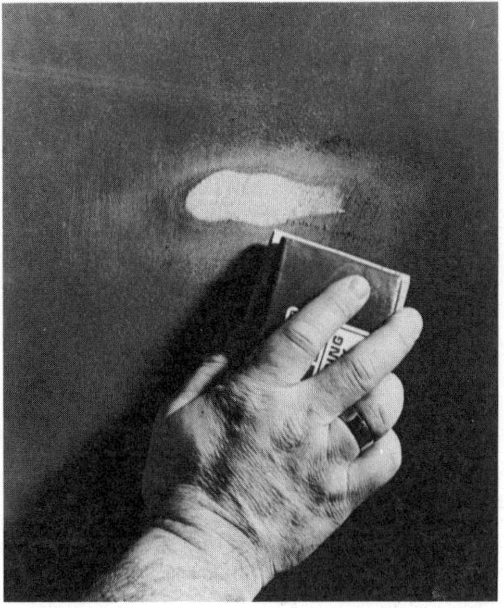

Hardening time for the putty depends on air temperature, how well you prepared the putty and how thick a layer of putty you applied. The thicker the layer and the lower the temperature, the longer it will take. Allow up to several hours on a cool day.

Once the putty is hard and dry, sand it down and shape it with coarse sandpaper on a sanding block. Do final shaping with medium paper (80 grit).

Apply a coat of primer paint. Use an aerosol type and hold the can at least eight inches away for even application. When the primer dries, sand the surface with wet very fine paper (240 grit) and wipe clean. Apply a second coat of primer and sand with wet extremely fine (400 grit) paper.

Again wipe the surface and apply coats of touchup paint (an aerosol is recommended). Several thin coats will produce a nicer result than one heavy coat.

After a week, rub the repaired area with a polish (not a wax). A month after the repair, clean and wax the entire car.

Deep body scratches can be filled with spot putty, a special compound that doesn't require mixing.

Begin by sanding the scratch down to bare metal with medium paper (80 grit). Mask the area and apply a coat of primer. When the primer dries, sand with wet very fine paper (240 grit) until smooth. Apply the spot putty to fill in the scratch.

When the putty dries, sand smooth with wet very fine paper (240 grit). Wipe clean and apply a second coat of primer. When the primer dries, sand to a smooth surface with extremely fine paper (400 grit). Wipe the surface clean and spray on the touch-up paint.

A week later, polish the repair. P.W.

See also: UPHOLSTERY.

Repairing Worn Ball Joints

In most cases, the injection of a resin compound can renew these key parts of your automobile's steering system

THE BALL JOINT is the pivot of the front suspension. If it is excessively worn, it creates handling and road wander problems. Wheel alignment is not the cure, for the wheels in effect are loose because of play in worn ball joints. Regardless of the alignment setting, the wheels can move in and out of alignment repeatedly as they wobble down the road.

A weekend mechanic can learn how to replace the four ball joints in the front suspension, but the job is extremely difficult under backyard conditions, and the investment in tools he would need is not usually worthwhile. Instead, worn ball joints now can be treated by injecting a special resin compound that hardens to take up play.

On most cars, the wobble and road wander should be noticeable long before the wear is beyond successful treatment with the resin. Note: many late-model GM cars have special ball joints pre-loaded with rubber inserts. On such cars, you may find very little play, but almost any steering play with this design is an indication of major wear within the joint itself.

Checking wear is made accurate and inexpensive with a cardboard gauge that is usually offered free from the marketer

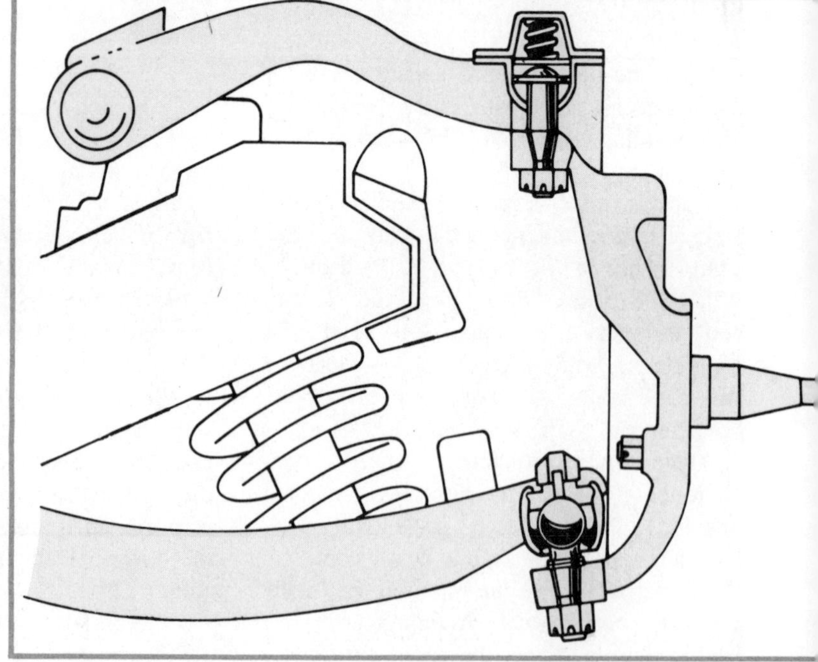

Typical front suspension. The wheel, not shown, is mounted on the spindle at the right. The part that the spindle is attached to is the steering knuckle. The knuckle has a ball joint at the top and another at the bottom. These join it to the upper and lower control arms. In this design, the lower ball joint is the load-bearing one. Usually, only the load-bearing ball joint receives enough wear to require treatment.

◄To check ball-joint play, first jack up car and block wheel with as much upward pressure as you can without lifting the car.

▼Attach cardboard gauge to fender and hubcap with tape. Then, remove block and allow wheel to fall.

◄Final step in checking ball joint play is to read gauge.

▼Resin compound is injected into ball joint through nozzle screwed into grease fitting hole. Warning: don't mix compound until the last minute. It will harden if you dally.

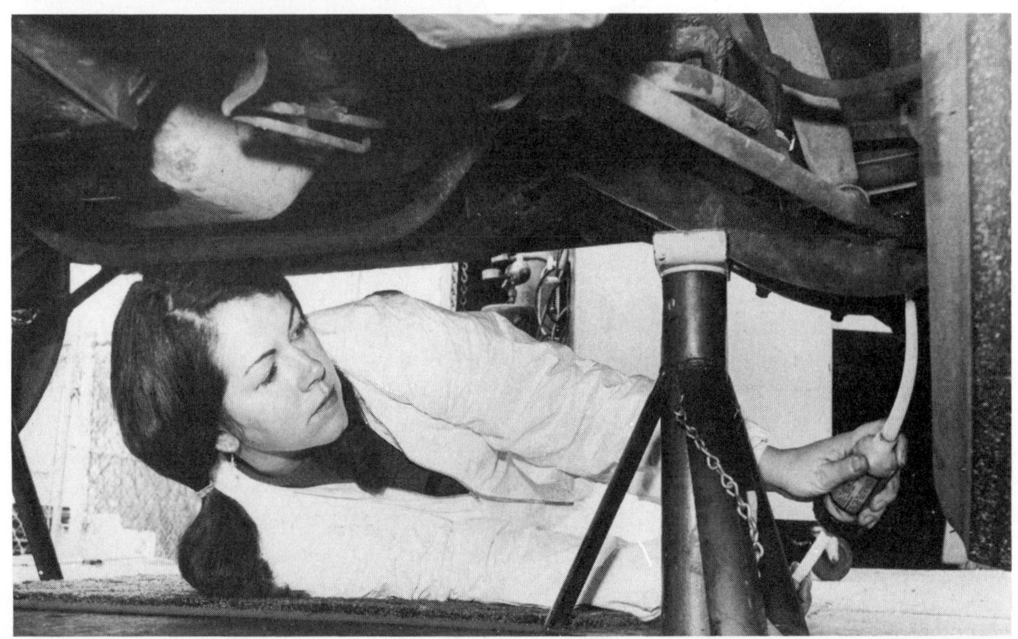

of the resin kit, anywhere the kit is sold, so that you can check the ball joints before you buy the kit. In any case, there is a gauge in the kit, and your car will need an injection sometime, so an investment in the kit should not be wasted. Use of the gauge is illustrated.

If wear exceeds the manufacturer's specifications, the resin kit is not guaranteed to work. However, if the kit will work with $\frac{7}{32}$-inch of play (one manufacturer's maximum specification) on one car, it also will work on another. The kit instructions say that if play exceeds manufacturer's specifications, the ball joints should be replaced. Engineers for one firm which makes the product, have said it will definitely not harm any worn ball joint, even if the wear is beyond specifications. Because replacement ball joints cost three to six times the price of the do-it-yourself kit, the kit is always worth a try.

Instructions furnished with the kit are detailed, but here are some additional pointers:

1. The resin is intended to be injected only into the load-carrying ball joints (the lowers on most cars, the uppers on Chevy II through 1967 and all Ford Fairlane, Comet, Cougar, Mustang, Meteor and Falcon, plus 1968-71 Torino, 1961-66 Thunderbird and 1960-69 International Harvester Travelall). The non-load carrying ball joints normally last the life of the car, particularly if greased every now and then. If they have a grease fitting or lubricating plug, however, they can be treated.

2. The instructions call for a couple of shots of grease to be injected into the ball joint first, so you'll need a hand grease gun. If your car has plugs instead of grease fittings on the ball joints, you'll need a fitting to inject the grease.

3. Make sure that the plastic injection nozzle furnished with the kit will thread into the plug or grease fitting hole after the plug or fitting is removed. If it won't a careful application of rust solvent to the hole's threads, plus turning the plug or fitting in and out should clean them up.

4. The grease fitting or plug hole may be at an awkward angle, making it very difficult to thread in the plastic injection nozzle. The nozzle is flexible, and you may find it easiest to thread it into the hole, bend it out and then onto the injection gun.

5. Never mix the resin compound before you have determined that you can get grease into the ball joint and thread in the nozzle. Once you mix the compound, it begins to harden—in a matter of minutes. If you are prepared, you easily can do both joints in under eight minutes, before the hardening is significant. Once hardening becomes measurable, you won't be able to inject the resin into the joint.

6. Hardening time varies with temperature, taking longer at lower temperature. If you're a methodical worker and want more time "just in case," do the job in lower temperatures. The instructions recommend installation in temperatures of 50 to 90 degrees. You can pick up several extra working minutes if you do the job at 50 instead of 90.

7. Although an overnight curing of the resin injected is recommended, you can hasten the cure if necessary by applying heat to the joint. Two minutes with a propane torch on the ball joint plug will speed the cure to 30 to 60 minutes at 70 degrees air temperature. A few minutes with a woman's hair dryer will reduce curing time to two hours at 70 degrees.

The ball joint compound kit is being marketed through mass merchandisers, where a discount of at least one-third off from list price can be expected. If you do not want to do the job yourself, the service is available in some tire stores and independent shops. P.W.

See also: BEARINGS; ENGINE; POWER BRAKES; POWER STEERING, AUTO.

➤ *This finished basement is typical of what can be done to transform that dank, lightless hole in the ground beneath your house into enjoyable living space. Major ingredients here are overlaid plywood panels, set out from the dark painted wall on 3/8-inch plywood frames and a floor of asphalt tile. Spiral staircase at left is a space saver.*

How to Take Care of Your Basement

If you've got an unfinished basement that's constantly damp, it can be restored to prime condition—or even finished for living

A DAMP CELLAR is a serious condition for any homeowner, especially when the basement can be converted into useful living space with the aid of attractive modern finishing materials like shag foam carpeting for the floor, wood grain wall panels that are immune to rot, and luminous ceilings that give the recreation room a pleasant daytime brightness. But only a dry basement is suitable for finishing as a family room.

Basement seepage can often be stopped or minimized with an application of waterproofing paint, or if there are leaking spots in the foundation wall, a dose or two of epoxy bonding compound, which is a two-part liquid adhesive that cures within 12 hours to form a permanent seal on poured concrete or cinder block walls.

Of course, a basement that is subject to heavy flooding or sewer problems may require an engineering study and extensive work; less extreme conditions possibly can be handled by installing an automatic sump pump, set into a pit in the basement floor. But the common variety of seepage through cracks in a poured concrete foundation wall, porous cinder blocks, and similar conditions usually are corrected with patching and coatings.

Concrete decks. The basement is a box in the ground. Below grade. The floor is a poured concrete deck or slab that caps or seals the foundation limits (the basement walls are built on the foundation or footings), for its part in keeping water and dampness out.

The earth outside is a different story. Some earth drains water, some earth holds water. Even when you don't see water, it is present as moisture. In addition to this ground water, there is ground pressure, the whole thing combining to close in on the intruder, the basement. Thus the basement elements, especially the concrete deck, must be structurally sound and free of faults. Poor construction, aging, earth changes, and nearby water tables can cause cracking, water seepage, moisture and flooding.

When cracks appear on the deck, there is pressure from below. If the cracking is minor, checks itself and does not worsen, the cracks may be treated with a cement patching compound, available in any hardware store. The technique is similar to spackling a plaster wall, and it will effectively plug anything from hairline cracks to moderately wide and deep cracks.

If the original cracks worsen or if new cracks appear after patching the old ones, the entire deck has to be strengthened with a new layer of cement—about two inches reinforced with wire. While this may be a job for a pro, it is possible to do it yourself with care. This new cap will also solve any "dusting" problems you may have had.

Basement walls. Basement walls are built on footings (the deck is poured after the walls are up) and consist these days of cement blocks; older homes will have poured concrete walls. The outer walls are coated with a sealer by the builder, then earth (and, frequently, building construction de-

Water, water everywhere. Getting your basement reasonably dry and keeping it that way is essential if you intend to refinish it.

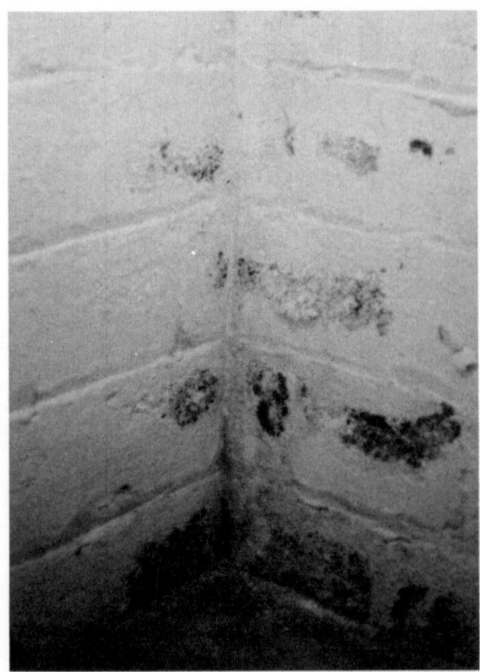

Seeping moisture has caused ordinary paint on this cinderblock basement wall to discolor and peel. Before the wall is resealed with basement paint or an epoxy sealer, the existing paint must be removed completely. This can be done with a wire brush. Oil paint can be burned off with a torch.

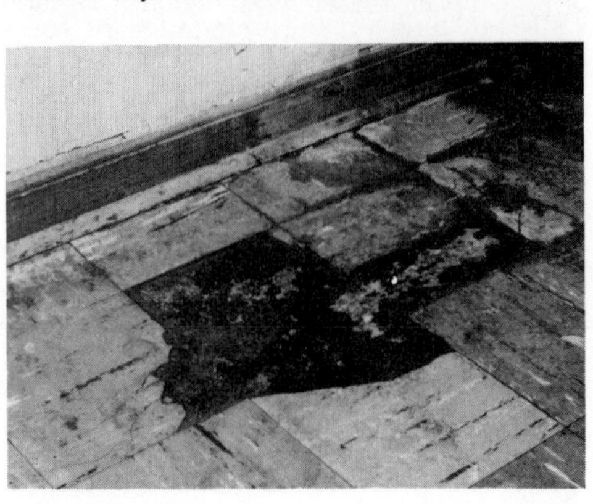

Baseboard and tile floor show heavy damage from water that has seeped into basement.

bris) is piled against the outside. Water in time works on these coatings and there are occasional breaks, but the more vulnerable spot is at the base of the wall where water collects in air spaces created by the old debris. Thus leakage will occur at the deck-to-wall joint. It may also build up and stain the lower section of the basement wall.

Recapping the deck, as described earlier, also caps this joint and solves the problem. If the deck is not recapped, the joint can be skinned over or sealed with one of the epoxy sealers, available in cans from the hardware store. There is also a cement curb which can be installed along the floor-to-wall line, but this requires forms which may prove too much a bother. The commercial sealers are good and convenient.

The alternative to this remedy is an enormous project involving the removal of earth from the outside of the house, the removal of the debris at the base of the foundation walls, the drying out of everything, and the recoating of the exterior wall. However, this waterproofing method is absolute. Perhaps it is a vacation project.

Dampness beyond any outright leakage can often be managed by proper ventilation. Humidity can be controlled with a humidifier, eliminating condensation when the warm air hits the cold deck. Exposed

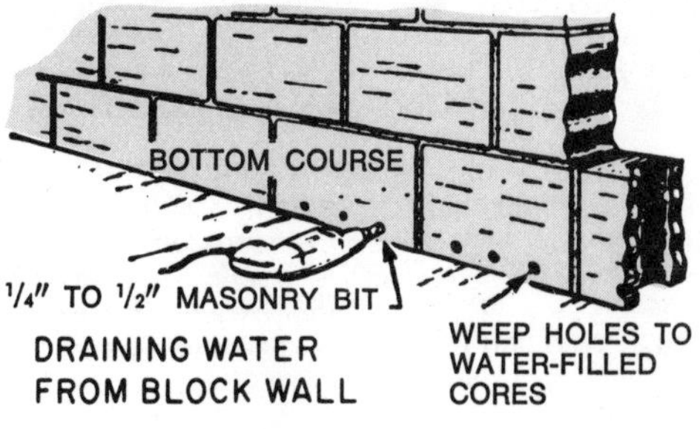

Sometimes ground water accumulates in the hollow cores of masonry blocks in the lower courses of basement walls. If you're using epoxy sealer, drain the blocks by drilling holes into the cores with a 1/4 to 1/2-inch masonry bit.

pipes can also be wrapped in felt and taped. Standard basement windows can be replaced with louvers—or one pane in a standard window can be replaced with a silent exhaust fan.

Assuming the basement is unfinished, much can be done to button it up in the way of improvements: finished walls and a tile floor are often all that's needed to make everything watertight.

Walls, for example, require simple stud framing (the air space), followed by an insulation material (such as sheet foam), followed by a vapor barrier (such as builder's paper), followed by the finished paneling. Some of these products come with the insulation and barrier layers bonded to the underside of the paneling; insulation comes with the vapor barrier bonded. Whatever the combination, the total effect is a triple layer that fights dampness, at the same time finishing off an unused or formerly unattractive space. If the basement wall also had asphalt paint on it, then that makes four layers of protection.

Tiling the floor is the equivalent of sealing the deck—and then some. The original cracks should be patched, then the whole deck buttered with bonding cement, followed by ⅛-inch vinyl tiles. That is a good seal.

Routine patching. There are other routine patching jobs. First, inspect all the basement windows, particularly the sealed area between the metal or wooden window frame and the foundation wall. Poke a nail in the area and test for softness, flaking, or crumbled bits. Clean the space thoroughly, dampen it with a sponge, and fill in with fresh mortar mix.

While at the window, also check for hairline cracks starting at the corners of the window installation. Clean and chip, as necessary, and fill these cracks.

Next, examine all of the points on the foundation walls where pipes or conduit enter or leave—the main drains, the water intake line, the natural gas intake line, the conduit for the power lines, the vent or exhaust pipes for the clothes dryer. These are all points of possible water entry and must be thoroughly sealed. So once again chip away old matter and butter the cavity with fresh mix.

Large chunks take a little more care. A hole on the flat will have to be built up in the same way a deep hole in a plaster wall is filled—a little bit at a time, let dry, then add more until it is flush with the surface.

Breaks at inside corners can be treated in the same way. However, missing chunks at outside corners need an extra step. Place a flat board against one side of the outside corner, propping it securely. Then fill the space from the other side. It is not necessary to fill all the way; it is better to do it partially, then after it dries, transfer the board to the other side and repeat the technique. Removing the board after the second step, there may still be surface im-

If using a roller to apply basement wall paint, cut in around ceiling, baseboards and corners with a two-inch brush, then roll paint on remaining area with back and forth strokes. Cross roll for better coverage, and finish by rolling all strokes in the same direction.

Wash down the wall with a light spray from a garden hose before applying waterproofing basement paint. If you're using an epoxy sealer however, do the opposite. Make sure the wall is dry before you apply it. Wait for several consecutive dry days to pass before doing the job.

When applying basement paint with a brush, start at the top and work down in three-foot sections. Work the paint into pits in the block, brushing it back and forth in a scrubbing motion. Use final vertical strokes that blend the paint into previously-coated sections.

perfections. These can then be covered with a third application, as with a minor crack.

Ideally, all patches should be sealed with a good sealer or concrete paint (such as asphalt paint). Overlap the patches liberally, spreading the paint onto unaffected wall areas as well as onto the pipe or conduit.

If dampness is minor, resulting only from seepage through a porous wall, waterproofing with a cement bonding paint may do the trick. One coat often will be sufficient, applied with a stiff bristle brush to the wall which has been sprayed lightly with the garden hose. The wall must be unpainted, or all old paint completely removed.

A more drastic solution is to paint the seepage area with a two-part epoxy sealer.

Leaks through cracks or other openings are sealed with epoxy cement. Timing and preparation are all-important to successful application. Surfaces must be absolutely dry. Any previous paint should be scraped and brushed off with a stiff wire brush. Pick a dry day to put on the epoxy, with the temperature above 45 degrees. For quicker setting, 70 degrees is better.

Dry out any wet spots, using a gasoline or butane torch, a photo floodlight, or sun lamp. If there is a persistent leak at any one spot, enlarge the hole a bit with a chisel and plug it with hydraulic cement, which can be used even when there is running water. Hold the cement in place until it has begun to harden.

Applying epoxy sealer. The epoxy comes in small containers for mixing batches small enough to be handled at one time without interruption—the cement hardens in 15 minutes and becomes unworkable. For mixing, open both containers—the resin and the hardener. Pour all the hardener into the resin can, so that there is the correct proportion of both parts, which is an important detail. Stir

If cement floor is treated with a hardener, it must be scrubbed with a muriatic acid solution. Rinse and let it dry thoroughly before starting to paint.

Use ordinary deck paint on stairs. Start from the top and work down. If there is no other exit, paint alternate steps. When these are dry, paint the remaining steps.

vigorously for two minutes with a clean stick or paint paddle.

Apply with an old paint brush—or buy a cheap 2½ or 3-inch nylon brush, which you can discard after use. Have some lacquer thinner at hand, which is the solvent for the epoxy, for cleaning up afterwards. Brush on in generous amount, covering not only the immediate area of the leak, but also about a foot beyond the margin. Hairline cracks that are too narrow to chisel should be given a generous coat of epoxy to form a surface seal.

You can apply a second coat if desired to reinforce the coating. However, if water returns before the epoxy sets, it will poke holes through the soft coating; in that event, wait until the area has completely dried, then put on a new coat of sealer. The epoxy dries to a shiny amber color, and may be painted with either epoxy or latex paint.

A final word about permanent flooding problems. Many homeowners have to live with periodic basement flooding whenever there is a heavy downpour. Their houses are situated on ground that promotes this condition despite efforts to keep things dry. A sump pump is a practical answer: basically a hole in the basement floor that collects water, then pumps it out of the house. Things are still damp, but they're not flooded.

▲ *Unlike ordinary basement paint, epoxy sealer requires a dry surface rather than a damp one for application. It's best to wait for a few consecutive dry days before starting to paint. Spots that are still damp can be dried by the flame of a torch.*

▼ *One method of handling water seepage is to install a pump, especially in areas where cellar flooding is common after heavy rains. The pump is installed in a sump cut in the basement floor. It operates automatically as water flows into the sump.*

Batteries come in many shapes, sizes, capacities, and construction features. This one has a prismatic cell cap for a visual indication of whether or not water is needed.

Guarding Your Car's Battery

Get more life and reliability out of your battery with a few simple maintenance procedures

PITY THE POOR car battery. At best it is ignored by its owner; at worst it is abused brutally. And yet it takes its punishment stoically, with hardly a complaint.

Toward the very end of its life, the battery tries to warn its owner in a tactful way—perhaps by sulfating its posts or by faltering momentarily when cranking the engine. At last, after perhaps two years of thankless toil, it abruptly expires. Has its owner learned his lesson? Hardly. He simply buys a new battery to abuse.

Fortunately, the battery manufacturers have given up on the average motorist and are busily developing permanently sealed batteries that will hold up. In fact, your car may have a sealed battery, but more likely it does not.

If it doesn't, you should give the battery some service. It requires very little—just keep it reasonably clean, satisfy its modest thirst, check its strength occasionally and extend a few other common sense courtesies.

To better understand a battery's needs, you first must understand what it is and how it works. To begin with, a battery doesn't manufacture electrical energy; it simply stores it, and then delivers it on demand. Energy is fed into a battery in the form of direct-current electricity, stored in the form of chemical energy, and released again as direct-current electricity. When a battery is accepting current, it is "charging"; delivering current, it is "discharging."

A battery consists of several cells, each containing two groups of plates made of unlike metals. These plates are immersed in electrolyte, a chemical solution that reacts with them chemically. In the lead-acid automotive battery, the positive plate is made up of lead peroxide; the negative plate is made up of a different form of lead oxide called sponge lead. Though both of these materials basically are lead, they react like unlike metals. When they are submerged in the electrolyte—a solution of sulfuric acid and water—a voltage is set up and electrical current flows when the circuit is completed. During discharge, the sulfuric acid combines with the active materials in the positive and negative plates and gradually changes both to lead sulfate. If this change is allowed to go on to completion, the battery no longer has two dissimilar metals, and electrical current no longer flows. The battery is then completely discharged.

A discharged battery must be recharged before it can deliver electricity again. This is done by applying direct current from an external source (the car generator or alternator, or a plug-in battery charger) to the battery terminals. From the terminals the current passes through the battery, in the opposite direction to the current flow when the battery is discharging. This restores the sulfated plates to their original forms—the positive plates to lead peroxide, the negative plates to sponge lead—while the sulfuric acid returns to the electrolyte. With two unlike metals in an acid solution, the battery is ready to deliver electricity again.

This cycle can't repeat itself indefinitely. Sometimes, as the plates turn to lead sulfate, large, hard crystals form that can't be broken down by recharging. Also, some of the plate material occasionally flakes off the plates and sinks to the bottom of the battery. If enough of this material accumulates, it can short-circuit a cell. Also, a battery can suffer internal damage from excessively high temperatures, rough treatment, and other causes.

Measuring a battery's strength. Acid is heavier than water. Thus, when all the acid returns to the electrolyte during recharging, the electrolyte becomes heavier. This change can be measured in terms of specific gravity—the weight of the electrolyte as compared with an equal volume of water. From this it follows that the specific gravity of the electrolyte is an excellent indication of the state of charge of a battery.

Here is where the hydrometer comes in. A simple, inexpensive instrument, it is a wise investment for any motorist. It consists of a calibrated float in a syringe-like glass or transparent plastic tube, into which a sample of the electrolyte in each battery cell can be drawn with a rubber suction ball. When specific gravity is high, the float rises higher in the electrolyte than when specific gravity is low.

At 80° F. the specific gravity of the electrolyte in a fully-charged battery should be 1.260 or higher; discharged, 1.160 or lower. (Deduct .004 from these figures for each 10° that the battery exceeds 80°; add .004 for each 10° below 80°.) All cells should test within .050 of each other. A greater variation indicates the battery must be replaced.

A discharged battery will freeze more easily in winter. For example, a battery with a hydrometer reading of 1.140 will freeze at 8° F., while a battery with a 1.280 reading will freeze at *minus* 92°. A hydrometer check every few weeks can help extend battery life and prevent annoying failures.

A small charger is helpful, especially in winter or whenever heavy demands are made on the battery.

Such home chargers, however, are not too effective for recharging a badly run-

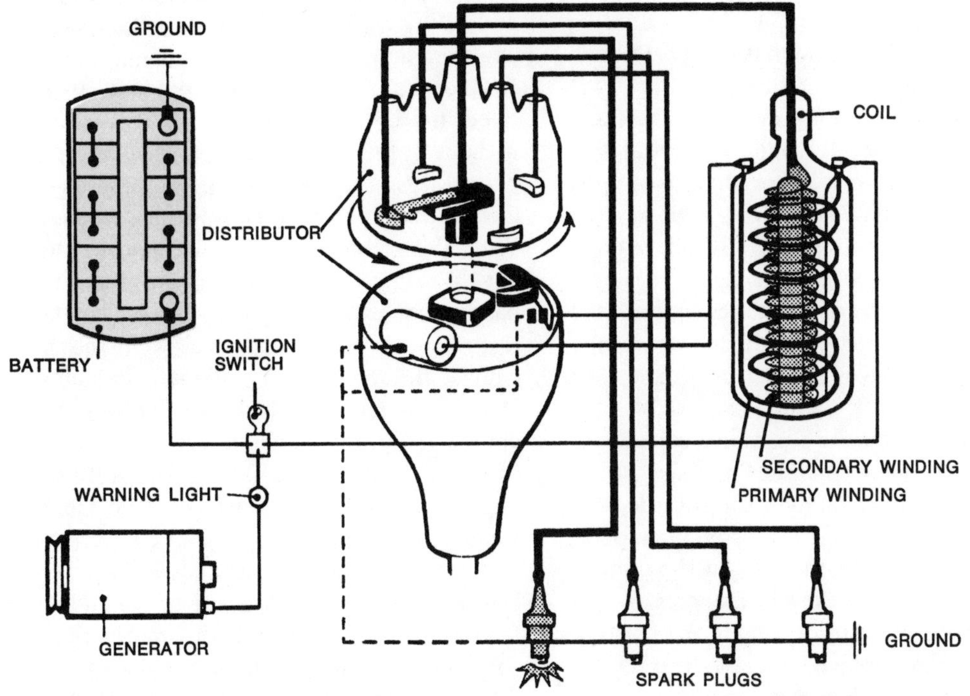

Heart of the ignition system is the battery, which supplies the spark that ignites the fuel mixture in the cylinders. While the engine is running, the generator or alternator generates electrical power.

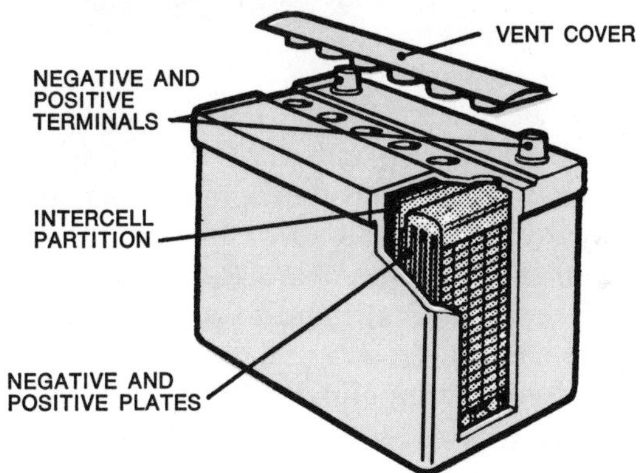

Basic battery components are shown here. Multiply the number of cells by two to determine voltage. The capacity depends on the size and number of the plates.

down battery. Here a larger commercial charger, as found in service stations, is needed. If possible, have the battery slow-charged; this may take from 12 to 24 hours. In cases of urgency, a fast charge (30 to 90 minutes) may be applied to get the battery up to about 70 or 80 percent of capacity. There is no risk of damage provided the battery is healthy and the current is reduced progressively. Careful supervision is necessary to make sure the battery temperature doesn't exceed 125° F. Excessive temperatures can buckle and ruin the plates.

Before placing the battery back in service, check the voltage regulator and generator or alternator output against the manufacturer's specs: too low an output causes discharging, while too high an output raises the battery temperature and increases chemical activity; either way the battery can suffer permanent damage.

Buying a battery. If your battery is defective and must be replaced, what should you look for in a new one? The first consideration, obviously, is outside dimensions. The new battery must fit the holder; a loose, improperly-mounted battery will quickly bounce itself to death.

Secondly, the voltage must be right. Each cell in a car battery puts out about two volts; thus a six-volt battery has three cells, a 12-volt battery has six cells. All modern domestic cars and practically all imports have 12-volt electrical systems.

For many years, batteries have been rated according to their ability, when fully charged, to deliver a specified quantity of electricity over a definite period of time (usually 20 hours). Basically, capacity is determined by the number and size of the plates and by the amount of sulfuric acid in the electrolyte. It is expressed in ampere-hours, a unit of measure obtained by multiplying the current flow in amperes by the time in hours during which the current flows. For example, a battery delivering five amperes for 20 hours has a 100-ampere-hour capacity.

Battery capacity also is rated in watts. The "Peak Watts Rating" is a measurement of starting power, with 3,000 the normally required Peak Watts Rating for the battery needed by the average car.

In fact, the Peak Watts Rating was the first successful attempt to supplant the amp-hour rating. After all, what you want is a measurement of starting power, not the ability of the battery to deliver a small amount of current over a 20-hour period. The amp-hour rating might be a convenient way of telling if your battery will have any juice left if you leave the parking lights on overnight, but that is about all.

There actually is a rating that gives you an indication of starting power. Called the "Five-Second Voltage," it indicates the number of volts the battery can maintain at zero degrees after a starting drain of 150 amps.

A good battery would have a rating of 9.4 to 10.2 volts. Of course, starting amperage draw is greater than 150 (more like 350-500 amps), but at least this rating tells you something.

Under a newer system, the battery is rated in amperes discharged in 30 seconds without voltage dropping to less than 1.2 per cell (7.2 for the battery)—high enough to start the car until perhaps the last second. With this system, a good battery would have a rating in excess of 375, a premium battery in excess of 450. To calculate reserve capacity, another newer rating counts the number of minutes a fully-charged battery at 80° F. will deliver 25 amps—indicating how long you can drive a car with a defective generator and still use important accessories, such as windshield wipers, lights, etc.

A replacement battery should have at least as great a capacity as the original one. If your engine isn't in the best mechanical condition and requires lots of cranking, or if you've added electrical accessories since buying the car, splurge for a greater capacity (heavy-duty) battery. An under-powered, bargain-basement battery is no bargain; it will give poor service right from the start, and will fail sooner.

Mounting the battery. Secure the battery hold-down straps snugly, but not so tightly as to crack the battery case. Examine the battery cables, and replace them if they are suspect. Remove corrosion from terminals by dipping them in a solution of sodium bicarbonate and water and then flushing with clean water. If necessary, wire brush the terminals and battery posts lightly for good electrical contact. If the terminals fit the posts too loosely, wind copper wire tightly around the posts. Attach the ground cable last to avoid short circuits. (When removing the battery, reverse this procedure and loosen the ground cable first.)

Once the terminals are on clean and tight, lightly coat them and the top of the battery post with petroleum jelly. Do not apply this coating to the sides of the battery

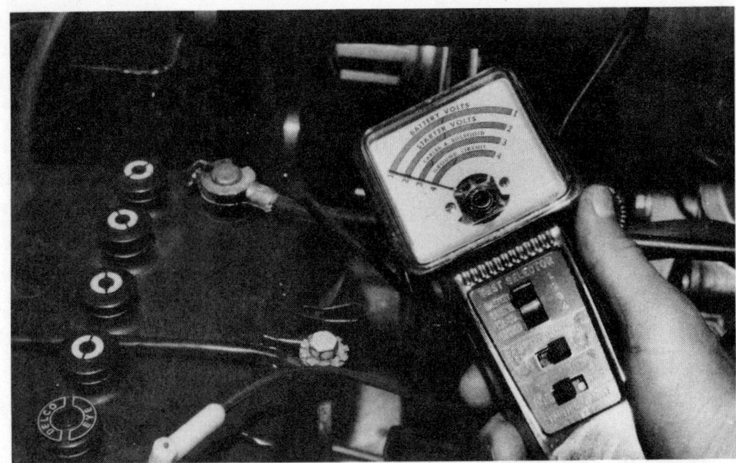

If a battery is questionable, it should be checked with a battery-starter tester. One shown is an inexpensive type that a weekend mechanic might consider.

posts before the terminals are attached, or you will impede current flow.

On General Motors cars with the sealed side terminals, the only service necessary is to occasionally check the cable terminal for corrosion and wire brush if necessary, making certain the terminal is tight. Don't grease anything.

Once the battery is installed, make sure connections are made properly. Turning on the headlights should show a discharge reading on your ammeter (if you're lucky enough to have one in your car) or, with ignition key on and the engine not running, should cause your generator warning light to glow. If the ammeter shows charge or the warning light doesn't glow, turn the battery around and switch the connections. Finally, smear the terminals and posts with petroleum jelly to reduce corrosion.

Keeping your battery healthy. Check the electrolyte level in each cell at least twice a month (more often during hot weather or fast, long-distance driving). As electricity passes through the cells, some of the water in the electrolyte is converted into hydrogen and oxygen gases and escapes through the vent holes in the battery caps. Normally a battery uses only a slight amount of water every few weeks. An excessive thirst indicates overcharging; check the electrical system.

Experts disagree on whether ordinary tap water may be added to a battery. Some say naturally soft, clear tap water is acceptable, but most recommend using distilled water (sold in auto accessory stores), rain water gathered in non-metallic containers, or clean melted snow. Rather than letting a service station attendant fill your battery, you'd be wise to carry your own plastic bottle of distilled water in the trunk. Never add acid to a battery; this subjects the plates to higher current densities, causing faster deterioration.

Check electrolyte level with a flashlight if necessary, but never with a match or other open flame; gases produced by batteries are highly explosive. Most batteries have markers to show proper electrolyte level. If yours doesn't, fill each cell no more than ⅜-inch above the plates. When the electrolyte level drops below the tops of the plates, the concentration of acid increases dangerously. Overfilling also is harmful. As battery temperatures rise, the electrolyte expands until it overflows through the vents. It then can form a bridge on top of the battery across which current can flow, draining the battery. Or it may damage the battery holder, body panels, and engine.

Special battery fillers are available that stop water flow automatically when proper electrolyte level has been reached. In a pinch, use your hydrometer to fill the battery. Pouring in water from a cup or bottle is unwise; the flow is hard to control.

In cold weather, add water only if you plan to run the car immediately afterward. Otherwise the water may freeze and crack the battery case. Also, do not take hydrometer reading immediately after adding water.

Those "miraculous" additives. Notwithstanding the fantastic claims made by manufacturers of various battery additives, none of these products has been proved effective in rejuvenating or extending the life of a healthy battery; more likely, additives will ruin your battery and void the warranty.

If the electrolyte level in one cell drops faster than in the others, suspect a leak. Small cracks in the battery case can be sealed with pitch or commercial sealer applied with a soldering gun. A large crack will necessitate replacement of the battery. Only when refilling a repaired cell should you use an acid solution. Check with a hydrometer to make sure you get the right concentration.

Besides checking electrolyte level, and state of charge and cleaning away corrosion, what else can you do to add years to the life of your battery? For one thing, you can keep your engine well-tuned and your starter motor in top condition to reduce current drain during starting. Also, remember the following driving hints:

Before starting the engine, shut off headlights and other electrical equipment. If you have a manual transmission, shift into neutral and hold the clutch disengaged. Cold, viscous transmission oil puts a considerable drag on transmission gears; but with the clutch (and transmission) disengaged, the starter motor has to crank just the engine.

On cold days, keep the battery warm, if possible. A fully charged battery at 0° F. loses 60 percent of the cranking power it has at 80°; and an engine at 0° requires two and a half times as much starting power as at 80°. That's why a weak battery may get you through the summer, but will fail during the first cold snap. Inexpensive battery warmers that plug into a household outlet are available.

In slow-moving, stop-and-go traffic, especially at night, when headlights are in use, avoid using other electrical accessories if possible. When traffic comes to a stop for a few minutes, switch down from headlights to parking lights (but don't forget to switch back when you start moving).

Jumper cables are good to have in your trunk—just in case. If you should have to use them, be sure you wire the posts of the two batteries from positive to positive and negative to negative; otherwise the wiring and other components may be damaged. The posts of most batteries are marked.

According to battery manufacturers, the average life of a car battery is 26 months. And yet some savvy motorists have squeezed five years' service from their batteries—evidence that a little tender loving care pays big benefits. P. W.

See also: ELECTRICAL, AUTO; ENGINE; SPARK PLUG; STARTER.

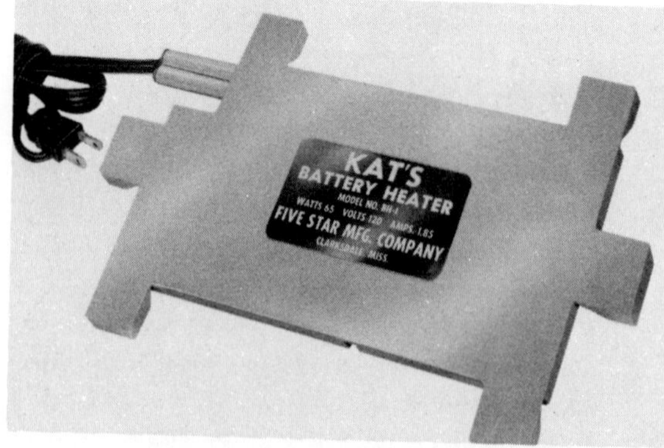

If you live in a very cold area, a battery heater can make winter starting easier. The battery heater is placed in the bottom of the battery case, the battery sits on it, and the heater is plugged into a household outlet.

Servicing Your Car's Wheel Bearings

Inspect these key parts regularly to keep your steering precise and prevent failure

▲ *Quick check for front wheel bearings is to grasp wheel at top and bottom and try to rock in and out. If you can feel play, wheel bearings should be inspected.*

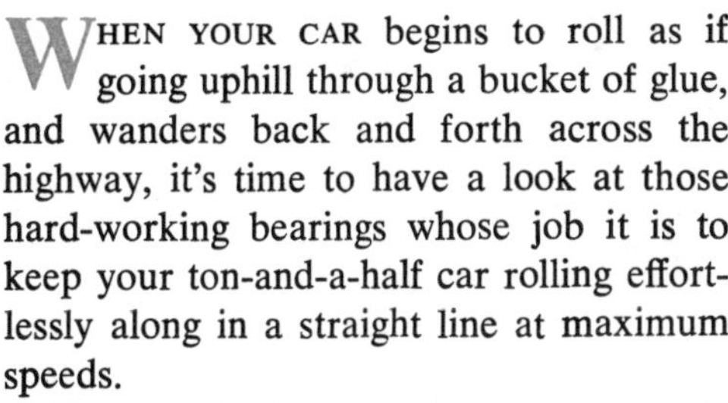

WHEN YOUR CAR begins to roll as if going uphill through a bucket of glue, and wanders back and forth across the highway, it's time to have a look at those hard-working bearings whose job it is to keep your ton-and-a-half car rolling effortlessly along in a straight line at maximum speeds.

These periodic inspections and adjustments are your best safeguard against bearing failure when you can least afford it. Only the front wheels need to be inspected because only they are adjustable. Rear wheel bearings are usually not disturbed unless there is some specific reason for removing them, and, once removed, they are replaced.

To inspect your front wheel bearings, first block the car so it will not roll, and then jack up a front wheel, supporting it so the wheel can be removed. Take off the wheel cover, dust cover, cotter pin, adjusting nut (be careful, it might be a left-hand thread), and flat washer. Then carefully remove the wheel, hub and bearings at one time.

Next, lift out the small bearings at the outer end of the hub and turn the wheel over to remove the rest of the bearing assembly. First pry out the oil seal and lift out the large bearing; then remove the bearing cups.

When the bearing is removed, note the color and odor of the grease. If it looks burned—almost black—or has an acrid odor, it is a dead giveaway that the bearing has been running hot. If the grease looks and smells normal, clean each part of the bearing assembly in solvent and allow to

Start by prying off metal dust cover.

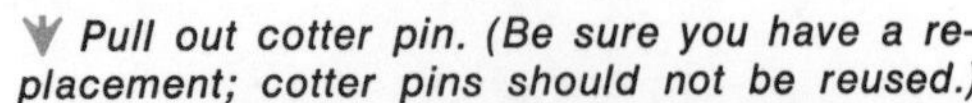

Pull out cotter pin. (Be sure you have a replacement; cotter pins should not be reused.)

Remove nut lock and then unthread castellated nut.

Pull out on wheel and outer wheel bearing will pop out as shown.

With wheel off, turn it over and pry out grease seal to gain access to inner wheel bearing. Parts in typical assembly are as shown.

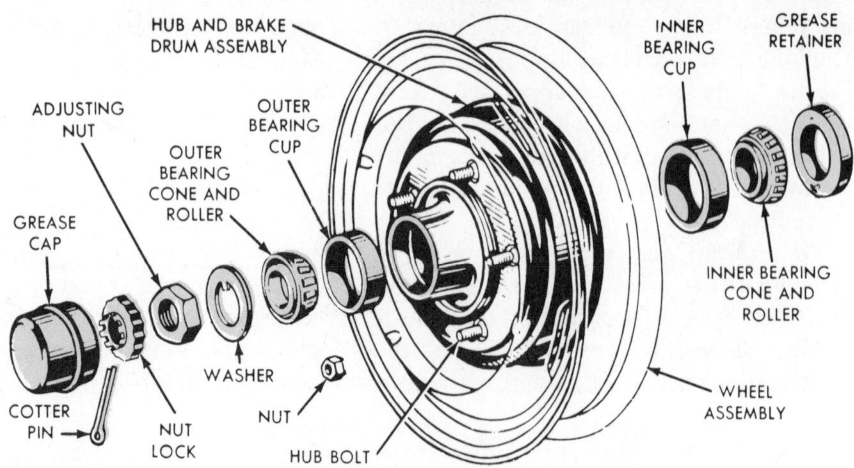

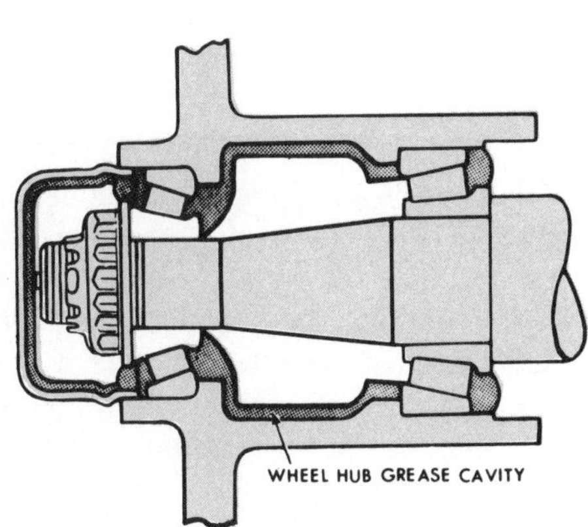

Wheel hub grease cavity should be cleaned with solvent and repacked. Best method is with special tool with bearings back in place. Otherwise, just coat cavity surfaces generously.

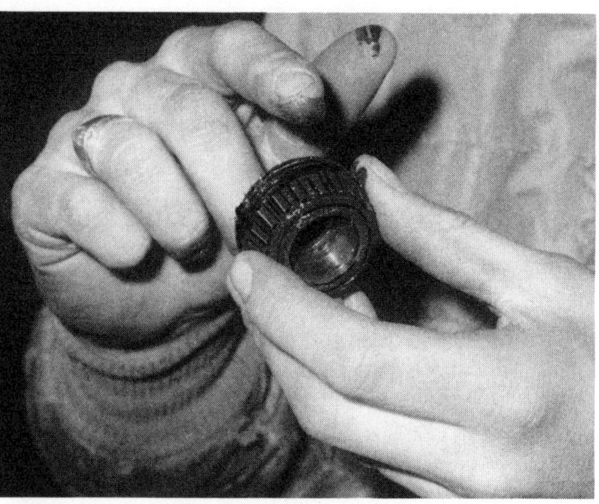

***Above:** Wheel bearings should be cleaned in solvent, and allowed to air dry; then coat with wheel bearing grease as shown. **Below:** Torque wrench in position for adjustment of wheel bearings to manufacturer's specifications.*

dry. Do not dry the bearings by *spinning* them with a blast from an air hose as it will drive grit into the bearings.

When the bearings and cups are clean and dry, check them for signs of *brinnelling* or *spalling*. These are just two of the several ways in which wheel bearings are damaged or worn. Brinnelling is a series of indentations where the rollers have slammed into the surface of the cup (caused by severe impact, such as when a wheel goes into a rut in the road). Spalling appears as chipping or crumbling on the small ends of roller bearings (caused by excessive clearance).

Fractures will appear as fine hairline cracks across the surface of the cup or cone. These are usually a result of forcing bearings onto oversize spindles, forcing cups into warped hubs, or improperly seating the cups.

Corrosion results in pits or pock-marks and appears similar to spalling, but is located at random along the bearings and cups. It is usually an indication that moisture or road chemicals have entered the bearing through a defective seal and have contaminated the bearing grease. It is also possible for corrosion to be caused by handling a bearing when all of the oil has been washed from its surface. Ordinary perspiration is often highly corrosive, so it is good practice to handle clean bearings with a dry, lint-free cloth.

End wear is also similar to spalling, but appears on the large ends of roller bearings. It is generally caused by too-tight bearing adjustments, resulting in insufficient clearance.

Dangerous dirt. If you find any of these defects, replace the entire bearing assembly. Never replace just one or two parts as the reason for failure in one part was very likely working on the entire assembly. Also, keep the workbench, tools, lubricant, and your hands free of dirt and grime when working with bearings. Grit is the mortal enemy of free-rolling, long-lasting bearings.

When installing replacement bearings, no on-the-spot lubrication is necessary. All new bearings are prelubricated to be used just as they come from the box. Old bearings that are in good condition should be repacked with special wheel-bearing grease.

Before refitting the bearings, clean out the bearing cavity with solvent. Make sure you have a tube of wheel-bearing grease to coat the bearing cavity. Coat the cavity, then install the bearings.

Reassembly. Check the replacement races and bearings against the old parts to be sure you have the right ones. Install the races and large bearing. Then dab the seal with clean oil and start it into the hub by hand, with lip positioned. The oil will make the seal slide on the spindle easily, preventing damage during reassembly, and will also make it soft and effective as a seal immediately. Never install a seal with just a hammer or use a steel punch which could damage the casing and cause leakage. Under no circumstances ever attempt to reuse a seal. Mount the wheel carefully to avoid tearing the seal on the spindle and install the outer bearing, washer, and adjusting nut.

Adjustment. The most common forms of adjustment are illustrated in this article. In all of these, the amount of tension applied on the thrust washer by an adjusting nut is set to the manufacturer's specifications, or according to feel for lack of free play and smooth rotation of the wheel. Adjustment by feel, although reasonably accurate and practical, should be done only if a torque wrench is not available.

Note: cars with tapered roller bearings should only be set with a torque wrench if the car maker specifies a torque setting to seat the bearings.

Tapered roller bearings can be damaged by improper installation very easily.

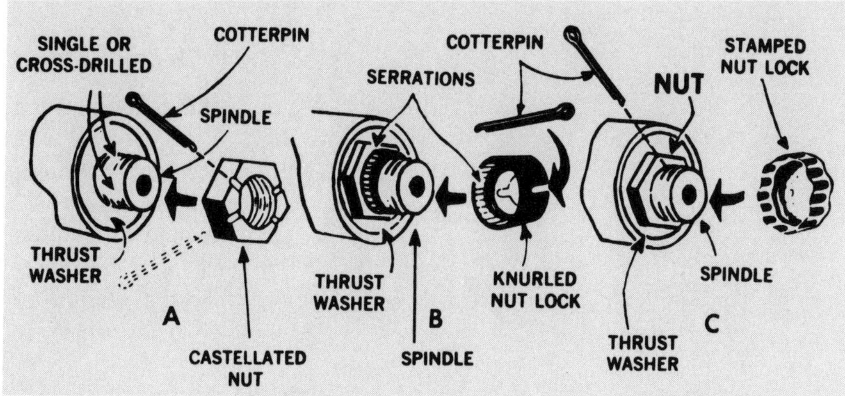

Different methods of retaining wheel and bearings are illustrated.

To adjust a bearing by feel, first seat the bearing assembly by tightening the nut with a long wrench until you feel a definite resistance while rotating the wheel. Then loosen the nut and run it up again finger-tight. Continue tightening it with the pliers, rotating the wheel and checking for free play constantly with your other hand. Stop tightening at the point where free play has just been eliminated. Be careful not to overtighten the bearing, mistaking looseness, at the ball joint for free play.

Now spin the wheel, stopping at several points to check for free play, and, if necessary, tighten the nut to eliminate it. Never back off more than one slot on the nut to get to the point where free play is eliminated. If the bearing becomes too tight, back the nut off to finger-tight and start over.

Torque wrench adjustment. The exact procedure for torque wrench adjustment varies according to make of car. Here are the procedures for popular late-model cars:

Ford products: With wheel rotating, tighten adjusting nut to 17 to 25 ft./lbs. Back adjustment nut off ½ turn. Tighten adjusting nut to just one ft./lb. Install the lock nut and a new cotter pin.

Chrysler products: Tighten bearing nut to seven ft./lbs. while rotating wheel. Position nut lock so that a pair of slots lines up with the cotter pin hole. Back off the nut lock (with the nut inside it) one slot, then install the cotter pin.

Chevrolet: Tighten bearing nut to 12 ft./lbs. while rotating wheel. Back off adjusting nut one flat and attempt to insert cotter pin. If the slot and pin hole do not line up, back off the nut until they do (an additional ½ flat turn or less should do it).

Not all car makers specify a torque wrench setting, and in some cases, the nut is never to be torqued.

Cars equipped with disc brakes on the front wheels pose a special problem insofar as wheel bearing service is concerned: the caliper and disc must come off.

This means that you must remove the wheel first by unbolting it from the wheel hub.

On older cars with fixed caliper disc brakes, removing the caliper may be a chore. If possible, hang the caliper with wire from the front suspension, so you do not have to disconnect a brake line (which would force you to bleed the brakes).

Under no circumstances should you let the caliper dangle by a brake hose. This is a sure-fire way to cause a premature brake hose failure.

If you find shims under the heads of the bolts that attach the caliper to the front suspension, you must refit them as they were, for they center the caliper over the disc.

Once the caliper is off, pull the dust cap from the disc and proceed as with drum brakes.

P.W.

See also: BALL JOINTS; POWER STEERING, AUTO.

How to Change Engine Bearings

This job is often easier than it sounds—it all depends on how hard it is to drop the oil pan—and doing-it-yourself can save a sizeable mechanic's bill

MOST WEEKEND MECHANICS think of engine bearings as little as possible, and then merely as the super-smooth supports for the engine's moving parts. The reasoning is that bearings are nothing for the weekend mechanic to worry about because they should last a long time, and if they don't, there is nothing he can do about it. But good maintenance practices will prolong bearing life, and if replacement is necessary for the most heavily loaded bearings—those on the crankshaft—the job often can be done by a weekend mechanic without exotic tools. Even if you have the work done by a professional, you should know what is involved and what types of crankshaft bearings are available for installation.

Let's review crankshaft properties:

Load-carrying ability. The downward pressure on the piston of the exploding gasoline mixture is transmitted by the connecting rod to the crankshaft. This pressure creates a load which must be carried by the bearings within the connecting rod and the crankshaft support caps (called the main bearing caps). The more powerful the engine, the greater the pressure developed by the exploding gasoline mixture, and the greater load.

High fatigue strength. The ability of the bearing to withstand the cumulative effect of a repeatedly applied force. In other words, the bearing can take a lot of pounding without getting "tired." (In the case of a bearing, when it gets "tired," it cracks.) The higher the fatigue strength, the longer the bearing will last under a certain load.

Slipperiness. When the engine is being cranked, and under other severe conditions, there is no oil film to provide lubrication. So the bearing surfaces must have a natural slipperiness, to avoid scoring the journals (the mirror-smooth round surfaces of the crankshaft, around which the bearings are fitted).

Corrosion resistance. As a result of combustion, corrosive agents are formed in the oil pan. The engine oil contains additives that neutralize these corrosive agents, but if the additives are used up, the bearing itself must be resistant to corrosion.

Ability to withstand high temperatures. Crankcase temperatures can exceed 200 degrees, which can affect the strength of a bearing material.

Conformability. Manufacturing tolerances prevent the bearing surface from being exactly parallel with the journal surface it supports. The ability of a bearing material to "creep" or "flow" to be reasonably parallel is called conformability.

Heat transfer. Both the oil and the bearings must transfer heat from the cylinders. The bearing must do its part of the job.

No one metal can do everything, so bearings are made of layers of different metals. The usual procedure is to use a steel backing for maximum overall strength and a top layer of babbitt, an alloy of tin and lead. Babbitt has superb natural slipperiness and conformability, making it an ideal bearing material in these respects. It also has good "embeddability," which means it can "absorb" dirt particles so they can't score journals. (With today's oil filters, embeddability isn't overly significant, but it's helpful in cases where the oil filter isn't changed at proper intervals.)

Unfortunately, babbitt has relatively low fatigue strength and load-carrying ability. So a layer of babbitt on a steel back would work only in light-duty applications. In such cases, either a lead-base or tin-base babbitt is used. The lead base has a slightly higher load-carrying ability.

Today's powerful engines use bearings with a layer of a secondary bearing material between a thin babbitt outer layer and the steel backing. This design serves two

These are the engine's main and connecting rod bearings. The eight sets of connecting rod bearings and five sets of main bearings are for typical V-8.

purposes: The thin babbitt layer (.0005 to .0015 inch) actually has a higher fatigue strength than a thick layer; that is, it is less prone to cracking. However, once the babbitt layer wears through, there has to be a reasonably suitable bearing surface. The usual choices for the second bearing layer are sintered (powdered) copper-lead, aluminum alloy, cadmium nickel and cast copper-lead. It is the second layer that essentially determines the bearing's load-carrying ability.

Cadmium nickel has better fatigue strength and load-carrying ability than babbitt, but isn't as slippery, doesn't conform as well, and has far less embeddability. It is sometimes plated with indium for greater corrosion resistance.

Aluminum alloy: a very satisfactory bearing material for medium to fairly heavy-duty use.

Sintered copper-lead: not as slippery as babbitt, but good fatigue strength and load-carrying ability; fine for medium-duty use.

Cast copper-lead: the super-heavy-duty material. It has the highest fatigue strength and load-carrying ability. A nickel barrier of 30 to 50 millionths of an inch separates the babbitt outer layer from the cast copper-lead, to prevent a metallurgical combination of the two layers, which would destroy them both.

Choosing a replacement bearing actually is easy. When in doubt, buy the next heavier-duty bearing; it won't cost much more. On older cars, the sintered copper-lead is adequate. On late-model cars with up to medium powered engines, the aluminum alloy design will do. On high-performance engines, buy the cast copper-lead.

Installation of replacement bearings certainly isn't in the category of minor tuneup, but it is not a job that is necessarily out of the question for the weekend mechanic. To decide whether or not it's a job you can do, check to see how the oil pan comes out, as this is the part of the job that can be the most "brutish."

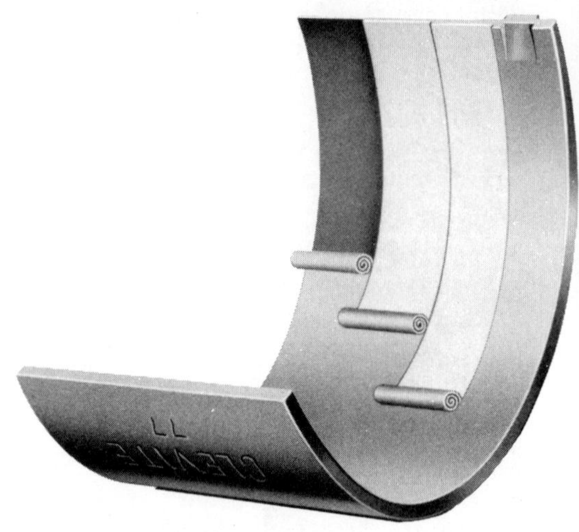

A bearing shell is a multi-layer part. Outer layer is soft babbitt; backing is steel. One or two layers in between vary according to manufacturer and load-carrying needs.

If part of the front suspension must be dropped to take out the oil pan, the job is going to be quite difficult under backyard conditions. The trouble comes when you try to bolt everything back in place, as it gets difficult to line up things.

If you have a pair of small hydraulic jacks (which sell for about $10 each) you can use them to keep the front suspension jacked up, and to assist in realigning everything when the job is ready to go back together. You'll definitely need a helper for the job.

If the engine has to be jacked up off its mounts to provide clearance for pulling the oil pan, another potential difficulty exists. You will need a floor jack to lift the engine, and probably a pair of safety stands to brace the engine in place. If you've got this equipment in your garage, you may be able to get the pan off. Once the job is done, the engine has to be raised off the safety stands (which then are removed) onto the hydraulic jack. You'll need a helper with a crowbar at this point. One man jockeys the engine up and down with the jack, while the other moves it from side to side with the crowbar, until everything lines up. It sounds difficult and often it is. The whole operation takes but a few minutes under favorable conditions, longer when conditions get tough.

The best situation is when the oil pan can be dropped simply by unbolting it and lowering it from the engine. In this case, the job is substantially easier. The category that your car fits into depends on engine, car model and year, and any breakdown would fill this book. A careful perusal of the car underbody and the engine compartment should tell you how easy or difficult oil pan removal is.

Once the pan is off, the bearing caps, bolted in place, are in plain view and usually quite accessible. Just unbolt a cap, and you've got half a bearing in your hand.

If you're trying to replace main bearings, insert a roll-out pin (which can be bought for pennies or made from a cotter pin) into the crankshaft oil hole. Turn the crank by hand and the other half of the bearing will be rolled out.

Removing a connecting rod bearing is even easier. Unbolt the cap to remove one half, and push the rod away from the crankshaft to provide clearance to pull out the second half.

Now the critical part. If the crankshaft journal is smooth, and the bearing itself is merely well worn, installation of new bearings poses no problem. If, however, the crankshaft journals are scored, installation of new bearing shells will eliminate knocks and improve oil pressure only temporarily. If only one journal is bad, it may pay to have it ground smooth with the engine in the car. This is expensive, perhaps $25 or more for a single journal, but for just one

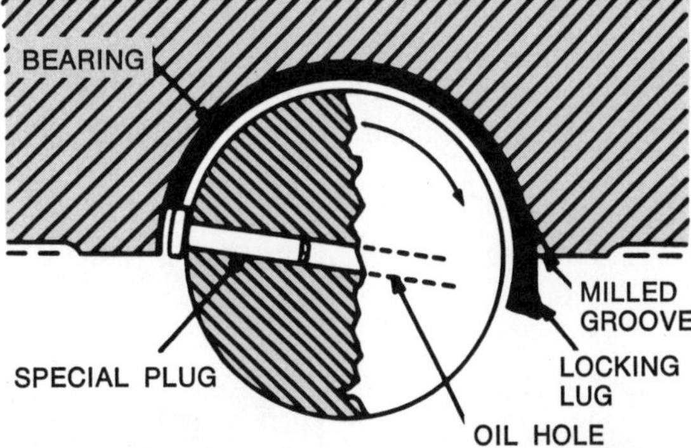

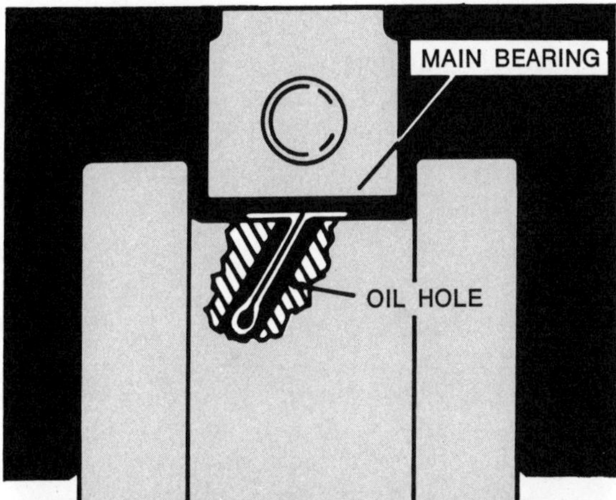

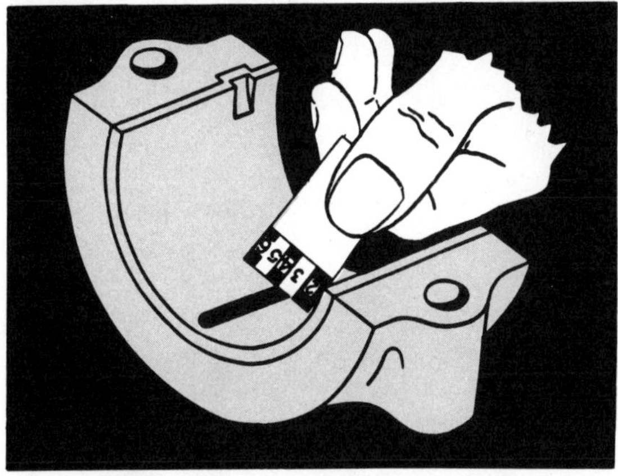

▲ *Top: Main bearings can be removed and replaced without taking out the crankshaft. Simple way is to use roll-out pins, which have a stem that fits into crankshaft journal oil hole and a head that rolls the bearing shell in or out. Middle: Cotter pin can be bent to serve as roll-out pin. Above: Checking bearing clearance with Plasti-Gage determines whether undersize bearings are needed.*

journal it's a lot cheaper and easier than pulling and dismantling the engine, and taking the crankshaft out. If a journal is ground, a standard size bearing will allow excessive clearance. You'll need an undersize bearing.

The most common situation is that some of the journals will have light scratches. In this case, installation of new bearings should prove worthwhile. There will be the elimination of knocks and improvement in oil pressure. And if a quality oil and oil filter are used, the bearing job should last long enough to pay for itself.

Important: Crankshaft and connecting-rod bearings must be precisely tightened, using a torque wrench (available for $10 to $12). Ask for the tightening specifications (given in foot-pounds) where you buy your bearings. There will be different specifications for connecting-rod and main bearings.

A common consideration is crankshaft journal wear. If the journals are worn more than about .002-inch, undersize bearings should be used. As a practical matter, however, if the journals are smooth, you can be sure they haven't worn significantly, and standard size replacement bearings can be used.

If you want to check, there are two ways. One is the use of Plasti-Gage, available in most auto parts houses. It consists of strips of plastic and permits very accurate measurement of bearing clearances. The plastic is laid across the bearing, which then is tightened to specifications and removed. The plastic will have been squashed to a certain width, which corresponds to a bearing clearance.

Another way is by use of a piece of feeler strip of desired thickness. Normally, the clearance with new bearing shells should be less than .004-inch (.001 to .002-inch is desirable). Get an .004 (or thinner) strip that is a bit less than the width of the bearing, and no more than a half-inch for its other dimension. Lay the strip so that the half-inch dimension is lengthwise. Torque the bearing to specifications and try to rock the crank (just an inch or so—no more). If the crank moves easily, undersize bearings are in order. If it locks completely or drags, install standsize bearings.

The whole job, under favorable conditions, is a one-day project, and if you do it yourself, you should save at least a $75 labor charge. P.W.

See also: ENGINE; OIL, ENGINE.

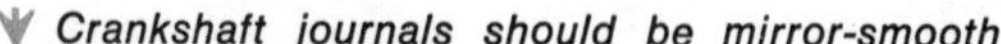 *Crankshaft journals should be mirror-smooth.*

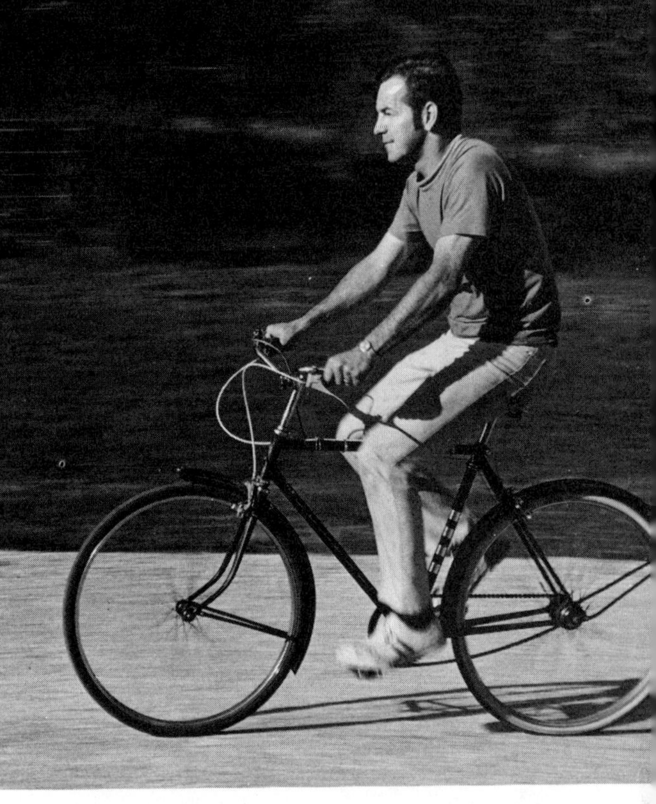

How to Fix Bicycles

Bike boom + bike shortage = do-it-yourself

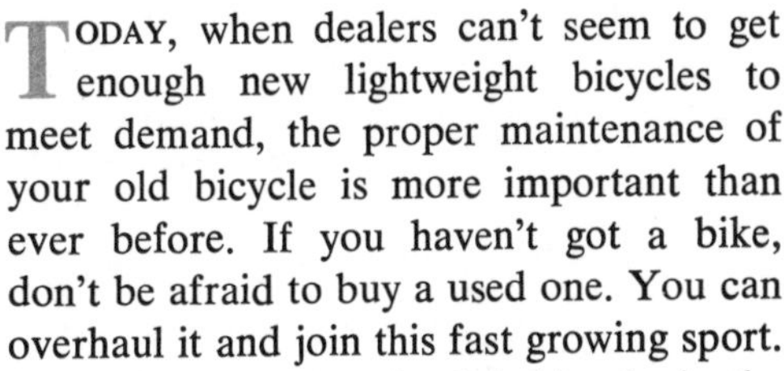

TODAY, when dealers can't seem to get enough new lightweight bicycles to meet demand, the proper maintenance of your old bicycle is more important than ever before. If you haven't got a bike, don't be afraid to buy a used one. You can overhaul it and join this fast growing sport.

A popular type of adult bicycle is the three-speed English lightweight tourist bike, often called, incorrectly, "English racer." European-made bikes, imported by some department stores, are similar in construction. Because of wide ownership, these bikes are frequently available in the used trade from bike shops or at giveaway prices from neighborhood garage sales. They are the Falcons and Valiants of the bicycle world; not quite as sporty as the ten-speeds, but far superior to the ordinary child's heavyweight. And they use parts and tires that are inexpensive and easy to find. As long as it's not rusted out or completely inoperative, you should be able to overhaul any bike you buy. Give it a test drive to be sure nothing is frozen stiff.

The only special tools that you will need are a spoke wrench, which costs about 35 cents, and a thin end-wrench to fit the wheel cones and pedals of your particular bike. An ordinary bicycle wrench will probably do the job. If it doesn't fit, buy a cheap end-wrench of the proper size and grind off one side of the jaws until it is thin enough to squeeze between a wheel cone and locknut. For other parts an adjustable wrench and a pair of water pump pliers will substitute for a whole tool kit.

Parts, if needed, can be purchased at your local bike shop, department store, or discount mart. While all parts of a bicycle need routine maintenance, those that contribute most to a free running bike are the wheels, chain, bottom bracket bearings, and pedals. Let's begin with the front wheel.

Remove the wheel from the fork; then back off the locknut and cone at one end of the axle. Remove the axle and bearings. English bikes have loose ball bearings, so a newspaper should be spread below the wheel to catch the balls. Clean the parts in kerosene and inspect them. Replace any

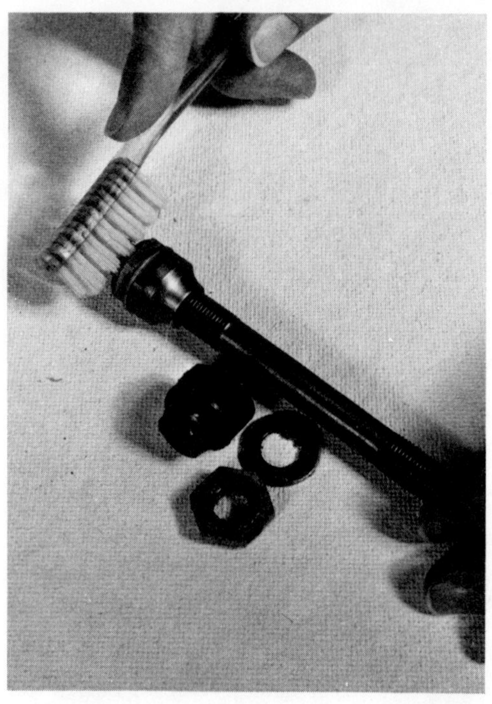

Tools needed include (l. to r., above) spoke and bike wrenches, old toothbrush, cycle lube, marking crayon, adjustable pliers and crescent wrench. After removing front axle and bearings, scrub cones with toothbrush dipped in kerosene (right). Note gunk on uncleaned cone, nut and washer.

bearings that show rust or pitting. Lubricate the hub with bicycle grease or any general purpose grease, and stick the ball bearings in the grease. Cover the bearings with more grease, and re-install the axle, cones, washers and locknuts. Tighten the cones against the bearings, then back off a cone about ¼ turn. The wheel should spin freely, but the axle should have no end play. Tighten the locknuts, if present, against the cones to hold the adjustment. On some bikes the cones fit tightly into the fork, and the outside nut locks the assembly.

Mount the wheel in the fork, and check it with chalk or crayon for out-of-roundness. Loosen spoke nipples where the rim radius is short, tighten them where it is long. Then check for side-to-side wobble. Loosen spokes from one side of the hub and tighten those from the other side to remove lateral "bumps." Cut out and replace rusty spokes that defy adjustment, but to avoid error replace one spoke at a time. Check the nipples in the rims for protruding spoke ends after adjustment. File off any long ends to protect your tube.

The rear wheel should also be trued, if necessary, and checked for bearing adjustment. But the rear hub should be dismantled only if it fails to operate and if you have a diagram of your particular unit. Three-speed hubs require periodic lubrication with SAE #20 motor oil and occasional adjustment of the indicator spindle. Frequently, a sluggish unit will gradually respond to nothing more than a good oiling plus use.

To release the chain, locate the master link and pry off the keeper. Soak the chain in kerosene to remove dirt and old grease or oil. Oil with SAE #20 motor oil and hang up to drain. Or use a special lubricant for chains. If your chain has no master link, brush it with a toothbrush dipped in kerosene, then wipe dry. Lubricate it lightly in place.

Set the bike upside down on the saddle and handlebar. Turn the pedals and cranks and listen closely. With the chain off the chain wheel, the bottom bracket should be quiet. Any clicking or grinding noise indicates dry bearings or gritty grease which should be replaced.

English and European bikes usually have three-piece cranksets which come apart for servicing. To remove the cranks, prepare a block of wood to support the crank and receive the tapered crank pins. Drill a ⅜-inch hole into one end of a 28-inch length of 2x4. The hole should be as close as possible to one edge. Back off the nuts on the pins and drive out the pins as shown in photo. Make note of the direction in which the tapered pin was inserted through the crank.

Pull off the cranks and pedals. Turn the bike on its right side to get at the left side of the bottom bracket. Loosen the lock ring, use a hammer and punch if necessary, and remove it. Remove the left ball cup, bearings, and axle. Use a newspaper to catch the loose balls, usually 11 on each side. Wash the parts in kerosene and inspect. Clean the inside of the bracket. The

Replace front wheel in fork and check for trueness by holding a crayon near the outside of rim and spinning the wheel. Wobbly wheel will pick up crayon marks.

After checking rim for up and down wobble, use spoke wrench to loosen nipples where rim radius is short or tighten where it's long. Then check for side-to-side wobble.

Clean hub and apply bicycle grease. Pack cleaned or new bearings in grease, install and adjust by tightening cone against bearing, then backing off ¼ turn.

right cup has a left hand thread and need not be removed unless it has been damaged.

Put new grease in the cups and install the clean, or new, bearings. Cover the balls with grease and install the axle, left cup, and lock ring. The long end of the axle should be on the right to hold the chain wheel. Tighten until the axle binds, then back off the cup about ¼ turn. Test for end play versus binding, and lock it in proper adjustment with the lock ring.

Check the pedals for noise or binding. If your bike has pedals with a removable dust cap on the outside end, you can dismantle them. Remove the dust caps, the locknut, the washer, and the axle cone. Hold the pedal axle itself in place until you have removed and counted the outside balls. Then pull out the axle and inside balls. Most pedals have more balls in the inside end of the pedal than in the outside end. Wash, grease, and replace the parts.

Pedals without removable dust caps may be oiled from the outside. If lubrication does not make them spin freely, they should be replaced.

Reassemble the cranks on the axle. The tapered pin on the right or chainwheel side should point in the opposite direction from that on the left side. If you failed to note the original position, check to see which end of the pin hole in the crank has the larger diameter. Start the pin from that end.

Next check the steering head. The fork should turn freely without binding or noise, but there should be no slackness in the bearings. If in doubt, service it. Loosen the handlebar stem bolt about ¼-inch and drive it down with a hammer to free the plug inside the bottom of the stem. Use a block of wood to protect the bolt head. Pull out the bar and stem. Loosen and remove the head locknut, washer and adjusting nut. Hold English bikes over a newspaper for this operation (loose bearings). If the head bearings are in a retainer, typical of German and American made bikes, note which side of the retainer faces upward. The retainer at the bottom of the head will be reversed to that above.

Pull out the fork, and collect all the parts. Clean and grease them. To reassemble, set the bike upside down and put grease in the bottom head cup. Stick the bearings in, and insert the fork with the lower cone on it. Invert the bike, holding the fork tightly in place until the top grease, bearings, and adjusting cone nut are installed. Adjust the cone nut for free movement without end play, and lock it. Replace handlebars.

Inspect the brakes for frayed cables, drag between caliper arms, and thickness

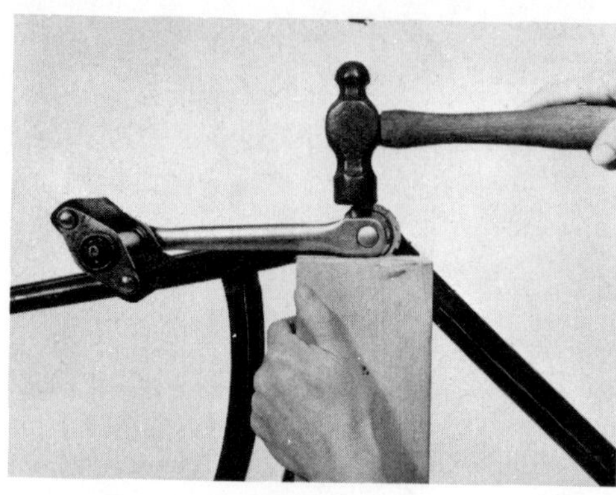

▲ *Use 2x4 block of wood with a 3/8-inch hole drilled in one end to support crank and accept tapered crank pin as you tap it out. Drill hole close to edge of block.*

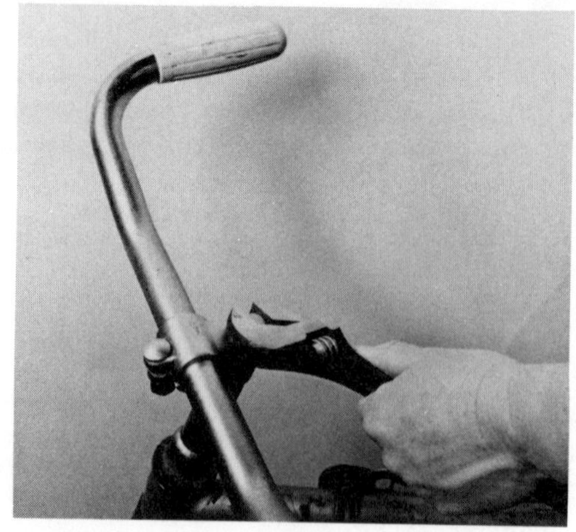

➤ *Fork should move freely with no binding or noise. To service it, remove handlebar by backing out stem bolt 1/4-inch.*

◀ *Drive stem bolt down with hammer to free the plug inside the stem. Use a block of wood to protect bolt head.*

▼ *To service fork bearings, loosen and remove the head, lock nut, washer and adjusting nut. Note position of bearing retainers on German and American bikes. On English bikes, catch loose ball bearings.*

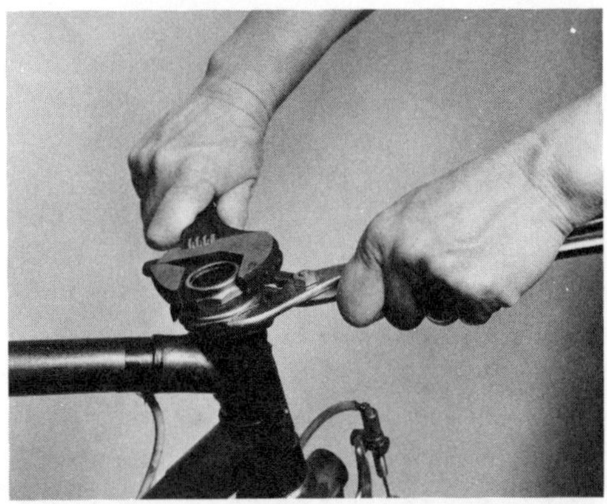

of pads. Replace cables and pads if necessary. Rusty brakes should be removed and scoured with steel wool or a wire brush to remove the corrosion. File off any bumps which restrict movement. When installed, adjust them for about ⅛-inch clearance between pads and the wheel rims. Test for slackness in lever action. Adjustment is made by loosening the locknut from its place against the ledge on a caliper arm and twisting the barrel (see photo). If the barrel adjustment does not take up the slack, loosen the anchor pin and draw more cable through it. Finally, check the pads for correct vertical placement to see that they engage the rim and not the tire.

The saddle height must be properly set to your leg length for efficient pedaling. With the pedal at the bottom position your leg should be slightly bent. The handlebar should be lowered so that you must lean forward a bit, even with a flat bar to reach the grips.

When you have finished the overhaul, don't forget to use the proper pressure in your tires. Low pressure is hard on the tires and on you. About 45 to 50 pounds is right for 26 x 1⅜-inch tires, the most popular size.

New bikes are great, but an old bike gives you two-way fun—rebuilding as well as riding. Now take off for a ride and see what a difference your work has made. D.W.

▲ *To adjust brakes, loosen lock nut (under finger) and twist knurled barrel (above finger) until brake pad clears rim by ⅛-inch. For further adjustment, loosen anchor pin and pull cable through.*

Repair Your Blender

If your blender doesn't work, use these techniques to spot the part to be replaced

THE BLENDER is a two-part appliance comprising a base or power unit and a blending container. All the work is done in the glass blending container.

Aside from cracking or breaking this glass container, the only things that can go wrong are damaged cutting blades or a leaky seal. These parts can be replaced easily if they don't function properly.

The base power unit contains the motor and electrical speed control switch.

The motor used is a series or universal type because it will deliver the high speed needed for complete blending or liquidizing of the material placed in the container. Operating speeds may be as high as 16,000 rpm.

Most blender power units are accessible for service by removing the base plate. This will expose the power cord connections and the brush end of the motor for electrical testing. The control switch is mounted on a front panel and in some cases the motor may have to be removed in order to make the switch accessible for test or replacement.

The greatest difference between blenders is in the method of motor speed control. They may have rotary switches, toggle switches or push button switches, each requiring a different electrical circuit.

Electrical testing is done with a volt-ohmmeter. This device is used to determine if voltage is available to the motor. The ohmmeter portion will indicate the condition of the switch and the electrical windings of the motor.

Before making any electrical tests, try

to turn the motor by hand, using your fingers to turn the drive lug. If it doesn't turn, the armature is frozen. Clean the motor bearings and lubricate them. If this doesn't solve the problem, continue trouble-shooting.

When using the volt meter section of the volt-ohmmeter, the blender must be plugged into a wall socket. The meter switch should be set at the 150-volt AC position.

During the tests a line voltage of about 115 volts should be obtained when the leads are connected to: (1) the wall socket —no voltage indicates a defective socket; (2) the connection of the power cord to the switch and motor—no voltage indicates a defective cord; (3) the motor connection of the power cord and the other side of the switch, with the switch turned on—no voltage indicates a defective switch.

If voltage is available up to the motor and the motor does not operate, it is probably defective.

Each electrical part can be tested individually with the ohmmeter. Follow the instructions with the meter to change over resistance readings. Turn the switch of the meter to the R x 1 position. *Caution:* unplug the cord from the wall outlet before making these continuity tests.

The line cord should show continuity (zero ohms) from each terminal on its plug to the end of its wire. The switch should show continuity from terminal to terminal when it is on and no continuity (infinity, shown by a sideways figure 8 on the dial) when it is off. The motor should show a resistance reading. No continuity would indicate it to be burned out. Any defective part should be replaced. Switches and motors of blenders are not ordinarily repairable.

The most commonly used tools are either a standard or Phillips screwdriver. A nut driver may be needed in some models to remove the switch or disassemble the motor.

Although defective parts will have to be replaced, an exception could be a loose or broken wire or a power cord that is broken at the plug end or at the point where it is clamped under the strain relief. The loose or broken wire can be resoldered

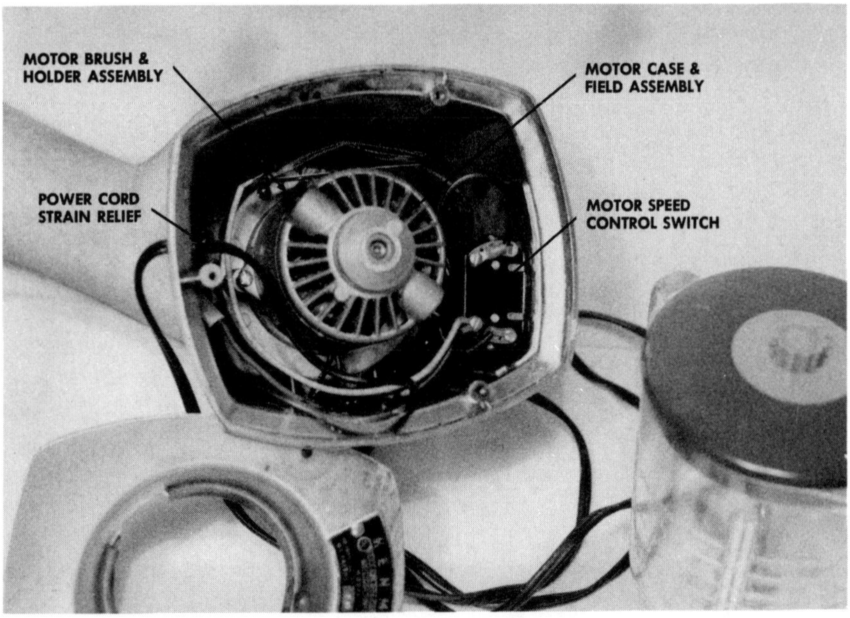

◀ Blender base power unit with bottom cover removed. Brushes can be examined by removing the caps from the brush holder. When replacing brushes, make certain curved end contacts armature commutator in exactly the same way as before it was removed.

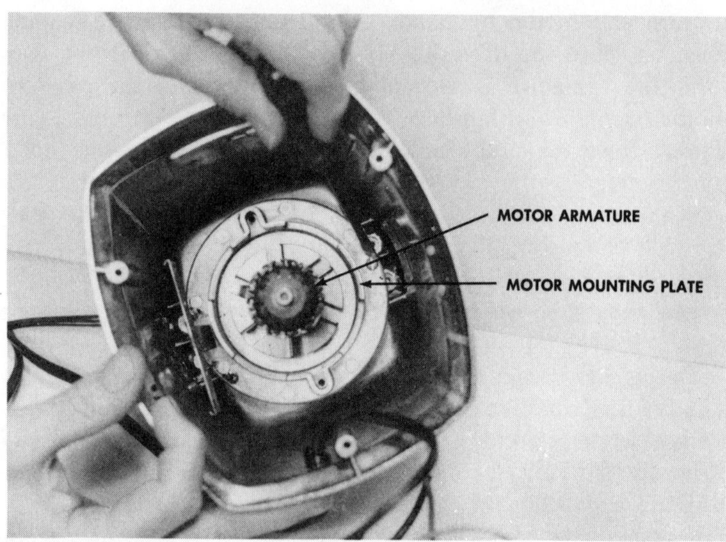

Motor armature is accessible after field coil and motor housing have been removed.

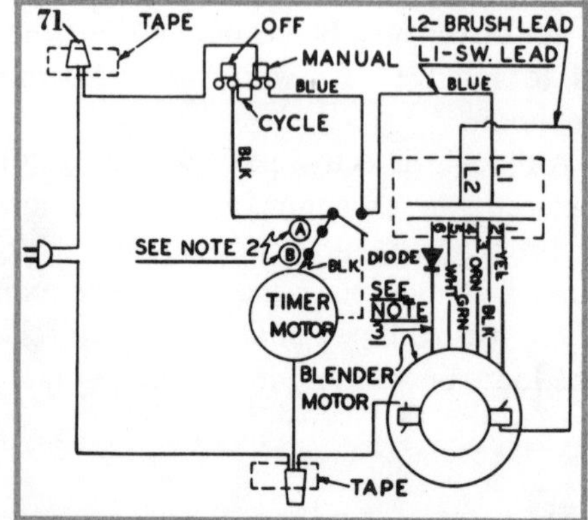

Several taps in the field winding and a diode inserted in the circuit provide 10 different speeds in this blender circuit.

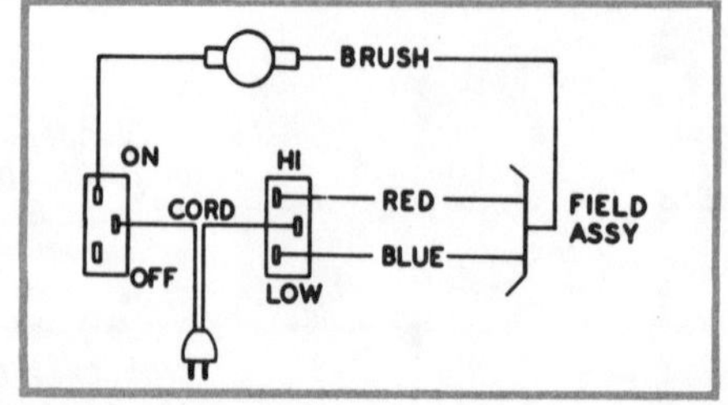

This simple two-speed circuit derives its speed change from a tap in the field winding.

and the power cord can be shortened and reconnected.

Parts should be available from a dealer who handles the particular make you have. If the dealer does not have the parts or says that he can not get them, try the manufacturer of the blender. Sources are usually listed in the yellow pages of your telephone book under "Electric Appliances—Small—Repairing." There are very few mail order parts outlets that might have all the special parts for the many different blenders in use. There are some very good small motor repair specialists who could repair or replace defective motors or any parts. These specialists are usually located in a major metropolitan area, listed in the yellow pages under "Electric Motors—Dealers & Repairing."

When reassembling the unit make certain some good light grade of oil is applied sparingly to the shaft and bearing. Be sure the armature turns freely by hand before applying power.

A word of caution—before getting too involved in a major repair, consider the cost of a new blender. Also consider the age of the unit requiring service and the potential cost of parts. Motors, armatures

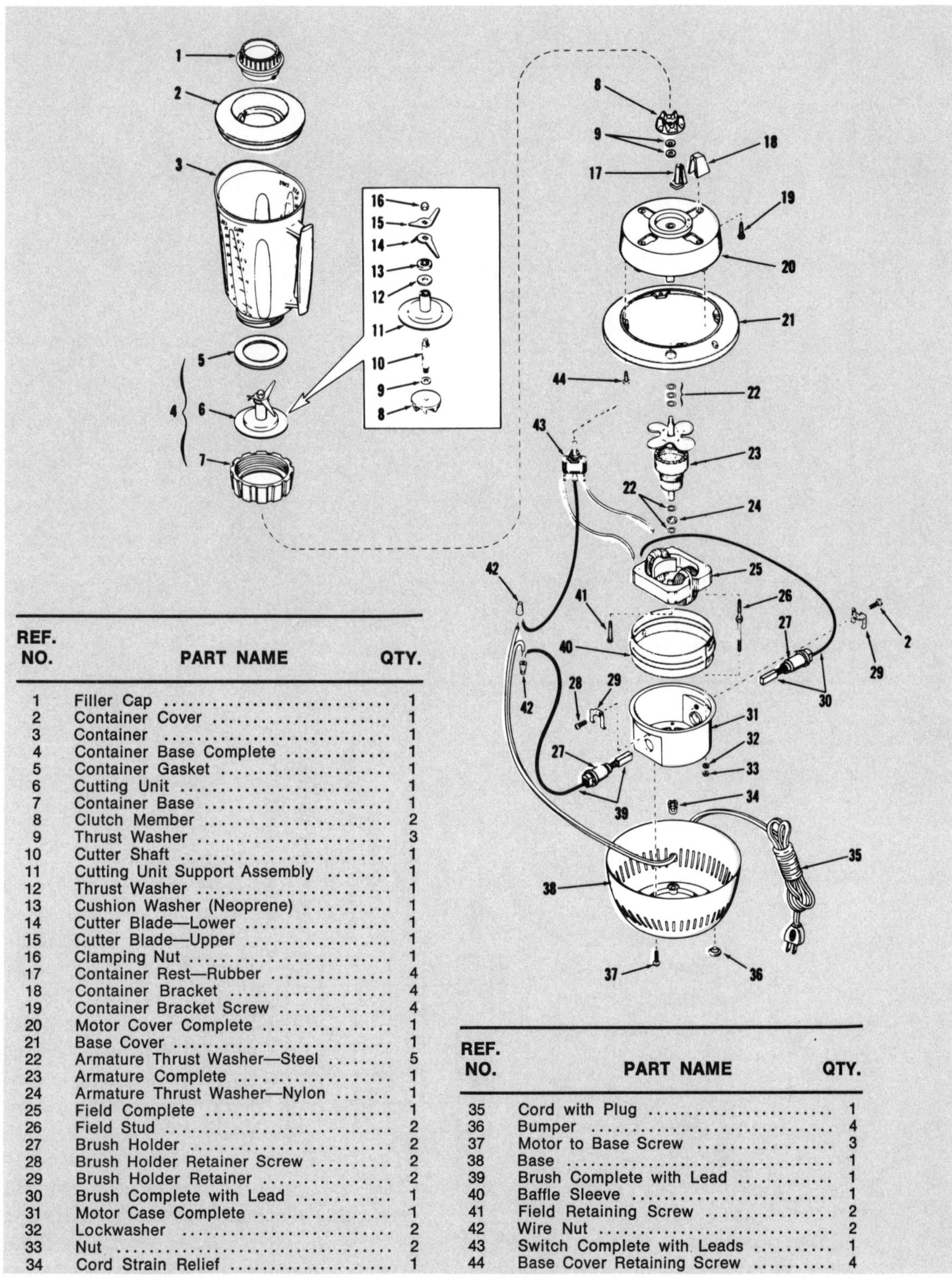

REF. NO.	PART NAME	QTY.
1	Filler Cap	1
2	Container Cover	1
3	Container	1
4	Container Base Complete	1
5	Container Gasket	1
6	Cutting Unit	1
7	Container Base	1
8	Clutch Member	2
9	Thrust Washer	3
10	Cutter Shaft	1
11	Cutting Unit Support Assembly	1
12	Thrust Washer	1
13	Cushion Washer (Neoprene)	1
14	Cutter Blade—Lower	1
15	Cutter Blade—Upper	1
16	Clamping Nut	1
17	Container Rest—Rubber	4
18	Container Bracket	4
19	Container Bracket Screw	4
20	Motor Cover Complete	1
21	Base Cover	1
22	Armature Thrust Washer—Steel	5
23	Armature Complete	1
24	Armature Thrust Washer—Nylon	1
25	Field Complete	1
26	Field Stud	2
27	Brush Holder	2
28	Brush Holder Retainer Screw	2
29	Brush Holder Retainer	2
30	Brush Complete with Lead	1
31	Motor Case Complete	1
32	Lockwasher	2
33	Nut	2
34	Cord Strain Relief	1
35	Cord with Plug	1
36	Bumper	4
37	Motor to Base Screw	3
38	Base	1
39	Brush Complete with Lead	1
40	Baffle Sleeve	1
41	Field Retaining Screw	2
42	Wire Nut	2
43	Switch Complete with Leads	1
44	Base Cover Retaining Screw	4

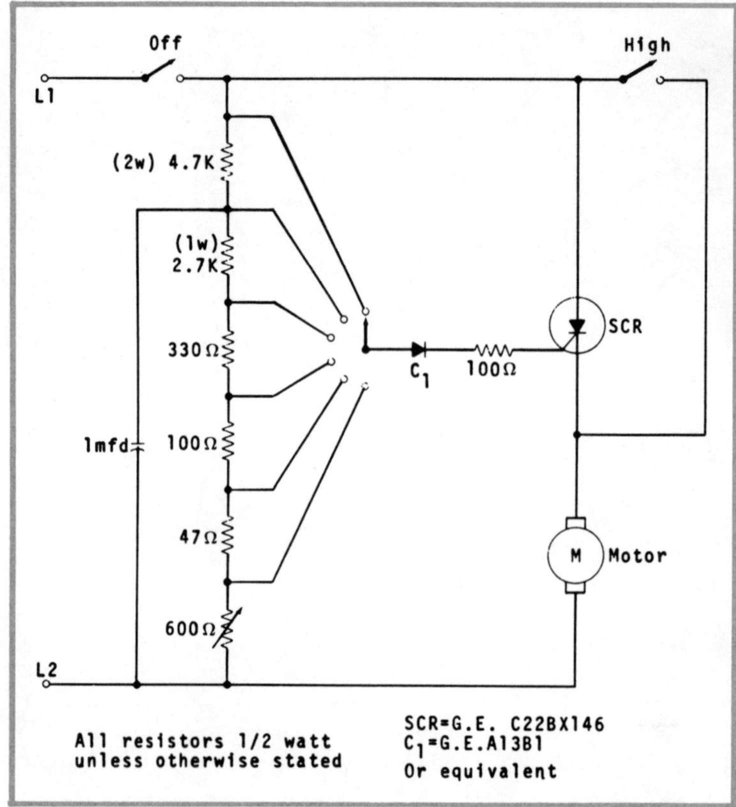

In this wiring diagram, the silicon controlled rectifier (SCR) controls the voltage available to the motor, reducing speed by about 2000 RPM per switch step.

BLENDER TROUBLE CHART

PROBLEM / POSSIBLE CAUSE	NO POWER	DEFECTIVE CORD	DEFECTIVE SWITCH	DEFECTIVE MOTOR	BAD BEARINGS	INCORRECT CONTAINER PLACEMENT	DEFECTIVE COUPLING	CRACKED CONTAINER	LEAKY SEAL	BENT BLADES	(LOOSE)
MOTOR WON'T RUN	√	√	√	√	√						
BLADES DON'T TURN						√	√			√	
HIGH SPEED ONLY			√								
LOW SPEED ONLY			√	√	√						
LEAKY CONTAINER								√	√		
ABNORMAL NOISE					√					√	√

and multiple contact push button switches are not cheap.

The accompanying check list should serve as a guide in locating a problem. The accompanying exploded view will serve as a diagram for locating parts.

G.M.

See also: INDIVIDUAL APPLIANCE LISTINGS.

➤*This combination porch wall and planter uses random stones for color contrast. See drawings for construction and method of filling the center of the wall, which becomes a planter 8 inches wide and 12 inches deep.*

"Homescaping" with Bricks

Use these photos, drawings and instructions to build walls, steps, patios, walks and planters

YOU DON'T HAVE TO BE a skilled mason to improve your home with decorative brick, stone or glazed tile.

The rules for doing good home masonry work are relatively simple. So are the tools and equipment required. And ideas for useful and colorful improvements are plentiful.

On this and succeeding pages, you'll find a selection of attractive masonry projects.

What you'll need. The most widely used common bricks measure 2½ x 3¾ x 8 inches. They are readily available at local building material yards, where you may also find other shapes, sizes, styles and textures of brick, cut stone and tiles.

In addition to the basic tools, you'll find either a metal wheelbarrow or a small mixing box helpful in preparing mortar and concrete mixes.

Mixing the mortar. The ideal mortar for strong brick work is a 1:1:6 mixture of 1 part Portland cement, 1 part lime and 6 parts sand. Use a small pail or box for measuring the ingredients. To prepare the mortar, first spread the sand in the box and then add the cement. Hoe these ingredients back and forth until a uniform color is obtained. Then spread on the lime and repeat the mixing process.

Add water gradually and hoe the mixture until the entire mass is soft and pliable. You have the proper consistency when the mortar oozes out from between the bricks without breaking away, and the bricks can be bedded in place with a light to medium tap of the trowel.

Try to mix only as much mortar as you can use up in about three hours, if the air temperature is around a normal 70°F. If the mixture hardens because of water evaporation, it can be re-tempered by adding more water and re-mixing.

Basic bricklaying technique. The step-by-step procedure in laying brick is shown in the accompanying drawings. Stretcher courses are laid one upon the other with the bricks flat and positioned end to end.

The patterns for both stretcher and header courses may be varied.

Another standard technique is that of angle-cutting bricks and laying them to form a sawtooth border.

Brick walls and planters. Before mixing your mortar, lay out the first course of brick to correspond with size of the wall or planter you are building, so as to come out with either full or half bricks at either end. Allow from ¼ to ½ inch for each joint, increasing or decreasing the spacing within this range so that you come out even with your planned dimensions.

Both brick walls and planters should rest on concrete footings at least half again as wide as the overall thickness of the work. For example, an 8-inch thick wall, 24 inches high, requires a footing 12 inches wide and about 5 inches thick.

For each additional foot in height, add 1 inch to the thickness and 2 inches to the width of the footing. As a general rule, planters or walls of only one brick in thickness should not be more than 24 inches high.

Footing mix. The proportions for a suitable mix for footings are 1:3:4 (1 part cement, 3 parts sand, 4 parts gravel). With a solid ground for the footing prepared at least 6 inches below frost line, pour the concrete mix in the forms in one operation. Your local building department can tell you the depth of the frost line.

For brickwork exposed to the weather, concave, weather or "V" joints shown are recommended. The concave or "V" joints are best made with a jointing tool. The pointing trowel is used for flush, struck or weathered joints. Raked joints can be made with a homemade raker; here the nail head removes the mortar to a uniform depth.

Laying the wall. Lay the end bricks first

◄ Ruffled bricks capped with glazed bricks form the combination tree and flower planter at left. Drawings show you how such a planter is constructed. Above, sawtooth-set bricks form a planter bordering a basket-weave style brick walk. The brick steps are topped with red-colored concrete. ▲

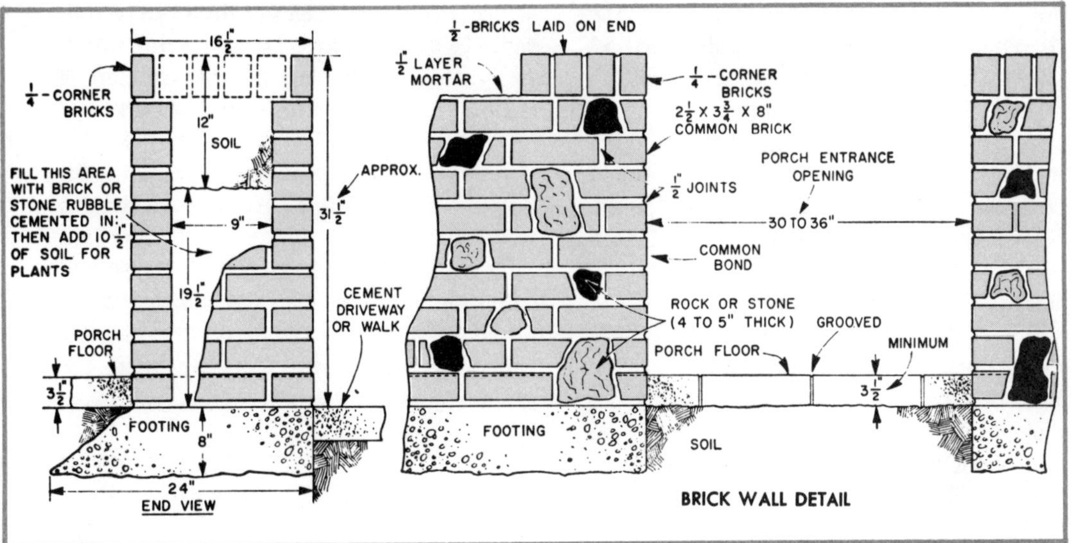

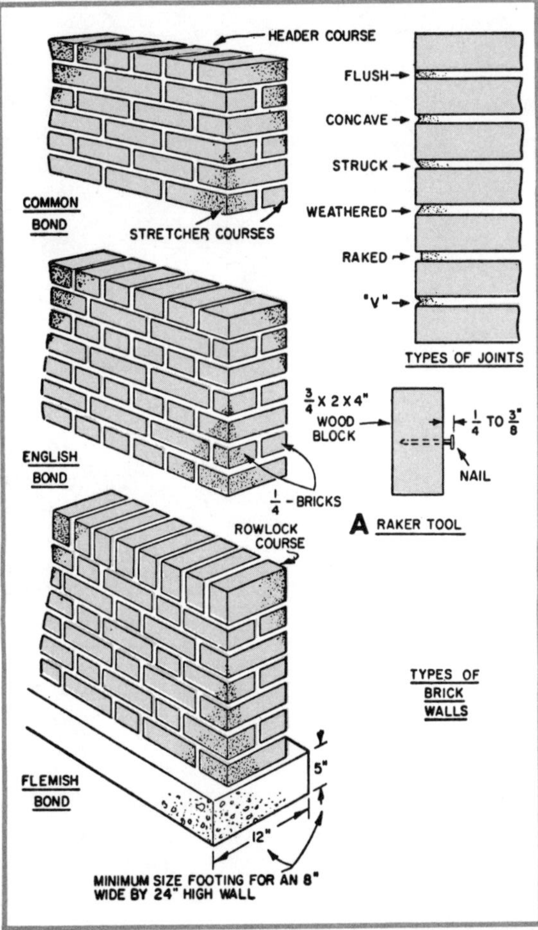

on a ½-inch bed of mortar. Then stretch a taut line aligned with the upper, outside corners of the end bricks, to serve as a guide for laying the remaining bricks in the course on a straight line.

Immerse each brick in a pail of water for one or two seconds before laying it; if you don't do this the dry brick will draw moisture from the mortar, resulting in a weak bond. Don't move a brick once the mortar has begun to set; it will produce a weak joint. If you have to reposition the brick, remove it, clean off the mortar, and re-lay the brick with new mortar which is still pliable.

As each course is laid, make sure the end bricks are all the same height from the footing, and aligned plumb with the brick below. After every third or fourth course, stop to tool all the recently-laid joints before the mortar hardens.

If you are building an 8-inch thick wall fairly high, so that two stretcher courses will be laid side by side using a common bond, be sure to top every fifth or sixth stretcher course with a header course, to keep the wall intact.

Planter combination. The specifications for the combination tree and flower planter are detailed in the drawings. For the stretcher course design, you'll need 32 bricks; for the soldier course design, 46 bricks. Each design is topped with 16 glazed bricks. The top edge of the wooden tree box (which has no bottom) is installed on a level with the glazed brick. Fill the outer (flower) area with soil up to 1 inch from the top; fill the box for the tree to within 5 inches from the top.

Porch steps. If you want to build brick steps, note the construction details in the appropriate drawing. Use the two-step design for porch floors 18 inches above grade level, or where you are allowed to fill in or remove the soil to the 18-inch level. This allows a 6-inch rise for the steps.

Install the footing forms. Allow ⅛-inch pitch per foot so step treads will drain properly. Pour in the same 1:3:4 footing mix specified earlier for wall footings. You can remove the forms in 24 hours and then lay the first two courses of brick. After the mortar hardens, fill with soil compacted to within 1 inch from the top of the bricks. Then add a 1-inch thick layer of concrete far enough back to form a footing for the second step or next two courses of brick. Add the soil and concrete fill as you did for the first step.

To make the colored concrete topping used on each step, you'll need the form setup shown in the drawings. Note arrangement of overhang supports; this allows the sideboards to be removed without disturbing the support boards when finishing the topping.

Seal the openings between the bricks and overhang supports with a cement and water paste; let this set for 5 minutes. Wet down the bricks and concrete fill and then pour a 1:3 (1 cement, 3 sand) concrete mix with coloring added to match the bricks. The powdered coloring, available at building supply yards, is mixed according to instructions.

Make certain the topping is well packed at the corners and edges of the form to prevent hollows. Remove excess mortar with a straightedge (strikeboard) manipulated in short side to side strokes while pulling it toward you.

After the topping has become quite stiff but is still workable, go over it with a wooden float which gives it a nonskid (sidewalk) surface. Round off the edges and carefully remove the sideboards. Then round off the lower edges of the topping and make the grooves. Touch up with the wooden float and finally remove the over-

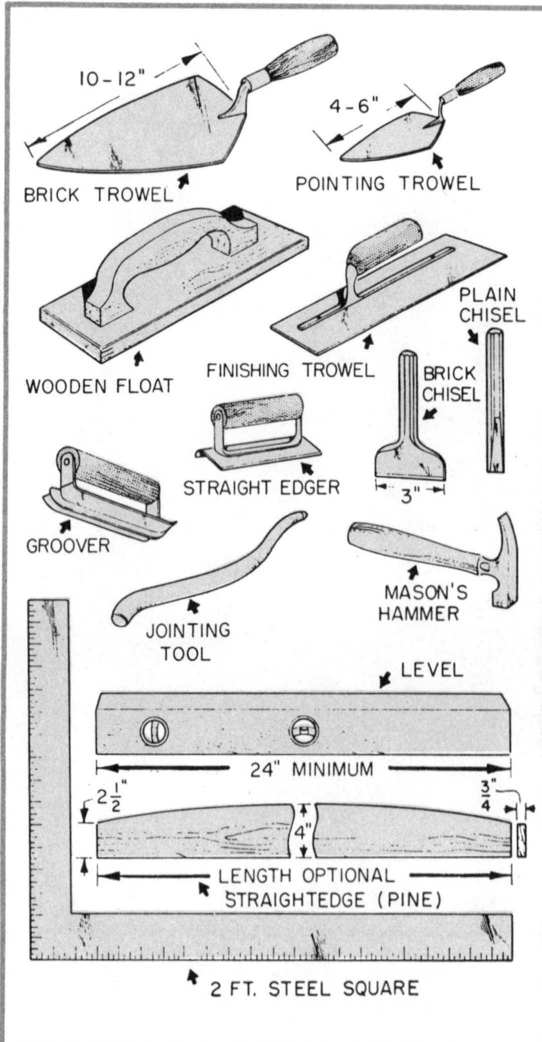

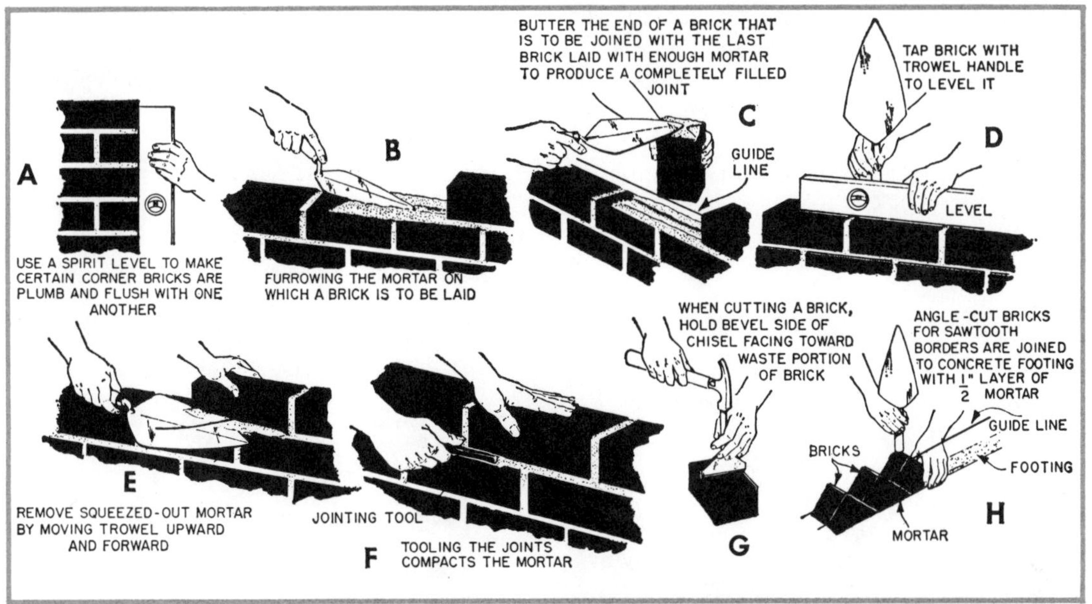
A
USE A SPIRIT LEVEL TO MAKE CERTAIN CORNER BRICKS ARE PLUMB AND FLUSH WITH ONE ANOTHER
B
FURROWING THE MORTAR ON WHICH A BRICK IS TO BE LAID
BUTTER THE END OF A BRICK THAT IS TO BE JOINED WITH THE LAST BRICK LAID WITH ENOUGH MORTAR TO PRODUCE A COMPLETELY FILLED JOINT
C
GUIDE LINE
TAP BRICK WITH TROWEL HANDLE TO LEVEL IT
D
LEVEL
E
REMOVE SQUEEZED-OUT MORTAR BY MOVING TROWEL UPWARD AND FORWARD
JOINTING TOOL
F
TOOLING THE JOINTS COMPACTS THE MORTAR
WHEN CUTTING A BRICK, HOLD BEVEL SIDE OF CHISEL FACING TOWARD WASTE PORTION OF BRICK
G
ANGLE-CUT BRICKS FOR SAWTOOTH BORDERS ARE JOINED TO CONCRETE FOOTING WITH 1/2" LAYER OF MORTAR
GUIDE LINE
BRICKS
FOOTING
MORTAR
H

▲ *Brick steps. Overhang supports are not removed until concrete has hardened thoroughly.*

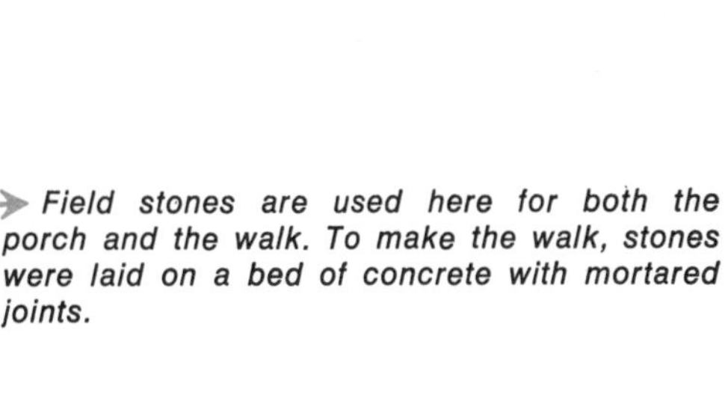

➤ *Field stones are used here for both the porch and the walk. To make the walk, stones were laid on a bed of concrete with mortared joints.*

hang supports. Make the topping for the lower step as you did for the upper step.

Adjusting for porch height. The step construction shown in the drawing is more flexible, in that it permits you to regulate the rise of the steps from 4 inches on up to 8 inches (average step height). Thus you can build steps for porch floors above or below the 18-inch level, merely by changing the vertical dimensions of the form boards.

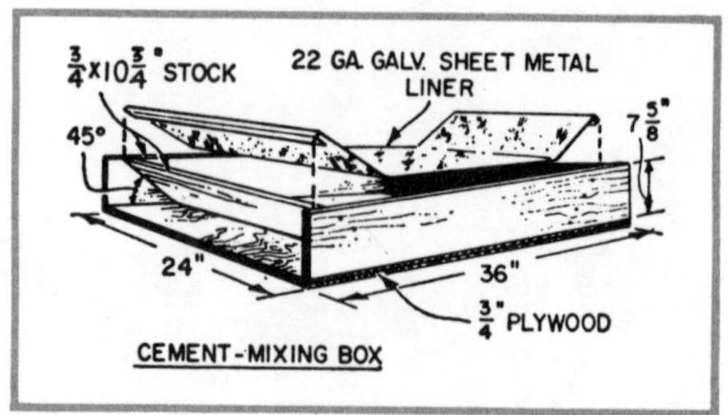

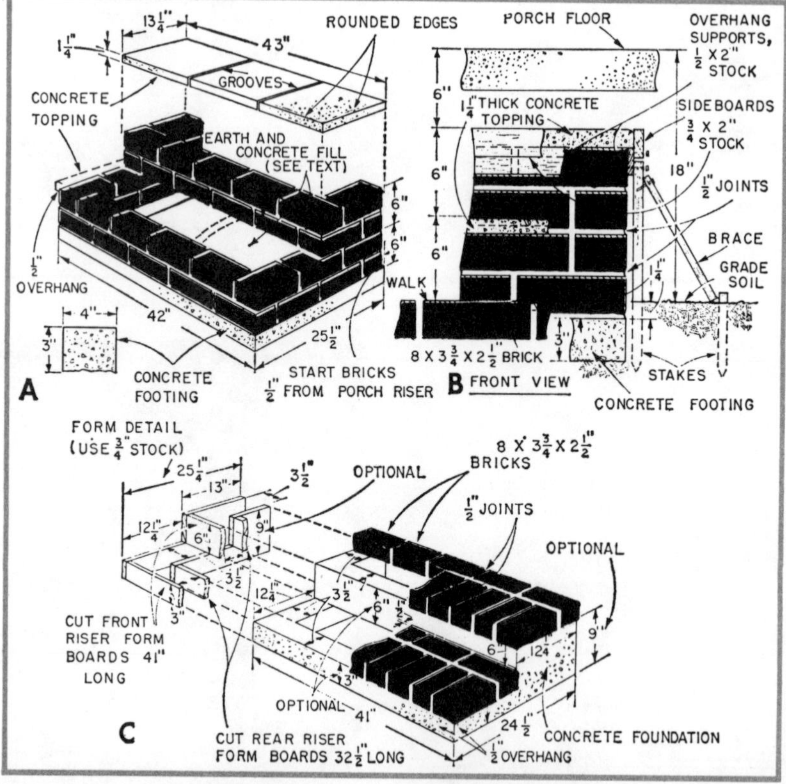

Let's say your porch is 21 inches above grade, for example. You'll need 7-inch high steps, each one-third the 21-inch distance. This means that you would add 1 inch to the 3- and 6-inch height dimensions, and 2 inches (1 inch for each step) to the 9-inch dimension.

To take another example, if the steps are to have a 5-inch rise for a 15-inch high porch, deduct 1 inch from the 6- and 9-

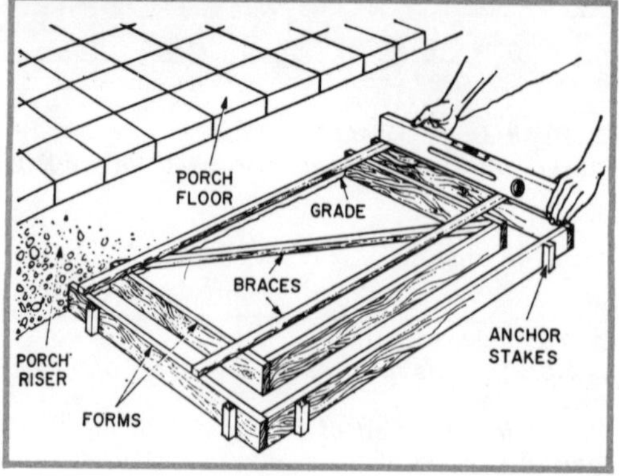

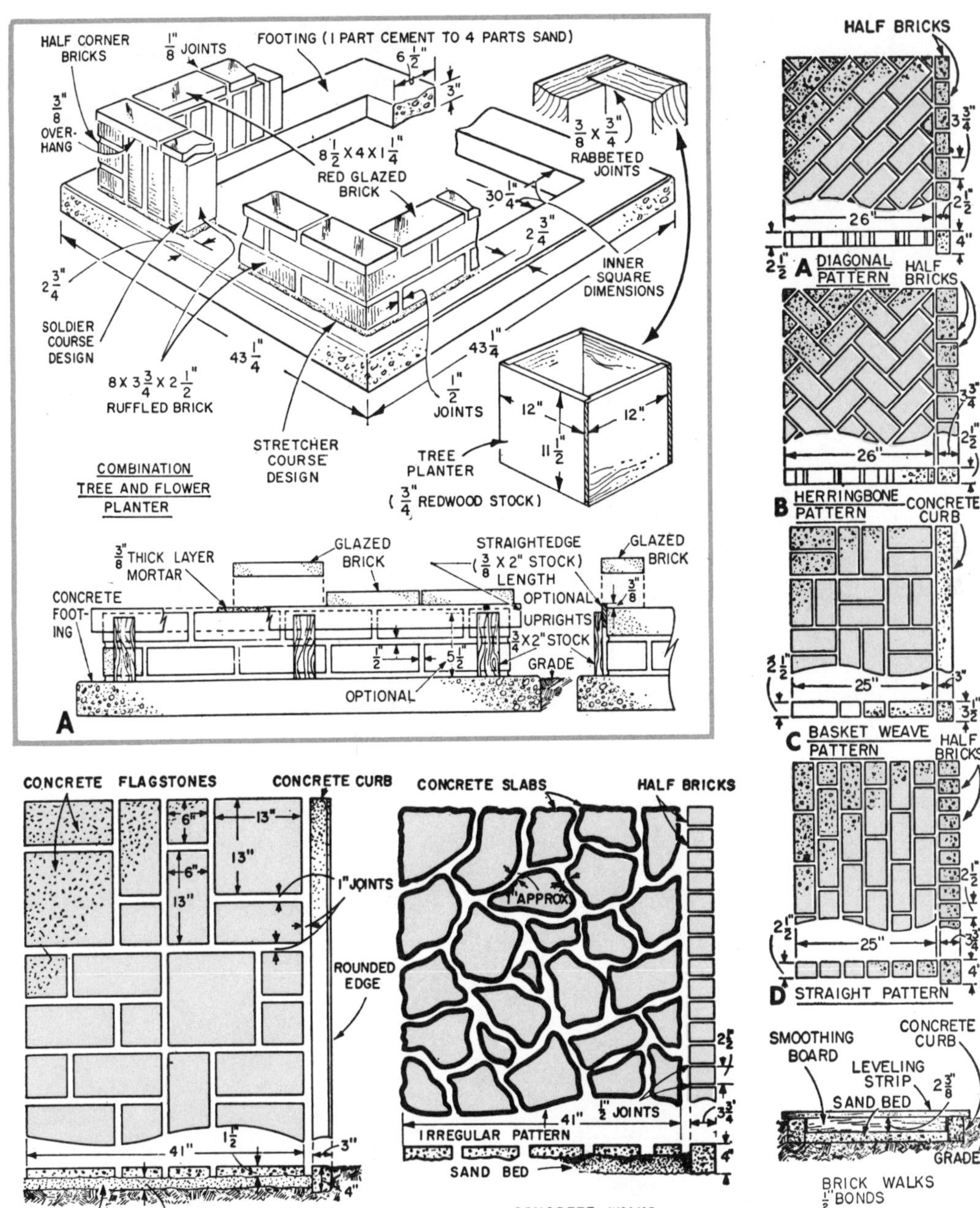

inch dimensions. Leave the 3-inch dimension as is and make a 1-inch deep excavation in the soil for the forms. Follow the same procedure for pouring the footing and adding fill described previously. But instead of the colored concrete topping, this time you will use brick treads laid on a ½-inch bed of mortar.

For the 21-inch porch, a walk would be laid 7 inches below the top of the first step; for a 15-inch high porch, 5 inches below.

Making brick walks. The brick walk

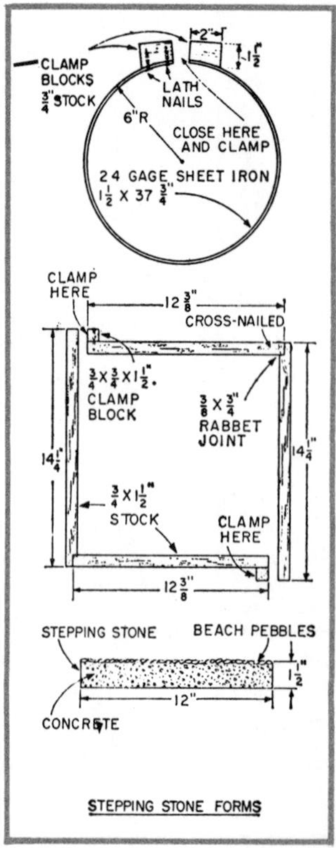

shown in the photo is the basket-weave pattern. Note that the walk is bordered on the outer edge with a concrete curb colored to match the bricks. The other designs shown use half-brick borders. Where a walk leads directly to porch steps, make the walk (complete with borders) the same width as the steps.

For walks with concrete curbs, lay out the walk location and install the forms (using ¾-inch stock) at the ultimate level the walk is to be. For curved portions of walks, curbs or concrete borders, you can use strips of ⅛-inch Masonite hardboard for forms. When installing forms for walks, allow at least ⅛-inch pitch per foot, either lengthwise or crosswise, for proper drainage. Compact the soil between the form boards and pour in a 1:3 mix (1 cement, 3 sand, with red coloring added) in one operation. Let set until surface water has disappeared, and then round off outside edge of outer curb. Let concrete harden 24 hours before removing forms.

Using a piece of ¾-inch plywood, long enough to span the concrete borders, to level the bricks. Medium taps with a hammer or mallet should seat bricks level with concrete.

An easy method for laying a brick walk is to place the bricks on a bed of sand, fill the spaces between them with a dry grout mixture composed of cement and sand, and then sprinkle the surface with a fine, watery spray. The grout absorbs the moisture to form a bond between the bricks.

If 2½-inch thick bricks are used, remove the soil between the form boards to a depth of 4 inches, and compact the bottom of the excavation. Dump in the sand and spread it evenly with a smoothing board 2⅜ inches from the top of the curbs. This allows ⅛ inch for seating the bricks even with the curbs, or wood forms. Make up a dry mixture of 1 part cement to 6 parts sand and sweep it between the bricks filling the spaces up to the top. Make certain, of course, that the mixture and the bricks are completely dry, so that none of the cement will adhere to the top surface of the bricks.

Remove excess grout with a soft bristle brush and then wet the walk down thoroughly with a fine water spray. Avoid flooding or a direct, sharp stream of water from the hose. Keep the walk wetted down to slow down the drying of the grout. Allow at least a full week before putting the walk into service.

Patios, terraces and flagstone walks. You can use the same dry grout method when laying patios or terrace floors consisting of flagstones or concrete flags. The irregular shapes shown are broken concrete slabs salvaged from a torn up sidewalk. These can sometimes be had for the asking if you don't mind hauling them home.

In place of the dry grout method, you can used colored concrete to accent the patterns. Or you can remove the sand from below the joints, replace it with soil up to ¾ inch from the top, and seed the soil with grass or low growing plants.

Making concrete flags. You can actually make your own concrete flags at less than half the cost of commercially made ones. Simple two-piece wooden forms, similar to the square type shown in the drawing, can be made in the three shapes and sizes shown as the patio pattern. Use a 1:3 mixture (1 part cement, 3 sand) with just enough water to form a stiff concrete mix. This permits the forms to be removed within two or three minutes and made ready for the next batch. Flags are best made on a flat concrete surface which is

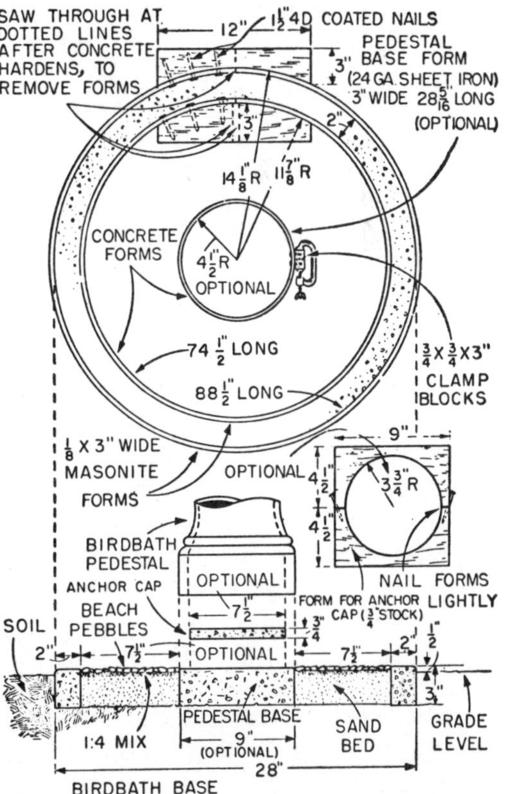

covered with a protective layer of black building paper. Coat the inside of the forms with linseed oil to keep concrete from sticking and give you smooth-edged flags.

Pebbled stone projects. Most masonry supply yards stock pebbled beach stones. These range from pea size to egg size, and add a decorative touch to an otherwise plain stepping stone. Use the 1 part cement, 3 parts sand mix and pour it to ¼ inch from the top of the forms. Completely cover the mixture with pebbles, leveling them with a stick of wood, as was done for the bricks.

Damp-moisten a soft bristle brush and go over the surface thoroughly to fuse the pebbles to the concrete. But don't use any more moisture—too much softens the concrete and causes it to crumble or break away from the edges when removing the forms.

If air temperature is around 70°F, you can remove the forms in about 5 minutes if you do it carefully. Any concrete picked up by the brush which adheres to the pebbles can be removed with a wire brush after the concrete hardens. Keep stones or flags wetted down and allow them to lay where formed for a full week before handling. Stepping stones can rest on a bed of sand placed in excavations made in the sod. They can also be bedded in pebbles.

As another use for pebbled beach stones, note the base for the pedestal-type bird bath shown in the drawings. The diameter of the pedestal base and anchor cap can be adapted to the size pedestal you have. To build this bath base, first excavate the soil to a 2½-inch depth and a 30-inch diameter. Anchor the forms with stakes and pour in a 1:4 mixture (1 cement, 4 sand). Round off the outer edges of the curbing after the cement has set for about one hour.

Give the concrete 48 hours to harden before removing the forms. Then fill the depression with sand to 1 inch from the top and add a ¾-inch thick layer of concrete topping. While this is still wet, place the pebbles as you did those used for the stepping stones. Finally, moisten the pedestal base and pour the concrete for the pedestal anchor cap if one is required.

Circular stepping stones, with egg-size, loose beach pebbles between them, arranged around a brazier. Large stones are seats.

Embellishing stepping stones with a layer of beach pebbles.

See also: CONCRETE; HOME IMPROVEMENT; MASONRY; STONEWORK; STUCCO.

Ten Steps to Cassette Player Repair

Trouble-shooting your cassette player will give you extra hours of enjoyment

CASSETTE RECORDERS come in every size and shape. They play on dry cells, AC line or operate right in the car. Generally, the portables are monophonic while table and console models are stereophonic. New cassette decks may feature "pop-up" cassette loading, level meter, remote control mike, push-button controls, tag-along speakers, and AC bias erasing system, to name only a few. After many hours of rough handling these cassette units will require servicing. This 10-step approach to trouble-shooting will give you an edge in cassette repair. H.L.D.

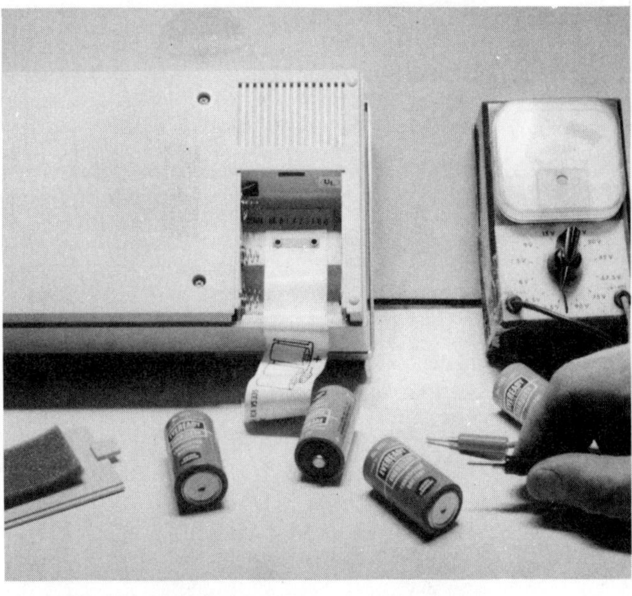

In case the recorder will not play, check the batteries. Check for corroded battery terminals or broken wires. Clean battery terminals with a knife or emery board. Disconnect one battery wire and insert VOM switched to low milliameter scale. No current indicates a defective on/off switch, bad battery connections or dead batteries. Excessive current indicates a short in motor or amp circuit. If unit works on batteries and not on AC suspect trouble in the power supply. A step-down transformer and rectifier produces this DC. Check AC voltage at rectifier and DC voltage at motor.

Low volume and background noise caused by a dirty tape head. Excessive oxide dust will accumulate and pack upon the tape head. Tape heads should be cleaned every sixty days to keep them in tip-top condition. Clean head with tape-head cleaner or just plain alcohol. Use a cotton swab, dip in alcohol and remove the oxide dust. A special tape head cleaning cassette can also be inserted in place of the cassette. Don't forget to clean around and under the tape head assembly. Always try to keep magnetized screwdrivers away from the tape head.

➤ *If the tape plays slow, suspect a worn or stretched drive belt. In case the tape won't move check for a broken belt. Oil on the drive belt or capstan pulley will result in slow tape movement. Clean the belt, idler, and motor pulleys with rubbing alcohol. If the speed is erratic (wow), check for oil on belt and capstan drive pulley. A belt partially off the track or a misaligned capstan assembly can cause wow conditions. Defective cassette or motor can produce erratic speed or wow conditions. After a good clean-up with alcohol, check the capstan flywheel for dry bearings. A drop of light oil on motor bearings will clear up a noisy motor. Some small motors are self-contained and do not require oiling. When you do use oil, just a drop will do; do not over-lubricate any bearing. Wipe off excess oil to prevent dripping upon drive belt.*

▲ *Suspect mechanical trouble when there is no tape motion and power is applied to the motor. Spin motor belt and see if the capstan drive wheel takes off. If not, remove the drive belt and see if the motor shaft is free. If not, clean out motor and bearings with alcohol, assemble and lubricate bearings. If starting is intermittent, remove drive belt and hold the motor pulley between fingers. Switch the power off and on. Sometimes under load, the motor armature will have a flat side and will not rotate. Replace defective motor. A frozen or binding capstan drive wheel will result in slow or no tape motion. Remove the capstan flywheel assembly, clean and lubricate. Wipe off excess oil. Especially, suspect dry bearings on plastic pulleys working on metal posts. Don't overlook a possible defective cassette.*

▼ *Most mechanical troubles are related to the drive or switch cassette mechanism. Remove the outside case of the cassette player so you can see the mechanical action. Check the sequence of operation and try to isolate the cause of trouble. For instance, if the record button will not stay down suspect a bent lever or locking pin. In some of these small recorders the thin levers are quite fragile and bend rather easily. Remove the lever and bend back in shape. Be careful not to compound the trouble. Many of these metal parts are rather difficult to obtain and you may have to repair them. Check for broken or loose springs. You can spot these springs rolling around in the case. They can fall out in removing the outside covers. Spring replacement is difficult unless you have an exploded drawing of the mechanism.*

◄ *A broken remote mike cable will result in intermittent or no power supplied to the cassette player. When hum or intermittent recording is noted, suspect a defective cable. These breaks are found where the wire enters the mike or at the male plug. If the remote unit will not shut off the recorder, check for a bent female plug or defective switch. Check to see if the cassette recorder will operate without a remote unit plugged in. If not, check shorting contacts of female remote-control jack. Continuity of the remote power switch can be checked with an ohmmeter. Cut off the broken section of cable and resolder mike or plug. Be real careful in soldering the small shielded cable so that you do not solder the shield to the shielded wire. Recheck continuity with an ohmmeter.*

► *If the unit will not record, check the microphone and mike jack. If the unit will play back a cassette, the amplifier and speaker are functioning. The trouble must be in the microphone circuit, play/record switch or switch transfer linkage. Clean and spray the play/record switch contacts. Then, check for poor soldered switch connections on PC board. Make sure the switch can be fully engaged and make contact. In case the unit will not play or record, turn volume wide open and touch the ungrounded wire from the tape head to the amplifier. You should hear a loud hum if the amplifier is working. If not, inject a signal from an audio generator at the volume control. Signal trace the defective amplifier by going from base to collector terminal of each transistor. Make voltage and transistor tests where the signal is lost. If you hear hum and the recorder will not play or record suspect the tape head.*

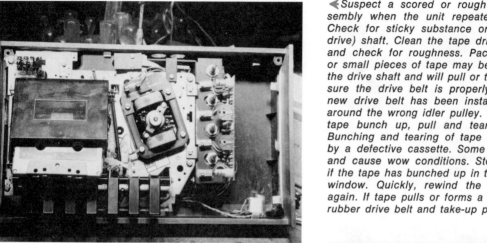

Suspect a scored or rough tape drive assembly when the unit repeatedly tears tape. Check for sticky substance on capstan (tape drive) shaft. Clean the tape drive with alcohol and check for roughness. Packed tape oxide or small pieces of tape may be wound around the drive shaft and will pull or tear tapes. Make sure the drive belt is properly installed. If a new drive belt has been installed, it may be around the wrong idler pulley. This will let the tape bunch up, pull and tear out the tape. Bunching and tearing of tape may be caused by a defective cassette. Some tapes will bind and cause wow conditions. Stop the recorder if the tape has bunched up in the small plastic window. Quickly, rewind the tape and start again. If tape pulls or forms a loop, check the rubber drive belt and take-up pulley.

Is your cassette player unusually noisy? Try to isolate the noisy condition in amplifier or tape head assembly. Make sure the tape head is clean and demagnetized. If the player is still noisy, see if the noise exists in a prerecorded tape cassette. Try a few prerecorded cassettes. Now, turn the volume down and see if noise is still present. Generally, noise produced in the amplifier is caused by leaky AF or driver transistors. Also, check for a poor ground on the PC board. The noisy transistor can be isolated by substitution or removing the collector terminal from the circuit. When the noise disappears you have located the noisy transistor or stage. A popping noise can be caused by a defective output transistor or burned resistor.

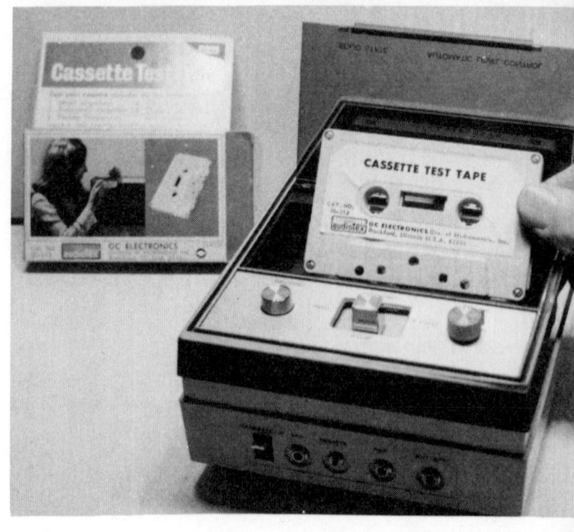

Two recordings heard at the same time indicate crosstalk. Excessive crosstalk and poor frequency response are caused by either poor erase or improper tape head alignment. Adjust the height and azimuth screws, located at the rear and side of the tape head, to correct. Use a cassette audio test cartridge in making these adjustments. Before performing these tests clean up the tape head. Connect a 40, 47 or 49 bulb across the speaker leads. Adjust the volume control so the bulb barely glows and then adjust the tape head height and azimuth.

How to Maintain Your Chimney

Keeping your chimney in good repair will cut fuel bills, keep your house cleaner

A GOOD DRAFT is essential for clean, efficient operation of your heating plant. Better heating, therefore, starts at the chimney where accumulated soot in the smokepipe or flue can prevent proper functioning of your furnace. When neglected for a period of years, as often happens, sufficient soot can pile up in the ash pit at the bottom of the chimney to restrict the draft.

Aside from the considerable waste of fuel and failure to provide sufficient heat, a blocked flue means dirty operation of the furnace and subsequent blowing of fly ash throughout the house, with the resultant soiling of upholstered furniture, draperies and ceilings.

Another cause of heating plant failure is an air leak in either the metal smokepipe, which connects the furnace to the flue, or in the chimney itself because of crumbling mortar in the brickwork. Tiny holes in the smokepipe are easily plugged with POP rivets, which are peened by means of special pliers. Pipes with larger holes, rips in the metal, or bent edges that prevent tight fitting of the pipe sections, should be replaced as such repairs are difficult and seldom satisfactory.

Caulking of the joint where the wall siding meets the chimney is an essential routine of home maintenance. The chimney stands on its own foundation, separately from that of the house itself, so there is a differential in expansion and contraction movements. The elasticity of modern caulking compounds provides some latitude to keep the seal, but the compound tends in time to split or separate from the chimney, leaving an open gap. Removal of the old compound is recommended to provide direct adhesion for the new caulking, although it is permissible to apply a new bead of compound over the old if it is securely bonded to the brick and the siding.

Another location that may require attention is the chimney pot, at the top of the chimney, which seals the ends of the clay flue. A very long ladder is usually necessary to reach that position. Damage to the cement seal is quite rare and would occur only as a result of an exceptionally heavy storm. At any rate, chimney pot inspection should be kept in mind whenever it is necessary to climb to the roof.

Cleaning the chimney. Do-it-yourself furnace cleaning is not a difficult job, though certainly it's a dirty one that must be followed by an immediate shower. It involves use of a vacuum cleaner, preferably the workshop type with a large five-gallon tank. You will also need a long-handled brush with stiff wire bristles. Wear your oldest clothes, including some form of cap, wrap a scarf or old towel tightly around the neck, tape a gauze pad over the nostrils to minimize inhaling fine soot.

Cleaning can be done at any time of the year, but is best after the heating season, thus eliminating soot that absorbs moisture and causes rusting. Be sure to switch off the burner.

Complete cleaning is done from both ends of the chimney—from the top by dropping a weighted sack down the chimney to dislodge soot from the walls of the flue, and from the ash pit at the bottom, through the cleanout door and by temporarily removing the smokepipe from the furnace connection. If the condition is not extreme, you might skip climbing a ladder to the top. Usually, just vacuuming the ash pit and smokepipe opening will be sufficient.

Loosen the smokepipe by rocking it side-to-side until the cement joint is broken, then separate the pipe sections. Avoid denting the flange edges so that the pipe can be replaced easily.

With the vacuum nozzle, pick up all loose soot around the chimney opening. Extend the brush into the flue as far as the handle will reach, dropping the soot into the ash pit. Finally, use the vacuum to completely clean out the ash pit. If there is a considerable amount of soot, you may have to empty the vacuum tank before the job is completed.

When replacing the smokepipe, examine it carefully for rust holes and repair or replace it if necessary. Make sure the pipe is properly assembled, the joints tightly fitted, then seal the joint at the chimney opening with asbestos cement mixed with water to a thick paste, applied like cement mortar.

The chimney itself should be inspected at least annually for any loose mortar between the brick. Rake out all loose mortar from the brick joint. Pointing the joints is done with a striking tool, a narrow steel bar used to pack the mortar deeply into the open space. R.T.

See also: BRICKWORK; CONCRETE; MASONRY.

◄Accumulated soot in the chimney ash pit may affect heating plant efficiency by restricting the draft, resulting in incomplete combustion and excessive fly ash throughout the house.

Cleanout door at bottom on chimney permits easy cleaning with vacuum hose. Use stiff bristle brush to clear sides of flue. The chore is dirty but not difficult.

Joint at house siding to chimney requires periodic caulking to close gap that results from separate foundation of house and the chimney footing.

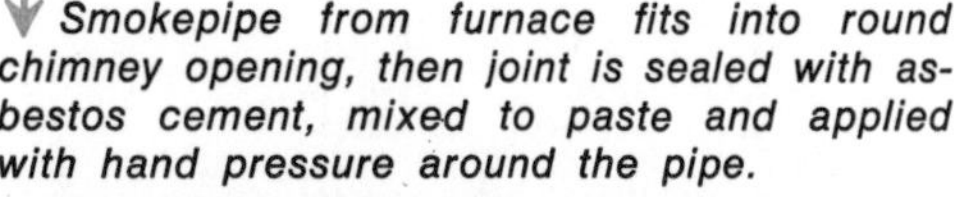

Smokepipe from furnace fits into round chimney opening, then joint is sealed with asbestos cement, mixed to paste and applied with hand pressure around the pipe.

Mortar pointing seals small openings that affect chimney draft. Use striking tool to press mortar tightly into the joints.

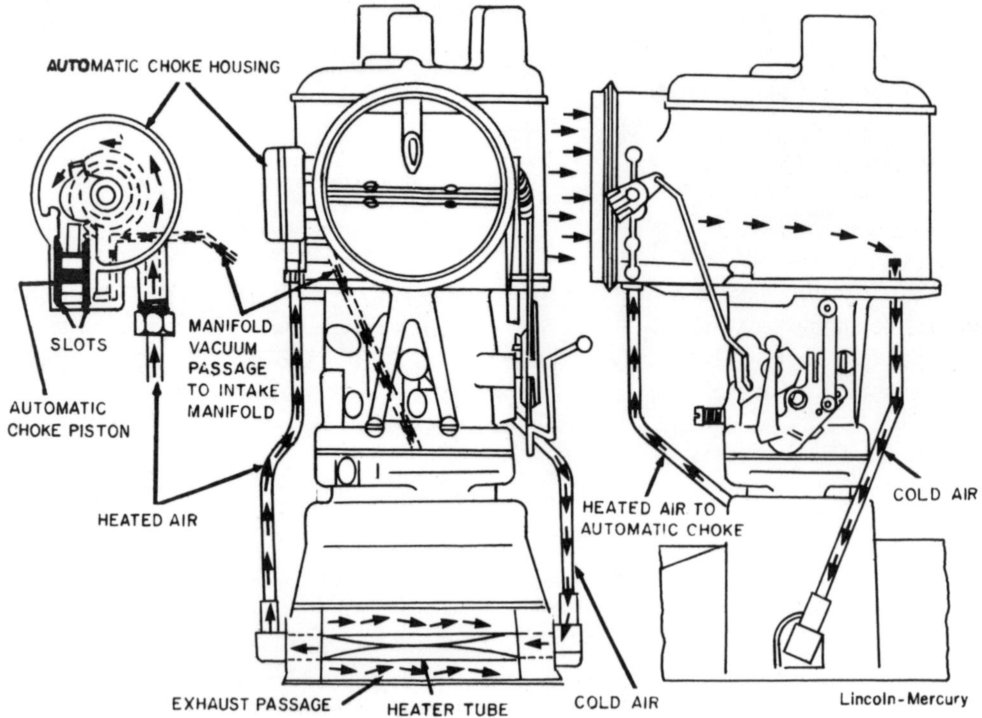

Drawing shows how the typical in-carburetor piston choke works.

How to Service Your Automatic Choke

Keeping your choke in shape can avert starting difficulties and prevent gasoline from harmfully diluting your engine's oil

WHEN THE ENGINE in your car is running at normal temperature, each part of gasoline has to be mixed with about 14 parts air in order to burn in the cylinder combustion chambers. But, when the engine is cold, it needs a richer mixture—more fuel and less air. The choke helps control this mixture.

It is likely, when starting a cold engine, that much of the fuel entering into the carburetor throat is in the form of small drops, and only a small portion of these will be properly vaporized by the time the mixture reaches the cylinder. By enriching the mixture and increasing the proportion of fuel to the proportion of air, sufficient vaporized gasoline can be delivered to the combustion chamber to start your engine and keep it running until the engine warms up enough to work on a normal fuel-air mixture.

Temporary changes in the fuel-air mixture are regulated by the choke plate in the carburetor throat. As the choke plate is closed, more fuel and less air is allowed down the throat.

The manual choke. On most older cars and even many late-model economy and sports cars and trucks, choke adjustments are accomplished manually by a pull knob on the dash. Pulling the knob out closes the choke, pushing it in opens the choke.

But manual choking has always been a

problem. It is simply too easy to overchoke the carburetor. The chance of overchoking has been removed by the automatic choke, a device which has been put on most cars since the late '40s and early '50s.

The automatic choke is a unit which reacts to the engine temperature. A temperature-sensitive metal coil opens and closes the choke plate in response to the action of the metal.

Automatic chokes today use some variation of the temperature-sensitive metal coil, and couple a vacuum-controlled piston or vacuum-controlled diaphragm to the choke plate linkage. Until the thermostatic coil becomes warm, its tension is relatively high so that neither the suction effect in the carburetor nor intake manifold is sufficient to overcome the tension, or the tension is high enough to overcome the downward pull of the piston. As the thermostatic metal warms, its tension decreases.

The vacuum-controlled piston or vacuum-controlled diaphragm or piston is connected to the choke linkage in such a way as to oppose the thermostatic coil. The coil tries to keep the choke plate closed; the diaphragm or piston, which is being drawn by engine vacuum, tries to pull it open.

As the thermostatic coil tension decreases, the diaphragm or piston pulls on the choke linkage, gradually opening the choke.

The thermostatic coil can be located in either of two places: a cast well in the intake manifold, or in the carburetor itself.

If the coil is in the intake manifold well, there is a rod from the coil up to the choke linkage on the carburetor.

Current design practice is to use a vacuum diaphragm with the well choke and a piston with the in-carb unit.

The vacuum diaphragm is mounted on the outside of the carburetor, where it can

➤*Keeping automatic choke's external linkage and choke plate clean is a preventive maintenance job that takes just seconds when using an aerosol solvent.*

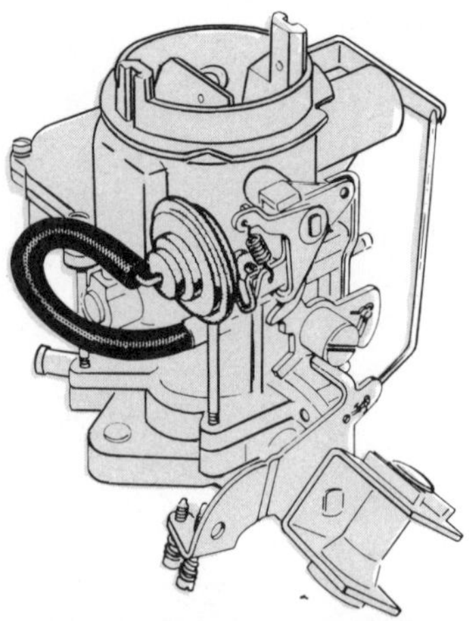

This is carburetor with vacuum diaphragm to pull open the automatic choke, instead of the in-carb piston.

In-carb piston is accessible through plastic cover, which is held on by screws. Before disturbing, note alignment mark on top of cover and what it matches up with on carb body.

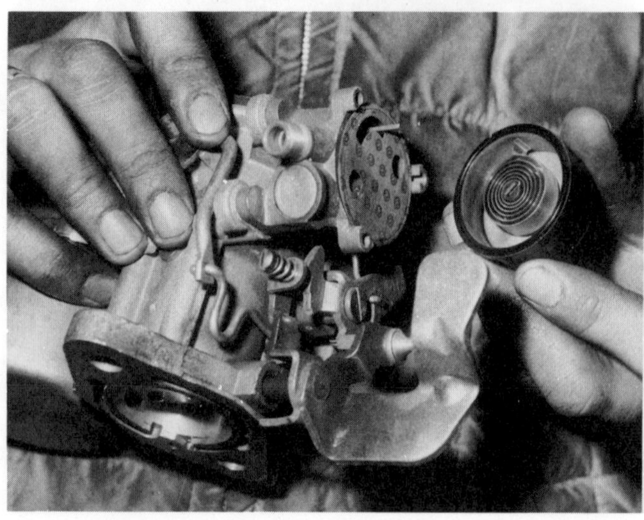

Cover off (note thermostatic coil in cover). Now remove gasket. Rod projecting from gasket is linked to vacuum piston. When cover is on, rod engages thermostatic coil.

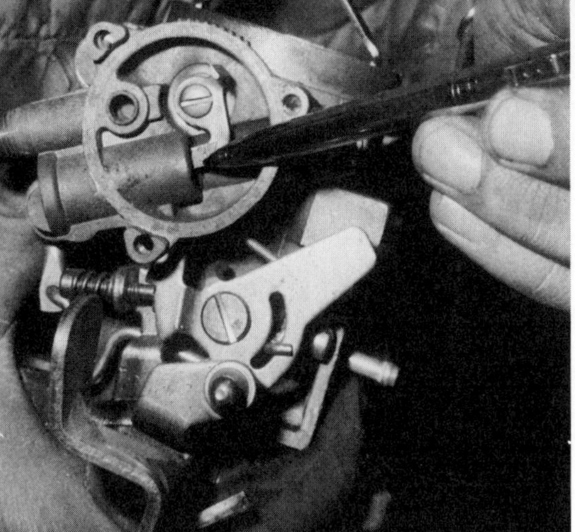

◄*Pen points to vacuum piston bore. Below: When putting choke together, be sure cover mark is aligned with marks on carb body.* ▼

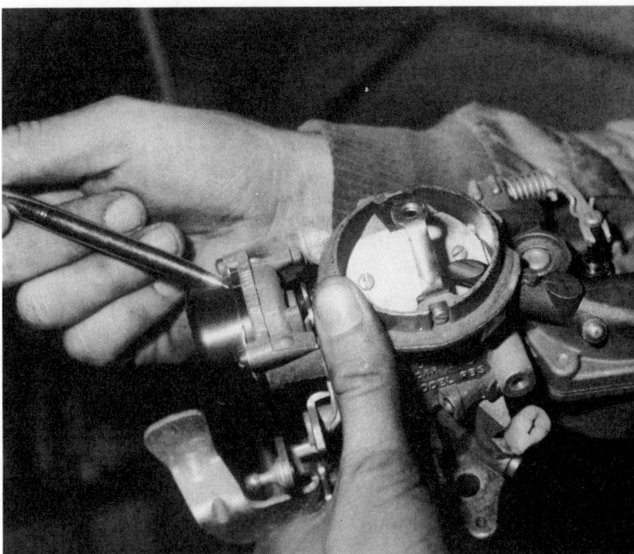

easily be checked and replaced. It is connected to the carburetor base or intake manifold (the source of vacuum) by a short hose.

The piston is inside the choke assembly, just back of the thermostatic coil. A passage in the carburetor runs from the back of the piston to the intake manifold, the source of vacuum.

The hose or tube you see on the outside of the housing for the in-carburetor coil choke is a heat tube. It runs to the intake manifold, and is the source of heat for the thermostatic coil.

Problems with an automatic choke. An automatic choke is anything but a foolproof item. Among the things that can go wrong are:

1. Sticking linkage.
2. Improper adjustment.
3. Weak thermostatic coil.
4. Seized thermostatic coil.
5. Stuck vacuum piston or defective vacuum diaphragm.
6. Clogged heat tube (in-carburetor coil chokes only).

If the choke fails to close, or opens too soon, the car will be very difficult, if not impossible, to start. If the choke sticks closed, the engine will stall and when it does run, the mixture will be overly rich—overchoked.

Overchoking is a very serious problem. Large quantities of raw gasoline enter the combustion chamber and the excess washes the oil from the cylinder walls, creating unnecessary cylinder wall wear. The extra fuel can flow past the rings and dilute the oil in the crankcase. Diluted crankcase oil may cause rapid wear of bearings and other fast-moving engine parts.

If you suspect trouble with the automatic choke, check its operation before you remove or replace it. Remove the air cleaner from the carburetor so you can see the choke plate in the carburetor throat.

When the engine is cold, the choke plate should be closed. Start the engine. The choke plate should open slightly and, as the engine warms, should open gradually. When the engine reaches the proper operating temperature, the choke plate should be fully open.

If the choke plate opens too soon or too slowly, you can compensate by adjusting the position of the thermostat spring cover. If the choke plate seems extremely slow opening, try this check before you remove the automatic choke. Accelerate the engine quickly, then release. The choke plate should remain in full open position. Close the choke plate with your finger, then release it. It should open immediately. If it does not, the trouble may be caused by a bent or sticky choke plate shaft or a vacuum piston or diaphragm rather than the automatic choke.

Adjustment. If the automatic choke opens too soon or too late, you should be able to make an outside adjustment rather than complete repairs.

Most automatic chokes of the in-carburetor coil type are provided with a system of cover adjustments to control the thermostat spring reaction to engine temperature. By loosening three screws enough to move the choke cover, you can turn the cover left or right and change the spring reaction.

On most covers you will find an arrow marked "lean" pointing to the left. If you move the cover to the left, or to lean position, you will cause the choke to open at a lower engine temperature. If you turn the cover to the right, you will cause the choke to open at a higher engine position. The proper adjustment of the choke for your engine normally is at the mid position, or one line "rich." But if your car experiences any starting problems, check manufacturer's specifications. On some cars the specifications were as high as four lines rich for very cold weather.

To replace well choke, start by disconnecting link. This one is held by push-on clip.

The well choke normally requires no adjustment. If you experience hard starting and cold stalling that seems to be accompanied by an early-opening choke, there is an adjustment on some Chrysler Corp. cars.

Undo the screw or screws that hold the well cover, disconnect the rod from the coil to the choke plate and take out the thermostatic coil assembly.

There is a locknut that holds two coil tension indexing plates together. Like the other type of automatic choke, this one has markings. One plate has a notch, the other has calibration lines. If you loosen the locknut, you can realign the marks to increase spring tension, which will lengthen the time required for the choke to open fully.

The normal adjustment is to align the notch with the center calibration line or one line toward more tension (toward the "R"). If the choke fails to perform with this adjustment, the coil should be replaced.

Regardless of the type of choke, this cannot be overemphasized: a thermostatic coil adjustment is not a cure-all for a weak coil.

Note: On some Chevrolets, the rod from the well coil goes into an elongated hole on the choke linkage. With the choke closed, the top of the rod should be even with the top of the elongaged hole on six-cylinder engines. On virtually all V-8s with an elongated hole, the rod should be even with the bottom of the hole.

All moving parts of the automatic choke should be dry and free of dirt. Never oil linkages; oil collects dirt and causes the parts to stick and eventually bind.

The best "tool" for automatic choke service is an aerosol can of choke solvent. As part of every tune-up, spray the external choke linkage clean. Remove the plastic cover on in-carburetor coil chokes and spray the solvent onto the piston and into its bore. Check the piston, which should move back and forth completely free.

With vacuum diaphragms, the only service is to check the operation of the unit. With the engine cold, start the engine and watch the diaphragm. If it is functioning, it will pull the link to which it is attached and crack open the choke. (The piston does the same thing.)

The cracking open of the choke by the diaphragm or piston gives an engine that has just been started enough air to run at fast idle.

If the vacuum diaphragm does not pull the link, pull off the hose and feel for vacuum. (Engine must be running.) If there is little or none, the hose is clogged or leaking, both very remote occurrences.

More likely, there is vacuum and the diaphragm has become porous, and the assembly must be replaced. This is a simple job since the assembly is held by screws.

The diaphragm or piston must crack the choke open only a specified amount. If the opening is too small, the engine will die for lack of air. If the opening is too great, the fuel mixture will be too lean and the engine will also stall out.

The initial opening of the choke is measured at its widest point, using a drill bit as a feeler guage (the drill should just fit in). The specification is referred to as the "choke vacuum kick" and varies according to carburetor.

The adjustment on carburetors with external diaphragms is on the link to the choke, which has a U-bend in it. Decreasing the bend lengthens the link and reduces the choke opening. Increasing the bend shortens the link and increases the choke opening. Just disconnect the link and make the appropriate bends with your fingers at the "U."

On in-carburetor coil chokes, there is a

▲ Rod slides out of well choke thermostatic coil. On cars so equipped, you could bend rod to change adjustment, but if choke coil is weak, it must be replaced.

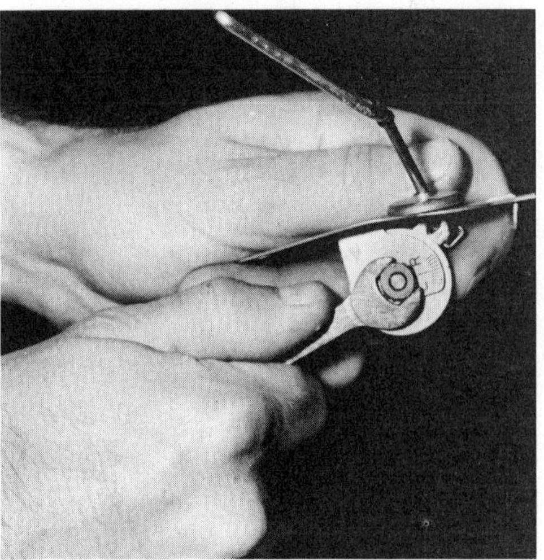

▲ On Chrysler products, you can loosen nut and adjust coil tension. "L" means lean, "R" means rich, and refers to mixture.

link from the choke plate shaft down to the thermostatic coil housing in which the vacuum piston is located. This link will normally have some form of threaded swivel on it to effectively change the length of the link. Lengthening the link reduces choke opening; shortening the link increases it.

Some Ford products with a water-heated choke (you will see the hoses going into it) have an internal diaphragm choke. On this design, there is a diaphragm housing on the side of the choke and an adjusting screw (normally with a cap over it). To adjust this design, remove the cap and turn the adjusting screw in or out as required. P.W.

See also: ENGINE; TUNE-UP, ENGINE.

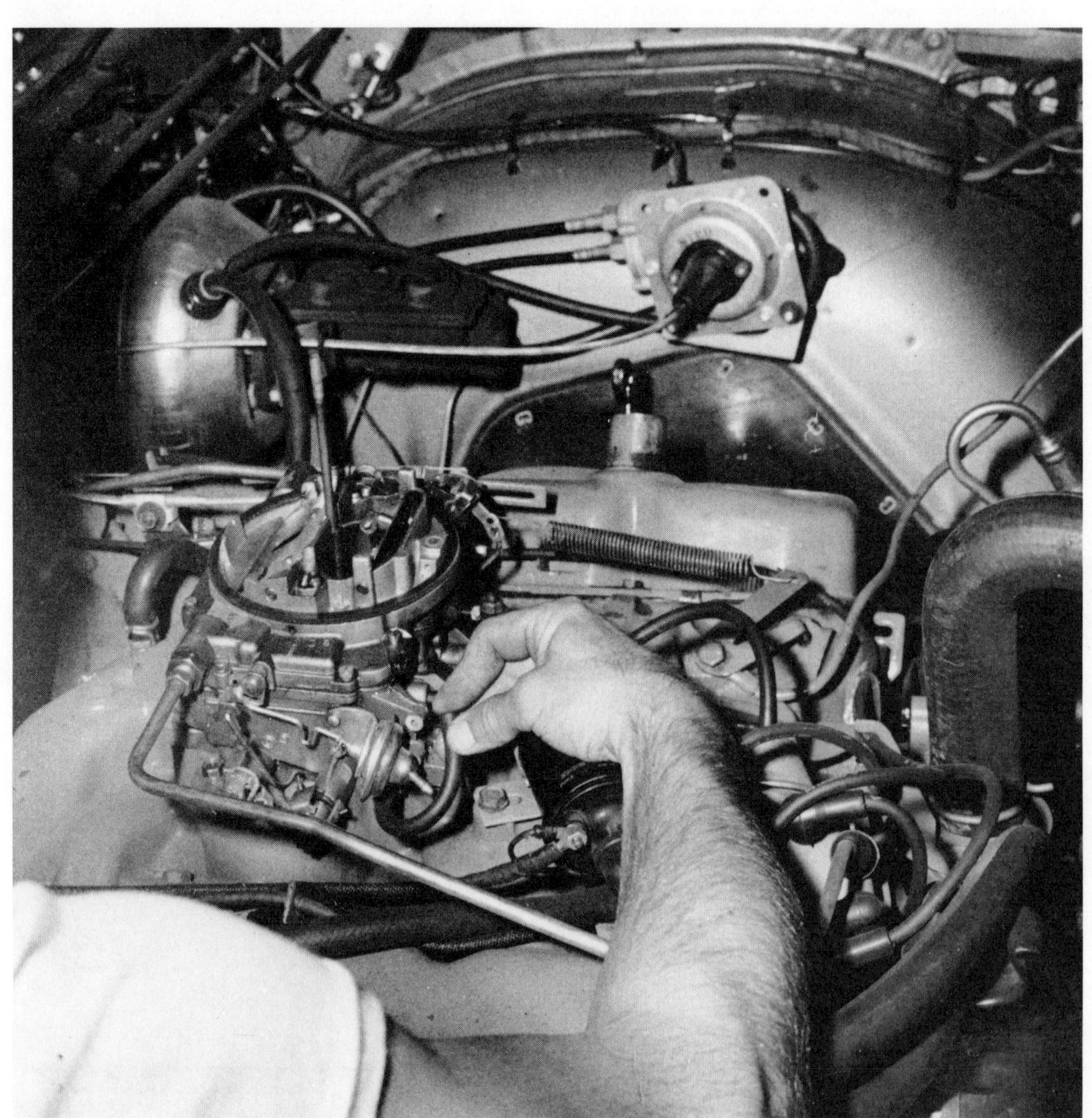

▲ *Checking vacuum action with engine idling and vacuum hose disconnected from choke vacuum diaphragm.*

Concrete Improvements Around Your Home

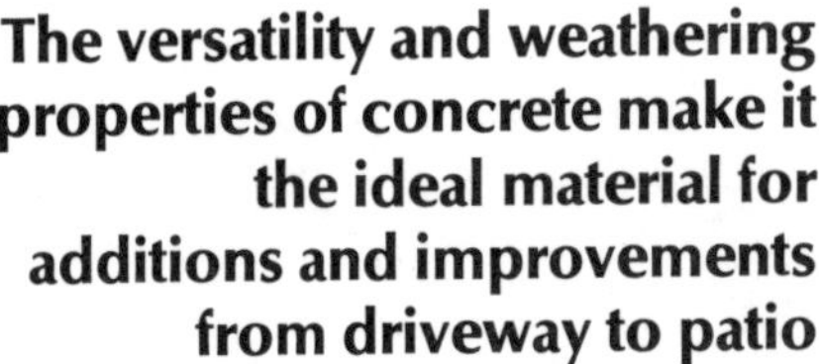

The versatility and weathering properties of concrete make it the ideal material for additions and improvements from driveway to patio

YOU CAN MAKE a dramatic change in the appearance of your home with one versatile and easily manipulated material: Concrete. Virtually every side of your home, from sidewalks and driveways in the front to patios and garden walls in the rear, can be improved by knowing how to work with concrete.

Some advantages of concrete are its superb weathering properties and the ease with which it can be maintained, so this makes it an ideal material for constructing a front sidewalk. Concrete walks provide easy access to the house in all weather and give the children a hard-surfaced play area. Not only are they serviceable in all types of weather, but concrete walks, whether plain, patterned or colored, lead a visitor's eye to the center of interest—your home.

The construction of a high-quality, durable concrete walk is surprisingly simple. You can place sections of the walk in easy stages at your convenience, but if ready-mixed concrete is ordered, you will want

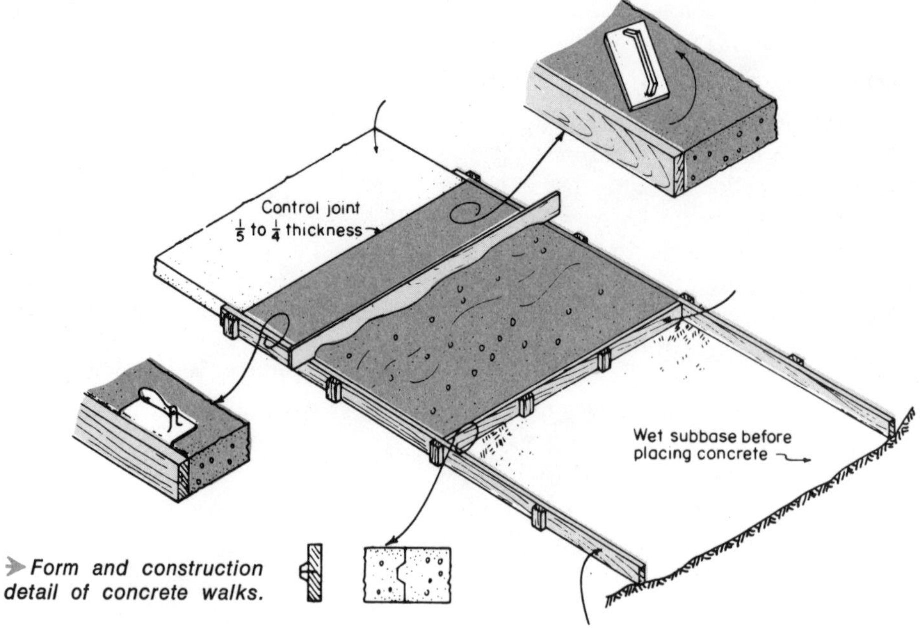

Form and construction detail of concrete walks.

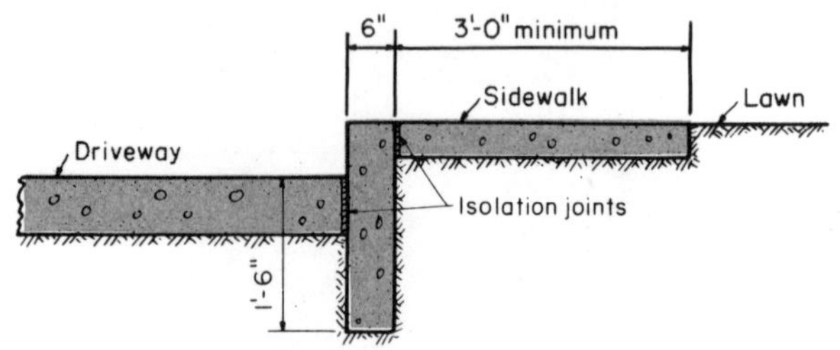

Curb and sidewalk detail.

to do the entire job at one time. This may also mean getting extra help.

Careful preparation of the area is most important if the finished job is to have the high quality you desire. The main walk should be at least three feet wide, and service walks a minimum of two feet wide.

All sod and debris must be removed to the depth of the walk. A subbase of crushed stone is used where the soil is spongy or the area is low and wet. Form boards (2x4-inch) are used and held in place by stakes. The cross-slope should be ⅛-inch per foot to drain away from the house or buildings.

For laying out pleasing curves in walks, a flexible garden hose can be used to mark off the curvature. Curved forms are easily made with two thin strips of plywood or hardboard. Bend the first strip to the proper radius by setting outside and inside stakes. Nail through the strip to the outside stakes, then place the second strip inside the first and nail the two together. Remove the inside stake and the form will hold its curved shape.

In making the walk, use quality concrete—one part portland cement, two parts sand and two and a quarter parts gravel with no more than six gallons of water per bag of cement. For a four-inch thick sidewalk, one cubic yard of concrete will be enough for 27 linear feet of a walk, three feet wide. Use asphalt impregnated joint material where the slab abuts foundations, curbs or steps. Control joints, which are weakened planes to control cracking, are cut with a groover four to five feet apart to a depth

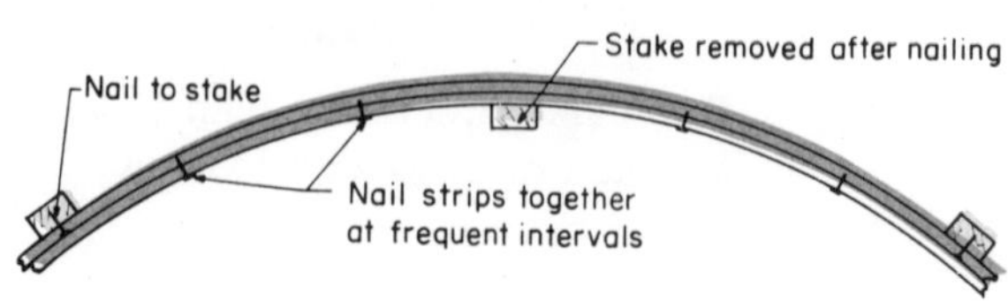

Usual method of forming curved sidewalk is shown.

of one-fifth to one-fourth the slab thickness.

If you wish to stop at any point, simply place a wood bulkhead at the point where you left off. Make the bulkhead from a 2x4-inch piece cut to the inside dimension of the walk forms. Then nail a beveled 1x2-inch strip to the 2x4 bulkhead so that future sidewalk slabs will always remain level with the previously cast slabs.

Place the concrete into forms after wetting the subbase. Screed the surface until it is even with the top of the forms and finish off with a wood or light metal float to give a gritty non-slip surface. Use an edger on all open edges to give a long-wearing and weatherable edge. If you wish to pattern the walk, be sure to do so before the concrete hardens.

Cover the walk with a sheet of plastic, sand, burlap, or other material and damp-cure it. This will give your walk sufficient protection until it has time to harden. Once hard, it will last for years and endure almost any possible extremes in the weather.

A durable material is also very important for driveways. In constructing a driveway out of concrete, you will find that the most attractive approach is one which will show off the home to the best advantage and provide year-round access under all conditions. The now easy availability of ready-mixed concrete makes the installation of a drive easier than ever before. Order ready-mixed concrete containing not more than six gallons of water per bag of cement and figure on six bags of cement per cubic yard and six percent entrained air.

Driveways designed for single cars should be eight to ten feet wide to allow passengers to step from the car onto the driveway. Where only passenger car traffic is expected, plan a concrete driveway four inches thick. When heavier vehicles such as trucks or tractors use the drive, it should be six inches thick.

The concrete is placed on firm earth or a gravel subbase using 2x4 or 2x6-inch forms. The cross slope or pitch should be

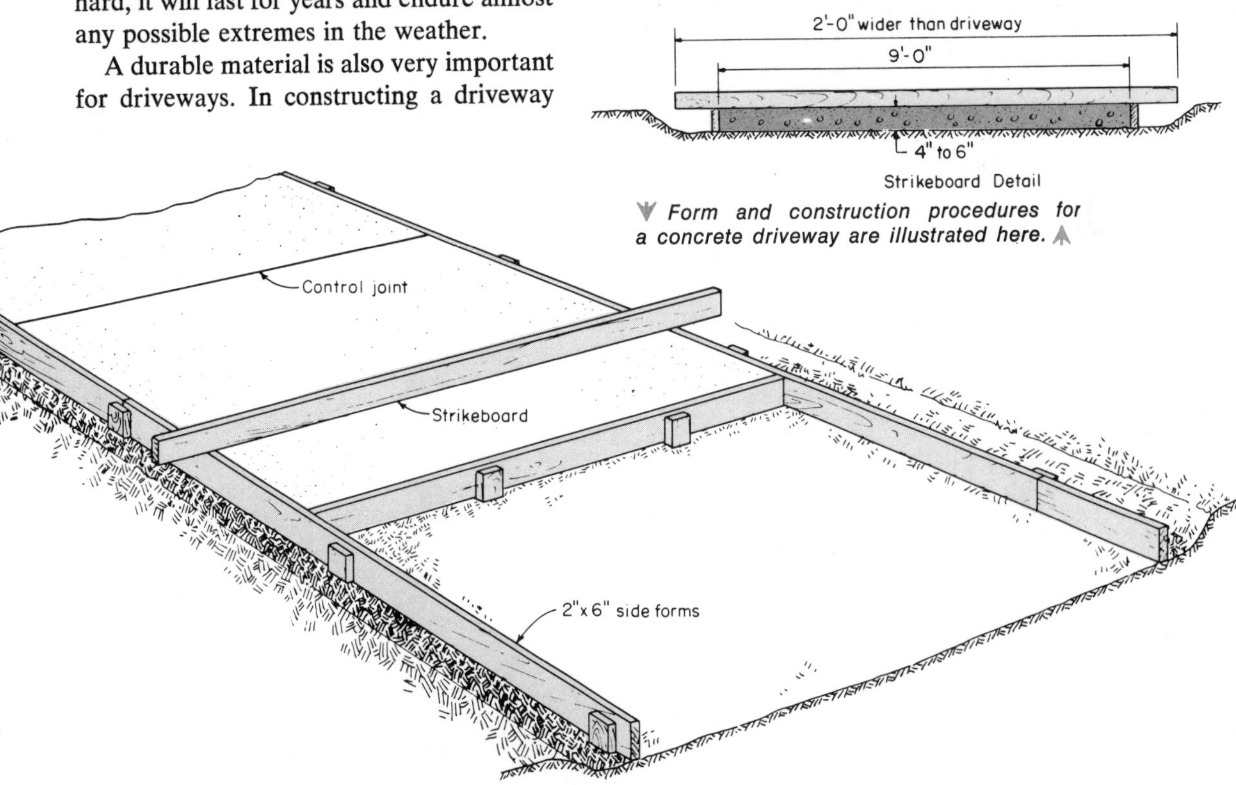

Form and construction procedures for a concrete driveway are illustrated here.

108

Form for concrete steps. A stepped ramp is often used on a long slope. Ramps should have a tread length to provide two easy paces between the risers.

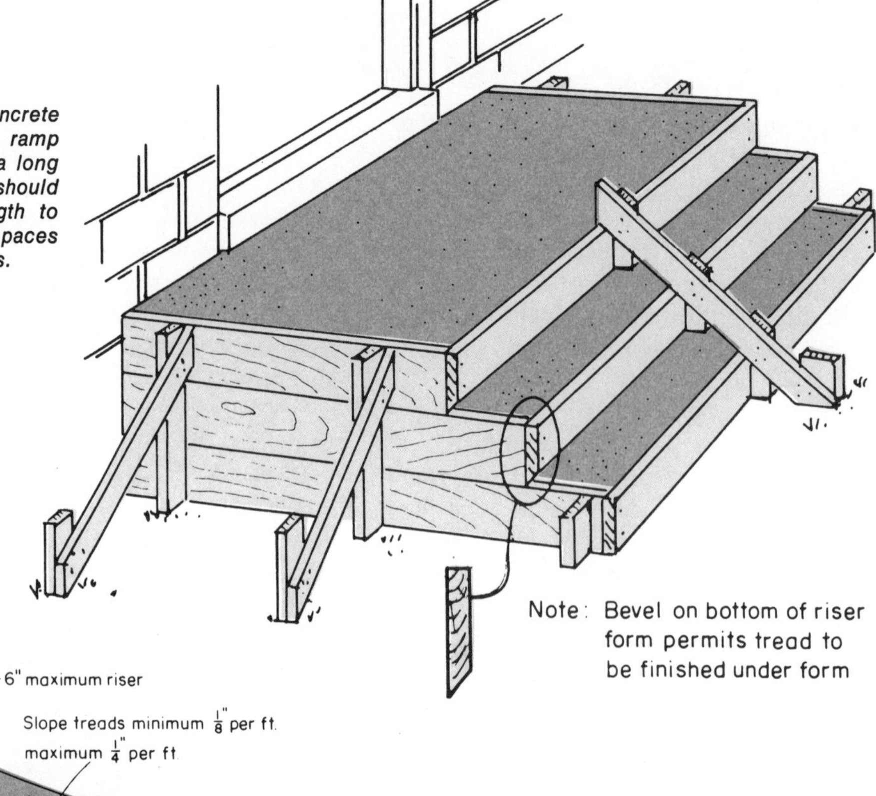
Note: Bevel on bottom of riser form permits tread to be finished under form

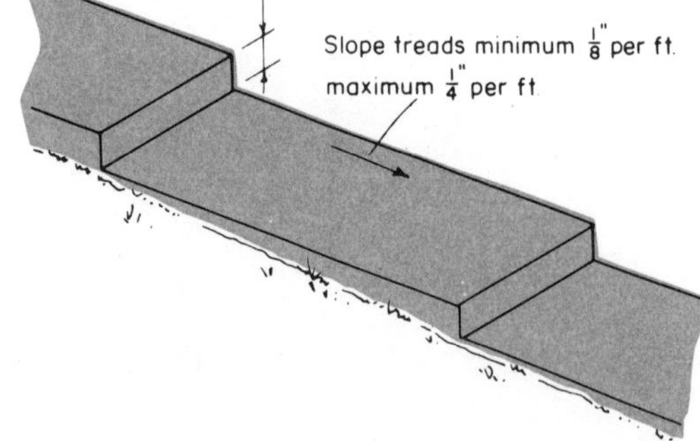
6" maximum riser
Slope treads minimum 1/8" per ft.
maximum 1/4" per ft.

A simple form for constructing stepped ramps.

Concrete steps and patio make a lovely setting for this attractive home.

Lacy, intricate patterns in screen wall add variety and beauty to your landscaping. Walls can be painted with cement paint, or left unpainted.

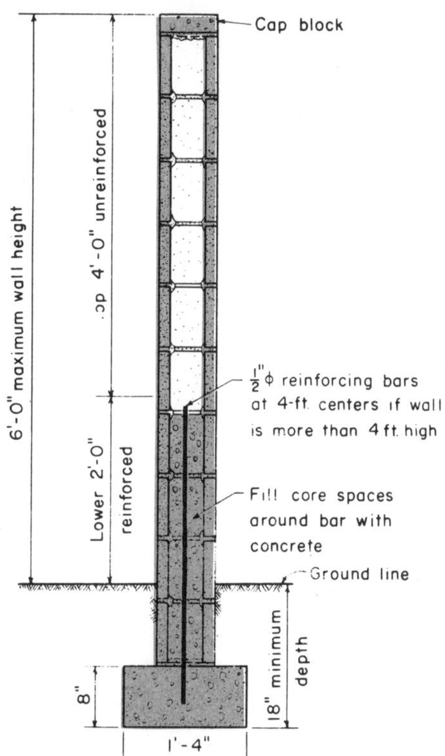

Easy method for construction of a solid masonry wall.

Attractive louvered walls can be built using precast concrete sections.

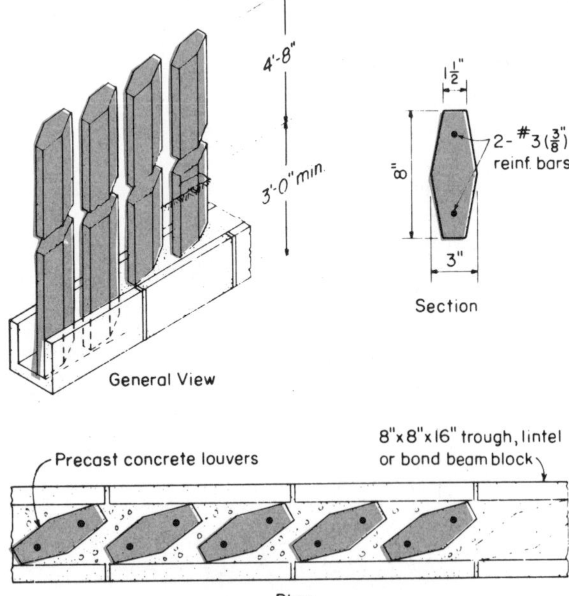

◀Start building a patio by removing sod and debris from area you wish to cover with concrete.

◀Set forms in prepared area. If desired, forms can be left in place, as in this patio, after the concrete has set. If you leave the forms in, use redwood or preservative-treated wood.

◀Fill completed forms with a two-inch layer of sand.

If you are leaving the form in place, cover the top with masking tape to protect the surface from wet concrete.

After the concrete is poured and spread, use a 2 x 4 to strike-off the surface, bringing it flush with the top of the form.

After strike-off, float surface with a wooden float.

Broom the surface to give it an anti-slip texture as well as an attractive design.

Cover finished job with plastic film while it moist-cures for at least five days.

a minimum of ⅛-inch for each foot of width. To level the concrete, use a long 2x4-inch strike-off board riding on each side form. Control joints, cut to a depth of one-fifth to one-fourth the thickness of the slab every ten to fifteen feet, will control cracking of the concrete. Moist-cure the concrete for at least five days.

Attractive patterns can be built right into the driveway surface. Light brooming makes a skid-resistant surface and, with a little imagination, you can make your own attractive and functional designs.

Because concrete does not rot and can be kept clean with simple sweeping or hosing down, it is the ideal material for building steps. They make a home approach much safer and more attractive, and when properly built, they are non-slip in wet weather and require no painting.

The steps should be at least as wide as the sidewalk, and all risers should be exactly the same height. A landing is only needed if there are flights more than five steps high. For safety and convenience, the thread should be at least 11 inches and all treads should be the same width. The rise for each step should be not more than 7½ inches with a ⅛-inch pitch allowance on each tread for drainage.

An economical way to keep steps from sinking is to dig 2-, 6-, or 8-inch diameter postholes beneath the bottom tread. The holes extend below the frost line and are filled with concrete. The top step or platform is tied to the existing wall with two or more metal anchors. Forms should be placed, braced, then oiled for easy removal. Well-tamped soil or granular fill may be used inside the forms to reduce the amount of concrete needed for the steps.

Place the mix of quality concrete into the post holes and the forms, starting at the bottom. Spade the concrete thoroughly around the form edges. Tap the forms lightly to release air bubbles, and screed off the concrete at tread level. Finish the treads with a float and then broom to create a non-skid surface. Moist-cure for at least five days, remove the forms and wire, and brush the steps to clean them.

High quality precast concrete steps are also available from many manufacturers. These steel-reinforced units may be obtained in several types. They are quickly installed and usually have built-in lugs to hold railings and grille work.

Outdoor living areas are also greatly enhanced by other concrete products. Attractive garden and screen walls which are well engineered and tastefully designed in concrete can add a new dimension to your backyard. From the simple 8x8x16-inch concrete block to the newest screen wall unit and grille block, concrete gives the beauty, the appeal, and the pleasing backdrop for a beautiful garden setting. Also, because concrete will not peel, warp, rot or decay in adverse weather, it will maintain its beauty for years.

Garden walls furnish privacy for your outdoor living area and around swimming pools. Solid walls of block can protect your area from chilling winds, yet with very little design change, block can be placed so air circulates freely through the wall.

Both solid and open-type garden walls are used as needs dictate. The many textures and patterns available in concrete help dramatize your landscaping ideas. Patterns of squares, rectangles, and strong diagonal lines add a feeling of movement to ordinary garden walls. Lacy, intricate patterns of screen block walls add beauty and an air of grandeur.

For a rugged appearance, extruded mortar or offset block in the garden wall lends a feeling of security. Split block and textured block capture shadows and highlights creating ever-changing shadow patterns and designs.

▲ *Concrete splash block carries downspout water away from wall.*

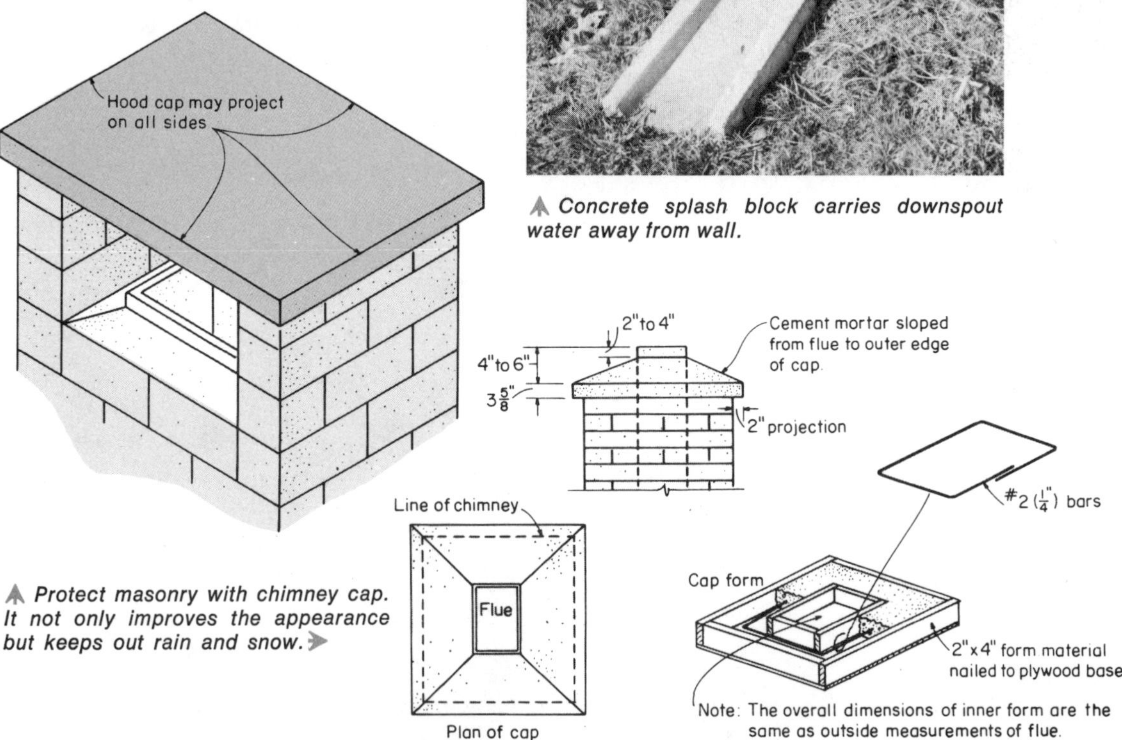

▲ *Protect masonry with chimney cap. It not only improves the appearance but keeps out rain and snow.* ➤

Garden walls need good foundations to keep them attractive for years of service. Lay out the wall in the desired line and dig a trench slightly wider than twice the thickness of the proposed wall. The trench should be a minimum of 18 inches deep or below the frost line in colder areas. Make the footing twice the width of the wall, and the same depth as the wall width. Thus for an 8-inch block wall, the concrete footing should be 16 inches wide and 8 inches thick. Then follow the same procedures mentioned earlier for laying block.

There is an old saying that, "Where you have the walls of a house, you have the start of a patio." This means you already have exciting possibilities for a garden terrace or an outdoor living room—and all your visions can be realized with concrete.

To build a cast-in-place patio, mark off the area and remove sod and soil to the depth desired. Most patios are formed with 2x4-inch wood forms. For circular borders, drive stakes on desired arcs and place two thin strips of wood around the stakes. By nailing the strips together, an arc is formed and can be held in place by outside stakes.

For dividers to be left in the concrete, use redwood or treated lumber placed to give the desired patterns. Where this is done, you will want to protect dividers by covering the top edge with masking tape before the concrete is placed. Set the forms with a slight pitch to keep water away from the house and to aid water run-off when hosing down.

One cubic yard of concrete will place 81 square feet of 4-inch thick patio. To allow for waste and irregularities in excavation, order 5 to 10 percent more concrete than actually calculated. Order a mix of six bags of cement per cubic yard with not more than six gallons total water. Specify six per cent air entrainment.

Be certain all forming is ready before concrete is delivered. Check forms and have finishing tools and enough labor on hand. If you have never finished concrete, consider hiring a concrete finisher. Spade the concrete well into the corners of the

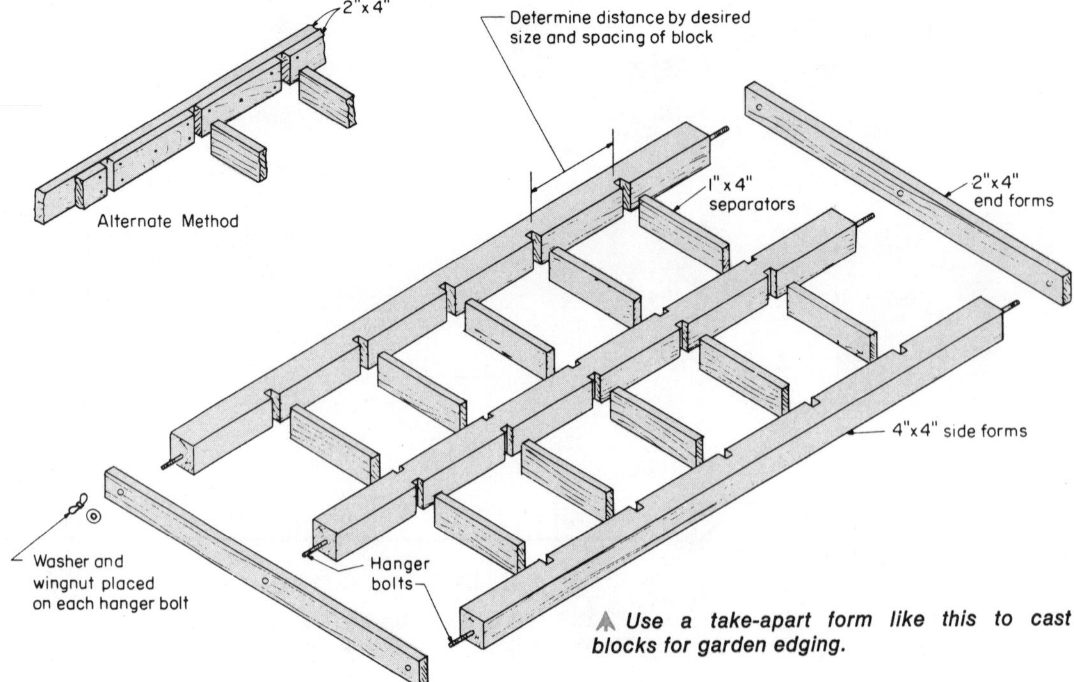

Use a take-apart form like this to cast blocks for garden edging.

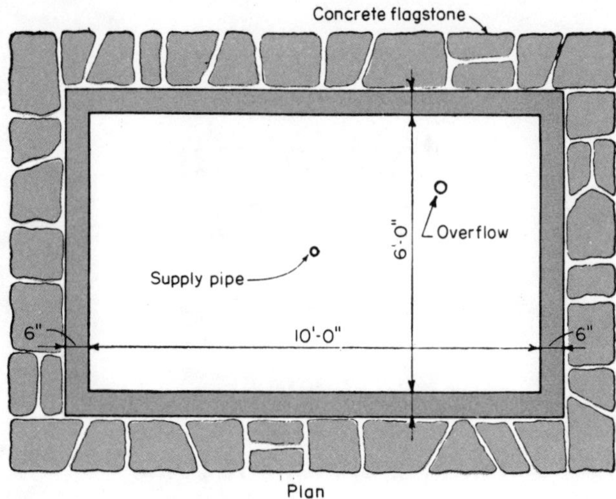

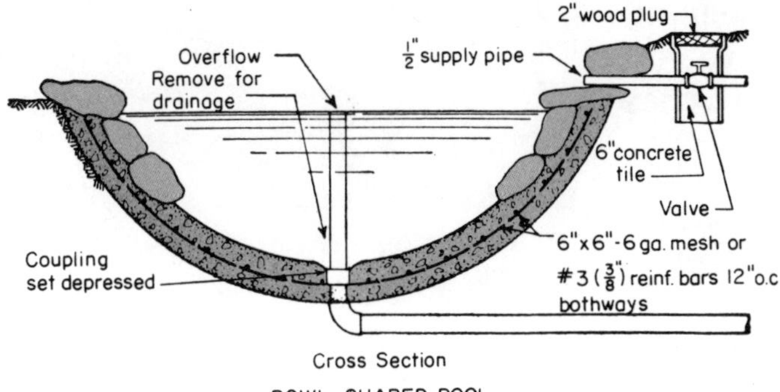

You can put a pool in your landscape scheme.

Shown are cross sections of designs for a bowl-shaped pool and rectangular pool.

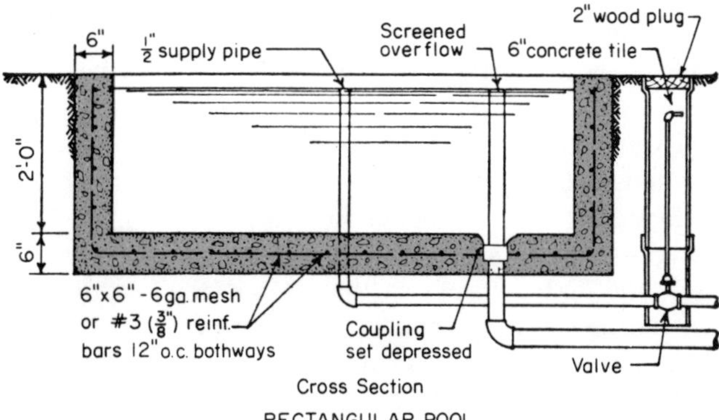

forms. Overfill the forms slightly, then screed with a straightedge.

Check the concrete frequently to determine when it is ready for finishing. Wood floating will give the concrete a rough texture; steel troweling is used for a dense smooth surface.

Moist-cure at least five days. M.E.F.

See also: ADDITIONS, HOME; BRICKWORK; HOME IMPROVEMENT; STONEWORK.

Maintaining Your Car's Cooling System

This system, which keeps your engine at the proper temperature is more complicated than it looks; understanding it and keeping it in good shape will save you many hot weather headaches

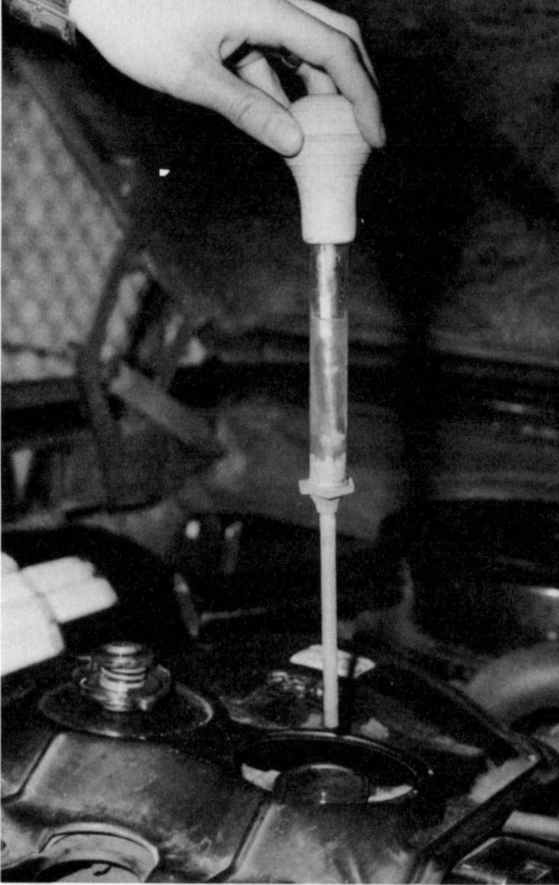

Using a hydrometer to determine antifreeze concentration.

THE COOLING SYSTEM is seemingly a very simple system. A pump driven by a belt draws water from the engine and pushes it through the upper radiator hose into the radiator, through which it flows, giving up heat to the air.

The coolant then flows through the lower radiator hose into the engine, where it picks up heat and the cycle starts all over again.

However, this apparently simple setup is anything but simple.

First, there is a radiator cap with two valves—one, a spring-loaded valve that seals the entire system so that as coolant expands the system becomes pressurized by as much as 17 psi (pounds per square inch), which raises the boiling point of the coolant.

The other valve is actuated by vacuum. As the coolant cools, it contracts, creating a vacuum in the system. If the vacuum valve did not open, the vacuum in the system would cause collapse of weaker parts, such as radiator tubes and hoses. The opening of the valve permits air to rush in and eliminate the vacuum.

Second, there is the thermostat, a temperature-sensitive device between the pump and the upper radiator hose. This unit closes to prevent coolant from reaching the radiator when the engine is cold, speeding up coolant warm-up.

As the engine warms up, the thermostat begins to open and some coolant can flow through the upper hose.

The thermostat then maintains a position that will send just the right amount of coolant through the radiator to hold overall coolant temperature at the desired level. Coolant that is kept from going through the upper radiator hose goes instead through a bypass passage or hose on the engine.

When the outside temperature is very high, the radiator cannot dissipate heat as well, and the thermostat is wide open.

The fan helps the radiator dissipate heat to the air at low road speed. Driven by a belt, it draws air through the radiator.

Many cars are equipped with thermostatic fans, another little complication. This type of fan is designed to free-wheel (thus requiring no real amount of power to turn) when the engine is running cool. When the engine is running hot, a thermostatic unit engages the fan.

In addition to all this, there are hoses to fail, hose clamps to come loose, gaskets to fail, and a water pump to go bad.

So our seemingly simple cooling system is really something you must pay attention to, and check and service carefully. Just an annual drain, flush and fill is not enough.

Most engines use one thermostat. Some V-8's with two hoses from radiator to cylinders use two thermostats—one for each bank of cylinders. The thermostat may be mounted in any one of several spots: in the block, at the radiator hose elbow, in a secondary hose connection, or even in the radiator. Instead of playing "find-the-thermostat," check your owner's manual or a nearby garage. In most cars, the thermostat —wherever it is—can be removed by loosening two bolts.

If your engine refuses to heat quickly on cold mornings or to cool quickly on hot days, the thermostat may be at fault. If it is mis-aligned, or the valve inside it is stuck open, it will allow water to circulate freely through the radiator even when the engine temperature is below normal, and the engine may never heat. If the valve spring is worn or stuck closed, it will force the water in the cooling system to bypass the radiator —even when it's boiling—and the engine may never get a chance to cool. The remedy is a new thermostat.

Getting the right one. All thermostats are not the same. Every auto manufacturer specifies the best type and the proper heat range for his car, and in some cases may even specify one thermostat for use with

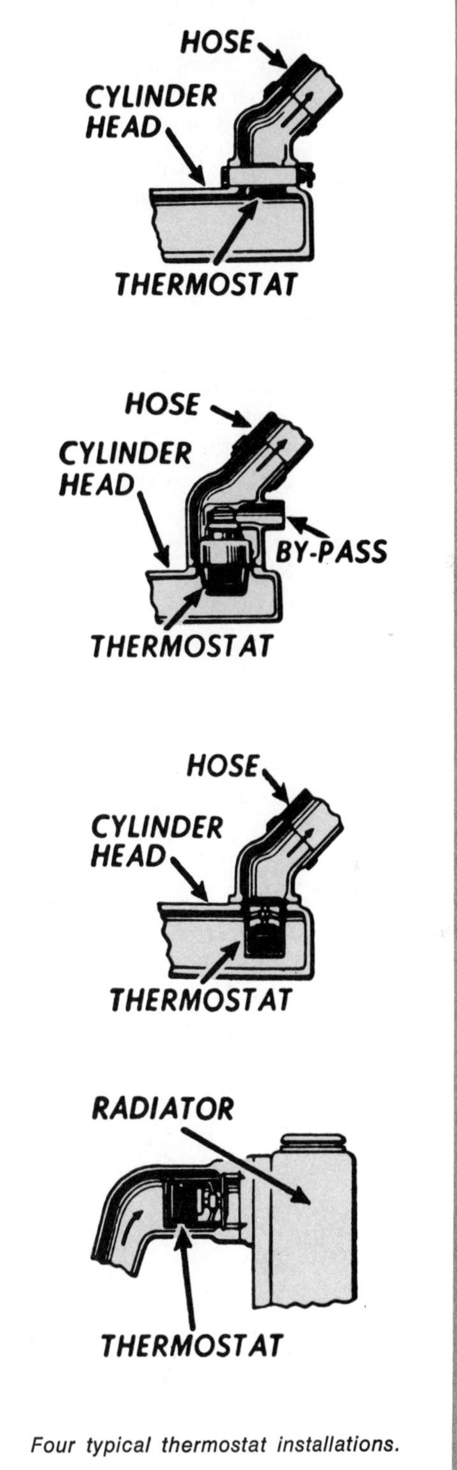

Four typical thermostat installations.

water and another for use with a permanent-type antifreeze.

Be sure to buy the right thermostat for your car. If you bought the car secondhand, don't go by the one now in the cooling system: it could be wrong. Check a thermostat catalog for the right model, heat range, and size.

Remove the thermostat, if you think there may be something wrong with it, and check for corrosion. If you can't see anything wrong, test it before you decide whether to discard it or to put it back in.

Many thermostats have their temperature ranges stamped on the casing. The lower temperature is the one at which the thermostat is supposed to begin opening, and the higher temperature the point at which it should be fully open.

To test the thermostat, heat water on the stove to a temperature 10° below the point at which it should begin opening. Suspend the thermostat in the water for a couple of minutes. If it starts to open, discard it. If it remains closed, heat the water to a point 25° above the opening temperature, and suspend the thermostat in the water again. At this point, it should open fully; if it doesn't, discard it.

It may be necessary to remove one or more radiator hoses to remove the thermostat. Check the hoses for breaks and splits while they are off the car, and when you put them back on, be sure to clean the connections. Before you replace an engine-mounted thermostat, coat the elbow or housing with sealing compound. If the gasket is torn or chipped, replace it. Tighten the hose clamps, start the engine, and check for leaks.

Danger signs. If your engine is running hot or using water, check the hoses in both the cooling system and the heater system. Since the system is pressurized, a poor hose in either system could mean trouble. A soft-walled hose may collapse inwardly, restrict-

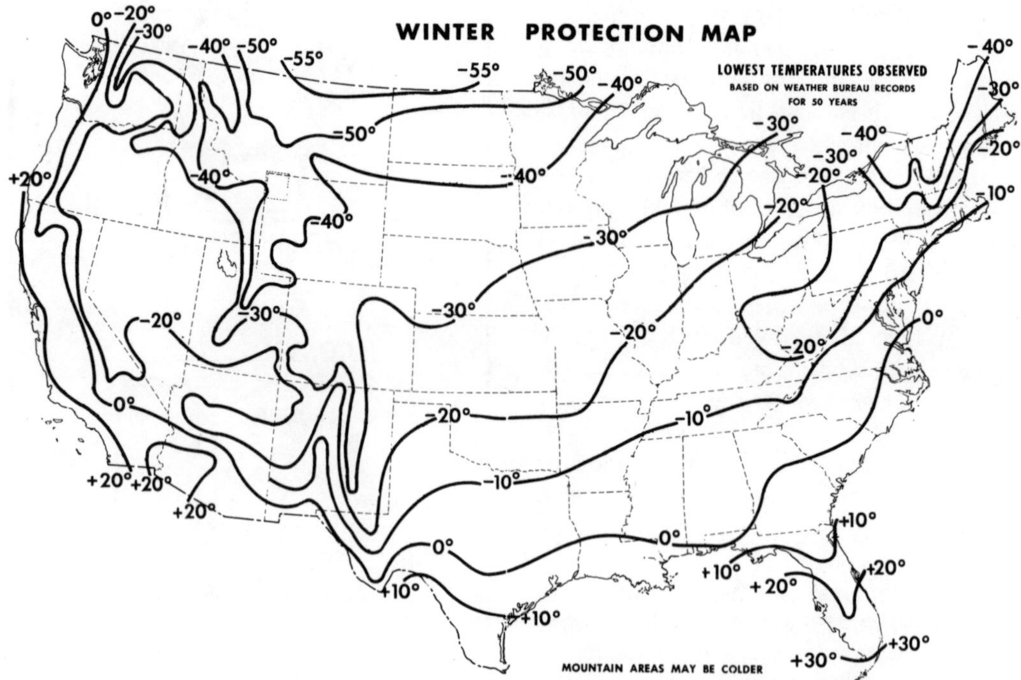

Use this map to determine how concentrated your antifreeze solution should be.

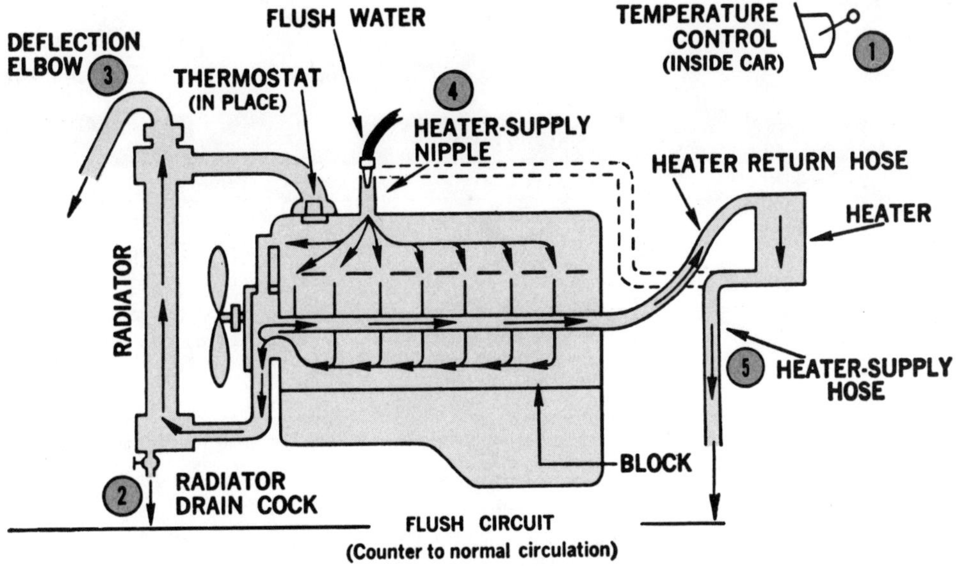

COOLING SYSTEM FLUSHING INSTRUCTIONS

A. Set heater temperature control (1) to high. (See Note #1 if car is equipped with a vacuum-operated heater valve.)

B. Open radiator drain cock (2).

C. Remove radiator cap and install deflection elbow in the filler neck (3). This prevents excessive splash into the engine compartment. (A clear, flexible plastic tube attached to the elbow permits viewing the coolant as it drains from the system.)

D. Remove hose from heater supply nipple at the engine block (4). Point this hose downward for an auxiliary drain (5). (See Note #2 if heater supply nipple is inaccessible.)

E. Connect water supply to the heater supply nipple (4) at the engine block. CAUTION: DO NOT CONNECT WATER SUPPLY DIRECTLY TO HEATER—THIS COULD CAUSE DAMAGE. Cool flush water may be supplied through an ordinary hose or a flushing gun (cool water necessary to prevent opening of thermostat during flushing). If flushing gun has provision for air injection, air pressure should be controlled to prevent damage. (Radiator cap pressure rating may be used as a guide.)

F. Turn on water. Flush for 3-5 minutes. During the last minute of flushing, squeeze the upper radiator hose to remove any trapped liquid.

G. Turn off water (see Note #3 if antifreeze is to be installed)—remove connection at heater supply nipple (4)—reconnect heater supply hose to nipple—remove deflection elbow from radiator—permit enough water to drain from radiator drain cock to accept antifreeze—close radiator drain cock.

H. Install antifreeze—replace radiator cap—start engine and warm to operating temperature —make final check of coolant level. Check for leaks.

NOTE 1:

If car is equipped with a vacuum-operated heater valve, start engine and run at "idle" during the flushing procedure. CAUTION: SHUT OFF ENGINE BEFORE TURNING OFF WATER (primarily Chrysler products).

NOTE 2:

If heater supply nipple on the engine block is inaccessible, remove heater supply hose at heater and connect water supply to flow into engine block—not into heater. Attach a short piece of hose at heater and point downward. CAUTION: DO NOT CONNECT WATER SUPPLY DIRECTLY TO HEATER—COULD CAUSE DAMAGE.

NOTE 3:

If antifreeze is to be installed, draining from the radiator drain cock should provide sufficient space for the addition of 50% antifreeze (—34°F. protection). When greater freezing protection is required, or if it is not possible to install sufficient antifreeze, AFTER FILLING THE SYSTEM the heater hose can be removed from the heater supply nipple (4) momentarily to allow additional water to escape from the system.

SERVICE DIAGNOSIS—COOLING SYSTEM

Condition	Possible Cause	Remedy
EXTERNAL LEAKAGE	1. Loose hose clamp	1. Replace the hose clamp
	2. Hose leaking	2. Replace the hose
	3. Leaking radiator	3. Repair or replace the radiator as necessary
	4. Worn or damaged water pump seal	4. Replace the water pump seal and impeller
	5. Loose core hole plug	5. Install new core hole plug
	6. Damaged gasket, or dry gasket, if engine has been stored	6. Replace gaskets as necessary
	7. Cylinder head bolts loose, or tightened unevenly	7. Replace the cylinder head gasket and torque head in correct sequence
	8. Leak at heater connection	8. Clean the heater connections and replace the hoses and clamps if necessary
	9. Leak at water temperature sending unit	9. Tighten the water temperature sending unit
	10. Leak at water pump attaching bolt	10. Tighten the water pump attaching bolts to factory specifications
	11. Leak or exhaust manifold stud	11. Seal and re-drive the stud
	12. Cracked thermostat housing	12. Replace the thermostat housing
	13. Dented radiator inlet or outlet tube	13. Straighten the radiator inlet or outlet tube as necessary
	14. Leaking heater core	14. Repair or replace the heater core
	15. Cracked or porous water pump housing	15. Replace the water pump assembly
	16. Warped or cracked cylinder head	16. Replace the cylinder head
	17. Cracked cylinder block	17. Replace the cylinder block
	18. Sand holes or porous condition in block or head.	18. Replace the cylinder block or cylinder head as necessary
	19. Faulty pressure cap	19. Replace pressure cap
	20. Loose or stripped oil cooler fittings	20. Tighten or replace as necessary
INTERNAL LEAKAGE	1. Faulty head gasket	1. Install a new head gasket
	2. Refer to causes 6, 7, 16, 17, 18, and 20 listed under External Leakage	2. Refer to corrections 6, 7, 16, 17, 18 and 20 listed under External Leakage
	3. Crack in head into valve compartment	3. Pressure test cooling system, replace the cylinder head
	4. Cracked valve port	4. Pressure test cooling system, replace the cylinder head
	5. Crack in block into push rod compartment	5. Pressure test cooling system, replace the cylinder block
	6. Cracked cylinder wall	6. Pressure test cooling system, replace the cylinder block
	7. Leaking oil cooler spring	7. Repair or replace the oil cooler
POOR CIRCULATION	1. Low coolant level	1. Fill radiator to correct level
	2. Collapsed radiator hose. (A bottom hose with faulty spring may collapse only at medium or high engine speeds)	2. Check radiator cap vacuum valve. If good, replace hose
	3. Fan belt loose, glazed or oil soaked	3. Tighten or replace the fan belt as necessary

SERVICE DIAGNOSIS—COOLING SYSTEM (Continued)

Condition	Possible Cause	Remedy
POOR CIRCULATION	4. Air leak through bottom hose	4. Reposition hose clamps or replace the hose. Check radiator outlets for dents or out-of-round
	5. Faulty thermostat	5. Replace the thermostat
	6. Water pump impeller broken or loose on shaft	6. Replace the water pump
	7. Restricted radiator core water passages	7. Flush the radiator thoroughly or rod out if necessary
	8. Restricted engine water jacket	8. Flush the engine cooling system thoroughly
OVERHEATING	1. Low coolant level	1. Fill radiator to proper level
	2. Blocked radiator air passages	2. Blow out the radiator air passages
	3. Incorrect ignition timing	3. Time the engine ignition system
	4. Low engine oil level	4. Add engine oil to the correct level
	5. Incorrect valve timing	5. Correct the engine valve timing
	6. Inaccurate temperature gauge	6. Replace the temperature gauge
	7. Restricted overflow tube	7. Remove restriction from the overflow tube
	8. Faulty radiator pressure cap or seat	8. Replace the radiator cap. Clean or replace seat
	9. Frozen heat control valve	9. Free up the manifold heat control valve
	10. Dragging brakes	10. Adjust the brakes
	11. Excessive engine idling	11. Set at faster idle or stop engine
	12. Frozen coolant	12. Thaw out cooling system, add anti-freeze as required
	13. Faulty fan drive unit	13. Replace the fan drive unit
	14. Faulty temperature sending unit	14. Replace the sending unit
OVERFLOW LOSS	1. Overfilling	1. Adjust coolant to the correct level
	2. Coolant foaming due to insufficient corrosion inhibitor	2. Flush the radiator and add anti-freeze or rust inhibitor as required
	3. Blown head gasket	3. Replace the head gasket
	4. Broken or shifted lower hose spring	4. Replace lower hose

ing the flow of water from radiator to engine. A worn hose, cracked or split, may leak water. A hardened hose may leak water around the connections. A leaky hose may also allow air to seep into the cooling system, and as the air bubbles form in the cooling system, they may promote rust. The rust, in time, can clog the radiator and the hoses.

In a recent survey, automotive engineers found that 15% of all cooling system complaints were caused by rotted or age-hardened hoses or by hoses with loose, leaking joints. The trouble may be in the age of the hose, but it can be in the quality of the hose itself.

Hoses are generally made with reinforcement, either an inner layer of fabric or an inner spiral of wire, or—in cases of extreme pressure—both. A hose without some kind of reinforcement can break without warning. In a recent test, engineers checked reinforced hoses against unreinforced types. Of all non-reinforced hoses, 54% failed during the test; only 15% of the reinforced types gave any sign of trouble.

To be safe, check the condition of hoses about every six months. Inspect them for cracks, splits and signs of leaks. Squeeze radiator hoses. Be sure they are springy and resilient, not spongy and lifeless. If any hose collapses under finger pressure and does not instantly spring back, it should be replaced. Hoses which are too hard may leak at the connections. Replace these. If the hoses seem in good condition and your engine still runs a fever, remove the hoses to see if they may be clogged with rust.

Replacing hoses. When you replace a hose, use one with the recommended internal diameter. If there is any doubt about the hose clamps, replace them.

There are many types of clamps used on cars.

The best is a worm-drive type, in which a worm gear engages slots in the clamping band. This band clamp applies the closest thing to circular clamping pressure. (The pressure is actually tangential.)

As a band design, it also has the advantage of not digging deeply into the hose, as the wire-type clamps do. And the greater area under the clamp means that it holds its tightness longer.

You can glue the new hoses to their connections with a thin coating of sealing compound if you wish, but this is not necessary when you use the right clamp. But whether you glue the new hoses to the connections or rely on clamp pressure, be sure to clean the connections before you fit the new hoses.

To replace the upper radiator hose, drain the radiator by opening the petcock at the bottom. Drain only enough liquid from the radiator to lower the coolant below the level of the upper radiator pipe.

To replace the lower radiator hose, drain the entire cooling system. Open both the petcock on the radiator and the petcock on the engine.

To replace the heater hose, check the intake and exhaust levels of the hoses. If they take off and empty above the upper radiator pipe, you will have to drain only part of the coolant from the radiator. If they fit to connections below the upper radiator pipe, it may be necessary to drain the entire cooling system to replace them.

After you have drained the system to the safe level (or empty, depending upon the car and the hose to be replaced), loosen the hose clamps and remove the worn hose. If the hose to be replaced is a straight section, you can cut a new length to match. If the hose is premolded, buy one to match. Use the old hose as a pattern. If the hose is a flexible type, be sure you have the right replacement.

Place two clamps over the new hose. Clean the two connections and slip the hose onto the engine connection first. Attach the other end to the radiator connection, bending the hose near the center to fit over the radiator pipe. Tighten the clamp at the engine connection, then slide the hose upward on the radiator connection as far as it will go. Tighten the radiator clamp.

Refill the cooling system with water (or anti-freeze) and start the engine. Check the hose for leaks, then retighten the clamps after the engine has warmed.

Other leaks. If there are traces of rust near any of the headbolts, remove the bolts (after the coolant has been drained) and wire-brush the threads clean. Then apply a film of nonhardening gasket cement to the threads and pull the bolts up to uniform tightness, using a torque wrench, if possible, to make sure the bolts are tightened uniformly. Refer to the engine or wrench manufacturer's specifications for the correct torque in foot-pounds, which may vary between 50 ft./lbs. and 120 ft./lbs., depending on the size of the headbolt.

If an expansion plug in the block is rusted, remove it by driving a sharp centerpunch through the plug about ¾-inch near its center and giving the punch a sharp tap sideways with a hammer. Scrape clean the recess in which the plug fits, using a screwdriver blade. Then drive a new plug into place, after applying a thin film of gasket cement to both the plug and the surface upon which it rests. Strike the domed side (which should always face *out*) a sharp blow with a machinist's hammer to cause plug to expand and form a tight fit in the block.

You will need a new cylinder head gasket if there is any sign of water in the crankcase oil. To check for leakage of exhaust gas into the coolant—and consequently the possibility of the leakage of coolant down into the engine—first remove the top hose from the engine and take out the thermostat. Then fill the engine with water and remove the fan belt. Carefully block all four wheels or set the emergency brake, then put the car into automatic drive. With a conventional transmission, shift into "high" and apply the load by slipping the clutch. Have an assistant start the engine and very quickly, before it has warmed up (which might create steam bubbles), accelerate it very briefly to rather high speed. If there is an exhaust gas leak into the coolant, you will see bubbles in the cooling system water in a matter of seconds. If bubbles appear, a new head gasket is in order. Before installing the gasket, be sure that head and block mating surfaces are clean.

The presence of a white deposit (lime) on the radiator core is a warning that water has leaked out and evaporated.

If you are using an antifreeze with a sealer, the leak is apparently serious, for this type of antifreeze will seal minor leaks. If you are not, try a can of sealer before going to the expense of having the radiator resoldered.

Water pump. If there is any sign of leakage at the water pump joint, try tightening the bolts. If this does not cure the problem, the pump will have to be removed, checked for a defective gasket and replaced if the gasket is good. (The problem is in the pump shaft seal.)

Note: do not confuse minor seepage from the pump vent hole with a leaking pump. The vent hole is supposed to permit the small amount of coolant that gets past even a good pump seal to drop out.

Radiator cap. The only sure way to test the radiator cap is with a pressure tester, a combination unit that also tests the ability of the cooling system to withstand the pressures built up by the cap.

If the cap holds specified pressure, it then can be physically inspected. The rubber seal should be in good condition. It and the inside of the radiator neck should be wiped clean of rust deposits. The vacuum valve should be checked by hanging a fingernail under it and tugging. It should open easily and spring back when released.

The system itself. Even if a system shows no apparent leaks, it should be tested to see if it will hold at least the pressure of the cap. If the system fails to hold cap pressure, check for loose gaskets and poor hose connections.

A pressure test of cap and system should always be made before draining, flushing and refilling.

Very few weekend mechanics are likely to have a pressure gauge. You will have to pay a service station a service charge for this test.

The anti-freeze and cooling system chemicals committee of the Automotive Division of the Chemical Specialties Manufacturers Association summed up modern practice in a detailed recommendation on cooling system care. The recommendation was distributed to the professionals, and is included here for weekend mechanics.

"The modern engine is designed to maintain efficient operating temperatures year-round with ethylene glycol (permanent antifreeze) solutions. New cars have factory-installed ethylene glycol antifreeze coolant which will afford freezing protection adequate for most areas of the country and which contains corrosion inhibitors to protect the cooling system. Under recommended service conditions, this antifreeze coolant will function for at least one year." (Goodbye to the semi-annual drain.)

"The antifreeze tester" (that's a hydrometer they're talking about—you can buy one for a dollar, although most of you probably have one already) "has now become a year-round service tool—check in warm weather months as well as winter for solution concentration and appearance. Maintain a minimum concentration providing 34° F.—50 percent—for adequate corrosion resistance and temperature protection."

The temperature protection is not only for winter. Antifreeze also raises the boiling point of the coolant and the entire cooling system is designed for this higher boiling point.

Most cars have temperature warning lights that go on at about 250° F. In a system with pure water and a pressure cap holding to 14 psi, the water would boil at 244°, meaning that you would have an over-heated engine with no warning.

And that would be with a 100 percent sound pressure cap. If your cap were only holding 11 psi, the coolant would boil at 235° with pure water, and 245° even with — 20° F. antifreeze protection.

All cooling systems leak to some degree. A perfectly good system will leak a pint in 1200 miles. If you just add water, the antifreeze concentration will soon drop to the point where over-heating protection is lost.

The new rules on cooling system service are:

1. Drain, flush and refill just once a year, but make sure the refill is at least 50 percent antifreeze. (Never exceed two-thirds antifreeze, as this is the highest percentage that will keep the freezing point down. As the antifreeze percentage is increased from two-thirds, the freezing point actually goes up. A 100 percent antifreeze solution will freeze at only — 8° F.)

2. When you top up the cooling system, do so with a 50-50 mixture of antifreeze and water.

Cooling system flushing. If the coolant is speckled with rust particles, you should add a can of flushing compound to the radiator and drive the car for about 100 miles to circulate it properly and give it a chance to work in.

The actual draining of the coolant can be done in either of two ways, but in any case should be preceded by a cooling system check.

1. You can open the drain cock on the radiator and remove the two drain plugs on a V-8 or open the drain cock on a six. Permit the coolant to drain out, run some water through the system, refit the drain plugs, close the drain cock(s) or whatever, and fill the system with a 50-50 antifreeze and water mixture.

This is a perfectly acceptable procedure and it will work nicely. The only problem is that the engine drain plugs on V-8s must be removed from underneath, and even the drain cocks on some sixes are not overly accessible.

You must have some way of safely jacking up the car. (After all, you will be getting underneath, and you don't really trust that bumper jack, do you?)

Even if you have a jacking setup, it is time-consuming to use. Most cooling system drainings are done in the soft earth backyard, not in the garage with its concrete floor. This can make the jacking somewhat difficult if not impossible.

2. You can use the flush and fill procedure illustrated. Although designed for use with an air pressure flushing gun, it will work acceptably with a garden hose.

3. You can install a flushing kit, an inexpensive set that includes the deflection elbow and a plastic tee that is installed in the heater hose. (The only tools necessary to

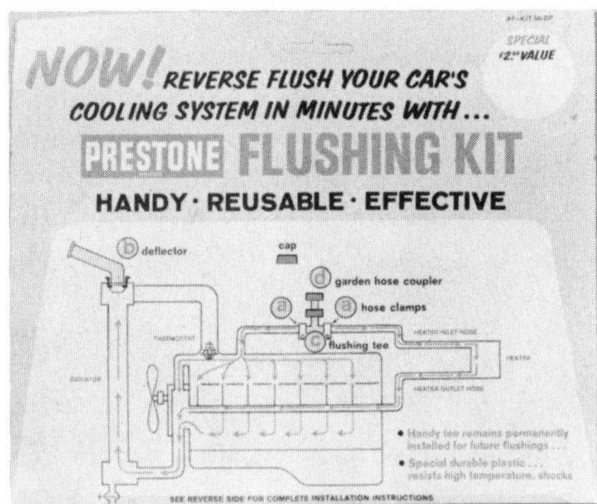

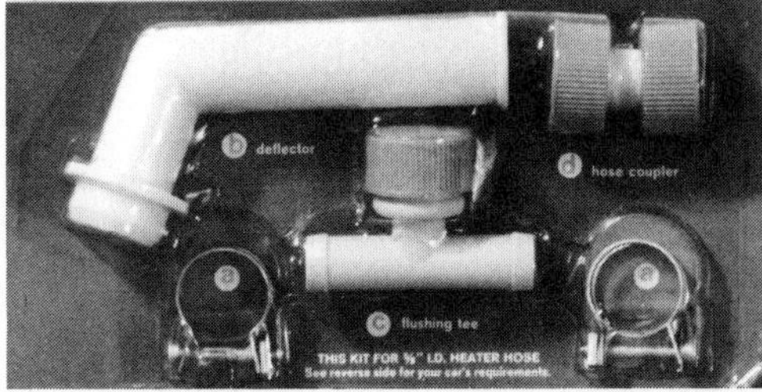

Inexpensive kit for flushing an automobile cooling system.

Water deflector of kit is fitted to radiator neck. This prevents flushing water from splashing into the engine compartment.

Kit's permanent tee-fitting is installed in heater hose.

Threaded tee of kit accepts garden hose for flushing. When job is finished, cap of tee is screwed on tightly.

install are a saw to cut the heater hose and a screwdriver for the hose clamps.)

The tee-fitting has a screw cap that is removed and a garden hose attached when you want to flush the system. Just turn on the water and the flushing procedure is essentially the same as with the illustrated procedure for the flushing gun.

See also: ENGINE.

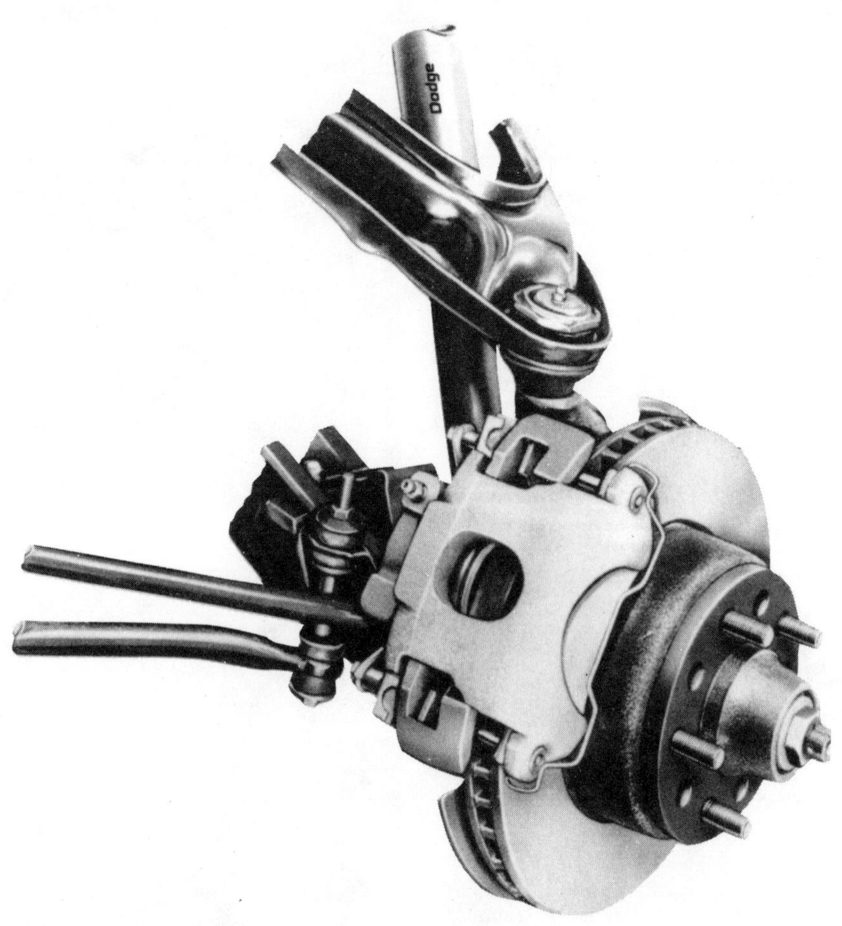

▲ *This is a typical floating caliper disc brake. Caliper floats along rods attached to brace. In this type, only one side of caliper has piston.*

Servicing Your Disc Brakes

They eliminate the problems of brake overheating and wet brakes, and new developments making the system easier to maintain give discs an added plus

DISC BRAKES can be installed on the front wheels of virtually all cars, and some cars even offer discs front and rear.

Instead of pumping fluid into wheel cylinders, the master cylinder of a disc brake pumps the fluid into a hydraulic piston device called a caliper. The caliper is much like a clamp. As pistons are pushed out by fluid pressure they squeeze a pair of friction pads against the sides of a disc. The disc is bolted to the wheel, just like a brake drum, and when the pads are clamped against it, the car is brought to a stop.

Because the disc is exposed to the air to keep it cool, the system is virtually immune to fade caused by heat, the brake system's number one enemy. The disc also spins off water, so driving through a deep puddle does not cause extended loss of braking efficiency.

The front wheels do two-thirds of the

brake work on a typical car, so the discs are usually installed on the front wheels. The old drum brake is better as an emergency brake, so many companies still fit drums to the rear wheels. The reason the drum does better as an emergency brake is the self-energizing effect, which is the wedging action of the shoes into the drum. This wedging action reduces the pedal pressure necessary for braking effort, and also the pulling action on the hand brake (or pushing action on the foot-actuated emergency brake). Because it has no self-energizing effect, the disc brake usually requires a power assist, particularly on larger cars.

In the drum braking system, return springs retract the shoes, so for fast response when you hit the pedal, a small amount of residual pressure is maintained in the hydraulic lines by that residual pressure check valve in the master cylinder. The disc system has no return springs, so it has no residual pressure check valve. It gets its fast response by keeping the friction pad lightly touching the disc or just a few thousandths of an inch away.

Because it does not retract the shoes, the disc braking system is self-adjusting. As the friction material on the pad wears, the piston pushes out further to press the friction pad against the disc. There is no spring to retract the piston, so it keeps its new position each time.

The absence of residual pressure in the lines keeps the brakes from dragging when you take your foot off the pedal. Some disc systems retract the piston mechanically (often with nothing more than a flexing seal around the piston) a few thousandths of an inch to eliminate drag of any sort. Others actually use a spring behind the piston to keep the friction pad and disc in light contact.

Two disc braking systems have been used. The first was the fixed caliper type. The caliper is bolted in position around the disc, and has one or two pistons on each side to push the friction pads against the disc. Most recent American cars use a floating caliper design. It has just one large piston.

The caliper floats a few thousandths of an inch along a bracket that is fixed over the disc. The single piston comes out, pushes the pad in front of it against the disc, and the caliper floats opposite to the direction of the piston. This movement pulls the other side of the caliper into the other side of the disc. The friction pad on this side then is pressed against the disc. The caliper moves very little in its float so there is really no obvious movement.

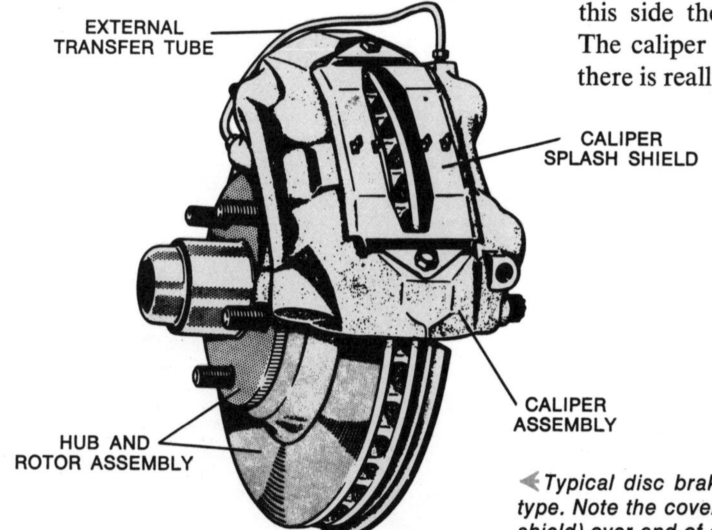

Typical disc brake setup of the fixed caliper type. Note the cover plate (called caliper splash shield) over end of caliper.

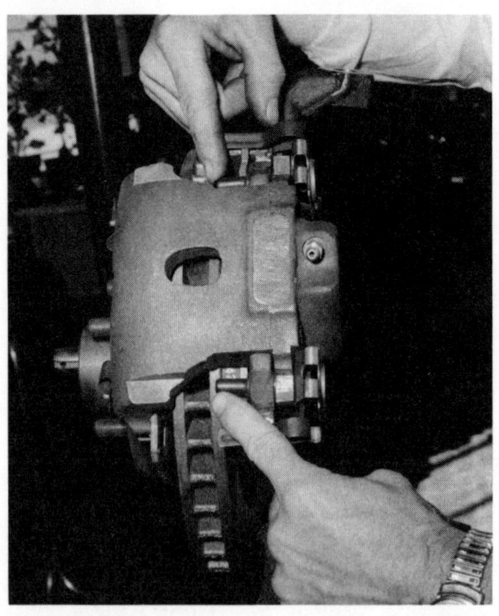

◄ This type of floating caliper disc brake has been used by Ford. Fingers point to bolts along which the caliper floats.

The basic repair on a disc system is replacement of the friction pads, the equivalent to fitting new brake shoes on a drum system. It is a job the weekend mechanic can easily do. The first step is to see if the pads need replacing. On most disc systems, you can see the condition of the pads simply by looking in through the end of the caliper. You may not even have to pull a wheel.

On most American fixed caliper systems, there are slots to a certain depth in the friction material, and when these slots are worn away, the pads must be replaced. The pads should wear evenly, and about the same on both sides, so if you can see what one pad looks like, you can safely assume the condition of the other. Pads on some floating caliper systems wear to a slight

▼ Disassembled fixed caliper. Notice four-piston design. Grooves in brake shoes are wear indicators. When groove wears away, it is time to replace shoe.

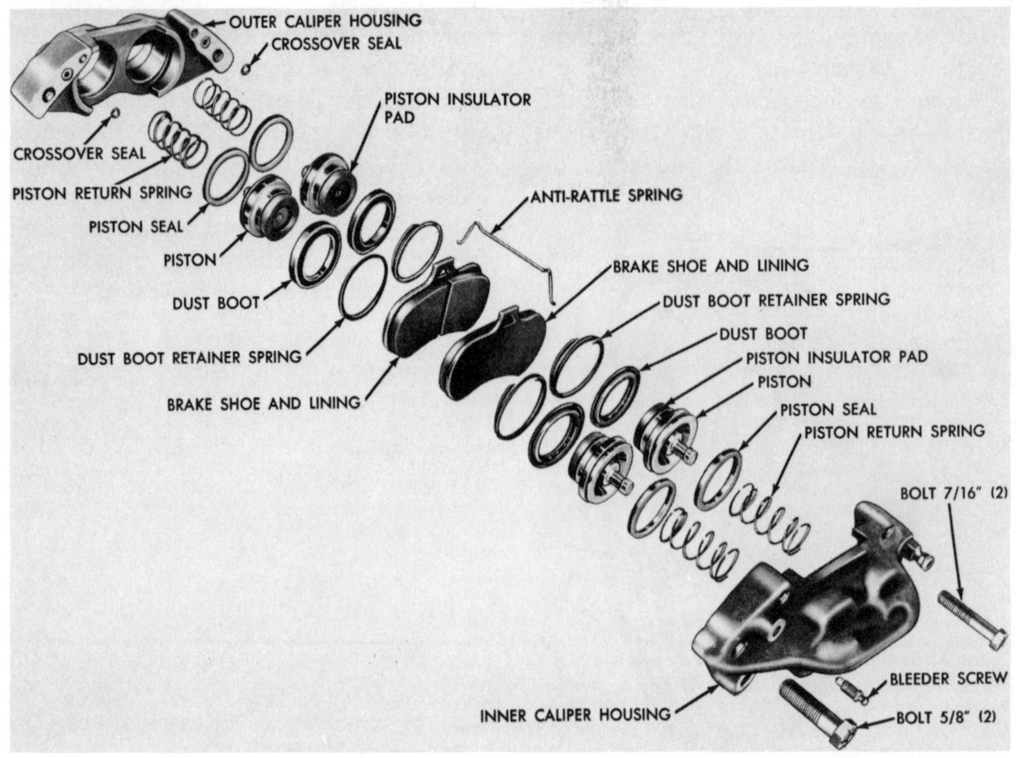

taper (normally a maximum of $\frac{1}{8}$-inch). In either system, the pad should be at least $\frac{1}{32}$-inch thick at its thinnest point.

Begin pad replacement by siphoning out a few ounces of fluid from the reservoir if it is full. Otherwise, when new pads are installed, and the pistons are forced further back into the caliper, they will displace fluid, pushing it up through the lines into the master cylinder, causing it to overflow. Discard the siphoned-out brake fluid. If the master cylinder was not topped up as the pads wore and the pistons projected out, there will be no need to drain out fluid.

The fixed caliper design is the easiest in which to replace pads. In virtually all cases, there is a cover plate (held by pins or screws) on the edge of the caliper. Take off the cover plate and pull out the old friction pads. You may have to work the pad back and forth a bit to gain the clearance to pull it out easily. Now push the pistons back in. (If they won't go back in, the caliper must be overhauled.) To gain the proper leverage, insert a small piece of steel and exert force against the steel with a large screwdriver (which will protect the aluminum pistons against scoring). Once the pistons are back, you can push the new pads into place. Refit the cover plate and the job is done.

The floating caliper design takes more time. One type has a caliper bracing plate (to and from which the caliper floats) attached to the spindle. Two bolts hold the brace, and once you remove these, the caliper and brace drop as a unit. If you are careful, you will lower the caliper onto a box and work at the wheel. Otherwise, you will have to disconnect a brake line and bleed afterwards. The friction pads may be held by guide pins or slots in the caliper. When you refit the brace, tighten the top bolt first. Each bolt should be tightened to factory specifications, normally 90-100 ft./lbs. using a torque wrench.

The other popular design has a bracket bolted to the spindle and the caliper mounts to the bracket on two bolts, along which it

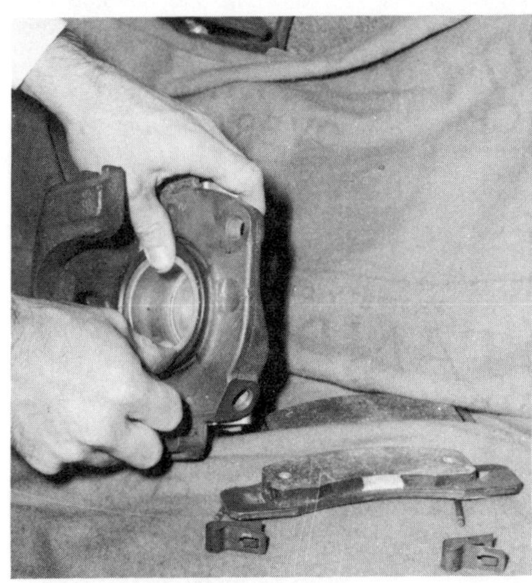

▲ Pads on that Ford system are easily removed once caliper is lowered. (It is shown on bench for illustrative purposes only.) Piston can be pushed back with thumb pressure.

◄ Fingers point to bolts which must be removed (on aforementioned Ford floating caliper discs), to pull away caliper and bracing plate for access to friction pads (brake shoes).

floats. To change friction pads, undo the bolts and remove them. This allows you to lower the caliper from the disc. With the caliper lowered, the new pads can be fitted into place. (There may be a spring between the caliper piston and the inboard shoe; if there is, be sure to reinstall it.)

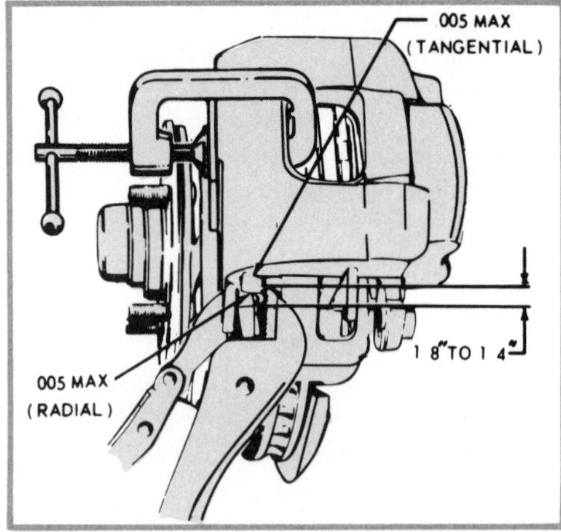

Outboard friction pad had to be aligned by clinching on early GM floating caliper disc brakes. Clinching was done by holding assembly onto disc with C-clamp and bending ears of the friction pad (brake shoe) with vise-type pliers.

This design of floating caliper disc brakes is simple to service. Clips are removed from end of float rod, then rod is pulled with pliers, permitting removal of caliper. Once caliper is off, float rod guides are slid out, freeing friction pads.

The sleeves and bushings through which the float bolts pass should be replaced when installing new pads, to be sure the caliper will continue to float properly. Lubricate the sleeves and bushings and the small ends of the bolts with a silicone grease.

Once the pads are in position (on some early models the outboard pad must have its ears properly lined up), begin a process called "clinching." This is done by starting the caliper with new pads back onto the bracket, so that the bottom edge of the outer pad is just resting on the outer edge of the disc. Clamp the outboard pad to the caliper with moderate pressure, using a C-clamp. (The caliper is cut out at the outer end, so you'll need a metal plate, such as an old brake pad, to span the opening.

With vise-type pliers, clinch the outboard shoe ears as illustrated. Locate the pliers ⅛ to ¼-inch from the outer edge of the ear. The clearance of the ear from each edge of the caliper should be no more than .005-inch, as illustrated.

Floating caliper discs were changed in 1970 to eliminate the need for clinching pads.

The condition of the disc itself is important, of course. But scratches .015-inch deep, which would certainly require refinishing of a drum, do not require attention on a disc. Previously, a badly scored disc had to be replaced, but the manufacturers of brake drum lathes now have attachments that permit perfectly acceptable refinishing of discs.

As you can see, there is nothing complex about disc brakes. In fact, when you compare them to today's self-adjusting brakes, with their complicated system of links and springs for self-adjustment, they almost look simple.

See also: DRUM BRAKE SERVICE.

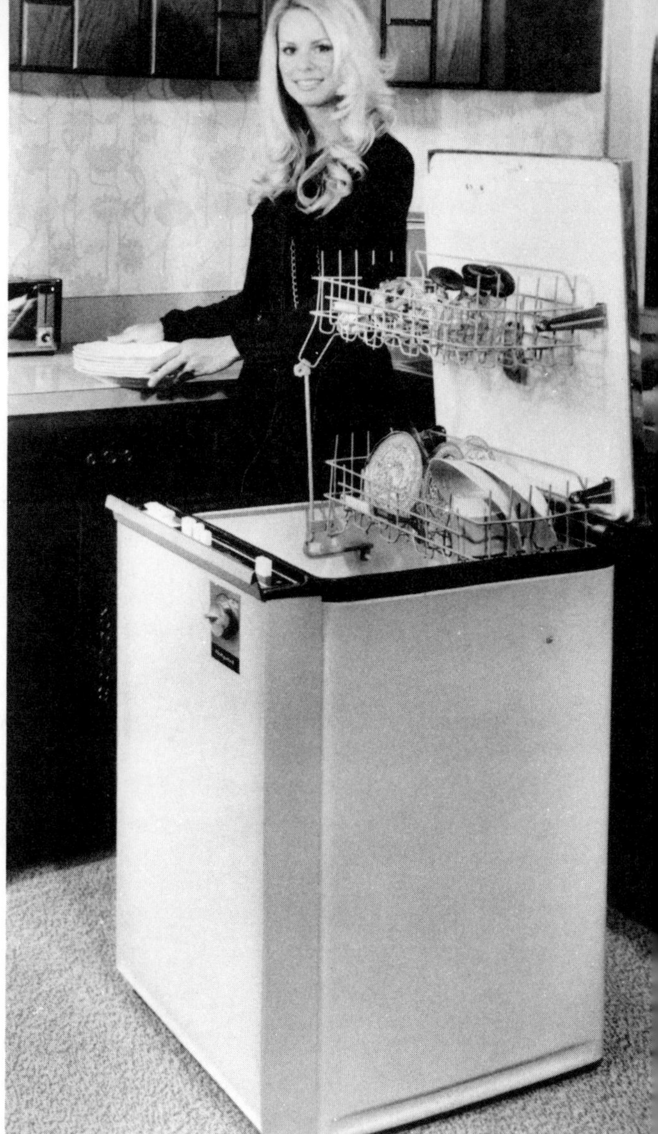

How to Repair Your Dishwasher

You can identify the causes of most dishwasher breakdowns. Save money by replacing the parts yourself

YOUR DISHWASHER is designed to wash, rinse and dry dishes automatically. When properly installed, used and supplied with suitable water it will do a better job than hand washing. As with other appliances, knowing your machine's capabilities and limitations will do much to give you more satisfactory results. Prepare your dishes as well as you would if you were doing them by hand!

Read your Owner's Manual. Incorrectly placed dishes will prevent good washing action in some areas of the machine.

Water. Poor water quality, resulting from dissolved minerals, can ruin an otherwise perfect dishwashing job. That cloudy film on glasses and the white spots on flat-ware are minerals from the water which remain when the water evaporates during the drying process. If you're in a "hard water" area check your water source before condemning your dishwasher for poor results.

Usually these white spots are calcium (lime) deposits and can be removed with a vinegar wash. Do it this way:

1. Run your dishes through a normal cycle up to the drying period.
2. Advance the timer to the wash cycle and allow the machine to fill.
3. Add two cups of vinegar—no detergent.
4. Allow machine to complete the cycle.

This should remove the lime deposit. If some still remains repeat the process.

A water softener may be the final answer to obtaining better quality water.

Installation. Another point to check before blaming your machine for poor results is the installation. Requirements are simple but must be met. Domestic dishwashers are designed to operate on a 115-volt, 60-cycle branch circuit provided with a 15-ampere time delay type of fuse. It would be a good idea to use no other appliance on this circuit at the same time.

Your dishwasher must be grounded to reduce shock hazard. Portable machines are grounded through a three pronged plug. If the wall receptacle is for the standard two pronged plug an adapter must be used. Be certain the adapter is properly grounded. A permanently installed machine is grounded through the wiring cable, or by a separate wire connected from the machine frame to a water pipe.

Water pressures greater than 120 pounds per square inch at the dishwasher may damage the fill valve or fill hose. A pressure

Exploded view of the water recirculating and drain system of a typical spray-arm type dishwasher.

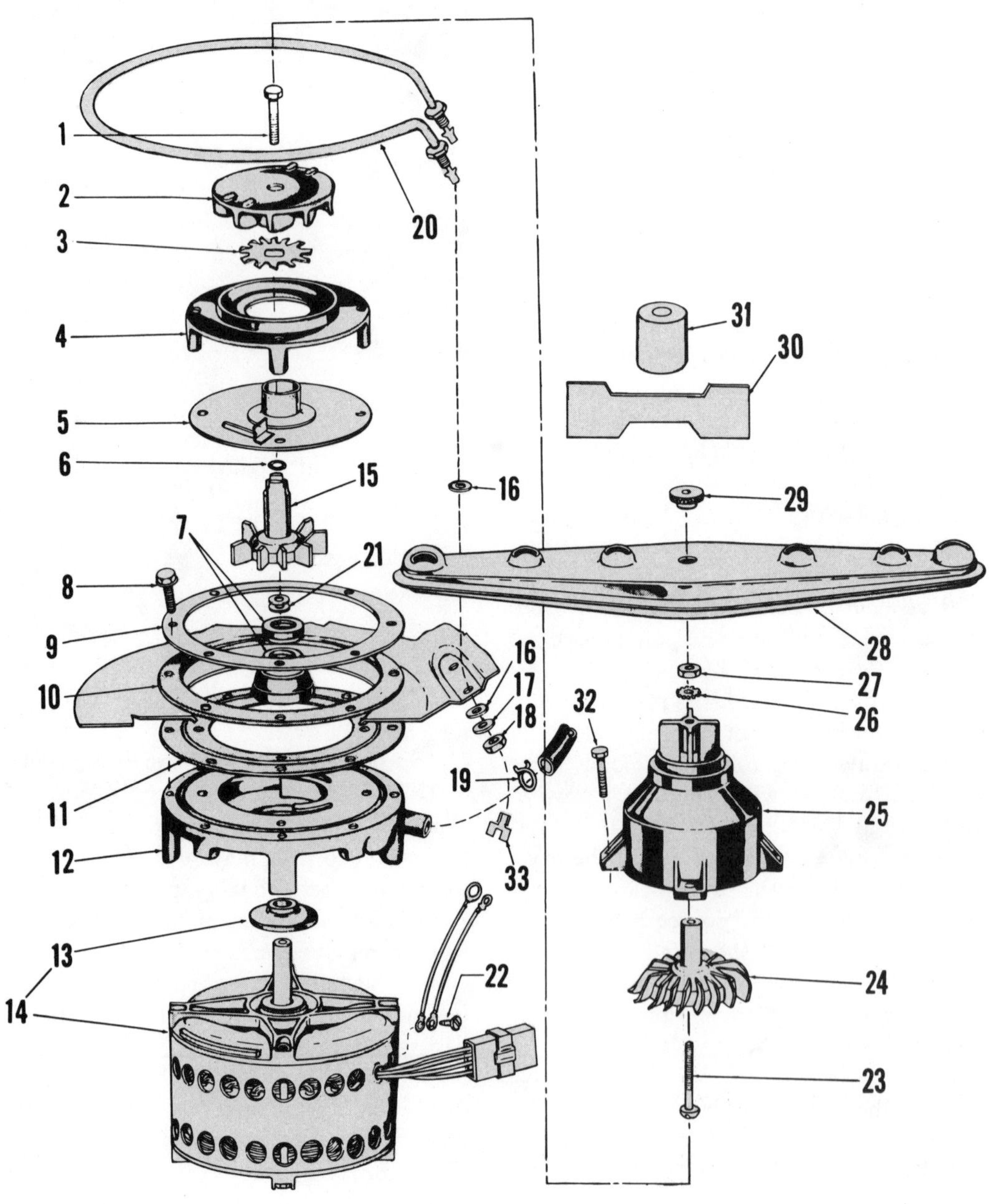

REF. NO.	PART NAME	QTY.
1	Number 10x1¼″ Hex Washer Head Stainless Steel Screw	1
2	Impeller—Upper	1
3	Blade—Macerator	1
4	Plate—Spacer	1
5	Plate Assembly—Pump	1
6	"O" Ring	1
7	Seal	2
8	Number 10—32x⅝″ Hex Washer Head Stainless Steel Screw	As Required
9	Cover	1
10	Gasket	1
11	Gasket	1
12	Pump Housing Assembly	1
13	Slinger	1
14	Motor Assembly	1
15	Impeller—Lower	1
16	Gasket	2
17	Washer	1
18	Nut ½″—20 Brass	1
19	Clamp	As Required
20	Heater	1
21	Shims	2
22	Screw	As Required
23	Number 10—32x2¼″ Hex Head Stainless Steel Machine Screw	1
24	Diffuser	1
25	Housing—Pump	1
26	Number 10 External Tooth Lockwasher	1
27	Nut 10—32 Stainless Steel	1
28	Spray Arm Assembly	1
29	Nut—Spray Arm	1
30	Shim Gage	1
31	Seal—Installation Tool	1
32	Number 10x1½″ Hex Washer Head Stainless Steel Screw	4
33	Terminal Adaptor	1

reducing valve should be installed in the water supply line entering your house to protect the entire water system.

Water pressure lower than 15 pounds per square inch will not allow enough water to enter the machine. Low water level will result in poor washing action and unclean dishes.

If your water supply can deliver a flow of three gallons per minute at the kitchen sink there should be no trouble on proper fill. Take a watch and a gallon jug and see whether the jug gets filled in 20 seconds or less. A two quart milk container should fill in 10 seconds.

A water temperature range of 140° to 160° in the machine is important. Detergents for dishwashers have ingredients that need this temperature to dissolve. You can't get clean dishes with cold water, nor will they dry. Proper drying requires that the dishes be hot at the beginning of the drying cycle.

Operation. To wash dishes a dishwasher sprays or splashes a hot solution of detergent and water over the dishes. Both methods are in general use. In both instances the force of water on the dishes knocks off the soils. The detergent then attacks the soils and holds them in solution.

Spray action is obtained by a rotating arm having a row of jet holes through which pumped water will spray against the dishes. Some of the holes are at an angle to provide a jet thrust for rotating the arm. These machines have a filter screen that separates particles of soil from the water, preventing them from redepositing on the dishes. It is important that these screens be properly fitted, otherwise large soil particles will clog the spray arm jet holes. Normally these large particles collect in a scrap basket which must be cleaned regularly. Sometimes foreign matter will collect under the spray arm bearing surface causing the arm to move slowly or stop. When this happens the arm must be lifted off the hub and cleaned.

Splash action is obtained by an impeller, partially submerged in water, at the bottom of the machine. This scoops the water upward and outward, slinging it against the dishes. These machines have no screen to prevent soil redeposition; therefore dishes must be more thoroughly rinsed before loading.

Operation of your dishwasher is programmed by a timer. There may be many combinations of time and cycles, with or without automatic detergent and wetting agent dispensers. At each cycle the machine must fill, run, drain, rinse and dry.

Your Owner's Manual will contain specific information about the operational cycles of your particular machine. Most dishwashers include a wiring diagram and cycle

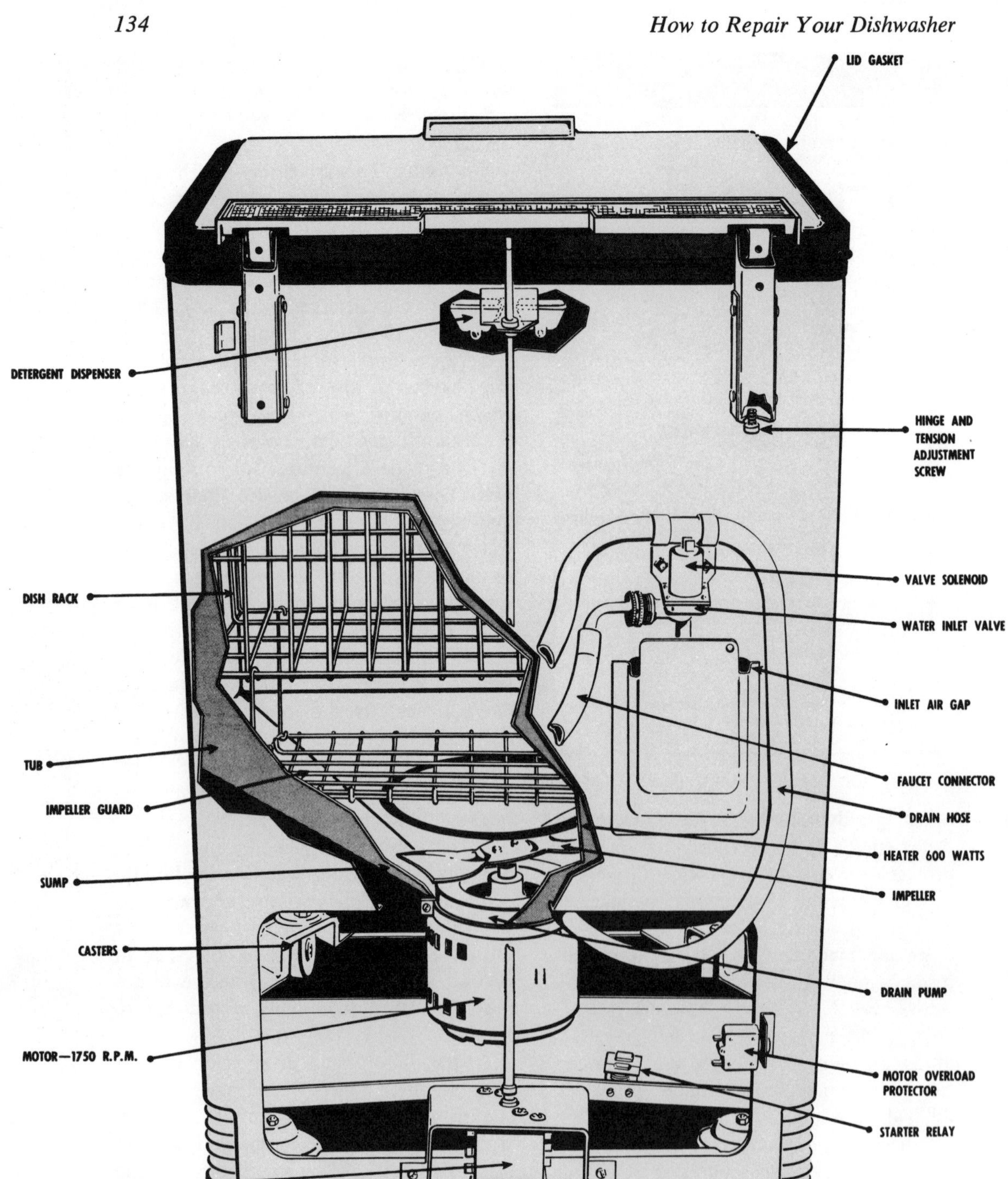

Parts location of a typical impeller-type dishwasher.

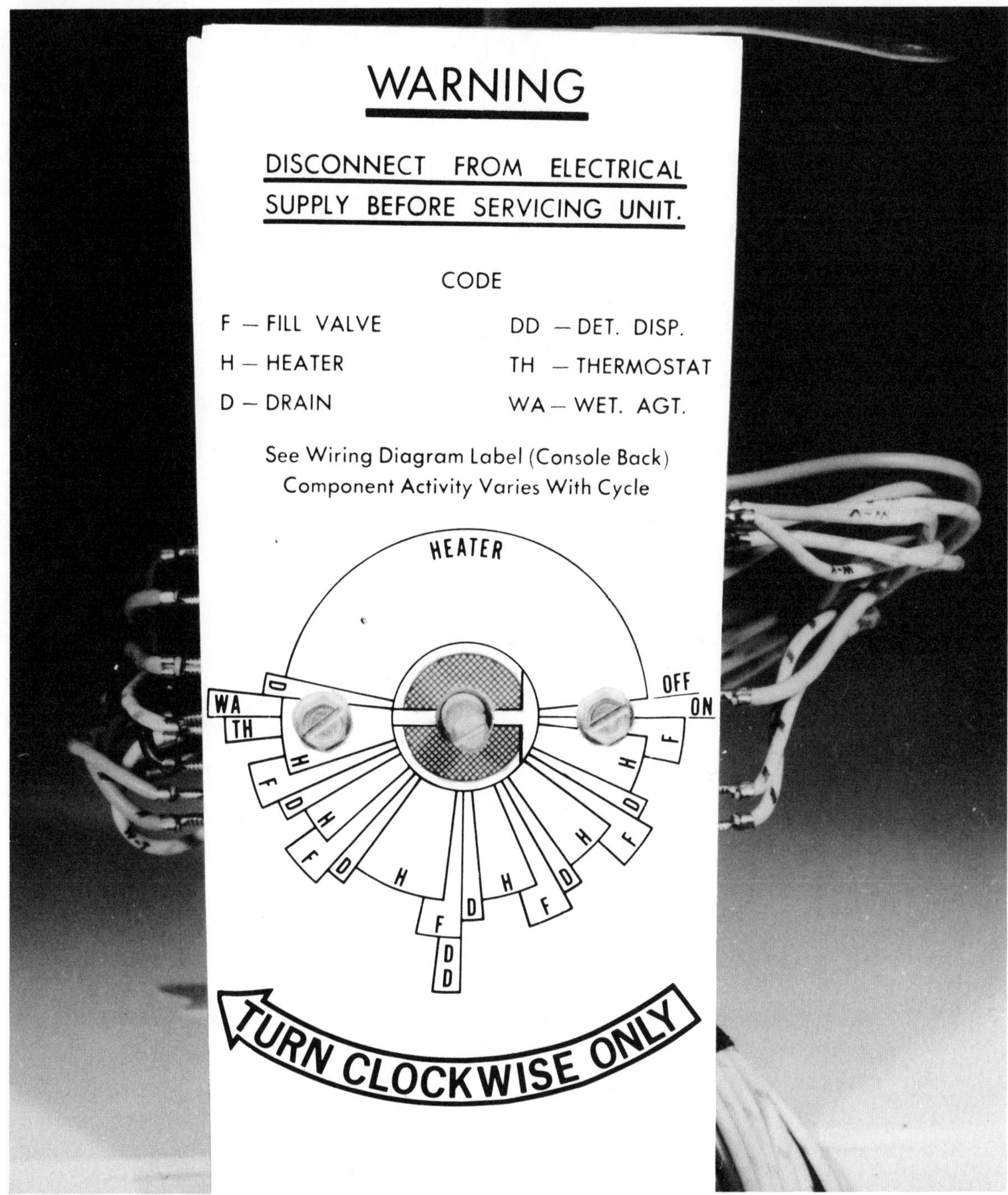

WARNING
DISCONNECT FROM ELECTRICAL SUPPLY BEFORE SERVICING UNIT.
CODE
F — FILL VALVE
H — HEATER
D — DRAIN
DD — DET. DISP.
TH — THERMOSTAT
WA — WET. AGT.
See Wiring Diagram Label (Console Back)
Component Activity Varies With Cycle
HEATER
OFF
ON
WA
TH
TURN CLOCKWISE ONLY

The timer can be advanced manually to any part of the cycle. The label is coded to show the active components.

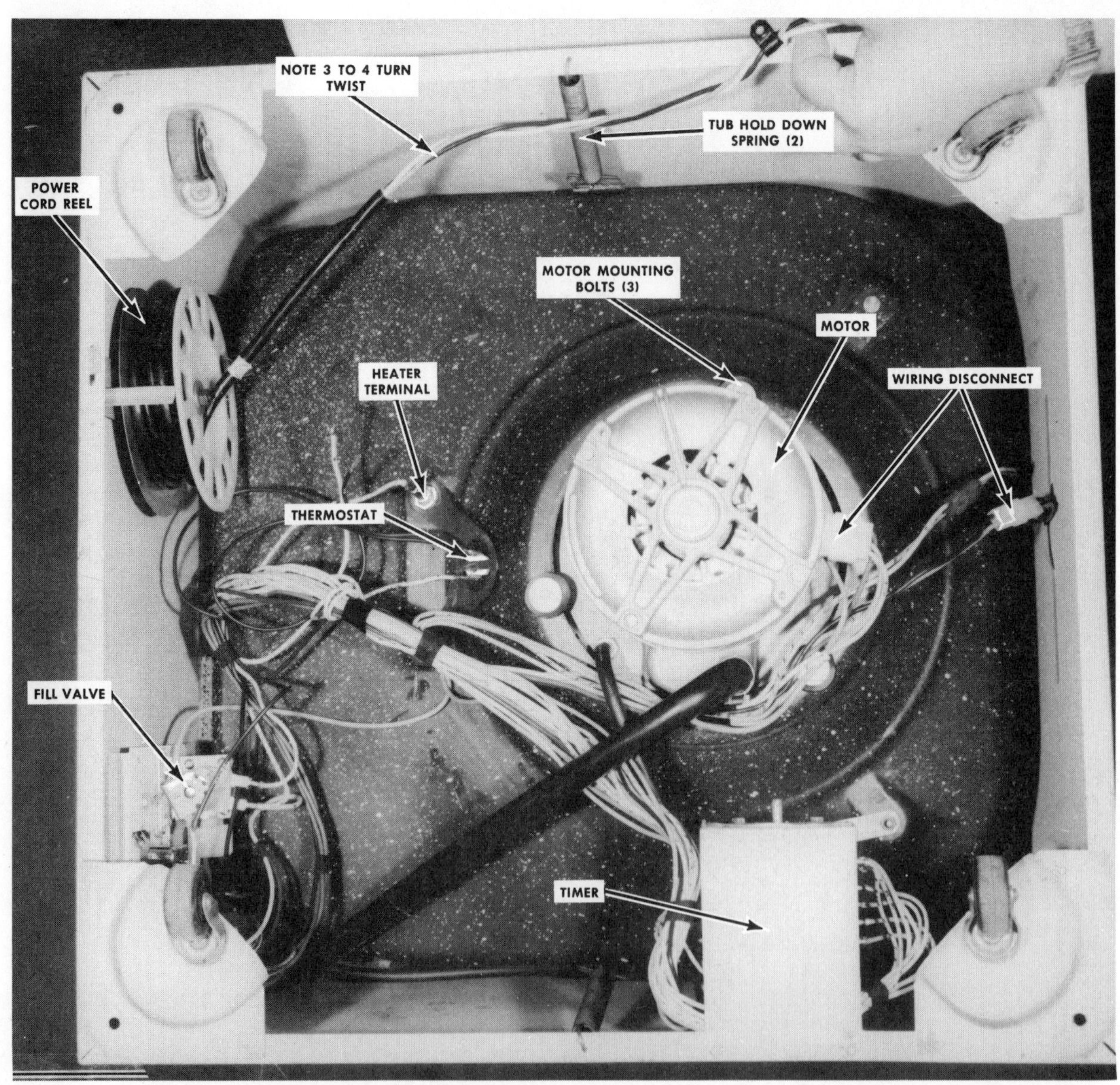

▲ *Location of major components of a portable dishwasher. Some machines have timer mounted in an upper console.*

chart pasted on the back or inside the access panel. This information will include the sequence of cycles and the length of time each one will require.

Up to now we have discussed the sources and resolutions of about 75% of dishwasher problems. Other failures will probably be mechanical.

Finding the problem. If your dishwasher is portable, remove the back to get at the working parts. If it is an undercounter machine, remove the access panel which is located under the door; or you may have to lay the machine on the floor in order to gain entry.

Much can be discovered by careful observation. Leaks, rust, physical damage and obviously burned parts will be clearly seen. Unusual noises, smells, squeaks, and/or rattles should be tracked down and eliminated before they develop into serious trouble.

All water inlet valves have a fine mesh screen to prevent specks of foreign matter from entering the valve. If this becomes clogged it will restrict the water flow. On portable dishwashers using the nylon bodied valve, the screen is accessible by removing the inlet hose connection and extracting the screen with tweezers or needle-nosed pliers. The screen can then be cleaned and put back—or replaced if cleaning doesn't seem to work.

Rear view of the control console of a portable dishwasher with inspection panels removed.

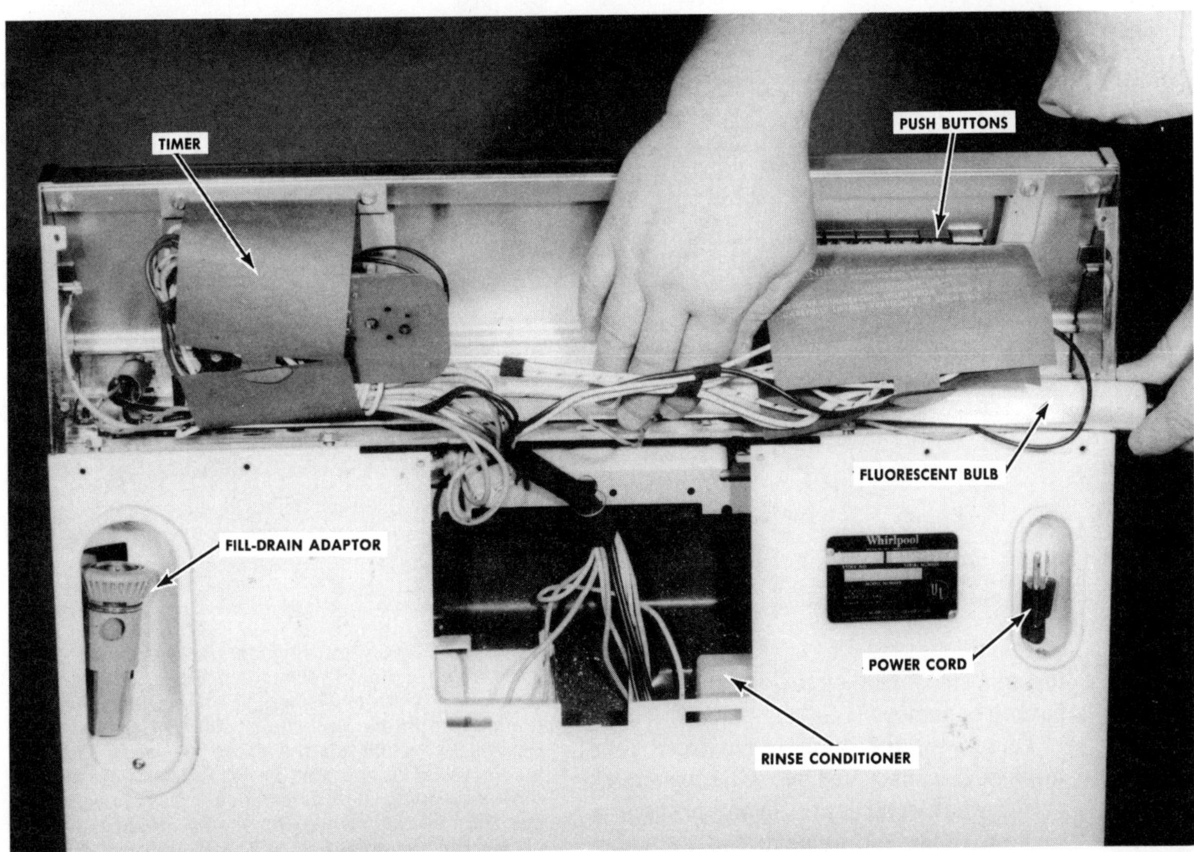

Built-in machines use a brass bodied valve. The strainer is removed for cleaning by unscrewing the large box cap nut on the underside of the valve. Make sure the water supply is turned off or you'll have a flood!

The drain for portable dishwashers is a hose that empties into the sink. Built-in machines require proper connection to the household plumbing system. Both machines must have the drain line rising from the machine at least 30 inches to prevent water from flowing out of the machine by the force of gravity. Make certain there are no kinks or foreign matter in this drain hose that will obstruct the water flow.

A drain pump can get jammed with heavy food particles, toothpicks, small pieces of bone, etc. The symptom of a jammed pump is water not draining from

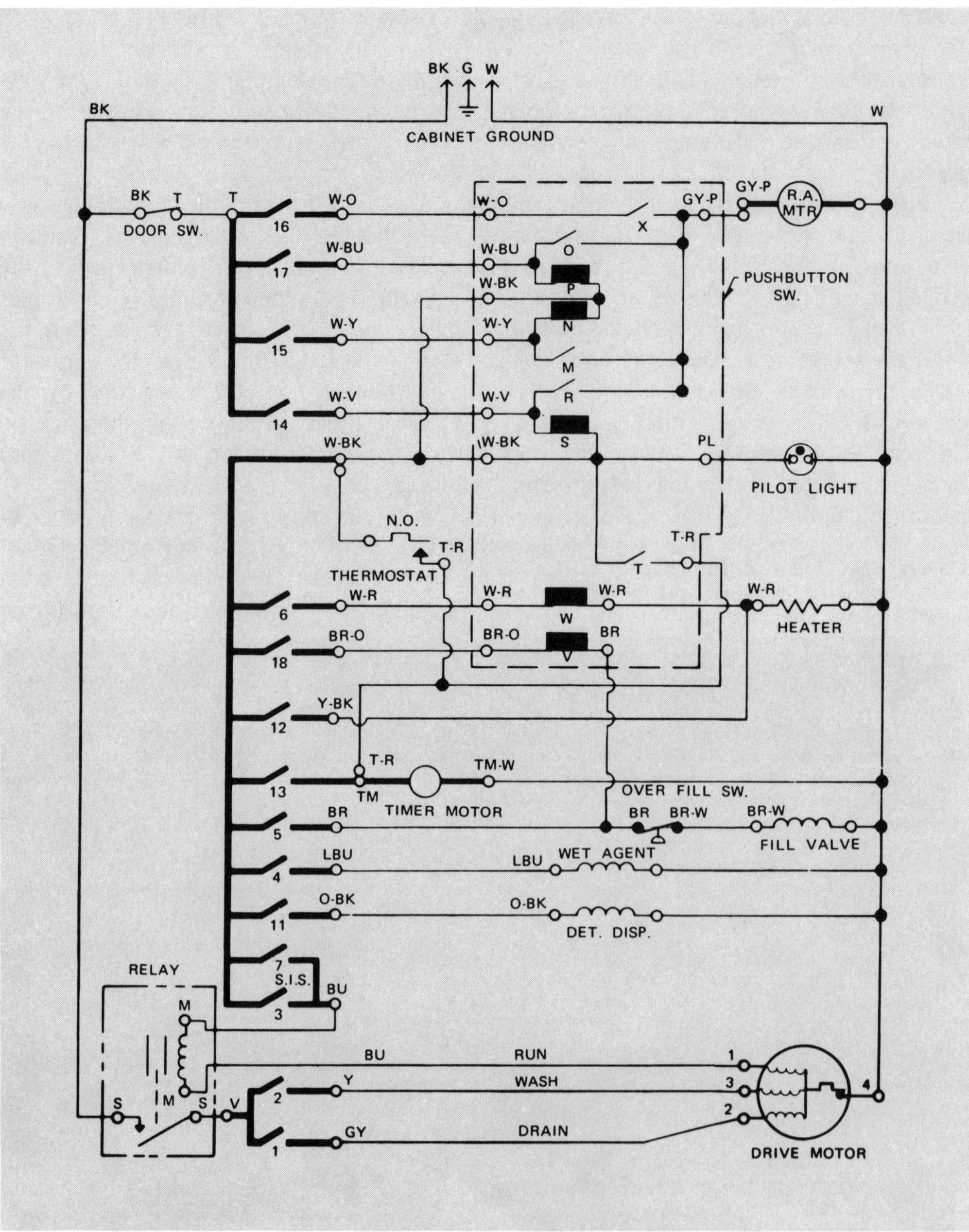

Wiring diagram for a typical dishwasher with a reversing motor. The motor operates the recirculating pump in the wash direction and the drain pump in the opposite direction. The timer determines which start winding is used. The starting relay is operated by the current flow to the run winding, and automatically disconnects the start winding when the motor reaches its proper running speed.

the machine. The offending particle will have to be removed.

To remove the drain pump from your machine disconnect the two wires, two hoses (catch what water is still in the hoses in a shallow pan), and remove the mounting

WHERE TO LOOK WHEN THINGS GO WRONG

PROBLEM / POSSIBLE CAUSE	NO POWER	LOOSE CONNECTION	DEFECTIVE DOOR SWITCH	DEFECTIVE TIMER	SUPPLY VALVE CLOSED	FILL VALVE DEFECTIVE	RESTRICTED WATER SUPPLY	PUMP JAMMED	DRAIN LINES RESTRICTED	DEFECTIVE HEATER	MOTOR NOT REVERSING	POOR DOOR SEAL	DEFECTIVE HOSE	DEFECTIVE PUMP SEAL
DOES NOT START	√	√	√	√										
DOES NOT COMPLETE CYCLE	√	√		√				√						
NO WATER IN MACHINE				√	√	√	√							
WATER DOES NOT DRAIN				√				√			√			
DOES NOT HEAT		√		√						√				
WATER LEAKAGE												√	√	√

Wiring diagram for a dishwasher with a separate drain pump. Note the timer function chart, which lists the active circuits by number for each timer increment. By connecting one lead of a test light or AC voltmeter to the L_2 wire, the other lead can be used to test for voltage at each active circuit. Don't condemn the timer for not delivering voltage to a functioning part until you know the timer is at the correct increment to do so.

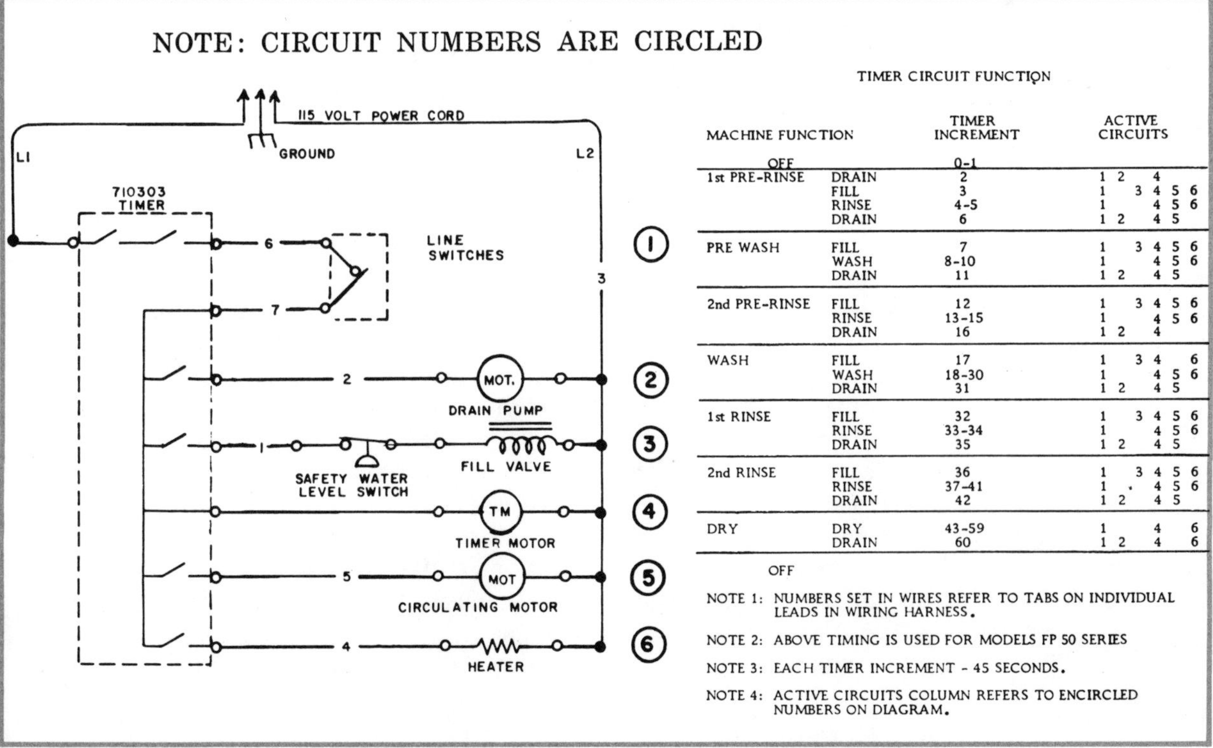

TIMER CIRCUIT FUNCTION

MACHINE FUNCTION		TIMER INCREMENT	ACTIVE CIRCUITS
OFF		0-1	
1st PRE-RINSE	DRAIN	2	1 2 4
	FILL	3	1 3 4 5 6
	RINSE	4-5	1 4 5 6
	DRAIN	6	1 2 4 5
PRE WASH	FILL	7	1 3 4 5 6
	WASH	8-10	1 4 5 6
	DRAIN	11	1 2 4 5
2nd PRE-RINSE	FILL	12	1 3 4 5 6
	RINSE	13-15	1 4 5 6
	DRAIN	16	1 2 4
WASH	FILL	17	1 3 4 6
	WASH	18-30	1 4 5 6
	DRAIN	31	1 2 4 5
1st RINSE	FILL	32	1 3 4 5 6
	RINSE	33-34	1 4 5 6
	DRAIN	35	1 2 4 5
2nd RINSE	FILL	36	1 3 4 5 6
	RINSE	37-41	1 . 4 5 6
	DRAIN	42	1 2 4 5
DRY	DRY	43-59	1 4 6
	DRAIN	60	1 2 4 6
OFF			

NOTE 1: NUMBERS SET IN WIRES REFER TO TABS ON INDIVIDUAL LEADS IN WIRING HARNESS.

NOTE 2: ABOVE TIMING IS USED FOR MODELS FP 50 SERIES

NOTE 3: EACH TIMER INCREMENT - 45 SECONDS.

NOTE 4: ACTIVE CIRCUITS COLUMN REFERS TO ENCIRCLED NUMBERS ON DIAGRAM.

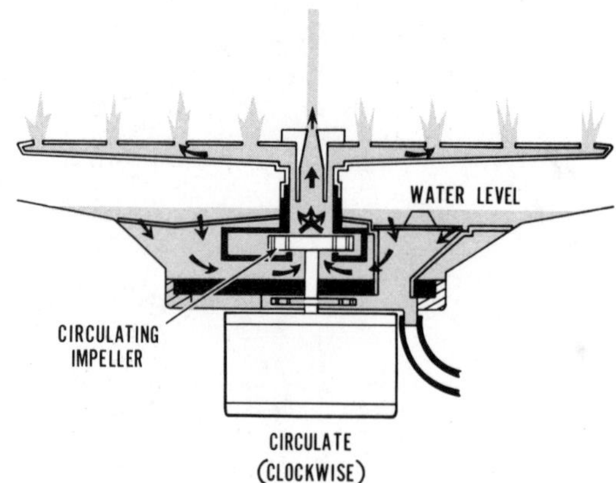

When motor runs clockwise, it drives the impeller to circulate water within the dishwasher. The center vertical stream impinges on the upper spray arm for distribution to the dishes on upper rack. When the motor turns counterclockwise, the drain impeller pumps water out of the machine.

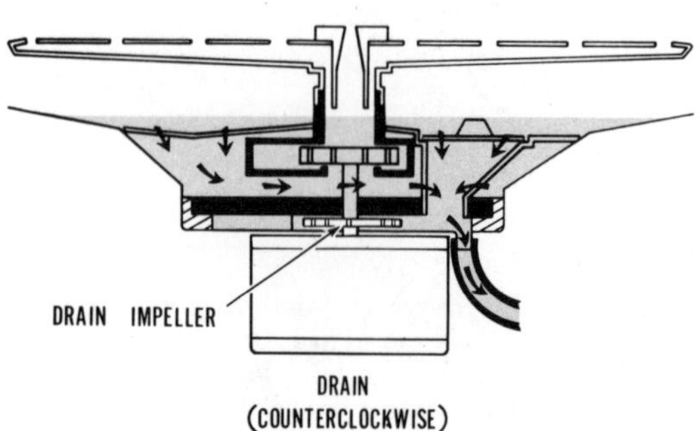

screws. To clean the pump remove the four Phillips head screws and pull off the pump body. This will expose the impeller and any foreign matter that may have collected there.

Mark the location of the discharge outlet with respect to the mounting frame so that, when it is reassembled, the outlet will be in its correct position to line up with its hose.

Some models use the same motor for pump out as for washing by reversing the motor's direction of rotation. This motor reversal is controlled by switching within the timer. So, if the motor fails to reverse, either from wash to pump out, or pump out to wash, replace the timer. Do not blame the motor! If this motor fails to start check its starting relay.

By following the wiring diagram and by using a test light or a continuity tester, any electrical part or circuit can be checked out. When using a test light be careful because the current is on. Use the test light to determine whether electricity is reaching the working part. If the bulb lights and the part doesn't function, then trouble is in the part. (Working parts for a dishwasher are: motors, fill valve, heater, and dispensing solenoids.) If the bulb does not light the trouble may be a loose connection or a defective timer switch. The wiring diagram and operations chart on your machine will tell you which circuits are supposed to be active at any given time.

Before condemning any working part or the timer, make sure that there is power in the machine and that the door lid switch is sound.

See also: INDIVIDUAL APPLIANCE LISTINGS.

Easy Installation of Doorbells

Changing or repairing your present doorbell system is an easy job with a little basic knowledge and the aid of wiring diagrams

The most common source of trouble in doorbells is the push button. Check it first by removing the cover and shorting the screw terminals with a screwdriver.

EVERY HOUSE requires some form of signal from the outside doors to an inside room, so that the presence of visitors can be made known. While the electric bell is used today to a large extent, chimes are also very popular. Stepdown transformers are taking the place of dry and wet cells for powering doorbell systems. These inexpensive units reduce the 115 volts AC to 8 or 10 volts for an ordinary bell and 12 to 16 volts for chimes. For the former, a transformer rated at 5 to 10 watts is generally sufficient, while good chime operation may require a 10 to 20 watt transformer. Lasting indefinitely, these small signal transformers are very good for the job and require no maintenance.

When installing a bell transformer, never secure it to a wooden or other inflammable surface, as it may become quite hot due to a short-circuit in the bell wiring, poor workmanship or design on the part of the manufacturer or other causes. Place it in or on a steel box or cabinet and protect it with 3-ampere fuses. When the box is attached to the existing fuse cabinet, the frame is effectively grounded and no danger of shock exists as when box is secured to an insulating surface.

Units are available which consist of a bell transformer, fuse block and 3-ampere fuses, mounted in a small metal box. Attach this box to the house fuse cabinet with a short conduit nipple, locknuts and bushings. Run #10 rubber-covered wires from the terminals of the fuse box, through the pipe nipple to the sub-mains in the house cabinet. In some cases there may be enough room inside the fuse cabinet for a transformer, in which case a transformer only is required. This should be considered when laying out a new wiring installation.

When making connections to the house sub-mains, be sure to solder the joints, after cleaning the wires well. It is often possible to extend the new wires from the sub-mains to the transformer cutout by splicing in the grooves of the main cutout blocks with soldered joints. If the sub-mains are quite short in their run to a safety switch or other unit, remove them and install new lengths which can run to the new transformer fuse block without splicing.

If the chimes are to be installed, it might be difficult to obtain a built-in transformer with a cutout and box which has a high enough voltage and watt rating to do the job. These are usually designed for operating bells. In such a case, obtain a chime transformer of the proper rating and install it with a cutout block in a small metal cabinet. Make the connections as in the other job.

If a spare circuit exists in the house fuse panel, mount transformer in this box, or attach it to the outside with short bolts, carrying the primary wires into the box through a porcelain bushing.

Wiring door bells and chimes is not difficult but the work should be carefully done and rubber covered #18 wire should be used. Do not use cotton insulated wire (annunciator wire or bell wire) since short-circuits can easily develop with this weak insulation.

Bell wiring in new houses is usually installed after the lighting circuits are in place and all partitions are up, but before lathing and plastering has been done. Electric door openers for the front and rear upper doors in a two-family house are installed in the door casings when the house is finished. They allow you to open the doors from upstairs by pushing a button. A common wire runs from one side of the transformer to one side of all outside units, while another common wire runs from the other side of the transformer to one side of all inside units. Connecting wires between them complete the circuit in each case. Solder and tape any necessary taps or splices in the wires. Many such taps can be eliminated by pulling a loop of the wire out and connecting it around a terminal of the bell or button. Avoid the use of metal staples or nails for supporting the wires, as they may cut into the insulation later and cause trouble. A few insulated staples may be used, if necessary, or a piece of wood can often be made to support the wires.

For carrying the wires up to a push button, in most house construction, use the small space between the door casing and first stud. A hole can be drilled through the outside finish board opposite this space, where button will be attached. Next drill a hole through studs as shown and another on a slant from the basement, through the sill. If the wiring layout is such that it is better to carry the wires up instead of down, bore plate at top of studs rather

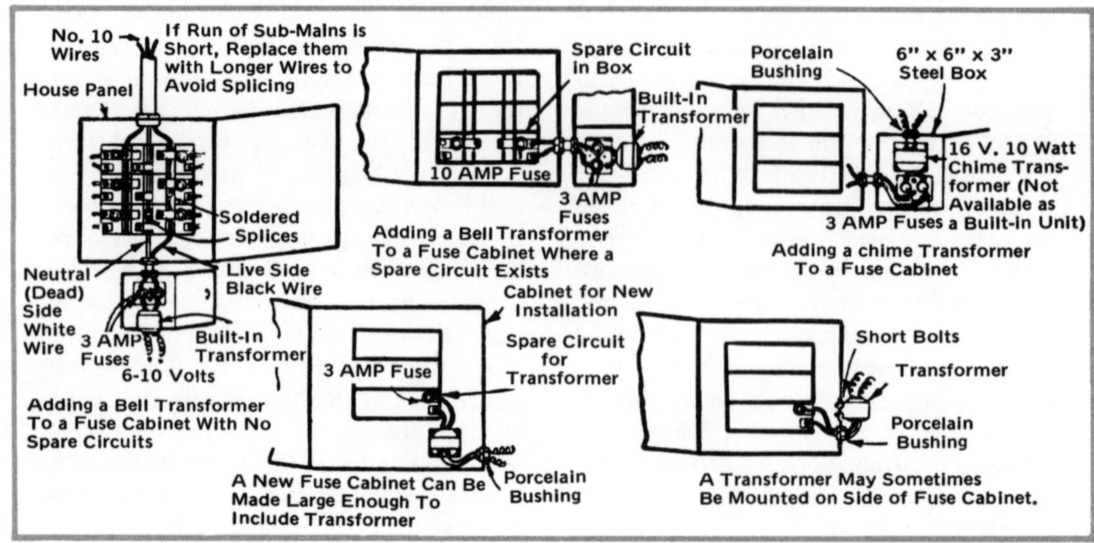

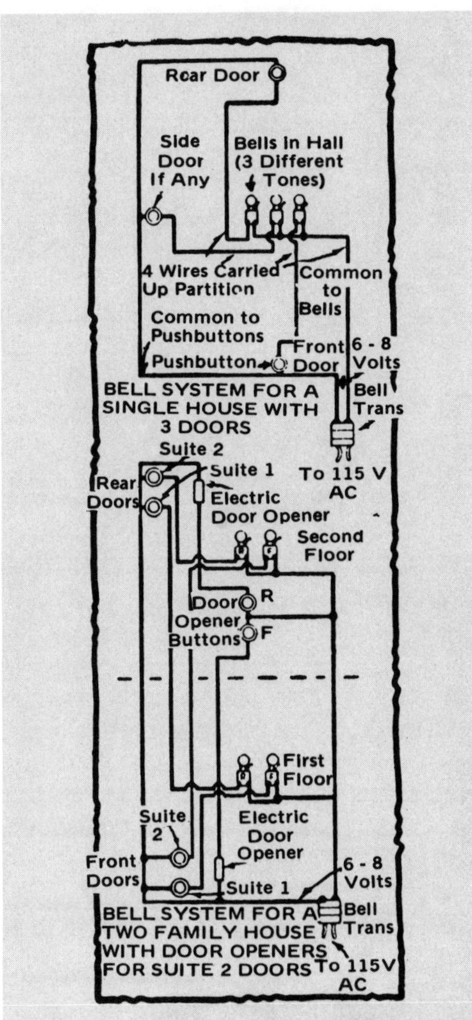

Two schematic drawings of double-bell systems, one for a single house and the other for a two-family home with electric door openers for the front and rear upper doors.

than sill, and direct wires towards ceiling to meet a line to bell location.

At the bell location in new work, set a board in between the studs to form a support for screws used in securing bells or chimes. This is necessary because the use of rock lath today usually replaces the older wooden laths and screws will not find a hold in it.

Bell wiring in old houses is usually done with the aid of "fish wires" or "snakes," narrow steel tapes that are used to pull wires up partitions and under floors. Heat the ends of the fish wires and form open hooks. Pass one wire through a hole bored as required and work up to the location of the bell or button, where another hole is provided. Use a second wire to catch the hook of the first one so it can be brought out the hole. Wrap bared ends tightly around hooked lower end of fish wire and draw them in.

The installation of chimes is not much different from that of bells. For a set of two-door tubular chimes, three wires are required, as with a pair of bells for two doors. One is a common wire and the other two run to the doors. Use wires with different colored insulation for quick identification. In some types of chimes a felt or rubber mounted bar is struck, instead of the long tubes, which is common construction with the lower priced chimes. These may also have short tubes for decorative effect or increased tone quality, although they are not actually struck. A solenoid is usually used with a plunger as the striking force.

In the long tubular chimes one type uses a single solenoid for both door signals. When the push button closes the circuit at the front door, the plunger strikes the shorter tube, producing the high note. Upon release of the button, a spring on the solenoid returns the plunger with enough force to strike the long tube for the low note. For the rear door signal, a built-in adjustable resistance prevents the plunger from striking the short tube, but the spring returns it from its restricted forward motion to strike the long tube. In the two-solenoid type separate units are used for each door, usually resulting in an improved sounding of the chimes. Chimes are also available that sound all eight notes of the Westminster chimes, at each press of the door

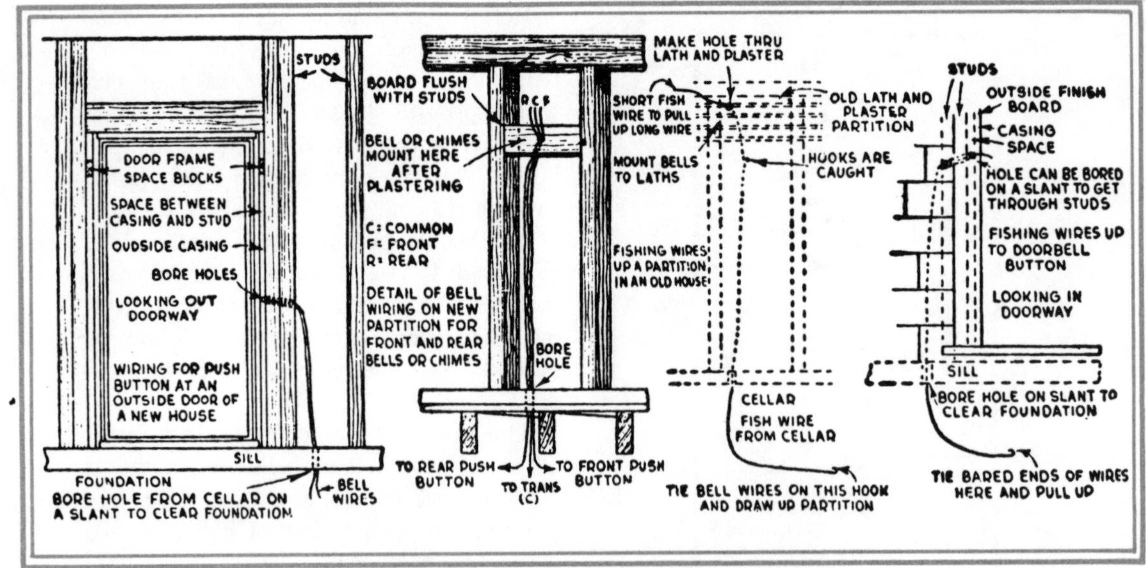

Diagram shows method of carrying wires from doorbell inside the home to a push button mounted on an outside wall. Method of securing bell wires inside the wall is also shown.

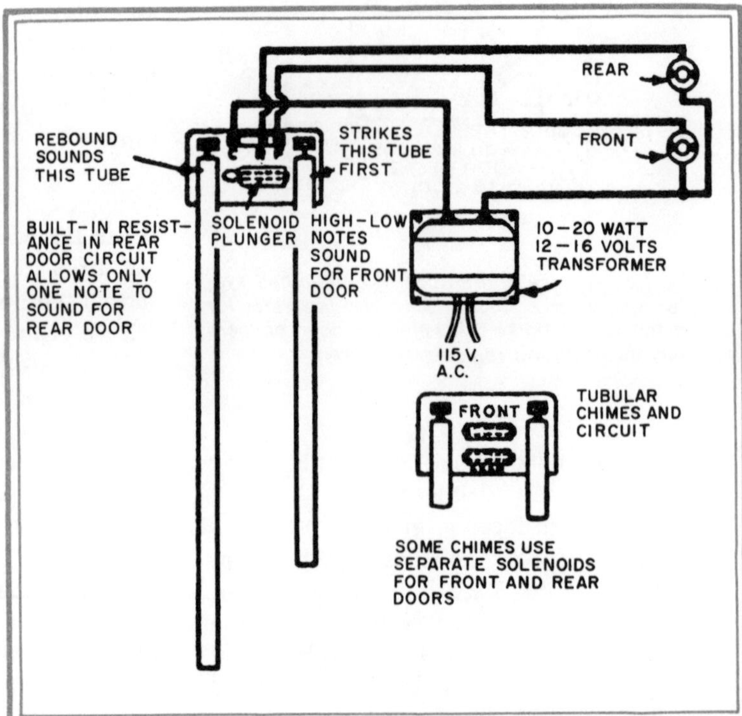

In push button operated chimes, the button closes the circuit at the front door causing the plunger to strike the short tube that produces a high note; when button is released, a spring on the solenoid returns the plunger to strike the long tube, producing the low note.

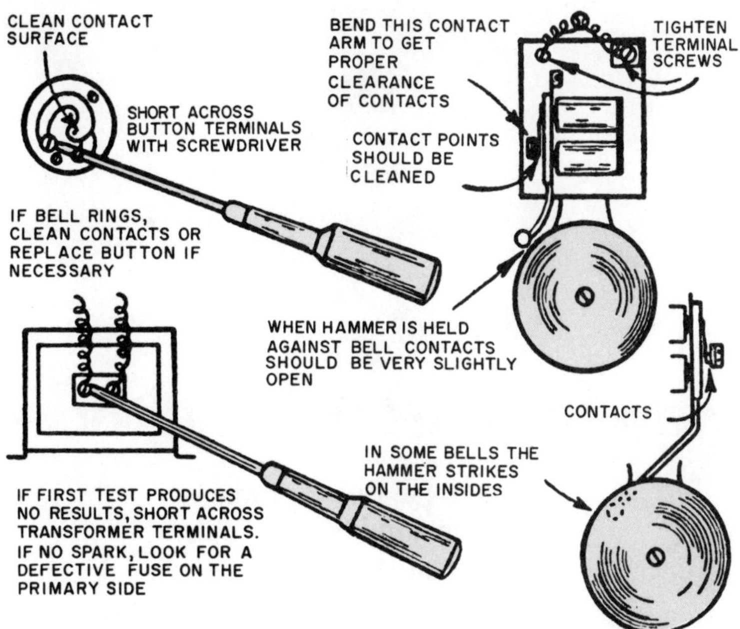
CLEAN CONTACT SURFACE
SHORT ACROSS BUTTON TERMINALS WITH SCREWDRIVER
BEND THIS CONTACT ARM TO GET PROPER CLEARANCE OF CONTACTS
TIGHTEN TERMINAL SCREWS
CONTACT POINTS SHOULD BE CLEANED
IF BELL RINGS, CLEAN CONTACTS OR REPLACE BUTTON IF NECESSARY
WHEN HAMMER IS HELD AGAINST BELL CONTACTS SHOULD BE VERY SLIGHTLY OPEN
CONTACTS
IN SOME BELLS THE HAMMER STRIKES ON THE INSIDES
IF FIRST TEST PRODUCES NO RESULTS, SHORT ACROSS TRANSFORMER TERMINALS. IF NO SPARK, LOOK FOR A DEFECTIVE FUSE ON THE PRIMARY SIDE

button. Full wiring instructions are usually included with the purchase of these more complicated musical units.

By far the most common source of trouble in doorbells is the push button, because of its location outside the house. Contacts corrode in time, making high resistance points. Check the button first, remove the cover and try shorting across the screw terminals with a screwdriver. If the bell rings, cleaning the contacts is necessary. Draw a strip of folded fine sandpaper between them, holding the top spring piece down for pressure. If inspection reveals extreme corrosion at the points of contacts, purchase a new button. If the bell still refuses to ring, check the transformer for output by touching a screwdriver blade across its secondary. A spark should be seen in this test, otherwise inspect the fuses. If they are working properly, the transformer winding may be open circuited.

If further search is required, have someone hold the button in contact while you remove the bell cover to see if movement of the flat armature with the fingers results in starting it to ring. The contacts may need adjusting or are not clean. To adjust a bell, hold the hammer against the gong. In this position, the contacts should be open slightly. Bending the fixed contact piece or adjusting a screw if one exists will allow proper adjustment to be made. Next, draw a piece of fine folded sandpaper between the contacts to clean them. Also, check for loose or broken wires at the terminal posts. The substitution of a bell known to be operative will determine if the trouble is in the bell.

With some of the lower priced bells, the wires from the magnets are wrapped around a projecting tab on the fixed contact terminal, and a wrapped joint is made at one of the main terminal posts. This is often the source of trouble, and a drop of solder on these two places will eliminate a poor connection.

Be sure to solder all joints. In time, unsoldered joints develop high resistance to the flow of current, and may prevent the bell from ringing. H.P.S.

See also: ELECTRICAL, HOME.

How to Free Sticking Doors

Use these tips to make your doors and latches operate faultlessly

HOUSE DOORS stick or bind either because damp weather has made them swell, or because the building has settled unevenly, throwing the door frame out of square. The simplest and obvious remedy is, of course, to plane down the edge of the door that rubs to provide clearance between door and door frame. This method is all right for the top or bottom edge of the door, however, since the paint or other finish on the lock-edge of the door is also removed while planing, you may wind up with a paint touch-up job requiring more work than if other methods were used.

So, before you plane the lock-edge of the door, look along the hinged edge of the door when it is closed to see if there is a gap between the door and frame. By reducing or closing this gap by shimming the hinges you may provide enough space at the top, bottom or lock-edge of the door to eliminate binding.

If door sticks along top edge or at bottom of lock-edge, first loosen screws in lower hinge leaf attached to door frame or jamb and shift door to lift back edge of leaf out of its mortise. Take care not to splinter the jamb at the end of the mortise. Then slip a ¼-inch wide strip of cardboard behind hinge, between screws and stop-edge of mortise, and retighten screws. If the door still rubs, also shim hinge leaf fastened to door.

If shimming raises a hinge leaf so it is not flush with door jamb or door edge, remove hinge pin, unscrew the leaves, and swing the door aside enough to chisel out a thin shaving from the bottom of the mortise. Then screw the hinge back in place. Such shimming, or deepening of the mortise, naturally is limited to closing the gap, if one exists, between door and jamb on the hinge edge when the door is closed.

If door sticks along the threshold or top of lock-edge, shim the upper hinge following the same procedure described above.

In rare instances the door may be "hinge bound" (hinge leaves coming together before the door is completely closed). This racks the door and tends to crack the paint at the joints. Reverse the shimming procedure and slip the cardboard shim behind

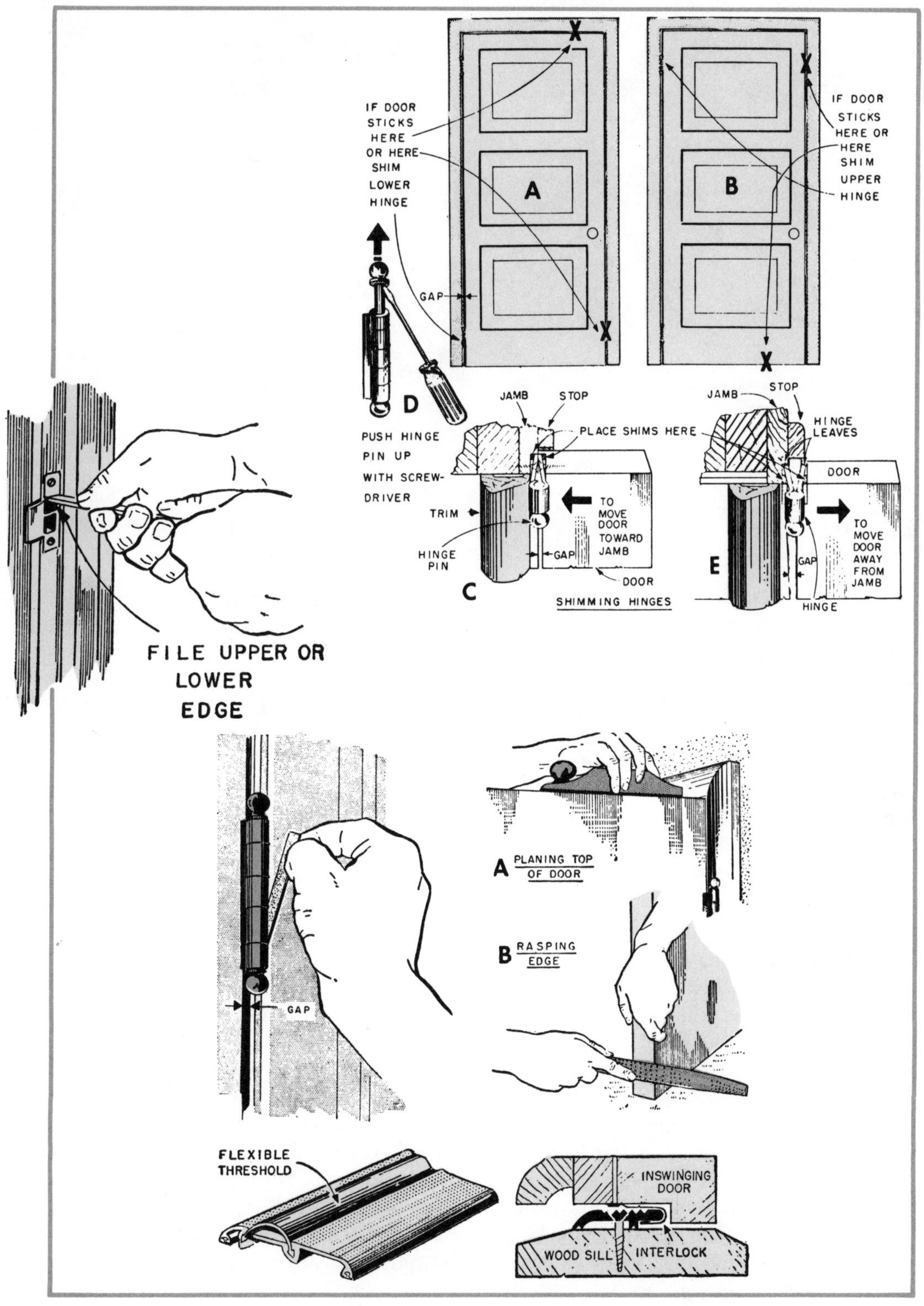
IF DOOR
STICKS
HERE
OR HERE
SHIM
LOWER
HINGE
A
GAP
IF DOOR
STICKS
HERE OR
HERE
SHIM
UPPER
HINGE
B
D
PUSH HINGE
PIN UP
WITH SCREW-
DRIVER
JAMB
STOP
PLACE SHIMS HERE
TRIM
TO
MOVE
DOOR
TOWARD
JAMB
HINGE
PIN
GAP
DOOR
C
SHIMMING HINGES
JAMB
STOP
HINGE
LEAVES
DOOR
TO
MOVE
DOOR
AWAY
FROM
JAMB
E
GAP
HINGE
FILE UPPER OR
LOWER
EDGE
GAP
A PLANING TOP OF DOOR
B RASPING EDGE
FLEXIBLE
THRESHOLD
INSWINGING
DOOR
WOOD SILL
INTERLOCK

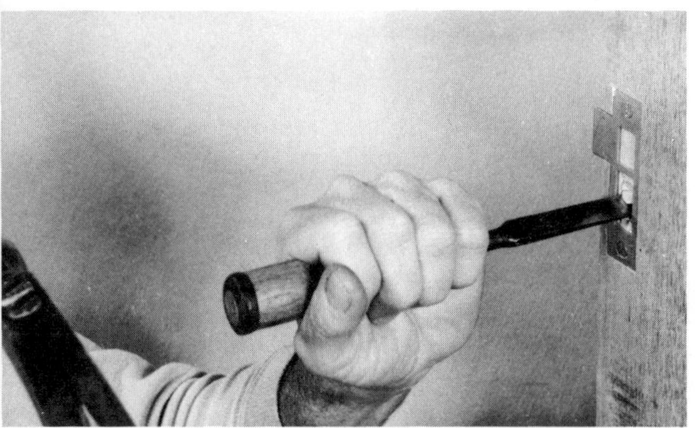

▲ *Installing a door latch keeper. After the keeper is bedded in its mortise, use a chisel to excavate recesses for latch and bolt.*

➤ *Replacing a cracked and unsightly door panel is a time-consuming task. It's easier to install a new panel, as shown here, right over the old one.*

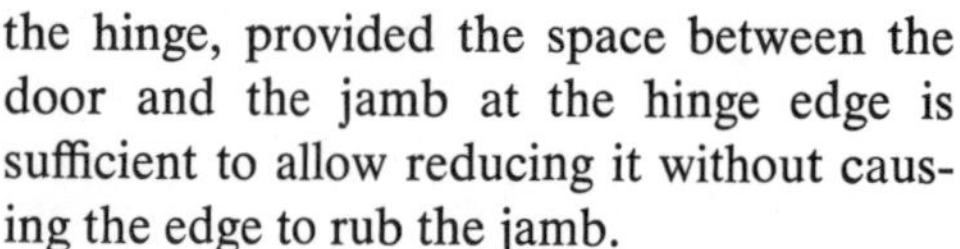

the hinge, provided the space between the door and the jamb at the hinge edge is sufficient to allow reducing it without causing the edge to rub the jamb.

Drawing in the upper hinge moves the top of the door at the lock-edge away from the jamb and raises it off the threshold because the door swivels a wee bit on the lower hinge. This effect is increased by shimming the lower by placing the shims at the front of the hinge. Although movement of the door by shimming the hinges is slight, it is sometimes enough to relieve binding without further treatment.

If the door still binds after the hinge-shim treatment, plane the offending edge or end, removing no more wood than is necessary and beveling it about $\frac{1}{16}$-inch toward the stop side to give closing clearance. Sand smooth and break the corners. In close quarters, as when dressing the top near the hinge edge or the lock stile at the bottom, a double-end block plane with the cutter set in the nose position is handy. Lacking this tool, use a wood rasp followed by a wood file and sandpaper. Postpone touching up with paint until the door is dry; then seal edges and ends and bare spots on the faces of the door.

If an outside door sticks or rubs at the bottom against the threshold it is probably due to moisture swelling the lower part of the door. Since this condition is likely to repeat, the best treatment is to lift the hinge pins, remove the door and cut off the bottom enough to apply weatherstripping, preferably the type having a metal threshold and interlocking member or flexible threshold.

Door latching troubles. Refusal of the lock bolt or knob latch to enter the keeper plate on the frame jamb is usually due to settling of the building. Hinge-shimming to lift or lower the lock-edge of the door may help. If not, file the lower or upper edge of the keeper to clear the bolt. If too much filing is needed, raise or lower the keeper by extending its mortise, plugging the old screw holes with a matchstick dipped in glue. Putty the surplus mortise and then finish by touching up with paint. E.M.L.

See also: LOCKS; PAINTING, HOUSE.

What to Do if the Drain Clogs

With a few special tools and a little know-how you can beat the high costs of plumber's bills and acquire an understanding of the plumbing in your home

WHEN THE WASTE WATER in your sink, lavatory or tub starts to run out slowly it is a sure sign an obstruction is building up somewhere along the drain pipes, and it is likely you will end up with a completely stopped-up waste pipe.

Get at the problem right away, before your line is completely blocked, with a can of chemical drain cleaner or even boiling hot water; it may save you the work and trouble of removing the waste trap pipe under the sink. (If you have a septic tank disposal system be sure to use the type of chemical drain cleaner that will not stop the bacterial action in the septic tank. Check the label on the can.)

Sink and lavatory drains. Grease from washing dishes is the major cause of a clogged kitchen-sink drain. Carried by the warm waste water, the grease solidifies on the bends in the cold drain pipe. Other waste particles become embedded in the hardened grease and before long an obstruction is built up. Chemical drain cleaners generate heat, when mixed with water, which softens the hardened grease so that it will run down the drain. Often a bucket of water heated to the boiling point on the kitchen range and poured slowly down the sink drain will clean out the solidified grease. Tap water is usually not hot enough to soften the grease.

If the drain is completely blocked so that water is left standing in the sink, do not attempt to ladle out some of the water and pour a chemical cleaner containing lye into the drain pipe. In most cases the cleaner will not reach the obstruction and it may form a hard crystallized deposit in the trap or waste pipe. Such a deposit is extremely difficult to remove and leaves you with a worse stoppage problem than you had in the first place.

Instead, first try to break through the obstruction with a rubber force cup or "plumber's friend." Even though you only get the water to drain slowly, it may be enough so that a chemical cleaner will then flow down to the place of the obstruction, where it can go to work.

When using a force cup on a double-bowl kitchen sink or laundry tub, seal the drain in the sink you're not working in with a sink stopper or a sponge-rubber ball held down firmly over the drain opening. Otherwise the force cup will merely raise the water in the other sink and not remove the obstruction.

The same holds true when using a force cup on the bathroom tub or lavatory drain. Here the overflow openings must be sealed by holding a damp washcloth tightly against the openings to prevent loss of pressure. If the lavatory or tub has a pop-up drain stopper, it should be removed before using the force cup. Most pop-up stoppers can be removed quite easily by first setting the stopper control lever or knob in the half open position, and then turning and lifting the stopper. If the stopper is the type that must have the lever disconnected before it can be lifted, remove the lever fitting located under the lavatory on the drain pipe.

Because pop-up type stoppers must have the opening and closing mechanism in the drain pipe, hair and lint collects on the mechanism and retards the flow of waste water. For this reason it's a good idea to remove the pop-up stoppers and clean them every few months.

When a clogged drain does not respond to the force cup treatment the only alternative is to remove the trap under the sink and use a soil-pipe snake. Be sure to place a bucket under the trap to catch the waste water in the line before loosening the trap coupling nuts with an adjustable wrench. After the trap is off, inspect the inside and clean it. Very seldom does the trap become clogged to the point where it stops the flow of waste water. Although small heavy objects accidentally dropped in the sink or lavatory drain may become lodged in the trap, the purpose of the trap in the drain line is to retain water in its V-shape at all times and thus provide an air-lock so that noxious sewer gas can not enter your home.

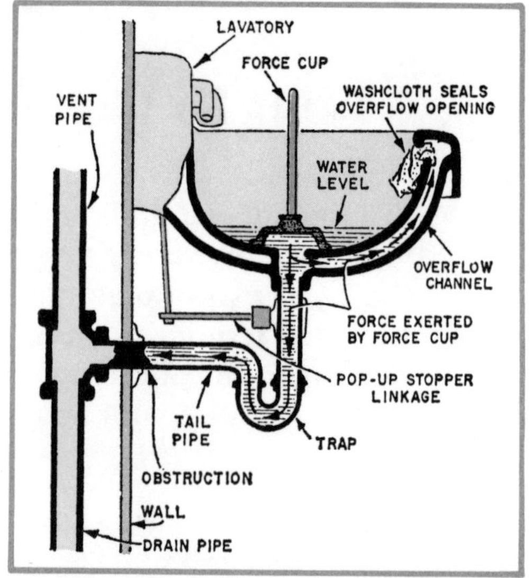

Using a force cup on a lavatory drain. It is important to close the overflow opening with a washcloth to seal in pressure.

Pop-up drain stopper, shown in left figure, has just been removed. Shown on right is removal of hair collected against sides of drain pipe by pop-up stopper.

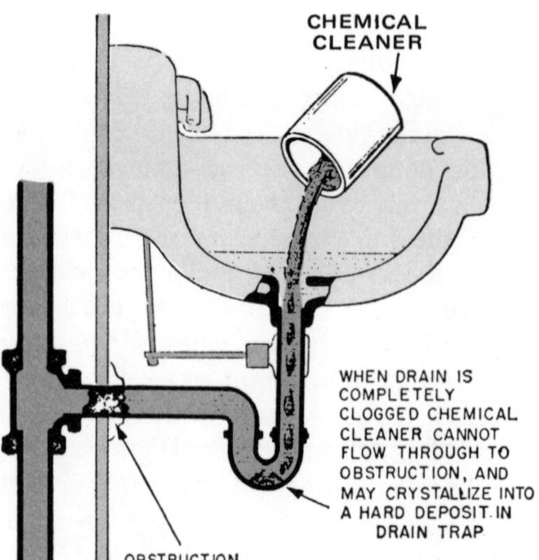

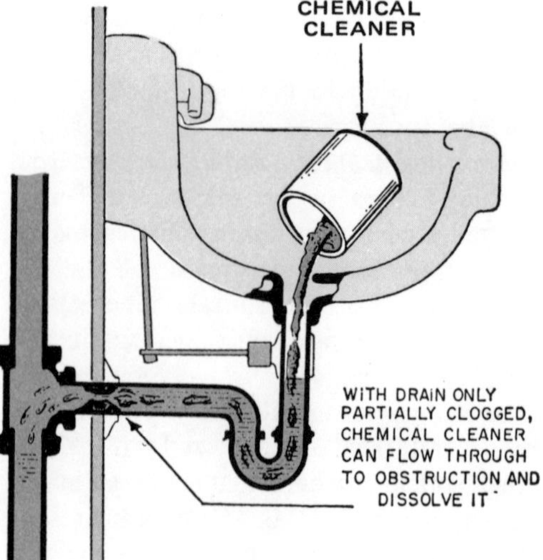

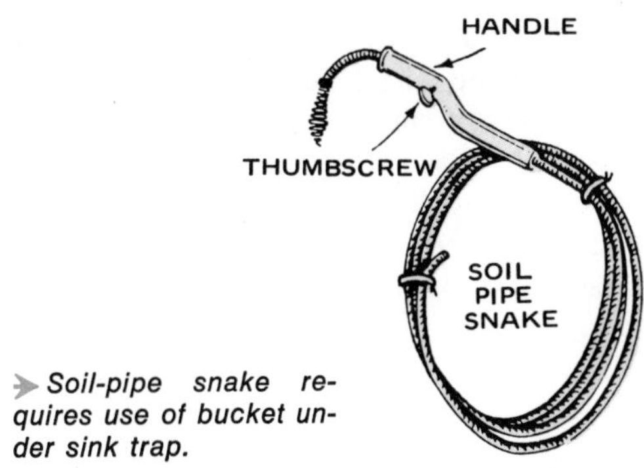

Soil-pipe snake requires use of bucket under sink trap.

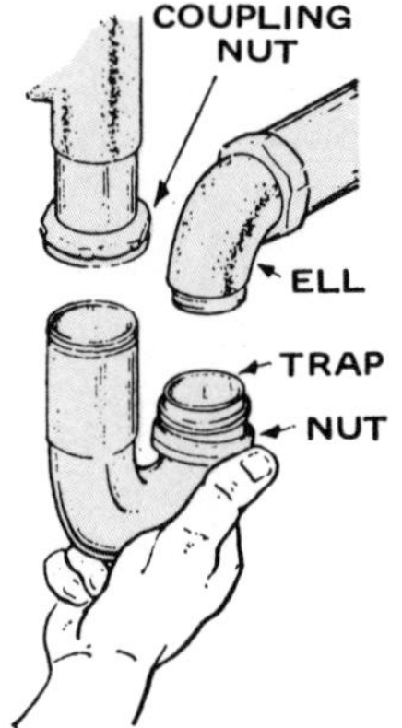

To remove the drain trap, loosen the drain coupling nuts with an adjustable wrench.

Usually the drain line obstruction is located somewhere along the piping within the walls of the house. And, that is where the snake, which is a long flexible, coiled spring-steel wire with a hook on its end, comes in handy. It will "snake" its way through and around the bends in the drain pipe.

Insert the snake into the drain pipe leading into the wall, twisting it clockwise with the crank handle as you do so. Loosening the thumbscrew on the handle will allow you to feed more of the snake wire through the handle into the pipe and at the same time keep the handle fairly close to the pipe opening. Work the wire in and out of the pipe slightly as you feed it in. If the wire becomes difficult to twist, or if you feel you have hooked something, pull the snake out slowly, continuing to twist the wire in a clockwise direction. Remove any matter on the hook and reinsert the snake working it as before.

Should the snake hit a solid obstruction 12 inches or so beyond the pipe opening and refuse to travel further, you are probably striking the vent fitting. A little in-and-out movement and twisting should send it around the bend of the fitting. If after making the bend, the wire goes in freely for 3 or 4 feet and yet you find no obstruction, the snake is probably going *up* the vent pipe.

When this happens back out the snake to the point where it strikes the vent fitting and try again. This time you may send it in the other direction or down the drain pipe. If the snake continues to go up the vent after several attempts, remove it and disconnect the drain tail pipe going through the wall. You then should be able to see the vent fitting and guide the snake in the right direction as you insert it.

When you have fished out and removed all the waste particles at the point where the obstruction was, you should be able to push the snake freely past this point and be fairly certain the line is now free of the obstruction.

Reassemble the trap piping and flush the drain line with boiling hot water or a chemical cleaner to remove particles still clinging to the walls of the drain line.

Bathtubs. Old style, leg-type bathtubs with an exposed drain pipe under the tub can be cleaned by following the methods described for a sink because the drain pipe can be removed. The obstruction can also be reached with a snake by merely removing the overflow strainer to admit the snake into the drain line. Some tub installations have a gooseneck-type trap which is under the floor and cannot be removed. With such a setup the snake must be forced through the trap bends.

Bathtub drain lines connected to a drum-trap simplify the problems of keeping the drain line free of obstruction. The only difficulty you may encounter will be in removing the drum-trap cover. A special wrench, which you can borrow or rent from your local plumbing shop, will be needed for the job.

Once the cover is removed, a snake may be run through the lines in either direction—up to the tub overflow strainer or toward the house waste line. If you cannot find the drum-trap, look for an access trap door located in the wall at the fixture end of recessed-type tubs. In some cases the trap door may be located in a closet of the adjoining room. Once you have removed the trap door, all plumbing will be exposed to view so you can work on it.

Bathroom water closets. The one thing to remember when the water closet in the bathroom becomes clogged is not to free it by repeated flushings. This only results in the bowl overflowing and a double problem.

A manual snake can be used when the drain tail pipe is left on, as on left, but the Miller Rod House will feed the snake into drain pipe when the tail pipe is removed.

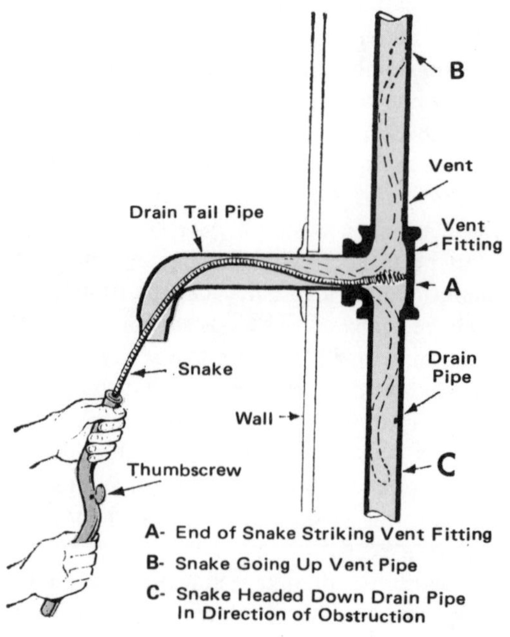

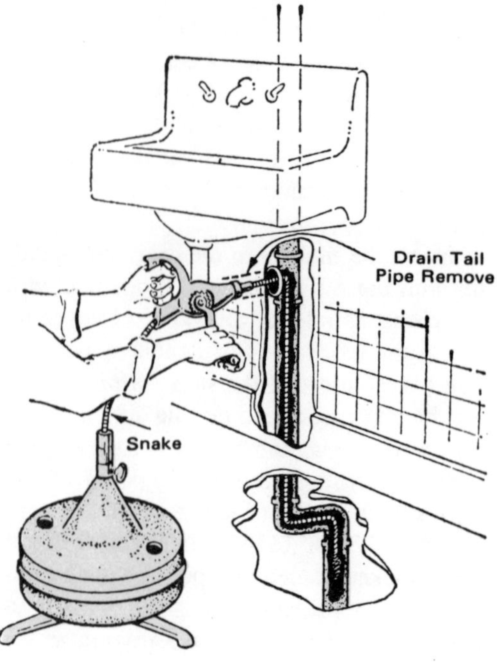

Instead, first try to force the obstruction through with a "plumber's helper" or force cup. Place it over the outlet in the water closet and work it up and down vigorously, then quickly lift the force cup from the outlet. If some of the water rushes down the drain with a swallowing noise you have probably forced the obstruction through the waste pipe to the sewer. Just to make certain, pour a pail of water down the water closet, and if it takes the water, test by throwing some crumpled tissue in the bowl and flush.

If you cannot dislodge the obstruction with a force cup, the stoppage is probably due to a plastic toy, bottle, small brush, towel or some such object that has accidently dropped into the water closet and becomes wedged in the closet trap. For this type of obstruction, two tools (closet auger and mechanical fingers) will prove helpful.

To use the closet auger, first pull the wire "snake" up through the tube by the handle so that only the hook tip protrudes. Place the bent end of the tube in the closet outlet.

The old gooseneck-type traps, as on left, cannot be removed so the snake must be forced through the bends in the pipes. For drum traps, as on right, simply remove the trap cover (located on floor) with special wrench.

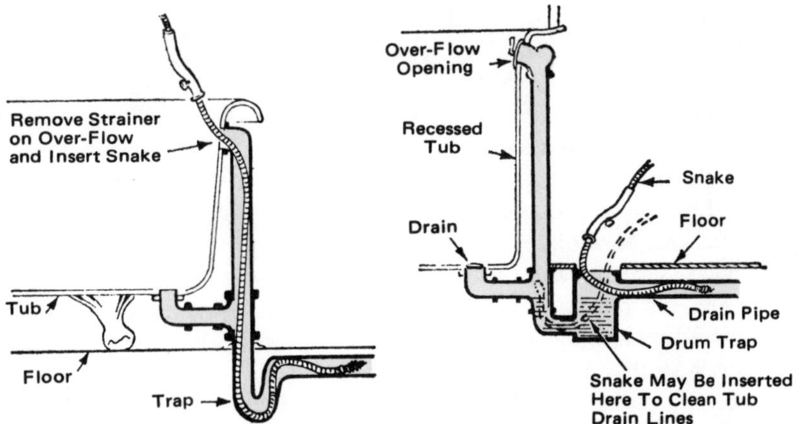

Cleaning Drain On Leg-Type Bathtub

Cleaning The Drain Lines Through Drum Trap

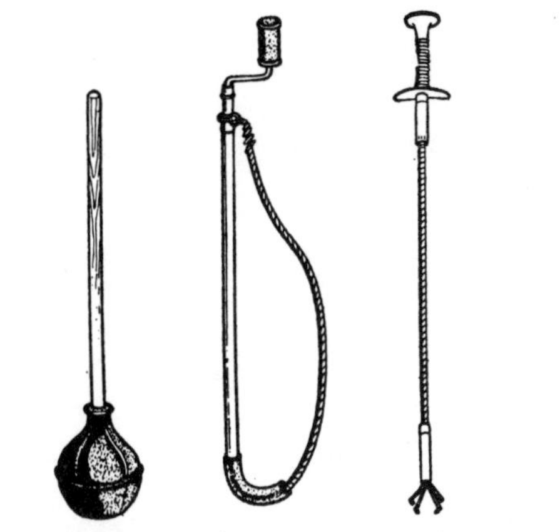

Then, grasping the tube near the top with one hand, start turning the handle clockwise with the other while slowly forcing the wire snake down the closet trap. The spiral hook at the end of the snake will become entangled in whatever is causing the obstruction and can then be withdrawn, pulling the obstruction with it. Repeat the procedure until you think you have removed enough of the obstruction to be able to flush the rest of it down with a pail of water.

An auger of this type works well for removing obstructions caused by fabric articles such as a towel or diaper or a wad of toilet tissue. The spiral hook, however, is not much good for grasping a hard solid object like a bottle, plastic toy or ball.

To remove this type of obstruction, the mechanical finger tool is superior. Its 36-inch slender flexible shaft can be forced down and around the water closet trap, and the fingers opened and closed by the knob at the hand-held end of the flexible shaft. The four hooked and sharp spring-steel fingers will grasp rigid plastic objects, as well as fabric and paper.

As a last resort the bowl can always be disconnected from the floor drain fitting to get at the obstruction from the other end of the bowl trap. To do this, first shut off the water supplying the flush tank and, with the tank lid off and your hand on the large rubber flush ball in the tank, allow the water in the tank to flow down into the water closet. If it looks like the bowl is going to overflow, quickly shut off the flow of water with the flush ball. Then ladle the water out of the bowl and into a pail with a tin can, and sponge out the remaining water in the bowl and tank.

If the water closet tank is the type that is fastened to the wall, loosen the coupling nut so that the tank-to-bowl piping will slide apart. If the tank is supported by the bowl, the tank will have to be disconnected and removed first. Then remove the nuts from the sides of the bowl at its base. Some of these nuts are covered with a ceramic cap which can be removed by very gently tapping the cap with the wooden handle of a hammer. This will expose the bolt nuts which can be removed with an open-end wrench.

Loosen these nuts alternately, a full turn at a time to avoid cracking the base of the bowl. Then jar the bowl loose with blows from the palms of your hands. Rock the bowl forward and backward over the floor drain outlet slowly to spill out any water left in the trap and set the bowl upside down on some newspapers spread on the floor. By inserting the mechanical fingers or closet auger into the bowl trap you can now reach and dislodge the obstruction.

Before replacing the closet bowl, inspect the sponge-rubber gasket used to make a water-tight seal between the bowl and floor flange of the waste pipe. If it was torn when the bowl was removed, replace it with a new one of the same type and thickness. If you do not find a rubber gasket, bowl-setting wax or putty was used to make the seal between bowl and floor flange. Scrape away the old putty and replace it with new bowl-setting putty available at your local plumbing shop. Apply putty around the bowl edges that contact the floor too. After pulling the bowl down to the floor flange with the two closet bolts, scrape away the excess putty that squeezed out around the edges of the bowl. Then reconnect the flush tank, turn on the water and test the fixture by flushing it several times.

Underground sewage drains. All waste water from sinks, tubs, lavatories and water closets in your house is carried away through a 4-inch waste pipe system to the main sewer pipe in the street or to your own septic tank system. The large black, cast iron pipe extending from the floor to the ceiling in your basement is part of this waste disposal system. When this line becomes clogged, the obstruction is usually somewhere in the horizontal run of the piping beneath the basement floor or underground between the house and the main sewer line.

The first indication of an obstruction in this line is slow and sluggish drainage of the basement floor drain or laundry tubs or overflow issuing from these drains following discharge of a plumbing fixture up in the house. If your town has a combination sanitary and storm sewer system, where the leaders from the gutters are also connected to the waste disposal line, the obstruction could cause the basement to flood due to backup of rain water during a storm.

Fortunately, stoppage in waste lines is anticipated when the sewer pipes are laid and one or more cleanout fittings are piped into the system. To run a sewer wire or snake into the line to dislodge an obstruction, the cleanout plug or cover must be

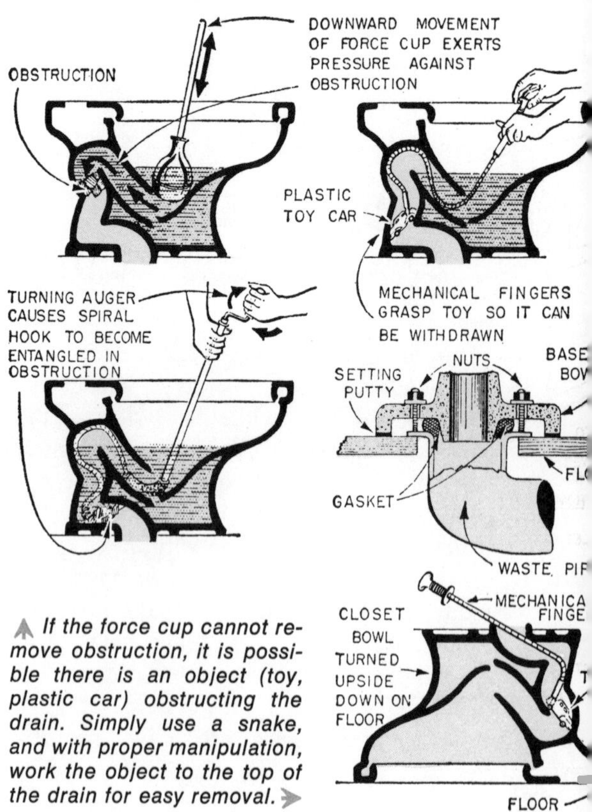

▲ *If the force cup cannot remove obstruction, it is possible there is an object (toy, plastic car) obstructing the drain. Simply use a snake, and with proper manipulation, work the object to the top of the drain for easy removal.* ➤

removed. This can frequently be a difficult job, especially if the plug is corroded. First tap the plug around the edges with a hammer and try to unscrew it with an 18- or 24-inch pipe wrench. A 2-foot length of pipe slipped over the wrench handle will give you more leverage. If you can't budge the plug with a wrench, nick the edge of the plug with a hammer and cold chisel, and drive it counter-clockwise until it loosens sufficiently to turn with a wrench.

When you remove the plug, some waste water standing in the vertical pipes may flow out on the basement floor. This is to be expected, so don't be too alarmed since it will only be a few pailfuls. Two types of sewer cleanout wires are available for rodding out the pipes. One is a flat spring-steel ribbon ½- to 1-inch wide and 50 to 100 feet long with a pointed spear having semispherical rollers on each side. The other is a ½-inch diameter coiled steel wire snake, similar to the smaller closet auger.

When working wire in and out of pipe in basement, increase pressure if it should buckle or seem to get stuck in a cleanout opening.

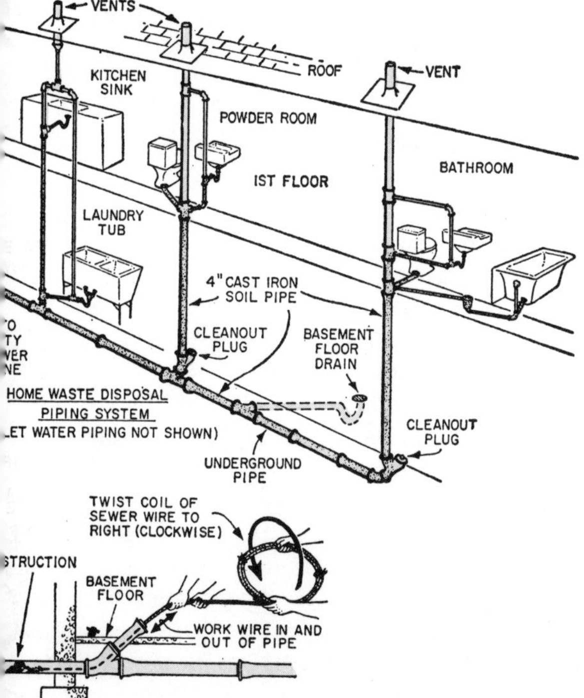

Feed the cleanout wire into the sewer pipe, and keep working it back and forth as you slowly inch it into the pipe. If you suddenly strike a barrier and the wire buckles at the cleanout opening, grasp the wire closer to the opening and continue working it into the pipe with increased pressure. This will often jar the obstruction loose, or send the wire around the pipe bend. Sometimes it is necessary to roll up the snake to within 5 feet of the cleanout; tie or wire the coil in several places and have someone slowly twist the coil while you continue to feed the wire into the pipe. This, too, will help to break up the obstruction or maneuver the wire around a bend in the pipe. Should the backed-up water begin to drain off, keep working the wire back and forth and slowly withdraw it. Remove any material adhering to the wire hook or spear and send the wire in again several times or until the waste water flows through freely.

If the wire hook extracts some tree roots, then your house sewer is probably of clay tile pipe and tree roots have wormed their way in through the joints. This type of obstruction could be very difficult to remove with a hand operated sewer wire and it would be wise to call in a plumbing contractor who has a motor-driven auger made especially for cutting out tree roots in sewer pipes.

Once the roots have been cut out, further root penetration may be prevented by monthly flushings of the sewer, through the cleanout, with a solution of copper sulphate (one pound to a pailful of warm water).

When replacing the cleanout plug, coat the threads with grease or petroleum jelly to make removal easy. Never use a pipe joint compound on these plugs.

See also: FAUCETS; TOILET.

Servicing Drum Brakes Yourself

You can check and repair your brakes safely and save ten dollars for every hour you work

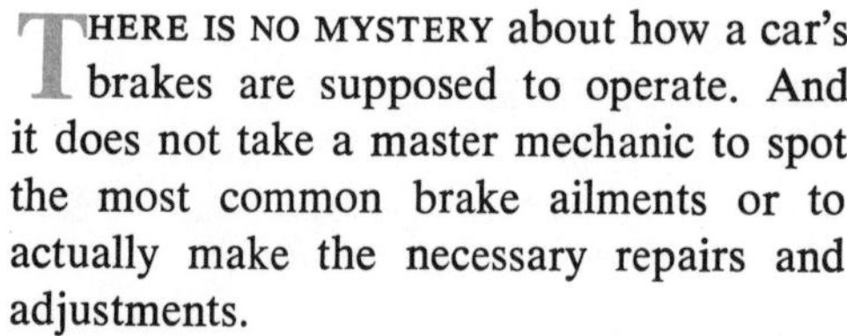

THERE IS NO MYSTERY about how a car's brakes are supposed to operate. And it does not take a master mechanic to spot the most common brake ailments or to actually make the necessary repairs and adjustments.

Working carefully, you can do a safe, sure job of brake repairing, and count on a savings in labor costs.

To determine whether your brakes need servicing, first check out their performance with this simple road test (performed in a deserted parking lot, if possible). While driving in a straight line at 15-20 mph, try a quick stop.

See if any of the tire marks in the gravel are heavier than others or if the rear wheels have swerved out of line. Try the same test again, but ease up on the steering wheel as you stop. If the wheel spins to one side, you know the brakes are not equalized and are dangerous on slippery roads. Now let the car coast and listen to the brakes while they are applied and release slowly. Carefully note any noise or faulty operation and then check the symptoms on the table for possible causes. You can locate the defect exactly by eliminating the most easily checked and repaired causes first.

Pedal clearance. Let the car sit a few minutes after the road test and then push the brake pedal down hard and hold it there. Then see how much clearance or *reserve* you have between the brake pedal and the floorboard. If this clearance is less than three inches, check the fluid reservoir at the master cylinder to make sure the fluid is within ⅜-inch of the threads on the filler neck. This reservoir is usually part of the master cylinder, or else it is a small tank connected to it by a line. If the fluid level is low, refill with a heavy-duty, nationally available-brand that is guaranteed to mix with all other brake fluids. Then repeat the pedal reserve test.

Free play test. Next, test the brake pedal for *free play.* Apply just enough pressure on the pedal with your fingers to move it. The pedal should move about ½-inch before you feel the resistance of the master cylinder piston. If there is less, the piston is not returning to its normal "brakes-off" position and is blocking the compensating port. Consequently, some of the fluid pressure may be retained, preventing the brakes from releasing completely. Adjustment for free play is usually made by loosening the lock nut on the push rod linkage between the brake pedal and the master cylinder. Then adjust the travel of the rod by turning it until the correct amount of free play is obtained. On some older Ford cars, the free play is adjusted by turning an eccentric bolt.

Adjusting the brakes. Virtually all American cars for some years have had self-adjusting drum brakes.

With this system, a cable is attached to the anchor pin, run around a flange on one of the brake shoes and attached to a lever which bears up against the familiar star wheel adjuster, described later.

When the car is operating in reverse and the brakes are applied, the outward movement of the shoe tugs on the cable and this actuates the lever, which moves the star wheel adjuster. Normally, no manual adjustment is necessary.

If, however, the system becomes corroded and freezes, it must be disassembled and penetrating solvent applied, or the parts need replacement.

Older cars and some high-performance cars of recent years have manual adjusting brakes, and they are described here.

The most common system, to which the self-adjusting mechanism has been added, is the star wheel.

To adjust this type of brake, raise the wheel, remove the oblong rubber rust plug from the back plate and insert a screwdriver or brake adjusting tool. By working the tool in a prying motion, you will be able to turn the star wheel inside

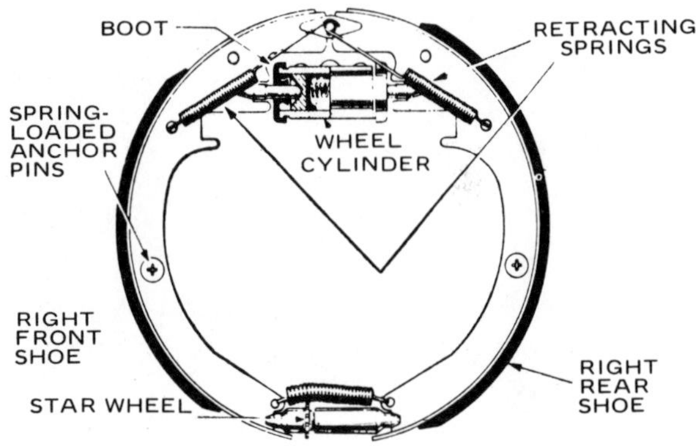

Modern self-adjusting drum brake is shown, below, with all components labeled. Note self-adjusting assembly which includes cable, guide flange on secondary shoe and lever assembly to actuate star wheel. Compare with manual adjusting setup, above, in which you see the simple star wheel and a tensioning spring over it.

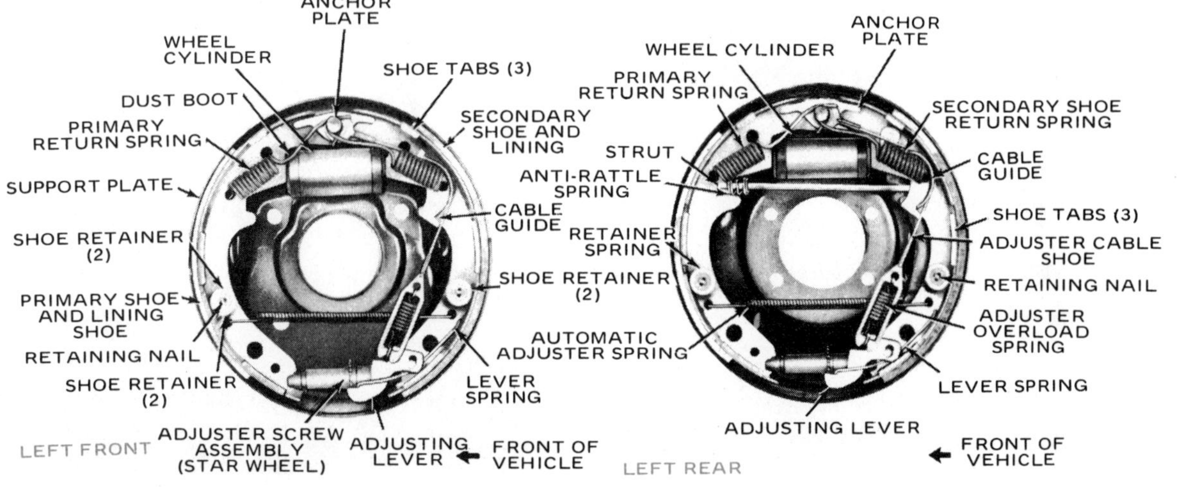

the drum until the shoes are expanded to their limit and the wheel is locked tight. Then, by prying in the opposite direction, back off the star wheel just enough to let the wheel turn freely. Apply and release the brakes several times, and check again for shoe drag by rotating the wheel. If there is any drag, readjust until the wheel turns freely. Be sure to replace the rubber plug.

The second type of adjustment is an *eccentric cam.* The cam adjustment may be made at the back plate with a wrench or through a hole in the front of the drum using a screwdriver. The adjustment is the same regardless of the method used to turn the cam. Working on one shoe at a time, rotate the cam until the brake shoe is tight against the drum and the wheel is locked. Now back off the cam just enough to allow the wheel to turn without the shoe dragging. Repeat the operation on the other cam and brake shoe and then check as with the star wheel system.

Hydraulic line inspection. Now with the car indoors, continue your inspection by getting under it with a flashlight to inspect the hydraulic lines. These lines should be firm and dry. Replace a line if there is the slightest trace of brake fluid or oil on the covering or if it shows signs of gumminess and softening.

Although they are less subject to damage or deterioration, the metal lines that connect the master cylinder with the flexible lines should also be checked carefully.

Pen points to access hole in brake backing plate. When rubber plug is removed, you can adjust manual adjusting brakes, or manually back off self-adjusting brakes that have overadjusted and prevent drum from coming off. In this case, however, both awl and adjusting spoon must be inserted in hole (awl to push away adjusting lever, spoon to turn star wheel).

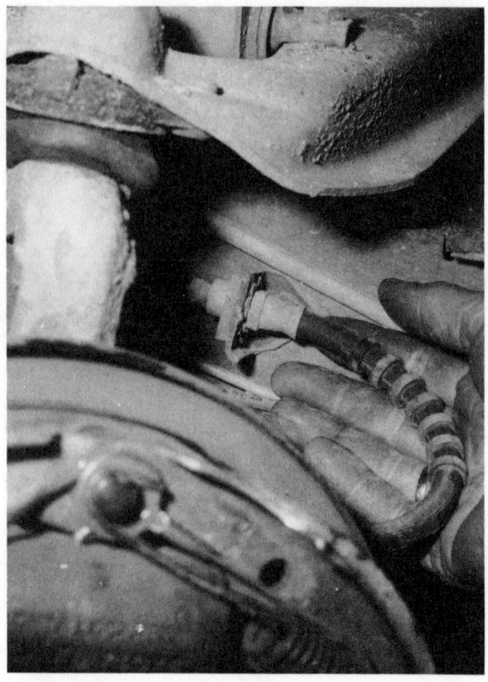

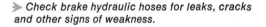

Check brake hydraulic hoses for leaks, cracks and other signs of weakness.

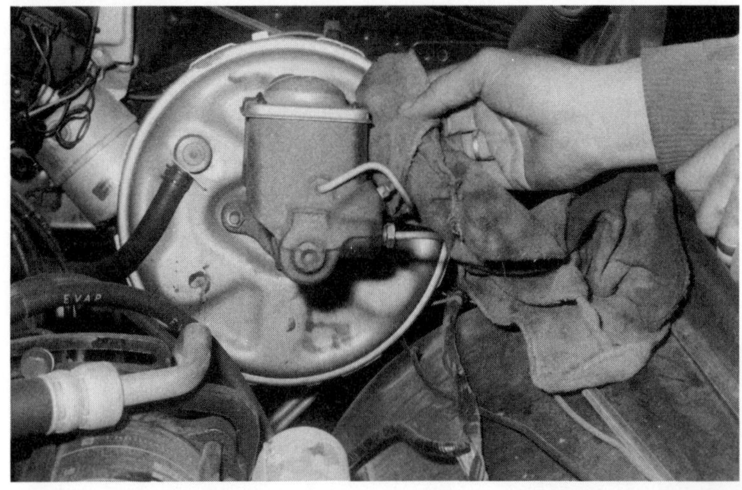

When you check a master cylinder for leaks, begin by cleaning it off thoroughly first, so you do not confuse road splash and engine oil with brake fluid.

Leaking wheel cylinder can be checked by pushing away dust cover at each side with a screwdriver and looking for signs of brake fluid seepage.

Check for leaking connections, dents, loose fastenings at the frame, and for signs of abrasion or wear on the guards where the line bends around the frame. While you are under the car, check the parking brake cables for wear and the inside of the wheels for bearing grease leaks. Such a leak can affect the operation of your brakes due to grease entering the brake drum and soaking the linings.

Now inspect the master cylinder closely for leakage. Leaks at the brake line connection can often be corrected by tightening, but if the fluid is coming from around the piston rod, the master cylinder is in need of overhauling and must be removed. To remove it, disconnect the brake line, remove the wires from the spotlight switch and unfasten the push rod from the pedal. Then remove the mounting bolts and lift out the cylinder for rebuilding as described later.

Continue your brake check by removing a front and a rear brake drum to inspect the linings and shoe mechanisms. Do not decide whether relining is necessary on the basis of a front or rear wheel alone. It is true that the front linings wear faster, but a poorly adjusted, dragging parking brake can put wear on the rear shoes in a hurry.

In the classified section of your phone book, locate an auto parts dealer who advertises pickup and delivery machine shop service. Go to see him to make certain he has all the parts you may need to complete the brake overhaul and get an estimate of their cost. Also, while you are there, you may have to borrow or rent a universal wheel puller to remove

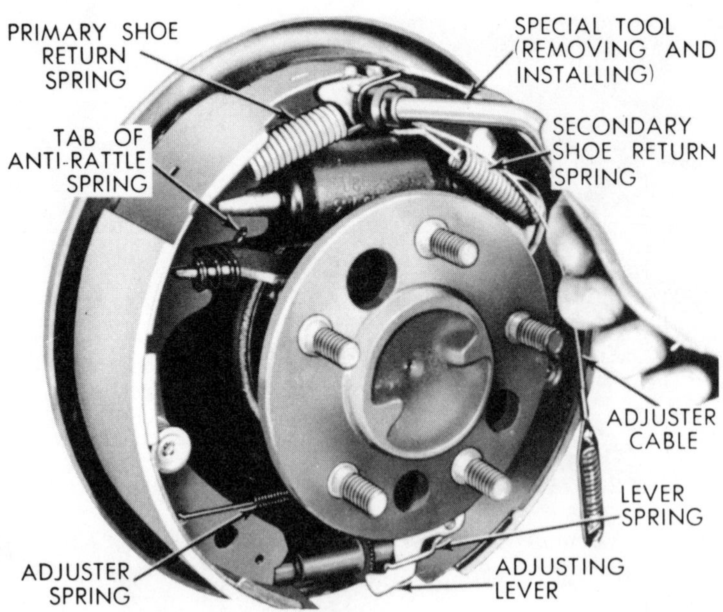

Disassembly of drum brake can begin with disconnection of self-adjusting cable on cars so equipped, and removal of brake shoe return springs. Taking off and refitting springs is easier with the special tool shown, but you can also use a screwdriver.

your rear brake drums. Occasionally, when accompanied by a parts order, there is no charge for the use of this tool.

Now block up the car and place a piece of wood under the brake pedal to prevent it from accidentally being pushed while the drums are removed. Remove the hubcap and dust cap from a front wheel and then, without removing the wheel, pull the cotter pin and remove the nut from the spindle. Get a good grip on the two sides of the tire, wiggle it a bit, and pull straight back. The tire, wheel, brake drum and wheel bearing should slide off easily as a unit.

To remove a rear brake drum, you may need the universal wheel puller. After removing dust cap, cotter pin and castle nut, fasten the three arms of the wheel puller under three lug nuts of the wheel and then turn the screw until it is against the axle shaft. Rap on the striking anvil with a hammer until the drum comes free.

Lining inspection. As soon as the drum is removed, brush the dust off of all parts and make a close visual inspection of the linings, brake drums and wheel cylinders. If the shoes are to be removed, label each one to show its location. Don't mark on the linings; when they are replaced, the marks will be lost. It may help you to remember the location of the springs and pins if you make a sketch of the assembly for a front and rear wheel.

If the linings are worn down to with-

With return springs removed, anchor plate can be taken out.

in $\frac{1}{16}$-inch of the rivets or shoe steel back, they must be replaced. For safety's sake, also change linings if they have become coated with brake fluid or grease.

To remove the brake shoes, first unhook the retractor spring. This spring is most easily removed with a special pliers that can be purchased for about two dollars. You can use an ordinary pliers, but it takes a powerful grip and extra care not to let the spring slip.

Tie a cord around the wheel cylinder or use the special clamp to keep the pistons from popping out of the cylinder when the shoes are removed. Then, if the shoes are held to the back plate by a spring-loaded pin, compress the spring, turn it 90° and release it to free the brake shoes.

When disassembling the rear brakes, remove both shoes, the parking lever, the shoe adjusting screw and its lock spring as a unit. Then disconnect the parking brake lever from the shoes and just let it hang from the cable.

Drum inspection. If the linings have worn down to the rivets and the drum is scored deeply enough to have made lengthwise marks on the shoes, have the drum reground at a brake shop. Brake drums should be replaced if there are any signs of cracking, warping or heat discoloration. The number of times a drum can be reground depends on the amount of metal removed during grinding. Since .060-inch is the maximum amount that can be safely removed, drums can seldom be reground a second time.

Check to see if there is a sharp shoulder at the back edge of the braking surface in the drum. This means the drum has been reground at least once and that if it is deeply scored now it is likely the drum must be exchanged. In either case, wire the labeled brake shoes and their drum together so they can be sent to the brake shop as a unit and the shoes fitted to that drum or its replacement.

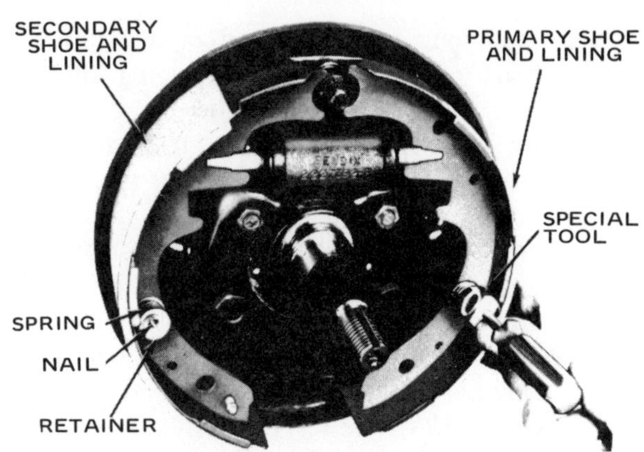

Retainer spring assembly is shown being removed with special tool. Job also can be done with screwdriver. Just press down spring with screwdriver and twist the retaining nail with fingers to free the assembly.

Shoes are pulled away from the anchor pin and lifted away from the backing plate.

Now turn up the edge of each of the rubber boots on the wheel cylinders to see if fluid has been leaking by the piston. Also check along the back plate for signs of leaking. If there is the slightest amount of leakage, all of the cylinders probably need service.

If your car is in need of a complete brake overhaul order a rebuilding kit for each wheel cylinder and one for the master cylinder, along with a hone for the cylinder bores. Also ask to have the brake shoes relined and, if necessary, have the drums reground. With this, purchase a quart each of heavy-duty brake fluid and a brake line flushing compound. Even if all of these materials are necessary, you will only have spent between $30 and $50 as the total expense for your brake overhaul; a fraction of the cost of having it done.

Since the replacement parts for rebuilding the cylinders may differ slightly in appearance from the original, check to see that there are instructions for assembling them in each kit. Also see that the brake shoes are still with the correct drums by checking the markings you made during disassembly.

Then remove the boot and brake shoe push rod from each wheel cylinder and gently press against one of the pistons until the opposite piston and its rubber cup are forced out of the other end of the cylinder. Remove the piston spring and push the remaining piston and cup out from the other side. If the brake system has two wheel cylinders, one end of each cylinder will be closed and the piston must be forced out by applying a light pressure on the brake pedal. On some models there is also an expander located between the end of the piston spring and the cup which should also be replaced.

WHAT'S THE MATTER WITH YOUR BRAKES?

Condition	Possible Cause	Remedy
PULLING CAR TO ONE SIDE	1. Tires unevenly inflated or worn unevenly	1. Replace with matched tires on each side and inflate evenly
	2. Shoes need adjustment	2. Adjust brakes
	3. Back plate or wheel bearings loose	3. Tighten plate; replace and/or adjust bearings
	4. Grease or fluid soaked lining on one wheel, lining charred	4. Replace linings and repair grease or fluid leak
	5. Moisture or mud on shoes	5. Clean out brake assembly with water if muddy. Drive slowly and maintain light pressure on brakes until friction dries lining. Replace rubber plug in back plate if necessary
	6. Drum scored or out of round	6. Regrind or replace drums
	7. Dissimilar linings on one side of car	7. Replace with matched linings
	8. Weak or loose chassis spring	8. Tighten or replace worn part
	9. Worn king pins	9. Replace worn parts
ONE BRAKE DRAGGING	1. Shoe clearance insufficient	1. Readjust dragging brake
	2. Hydraulic line clogged or crimped	2. Flush system or replace line
	3. Loose wheel bearings	3. Tighten or replace bearings
	4. Weak or broken shoe return spring	4. Replace spring
	5. Shoe sticking on anchor pins	5. Lube anchor pins and other contact points
	6. Wheel cylinder pistons sticking	6. Hone cylinder and replace piston

WHAT'S THE MATTER WITH YOUR BRAKES?		
Condition	**Possible Cause**	**Remedy**
HARSH OR GRABBING	1. Linings are wet or damp	1. Drive car slowly while maintaining light pressure on brake pedal until friction dries linings
	2. Back plate loose	2. Tighten back plate screws
	3. Charred, grease soaked or improper linings	3. Replace linings
	4. Drums scored	4. Regrind or replace drums
SQUEAKING	1. Loose wheel bearings	1. Replace and/or adjust bearings
	2. Metallic particles or dust imbedded in lining, worn lining	2. Replace lining
	3. Bent back plate	3. Repair or replace back plate
	4. Bent shoes	4. Check installation and replace shoes
KNOCKING	1. Roughly finished or warped drum	1. Replace or regrind drum
	2. Adjusting slot in shoe is not square	2. Repair or replace shoe
INADEQUATE RESERVE CLEARANCE AT BRAKE PEDAL	1. Low fluid level in master cylinder	1. Add fluid
	2. Pedal and/or shoes need adjustment	2. Adjust pedal and shoes
	3. Air or fluid vapor trapped in system	3. Bleed system
	4. Fluid leak in system	4. Repair or replace defective lines or cylinders
	5. Worn lining	5. Replace lining
BRAKES DRAG AFTER ADJUSTMENT	1. Vent in filler cap is clogged	1. Clean vent
	2. Inadequate freeplay at pedal	2. Adjust master cylinder push rod or brake pedal eccentric bolt
	3. Brake lines clogged or crimped	3. Replace line and/or flush system
	4. Rubber pistons swollen	4. Check and replace brake fluid

Note that wheel cylinders can only be rebuilt if the cylinder bores are in good condition. Very light scratches and corrosion can be cleaned with crocus cloth. If there is any question in your mind, replace the wheel cylinder.

The practice of honing out wheel cylinders that are moderately scored is of questionable value. A replacement cylinder is little more expensive than one that is professionally honed and rebuilt by you. Your safety is worth the small extra expense.

If the cylinder bore looks bright and free from scratches, wipe it thoroughly with a soft clean cloth dampened with brake line cleaner. Then insert one of the new pistons and check the clearance between the piston and the cylinder wall with a feeler gauge. This clearance must not be more than .004-inch. If it is over .004, which is very unlikely, you will have to replace the cylinder housings.

Master cylinder overhaul. Mount your master cylinder in a vise and clean the outside of it thoroughly before beginning disassembly. Position the cylinder so the push rod from the pedal is toward you and you will see either a retaining wire or a metal collar held with a pair of capscrews. Remove this retainer first so you can take out the piston, piston cups, spring and valve from the cylinder. Lay these parts out in order for reference when assembling the new parts, but do not under any circumstances use them when reassembling the cylinder. The exact number and style of the parts will differ with each make and year of car.

Some Buick cars in the late 1950's had a unique master cylinder in which the piston did not fit against the cylinder walls. This cylinder is serviced by separating the cast housings and removing the retaining wire to expose the long, rod-like piston.

Check the bore and the valve seat at the end of the bore for rust or corrosion and clean, if necessary, with crocus cloth or a commercial rust remover. Follow the same procedure for the master cylinder as was used on the wheel cylinders if the bore is pitted or scratched. Then reassemble the cylinder with the new parts from the kit, following the enclosed instructions.

Install the master cylinder in the car, connecting the lines and the stoplight switch and checking to be sure that the push rod is lined up to work freely before tightening the mounting bolts. Adjust the free play as described. If it is necessary to replace any of the hydraulic lines, do so now. No sealer of any kind is necessary or desirable here as the brass fittings will make a very tight seal under moderate pressure.

Brake line flushing. Pack each wheel cylinder with a clean cloth and fill the master cylinder with the brake line cleaning fliud. Then remove the cloth from one cylinder at a time and flush the brake line by pumping the fluid through it with the brake pedal. Refill the reservoir and continue this until the distinct color of the cleaner can be seen when it is forced out at the wheel cylinders.

Pump the cylinder until the system is empty and then reassemble the wheel cylinders according to the instructions in the kits. Lubricate all the new parts with brake fluid before assembly and insert them from the end of the cylinder in which they will operate. Do not try to push the cups through from one end as the rubber parts may snag on the bleeder or inlet hole and be damaged. If trapped air forces one piston out when you insert the other, open the bleeder valve to relieve the pressure.

If any of the parts become dirty while they are being assembled, rinse them in the brake line cleaning fluid, allow them to dry and then dip them into fresh brake fluid again. Do not use the brake fluid that has been used for lubricating these parts or the hone to refill the master cylinder as it will contain grit and air bubbles. Also, do not allow any oil or grease to come into contact with the cylinder assembly as it will deteriorate the rubber parts. When the wheel cylinders have been completely assembled, snap on the boots and push rods and secure them temporarily by tying or using clamps.

Brake shoe assembly. Before installing the brake shoe assembly, coat the threads and contact surfaces of the adjusting screw with a high temperature fiber or silicone grease. Also coat the raised shoe guides on the back plate with this grease.

Then mount each brake shoe on the anchor pin and set it in the cylinder push rod slots. On Bendix type brakes, screw the adjusting screw all the way in, that is, make it as short as possible and fit it between the lower ends of the shoes. Assemble the hold-down pins by placing the plates over the spring and pin, compressing the spring and turning the assembly 90°. On other type brakes, turn the eccentric cam adjustment so its low point will be against the shoe. Finally, secure the entire assembly with the retracting springs and attach the self-adjusting mechanism.

Star wheel should be inspected carefully. It must thread in and out easily, or threads should be immersed in solvent to remove rust and then be coated with silicone lubricant. Teeth of star wheel should not be damaged. This is particularly important on self-adjusting brakes, which have 24 small teeth per star wheel, compared with 12 larger ones for the manual adjusting brakes.

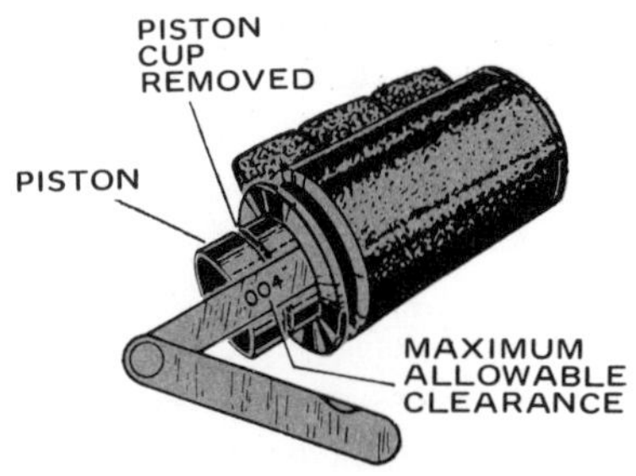

To check wheel cylinder bore, take piston with sealing cup removed and insert in bore. Try to insert an .005-inch feeler gauge. If it can fit in, the bore is too large and the wheel cylinder should be replaced. A clearance of .004-inch between piston and bore, measured with a feeler gauge, is maximum permitted. With everything off the backing plate, it should be cleaned and the raised shoe contact areas (six on the backing plate illustrated) should be coated lightly with silicone grease.

Brake drum surface that comes in contact with brake shoes should be smooth. If you can hang a fingernail on a score, drum must be resurfaced or replaced. Minor scratches can be removed with crocus cloth.

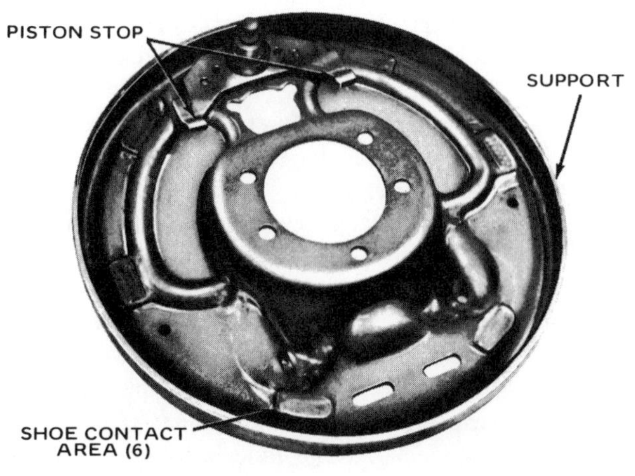

Be sure to replace the parking brake lever on the rear wheel by connecting it to the shoe with the pin and then crimping the horseshoe washer over the pin end. Repack the front wheels and replace the grease seals in the hubs if necessary. Then fit the drum over the shoe assembly. On brake assemblies where both ends of the shoes fit in slots, it may be necessary to center the shoes somewhat to install the drum. Do this by moving each shoe in the right direction by hitting it with a soft-mallet or the heel of your hand.

Be sure to replace the key and lock washer on the rear drum and then draw all of the hubs up tight. Back off the front axle nut to the next cotter pin slot, insert a new pin and replace the dust cover. If the rear brake drum is fastened to the hub with sheet metal nuts, use new ones when reassembling.

Bleeding. Before replacing the wheels, bleed the entire brake system of air. The principle of operation in a hydraulic system is built around the fact that fluids are not compressible. The presence of even a small quantity of air, which is easily compressible, will seriously affect its efficiency. Your car is equipped with bleeder valves which allow this air to escape when they are opened, but it is up to you to see that air is not drawn back into the system.

You can bleed your brakes by having a helper operate the brake pedal while you control the flow of fluid through the bleeder valves. First close all the valves and then fill the master cylinder. Replace the cap and have your helper pump the brake pedal a few times. Then check the level of the fluid again and add more if necessary. Now have him hold a steady pressure on the pedal while you open the bleeder valve with a small wrench.

Check the color of the fluid that escapes to be sure the cleaner is completely expelled. The fluid will squirt through the valve with a sputtering sound until there is no more air in the line. This may take two or three pumps of the pedal. Your helper should let you know each time the pedal is just about to the floorboard so you can close the valve while there is still pressure in the line. Check the master cylinder reservoir after each wheel is bled and keep it filled to the proper level.

Bleeding attachments are available which will allow you to do this job by yourself. These will usually have three fittings to adapt to all cars and will have a ball-check valve to prevent air from being drawn into the system when the pedal is released.

When all points have been bled, the pedal action should be firm and should maintain the correct reserve clearance under continued pressure. On the second pump of the pedal the reserve should be no greater than on the first pump. If this is not the case, repeat the bleeding operation. If the second bleeding still does not provide the proper pedal action, check for leaks that may have been overlooked during assembly.

The next step is to adjust the brakes. On the typical late-model car, all that is necessary is to drive in reverse at low speed and apply the brakes, and they will adjust automatically.

Brake shoes, like most equipment on your car, should be broken in carefully for long, trouble-free use. Allow the shoes about 100 miles of moderate use before attempting mountainous roads or frequent fast stops. After 100 miles make another adjustment as before and recheck the lines for leaks.

Then, with these service adjustments and inspections at 5,000-mile intervals, the brake system overhaul as described will provide safe, carefree service for 30,000 miles. P.W.

See also: DISC BRAKES.

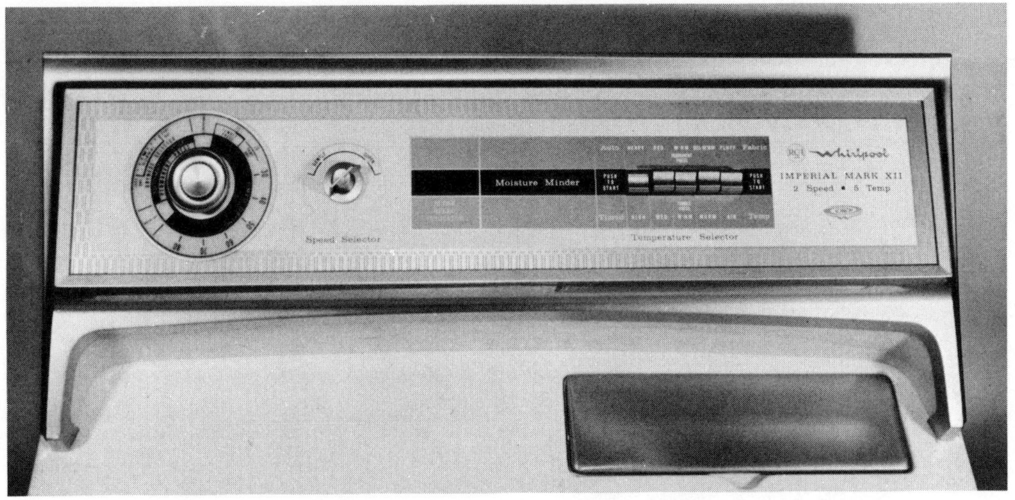

▲ *Dryer control panel. Small access door at right is for lint screen removal. To remove the top of the dryer, open the lint screen access door and remove two screws that hold the screen fixture in place. Then, merely pull the whole top forward and upward. It is hinged at the back.*

How to Repair Your Clothes Dryer

This is a relatively simple appliance and, except for the burner in a gas dryer, you can do most of the work yourself

YOUR AUTOMATIC DRYER is not a very complex machine. It simply tumbles the clothes in a stream of warm air which removes the moisture from the clothes and blows it outside.

The tumbling action occurs in a revolving drum driven by an electric motor which also drives the fan that produces the air motion. The heat is obtained from either an electric heating element or a gas burner, depending on whether you have an electric or gas dryer. The drying time is controlled by a timer; the temperature by a thermostat.

Some dryers have an electronic sensor to control the degree of clothes dryness. In some models the electronic sensor operates with a timer and in others there is no timer.

Most dryers have a wiring diagram posted on the back. Use it when you are looking for trouble.

Know what the dryer can do. Before doing any service work on a dryer (or any other appliance), read the owner's manual to familiarize yourself with the proper operation of the machine and its limits. You should know whether or not the machine has two tumbling speeds or if there is a cool-down period at the end of the drying time during which the clothes tumble. Don't blame the dryer for wrinkled permanent press clothes if they are allowed to remain in the dryer drom after it has stopped tumbling.

Normal operation of the dryer is reasonably quiet. Any random noises could be due to free moving hard objects being tumbled with the clothes; they must be removed. A lipstick could quickly ruin a load of clothes;

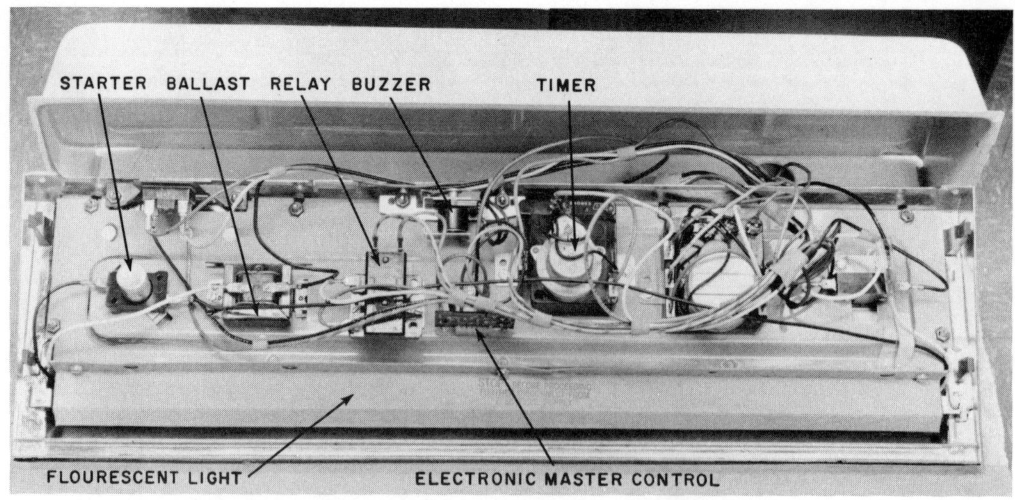

Rear view of the control console of a Whirlpool dryer.

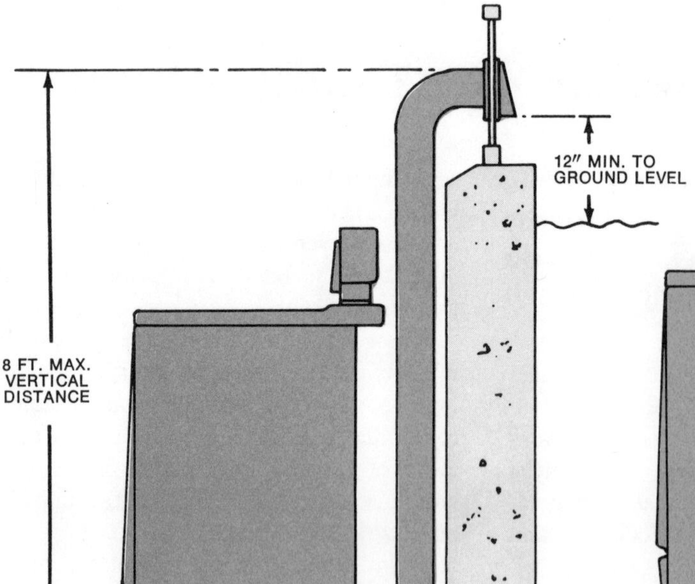

12″ MIN. TO GROUND LEVEL

8 FT. MAX. VERTICAL DISTANCE

OUTSIDE WALL

Basement installation. The exhaust ducting can be directed from the rear or side of the dryer through a basement window or wall above ground level.

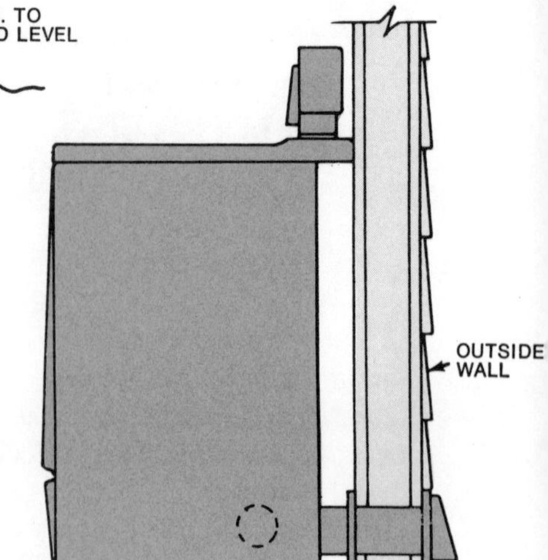

First floor installation. The exhaust ducting can pass from the rear or side of the dryer through the outside wall.

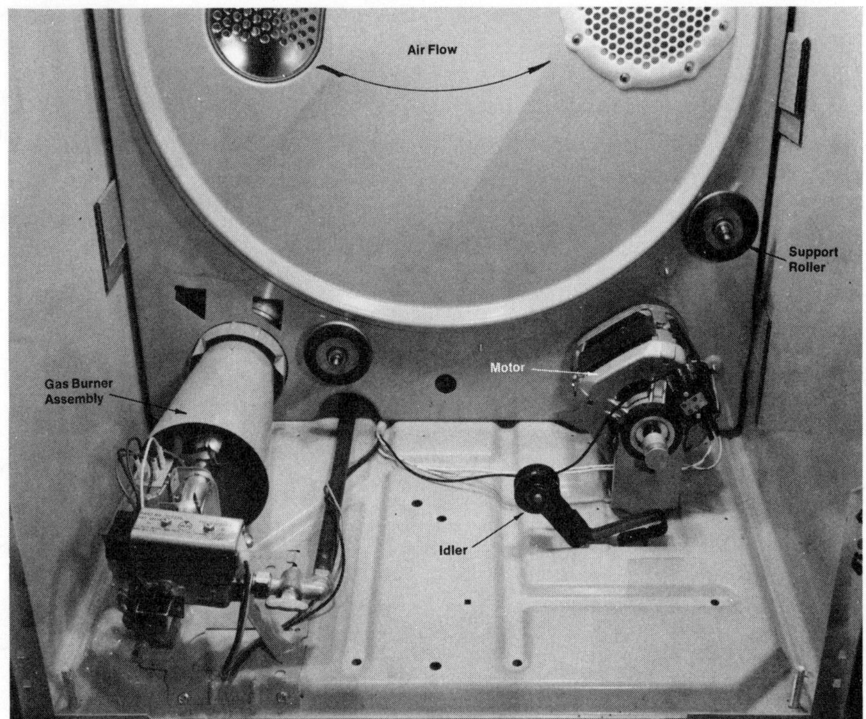

Removing the drum makes it easy to get to the motor, support rollers and gas burner (in this model), or electric heating unit. While the drum is out, check the idler and support rollers for lubrication. They should turn freely, but do not overlubricate; excess oil will collect lint.

bobby pins and nails could damage the drum or the electric heater element.

The air drawn through the machine is usually exhausted outside the house through a 4-inch duct. You should have some feel for the proper air flow for your dryer. Any decrease in air flow will indicate an obstruction in the duct. This may be due to an accumulation of lint in the system or failure to clean the lint trap. This lint filter should be cleaned after every load.

The installation should be close to an outside wall in order to keep the exhaust duct as short as possible. Long ducts decrease air flow and collect lint. The machine should be level and firmly set on the floor. Dryers are equipped with leveling screws which can be adjusted so that each leg is in secure contact with the floor. Most electric dryers must be connected to a 240-volt AC power source with a No. 10 three-wire cable protected by a 30-ampere fuse.

A gas dryer requires at least a 15-

Dryer front can be removed easily, once the top has been lifted. Some models may have two screws near the top of the cabinet, while others may have six—two on each side near the top and one at each door hinge in models with drop-down doors. On all of these machines, the ring around the drum opening serves as a front bearing for the drum.

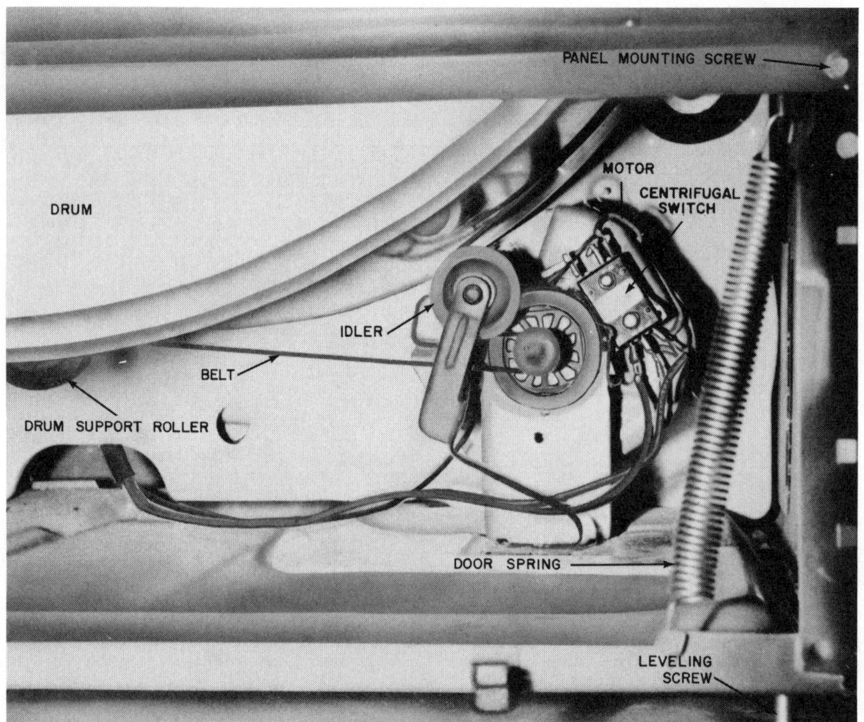

Note the method of threading the belt through the idler carefully. The belt passes around the entire drum, which the motor turns at about 55 rpm.

An older model dryer with the back panel removed. Note the dangerous accumulation of lint, which must be cleaned out (use a vacuum cleaner) before the machine is serviced. The motor and fan assembly are accessible from the rear. The drum drive pulley is often held to the shaft with two setscrews, one locking the other in place, so don't try to force it off after removing only one screw.

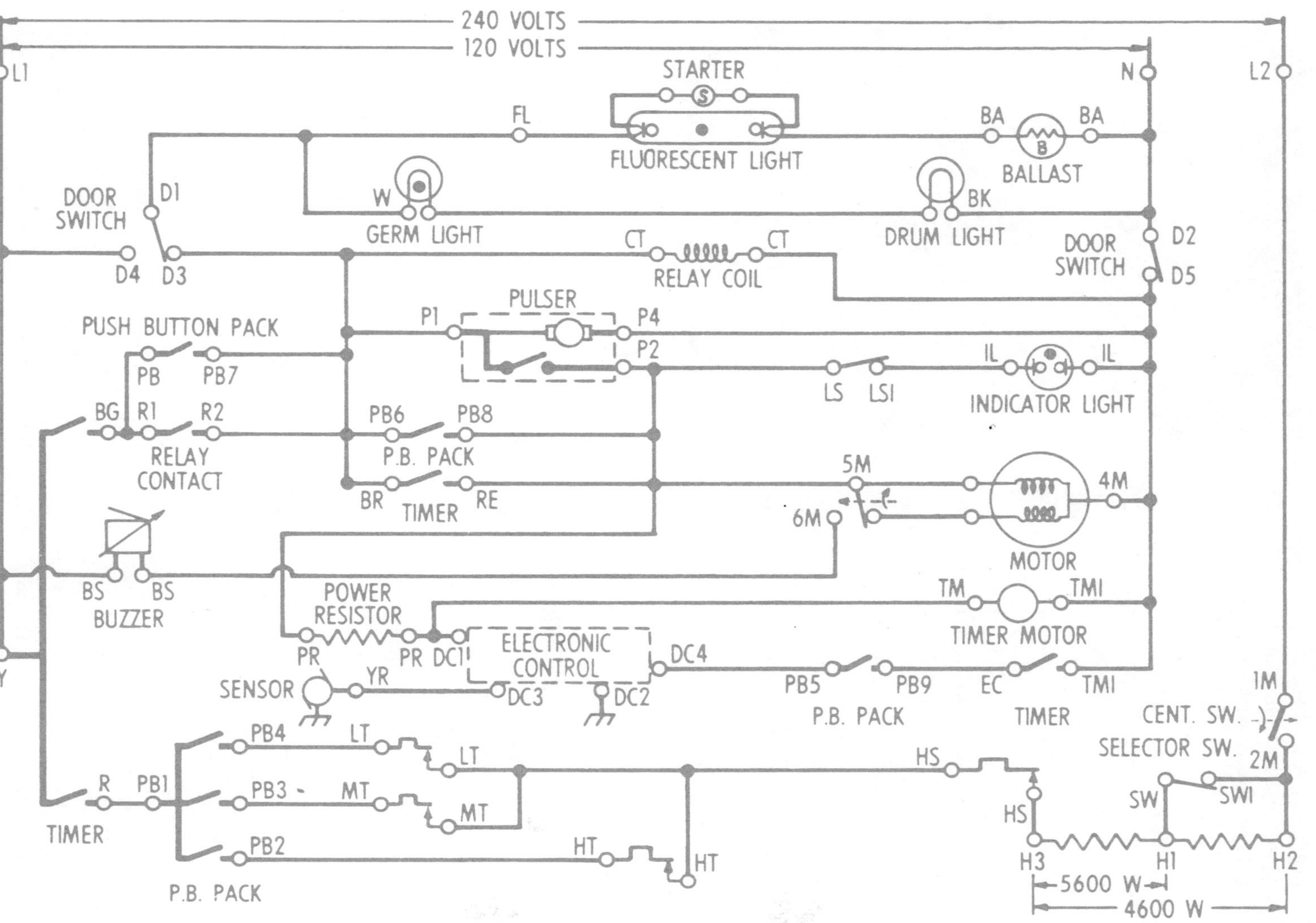

▲ *Most dryers have a wiring diagram attached to the back. Use the diagram for your machine while making tests.*

ampere, 120-volt power supply to operate its motor and controls; a 20-ampere circuit wired with No. 12 wire would be better.

A gas burner is typically rated at 25,000 B.T.U.'s and should be supplied by a ½-inch pipe if not over 20 feet from the meter. A longer run would require larger pipe. In either case there must be a gas shut-off valve near the dryer. If you have to do any work with a gas burner, make certain this valve is shut off. When reassembling the burner check the fittings for leaks with a soap solution. Any movement of soap bubbles would indicate a gas leak.

Service. Servicing the dryer may be done from either the back or the front, depending on the model. The back panel can be removed to expose the electric heater wiring, duct, thermostats and, on some models, the drive belts and pulleys. From the front, an access cover under the door can usually be removed to expose the gas burner, and in some models, the motor and belt drive.

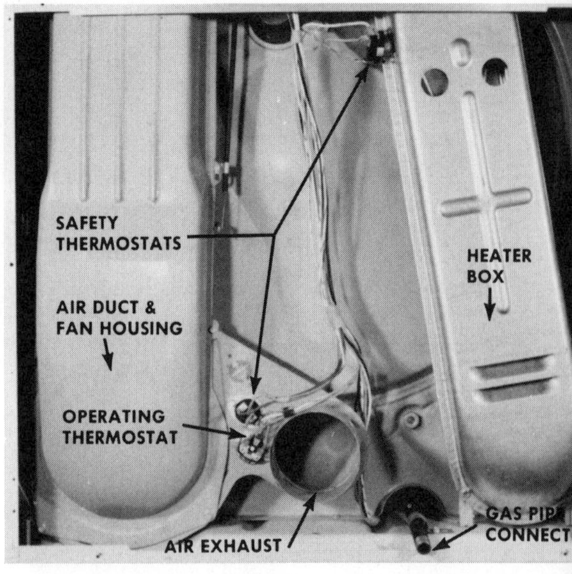

Both electric and gas dryers have safety thermostats. These are located at the top of the heater box and the exhaust fan housing assembly. They are ordinarily closed and open only if a malfunction causes overheating.

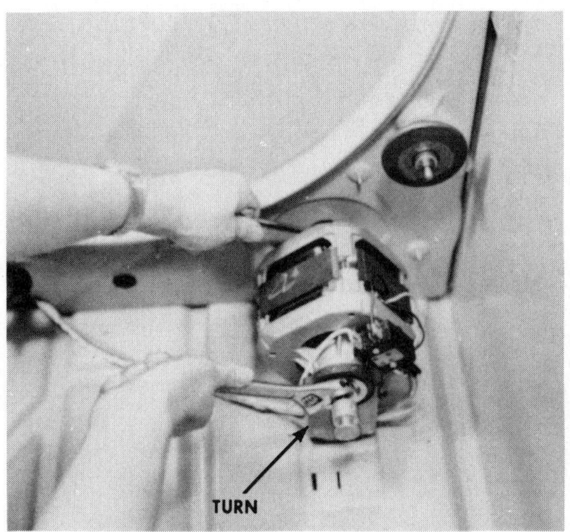

Remove the blower wheel to service the motor. Remove it from the shaft with an 11/16-inch open-end wrench at the blower hub and an adjustable open-end wrench on the flat on the shaft behind the pulley. Hold the wrench stationary on the hub and the turn the shaft clockwise. The centrifugal switch can be removed, if necessary, without removing the motor from the machine. When replacing the motor, make sure that the dimple on the motor mounting hub mates with the slot on the support.

To replace a belt on these models it will be necessary to remove the front panel and top.

Removing the top on Whirlpool and Kenmore dryers involves removing the screws that hold the lint filter chute to the top and removing the lint filter, then pull the top forward and lift. It is hinged at the rear and can be folded back to lean against the wall. This will expose the door switch, its wiring and the screws that hold the front to the sides. After the front is removed the drum can be lifted out.

Anytime you work on a dryer, clean it out; remove the dust and lint. A vacuum cleaner does a good job on this.

Before servicing a dryer make certain that electricity is available at the dryer terminals. There must be 208 to 240 volts at the two outside terminals of an electric dryer and 120 volts from the center terminal to either outer terminals. This test can be made with either an AC voltmeter or a test light consisting of two 120-volt bulbs connected in series. Make certain the dryer is turned off when making this test or else you may get a false reading. It is possible for a fuse to blow in one line allowing the motor and controls to work but there would be no heat.

A study of the wiring diagram will show that the heater circuit includes several safety switches and thermostats. The timer-operated switch controls the length of time the heater is on. The high limit or safety thermostat is normally on and turns off only when the exhaust air gets too hot. The operating thermostat cycles on and off to maintain a preset drying temperature. The centrifugal switch is operated by the motor and is ON only while the motor is running and the fan is moving air through the dryer. Thus, there are at least four controls in series with the heater element.

The motor is controlled by the timer and/or some other ON-OFF switch and the door switch. The motor will not start unless the door is closed.

Any electrical testing can be done with either a test light or a volt ohmmeter and a wiring diagram. Follow the diagram and test from point to point in an orderly and logical manner. The Trouble-shooting Chart will serve as a broad guide to locate an area in which to start looking for the problem. Any defective electrical part will have to be replaced. A loose or burned connection will have to be cleaned and tightened. Make certain that all wiring is secure so that it will not rub against a moving part or chafe its insulation on a sharp corner.

The gas burner. There are many different types of gas burners and automatic ignition methods. Each requires a different service approach and, in some cases, special tools and test equipment.

Clean and check the dryer for all other troubles, making certain electrical power is available to the gas burner. Then, if the burner doesn't operate, call a service technician who is qualified to work on your particular make of dryer.

See also: ELECTRICAL, HOME; INDIVIDUAL APPLIANCE LISTINGS.

AUTOMATIC CLOTHES DRYER TROUBLE-SHOOTING CHART

PROBLEM / POSSIBLE CAUSE	NO POWER	LOOSE CONNECTION	DEFECTIVE DOOR SWITCH	DEFECTIVE TIMER	DEFECTIVE MOTOR	DEFECTIVE HEATER ELEMENT	HEAT SWITCH "OFF"	DEFECTIVE THERMOSTAT	DEFECTIVE BELT	FROZEN BEARING	CLOGGED LINT SCREEN	LEAKY DOOR SEAL	CLOTHES TOO WET	INCORRECT CONTROL SETTING	CLOGGED EXHAUST DUCT	GROUNDED WIRING
WILL NOT RUN	√	√	√	√	√											
WILL NOT HEAT	√	√		√		√	√	√								
DRUM WILL NOT ROTATE									√	√						
WILL NOT SHUT OFF				√												
CLOTHES NOT DRYING							√	√			√	√	√	√	√	
TIMER FAILS TO ADVANCE		√	√	√												
BLOWS FUSES																√

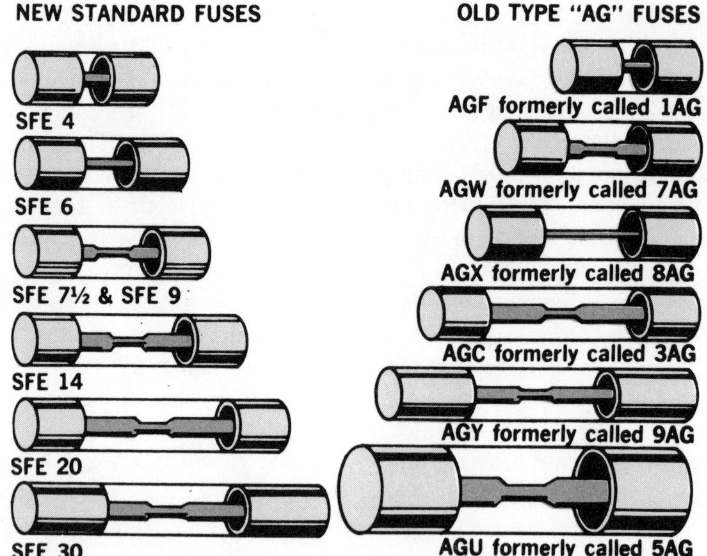

Servicing Electrical Controls in Your Car

If the cigarette lighter is broken or you are having trouble with the radio, it may be the fuses. These few simple checks can test the circuits of the entire electrical system in your car

MOST CAR OWNERS have experienced blown fuses in their homes and know where to go and how to remove the damaged fuse and replace it with a good one. Your car's light and electrical-accessory wiring system is not very different from your home's and if you carry several new fuses—and know where the fuses are located—the job of handling a blown fuse is simple.

Correcting the trouble that was responsible for the fuse blowing, however, is not always so easy. Besides, an electrical system, such as wipers or a clock, may be protected with a "circuit breaker," which, unlike a fuse, does not "blow," but intermittenly opens the circuit to reduce the current and serve as a warning that a "short" exists and something must be done about it.

The small fuses used on cars are of the cartridge type and slip into fuse clips or in-line retainers. Do not attempt to remove fuses with a screwdriver; you may touch one clip with the screwdrivers blade and at the same time ground the blade on nearby metal. The resulting sparks may not only startle you badly, but on a 12-volt system could instantly burn out every wire under the instrument panel, since the overload factor inherent in the older 6-volt systems is missing. Use a small wooden stick to remove the fuses. Better still, purchase a small, inexpensive plastic or hard-rubber fuse puller that permits you to get a good grip on a cartridge fuse. It must also be completely insulated. Such pullers are available at auto supply stores.

Suppose that the electric clock in your new car does not work. You go about trouble-shooting it as you would if the lights in your home go out. You look for a blown fuse. A chart that tells you the size, type and location of car fuses is available. Once the fuse is located, you can tell by looking at it that the link inside the glass casing has melted to interrupt the circuit. Occasionally, clock fuses are in the line and you have to undo the bayonet lock on the fuse housing to drop out the fuse. If the fuse is blown, replace it with one of correct type and size. Correct fuse amperage is important. Installing a fuse of greater capacity than specified may damage the unit it is intended to protect.

The single-wire system, wherein the metal parts of the car serve as a return wire or ground, is universally used on cars. With the switch on a car lamp closed, the circuit to and from it is complete and, consequently, the lamp lights. If a connection to the lamp loosens, becomes corroded, or begins to chafe, resistance is set up in the circuit, heating occurs, the lamp burns dimly and—if the wiring grounds—the battery will discharge. Heavy discharge reading on an ammeter would warn of this, but if a light is used instead of an ammeter (as is common with later model cars) a very heavy short would be required to cause the lamp to glow.

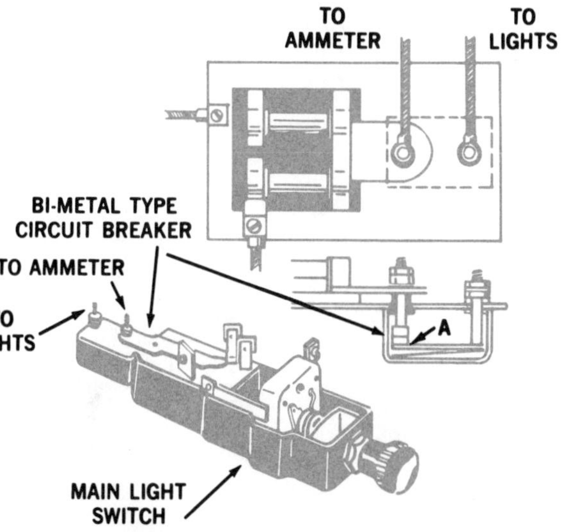

Circuit breaker has been used for lights, and is now primarily used for accessories, such as windshield wipers. Cutaway and schematic show how it works. Circuit breaker is usually built into a switch, as illustrated.

If such a simple circuit is protected with a fuse, however, any of the conditions mentioned above will melt the fuse link, breaking the circuit, thus protecting the units and wiring and preventing danger from fire.

To locate the cause of a blown fuse, always check wiring terminals for tightness first. Look for spots where a wire is rubbing against a sharp metallic surface. And if you do put in a new wire, don't let it hang loosely. Tape it wherever possible to a bracket, or insert it in the regular clips made to hold it.

If any of the car lamps fail to light and the bulb is known to be okay, then it can be due to a blown fuse and replacement often restores the circuit. If a second fuse blows, the trouble lies elsewhere in the circuit. A vibrating circuit breaker always means a short which you must find and correct. To do this, disconnect the switch wires one at a time until the relay stops vibrating. That is the line or wire in which the trouble will be found. If you get no light and the lamps are working properly, the circuit breaker contacts could be disengaged. Replace an open circuit breaker. You will also find that electrical circuits will work better if you occasionally take out the fuses and clean the fuse clips and the ends of the fuses to remove corrosion.

The lighting system is the largest and most involved in wiring and the likelihood of shorts or grounds. The circuit basically includes head lamps, parking lamps, taillights, spotlights, directional lights and interior lamps. It is often supplemented by spotlights, back-up lights and fog lights; all of these circuits usually being fused. Fuses are also used in the accessory circuits such as heaters, radio, underhood lights, hand brake lights, cigarette lighters, overdrives, trunk lights, air conditioners and many other units.

Fuses are seldom used for headlamps, except in very old cars and trucks. Protection for headlamps, taillamps, parking lamps and instrument lamp circuits on most older cars is through a thermostatically-controlled limit relay or a bimetal type circuit breaker, usually attached to the main light switch. On most cars built in the last few years, all circuits but the headlamps have been removed from the circuit-breaker line and are fitted with separate fuses. The reason for this is that the headlamps and taillamps are used the most, and are the most important in the operation of the car.

Headlamps, generator and the entire battery system on today's cars are protected by "fusible links." A fusible link is nothing more than a piece of wire that is spliced into a circuit in which the wiring is one or two standard thicknesses larger. For example, a piece of 14-gauge wire is spliced in, to protect a 10-gauge wire circuit.

This piece of wire is often covered by a plastic sheath of special shape for easy identification.

If the circuit is overloaded, the higher-number (thinner) wire burns out and separates, just like a fuse.

The location of these links varies according to the make of car. On late-model Chevrolets (except Corvette), for example, there is a 16-gauge black fusible link to protect all unfused wiring of 12-gauge or thicker. This link is at the horn relay.

The generator warning light and gener-

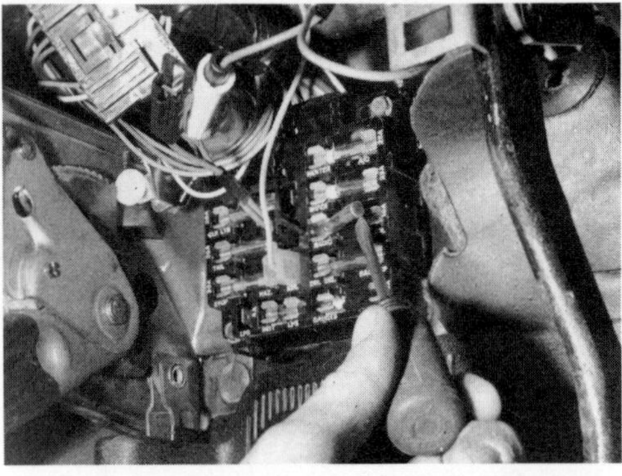

Removing a fuse with a screwdriver is risky, as screwdriver might touch another fuse's clip or an electrical ground and cremate some car wiring. A wooden stick, such as from an ice cream pop, is the best choice.

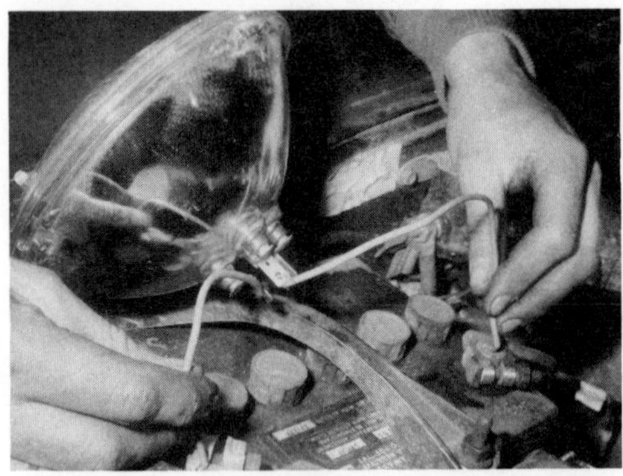

Headlamp is checked by connecting two or three terminals to battery posts, using jumper wires. By trying all three possible combinations, you should get low and high beams to work.

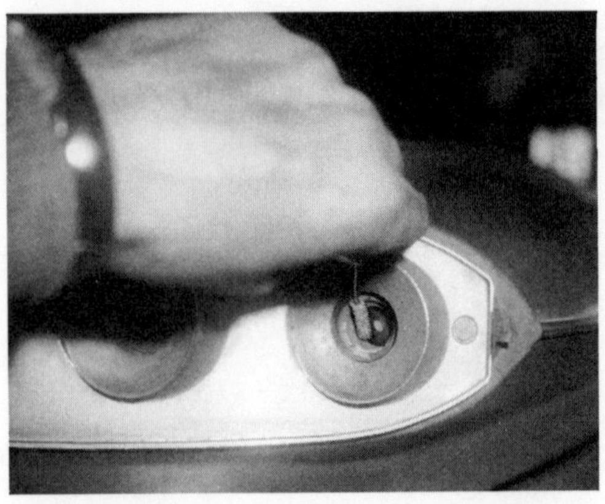

Corrosion and rust are usual causes of socket failure. Clean with a wire brush.

ator field circuit, which is 16-gauge, is protected by a 20-gauge fusible link, also at the horn relay.

If a fusible link breaks, the repair (after correcting the cause) is to splice in a new piece of the appropriate gauge wire, solder or crimp-connect the terminals and tape over with plastic electrical tape.

Remember that the wiring circuits in your car are like those in your home. If you have too many lights and appliances on one circuit, a blown fuse will result. The same thing is true in a car. Using a larger capacity fuse will prevent a blown fuse, but trouble is built in. The best method is to run a new circuit, with its own proper capacity fuse, to protect the new spotlight or other accessory. In some cases there is a junction block wired to the ignition switch that has spare connections that can be used. This heavy-duty circuit will handle the additional electrical load, and also has the advantage of shutting off the current when the ignition key is turned off.

Although sophisticated electrical troubleshooting is for the professional, most problems are not all that sophisticated.

If a bulb circuit fails to operate, there are five possible causes:

1. Bad bulb.
2. Poor connection at the socket or bulb terminal.
3. Defective wiring.
4. Defective switch.
5. Blown fuse (if the circuit is fused).

Clearly, a wiring problem is only 20 percent of the possibilities, and in actual practice, occurs perhaps five percent of the time.

Checking a bulb is simple. Attach a jumper wire to one terminal of the battery. Sit the bulb on the other battery post, holding it so that its bottom terminal is in contact. With the jumper, touch the metal side of the bulb. If it is good, the bulb will light.

To check a headlamp, which has three terminals, the procedure is similar. Connect any two terminals to the battery posts in the three different combinations possible and you should get a low beam and high beam.

A socket can be checked with a test lamp. With the appropriate switch on, one lead goes to the metal tab contact in the center, the other to the cylindrical metal side. If the lamp lights, the socket is good.

Corrosion and rust are the usual causes of a socket failure, and if you see any, clean with a wire brush.

Corrosion not only affects sockets, but fuse contacts as well. If you see a white corrosive coating on the fuse contacts, also clean with a wire brush.

Wire and switch terminals are still another area corrosion can affect, causing a poor electrical connection. You are probably familiar with the effect of corrosion on the battery cable connections, and how this can interfere with engine starting by restricting the flow of current.

Plainly, if current cannot get to a light or accessory, it will not work. Even if a connection is physically tight, it may be electrically weak if corrosion is present.

Poor connections can also be caused by loose terminals which you can physically feel, particularly on a switch.

A switch may also have an internal break. This can be checked, but like the defective wiring problem, is best left to an expert. If you can get a replacement switch on a "return it if I don't need it" basis, you can check the old switch by substituting a new one. P.W.

See also: BATTERIES; ENGINE; SPARK PLUG; STARTER; TUNE-UP, ENGINE.

WHERE TO FIND IT

A chart that tells you the specified size, type and location of car fuses for all makes and models of cars for the last 15 model years is available from Bussmann Mfg. Division, McGraw-Edison Co., University at Jefferson, St. Louis, Mo., 63107.

How to Work Safely with Electricity

A few simple rules and keeping your mind on what you are doing can save you costly repairs of damage and prevent tragic accidents

A LITTLE KNOWLEDGE can be a dangerous thing. Do not prove this adage by assuming that simple electrical jobs can be done hastily. Work only when there are no distractions, when you feel alert, and when your mind is fully on the job at hand. Here are a few basic safety guidelines. Your common sense will discover more as you gain electrical work experience.

Anyone can rewire a table lamp, install a battery-operated alarm system, or handle any other such "safe" electrical job without a great deal of electrical experience. Yet such a simple operation as boring a hole through a wall for a bell wire can be risky if the wrong tool is employed. The addition of new lighting fixtures, the installation of extra wall receptacles, and any other work involving the main power lines of a home can be hazardous. The novice should study a house wiring guide thoroughly before starting work. For example, a newly installed fixture may appear to function perfectly, but improper wiring may defeat the grounding system and make the new receptacle or fixture a potentially lethal boobytrap.

Even those who know the basics of house wiring sometimes take unnecessary risks. They use power tools that are not properly grounded, use them on circuits that are assumed to be grounded but are not, or use them when manual tools are safer. Familiarity with electricity should not be allowed to breed indifference to sensible safety practices.

Safe tools. There is simply no excuse for anyone to use ungrounded power tools. New tools of reputable make have three-wire cords with grounding plugs. And it is easy and cheap enough to add a grounding cord and plug to an old tool not so equipped. Just open the tool and replace the old cord with a three-wire lead of adequate current-carrying capacity. Attach the third, ground wire to the shell of the tool, taking care to keep it well insulated from the power leads.

While you are at it, get enough of the three-wire cord to make a grounded extension cord. It will double the usefulness of the tool.

The three-pronged plug of course needs to be used in grounding receptacles. If you have none at present, use an adapter. But make sure that the adapter pigtail is

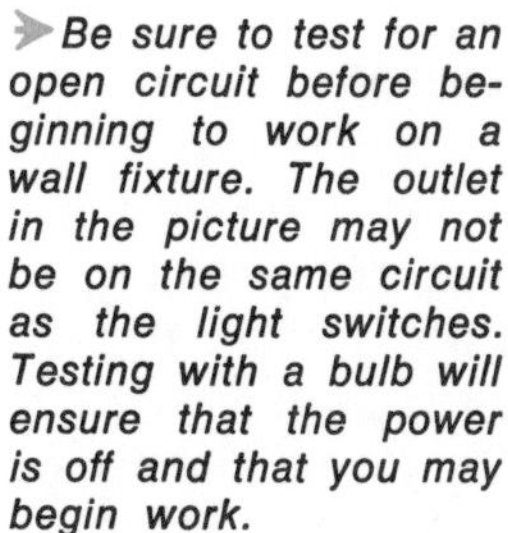

Be sure to test for an open circuit before beginning to work on a wall fixture. The outlet in the picture may not be on the same circuit as the light switches. Testing with a bulb will ensure that the power is off and that you may begin work.

fastened to the screw holding the receptacle plate, and that the plate is properly grounded through the house power lines. Test with a trouble light to make certain.

You should be able to use your grounded tools anywhere in the house without fussing with adapters which should be considered only as emergency conveniences. Choose a number of conveniently scattered receptacles and replace them with polarized receptacles that will accept the grounding plugs. For example, one such grounding receptacle in the kitchen

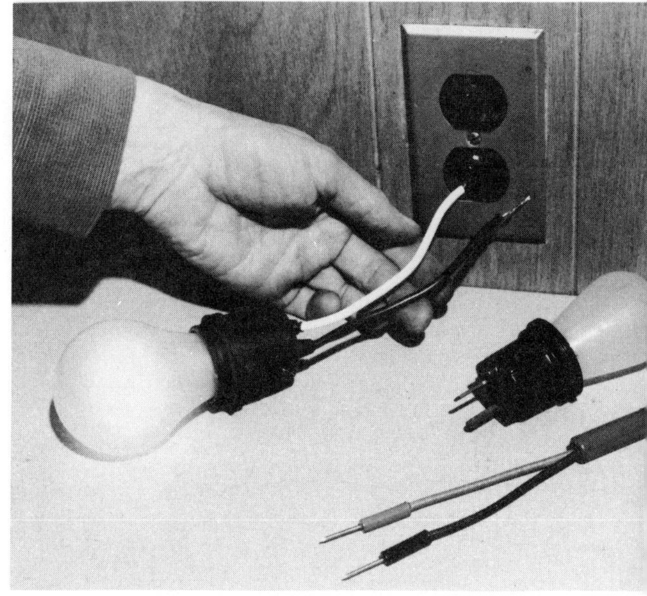

When testing for a live circuit, a neon tester and two types of bulb sockets—one with leads, one plug-in—come in handy. To test for a grounded circuit, touch a lead to the cover plate; the bulb should light when other lead is pushed into socket.

Only fifteen seconds are needed to fasten this grounding adapter into place. Unless pigtail is attached and tool cords have three-pronged grounding plugs, adapter is useless.

may serve several adjacent rooms as well if your extension cord is long enough. You may need another in the bedroom area, one or two in the basement (many local codes now demand that all basement outlets be of the polarized type), another in the garage, and elsewhere in the home.

Use tools safely. A power drill can greatly speed work when, for example, many holes must be drilled through beams and studs for BX cable. But the power drill should be used only on exposed structural members; it is dangerous to drill blindly into walls, floors and ceilings that have already been covered because a power drill can quickly cut into unseen power lines. The operator of the drill may be killed and the house may be set afire. A manual drill or bit and brace should always be used when boring holes in such places.

Before using a saber saw to cut a hole in a wall for, say, a new receptacle box, hand bore a pilot hole that is large enough to permit inspection for power lines. Even if you feel that the saber saw cannot cut through an armored cable without your knowing it, there may be other good reasons for avoiding blind sawing. For example, if your home has a low-voltage switching system, you may cut into these unarmored lines. You will not be killed, but why risk avoidable repair jobs?

Use a manual bit and brace when drilling holes in walls. A power drill may damage hidden wiring and cause shorts or shock.

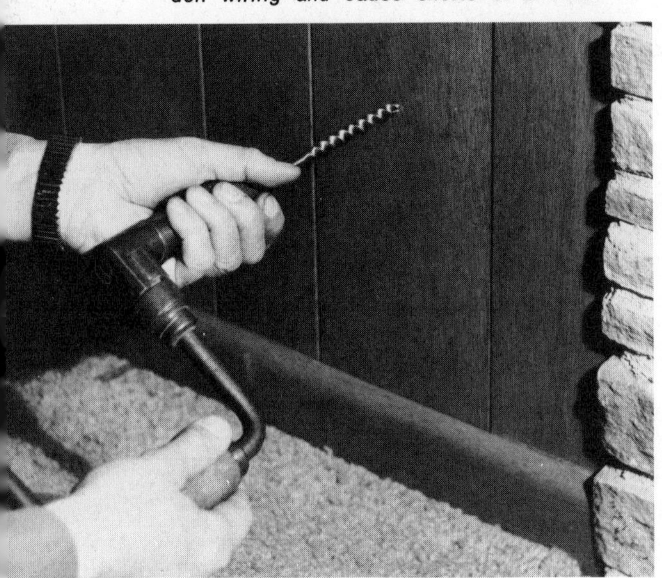

Safety tests. For some reason, most people fear rattlesnakes more than they do defective electrical fixtures although many more people die each year from electrical shock than from snakebite. Remember that house current is deadlier and faster than snake venom, and often there is no time for first aid.

Take nothing for granted when doing electrical work. Do not assume that every receptacle box in your home is properly grounded, especially in older homes. Test each box with a trouble light such as a neon tester or a low-wattage bulb screwed into a rubber covered "pigtail" socket having short wires with bared tips that serve as probes. To test for proper grounding, touch one probe to the receptacle cover plate, and the other to each of the receptacle openings. If the bulb does not light with either side of the receptacle, there is no ground.

Do not work on a receptacle or fixture without first testing to make sure that power in the circuit has been cut off by removal of the proper fuse or pushing the right circuit breaker. After opening the box and removing the enclosed fixture, remove the wire nuts and again use the trouble light to double check that the bared wire ends are not alive.

If you know that several wall receptacles are on the same circuit, plug a bulb into one receptable not being worked on. Use a pronged socket of the type shown. The light will alert you to a live circuit in case you turn on the power to test your new work, and then forget to turn it off again before resuming work.

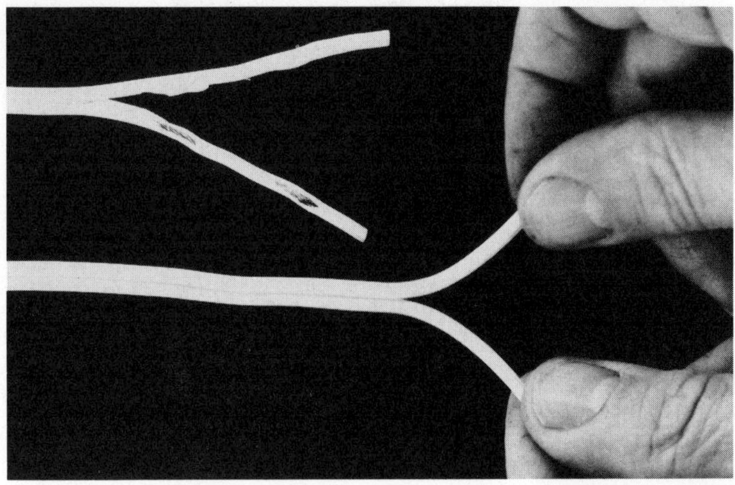

Lamp (zip) cord should always be separated by pulling the two halves apart by hand. Cutting it with a knife or metal tool often exposes some bare wire.

Do not assume that electrical fixtures are on the same circuit simply because they happen to be in close proximity to each other. For example, a wall outlet may not be on the same circuit with a nearby switch controlling ceiling lights. Test to make sure.

Unhurried work. Adopt a craftsman's attitude when doing electrical work. This means an unhurried approach, and attention to proper working techniques.

Learn how to strip wires properly. The metal wire in a BX cable looks stronger

Watch that soldering iron. It stays hot enough for a while to burn through cord insulations.

Be sure power has been turned off before prying frozen or damaged plug from a receptacle with metal tool.

than it is. If you knick the copper wire when removing insulation, you create a weak spot that may become weaker when you twist the bared ends of wires together to form a splice. Then when the wires are crammed into the receptacle box, the added strain may be just enough to snap the wire or make it so thin an electrical path that it will burn out when power is applied.

When separating the two halves of lamp "zip" cord, do not use a knife except to start the separation which should be completed by pulling the halves apart by hand. Cutting with a knife not only takes longer, but it often bares wire where it should not be bared.

When connecting wires to lamp sockets or plugs, make neat connections having no splayed wire strands that can cause short circuits. If the plug has a cardboard terminal cover—use it.

Common sense. Many electrical accidents could be avoided just by using a little common sense. Like standing on a rubber mat or dry plywood when changing fuses in a damp floor or ground area. Like keeping small childen out of the work area; not only are the children endangered, but they may distract you into an accident.

The plugs on lamp and appliance cords sometimes corrode or for other reasons jam in wall receptacles. Or the plug may break when it is removed, leaving a prong in the outlet. Never use a screwdriver or pliers to remove the defective plug until power in the circuit has been cut off. Even if the tool has an insulated handle, its use in a live fixture is not entirely safe. At the very least, the metal part of the tool may cause a short between the defective plug and the receptacle cover plate and give you a good fright.

Watch what you do with your soldering equipment. For example, the tip of a soldering gun remains hot for some time after the gun is put down, it could easily burn through the insulation of the gun's own power cord.

And do not use a torch when soldering inside wall or ceiling fixtures. Fine dust behind the metal box may smolder unobserved and burst into flame hours later when you are asleep.

Shop for safety. A plethora of new electrical gadgets are flooding hardware and department store counters. Some of these "convenience" devices are good, others are of dubious worth. If an item that attracts your eye does not carry the Underwriters' Laboratory (UL) label, buy with caution.

For example, a number of different wall receptacle adapters are now available that convert a standard duplex outlet into one having as many as eight outlets. Admittedly, some of these devices are improvements over older types of multiple-outlet adapters because they are sturdier and flatter.

But some designs are clearly too hazardous for many of the applications advertised. One style of multiple outlet has two parallel slots through which the two ten-inch long terminals are clearly visible. Such a device would be extremely hazardous in a child's room though the device is advertised as handy for plugging in electrical toys. Nor is it suitable for another proposed use—the workshop because it defeats the primary safety need in any workshop—grounded outlets.

Leave such gimmicks for others. If you need a multiple outlet, put in a bigger box and add another standard receptacle, preferably a grounded type. It will last longer, be cheaper in the long run, and above all much safer.

See also: ADDITIONS, HOME; BLENDERS; DISHWASHER; DOORBELL; DRYER; HOME IMPROVEMENT; IRONS; MIXER; REFRIGERATOR; TOASTER; TOOLS; TRASH COMPACTOR; VACUUM CLEANER; WAFFLE IRON/GRILL; WASHING MACHINE.

Adding a Circuit

Increased demand caused by more appliances can be supplied by tapping reserve power

THE ELECTRIC SERVICE in many homes was planned for future expansion of the branch system and not all the circuits that could be used were installed. Where this is the case, you can tap off additional circuits to handle the load of newly purchased appliances.

A quick look at your main circuit panel will tell you whether there is reserve power that can be utilized. If there are any empty fuse sockets, that means that those terminals in the box are not in use, either because no wiring has been connected to those terminals, or there is a "dead" circuit that's been abandoned.

Also, look to see if there is a burned-out fuse in any of the sockets, because it is possible that an "empty" was covered that way. You can distinguish a burned fuse visually by the blackened color under the glass, and the fact that the thermal strip inside has parted or burned away.

Another way to check for unused circuits is to count the number of circuit cables entering the sides of the box (in addition to the power feed cable from the main switch) and compare with the number of fuses or circuit breakers.

You may find that the box has provision for 12 circuits, but only 10 cables enter the box. Unless they are already taken by three-wire circuits, two additional branches can be tapped. This is based on the assumption that the right size panel box was installed originally, conforming to local power company or R.E.A. (Rural Electrification Administration) requirements.

Parts of the system. Before coming to conclusions about the possibility of having additional circuits, you should know the arrangements and parts of the electric system. The service entrance is the power feed from the utility company which may come into your house through overhead wires, or through underground conduit in some cities.

The utility company lines end at the meter. From there on, the system is part of the house. Wires from the meter may go through a separate main switch box which also contains a main fuse that is of the correct ampere rating for that service.

Then the power lines go into the circuit box, sometimes called the fuse panel, or cabinet. In modern installations, the main switch and fuse are part of the circuit box, so the separate switch and fuse box are eliminated. The circuit box has a number of fuse sockets or circuit breakers, each intended to serve an individual branch circuit.

A 60-amp. box has from four to six fuses, while a 10-amp. service has from eight to twelve fuses. Homes with electric ranges and electric water heater may have 150- or 200-amp. service, with up to 24 circuits.

Another factor determining the total number of branches is the "size" of the circuits, or rather the purpose for which

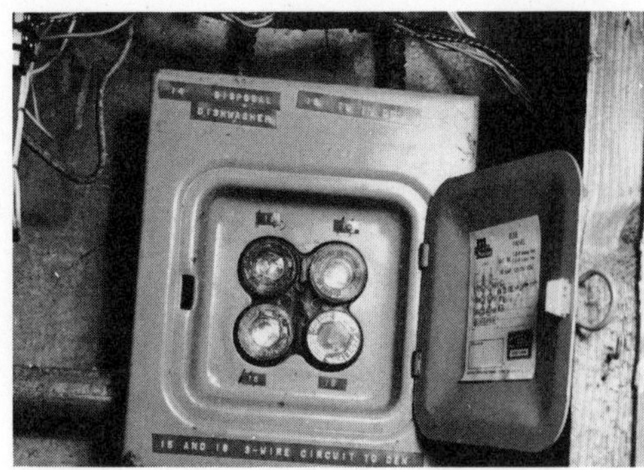

▲ *To add extra circuits to your present system install a four-fuse sub-panel that can be attached to the main cabinet.*

they are used, whether for lights and small appliances, or for major appliances and heaters that draw considerably more wattage.

With these considerations in mind, you can tell whether there is room for putting extra circuits into the panel. If there is any doubt in your mind, get in touch with the utility company which has a record of the type of service installed at your house.

Adding a fuse cabinet. The wiring in your home may have been badly planned to begin with, resulting in inefficient distribution of the power. There may be only one circuit in the kitchen where there are a number of appliances. In addition to the refrigerator, some of them simultaneously are in use like a toaster and skillet, while other circuits to the bedrooms are used only for a few lights. You could correct this to some extent by redistributing the load with an extra circuit if it is installed in conformity with National Code standards and local ordinances.

The new circuit won't add a bit to your total electric capacity, but can help prevent special overloaded situations. In the above case, a separate circuit for the refrigerator may make the present wiring in the kitchen more reliable, prevent blowing of fuses.

If there are just six fuse plugs, and all are in use, you will need an extra box for the additional branch. A small box for surface mounting, with two fuse plugs, should be purchased. This is called a sub-panel.

The switch panel and sub-panel should be close together and joined with a short pipe nipple through knockout holes at the sides. The wires run from the switch panel through the nipple to the fuse lugs and the circuit wires connected at the terminals.

Mounting the box. The sub-panel box must be separately attached to the wall, or to the same board that holds the main panel. Pry out the knockouts in both boxes, get a pipe nipple to fit the opening and long enough so there is about ½-inch of thread on the inside of each box.

Usually, there is ample clearance inside the boxes, but check on this first to select the best knockout position in the main box so the nipple can be easily joined on the inside with a locknut. Remember to use bushings on the nipple threads. Avoid making any extra holes in the box beyond the ones needed for the actual connection. Strip the enamel on the box around the holes so there will be good ground contact for the nipple locknuts.

When the box is mounted, shut off the power by pulling the main fuse. This may be the blade type, held in copper spring catches, and can be gripped at the center and pulled out. As a safety measure, it's a good idea to stand on a rubber mat or wood plank and avoid touching anything with the other hand.

Use #12 wire for an appliance circuit. Measure the wire beforehand to correct length and strip the ends.

Making connections. When the boxes are solidly joined with the nipple, slip the wires through. First connect them to the fuse lugs, then make the connection in the main box. The terminal connections are just as simple as any other, except that utmost care should be exercised to get the wires on the correct lugs. That is, the white wire on the common ground (neutral) side, and black wire on the "hot" side.

Also, avoid changing the wires of the existing circuits in the box, and be sure not to touch the service entrance wires if the main fuse is in the same box, as they would be "live" even though the fuse is pulled. Go over the terminal connections to make sure they are tight.

Replace the panel cover and turn the main switch back on. The fuse plugs in the new box now have current and are ready for connecting the new circuits. If you want to test them, just screw a light bulb into the sockets. Don't leave the sockets empty, but rather put in burned out fuses right away.

For connecting an appliance circuit use #12 cable. Make the outlet box installation first, working back toward the fuse box. This is the general practice in almost all electrical work. Connect the wires into the appliance outlet box, then run the cable back to the panel box. If possible, use a continuous run of cable without splices.

At the fuse box, with power shut off, bring the cable through a knockout opening, lock it in tightly with a connector, and make the connections to the terminal lugs. Replacing the fuse and turning on the main switch puts the circuit into service.

Snaking wires. The big task in circuit wiring is getting the cable to the final location. That's easy enough when connecting an outlet in the basement laundry room for a washing machine, as the location is probably not far from the fuse box and there is no need for concealed wiring. Even appliance wiring for a kitchen is usually without complications because the cable is simply brought up through the basement ceiling behind the wall cabinet or the sink.

But it's a different matter when bringing wires to an upstairs bedroom for an air conditioner or to the living room or den where there can be no breaking of walls.

The basic technique is snaking wires through the walls, or wherever there is the slightest opening. Cables can be brought from the basement all the way to the attic for a cooling fan, by fishing it up along the the plumbing soil stack.

A fish tape is the chief tool in the electricians' bag of tricks. Also known as a snake, it is used to find the trail and pull wires inside walls, through floors, along the joists, and through long runs of conduit.

This tape is a tempered flat steel wire, 1/16 x 1/8-inch, comes in coils of 50, 75 and 100-foot lengths, and is sold at electrical supply stores. Ordinary steel baling wire sometimes is a satisfactory substitute, though it lacks the springy temper and stiffness that straightens out the tape after it hits an obstruction.

Before using the tape, make a loop at the tip so the wire won't snag, and to form an eye for threading the cable wires. As the tempered steel may snap when bent, the end should be heated red hot with a torch or over a gas stove. Some tapes come with a knob at the end for use with a special "eye ball."

A drill bit extension is also valuable for drilling through from floor-to-floor, or where there is unusual thickness. A bit extension is 12, 18 or 24 inches long, with a

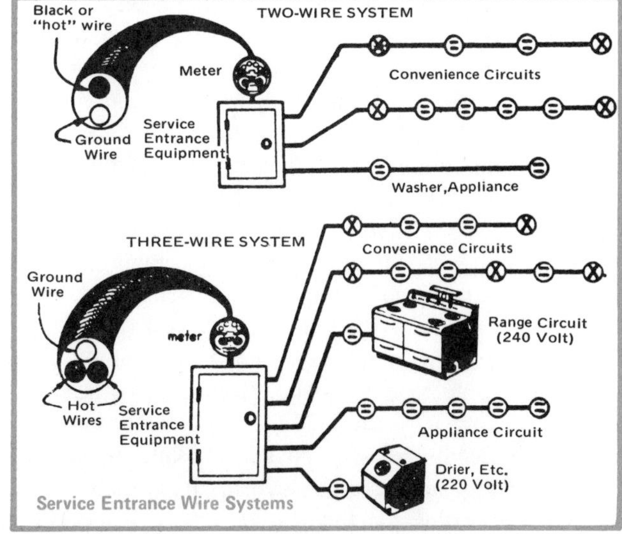

Service Entrance Wire Systems

square chuck at one end for clamping the bit shank. The other end is fitted into a standard drill brace.

Because the extension chuck is 5⁄8-inch diameter at its largest part, the bit used with it must be at least 1⁄16-inch larger to permit the extension to follow through in the hole. This extension is sold at hardware stores.

Fishing tricks. Fishing for an opening inside walls is slow work and may exhaust your patience unless you know there's a good chance to get through. The "light test" gives encouragement to keep at it. For example, if you need to push the snake a long way between beams, place a drop lamp or flashlight at the far end of the run; a glimmer of light at your end is a sign that the way is clear.

When the tape is stuck because of a sharp bend in the wall or other obstruction, it sometimes can be brought in by sending a second tape from the other end to help pull it through. One of the wires is rotated while it is moved back and forth until both hooks catch, then one tape is pulled back carefully, bringing the other with it.

If the snake is blocked by a "cat" or header in the wall, the position of the obstruction is found by sticking a bit of electrical tape on the snake at the point where it enters the wall opening. Measuring the length from the marker to the end of the snake will show where to cut into the wall and notch out the header to clear the way.

Make a safe tie. When the tape reaches its objective, it must pull the wire cable after it. There may be tough going around curves and through small openings, so the cable must be securely fastened.

Strip about 12 inches of armor off the cable to expose the wires. Both wires go part way through the tape hook or eye. Bend one wire back and wind it tightly around the other cable wires, then bend the others so they can be turned around the steel tape. Another way is to separate the cable wires, putting one through the tape hook from one side, the other wire from the opposite side. Then bend both wires back and wind them tightly around the pair of wires. For extra security, bind the tie with electrical tape.

Fishing holes should be located, when possible, behind baseboards and moldings, and inside closets. Small holes are punched in room walls and ceiling only as a last resort and then damage is minimized.

For example, if the wall is papered, the section of wallpaper is peeled back so it can cover the patch later. To do this, make several slits with a razor blade, then moisten the paper with a sponge until it softens and can be peeled back. Ceiling holes are easy to patch. The paint usually is white, or a light color that can be matched. At the very worst, painting of an entire ceiling is simple.

A valuable "coverup" scheme is to place a new outlet at the location of a fishing hole. The opening is planned at a logical place for the outlet, which will be part of the new circuit wiring. This method helps also to simplify the installation, as the outlet serves as a splice box and thus, a shorter stretch of the cable need be used from the circuit box.

The new outlet also offers opportunity to distribute the circuit for additional purposes. This outlet connection should meet the requirement that cable splice boxes be solidly mounted and always accessible.

Additional ways to bring cable across a room are under the floor and along the basement ceiling (in a one-story house), or between the floor beams, if they run in the right direction. In the first method, holes are drilled up from the basement through the floor plates at both receptacle locations. The cable then is run underneath between both points.

Running the cable across the floor joists is a bit more tricky, as this requires lifting a length of finish flooring, by slicing the tongue at both sides, with a three-inch flooring chisel. A narrow strip of sub-floor can be cut with a portable saw to recess the cable.

Second story job. One way to get a new circuit cable to a second-story bedroom is to start from the top—that is, up in the attic alongside a vertical plumbing line, such as the vent stack. House framing and flooring do not fit closely at such installations, so there's a chance to snake all the way through to the basement. This takes patient fishing, but is frequently successful.

Once the tape gets through, pull the cable all the way up to the attic, then lower it inside the wall to the floor below through a hole in the top framing plate, and fish it out through the new outlet opening.

The standard procedure for bringing cable floor-to-floor is to drill inside the wall.

Directly below the second-floor opening, drill up from the basement into the first floor plate. Now push a snake up from below, and send another down from the second floor.

This is a long-shot chance, but the tapes must stay within the narrow area between two studs and if one of them loops over, the other hook will slip under it and ride along until the ends meet and hook together.

If repeated efforts fail, the situation is solved by opening a hole for an extra outlet. A cable through the bottom hole is spliced inside the outlet box, from which a second cable is easily brought upstairs.

A chief obstacle may be a header in the wall frame. The choice then is to shift operations to the next stud, which may be clear, or to open a hole and notch the header.

An alternative method for reaching the upper floor, particularly for homes with metal lath or solid walls, is to bring the weatherproof wires outside the house, through rigid conduit. The conduit is passed outside a hole drilled in the exterior wall above the foundation sill, then bent in the upper story. Bending is done with a hickey.

Use utmost care when connecting wires to fuse lugs making sure they are attached to the right terminal.

One place to consider snaking the fish tape is between studs where an opening sometimes exists.

Conduit is available in 10-foot lengths, and joined with couplings. The wall openings must be properly caulked and conduit securely strapped to the wall. Pull the wires through with a snake after the conduit is installed.

See also: ADDITIONS, HOME.

Engine cleaning can be done with an aerosol degreaser. Air cleaner should be removed and carburetor opening covered with plastic wrap. Distributor should also be plastic-wrapped.

Taking Care of Your Engine

A little attention at the right time can head off trouble, save repair costs and add miles to the life of your car

YOUR CAR'S DRIVING power starts with its engine, and just as long as cars continue to utilize internal combustion engines, engines will continue to receive the greater share of car maintenance. This is so because the engine, in addition to its own mechanical structure—block, head, oil pan, oil pump, crankshaft, pistons, rods, bearings, flywheel and timing gears—takes in the all-important ignition, carburetion, and cooling systems. And on today's smog- controlled cars, there is even more, such as Positive Crankcase Ventilation and special ignition timing controls.

If each of these individual units is kept up to standard, your engine will perform substantially as it did when new, even after thousands of miles of operation. But car owners usually become somewhat careless; when the thrill of new-car ownership has worn off, they tend to take their car and its engine for granted. Only when trouble shows up do they realize that a little attention at the right time would have forestalled trouble, saved them repair costs and —as a plus factor—made their car last much longer.

When you get your new car, every unit in it is brand new, and moving parts fit with just the right clearance. Then, in time, the engine parts gradually become worn so that clearances between rubbing metal enlarge, components in the ignition system become so worn that timing is late, spark plugs wear out and erosion of the plug electrodes widens the gaps so that plug performance falls off. Other parts loosen or disconnect. Dirt and other foreign matter impedes the operation of the fuel, lubrication and cooling systems, the power and zip of the engine falls off: in short, the engine ceases to purr. . . . Periodic attention could have prevented all of this.

Keep your engine clean. It doesn't take a "mechanically minded" person to keep the outside of the engine clean. And keeping the outside of the engine clean is the

After solvent has had a chance to work, spray it off with a garden hose.

This is the same engine as in the first illustration. The car is old, but the engine doesn't show it.

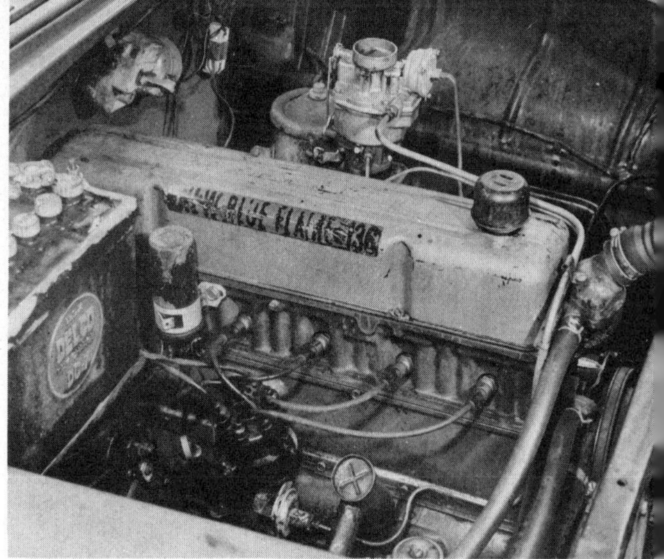

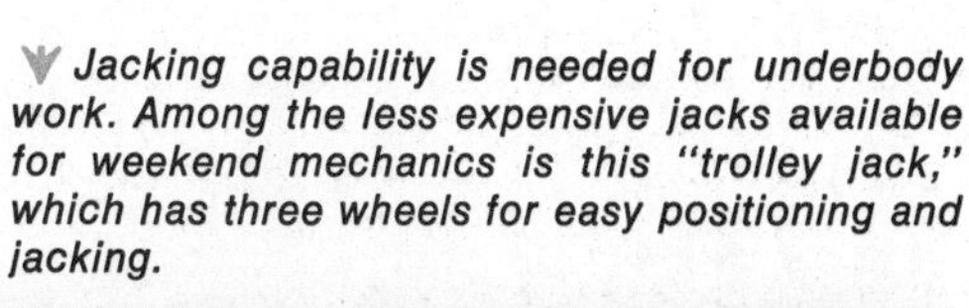

Jacking capability is needed for underbody work. Among the less expensive jacks available for weekend mechanics is this "trolley jack," which has three wheels for easy positioning and jacking.

Once car is raised, safety stands should be placed under lower A-frames. You don't need expensive ones. The 5000-pound capacity stands illustrated are inexpensive.

first step toward getting the longest possible life from your engine.

Excess operating heat from your engine is dissipated by being passed to the atmosphere through the radiator core, the engine oil pan, and to some extent through other surfaces such as block, cylinder head, and manifold. If you keep the outside of your engine clean, its operating temperature will have a better chance of remaining normal at all times. A dirt-caked oil pan, on the other hand, will not permit excess heat to escape and the bearings, crankshaft, pistons, rods and other parts will operate at higher than normal temperatures. The oil itself may overheat, oxidize, become black and lose much of its lubricating value.

▲ When making compression test, make sure all plugs are out, engine is warm and throttle is blocked open. Watch action of compression gauge needle for indication of condition of valves.

➤ Fuel pump capacity test is made by cranking engine with fuel line end disconnected from carburetor and aimed into can. Pump should deliver a pint in 30 seconds on V-8, 45 seconds on a six.

Dirt and road film can also cause carburetor linkage to stick, mask an oil leak while it is still easy to cure, enter the brake master cylinder and contaminate brake fluid, and create electrical short circuits.

If you clean your engine just once a year, or twice a year in areas where winters are severe, you can greatly extend the life of many components.

You don't need an expensive steam-cleaning system to do the job correctly. For a few dollars you can buy an aerosol can of engine-cleaning solvent, and it will do an equally good job.

Just remove the air cleaner assembly and with clear cellophane household wrap, cover the generator end plate, top of the carburetor and the distributor body. (These must be cleaned separately with kerosene and a wire brush to keep dirt and water from entering these units.)

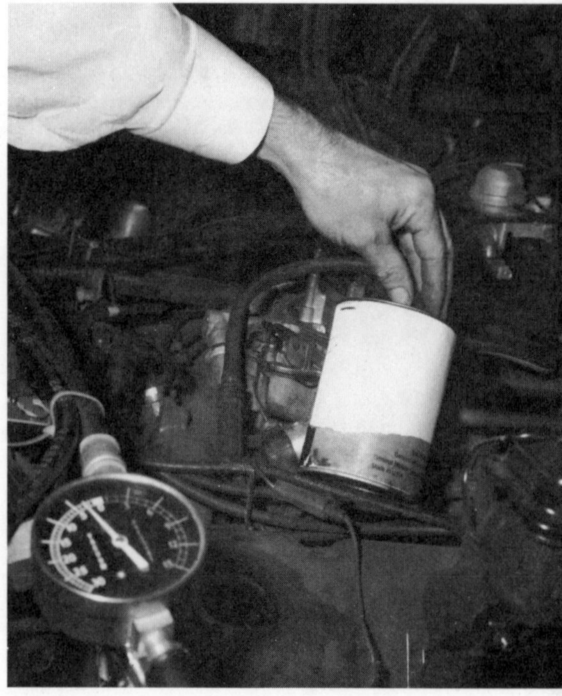

Spray the engine with the degreasing solvent, using a repeat spray on areas with caked-on film. If the cake of dirt is really thick, you may have to scrape it off. The solvent works best when the engine is warm.

Allow the solvent to work in for about fifteen minutes, then wash it off with a garden hose.

A clean engine has the additional advantage, to a weekend mechanic, of being much easier to work on. Adjustment screws are easier to regulate when they are clean, and nuts and bolts can be tightened properly only when clean. (Dirt causes thread friction that gives a false sense of tightness.)

Keeping the engine clean means keeping *all* of it clean. In addition to brush-and-solvent cleaning of the generator, top of carburetor and distributor, also brush out well around the spark plugs, so that when they are taken out, no foreign matter will fall into the plug hole. Such dirt could lodge under a valve seat to prevent its seating, and it would take a very short time for the valve and seat to burn, which would require an expensive and time-consuming repair.

Some other simple steps. Over the miles, engine performance falls off gradually—but few engines ever have to have all adjustments and tune-up work done at one time. If your engine seems to be ailing, look first for one of the relatively simple sources of troubles listed in the table, "Simple Engine Troubleshooting."

With the possible exception of bringing the ignition distributor up to standard specifications, you can, with no special equipment, easily make all of the adjustments and repairs listed in the table.

You will be helped considerably in your efforts to keep the engine at its best by buying a set of socket and open end wrenches. If you cannot get these at a hardware store, you can at an automotive parts and equipment jobber. With a set of such wrenches you can go over all the various nuts in the engine, tightening those at such parts as intake and exhaust manifolds, carburetor joints, valve cover plates, timing gear cover, oil filter brackets, fuel lines, oil lines, oil pan—in fact, wherever the nuts are accessible. Be careful of the nuts on the cylinder head. These should be tightened with a torque wrench (a wrench which shows the exact amount of tension being placed on the stud upon which the nut is being tightened).

Jacking capability. If you presently have your car lubricated and the oil filter changed at a service station, you may wish to have underbody bolts and nuts, particularly oil pan bolts, tightened by the station attendant while the car is on the lift.

But if you have a late-model "lubricated for life chassis" you should consider changing the oil and filter yourself. You can normally buy the oil and filter at discount houses and auto supply stores for less than the list price the service station charges.

Most cars have spin-on filters which require only an inexpensive wrench to replace. The oil pan drain plug requires only a simple box or open-end wrench. The elimination of the chassis lubrication means that you do not need to use an air-pressurized grease gun or struggle with a small hand grease gun.

You will, however, need good jacking capability to do this work. But you will need this for many routine underbody jobs, including underbody nut and bolt tightening, which you will then be able to do yourself.

Using a vacuum gauge. A vacuum gauge is a handy and inexpensive instrument that can tell you much about engine condition. When an engine is performing properly, the downward stroke of the pistons creates a healthy vacuum in the intake manifold. Engine malfunction often shows up as changes in intake manifold vacuum, which you can measure with the vacuum gauge.

The vacuum gauge is easily connected to either the base of the carburetor or to the intake manifold itself. (The intake manifold is the tubular unit that sits below the carburetor. It carries the fuel mixture into the cylinder head.)

Testing compression. Good operation of your engine depends to a great extent upon having uniform compression in all the cylinders. A compression gauge tests for this. Before removing spark plugs from all cylinders to make such a test, the engine should be operated long enough to bring it to its normal operating temperature. Next, loosen all plugs two turns to crack internal carbon, then start and "gun" engine to blow out this carbon. Now you can remove the spark plugs, open the carburetor throttle valve wide and block the accelerator pedal if necessary to hold it in this position. Also make sure that the carburetor choke valve is wide open. Place the compression gauge in the plug hole of the first cylinder (hold it firmly in place), and with ignition disconnected (pull center wire from coil) have someone crank the engine. Watch the pointer of the compression gauge and count the number of revolutions necessary to bring the hand to its highest indication. Actually, you do not count the engine revolutions, but rather the *whrr whrr* of the starting motor. Jot down the reading and do the same with the remaining cylinders.

If you have the correct grade and amount of oil in the engine and if pistons, rings, cylinders, valves and gaskets are in good condition, the highest readings on all cylinders should be within 25 percent of the lowest readings. If there is a greater variation, there is an engine mechanical problem, and normal tuning will have very limited effect. Example: if the highest compression reading is 160 psi, the lowest should be 120.

The important thing to watch for in this test is the action of the compression gauge pointer. For example, if the pointer does not climb steadily, but remains at rest during the cranking process, indications are that the valve of the cylinder on test is holding open. Or, if on the first turn of the starting motor the hand goes to 35, for example, then remains at 35 on the next turn but climbs higher on succeeding strokes, it is likely that the cylinder has a sticky valve. Such a valve condition will show up on the first few revolutions during the test.

Note: On many V-8 engines, it will be impossible to hold the compression gauge in the spark plug hole as required, and still be able to read it as the pointer rises. If you have a V-8 and this is the case, you will need a compression gauge with a hose. One end of the hose has a threaded fitting for the spark plug hole. The other end has the gauge, which can be held away from the plug hole and read easily.

Head gaskets leakage is generally indicated by low compression readings on adjacent cylinders. If the readings you have jotted down show definite lack of uniformity between cylinders, you can often restore normal conditions by using a special gum solvent or similar preparation sold by auto supply stores for this purpose. Valves and piston rings freed in this way may again seat firmly to restore compression; but if the valves are burnt, the obvious remedy is replacement of the old valves with new.

The cooling system dissipates the excess heat from the engine. It must always be kept in the best of condition. At one time it was necessary to drain the system twice a year—once in the spring, again in the fall.

But today's cooling systems are designed differently. They require only once-a-year draining, and year-round use of antifreeze.

The fuel pump draws gasoline from the tank and forces it up into the carburetor, usually through a gasoline filter. It is a simple unit that normally functions for up to 50,000 miles or more without giving trouble.

The pump has two valves, both spring-loaded but in different directions, and a diaphragm that is connected to an arm. The engine camshaft has a lobe that moves the arm to flex the diaphragm.

As the diaphragm flexes downward, it creates a suction that pulls open one of the two valves, called the inlet. The suction also draws in fuel from the gas tank.

As the camshaft turns, it relieves the pressure against the arm, and a spring pushes the diaphragm up. The spring pressure against the diaphragm forces the fuel against the other valve—the outlet—opening it and pushing the fuel out of the pump and up the tubing to the carburetor.

Eventually, however, the diaphragm may become punctured by dirt in the gasoline, or porous, and insufficient fuel will be pumped to the carburetor. And over a period of time, the diaphragm arm may become excessively worn.

Fuel pumps can be tested with a pressure gauge that reads to about nine psi. All vacuum gauges sold for engine troubleshooting also have a pressure gauge built in, so you need not purchase an additional test instrument.

The pressure gauge is normally connected to the end of the fuel line at the carburetor. The engine is cranked, or even started (and operated for a moment on the fuel in the carburetor), while the pump output pressure is read on the gauge.

The correct pressure varies according to the make of car. In general, a six-cylinder pump is satisfactory if it develops 2.5 to 4 psi. A V-8 pump normally develops 3 to as high as 8 psi. Inadequate pressure causes fuel starvation; too much pressure causes carburetor flooding.

In addition to a pressure check, a volume check should also be made. This is done by cranking the engine and holding a can to catch the flow from the fuel line, and is most conveniently performed immediately after the pressure check. A six-cylinder pump should deliver a pint into the can in 45 seconds at most. A V-8 pump should deliver a pint in 30 seconds.

If fuel pump delivery is not up to specifications, the problem may be caused by a clogged gasoline filter. On many cars, the fuel pump is a sealed assembly and must be replaced if defective; on others, it can be rebuilt.

The carburetor. Modern carburetors can be complicated units, particularly if they have two or four barrels. You can, however, do some carburetor service work yourself even with little experience.

Light carburetor service is limited to the following:

1. Adjusting the carburetor. You will need a tachometer for this. The tachometer, which is an engine speed indicator, is normally sold as a combination unit with a dwellmeter, which is needed for checking ignition point adjustment.

Inexpensive tach-dwellmeters for weekend mechanics are sold by discount and auto accessory stores. You should not buy the least expensive, for these will be very difficult to read accurately. Unless the tachometer has scales at least 2½ inches wide, and the dwellmeter preferably about three inches, neither will be readable. The tachometer should have two scales for versatility: 0-1000 rpm and 0-5000 rpm. The better tach-dwellmeters (also called dwell-tachometers) have chrome metal cases and cost two to three times as much as the ones with small scales and plastic cases. You may be able to get units with plastic cases and readable scales for a price somewhere between the lowest and highest. These are a good choice; you do not need the durability and ruggedness of the chrome case.

Connect the tachometer as specfiied by

the instrument manufacturer (normally to the thin-wire "CB" or minus sign terminal on the coil, and to an electrical ground, such as a cylinder head bolt).

With the engine fully warmed up, you should adjust the idle mixture screw. This screw is near the base of the carburetor. Turn it clockwise until the engine starts to falter, then counterclockwise one turn.

Note: On late-model cars with emission controls, the idle mixture screw may have a plastic cap that limits how much it can be turned. Somewhere within this range of adjustment, the engine should idle smoothly. Otherwise, the plastic cap may require removal and the carburetor adjustment by a professional shop with an exhaust analyzer.

Once the mixture is set, you can adjust the idle speed. This is controlled by a screw against the throttle linkage, which you can identify by its return spring (or by stepping on the accelerator pedal and seeing what moves).

Fuel pump pressure test is made with fuel line end disconnected from carb and vacuum-pressure gauge attached. Check manufacturer's specifications which will tell you what pump output should be.

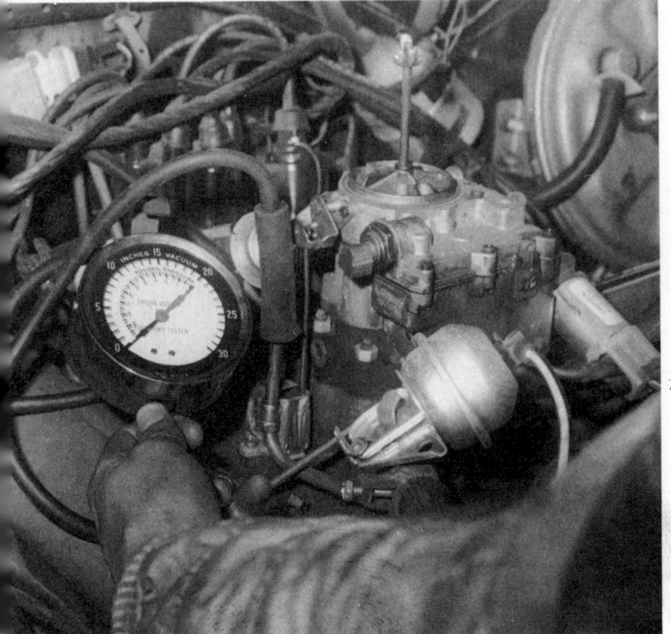

Turning the screw clockwise increases idle speed; turning it counterclockwise decreases it. On most automatic transmission cars, idle speed is set with the emergency brake applied and the transmission shift lever in "drive" position.

A satisfactory idle speed is normally about 500 rpm for a V-8, 600 rpm for a six-cylinder, although on a somewhat older engine, you may have to increase the speed 150 rpm to obtain a smooth idle.

There is a limit to how high to set the idle speed on automatic-transmission-equipped cars. Most automatics will creep if the idle is too high, an inconvenience most motorists will not accept.

2. Checking the accelerator pump. Most carburetors have an accelerator pump, which squirts extra fuel into the air horn when you floor the accelerator suddenly. The extra fuel prevents fuel starvation under hard acceleration, which could cause "flat spots." If your engine hesitates on hard acceleration, remove the air cleaner with the engine turned off, and have someone pump the gas pedal while you peer into the carburetor air horn. With the pedal being pumped, there should be squirts of fuel into the air horn.

If there are none, the carburetor requires disassembly and replacement of the accelerator pump. If the squirts are very weak, perhaps the problem is that the pump arm is not connected to the correct hole of the external linkage. For maximum pump stroke, the pump linkage (which you can identify by watching what moves on top of the carburetor) should be connected to the top hole if there are more than one. To change the rod adjustment, take off the retaining clip, move the rod to the top hole and refit the clip.

The pump must have its longest stroke in winter, its shortest stroke in summer.

Adjustment of carburetor idle mixture on late model cars is restricted by plastic idle limiter. However, you should be able to get an acceptable idle within its range.

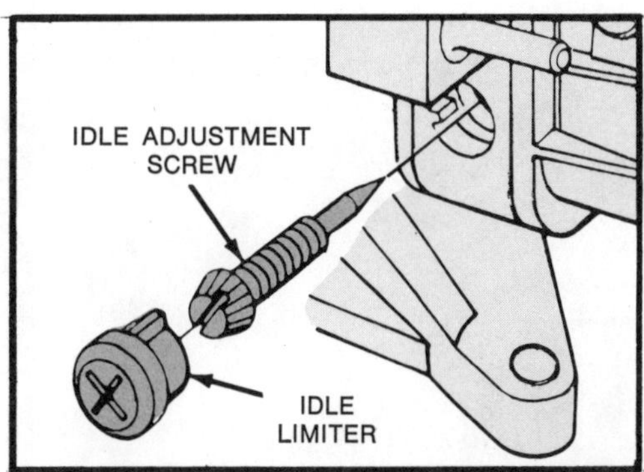

Drawing shows that limiter is nothing more than a plastic cap over the conventional idle mixture adjustment screw.

3. On some older Holley-brand carburetors, you can also check the fuel level in the carburetor bowl. If you see a plug threaded into the side of the bowl, remove it with the engine running; fuel should just dribble out. If no fuel comes out, or if the fuel really pours out, the fuel level is too high and the top of the carburetor must come off.

Thermostatic controls. Modern engines use either of two means (and occasionally both) to warm up the incoming air mixture for better fuel vaporization (and better combustion) when the engine is cold.

The most popular system over the years is the manifold heat control valve, also called a "heat riser."

On late model cars, a "thermostatic air cleaner" is used. This is nothing more than a valve in the air cleaner snorkel and a duct over the exhaust manifold. A thermostatic control ducts air warmed by the exhaust manifold into the engine during cold operation. As the engine warms up, the valve pivots to close off the exhaust manifold duct and open the snorkel to intake air flow.

Valve adjustment. The valves in your engine may be adjustable, even if the valve lifters are the "hydraulic" type. In addition, all valves with mechanical lifters are adjustable.

Most foreign cars, most six-cylinders and most Ford and Chevrolet V-8s have adjustable valves, whether hydraulic or mechanical. Valve adjustments are well within the ability of the weekend mechanic.

Valves should be adjusted at least once a year. Wear in the valve train creates the need, and periodic adjustment makes certain the valves open and close at exactly the right times for good engine performance.

The ignition system. Periodic checking and replacement of the spark plugs will not only prolong engine life, but will help you to get maximum fuel mileage. Spark plugs when correctly chosen for the engine operate for a long period, but eventually lead in gas, oil and combustion heat cause gradual loss of efficiency. The insulators accumulate deposits and the result is that the spark electricity tracks along the insulator up inside the plug rather than across the intended gap. The electrodes, too, become eaten away so that the gap becomes wider than the normal setting called for.

In adjusting electrode gap, always bend the outer, never the center, electrode. Gaps vary from .022 to .040 inch, the average being about .035 inch. Spark plug makers and service stations have specifications listing all makes of cars and the correct gap setting for each model. When the plugs are installed, tighten them only enough to compress the gasket. When buying new plugs, be sure they are of the heat range specified for your engine. Plugs are classified hot or cold according to the exposed interior length of the insulator. A hot plug does

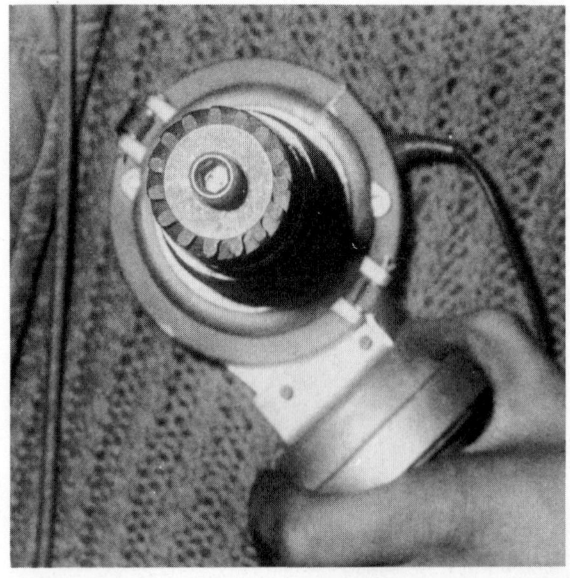

End view of Ford distributor shows the problem of installation. Note hexagonal hole in center and gear that must be engaged.

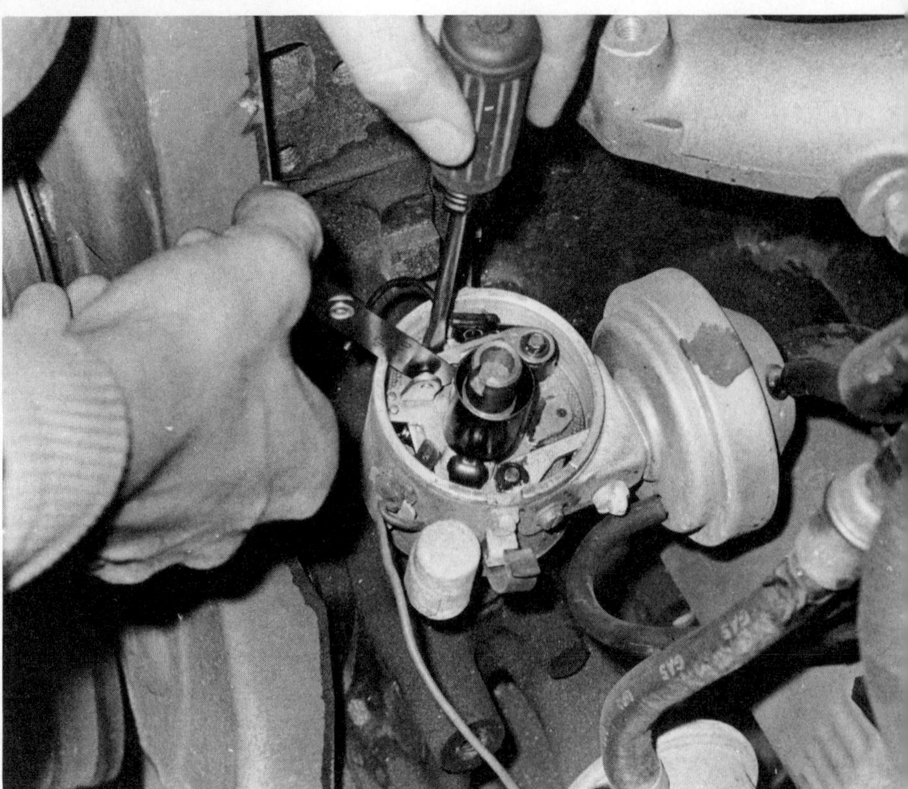

Normally, ignition points can be replaced and adjusted without removing distributor.

SIMPLE ENGINE TROUBLE-SHOOTING		
Condition	**Possible Cause**	**Remedy**
Low gas mileage.	Dirty air cleaner.	Replace paper air filter. For other types, see section on filters.
Starter works too slow; lights almost go out when starting; engine does not start; lights brighten when engine speeds up.	Battery at low charge.	Have battery charged and tested for condition of cells.
Sluggish starting motor; engine starts hard, lights dim with engine not running.	Loose, corroded, frayed or broken battery cable or ground strap.	Clean and tighten terminals or replace old cable and ground strap with new ones.
Water dripping when car is at rest.	Leaking water hose connection, defective water pump or radiator cap.	Tighten hose clamps or replace hose with new one. Have professional shop check pump and cap.
Engine overheats; water in cooling system boils.	Loose or broken fan belt or defective radiator cap.	Adjust tension of belt or install a new belt. Have professional shop check cap.
Engine starts hard or fails to start; poor gasoline mileage.	Choke sticking partly closed.	Remove air cleaner and free choke valve or linkage with kerosene or aerosol solvent.
Slow acceleration when "stepping on gas."	Wrong seasonal setting of carburetor.	Make correct setting of seasonal adjustment for cold, hot or normal temperature.
Misfiring; rough operation; poor gasoline mileage; hard starting.	Worn out or wrong type of spark plugs.	Replace plugs with a new set of correct type and heat range.
Flooding carburetor.	Dirt or chip stuck under carburetor float valve.	Remove carburetor float bowl cover, remove float and float valve. Look for foreign matter on valve or its seat.
Rough engine operation; misfiring; hard starting.	Pitted or wrongly spaced distributor contact points.	Install new points if old are badly worn.
Low gasoline mileage; engine lacks power and pick-up.	Heat control valve sticking.	Squirt aerosol solvent on shaft and tap lightly with hammer until free.

not have a "hotter spark." Hot plugs burn off fouling deposits in low-speed driving. Cold plugs prevent insulator blistering from the heat generated in high-speed driving.

As far as the ignition distributor itself is concerned, it should not be removed from the car unless absolutely necessary, as for replacement. Ford distributors, for example, have a gear and a hexagonal slot on the shaft, and engaging both properly can be a very difficult job.

Most routine checks of the distributor can be made on the car, as can replacement of the ignition points and condenser.

Muffler and tail pipe. A badly corroded muffler, broken or disarranged baffle plates, together with a kinked pipe, may produce enough back pressure to offset all of your other good work. P.W.

See also: BATTERIES; BEARINGS; CHOKE, AUTOMATIC; COOLING SYSTEM, AUTO; FILTERS; GASKETS; OIL, ENGINE; SPARK PLUG; STARTER; VALVES.

➤ *Replacing carburetor begins with removal of complete air cleaner assembly. On late-model cars this involves several hose disconnections and perhaps loosening or removing bracket(s).*

How to Change Engine Parts

Slice a healthy chunk from your auto repair bills by exchanging worn out parts for rebuilts and installing them yourself

WHEN YOUR CAR needs a new generator, starter, fuel pump, carburetor, transmission, or engine, you can replace it with an exchange unit, doing the removal and installation yourself to save a big part of the repair bill. Buying rebuilts is convenient when you don't have the time, tools and/or know-how to rebuild your own.

In addition, many parts houses give discounts from list price to weekend mechanics, though professionals do, of course, receive large ones.

The exchange unit is a rebuilt. At one time, rebuilts were very risky purchases. But today, there are excellent assembly-line and semi-custom, rebuilders all over the country, and their products are reliable.

There also are poor rebuilts. Take a carburetor for example. A "cheapie" rebuilder will merely clean out the old carburetor, replace the gaskets and perhaps the needle valve and seat assembly. A quality rebuilder will replace power valves, jets, accelerator pump and choke too.

With a fuel pump, the cheapie rebuilder will just replace the pump diaphragm. The quality rebuilder will change the diaphragm spring, and also check valves and pump arm, if worn.

How can you be assured of a quality rebuilt? The answer is to buy from the auto parts houses that the professionals patronize, and not from the stores that also sell toys and garden hoses.

Carburetor replacement. One of the most frequent troublemakers is the carburetor. Remove the air cleaner and disconnect the throttle, choke linkage and the fuel line from the fuel pump. Two to four studs hold the carburetor body to the flange. Buy an exchange carburetor to fit your car from your rebuilt parts dealer. The carburetor represents a real savings. A new four-barrel carburetor costs around $75 to $110, while the price of a rebuilt is perhaps half that, including the trade-in of your old carburetor.

The new carburetor, depending on the rebuilder, will often require transfer of some pieces of linkage from the old carburetor to the new. So before you hand in your old carburetor, place it side by side with the new and determine what parts must be transferred.

Installing a rebuilt carburetor is the reverse of pulling the old one, although it is

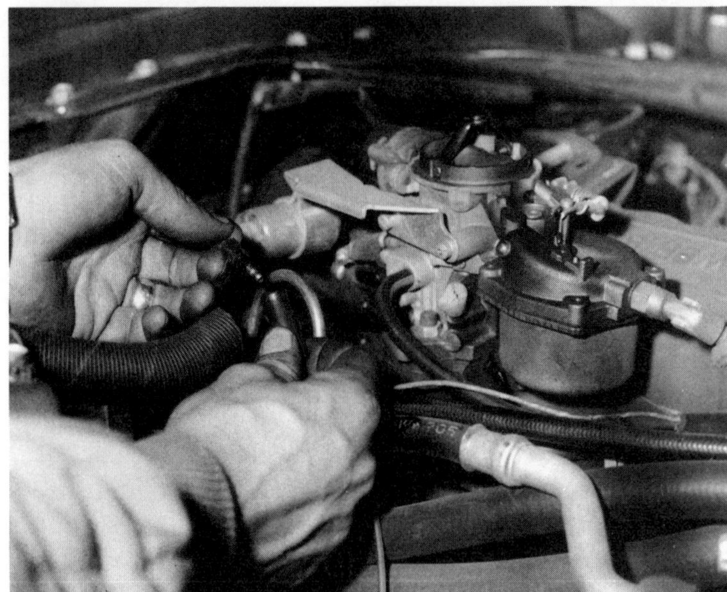

Most late-model cars have an electric solenoid to regulate the precise position of the throttle. Solenoid holds throttle open slightly for idling and when engine is shut off, allows it to close completely so engine does not run on. Disconnect solenoid wire.

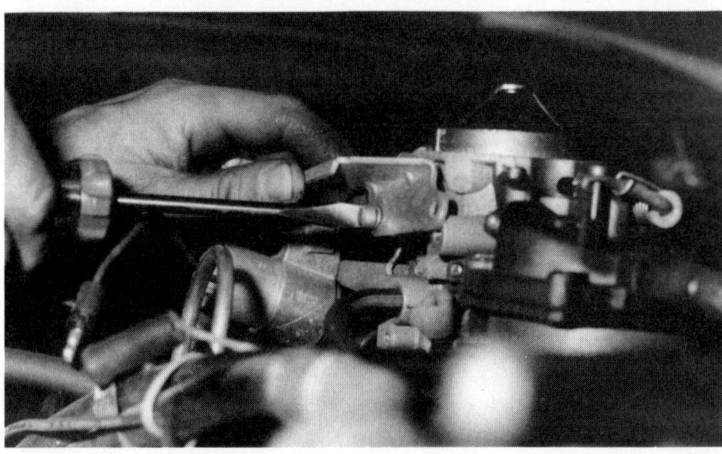

If new carburetor does not come with throttle solenoid, remove old one for transfer.

Disconnect automatic choke heat tube on carbs with incarburetor coil. On carbs with well choke, disconnect link from coil to choke plate.

good practice to install a new gasket between the carburetor and the intake manifold.

To get a precise adjustment, you can use a vacuum gauge. Turn out the mixture screw or the two screws, in the case of a two- or four-barrel carb, until the engine idles smoothly without rolling or galloping. The indicator on the vacuum gauge should remain stationary, but if it oscillates in a slow floating motion, keep adjusting the idle-speed screw along with the idle-mixture screws until the gauge shows the highest vacuum without vibration. Then adjust the idle-speed screw alone for the best idle speed before the engine warms up thoroughly. On cars with automatic transmissions, it may be necessary to readjust the idle speed somewhat lower if the car tends to creep too much at a traffic light.

If the engine will not start after installation of the rebuilt distributor (and it was running, even poorly, before), chances are you have installed the distributor incorrectly and ignition timing is far off.

Many distributors will go in only one way, but many more will go in any number of ways, but the timing will be wrong and the car won't start.

The best procedure is to prevent an error by carefully marking the distributor body and the engine adjacent, and noting the position of the rotor.

If you have made an error, here is a procedure to get the engine timed close enough to get it started, after which you can use a power timing light to set timing accurately.

With the distributor removed, crank the engine in very short bursts until the timing mark on the crankshaft pulley or damper is lined up with the timing indicator on the front of the engine.

At this point, the ignition system should be ready to fire either No. 1 cylinder or its companion, No. 6 (on a six-cylinder or V-8 engine). On a four-cylinder engine with a firing order of 1-3-4-2 or 1-2-4-3, the companions are 1 and 4. On a four-cylinder with a firing order of 1-4-3-2, the companions are 1 and 3. Note: except for in-line engines, which are numbered front-to-rear, car manufacturers number the cylinders differently, and you will have to learn which is which by checking a general repair manual.

Put the distributor partly back in, lining up the body as close as you can remember to its original position. The location of the vacuum hose or tube to the distributor vacuum advance may assist your memory.

Swing the distributor cap back into position, but do not fasten it down. Just note the location of the No. 1 and No. 6 spark plug wires and aim the tip of the rotor for either of them. With the rotor so aimed, slip the distributor back in all the way. (This may take time on such as Ford products, where the distributor shaft must engage both a gear and a hex fitting.)

Refit the distributor cap and try to start the engine. If the engine seems to be trying to start, move the distributor body in short arcs, and if the engine starts, you are now ready for precise timing with the power timing light.

If it shows no sign of starting, take out the distributor and re-install, aiming the tip of the rotor for the other cylinder. Refit the distributor cap and again try to start the engine, also moving the distributor body in short arcs if the engine seems to be trying to start.

If the term "trying to start" is unfamiliar, here is what is means: the engine will fire then die immediately. This is an indication that ignition timing is close, but not close enough.

Special technique. Here is a technique that you can use to determine which cylinder (No. 1 or No. 6) is ready to fire when the timing marks are lined up. It eliminates the 50-50 odds you face otherwise.

Remove the No. 1 cylinder spark plug and watch the timing mark on the crankshaft pulley or damper. When it is several inches from the timing indicator on the engine, insert a compression gauge into the No. 1 spark plug hole and continue cranking until the marks are very close. Remove the compression gauge and see if there is a reading on it. (It won't be a normal one, but it should be something if No. 1 piston is coming up on compression.)

If there is no reading, No. 1 piston is coming up on exhaust and No. 6 is coming up on compression. The rotor tip should be pointed toward No. 6.

Generator and voltage regulator. The generator (whether an older DC type or the newer alternator) can be confidently replaced with a rebuilt, at a saving that could exceed 60 percent over a new unit.

The voltage regulator is integral with the alternator on many new cars, but it is a separate unit on most others, and has always been a separate unit with DC generators.

Never install a rebuilt conventional voltage regulator. There are many reasons a voltage regulator can fail, and the rebuilding jobs are limited to replacement of the vibrating contacts.

Fully-electronic regulators have no moving parts and seldom fail. Rebuilt units of these are not readily available, although they should soon be, and will be worth considering. Note: some alternators have the regulator built in. When this type is remanufactured, a new or rebuilt regulator is included as part of the overhaul process, when necessary.

It is important that you definitely determine that the trouble is in the generator before you replace it. Broken connections, a faulty regulator and a slipping fan belt are far more likely problems.

Disconnect fuel line from carburetor.

Disconnect throttle linkage. The arrangement from one carburetor to another varies, so you will just have to see what is used. On this particular carb, pushing off a spring clip does the job.

Disconnect vacuum hoses to the carburetor.

Replacing a generator is a very straightforward job, but there is one precaution: always disconnect the battery ground cable before you start.

Two or three bolts and nuts will hold the generator, and there are two or three electrical connections. If the terminals are not sufficiently different, make a sketch showing where each wire goes before you remove anything.

Undo the nuts or bolts that hold the carburetor to its base, and remove.

Fuel pump. When a fuel pump fails, replacing it with a rebuilt is a simple job.

The typical fuel pump is a mechanical unit, driven by the engine. The only exceptions are some foreign cars and the Chevrolet Vega, which have electric pumps.

Tht mechanical pump is held by two bolts or studs and nuts. To replace the pump, just undo the two fuel line connections (one inlet line from the gas tank, the other an outlet line to the carburetor).

Then remove the two bolts or nuts and pull the pump straight out. On cars with a flexible hose or hoses, it may be easier to take out the bolts or nuts first and lift the pump to a position where the hose connection is easier to get at.

Warning: on Chevrolet engines, the fuel pump arm is moved by a cylinder that is in contact with the camshaft. This design can make it difficult to install a replacement pump. There are special tools available to hold the cylinder up and in its bore, so that the replacement pump can be fitted. If you don't have this tool, you can do the job with a piece of stiff wire and patience.

Virtually all Ford products have sealed

The carb is ready for removal. Just lift it up and out. Installation is a reversal of the removal procedure.

pumps, so they cannot be rebuilt except at a factory. Even if your pump is rebuildable, the low price of a factory rebuilt makes it the best choice for time-saving repair.

On Chevrolet Vega, the only American car with an electric pump, the pump is in the gas tank, which is held by two straps. To get at this pump, undo the strap nuts at the rear of the tank, lower the tank and remove the pump from its bracket.

Engine. When the engine in your car is so badly worn that it needs a complete overhaul, such as reboring, new pistons and rings, engine bearings, crankshaft regrinding, valve job, ring gear on the flywheel, etc., a rebuilt or used engine is the best answer.

You can save at least $200 by buying a rebuilt instead of a new engine, even if you could get a new engine. The rebuilding art is so highly developed in the engine field that few car makers even supply complete new engines. In many cases, all they supply are short blocks, which are engine blocks with crankshaft, connecting rods, pistons and rings. To get a complete engine, you have to buy all the accessories and cylinder heads.

Even if the car maker lists a complete engine, it will not be easy to get. The few that are made are for warranty use.

So your choice is either a factory rebuilt, a semi-custom rebuilt or a used engine from a wrecking yard.

If you can obtain a late-model used engine from a wrecking yard, this is the most economical choice. There is very little risk if you buy from a reputable wrecking yard, for it surely will have run the engine before it was pulled from the chassis, and therefore will not sell it if it burns oil or has piston slaps or bearing knocks. It also will advise you of the mileage on the engine.

The rebuilt engine offers a bit more security, for it comes with a firm guarantee. In the rebuilt area, there are two choices:

1. The factory rebuilt. This is an engine

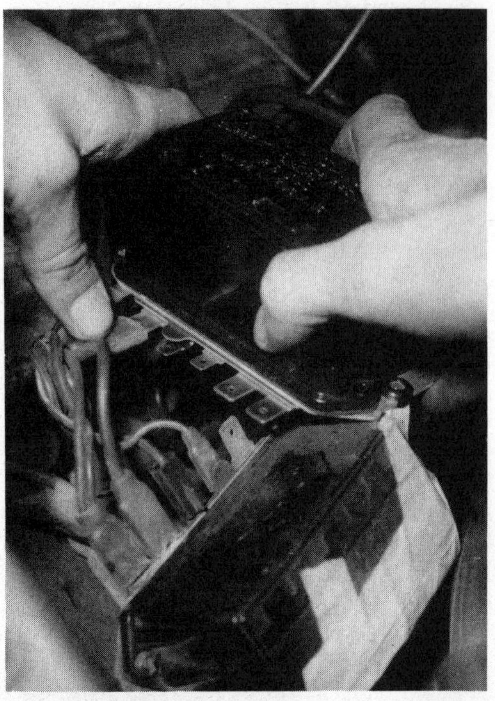

Replacement of a regulator is simple. Regulator is held by two or four screws. Hold replacement regulator next to defective unit and transfer one wire at a time.

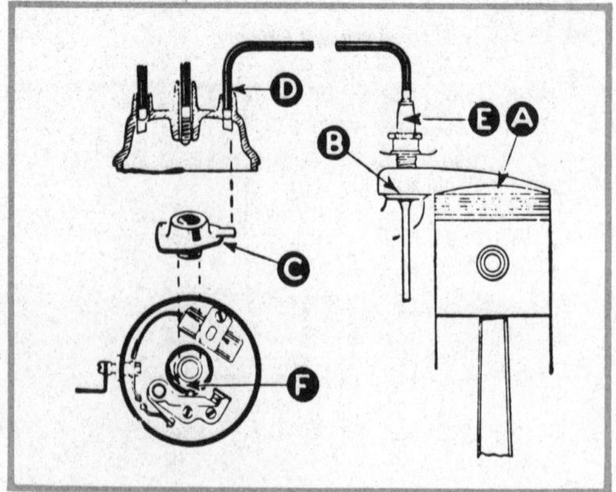

If you make a mistake while replacing a distributor, drawing shows how to set up ignition timing close enough to get engine started, at which point timing light can be connected. Piston (A) of No. 1 cylinder is at top dead center of cylinder on compression stroke. Rotor (C) points to No. 1 spark plug wire in distributor cap (D). Lobe on cam (F) is about to open breaker points. E is the No. 1 spark plug about to fire. Intake valve (B) should be closed.

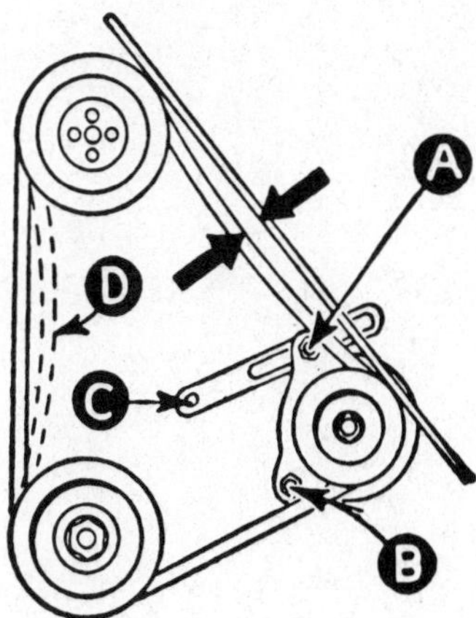

Replacement of a generator is difficult only if the generator is inaccessible. Normally it is held by two or three bolts and is removed by taking out bolts A and B, pushing generator in along pivot C, and removing belt D. There are two or three electrical connections on the generator and if they look the same, make a sketch and tag them so you can refit them correctly.

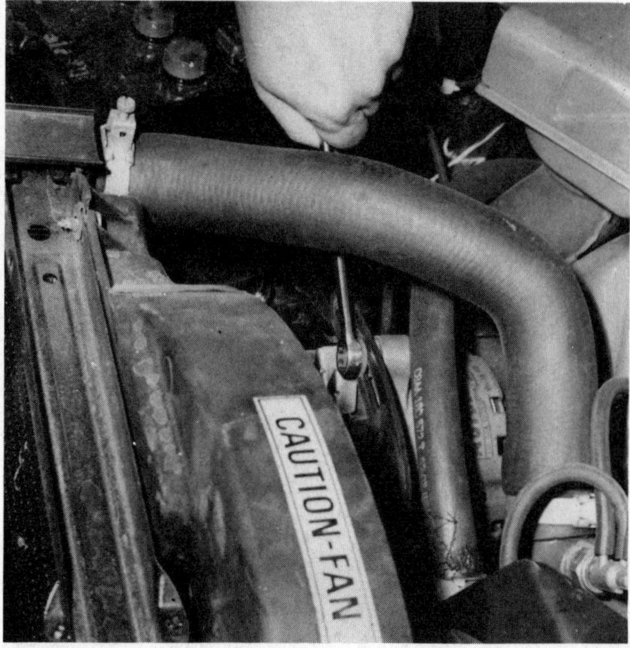

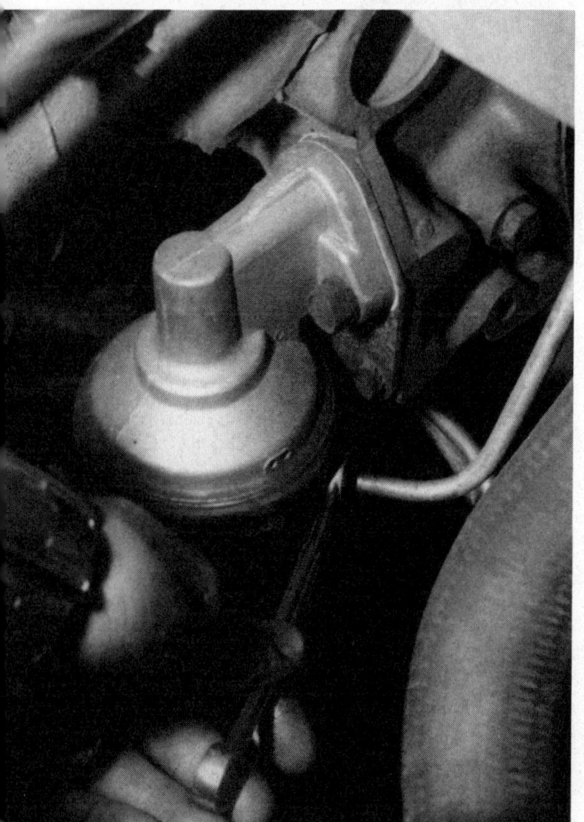

that went down an assembly line much like the one that put it together.

2. The semi-custom rebuilt. This is an engine that was rebuilt in a smaller shop with a lot more human inspections. It is 10 to 20 percent more than a factory rebuilt.

If you have an older car, or one that just wasn't a big seller, the factory rebuilt engine may not be readily available. The semi-custom rebuilding job will be done on your engine, and your car may be out of action less than a week.

Engine removal. There are no complete sets of hard-and-fast rules that will cover engine removal on all cars. Some general information, however, may help you:

1. You will need a chain or cable hoist,

Replacing fuel pump is normally not difficult if the pump bolts are accessible, and they usually are with ordinary tools. First step is to disconnect the fuel lines. In the case of this pump, only one line has to be disconnected, as other is a hose which can be swung up with the pump and removed from the top of the engine compartment more easily.

➤ *Socket wrench makes short work of the two fuel pump bolts.*

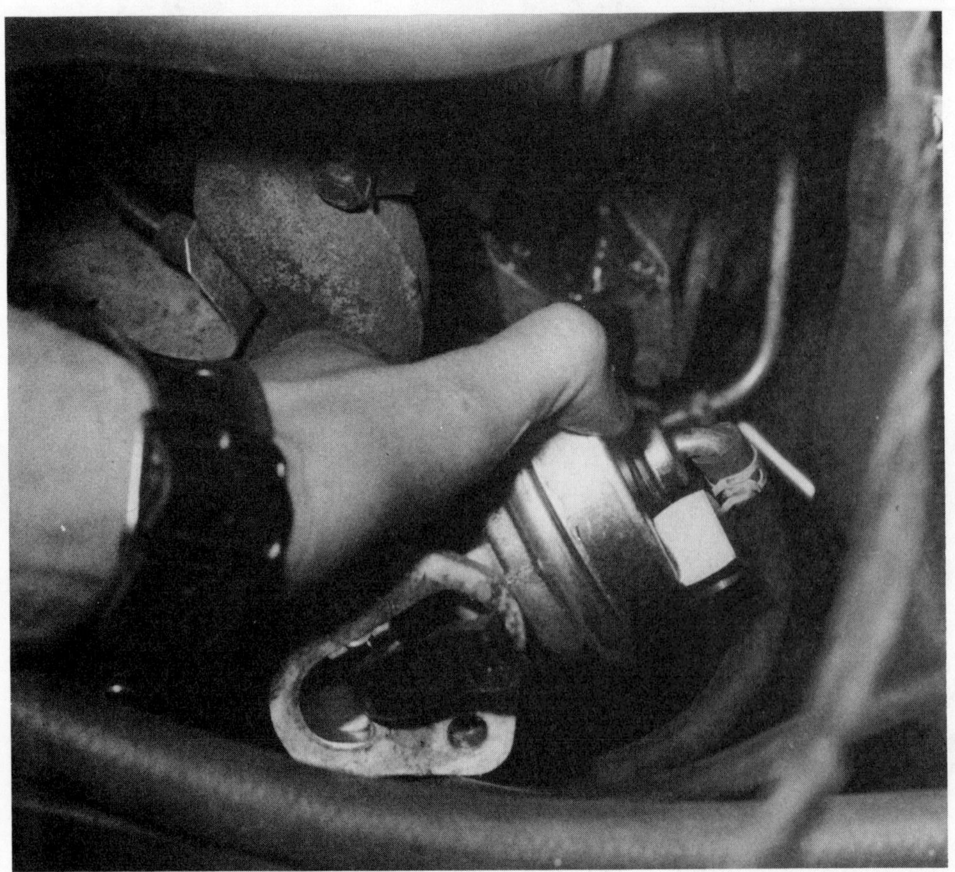

➤ *Pump can now be lifted up and hose connection taken off. This particular pump is from a Chevrolet, and a special tool is very helpful in refitting the pump so that the pump arm will properly be under an actuating cylinder.*

Chevrolet Vega has an electric fuel pump in the gas tank. When pump goes bad, you undo two strap nuts shown, drop tank and discard pump which is sealed unit.

and this can be rented for a day for a few dollars.

2. You will need something from which to hang the hoist. A heavy beam across the top of your garage or a sturdy basketball backboard normally are acceptable.

3. When you make disconnections of either tubing or wiring, tag everything so you'll know where it goes when the replacement engine is ready for installation.

4. The engine on all front-engine-rear-drive cars comes out from the top of the engine compartment, so the hood may have to be removed. Inasmuch as hood re-installation and alignment is a time-consuming procedure, you may be able to reduce it by scribing around the bolts or nuts in elongated adjustment holes with a sharp instrument.

5. Do not try to do this job without a complete set of wrenches. You will need a complete socket set (preferably both ½-inch and ⅜-inch drive), in addition to open-end and box wrenches.

6. If the car is a manual transmission, you will have to align the clutch. Inexpensive but satisfactory wooden alignment tools are available. Don't waste your money on the expensive professional-type alignment tools.

7. Although engine removal is often a one-man job, installation is never so. Have a husky friend lined up for the day you install the replacement engine. Better still, have two husky friends.

8. Keep related parts and nuts and bolts together, using envelopes appropriately marked or muffin tins. It is very easy to become impatient when pulling an engine, and just pile up nuts and bolts. But when the job of installation comes later, one misplaced nut or bolt could hold you up for an hour or more.

9. Rebuilt engines are supplied stripped of accessories, but including all innards. It's best to equip the rebuilt block with rebuilt carburetor, distributor, fuel pump, generator and other parts subject to wear.

10. If you can, obtain a factory shop manual. It won't make the job that much easier, but it may keep you from breaking something.

11. If the engine seems to be stuck, either coming out or going in, look for a reason instead of applying heavy force. And be very careful not to pinch tubing or lines.

12. On virtually every engine pull, you will have to do the following:

a. drain engine oil and cooling system; disconnect hoses.

b. disconnect ignition system at the coil's "SW" or plus terminal.

c. disconnect the fuel system from the tank. Because of clearance problems, you may also have to pull the fuel pump and carburetor.

d. disconnect the exhaust pipe from the exhaust manifold, and if clearance is limited, remove the exhaust manifold.

e. disconnect the electrical ground strap from the chassis to the engine. On late-model cars, a split ground strap is sometimes used, with one part going from battery to chassis, the other part from battery to engine. If your car doesn't have this, look for a separate strap from engine to chassis. It may be buried underneath, and would, if left connected, keep the engine from coming out.

f. disconnect the engine mounts. Most cars have two (there is a third support at the transmission).

13. If the engine compartment looks a bit crowded, remove any accessories that are reasonably easy to get at, such as alternator, oil filter, possibly the starter.

14. The last item on this list should actually be the first on yours: always disconnect the battery cables before you start working. In fact, removing the battery and both cables will not only give you more room, but in part is necessary for engine removal (the cable to the starter has to come out).

With the engine out, clean the compartment of all grease and mud with a putty knife and rags soaked in solvent. Examine the rubber engine mounts and replace them if they are flattened, broken or uneven. It it inexpensive insurance to replace the mounts, as they will have become worn by the time the engine needs replacing.

Once you install your practically new engine, use a new fan belt, ignition wiring, battery cables and hose connections to complete the installation. Install new spark plugs of proper heat range and gapped for your engine. (Check with your service station to determine the correct gap for your engine. Most older cars use a .025 inch plug gap; all recent cars use a gap of .035, and most plugs manufactured today are sold with the wider gap.)

Installing replacement parts is not limited to engine parts. Replacement transmissions, universal joints, muffler and exhaust pipes, brakes, front suspension parts and shock absorbers are available. Some are rebuilt, some new. P.W.

See also: BATTERIES; BEARINGS; CHOKE, AUTOMATIC; COOLING SYSTEM, AUTO; FILTERS; GASKETS; OIL, ENGINE; TRANSMISSION, AUTO; TUNE-UP, ENGINE; VALVES.

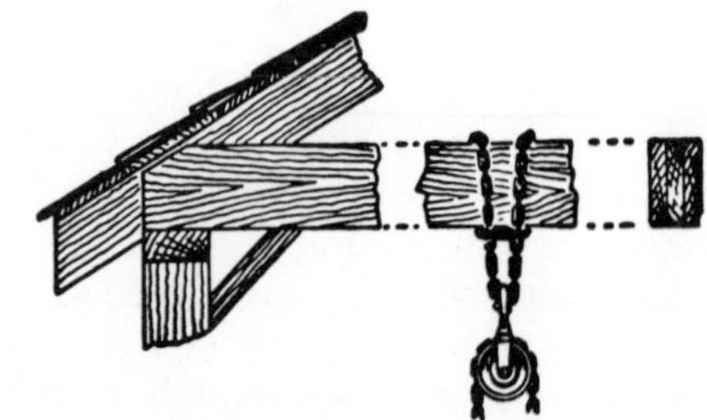

Chain sling over built-up beam across caps of garage walls supports chain hoist to lift out engine.

Many engines have lifting hooks, which makes the job of removing them a bit easier. There are two on this V-8, one on each side between second and third spark plugs.

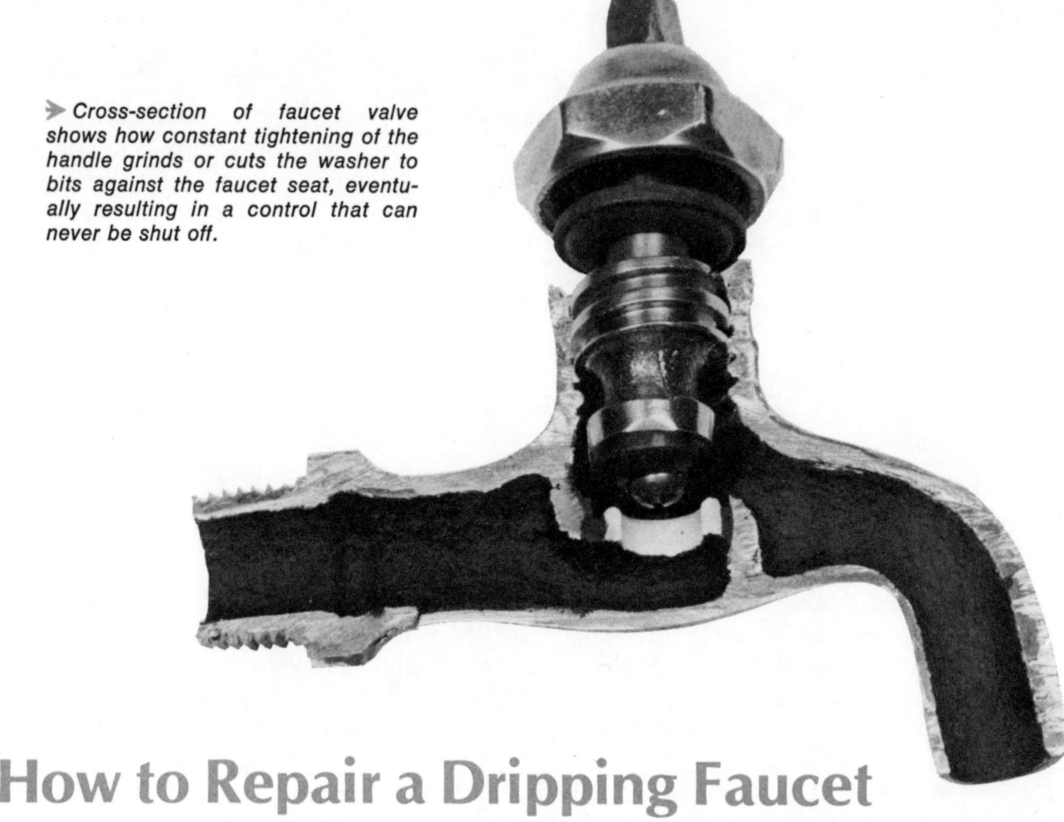

Cross-section of faucet valve shows how constant tightening of the handle grinds or cuts the washer to bits against the faucet seat, eventually resulting in a control that can never be shut off.

How to Repair a Dripping Faucet

If leaky faucets are keeping you up nights, try these simple, speedy repairs and rest peacefully from now on

SOME FAUCETS keep going year after year in perfect working order without the slightest attention. Others act as if they are pixilated—they gulp washers galore without showing any appreciation, drip constantly, are hard to open and still tougher to shut off.

It requires little effort to get all the faucets in your house to perform properly, which means that they open and close smoothly and without effort, control the flow of water to the degree that you want it, make no objectionable noises, and keep going for long periods without any attention.

New styles. Faucets are becoming more attractive in appearance, more efficient—and more complicated. Formerly a faucet disassembly required merely removing a single lock nut and the entire works came out, consisting of a worm-thread stem with a washer cup at the bottom.

Now we have one-arm faucets, dish spray hoses, three-valve shower diverters, kitchen counter-sets, and a whole array of new styles, some of which have 15 to 20 separate parts that must be put together in the right order.

The fundamental process of washer replacement applies to nearly all faucets except the one-arm kitchen model.

Often, replacement of washers is neglected because it involves shutting off the house water main and draining the lines. This problem is completely eliminated by having separate shut-off valves at every fixture. These are easily installed at lavatory sinks, as described later.

Replacing washers. Use a monkey

wrench, or channel lock pliers with smooth jaws to loosen the bonnet nut. In most cases, this will permit removal of the stem just by twisting the faucet handle.

In some models, it is necessary to lift off the handle after turning out the screw at the center. (If there is a plate covering the screw, remove the plate.)

When working with the decorative faucet parts, use care not to scratch or dent the chrome surfaces. If necessary, protect the finish from the wrenches with a cloth or masking tape.

The washer is at the bottom of the stem. Remove the screw that holds the washer in place, being careful not to snap it off.

If the screw slot is corroded, or partly broken, ease it loose with pliers. If screw head is gone, pry up the washer, exposing a part of the screw stem that can be gripped with the pliers.

Remove the washer from its brass cup. Clean out the cup with a brush or knife, and select a new washer to fit.

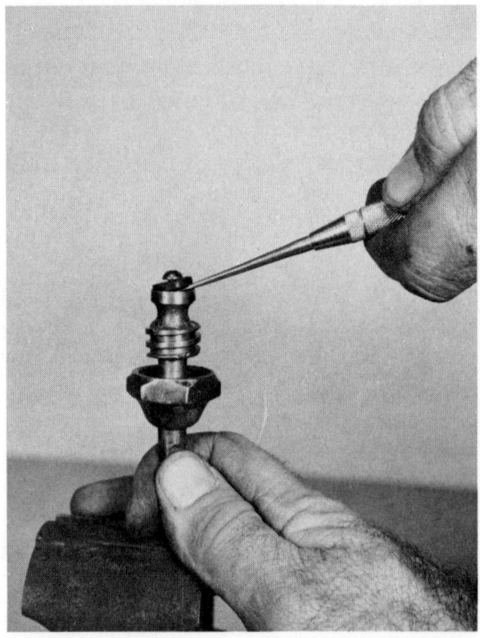

Faucet stem has cup at the bottom, into which the washer is held with a brass screw.

There is no practical difference between the black, white, gray, and red washers—the colors are only for merchandising purposes. Select a neoprene or hard rubber washer for a snug, but not tight, fit. It may not be possible to tell the size from the original washer because of distortion.

Make certain the brass screw is turned in tightly so it can't work free and drop out. Also, a loose washer will cause chattering of the faucet when water is turned on. Use a new brass fastener each time you make a washer replacement. Put the stem back into the faucet body, tighten the bonnet nut, and the job is done.

Turn the faucet handle tightly a couple of times to help seat the washer, then open the water valve.

Washer sizes. While you are at it, make a note of the size washer used for the fixture, so you can buy replacements to keep on hand. It is not worth buying the usual hardware store assortment because most of the washers included will never be used.

Once you list the needed sizes for your house fixtures you can stock up with only the sizes required.

There are several types of washers, some offered as a panacea for every faucet trouble. The domed type usually functions better than the flat because it compresses against the lip of the seat as well as on the flat surface, though you will find these washers flatten out eventually in use.

Non-rotating washers have an advantage because they move up and down with the stem rather than being twisted at the point of compression. The non-rotating type with a stem that fits into the washer screw hole is better because it can be removed when necessary, while the free-floating type may become jammed against the seat, making it difficult to reach for removal.

Smoothing faucet seat. If the faucet still drips after the washer is replaced, it indicates that the washer seat is nicked or scratched. This happens sometimes because of a particle of sand or some other matter in the water line.

A low-cost seat dressing tool will quickly smooth the seat for better closure.

Open the faucet as before, take off the handle, slide up the bonnet nut, and remove the stem. Place the dressing tool into the faucet body, with the knurled nut adjusted to permit threading of the bonnet nut back into position. The bonnet nut holds the dressing tool shaft straight and exerts slight pressure while it is rotated. Make just one or two turns, then remove the tool.

Before reassembling the faucet stem, open the water valve just for a moment to flush out brass chips left by the dressing operation. Then replace the stem, reassemble the bonnet nut and handle. Try the faucet to see if the drip has stopped.

Continuation of the drip means that the washer seat is badly corroded or chipped. Most better-quality faucets have replaceable seats which look like shallow brass rings with threaded base, rounded at the top. These seats are turned out with a narrow-blade screwdriver or an Allen wrench.

A parts catalog from the manufacturer of the faucet will show whether the seat is removable and indicate the part number for replacement. If possible, get the new washer seat before removing the old one so it can be replaced immediately without tying up the faucet. You may be able to match the seat at a plumbing supply dealer who stocks these parts.

Faucets that do not have a replaceable washer seat sometimes can be repaired with a special insert of soft brass which is placed over the old seat to provide a new smooth surface. This may work for a while, but will deteriorate quickly under the constant rotation of the washer.

The best correction, then, is to replace the troublesome faucet with a new one—of the latest type.

Worn faucet stems. When force must be exerted on the faucet handle to shut off the water completely, it indicates that the stem gear is worn.

Cutaway of faucet section shows how Allen hex wrench is used to remove washer stem.

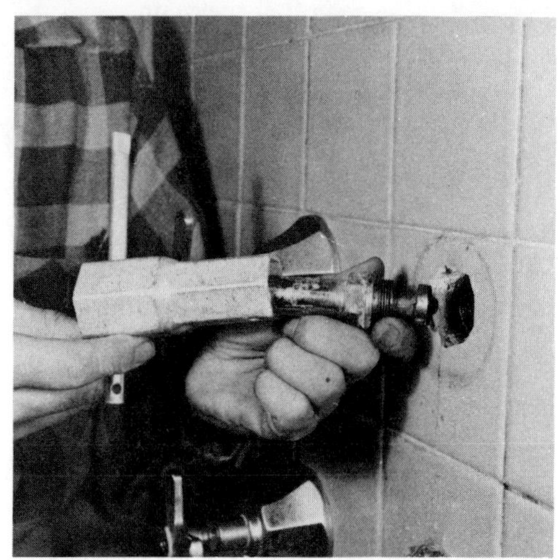

Gain access to tub and shower controls by removing the escutcheon plate which covers the faucet stem.

Most hardware dealers carry a large selection of faucet stems and probably can match yours. If unable to get one locally, write to the manufacturer for a source.

The packing washer around the stem may become worn or enlarged so water seeps up around the stem when the faucet is open. Remove the old packing, stripping it away in sections, and press on a new washer of proper size.

If a washer cannot be obtained, wrap graphite-coated wicking around the stem and tighten with the bonnet nut to stop the leak.

Some bathtub and shower faucets are recessed into the wall tiles, and are removed only with a deep socket wrench, after taking off the handle and escutcheon plate.

Adding sink valves. Individual valves are easily installed at fixtures with the aid of a valve set. These sets consist of a small angle valve, flexible inlet riser tubing with compression fitting, and a reducer bushing.

A valve installation for a bathroom sink can be done in the following manner, once the water is turned off at the main.

Remove old connection pipe from wall to sink faucet. If the sink is of modern type, a special basin wrench will be needed to loosen the connecting nut underneath the faucet. The water entry line, in most cases, ends close to the wall. When the top nut is loosened, turn the pipe out of the right angle elbow, then remove the horizontal section connecting to the entry pipe.

Install a coupling on the entry pipe. If pipe is ¾-inch, use a ½-inch reducer coupling. Turn the angle valve on a nipple which is of a length that, when turned into the entry coupling, will bring the valve riser directly under the faucet opening below the sink. Put escutcheon plate over the horizontal nipple before installation.

Measure the flexible riser in position against the valve and cut to length with a tubing cutter.

Push riser into valve part and tighten the slip nut. Force the other end into the faucet opening (there is sufficient flexibility of the tube for this) and tighten the compression nut.

At a nominal cost, the faucets now have an individual shut-off valve that saves considerable trouble whenever repairs must be made. Each lavatory, sink, water closet tank and shower should be equipped with individual valves for the hot and cold water lines.

▲ *Deep socket wrench might be necessary to remove faucet stems that are recessed in the wall.*

Valve repairs. There are a number of valves used in the average home system. Gate valves are usually for the service entrance and the main water branches, as they allow direct passage of the water with minimum drop in pressure. These valves are intended only for infrequent use, and generally are kept fully open.

Globe and angle valves are used to control the flow of water (for example, the mixing valve at a water heater) and thus are adjusted quite frequently.

Globe valves may leak at the stem, which will require repacking. This is done by loosening the packing nut so it can slide up on the stem sufficiently to allow threading the graphite packing underneath. Pressure of the cap usually seals the space and stops leaks.

When the washer must be replaced, the water main is closed down and the lines drained. The stem is removed similarly to a faucet by turning off the packing nut and

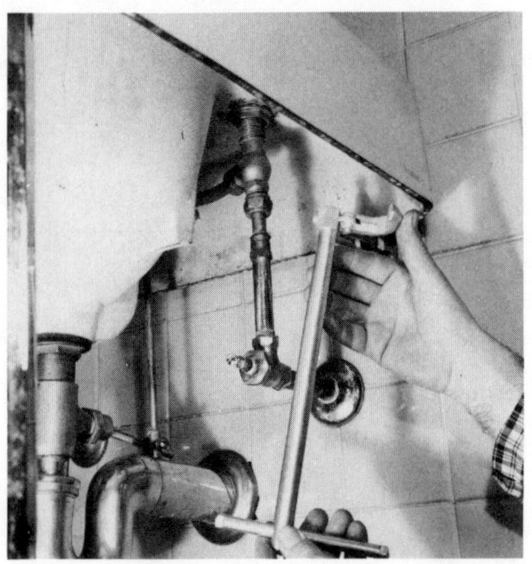

When replacing lavatory faucets, use a basin wrench to remove retainer nut from underneath.

Wrap lamp wicking or apply plumbers compound to the stud to provide a watertight seal for temporary leak repairs.

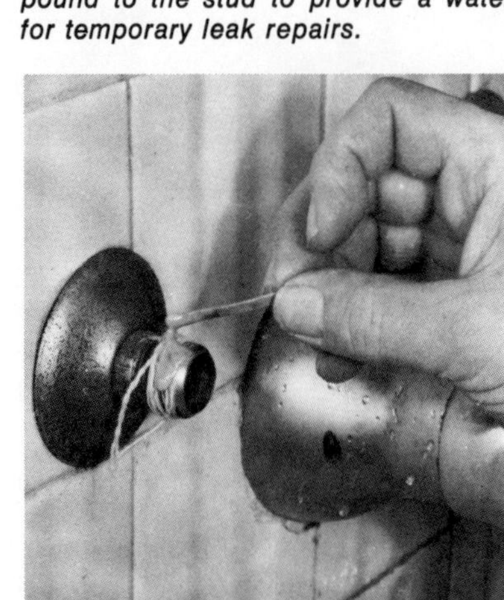

After the nut is started, tighten tube to valve by turning compression nut with wrench.

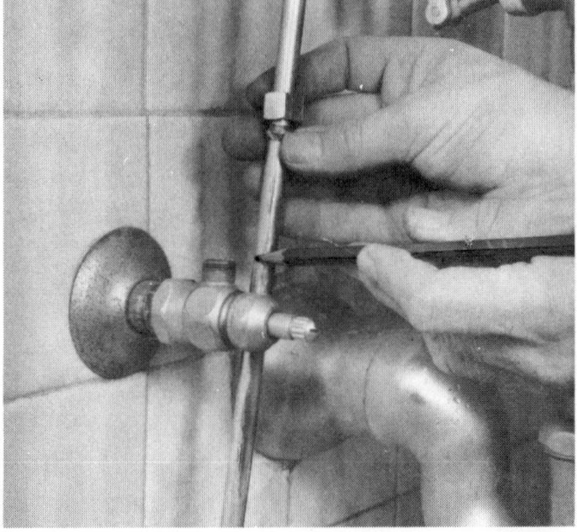

Measure and cut the riser tube to required length. Leave enough stock to go into the fitting.

bonnet. A composition fiber washer is fitted into the stem cup, held with a brass screw.

Globe valves should be installed so that when closed, the pressure will be against the stem so the packing can be replaced while there is pressure in the line.

Pipe hangers should be placed on each side of the valve so no strain or weight of the pipe is carried by the valve. A bowed condition will result in unequal strain on the threads and, in time, result in a leak that can only be checked by replacing the valve, pipes, or both.

Globe valves should be set with the stem in a horizontal position when possible. Gate valves should be set with the stem in a vertical upward position, or at a 45° angle so scale and sediment will collect on the bottom.

See also: DRAINS; TOILET.

Three Easy-to-build Fence Designs

Once you have determined exactly what your fence needs are, and checked your town's regulations regarding fence size, you can begin construction on these simple but beautiful fences

FENCES ARE erected on residential properties for safety, convenience or decorative reasons. Some of the main purposes are to prevent other people or their pets from encroaching on the property owner's private domain, to keep ones own children and pets confined, or both. If the fence is made higher than eye level, the added objective may be to ensure privacy by blocking the view of neighbors or of passersby on the street, or to help muffle street sounds.

To these time-honored convenience reasons also add: to protect a garden area, particularly a vegetable garden, from the ravages of children, dogs, rabbits and other domestic or wild trespassers; to provide a wind baffle to protect a terrace, patio or other outdoor living area from unwanted winds; or conversely, by strategic orientation of the fence in relation to the prevailing wind, to divert cooling breezes into the same types of outdoor living areas.

Safety considerations that dictate the erection of fences most often relate to the protection of childern, pets and plants. A fenced-in play area for very young children relieves a mother of minute-to-minute supervision because the tots are confined to a safe area and because they are safe from the harassment of wandering dogs. A fence around a vegetable patch not only protects the plants, but keeps small children from spray-contaminated crops. In many areas, fences around swimming pools are required by law; even if your local regulations do not prescribe such mandatory fencing, it should be added anyway to keep wandering children from falling into the pool and to keep the poolside area free of contamination by roaming animals.

Fences are sometimes erected even when there are no compelling safety or convenience considerations just to add decorative touches to the property. A fence along the sidewalk or roadside can add dramatic impact to the home and law just as a picture frame can enhance a painting. Just be sure to choose a fence design having proper empathy with the basic styling of your home so that it adds to, rather than detracts from the overall effect. In the garden a short fence that actually encloses nothing may be used as a support for climbing roses or other plants, or to serve as a contrasting textural background for other plantings. The same or separate fences may also be used to hide such necessary eyesores as a wood pile, compost heap or garbage cans.

Before you erect any kind of fence, check your town ordinances for any regulations concerning the heights and types of fences that may legally be used in your residential area. Also make some effort to determine whether your intended fence will be accepted by neighbors as a contribution to neighborhood aesthetics, or at least be gracefully tolerated because it does not detract from the appearance of the neighborhood. In some residential areas fences are taken very much for granted. Where lots are small, and houses are close together, erecting a fence may be the only practical way to ensure mutual privacy. In an area where the lots are an acre or larger in size, the prevailing community desire may be to keep fence construction at a minimum to maintain an open and uncluttered atmosphere. But even in such an area there may be no neighborhood objections if you leave the front yard unfenced and limit enclosures to the side and rear yards.

Above all, be very sure that your fence is of safe design. It must have no sharp components on which running children could fall or otherwise impale themselves, nor should it have projecting nails or other sharp hardware on which people might scratch themselves. In particular, avoid those precious little picket fences that are only a foot or so high; they keep nothing out or in, and they serve only to trip the unwary.

Attractive and highly functional fences may be made of many different kinds of materials including wood, metal, brick, poured or block concrete, stone or plastic. Wood is a favorite material because it is easy to cut and assemble, looks attractive if properly maintained, and is one of the least expensive fence materials. Three different general-purpose fence styles are discussed here. The construction costs can be as low as $20 per standard 5 x 8-foot unit if you do the work yourself.

If neither the town nor your neighbors object to your fence plans, consider what type of fence design would be most appropriate for your purposes. Then decide what type of wood would be best and within your budget. Woods suitable for fencing include: Douglas fir, Engelmann spruce, Idaho white pine, lodgepole pine, cedar, sugar pine, ponderosa pine, Sitka spruce, western hemlock, western larch and white fir. All of these woods possess three desirable properties: durability, straightness and workability. Posts and framing should probably be of *standard* or *construction* grades. Usable board grades include *commons* if you want a knotty appearance, or *select* for clearer effects.

While you await delivery of the lumber, go over your property carefully to make certain that you really know where your property lines run. Anticipate any problems you may encounter, such as erecting posts where bedrock is close to the ground surface. If you have decided to cut down on materials costs by by-passing such rot-resistant post woods as heartwood of cedar, or other woods pressure treated with preservatives, shop around for wood preservative materials you can apply to the lower ends of the posts yourself. Your local lumber dealer can probably advise what type of wood preservative is most suitable for soil conditions in your area.

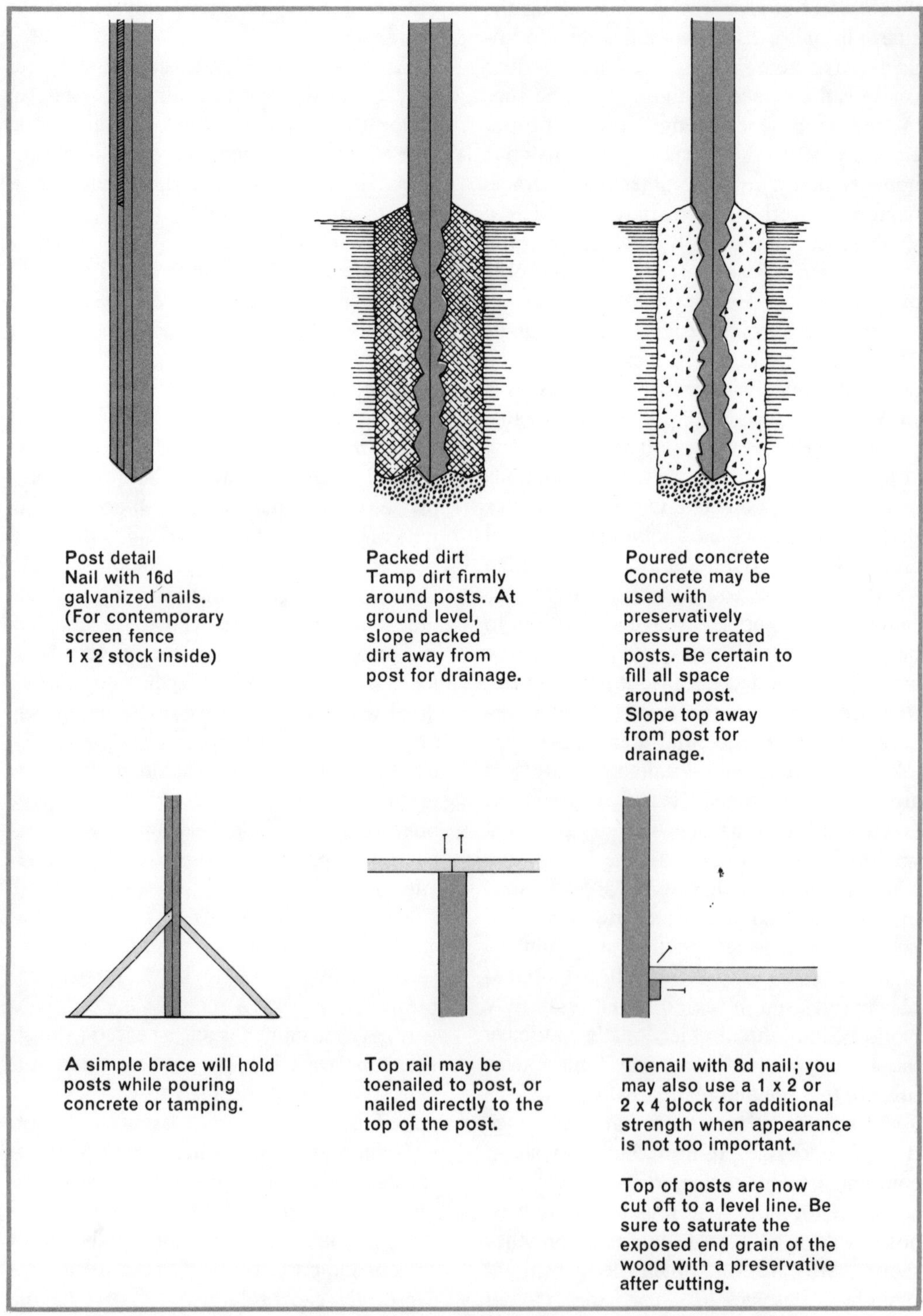

Post detail
Nail with 16d galvanized nails.
(For contemporary screen fence 1 x 2 stock inside)
Packed dirt
Tamp dirt firmly around posts. At ground level, slope packed dirt away from post for drainage.
Poured concrete
Concrete may be used with preservatively pressure treated posts. Be certain to fill all space around post. Slope top away from post for drainage.
A simple brace will hold posts while pouring concrete or tamping.
Top rail may be toenailed to post, or nailed directly to the top of the post.
Toenail with 8d nail; you may also use a 1 x 2 or 2 x 4 block for additional strength when appearance is not too important.
Top of posts are now cut off to a level line. Be sure to saturate the exposed end grain of the wood with a preservative after cutting.

Diagram shows variety of ways to sink and secure fence posts. If you plan to dig the holes and wait to sink the posts, be sure to cover the holes to avoid mishaps.

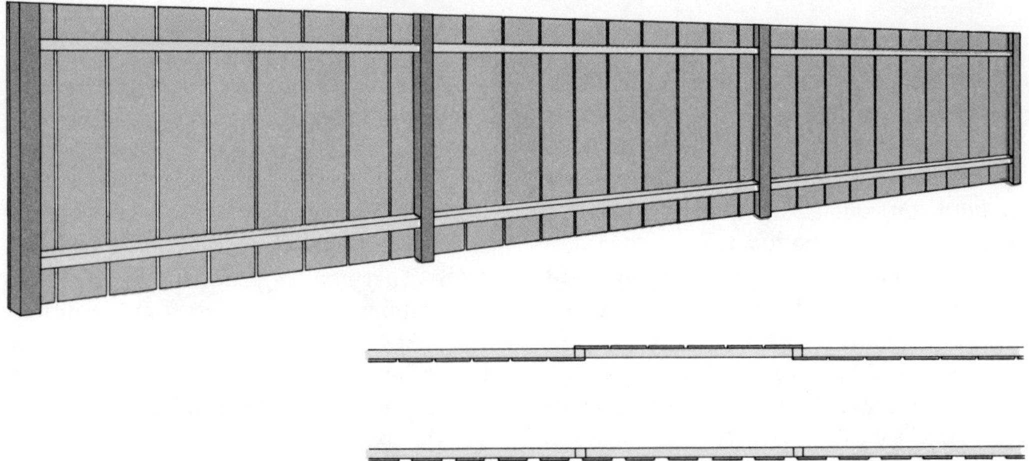

This board fence is probably the easiest of the three to build because the boarding is simply nailed to the top and bottom rails. You can add a dramatic affect by alternating the boards from one side to the other as shown in top diagram.

Use strong cord to lay out the fence line, locate the post holes (normally 4′ or 8′ apart), and dig the holes which should be about three feet deep. If the fence is to be higher than five feet, increase the underground section of each post proportionately to ensure stability. Buy or rent a post hole digger if there are many holes to be dug; the digger resembles two ordinary long-handled shovels joined face to face by means of a hinge. If the posts are not to be put into the holes immediately, cover the holes so that no one will be injured.

Drop the posts into the holes and use scrap wood braces to hold them erect and plumb. Use a carpenter's level to make sure they are plumb, and sight along the tops to see that the line of posts is straight. Do not worry if the tops are not all exactly the same distance above the ground (this could happen if a stone prevents planting a post as deep as the others). You can quickly top the longer poles with a hand saw after the boarding has been added.

The quickest and easiest way to set the poles is to tamp dirt into the spaces around the posts, using a metal or wood tamper. After you have pounded in all the dirt possible, add a little more to make a mound around the base of the post to shed rainwater away from the post. If the soil is structurally too loose to hold the posts firmly, fill the holes with poured concrete, making sure that all spaces are filled. It is best to use wood pressure treated with preservatives. Slope the concrete at the top to divert water from the post.

To further stabilize the posts, immediately add the top rails which may be toenailed between the posts, or in some cases nailed directly to the tops of the posts, depending on the type of fence to be made. In like manner, toenail the bottom rail to the posts using eight penny galvanized nails. These rails can be additionally supported by the addition of 1 x 2-inch or 2 x 4-inch block nailed to the posts, just under the rail ends.

Conventional solid, square posts measuring 4 x 4 inches are used for the board fence and for the horizontal siding fence to be discussed. The contemporary screen fence posts are made up of pairs of 2 x 4 components separated by three-foot lengths of 2 x 4 stock at the lower ends, to form slots into which the horizontal members can be added. To make the posts, nail the two outer members to the inner member using 16 penny galvanized nails.

Board fence. This traditionally styled

fence is the easiest of the three to build because the boarding is simply nailed to the top and bottom rails. If the fence is much over five feet high, it would be wise to add a third horizontal rail in the middle, between the top and bottom rails.

The surface boarding can be any width of one-inch thick board, spaced an inch apart. To make a standard height fence, use boards about five feet long. Note that you do not have to put all the boarding on the same side of the fence. For a bolder visual effect, alternate the boarding from one side of the fence to the other from one section to the next.

Horizontal siding fence. This type of fence is especially appropriate if your home is finished with siding. For example, if you use a ¾-inch beveled siding for the fence, to match the house siding, you can create a long, luxurious look that could be the envy of your neighborhood. This fence features an optional top cap made of 1 x 6-inch boarding. When installing the boarding, use a one inch overlap whether you use beveled or standard boards.

If the fence is to be a property divider, your neighbor may be interested in a joint project to make it a double-beveled fence which has the same finished look on both sides. This type of fence has many other applications, other than as a property line fence. It can serve as a connector between the garage and house, as an exterior space divider, or as a screen to hide garbage cans and the like.

Contemporary screen fence. The construction of the special fence posts needed for this fence has already been described. To make the horizontal strips rip 1⅝-inch wide strips from larger boards or buy the 1 x 2 inch stock from the lumber company. Treat these strips with preservative and paint before you assemble them, to make the job much easier.

Start assembly by nailing 8-foot bottom rails (2 x 2 inch) between the posts. Now stack the three different lengths of 1 x 2 inch

Horizontal siding fence is especially appropriate if your home is siding-finished. Bottom two drawings show fence side view with optional caps made of 1 x 6-inch boarding.

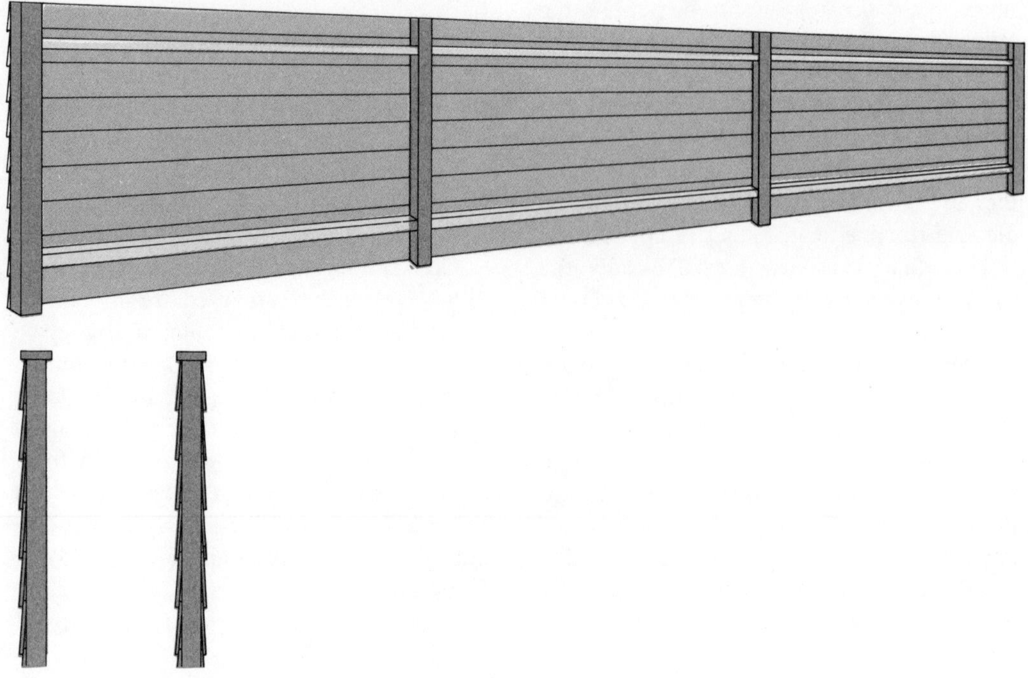

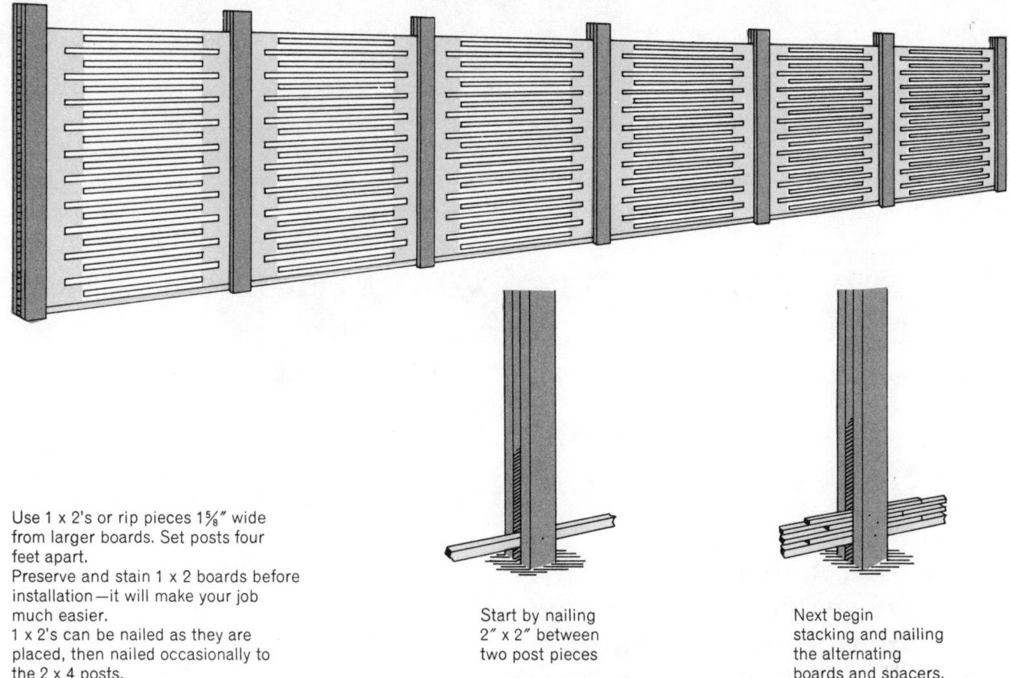

Use 1 x 2's or rip pieces 1⅝″ wide from larger boards. Set posts four feet apart.
Preserve and stain 1 x 2 boards before installation—it will make your job much easier.
1 x 2's can be nailed as they are placed, then nailed occasionally to the 2 x 4 posts.

Start by nailing 2″ x 2″ between two post pieces

Next begin stacking and nailing the alternating boards and spacers.

stock in the proper sequences to form the indicated pattern. Note that the two different length shorter pieces of stock are used as fillers between the full length strips to create the alternating short and long open spaces.

Place an 8-foot length between the post pairs, atop the rail. Next insert a 15⅝-inch strip into each post slot so that it projects the same amount on both sides of the post. Now add another 8-foot length, then the shorter spacer (9⅝-inches long). The pattern is thus built up of the following sequence repeated a number of times: long, medium, long, short.

Note that there is no "front" or "back" to this fence since both sides have the same finished look.

There is only one way you could go wrong when building this fence, and that has to do with spacing the posts. If you are to use 8-foot lengths for the longest strips, without wasting lumber, the posts must be placed 8 feet apart *on center*. Otherwise the long strips will not reach from the center of one post to the center of the other. When making the two other types of fencing you can similarly space the posts 8 feet apart on center, and cut a few inches off each rail. This might be safer than trying to make the space *between* each pair of posts exactly 8 feet to accept the stock length uncut.

▲ Spacing of posts is the trickiest part of building the contemporary screen fence, one of the more attractive wood designs. If you are using eight-foot lengths for the longest strips, you must place posts eight feet apart on center, otherwise strips will not reach.

▼ One of the nicest features of the contemporary fence is there is no front and back. And being identical, both sides are attractive.

One final tip: Maintain your fence by either painting or otherwise weatherproofing it periodically to preserve its beauty as long as possible.

See also: BRICKWORK; CONCRETE.

Changing oil filter requires a special wrench, but it is not expensive.

How to Change Your Car's Filters

Get started as a weekend mechanic by servicing the devices that clean the air, fuel and oil in your car

SERVICING YOUR CAR'S FILTERS is an excellent beginner's job for anyone interested in becoming a weekend mechanic.

Filter service is simple—no complicated disassembly required.

It is also the most frequently needed service on a car. Oil filters are normally replaced three or four times a year, air filters once a year and gasoline filters once a year.

Name brand filters you can trust are available at discount prices (40 percent off list) in auto supply stores and the auto departments of discount houses.

The leading brands are: Purolator, AC, Fram and Wix. Stick to a name brand when buying filters. A poorly made filter is no bargain at any price.

Oil filter replacement. For this job you need a filter wrench (an inexpensive tool) and jacking capability.

Jacking capability is necessary to raise the front of the car several inches off the ground so you can get in underneath.

Although the oil filter may be accessible from the top of the engine compartment, the filter is replaced as part of an oil change. The engine oil drain plug is underneath and you've got to get underneath to remove it.

The car's bumper jack will raise the car, but it is hardly safe enough. The car should be supported on safety stands.

If the car's bumper jack is so inadequate that it will not raise the car high enough to slip the safety stands under the front suspension's lower control arms, then you need a better jack (there is no bumper jack worth talking about anyway, so you really should have something better).

An inexpensive choice is a scissors jack. This can be slipped under the front crossmember and will raise the frame (and carry the suspension with it) high enough to get the safety stands in position.

For two to three times the price of a scissors jack you can get a trolley jack, which is similar to the scissors jack but has a tricyclic stand, making it very easy to position and safer to use.

The easiest to use jacks are the hydraulic types. The inexpensive hydraulic jacks (about the price of a scissors jack) have very limited use, because they cannot get under most parts in the car's underbody (typical jack of this type is nine inches high when shaft is down to bottom).

The best choice is the hydraulic floor jack, which is the type you see in most professional shops. It can get under anything, and it is very easy to use. It was once far too expensive for the weekend mechanic, but imported units are now available at moderate prices. The 1½-ton unit is all you need for even a full-size car, and a 1- or 1¼-ton is adequate for American compacts.

Still another option is the ramp. A pair of ramps, which the car is driven onto, will raise the car a foot to a foot and a half, depending on the model purchased. Ramps are relatively inexpensive; so shop around for quality, looking for such features as non-skid designs.

Ramps have the advantage of requiring no additional support. Even with a quality hydraulic floor jack, the car must be supported with safety stands.

You will also need a drain pan (which you can make out of a flattish container of at least one-gallon capacity; or you can use an inexpensive plastic wash basin). The drain pan must be large enough to hold the oil you will drain from the engine and most engines have a five-quart capacity. However, only four quarts at most will come out when you pull the drain plug.

With the car safely raised, remove the drain plug and allow the engine oil to drain out. For best results, the oil should be hot (it takes a fifteen to twenty mile drive to heat up the oil).

After the oil has finished pouring out of the drain hole, the oil filter can be removed. The wrench, as illustrated, wraps around the filter body and you just apply counterclockwise pressure.

Before installing the new filter, lubricate the filter's rubber gasket with clean engine oil.

Hand tighten the filter—do not use the wrench.

Cartridge filters. Some foreign cars have replaceable cartridge filters (American cars dropped this design many years ago in favor of the easy-to-install and replace spin-on unit).

With the replaceable catridge type, you must clean the container to remove sludge. Use a general purpose automobile solvent (such as the type used to clean carburetors).

The through-bolt that holds the container has one or more sealing O-rings on it, and these should be checked for a tight fit, and replaced at least every fourth oil change.

The filter container seals against a rubber gasket, which should be replaced every time the element is changed.

Air filter replacement. On most cars, there is nothing simpler than replacing an air filter element. A wing nut holds the filter cover; just remove it, pull out the old element and install the new. Some cars have spring clips to hold the cover, but that doesn't really make things any more difficult.

On some cars, however, the filter is cleaned, not replaced. Most Volkswagens have oil bath, wire mesh air cleaners, and many GM products have polyurethane foam filters.

Servicing oil bath. Remove the entire air filter assembly. Undo the wing nut that holds the wire mesh and remove it.

Inside you will see the oil reservoir. Dump out the old oil, clean the reservoir with solvent and refill to the level mark with clean engine oil. Dunk the wire mesh assembly in solvent, agitate, remove, and allow to air dry.

Refit the reservoir assembly, then bolt the wire mesh assembly to it.

Servicing polyurethane foam. Gently remove the foam from its metal cage, soak in solvent and gently squeeze dry (do not wring). Allow to air dry and dunk in clean engine oil. Gently squeeze out the excess oil and refit to the cage.

Replacing gasoline filter. There are three popular gasoline filters used in recent years: one is an element type on the fuel pump;

a second is in the carburetor fuel inlet boss; and the third (and most popular) is in the fuel line between pump and carburetor.

The fuel pump type is replaced by simply unscrewing the cover, lifting out the element, installing a new one and refitting the cover.

The type in the carburetor fuel inlet boss requires undoing the fuel line fitting. Pull the fuel line out of the carburetor inlet boss and inside you'll find the tiny element, made of sintered bronze or pleated paper. You will also find a filter positioning spring.

This type of filter is best discarded completely. If it is sintered bronze, it has poor filtering ability and will pass dirt particles 10 times larger than a good paper filter. If it is paper, it's so small it will clog in only a few thousand miles and the constant replacement is a nuisance.

The discarding of the carburetor boss filter doesn't mean you have to leave your fuel system unprotected. You can install an in-the-line gasoline filter, which will last a year because it is so much larger. Many cars are factory equipped with this type, but it does cost more than the smaller one, and Detroit has its penny-pinchers.

In-line gasoline filters. This type of filter is available in kit form, for installation on cars with no fuel filtration or with the inadequate carburetor boss type.

The kit differs from the replacement filter only in the inclusion of two short hoses. The boxes for both contain four spring clamps.

To replace the filter on a car so equipped, remove the clamps. The original equipment clamps are a pry-off type that you discard. Pull the hoses from the filter necks, and discard the filter.

Replacing most air filters is simple. Take off the cover, lift it out and put in a new element.

To service oil bath air cleaner, remove cover, which contains wire mesh. Clean wire mesh in solvent and allow it to air dry.

Fill oil bath reservoir to the mark with clean engine oil.

Polyurethane foam filter is removed from cage for service. Dunk it in carburetor solvent, agitate and gently squeeze. Allow to air dry.

Oil polyurethane foam with clean engine oil.

Squeeze out excess oil (gently) from polyurethane foam element and refit to cage.

➤ *Pump-type gas filter is replaced by removing cover, taking out old element and installing new one.*

➤ *This is a sintered bronze filter in carburetor boss, accessible after removing fuel line (on some cars, filter is accessible after removing plug in carb side).*

➤ *Installing in-line gasoline filter begins with disconnection of fuel line at carburetor.*

Fit a spring clamp onto each hose. This can be done by spreading the tangs of the clamps with a pair of ordinary pliers, but it isn't easy. By filing a notch in the center of the top edge of each jaw, you will be able to hold the tangs for easy spreading. Or you can purchase a pair of hose clamp pliers, which are designed for the purpose. Such pliers are available in combination forms with tubing cutters, and if you are planning to install a kit, they are a worthwhile purchase.

Then cut out six-inch section of fuel line with tube cutter. Type used in illustration is combination tube cutter and hose clamp pliers.

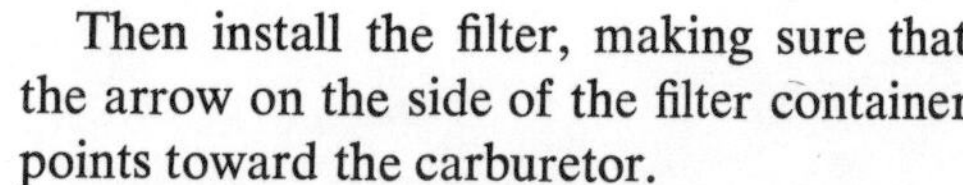

Then install the filter, making sure that the arrow on the side of the filter container points toward the carburetor.

With the hoses firmly in place spread the tangs of the clamps and move the clamps to positions on the hoses over the filter necks.

Installing the kit. The kit takes about 15 minutes to install and requires a tubing cutter, such as the type that is built into some hose clamp pliers.

Find a six-inch section of fuel line between pump and carburetor that is reasonably straight and accessible, and with the tubing cutter, chop it out. You may find it easier to brace the fuel line by disconnecting it at the carb and holding it.

Fit a short hose on to the necks of the filter and secure with a spring clamp.

Position the entire assembly in the gap in the fuel line and secure with the remaining clamps. (Slip the clamps onto the line before you put the hose on; that's the easy way.)

After you have changed oil and a few filters, you will begin to feel more comfortable about working on a car, and can tackle other jobs. P.W.

See also: ENGINE; TUNE-UP, ENGINE.

Fit short hoses and secure with spring clamps furnished with kit.

The finished job. Run engine and check for leaks.

How to Remove Stains from Floors

Whether the floor is tile, wood, cork or stone, there's a method to remove stains. This guide tells you what that method is

THE METHOD RECOMMENDED FOR removal of a stain may be effective on the stain but may be injurious to the floor. For instance, most solvents dissolve asphalt tile, acids etch marble and terrazzo, and strong alkalis destroy linoleum and cork and damage the grouting in ceramic tile. The accompanying chart lists common stains, and numbered references are made to the list of removal methods for specific stains. A method specifically prescribed for one type of floor should not be tried on another type floor because it will damage the floor.

Try the methods in sequence as they are listed in the three columns of the chart progressing to the next proposed method only if the first one listed does not work. For example: In removing ink from an asphalt tile floor, try (1) synthetic liquid detergent and warm water first and if this will not work, then try (16) ink remover; if this won't work, try (4) oxalic acid in water.

Make a small test first to determine if a

Those "impossible" floor stains can be removed, when you know what to use.

particular method will work. Begin at the outer edges and work toward the middle to prevent the spread of the stain.

Apply a poultice about one-half inch thick. Poultices, in drying, absorb moisture that has penetrated the stain and draws the stain out with the moisture.

See also: SPOT REMOVAL.

STAIN REMOVAL CHART

Stain	Resilient Tile	Wood or Cork	Nonresilient Floors
Alcoholic Beverages	1, 10, 4	1, 10, 4	1, 10, 5
Blood	11, 12	11, 12	11, 32
Candy	1 and 3	1 and 3	33
Chocolate	6	6	6
Coffee	7, 8, 9	7, 34, 9	7, 34, 9
Dyes	13, 14, 9	13, 14, 9	13, 5, 9
Fruit	2, 4	2, 4	2 and 15
Grease or Oil	1	29	30
Ink	1, 16, 4, 17	1, 16, 4, 17	1, 21
Iodine	18, 19, 20	18, 19, 20	18, 19, 20
Lipstick	1 and 3, 4	1 and 3, 4	1 and 3, 5
Paint	1 and 3	4	31
Rust	22	22	22
Soft Drinks	4	4	5
Soot	23, 1 and 3	23, 1 and 3	23, 1 and 3
Tar	24, 25, 26	24, 25, 26	24, 25, 26
Tobacco	27, 5, 9	25, 5, 9	27, 5, 9, 28
Urine	9, 5	9, 5	9, 5
Varsol	35	35	35

STAIN REMOVAL METHOD

Method	Stain
1. Synthetic liquid detergent and warm water	Alcoholic beverages, candy, grease or oil, ink, lipstick, paint, soot
2. Synthetic powdered detergent and warm water	Fruit
3. Grade 00 steel wool	
*4. Tablespoon of oxalic acid in pint of water	Alcoholic beverages, fruit, ink, lipstick, soft drinks, paint
*5. Absorbent cloth soaked in hydrogen peroxide laid directly over stain; an ammonia-saturated cloth on top of this	Alcoholic beverages, dyes, lipstick, soft drinks, tobacco, urine
*6. Use ammoniated alcohol: 9 parts denatured alcohol and one part stronger ammonia (26%)	Chocolate

STAIN REMOVAL METHOD (Cont.)

Method	Stain
7. Saturate an absorbent cloth with solution of one part glycerin and three parts water and lay over spot	Coffee
*8. Apply a poultice made of one part chlorinated lime and three parts washing soda and calcium carbonate. Allow to stand until dry. *Do not use on linoleum.* Use poultice of hydrogen peroxide and whiting	Coffee
9. Poultice of abrasive powder and hot water	Coffee, dyes, tobacco, urine
*10. Follow with denatured alcohol if necessary	Alcoholic beverages
11. Try cold clear water first, then add a few drops of ammonia	Blood
*12. For old stains try 2 ounces salt and 2 drams formic acid in pint of water. Soak stain for an hour or so, then rinse and blot up with absorbent cloth	Blood
*13. Try a chlorine bleaching agent	Dyes
*14. Apply solution of one tablespoon permanganate of potash to pint of water. When dry apply solution of one tablespoon oxalic acid to pint of water.	Dyes
15. If rough spot results rub with powdered pumice stone under a block of wood	Fruit
16. Ink remover	Ink
17. If a brown stain remains, treat as a rust stain	Ink
*18. Apply ammonia	Iodine
*19. If stain is old or deep, apply ammonia-saturated cloth	Iodine
*20. Poultice of denatured alcohol and calcium carbonate	Iodine
*21. Poultice of two tablespoons sodium perborate in pint of water mixed into a paste of calcium carbonate	Ink
22. Poultice of calcium carbonate mixed with one part sodium citrate crystals to six parts water added to an equal portion of glycerine. Allow to stand 2 or 3 days	Rust
23. Cover with salt or rub in calcium carbonate and rub off. Wash with synthetic detergent and water	Soot
24. Poultice of synthetic powdered detergent and whiting	Road tar
25. Stoddard solvent on any floor *except* asphalt and rubber	Roofing tar
26. Freeze to brittleness with dry ice. Scrape off	Roofing tar
27. Lemon juice in water	Tobacco
28. Equal parts alcohol and glycerine	Tobacco
29. Pour kerosene on spot. Soak for 5 minutes. Wipe dry with clean cloth. Wash with synthetic liquid detergent and water	Paint
30. Pour Stoddard solvent on spot. Rub with clean, soft cloth	Paint
31. One pound synthetic powdered detergent in one gallon water. Scrub and rinse with clear water	Paint
32. Wet spot with lukewarm water and sprinkle with powdered malt. Let stand an hour and rinse	Blood
33. Use synthetic scrubbing pad and synthetic detergent	Candy
*34. Poultice of hydrogen peroxide and calcium carbonate	Coffee
35. Poultice of synthetic powdered detergent	Varsol

PRECAUTIONS: Wear rubber gloves when working with these materials. Always pour acids into water. Wear face shield to protect eyes and face against splashing fluids. Wear chemical resistant gloves when working with materials marked with an asterisk(*).

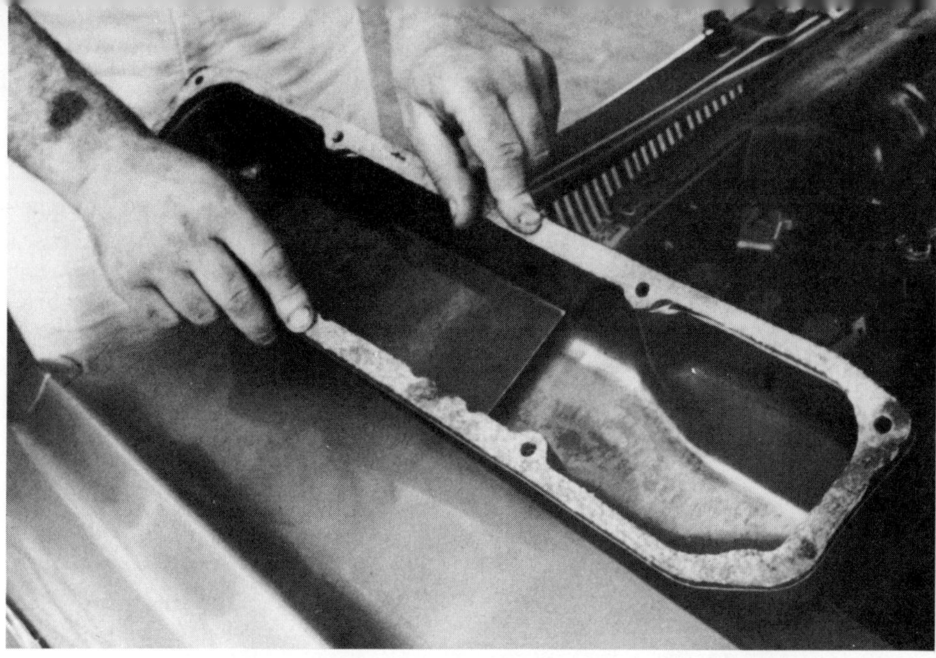

Cut Down on Gasket Replacements

Faulty gaskets are very rare. Correct application cuts down on replacement and gives you a cleaner engine and better gas mileage

MANY GASKETS, particularly engine cylinder head gaskets, "blow." Maybe it has happened to you, and maybe you thought the fault lay in the quality or construction of the gasket. Actually, gaskets usually blow because of incorrect application. It is the way you do or do not prepare the surfaces to be sealed together that counts, and counts heavily. The gasoline mileage you get, the engine's cooling efficiency, compression, lubrication, silencing of the exhaust, tightness of the rear axle housing and other performance factors depend on the ability of gaskets to seal well; to maintain pressure; and to keep out dirt and water. The oil, water or fuel that drips on your garage floor overnight may indicate leaky gaskets. The leakage may be worse when the car is running because parts get hot, metal expands and the gasket-packed joints widen, creating greater leakage. If you want to track down guilty gaskets, first inspect the car's engine carefully. If you see rusty and gooey-looking seepage around the cylinder block and head joint, your engine needs a new head gasket. The same evidence around the crankcase and oil pan joints, the water inlet elbow flange and head, the fuel pump connection to crankcase, the front end chain housing cover, and the water pump flange and manifolds is a sign that gasket trouble has arrived.

It is always a good rule to install a new gasket every time a joint is opened. The old gasket might "look good" but it has done its job even if it has not "blown," so toss it out and use a new one. There is always the temptation to use the old cylinder head gasket, for example, especially if it comes off clean, stays flat and has that nice shiny copper color. But you cannot reseal the joint adequately with the old gasket. In the first place, the joining surfaces between the cylinder block and head, while "milled" to substantially smooth surfaces, are never completely smooth. Under a microscope, you see a lot of hills and valleys. When the head is bolted down tightly, the copper of the gasket (usually made of asbestos between two thin layers of copper or steel) squeezes into the tiny imperfections of the metal and with the asbestos filler makes a tight seal against compression and coolant losses. Obviously, this compression of the gasket flattens and conforms it to irregularities of the block and head, so that if the head is later removed, it is practically impossible to replace the gasket (which has lost much of its compressibility) and get a perfect seal against all the little irregularities again.

Also, the old gasket may be bent while removing it so that the asbestos filler breaks when the gasket is straightened for reuse—and the gasket is liable to burn through at this weak spot and lose its effective seal.

Cylinder head gaskets. You can find out whether you have a broken and leaky head gasket by checking these points. If the coolant boils at normal atmospheric temperatures and your radiator takes a lot of water, it could indicate a broken gasket. When you make a cylinder compression test and find two adjacent cylinders reading much lower than the others, the gasket may have blown at the spot between the two cylinders. Sometimes you can see bubbles in the top of the radiator, which can be from a blown gasket. An inexpensive air hose adapter is available that threads into the spark plug hole. You can use it to find out whether the head gasket is faulty and allowing leakage into the coolant. To use it,

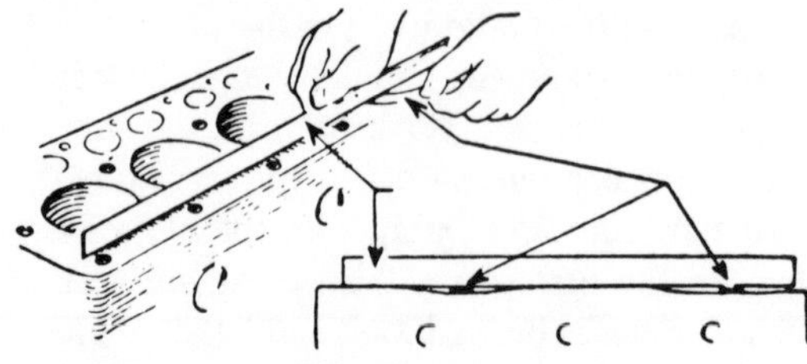

Checking block with a straightedge and a feeler gauge. Same procedure can be used for cylinder head gasket surface.

fill the radiator to the top with coolant, run the car until it reaches normal operating temperature, then remove the spark plugs and test each cylinder in this way. Take off the distributor cap so you can watch the rotor. Turn the engine slowly (with fan belt or by jacking up one rear wheel with the transmission in gear), until the rotor is lined up with one of the cap electrodes if the cap were in place. The valves of that cylinder will then be closed. Screw the tester into the spark plug hole of that cylinder and from a hand pump or air supply, apply air to the tester valve. If there is gasket leakage you can see or hear the bubbles at the radiator neck with the filler cap off to allow you to look in.

To replace this gasket, you will have to strip the engine of such parts as the air cleaner, carburetor, spark plugs and wiring harness, perhaps the oil filter bracket, the hose connection at the water inlet elbow and other parts depending on the make and type of engine. Then you take out the head bolts or loosen the nuts on the block studs so you can lift off the head. But before you loosen the nuts and bolts, let the engine cool to the surrounding temperature of the atmosphere or room.

Next, clean the block and cylinder head of all carbon deposits by scraping, wire brushing, and with a metal parts cleaner. You can use an ordinary hand tire pump to blow out any foreign matter on the piston heads, bolt holes and water passages. Also, blow out the passages inside the cylinder head to prevent any carbon particles from dropping on the new gasket (such particles can form pockets in the gasket and cause leakage). With the block and head surfaces clean, check the surfaces with a straightedge for indications of distortion or warping.

Since the cylinder head gets hotter than the block, warpage is more likely to occur in the head. If you run into such a condition, it is best to have an automotive

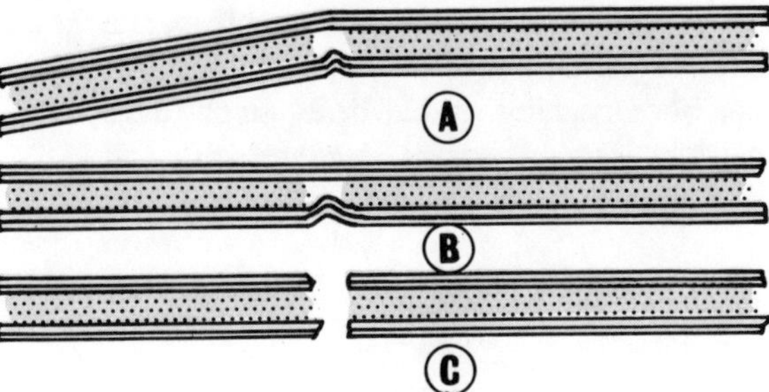

If a cylinder head gasket of the copper asbestos type is bent, the asbestos filler may break (A). If the gasket is then straightened (B), it may look all right, but later burn through and "blow" at the break in the asbestos (C).

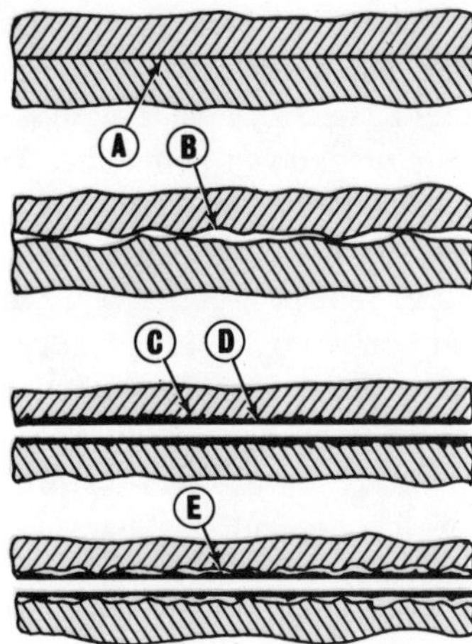

Instead of an unobtainable perfect joint (A) between the machined surfaces of a cylinder head and engine block, there is a series of microscopic hills and valleys (B). Note how the metal of the gasket (C) fills the irregularities of the block and head, making a tight joint. (D) is the asbestos filler. After a head gasket has been compressed, it is almost impossible to seal the irregular surfaces (E) again.

machine shop true the surface of the head on a surface grinder. This removal of metal, however, should be held to a minimum as it increases compression ratio—perhaps more than is good for the engine. On old engines, especially, if the cylinder has been re-machined more than once, it is wise to replace the head with a new one.

Make a careful inspection of the cylinder head studs in the block (or the bolt holes, if the head is held down with bolts). If you find there is a buildup of metal around the studs or bolt holes, you can use a chamfering tool to trim enough off so the studs or bolts can be firmly tightened with clearance for the gasket. But make sure you do not remove too much metal with the chamfering tool, particularly where a stud is located very close to two cylinders (removing too much metal in such places may cause gasket to blow). Some mechanics prefer to dress the block with a large file, which also removes the rough spots.

Now check the new gasket for correct fit on the cylinder block. Some gaskets are marked "Top," "Front" or "Up." Check for these markings before installing and follow the directions they indicate. All of the water holes and bolt holes should tally with those in the block. On some engines like the older 6-cylinder Ford, be sure that the gasket is positioned with the cut-off corner at the left front corner of the cylinder block; otherwise water will leak externally at the left rear corner of the engine between the cylinder head and block. Never enlarge any of the water passage holes in the gasket, as the rear cylinders might overheat. Watch out for a bent gasket. The method of applying the gasket depends on the type of gasket material. The steel and the asbestos head gaskets usually have a sealing coat put on them by the gasket manufacturer. This clear coating ordinarily does not require any additional gasket cements. But if this type of gasket does not have a coating you can use a non-hardening gasket compound. This is a liquid material applied with a brush which changes in a few seconds to a paste. It produces a non-drying elastic, adhesive, heat-resisting seal. You can also use it with copper asbestos gaskets.

If you wonder why both steel and copper

asbestos gaskets are used, each has certain advantages. For example, where high octane fuel is used and detonation is likely, steel resists breakdown better than copper. But this advantage is offset to some extent by the superior heat conductivity of copper. Copper also makes a better seal with less likelihood of compression leakage that might cause burning of the gasket back of the edge of the cylinder opening. Steel has a natural tendency to corrode when exposed to the coolant at water holes or where the gasket itself is exposed to the coolant. Some steel gaskets are made with copper grommets at the water holes. Remember, however, that gaskets with copper ferrules must never be used with aluminum heads.

Some cars use an embossed type of steel cylinder head gasket. This is said to provide an even and uninterrupted flow of heat between the cylinder head and engine block. The design and formation of the embossing makes the flow of metal under compression even, producing a good seal.

If you do not want to blow your new gasket, better check for clearance of the new gasket around the cylinder bores. The engine may have been rebored and fitted with oversize pistons. In this case, the edge of the metal around the gasket might be very close to, or even slightly overlap, the cylinder bore openings. Thus, on the upstroke, the pistons might strike the head of the gasket, causing early gasket failure or blowout. The minimum clearance from the edge of the gasket to the edge of the cylinder bore opening should be $\frac{1}{32}$-inch. This permits correct gasket compression and prevents direct flame contact burn-out. If

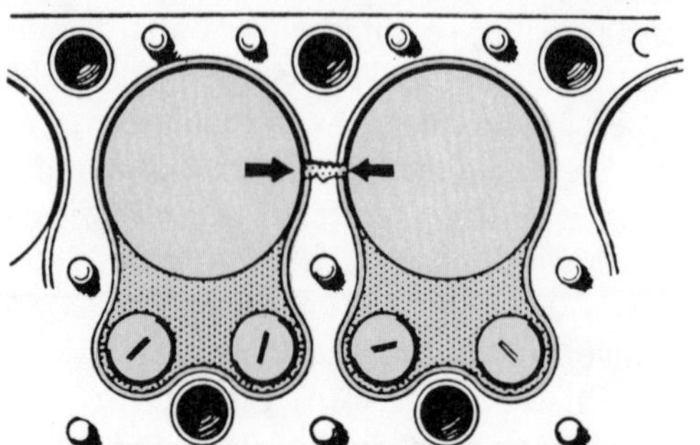

Occasionally a cylinder head gasket breaks at a point between two adjacent cylinders, shown by the heavy arrows.

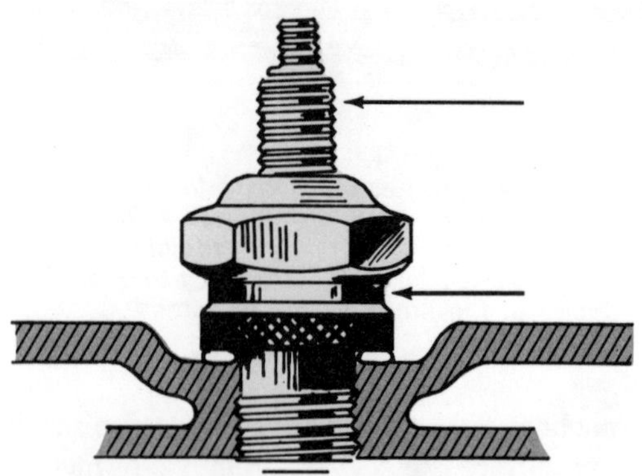

A handy tester to check for a blown gasket can be made by brazing a tire valve into a spark plug shell. You also can isolate a blown head gasket of the two-adjacent-cylinders type by compression testing. If you prefer the air pressure test, but have no brazing equipment, you can buy the equivalent of the plug shell and tire valve tool at auto supply stores.

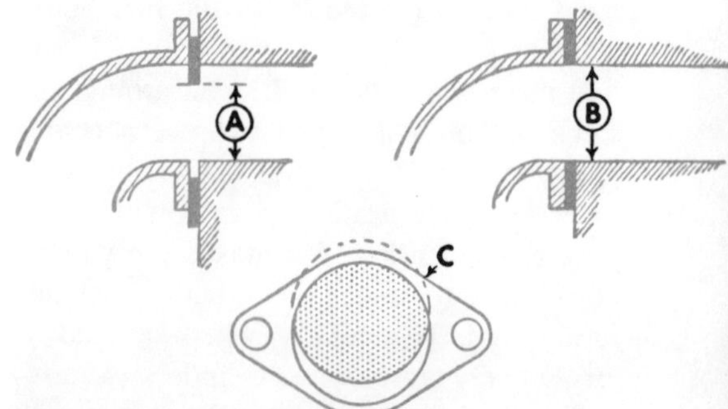

Intake and exhaust manifolds must have their gaskets in alignment; otherwise the port openings are reduced. Note the small opening (A) compared to what it should be (B). The effect of misalignment on port opening is shown at (C).

you find you cannot get this clearance, check the tops of the pistons for a number such as +.010 which indicates an oversize piston, and buy a gasket to match it.

Make a final check to make sure that the gasket is correctly centered. If the head is held by studs, this is easy. But if long cap screws or bolts are used, buy a couple of longer bolts, cut off the heads and screw these into a couple of holes at the end of the block. These will serve as pilots. After the head has been dropped and a half dozen or so of the head bolts inserted finger-tight, remove the pilot bolts with pliers.

You are now ready to tighten the head, which must be done with a torque wrench, to factory specifications.

After you have replaced the accessories you previously removed, run the engine for 15 or 20 minutes at a fast idle and then go over the head bolts on the cast-iron head again, once more tightening them about a quarter turn. On aluminum heads, the engine must first be cooled to room temperature before tightening the bolts down. You should tighten again after about 300 or 400 miles of operation, using the same recommended sequence.

▲ *Note that some of the bolt holes in this transmission oil pan have gasket residue. It must be cleaned out (also gasket surface and pan itself), before fitting a new gasket.*

Manifold gaskets. When you install intake and exhaust manifold gaskets, alignment is important. If the gasket does not line up with the port holes, the reduced port opening area cuts down on engine power and, in the case of the exhaust, might cause engine overheating. On manifold gaskets, the gaskets are positioned by the bolts holding the manifold on the head. On overhead-valve V-8 engines, tighten the bolts holding the intake manifold. If they are loose, air is pulled into the manifold, making a lean mixture, and also ruining the gasket.

Intake manifold gaskets are additionally important on some V-8 engines, where they seal off the valve tappet chamber. A poor gasket seal in such a situation could cause the engine to leak oil.

Other gaskets. Although the cylinder head and intake manifold gaskets involve a great deal of work and care, there are other gaskets that are more prone to failure. These include the rocker cover, oil pan, fuel pump, thermostat housing, timing chain cover, rear axle cover, and transmission pan.

There is nothing complicated about gasket replacement, but unless you do it correctly, you can find yourself with an expensive comeback. Clearly, a gasket is supposed to seal, and if it leaks, something is wrong.

To insure a leak-free seal, regardless of what gasket is being replaced, takes just a bit of care and know-how.

Start by making sure that if the bolts that hold the cover or part are of different lengths, you know exactly where they go, so you can refit them properly. A simple technique is to push them through a piece of cardboard in the pattern that they go on the engine or transmission.

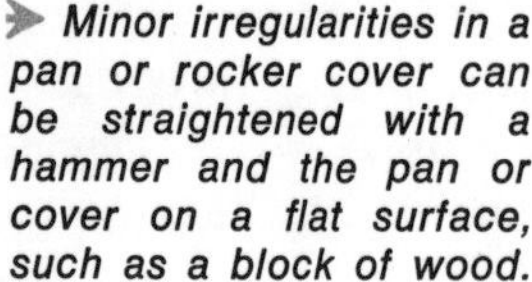

➤ Minor irregularities in a pan or rocker cover can be straightened with a hammer and the pan or cover on a flat surface, such as a block of wood.

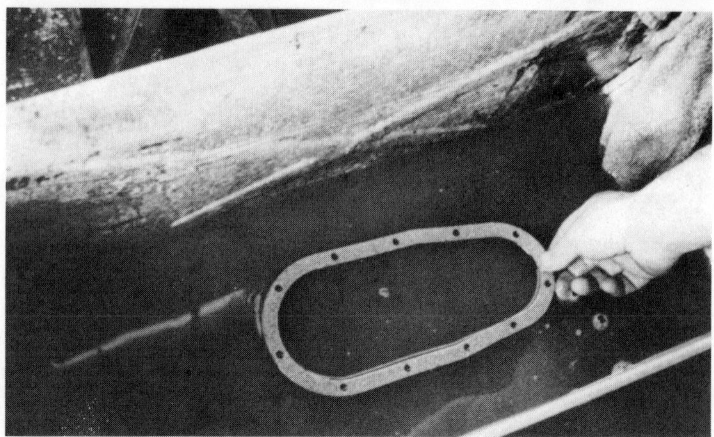

➤ If a cork gasket has shrunk, it can be soaked in warm water.

When you remove the cover, pan or part, scrape all gasket particles from both gasket surfaces, using a scraper. A screwdriver often will do the job, but it is a blunt instrument and you may gouge a gasket surface using it. This is particularly true of an aluminum part, such as a thermostat housing. Aluminum is quite soft and it does not take much to damage it.

On sheet metal parts with a narrow groove in the gasket surface, however, a thin screwdriver is about the only practical way to clean the groove, particularly if the gasket is cork or if a coating of sealant was applied.

Cleaning out gasket material from bolt holes is very important. Pieces of gasket material can prevent the bolt from seating properly. Remove large pieces with an awl and blow out small pieces with compressed air.

At this time, inspect the bolt holes. If any go through to water jacket or oil passage, the bolts will have to be coated with thread sealer when you reassemble.

Once the gasket surfaces are absolutely clean, you can fit the new gasket.

There are four common choices in gasket material for sealing fluids under low pressure: cork, composition cork, neoprene and treated paper.

Treated paper has little resiliency and does a relatively poor job of compensating for any warpage in parts. It should not be used except in emergencies when nothing else is available.

Cork has been a popular gasket material for many years. It does a fine job of compensating for irregularities in sealing surfaces, but it is somewhat brittle and it shrinks when stored in a dry place for some time.

Composition cork is a combination of cork and other fibers. It is less brittle than cork, less prone to shrinkage, and is almost as resilient.

Neoprene is the best material. It is the easiest to handle, does the best job of sealing, doesn't shrink and doesn't break. If you can get a particular gasket in neoprene, this should be your choice.

Unfortunately, you do not always have a choice. Some gaskets for certain cars are only available in cork, or composition cork, or perhaps just treated paper.

If a cork or composition cork gasket has shrunk, do not try to force it in place, or it will probably break. Soak it in warm water for fifteen minutes and it will stretch to properly cover the gasket surface.

If the old gasket was leaking badly, don't just install a new one. See if the gasket flange is distorted by lining up a straight edge against it.

A mildly-distorted flange can be straightened with a hammer, as illustrated, by holding the flange against a flat wooden surface. Do not try to straighten one that is badly cocked; replace the part.

Many pans and covers have retaining features for the gasket, such as cutouts for gasket tabs. With such designs, a sealant is frequently unnecessary.

If a sealant is necessary to hold the gasket in place, or to provide additional sealing for a hard-to-seal surface, only apply the sealant to the cover or pan, not to the engine or transmission. That pan might have to come off again some day, and if the someone who has to do the job is you, you won't want to scrape sealant and gasket off two surfaces.

Gasket shellac is a glue that will keep a gasket from shifting position during installation in a tight spot. It is not as good a sealant as the flexible setting type and should be avoided. It certainly is difficult to scrape off completely.

Never overtighten a gasket. Excessive tightening is the major cause of distortion of a cover or pan. If a leak won't stop with a new gasket, coating of sealant, and tightening to specifications—something is wrong, probably a warped pan or cover.

Do not leave out the bolt washers. Many pans and covers rely on the washers, which often are specially shaped, to distribute the bolt tension evenly and contribute to a good seal.

You can buy sheet cork and treated paper and make your own gaskets. This procedure is recommended for emergency use only. Gaskets are cheap, and although with care you could make one that is almost as good, you also might not.

On many cars, replacing the oil pan gasket is anything but easy. To avoid removing the pan, which requires jacking the engine well up off its mounts for clearance on many cars, you will be working in tight quarters with the oil pan hanging down just a few inches. Be sure you take the time to scrape off the old gasket completely, clean the side packing grooves and check the mating surfaces in the engine for any burrs, which can be smoothed with an oil stone if not deep. P.W.

See also: ENGINE; TUNE-UP, ENGINE.

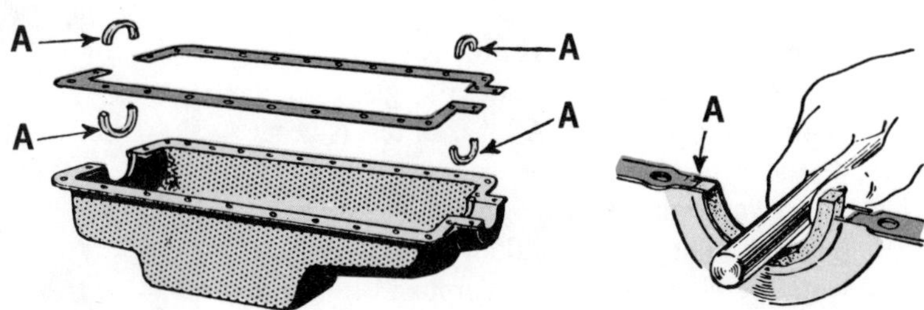

Engine oil pans usually have two cork gaskets. When they are replaced, the crankshaft oil seal packings (A) should also be replaced, as illustrated. The oil seal packings should be rolled in place.

How to Cut and Install Window Glass

Replacing a window pane is a relatively simple job, and it can be done with a few inexpensive tools and materials

SOONER OR LATER, you'll probably have to replace a piece of broken glass, or at least, cut a piece of glass. This job can easily be done by the layman—there are just a few secrets to be mastered first.

The tips pictured here apply to all except safety glass, which you are not likely to break or have to replace anyway.

The big trick—and this takes practice—is to get a smooth, even cut with the scorer or glass cutter. This weakens the glass along one line and focuses all breaking tendencies along one path.

Don't wait too long after scoring your cutting line before actually breaking the glass in two. Glass, strangely enough, has recuperative powers and the break may not come as easily if you delay.

The first step is to wipe the glass clean to eliminate dirt or film which might interfere with a uniform cut. If the glass is new, remove any stickers. Place the glass on a soft, uniform surface. A layer of felt is best, but a layer of newspaper is serviceable.

Use a yardstick or a long metal rule as a guide for cutting. The rule will stay in place without slipping if you dampen it. Hold

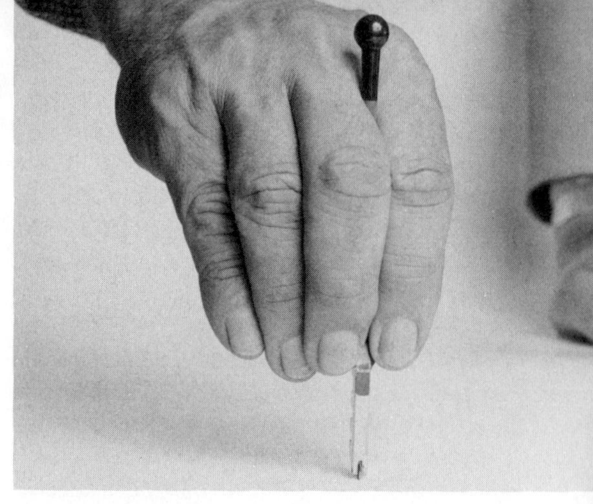

▲ The correct grip. The cutter is held between the first two fingers with the thumb pressed against the underside.

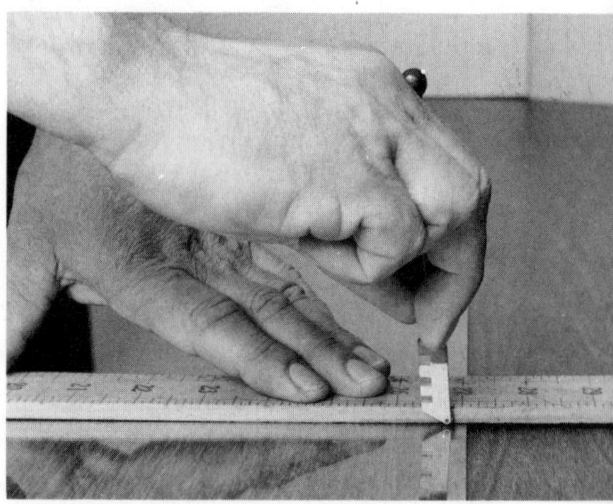

▲ Be sure to hold the cutter upright. Draw it along the straightedge guide with a continuous motion. Use firm, even pressure, but remember, you are trying to score the glass, not cut through it.

▼ Bend the waste side of the glass down and away from the score in a quick, even motion.

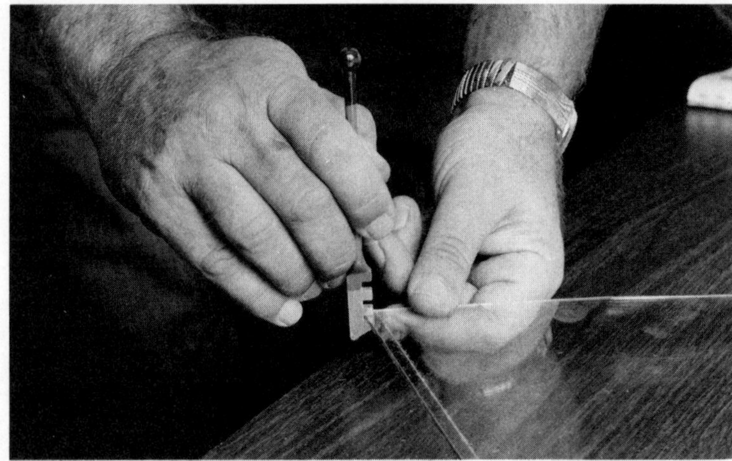

Narrow edges can be broken away with one of the grooves on the cutter, or ordinary pliers can be used.

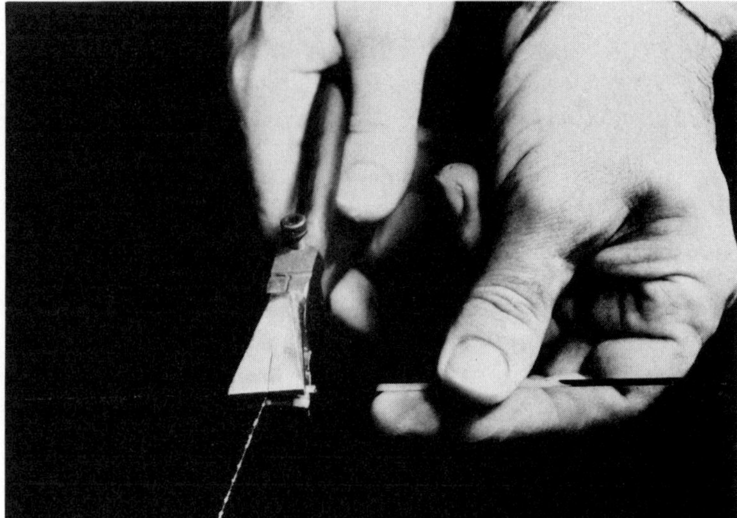

Cut-running pliers, like this, is used to break plate glass.

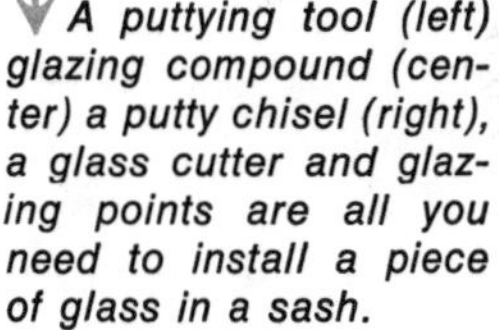

A puttying tool (left) glazing compound (center) a putty chisel (right), a glass cutter and glazing points are all you need to install a piece of glass in a sash.

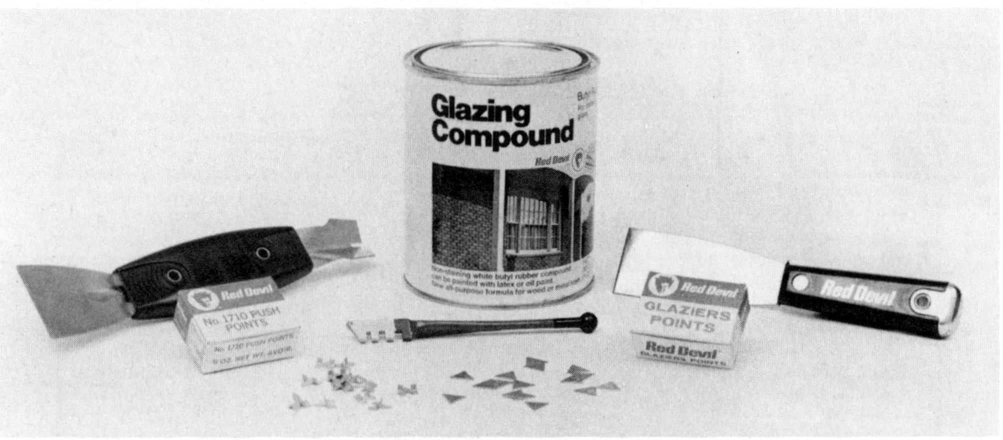

the glass cutter between the first and second fingers with the thumb on the underside of the handle.

Press the cutter gently, but firmly, against the glass about ⅛-inch from the farthest edge. Be sure to hold it upright. An angle will give you a poor cut. Draw the cutter across the whole surface and off the edge of the glass in a single, continuous stroke, using the straightedge as a guide. Practice beforehand on a piece of scrap to get the feel for the correct pressure and stroke.

After the cut is scored, hold the glass firmly on both sides and break it apart with a quick bending motion, away from the cut. Another way to do this is to slip a straightedge beneath the score and break away the waste.

To break away narrow strips, you can use the slot in the glass cutter.

Another tip: tap the underside of the glass opposite score with the round end of the cutter. This will make the glass break more easily.

To snap plate glass up to ¼-inch thick, use cut-running pliers. This special angled pliers has a sight line that is aligned with the score on the glass. A firm squeeze separates the glass cleanly.

Cutting curves in glass is done by marking the curve on paper and putting it beneath the sheet of glass. Then, with the same continuous motion used in straight cutting, follow the guide line with the cutter.

You may wish to use clear acrylic sheeting, such as Plexiglas, rather than glass, especially where there is a danger that people may break it—in doors, for example, or in full length windows near doors that could be mistaken for entrances, or other hazardous locations.

Clear acrylic glazing material is handled much like glass, except that a special cutter is used to score. After it is scored, the acrylic sheet is snapped apart just as glass is, or it can be placed over a dowel and broken at the score.

Cut the pane of glass slightly smaller than the size of the sash in which it is to fit. Use a heavy-duty putty chisel with a beveled edge to scrape away old putty and smooth the surface of the sash.

When the sash is clear of old putty, insert the new glass and hold it against the wood, while inserting glazing points. The points can be pushed in with a putty knife or a screw driver. Some points come with a driving tool. Special sash clips are needed for steel sashes.

When several glazing points on each side of the glass are holding it in place, apply plain putty or glazing compound. These come in cans from one-half pint to five gallons.

Apply the glazing compound evenly all around with the putty knife. Clean up any excess putty or compound and the job is done. F.C.

See also: SCREENS AND STORM WINDOWS.

HOW TO CHOOSE A GLASS CUTTER

Today you can choose among several different types of glass cutter. Most popular are the ones with steel wheels for general use and diamond-hard carbide wheels for longer life.

Choose superhard carbide wheel cutters for maximum life, easiest cutting and true economy. Precision cutters feature pre-lubricated, low-friction bronze axles and perfect wheel position for clean effortless cutting.

You may also discover turret-head cutters, in the head of which are six different wheels, each of which can be locked into cutting position. Or "refill" wheel cutters, some with magazines in their handles holding six spare replacement wheels.

Plate, polished, laminated or heavy glass is best cut with wheels that have blunt wheels. Extra hard glass is more easily cut with sharp-angle wheel models.

How to Install Acrylic Safety Glazing

Use this strong, clear, shatterproof material where children play or in other danger spots, such as patio or storm doors

THE WINDOW THAT lets light into your home or the glass door that gives you a view of patio or lawn can also be a nearly invisible menace waiting for the unwary adult or running child to smash into it.

One way to reduce the hazard of broken windows—not to mention the expense and trouble—is to replace the glass in high-risk areas with clear acrylic glazing materials.

If you bump into an acrylic window you might get a bruise, but there will be no sharp, jagged shards to send you to a hospital emergency room.

Acrylic sheeting resists impact better than glass, and, when it is struck hard enough to shatter, it breaks into large dull-shaped pieces that rarely cause injury.

The safety features of acrylic sheet make it a suitable material for danger areas—children's rooms and playrooms, storm doors, patio doors and full-length windows—wherever there is a strong chance that someone might have an accident.

Working with acrylic sheeting is easy. With two exceptions, you can install a sheet of acrylic in the same way you would a pane of glass.

The first exception is in measuring the material. Acrylic expands and contracts more than glass, so it must be fitted somewhat more loosely. To do this, measure each dimension of the opening exactly. Then subtract 1/32 of an inch for each foot for each dimension. This factor gives the acrylic room to expand. For example, if an opening is two feet wide and four feet high, subtract 2/32 of an inch from the width and 4/32 of an inch from the height. The result will give you the dimensions of the panel required to fill the space.

The second exception is cutting. Glass can be cut only with a glass cutter, and it can be a tricky operation for a beginner. Acrylic sheeting can be cut with ordinary power tools or with an inexpensive cutter that is available from the same hardware stores and building supply houses that sell the glazing material.

To replace a broken pane of glass in a storm door with an acrylic panel, first take out the drop-in sash frame and remove the broken glass carefully. Then, take out the rubber gasket and clean it. If it is in good shape, put it aside for re-use. If it is cracked or torn, throw it away and buy a new one.

Measure the opening in the drop-in sash exactly. Then subtract the expansion factor—1/32 of an inch for each foot in each dimension.

The next step is to order the acrylic sheet—Plexiglas is one type. For a drop-in sash or other applications that require a thin sheet, use material 0.08- or 0.10-inch thick, and be sure it has a label inscribed in the material itself. The label identifies the material as acrylic safety glazing and gives the brand name, manufacturer's name and U.S. code number.

To replace a glass storm door pane, first remove the drop-in sash frame, carefully clean out all the glass and remove the rubber gasket. Measure the opening exactly and substract an expansion factor of 1/32-inch for each foot in each dimension.

Acrylic glazing material can be cut with power tools or an inexpensive cutter. With the protective masking paper in place, score thin material five or six times with the cutter; thick material eight or 10 times.

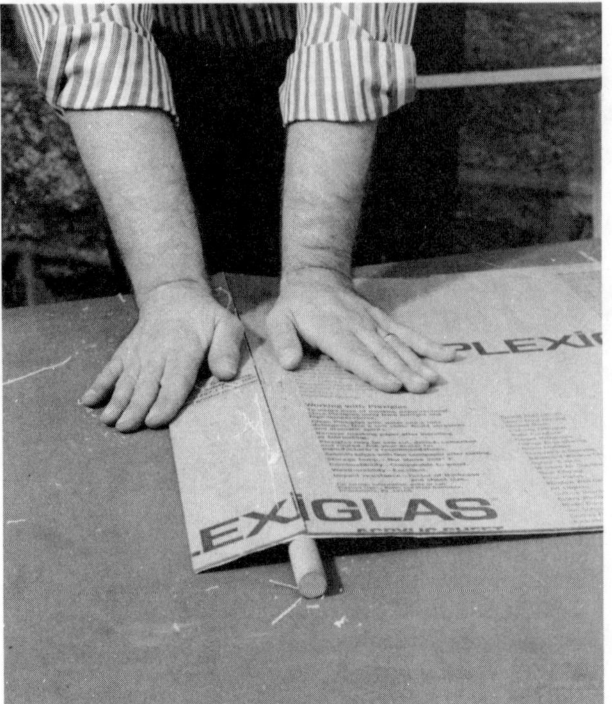

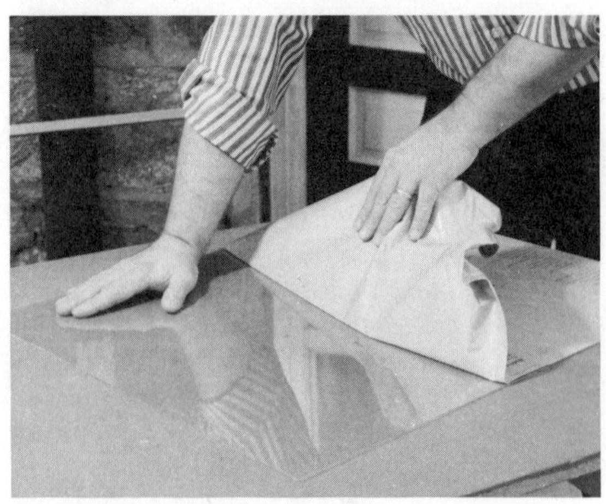

After the edges of the acrylic panel have been smoothed with medium grit sandpaper and you are sure of the fit, peel off the masking paper that covers each side.

Place the material scored side up over a 3/4-inch dowel. Hold the long end on the surface and press the short end down. If the score is over the dowel, the material will snap apart easily along the score.

Use a putty knife to force the rubber gasket back into the channel of the drop-in sash frame.

For a stronger window, discard the drop-in frame and measure the door opening for a panel of 3/16- or 1/4-inch thick acrylic. Figure the expansion factor the same way as for a drop-in frame—1/32-inch per foot.

Once the panel is cut, smooth the edges with medium grit sandpaper.

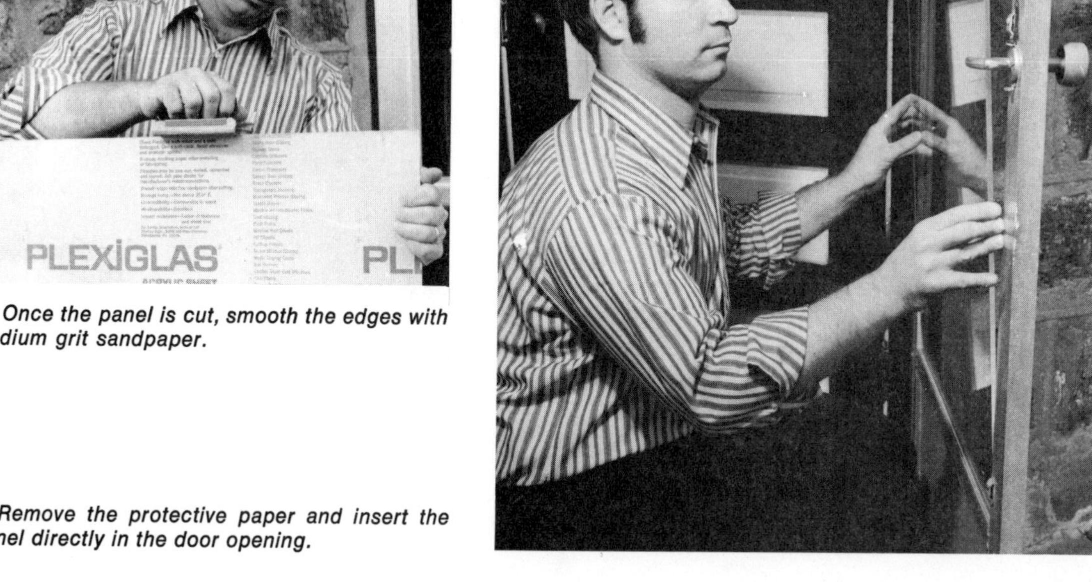

Remove the protective paper and insert the panel directly in the door opening.

Some dealers will cut the material to exact dimensions for you, but you can cut it yourself with little difficulty.

Acrylic sheeting of the type ordinarily used for windows comes with protective masking paper covering each side. Leave this paper on while cutting, sanding or performing any similar operations.

To saw it, use a straightedge to mark a line on the masking paper, then cut along the line with a circular saw or powered jig saw, using the same kind of blade that is used for fine finish cuts in plywood or veneer.

Or, you can purchase a special cutter where you buy the acrylic sheet. To use this, simply score the material deeply with the cutter. Again, the masking paper should be in place. Score thin sheet with five or six passes of the blade. Use seven to 10 passes for 3/16- or 1/4-inch thick material. Lay the sheet over a 3/4-inch wooden dowel with the score on top of the sheet and directly over the length of the dowel. Press each side down and the acrylic will snap along the score.

After the cut is made, smooth the edges with medium grit sandpaper and round the corners and edges slightly. Leave the masking paper on while you sand.

▼ Tighten the clamps as firmly as you would for a drop-in frame. If the panel is too thin to be held firmly, insert wood spacers between panel and clamp, or use spring-loaded clamps.

Check to make sure the panel fits the opening. Remove the masking paper and slide the acrylic panel into the sash. Use your fingers or a putty knife to force the rubber gasket into the channel. Soaking the gasket in warm soapy water will make it easier to install.

You also can eliminate the drop-in sash and install an acrylic panel 3/16- or 1/4-inch thick directly in a door.

Cut the panel to size—remember to subtract the expansion factor of 1/32-inch per foot—sand the edges, remove the protective paper and insert the panel in the door.

Tighten the clips just as you would for a drop-in sash and the job is done. If the material is too thin to be held firmly by the clips, insert thin wood spacers between the acrylic and the clips, or use spring-loaded clips.

Acrylic window panes can be cleaned with a one percent solution of liquid dishwashing detergent in water applied with a soft, clean cotton flannel or jersey cloth. Periodic waxing with automobile paste wax —use wax only; not a cleaner-wax combination—will fill most minor surface scratches and maintain luster. Apply a thin coat and buff with a soft, clean cotton cloth.

When glazing ordinary frame windows with acrylic sheeting, follow the same rules for measuring and cutting acrylic storm door panels. Be sure to use a non-hardening glazing compound or putty that will yield slightly when the acrylic expands or contracts.

Apply a thin bead of glazing compound around the frame before inserting the acrylic panel. Press the acrylic in place against the bead, insert glazing points around the frame and apply a covering bead of glazing compound as you would for an ordinary glass window pane.

See also: SCREENS AND STORM WINDOWS.

Servicing Hi-fi's, Radios and Television Sets

You can repair them yourself and save on total labor costs, or partially save by diagnosing the trouble before the technician gets there

YOU CAN OFTEN DIAGNOSE and repair troubles in your radio and television receivers, or hi-fi system. There are some repairs that should be tackled only by a competent technician, but since it costs money to have a technician diagnose the trouble, it would still be cheaper if you were to do the preliminary diagnosis and perform the easy and simple repair tasks.

The only test equipment you need is a volt-ohm-milliammeter, called a VOM by engineers and technicians. It is a multipurpose meter that will measure AC and DC volts, current in milliamperes and resistance in ohms and megohms.

AC/DC radios. Most radio sets, except transistor portables, are of the so-called AC/DC type. The AC/DC radio was devised some 30 years ago when there was a need for a radio that could be operated either from AC house current or DC power, which was still in use in some cities at the time. Today, nearly all homes and apartments have AC power and the AC/DC radio still exists mainly because it is cheaper to build, since a power transformer is not used.

Tubes don't light. In radios of the AC/DC type, the heaters (filaments) of the tubes are connected in series in Christmas tree light fashion. If one tube burns out, none will light. This is the most common cause of failure.

If your radio fails to play when turned on and plugged in, and no hum is heard when your ear is held close to the loudspeaker, suspect a burned out tube. If the set is left turned on for several minutes and the cabinet does not get warm, and you see no light at any of the tubes (dull red glow), the trouble can be a defective switch, broken connection at the power plug, or a burned out tube.

Disconnect the power plug and connect the leads of an ohmmeter (volt-ohm-milliammeter set to measure ohms) to the prongs of the power plug. With the switch turned on, the meter should indicate less than 1000 ohms. If it indicates that the circuit is open (meter needle does not move), examine the power plug to determine if one of the wires has been pulled loose from its prong. If this is the case, cut the cord an inch or so from the plug and install a new plug.

If this does not cure the trouble, remove the set's rear cover carefully, the chassis holding screws and the knobs, and remove the chassis from the cabinet. With the power plug disconnected, connect the ohmmeter leads to the ends of the power cord inside the chassis, and short circuit the power plug prongs with a screw driver blade with the switch in the "off" position. The meter should now indicate zero ohms (full-scale meter deflection). If this does not happen, the cord is defective and should be replaced with a new one. If the cord is OK, you are ready to check the on-off switch by connecting the ohmmeter across its soldered terminals. With the switch turned on, the meter should indicate zero ohms.

The ohmmeter is the best instrument for checking out the appliance's open line cord. Wire breaks are common. Look for weak spots in wire near chassis and close to plug.

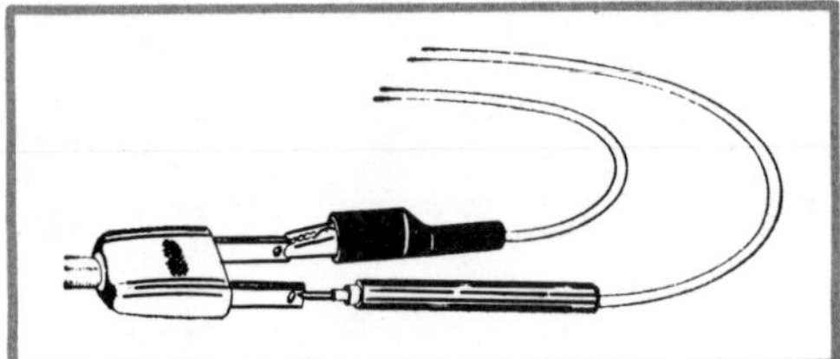

Depending upon which is handier for you, take the tubes out of their sockets and have them tested, or use the ohmmeter to measure the continuity of the heater of each tube with the tubes in their sockets. You have to know which socket terminals to check.

The terminals may be numbered. If not, you can tell the numbering arrangements used for common types of tubes by looking at the bottom of the socket.

Touch the ohmmeter leads to the heater connections of each tube, one at a time. If you get an open circuit reading (meter needle does not move) at one of the sockets, the tube in that socket is apparently burned out. Replace the tube with one of the same type. Now, you should not get an open circuit indication.

Turn on the radio switch and plug in the power plug. The tubes should light and, if nothing else is wrong, the set should operate. Make sure that the set chassis does not make contact with any metallic grounded object. Do not touch the chassis unless you are standing on a dry insulated surface, in order to avoid possible shock.

To test the set while it is out of its cabinet, put the knobs on the shafts (with power plug disconnected) and touch only the knobs when adjusting the set. If it works properly, disconnect the power plug and reassemble the set.

On the other hand, if you choose to take all of the tubes out for testing, make a chart noting which tube belongs in which socket so you will know where to reinstall them after testing.

Pilot lamp. Most AC/DC radios no longer have a pilot lamp which glows when

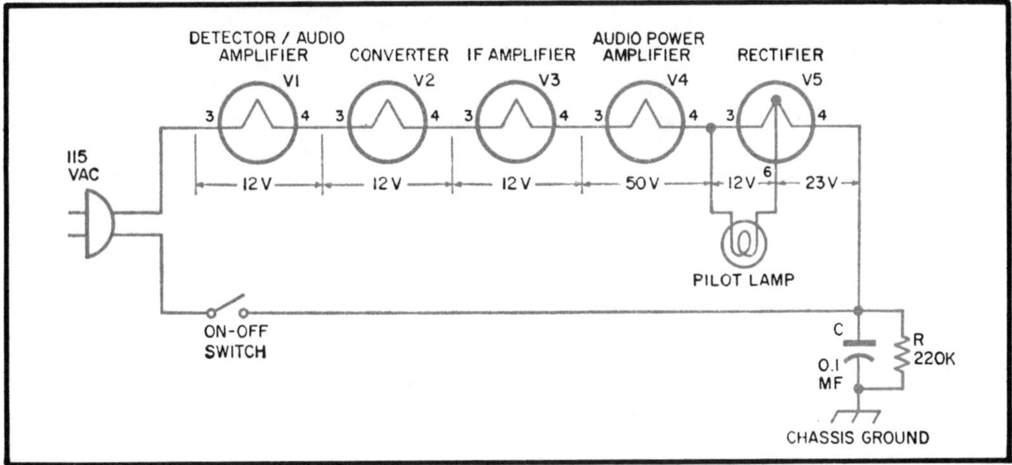

▲ *Filament line-up for most "all American five" AM superhet radios. Pin 3, of V1 is often connected to chassis ground to keep hum voltage to V1's cathode low.*

the set is turned on. When a set is equipped with a pilot lamp is is usually connected, across part of the heater of the rectifier tube. The set will continue to play even if the pilot lamp burns out since the series circuit is not broken, although slightly changed in total resistance.

The pilot lamp should be replaced only with one of the same type number as originally installed in the set by the manufacturer, usually a number 47 lamp. When the set is first turned on, the lamp may glow brightly and then dim as the tubes warm up. The resistance of a tube heater is quite low when it is cold compared to its resistance after it has reached operating temperature.

Tubes light—set doesn't play. While a burned out tube is the usual cause of trouble, there are many other defects that can prevent a radio from operating. A tube can be defective even if not burned out. So, have them tested and replace any bad ones.

If the tubes light and the cabinet gets warm, listen for a slight hum in the loudspeaker. If none is heard, disconnect the power plug and pull the chassis. Momentarily connect a 1.5-volt flashlight cell across the speaker terminals. A click should be audible as the battery leads touch the speaker terminals. If no click is heard, the speaker voice coil circuit is probably open and the speaker should be replaced with one of the same physical size and impedance rating.

Presence of hum indicates that the speaker is live and that the trouble is elsewhere. With the chassis out of the cabinet, the power plug connected, the switch turned on, and the volume control set wide open, touch a test lead (not connected to anything) to the center volume control terminal. A buzz should be heard. If not, the trouble is in the audio section of the receiver, in any one of the many components, including either of two tubes.

Among the possible troubles in the audio section are an open coupling capacitor from the plate of the first amplifier tube to the grid of the audio power amplifier, a shorted capacitor across the primary of the output transformer or an open first amplier plate resistor or open power amplifier resistor.

A buzzing sound caused by touching a test lead to the center volume control terminal indicates that the trouble is ahead of the audio amplifier. If the set cannot be made operative by replacing one or more

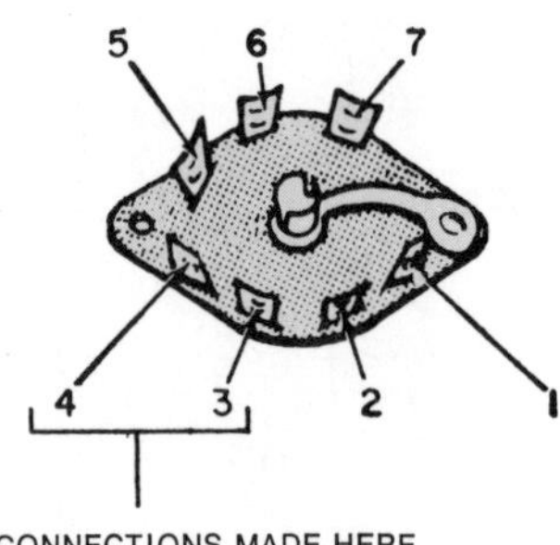

Bottom view of a 7-pin miniature wafer socket. Printed-circuit sockets are similar.

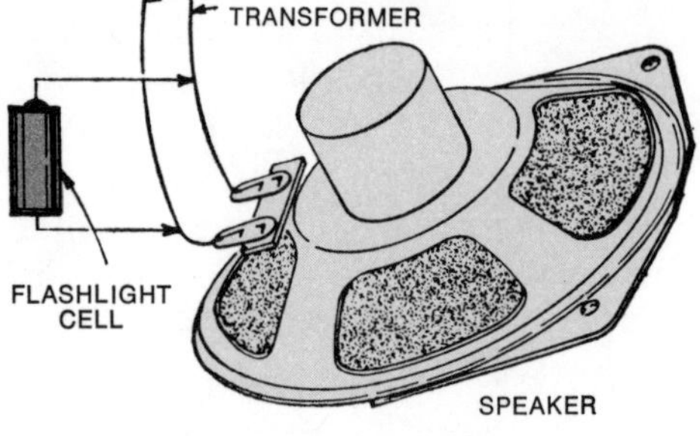

An ohmmeter, or leads connected to dry cell, will make a "good" speaker thimp or click.

tubes, further diagnosis should be made by a technician, unless you want to attempt it yourself. But, do not touch the IF transformer alignment screws since you will need a signal generator to get them back on the correct frequency.

Look for a charred resistor and for swollen capacitors or chemical oozing out of a capacitor and replace such components with exact equivalents. In the case of a charred resistor, a capacitor in the same circuit may have blown causing the resistor to overheat.

Excessive hum. A loud hum may be caused by a shorted tube or a dehydrated filter capacitor. The set may or may not play. The first step is to test the tubes and replace defective ones. If the hum persists, chances are the filter capacitors need replacement. Note the ratings marked on the filter capacitors and buy an exact equivalent. Unsolder and remove the old ones and install the new ones, being careful to observe color coding or polarity marks. If this was the cause, the hum should be gone or diminished. After the set has been played a while, the hum may get weaker as the capacitor forms.

Distortion. Highly distorted sound, often accompanied by hum, is often caused by a shorted tube or electrically leaky coupling capacitor between the plate of the first audio amplifier and the grid of the power amplifier. Disconnect the old one and solder in an exact equivalent. At the same time, as added insurance, replace the capacitor between the plate and screen of the audio power amplifier tube (bridges output transformer primary).

Lack of sensitivity. Inability to pick up as many stations as in the past may be due to aging tubes, dehydration of filter capacitors or change in the characteristics of a resistor or capacitor. Test and replace weak tubes first. If the set hums, replace the filter capacitors. These steps usually restore performance. Further diagnosis should be made by a technician.

Fading. The sudden rise or fall in the volume of a radio is often caused by inadequate pick up by the built-in antenna. In some cases, the volume drops or falls when a light switch is turned on or off. The lighting circuit changes its characteristics as a switch is opened or closed, and may reinforce or attenuate the level of the signal reaching the radio's antenna. The simplest cure is to move the radio to another location in the room, or to re-orient it to change its antenna position with respect to the stations to be received.

A loose connection inside a tube or capacitor can also cause sudden changes in volume. Slow fades on all stations are generally caused by a tube with an intermittent heater. Fading of volume when listening at night to stations more than 50 miles away, but with nearby programs remaining steady, is due to cancellation of the ground wave radio signal by its sky wave, which is not the fault of the radio.

Transformer type radios and hi-fi tuners. Nearly all hi-fi radio tuners and some radio receivers employ power transformers, particularly those inside of large console cabinets, and particularly those that were manufactured several years ago. In these sets, the tube heaters are generally wired in parallel and the plate and screen voltages are usually much higher than in AC/DC radios.

Tubes don't light. Failure of the pilot lamp to light when the tubes light is generally due to a burned out pilot lamp. Failure of all the tubes to light is most often caused by a blown fuse, if the set has a fuse. Generally, the fuse is at the rear of the chassis and can be replaced by merely turning the fuse holder counterclockwise and pulling it out. It can be checked with an ohmmeter to determine if it is open, if it is not obvious when looking at it that it is burned out. Replace the fuse only with one of the same type and rating as specified by the manufacturer of the set.

Should the fuse blow when the set is plugged in and the switch is turned on, there is trouble inside the set.

If the fuse is all right, or a new fuse does not blow, pull out the power plug and connect the ohmmeter leads to its pins with the radio switch turned on. If an open circuit condition is indicated, inspect the power plug connections to the cord and replace the plug if one of the wires has pulled loose from its prong. Pull the chassis if the trouble is not at the plug.

Touch the ohmmeter test leads to the ends of the power cord inside the chassis and short the power plug prongs with a screw driver blade with the switch in the "off" position. You should get a short circuit indication. If not, replace the cord and plug. Now, check the switch with the ohmmeter. A short circuit (zero Ohms) condition should be indicated when the switch is in the "on" position, and open circuit when in the "off" position.

Then connect the ohmmeter leads to the power transformer primary leads. One is usually connected to the fuse (or to one wire of the line cord when there is no fuse), and the other to one terminal of the switch. An open circuit reading indicates that the power transformer primary is open, which means that the transformer must be replaced by an exact equivalent.

New fuse blows. Blowing of a newly installed fuse of the proper rating usually indicates that there is a short circuit within the set. If the set is connected to an external ground, remove the ground connection. Now, if the fuse does not blow when the set is plugged in and turned on, chances are that one of the line filter capacitors is shorted. Disconnect the power plug and touch one ohmmeter test lead to the chassis and the other to either power transformer primary lead. You should get an open cir-

Electrolytic capacitors are of two basic types. Tubular units (extreme left) and miniature units for transistor circuits usually have wire leads. Can types may have one, two, three or four sections. The can does not have to be grounded—it can be mounted on a phenolic wafer and be "hot." Cardboard-sleeve insulators are often left off during replacement.

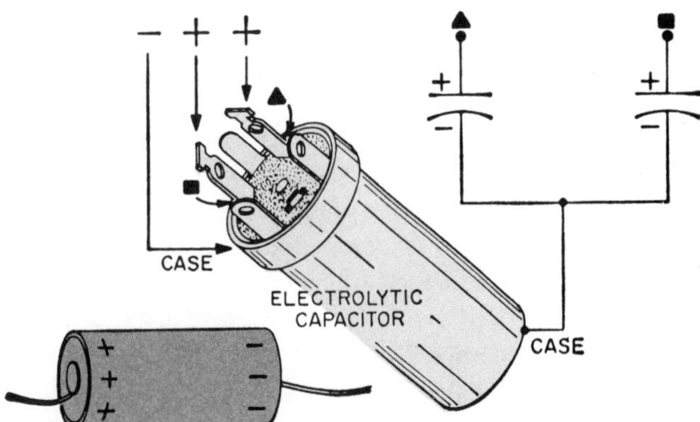

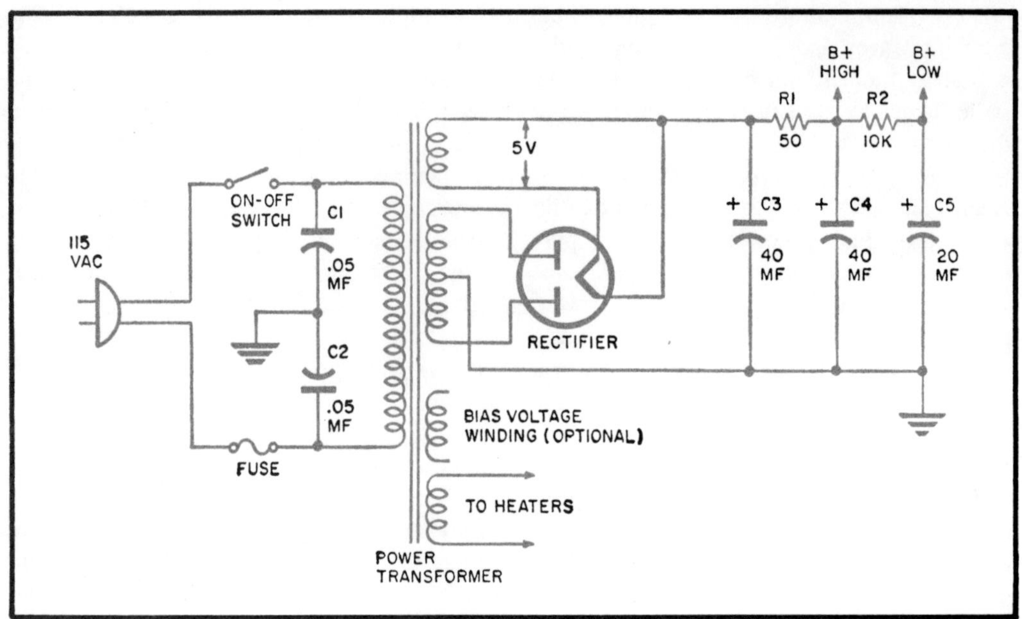

▲ *Typical full-wave rectifier circuit, used in vacuum-tube hi-fi, is just about identical to those used in first transformer-powered radios more than 30 years ago.*

cuit indication. If not, replace the line filter capacitors with new ones of equivalent value and rating. However, if you still get other than an open circuit reading, the power transformer primary winding may be grounded to its core and replacement of the transformer is indicated.

Trouble on the other side of the power transformer, which causes the fuse to blow, could be due to a short or ground in one of the transformer secondary windings, or a short circuit or ground in the tube heater winding. Pull out the rectifier tube and turn the set on. If the fuse does not blow now, but does blow when the rectifier tube is reinstalled, the trouble is probably due to a shorted filter capacitor.

The shorted filter capacitor can be identified by measuring the resistance with an ohmmeter from the hot terminal of each filter capacitor to the chassis. Sometimes two or more capacitors are inside the same container. If a very low resistance or short circuit condition is found, disconnect the wire at the capacitor terminal and check it again with the wire removed. If the short isn't cleared now, replace the capacitor with an equivalent type. Observe color coding or polarity marks.

Tubes light—set doesn't play. When the tubes light, but the set is inoperative, any of dozens of components could be defective. If there is an odor and the power transformer gets hot, it could be transformer trouble or a short circuit elsewhere. Look at the rectifier tube for reddening of its plates which is indicative of a shorted filter capacitor.

On the other hand, if the set does not give off an odor and does not seem to overheat, the trouble could be a defective tube. All should light. The light in some may be difficult to see. After the set has been turned on for a while, all tubes should feel warm to the touch. Nevertheless, have all the tubes tested and replace any defective ones. Check the loudspeaker as explained earlier about AC/DC sets.

Other troubles, such as hum, distortion,

lack of sensitivity and selectivity, and fading can be due to the same causes as explained earlier, regardless of whether the set is of the AC/DC type or transformer type.

Hi-fi amplifiers. The power input circuits of hi-fi and other audio amplifiers, as well as AM/FM tuners, are similar to those of transformer type radios and the same check-out procedures can be used.

Excessive hum. Some amplifiers are equipped with a hum control at the rear or top of the chassis which can be adjusted with a screwdriver. With the volume control turned to minimum volume, adjust the hum control slowly for minimum audible hum. If the hum cannot be reduced to a satisfactory level in this manner, have the tubes tested and replace any defective ones.

The audio power amplifier tubes may have to be closely matched in order to minimize hum and distortion. When buying new tubes, have them checked and take those which check most alike.

While it may not be specified in the user instruction book, a ground connection may reduce hum level. Get a ground clamp and fasten it to a freshly cleaned spot on a cold water pipe and run a wire from it to a screw on the chassis. (Do not do this if the amplifier is of the transformerless type).

The hum could be caused by dehydrated filter capacitors. This can be checked out by turning the chassis over to gain access to the wiring. Take a 20-ufd, 450-volt tubular electrolytic capacitor and temporarily bridge it across each filter capacitor or section, one at a time, making sure that the positive (+) terminal of the test capacitor is connected only to the positive terminals of the capacitors in the amplifier, and note any reduction in hum. Be careful to hold the test capacitor by its insulated housing and avoid touching any of the wires, terminals or test capacitor leads, to avoid shock.

An appreciable reduction in hum level, when the test capacitor is tried, indicates that the filter capacitors should be replaced.

Hum, which increases in intensity when the volume control is turned up, in any position of the function selector switch (phono-tape-tuner, etc.) indicates amplifier trouble. It could be an improperly seated tube shield or a defective tube.

However, if the hum rises when the function selector switch is set to one particular position, the trouble could be in the particular pre-amplifier selected, in the lead from the selected input device (tuner, record player), or in the input device itself.

Check the amplier input lead and plug, looking particularly for a broken shield at the plug at each end of the lead. Make sure that the plugs are firmly seated in their sockets.

When separate line cords are used for each hi-fi system component, try reversing the positions of their respective power plugs in their sockets.

Record changers. A record changer is an intricate and touchy mechanism which should be adjusted only by an expert. However, it can be lubricated by anyone who has available an instruction book spelling out when and where to lubricate and what kind of lubricant to use.

Rubber rimmed drive wheels and idlers wear out and cause rumble. Replacements can be purchased at radio parts stores. You can install them, if you exercise care not to disturb other parts of the mechanism.

The stylus of many types of stereo and mono cartridges can be easily replaced. The new stylus is generally furnished with specific installation instructions. Sometimes it is necessary to replace the entire cartridge, or you may want to replace your cartridge with one of a type more suited to your requirements.

Portable transistor radios. Servicing portable transistor radios is a job for an expert with the proper tools, test equipment and spare parts. The most common trouble is worn out batteries, which you can easily replace. Symptoms of worn out batteries are lack of volume, a motorboating sound or a rapid fade out shortly after switching on.

Replace the battery or batteries (all of them at once) with exact equivalent types, being very careful that the new ones are inserted or connected in the same polarity as the original ones. If necessary, clean the contacts with a pencil eraser and bend the clips slightly to ensure firm contact.

Television sets. Numerous books have been published about how to repair your own TV sets. While many professional TV service shops have initially lost business as a result, they have gained additional revenue undoing the damage done by some do-it-yourself TV owners.

When your TV set acts up, it will cost you several dollars to get a pro to come to check it over, quite a few dollars to get it repaired if more than a new tube is required. Some shops charge a minimum to look over your TV set even when you bring it to the shop.

There are several things you can do before you call in an expert. Before touching the TV set, as long as it is operating, even if not satisfactorily, check out the antenna system. Look for loose, bent, broken and corroded elements and carefully examine the connections to the twin-lead transmission line. If the antenna has been in use more than five years, it might be a good idea to replace it and the transmission line, which gradually deteriorates, downgrading reception as it does. Also check the antenna connections at the set.

No picture—no sound. Sudden failure of a TV set to operate is usually due to a burned out tube or fusible resistor inside the cabinet. The first step is to remove the rear cover. The power cord is automatically disconnected when the cover is removed.

Before you take out the tubes for testing, look for the label that shows the locations of the various types of tubes. If there is not a label, make one noting the locations of the tubes and the number of each tube as you remove it from its socket. Have the tubes tested and replace any defective ones.

Many TV sets have their tubes connected in series as in AC/DC radios. Hence, one burned out tube can prevent the others from lighting. Also, the fusible resistor in such sets, if burned out, can prevent the tubes from lighting. Usually, the fusible resistor is a two-wire plug-in device which can be pulled out of its sockets and replaced with a new one of the same value. You can check it with an ohmmeter.

Picture troubles. Vertical and horizontal picture instability can often be corrected by adjustment of the horizontal and vertical controls. Sometimes, replacement of a weak tube will cure the trouble. Absence of a picture, but with the screen lighted, is often caused by a defective tube. Unclear pictures and ghosts are usually caused by antenna trouble, improper tuning and antenna orientation.

Sound troubles. One of the troubles is buzz in the sound which can be due to any number of causes. A screwdriver adjustment is provided in some sets which is set for minimum buzz. There is also a tuning slug in the gated beam detector coil which can be adjusted with a special tuning wand. But, both of these controls are usually inaccessible unless the rear cover is removed, and adjustment cannot be made satisfactorily unless the set is turned on.

Tuner troubles. After a few years of use, the contact points inside the tuner (controlled by channel selector switch and fine tuning knob) get dirty causing unstable picture and sound. You can get a can of TV tuner cleaning fluid which you can spray into the tuner through the holes, with the set's rear cover removed. Rotate the channel selector knob as you spray.

See also: ELECTRICAL, HOME; INDIVIDUAL APPLIANCE LISTINGS.

A New Face for Your Old Home Front

These easy-to-build and install home fronts can add to the value of your home

REAL ESTATE AGENTS indicate that dêsigning a new "face" for an old home may increase its value. It will certainly be easier to sell.

The low-cost design improvements shown here provide considerable latitude —they may be used singly or combined with each other, as long as the selections harmonize with the architectural style of the house. Dimensions given may also be altered to suit. To simplify construction, specified thicknesses and widths are confined mostly to standard mill runs which need be cut to length only.

Fences and gates. To make sure any fence or gate design you select will harmonize, it's a good idea to sketch or paint it on a photo of your house beforehand.

Picket fences are old favorites, particularly for colonial-style homes. Rail fences, which are easier to build and care for, run a close second. The louver fence, increasingly popular, can be built in sections to screen off entrance doors from the street, or unattractive parts of the yard.

The basket-weave, a relative newcomer, is also finding favor rapidly. You can make it with posts spaced up to eight feet apart and adjacent rails crisscrossing to opposite sides of posts. Posts should be imbedded in concrete—at least 18 inches below grade if for a fence three feet high, and two inches more for each additional foot of height.

Fencing should be kept well painted. A good grade of pine will do for all parts except the posts, which ought to be redwood or cypress. Before installing, treat below-ground sections of posts with two or three soaking coats of creosote.

No fence is complete without a suitable gate. One of the most substantial is the solid colonial type made up from three ¾ x 11½-inch boards (known as 1 x 12s in dimensional size). To assemble, glue-join the boards with a waterproof adhesive. Cut the facing boards for each side out of ¾ x 4⅝-inch stock (1 x 5s), except wider pieces at the bottom which could be ¾ x 9½ inches. If possible, use a shaper to make the stop-chamfers. Apply framing on one side of the gate with four penny coated common nails, then turn up other side and frame with six penny nails.

Prepare a cardboard template from graph squares to scribe cutting line for the pediment and cut with a band saw or coping saw. Shape the fillet, cap and

Archway with recessed gate.

turned finial, and install. Many lumber yards will furnish the finial if you do not have a lathe to turn it out yourself.

The archway-gate goes hand in hand with a picket fence. Assemble posts, stretchers and lattice strips. Cross-brace the front and back posts until unit is cemented into the ground.

Prepare two laminated sections for the arch, using ¾-inch stock. Join segments with waterproof adhesive and four penny

FIVE WAYS TO "LIFT" OLD HOMES:

Corral gate for a ranch look.

Outdoor room in breezeway.

Rails and trim between posts.

Oriental divider planter.

nails, then position the sections in the post notches the same way. Add crosspieces, set posts in concrete and remove bracing.

You can adapt this archway to brick posts by anchoring it to bolts imbedded in the mortar.

A wagon-wheel gate is appropriate for ranch homes. Wheels are usually available at antique, second-hand or junk dealers and discarded croquet balls will serve well as post balls.

The anchor gate is a natural for seashore residences and beach cottages. The corral-type gate is built in the same manner.

Porch improvements. Ornamental iron work can replace a wood post and trim. When making a similar conversion, be sure the porch overhang is amply supported before removing the old post. You can obtain such ornamental posts and trim from dealers listed in phone books under "Iron Work" and from some hardware dealers. They are usually custom-made to your specifications.

For a simple, inexpensive porch railing you can use 1⅝ x 2⅝-inch stock (2 x 3s). Or, using the same wood, you can install open-effect vertical dividers.

Breezeway walls. Enclosing the covered area between your home and garage adds, in effect, an outdoor room with whatever amount of privacy you wish. If you make it harmonize with the siding, your house will appear larger.

An easy way to improve your breezeway is to build a low-wall partition with center gate and lattice work. Two posts installed for the gate are the only heavy pieces needed. You can nail up wall plates to garage and house siding and run grooved cap rails between posts and plates for vertical board siding.

First toenail the lower grooved cap to wall plates and posts with ten penny nails.

▲ *Louvered fence panels provide front entry with effective shield from nearby walk.*

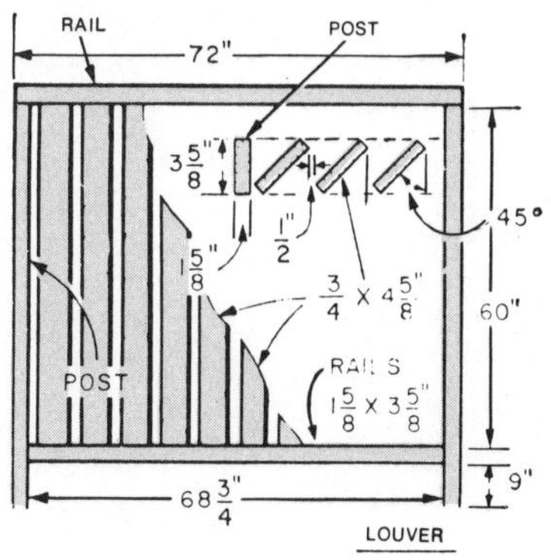

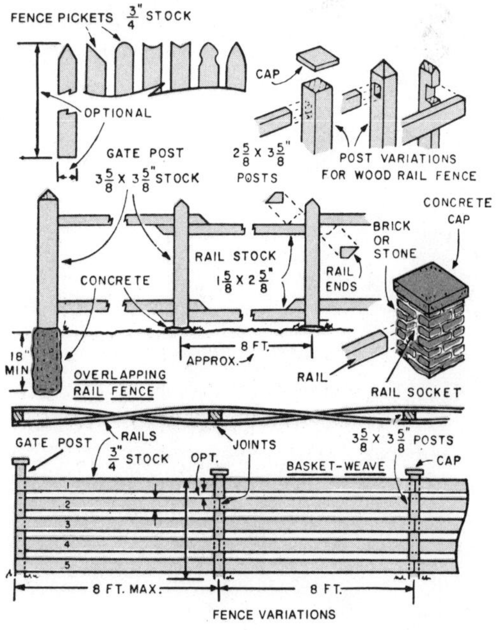

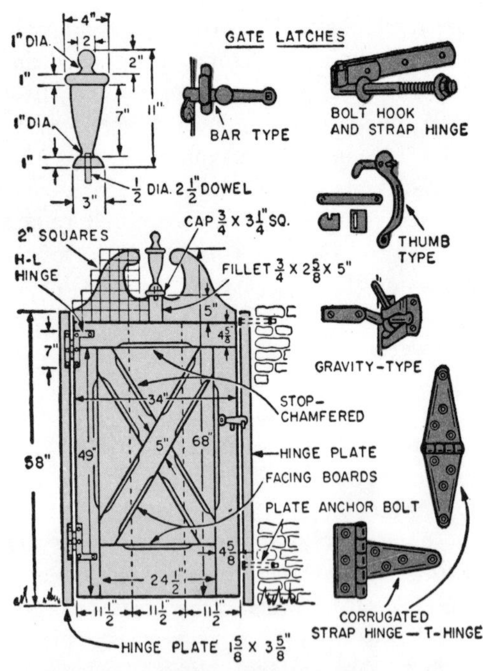

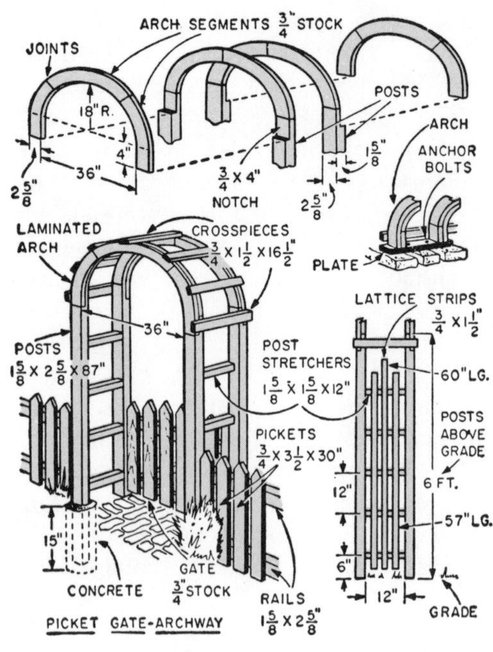

Solid, high gate adds much to the privacy of a yard or garden area.

Then install boards in the grooves, fit top cap to the boards and toenail in place to posts and plates. Nail battens on both sides to conceal board joints and cover joints where boards meet posts and plates with quarter-round molding. Toenail ends of light lattice strips in place and reinforce them where they cross with #18 x ¾-inch wire nails.

Ornamental iron work is easy to install on porches but, unless you are building a new work to fit standard, you may need to have parts made to order.

➤ *The addition of the ledge and cornice makes this window outstanding.*

▼ *Simple breezeway improvement uses stained redwood board and batten siding to match that of house. Light lattice-work above is positioned so screens can be installed inside. It can be removed quickly for future installation of windows.*

The breezeway matches the clapboard siding of the house and uses 1⅝ x 3⅝-inch vertical and horizontal members (norminal 2 x 3s) to form shelf frames for small potted plants.

See also: ADDITIONS, HOME; BRICKWORK; CONCRETE; FENCES; STONEWORK.

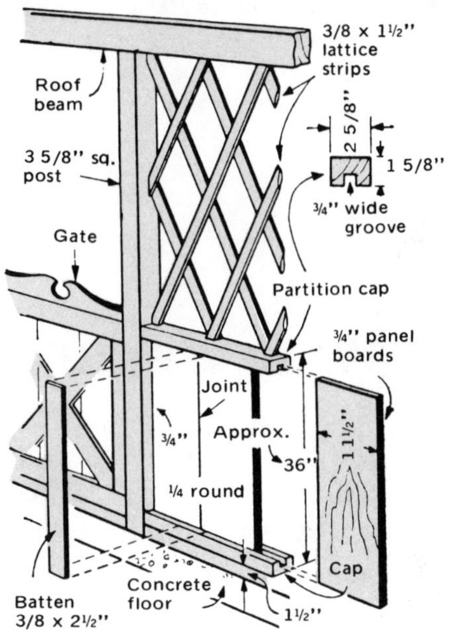

BREEZEWAY PARTITION

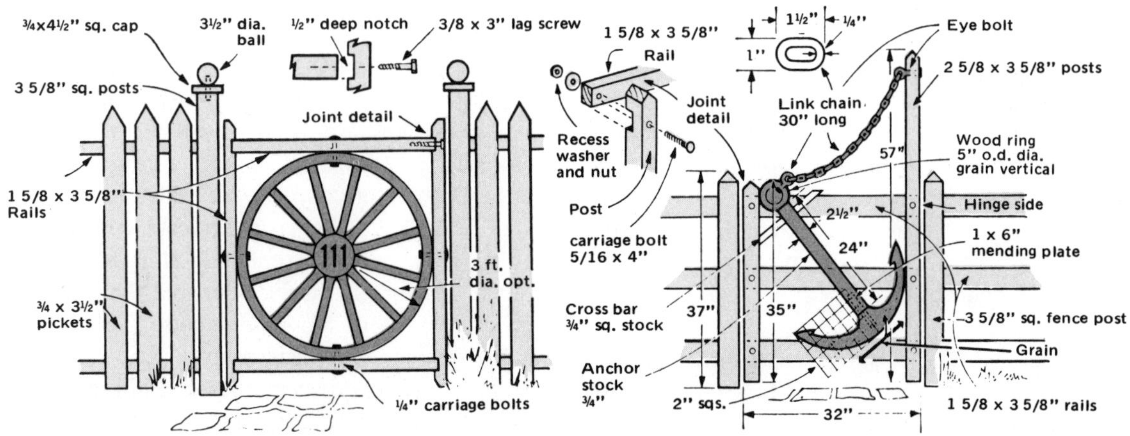

How to Repair Steam or Dry Irons

You can check out your iron yourself, rather than call a repairman. But, remember, anything more than replacing a damaged handle or cord may cost more than the iron is worth

THE ELECTRIC IRON is a hard working appliance often used by someone who is in a hurry and expects instant results. We take its existance and rugged construction for granted.

Most electric iron troubles result from careless use or accidents. The most frequent complaints are broken cords, handles or sticky soleplates.

CAUTION: Before working on an iron make certain it is disconnected from the electrical outlet.

Basic service. A cord can be tested for continuity with a test light or an ohmmeter by connecting the tester to the attachment cap (plug) terminals, turning the switch on and wiggling the cord by alternately pushing and pulling it as you move your hands along the length of the cord. Any flickering of the test light or movement of the ohmmeter needle will indicate a break in the cord. In extreme cases, a visual check will show where the cord is broken or the insulation worn. A defective cord should be replaced. They are usually available at the electrical counter of your local super mart or hardware store.

A broken handle is usually not repairable and should be replaced. It must be obtained from the dealer who sold the iron or directly from the manufacturer. There are no universal replacements.

Sticky soleplates occur when the iron is too hot for the material being ironed. The

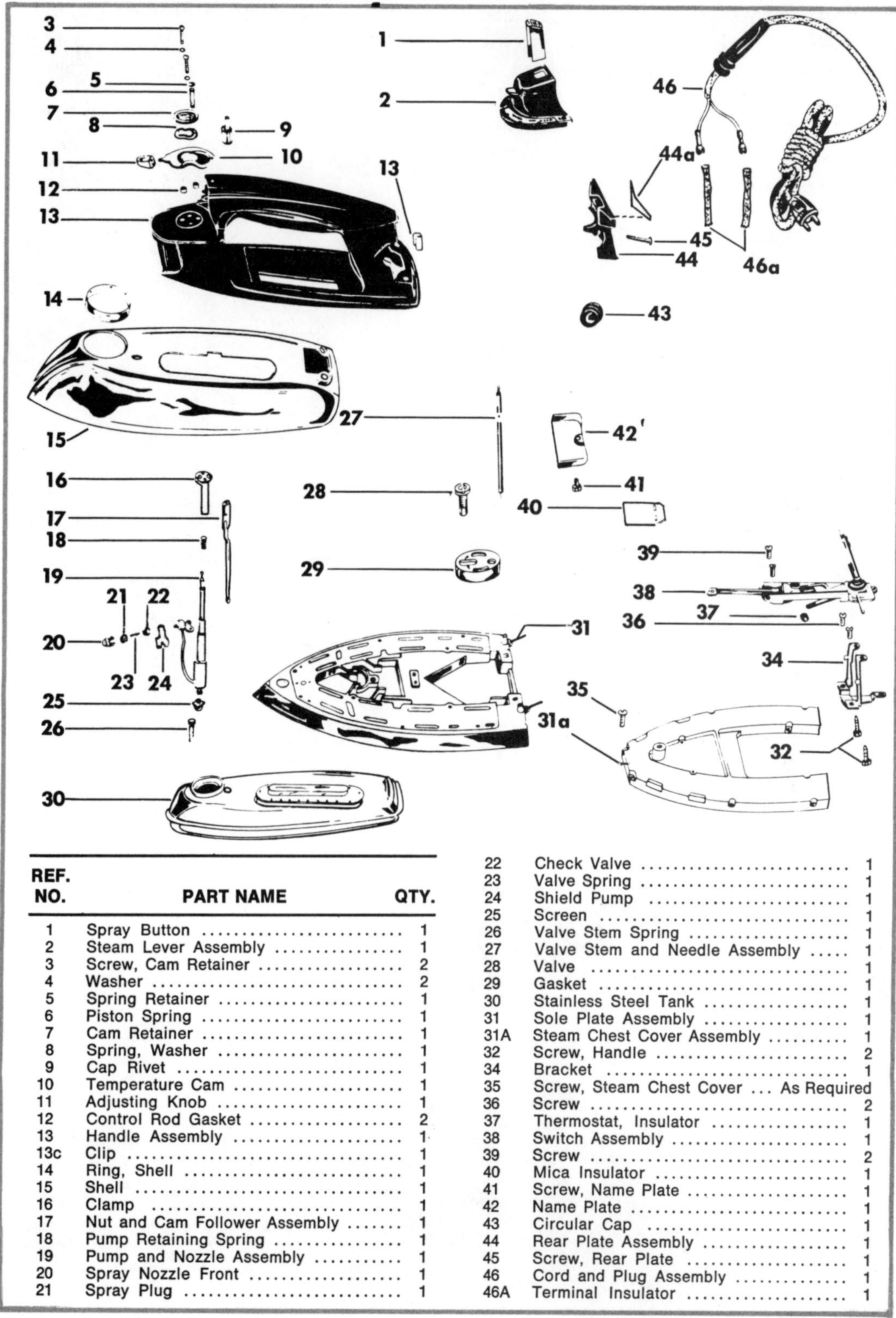

REF. NO.	PART NAME	QTY.
1	Spray Button	1
2	Steam Lever Assembly	1
3	Screw, Cam Retainer	2
4	Washer	2
5	Spring Retainer	1
6	Piston Spring	1
7	Cam Retainer	1
8	Spring, Washer	1
9	Cap Rivet	1
10	Temperature Cam	1
11	Adjusting Knob	1
12	Control Rod Gasket	2
13	Handle Assembly	1
13c	Clip	1
14	Ring, Shell	1
15	Shell	1
16	Clamp	1
17	Nut and Cam Follower Assembly	1
18	Pump Retaining Spring	1
19	Pump and Nozzle Assembly	1
20	Spray Nozzle Front	1
21	Spray Plug	1
22	Check Valve	1
23	Valve Spring	1
24	Shield Pump	1
25	Screen	1
26	Valve Stem Spring	1
27	Valve Stem and Needle Assembly	1
28	Valve	1
29	Gasket	1
30	Stainless Steel Tank	1
31	Sole Plate Assembly	1
31A	Steam Chest Cover Assembly	1
32	Screw, Handle	2
34	Bracket	1
35	Screw, Steam Chest Cover	As Required
36	Screw	2
37	Thermostat, Insulator	1
38	Switch Assembly	1
39	Screw	2
40	Mica Insulator	1
41	Screw, Name Plate	1
42	Name Plate	1
43	Circular Cap	1
44	Rear Plate Assembly	1
45	Screw, Rear Plate	1
46	Cord and Plug Assembly	1
46A	Terminal Insulator	1

synthetic fabrics are sensitive to heat and in melting will stick to the soleplate, so will excessive starch. Besides being hard to push, a dirty soleplate will soil the articles being ironed. To clean the soleplate, first try a cloth and warm water; if that doesn't clean it, (Caution: Don't try the following on a Teflon coated soleplate), use a scouring pad or fine steel wool. Don't overdo it and scratch the soleplate so as to raise a burr which can tear cloths.

Light scratches on the soleplate will do no harm since they can't get caught in the fabric being ironed. However, nicks, burrs and other sharp projections can pull the fabric. These should be filed down to the level of the rest of the soleplate.

Steam irons. This general maintenance holds for both dry and steam irons. Steam irons have added problems due to the water used. Careless filling will cause rust on thermostat parts and using tap water instead of distilled water will allow mineral deposits to collect in the steam passages. Fortunately, most of the mineral deposit resulting from hard water usage is lime, which can be dissolved by pouring vinegar in the tank and allowing it to stand overnight. Make certain the control is in the steam position to allow the vinegar to drip into the steam chamber. The tank should be rinsed out before using the iron.

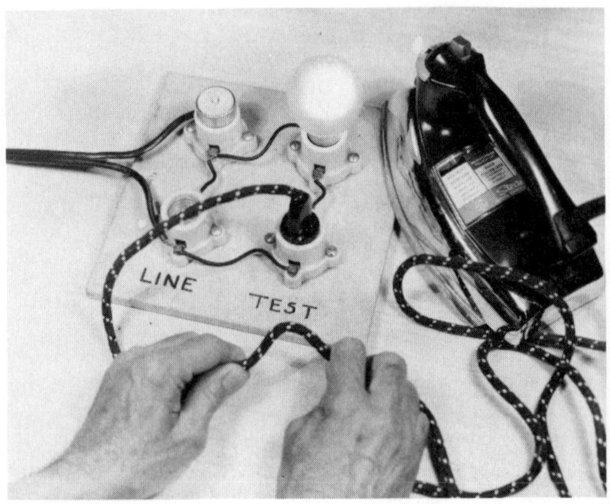

Erratic iron performance could be due to a break in the cord that opens and closes intermittently. Check for this by turning the iron on and hooking it up to a test light rig. Push and pull the cord and shake it a section at a time. If the light flickers or goes out, there is a bad spot in the cord. Usually, if there is a break, it will appear at one end of the cord or the other. If the defect is in the iron, the light will not go on under any circumstances.

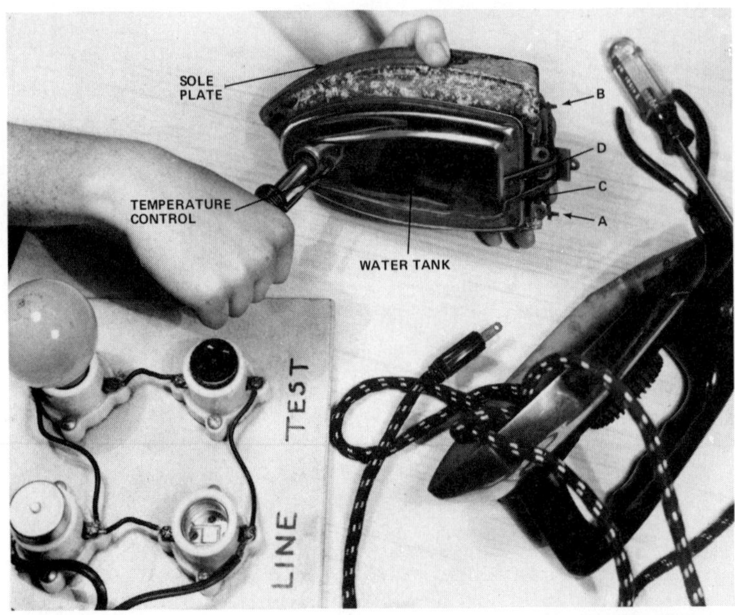

Removal of the handle and shell exposes the water tank and the sole plate and thermostat terminals. No continuity between A and B indicates an open heater element. No continuity between C and D indicates an open thermostat circuit. Any further examination requires removal of the water tank. Before removing the water tank, remember that many persons believe it is cheaper to buy a new iron than to repair anything more than a damaged handle or cord.

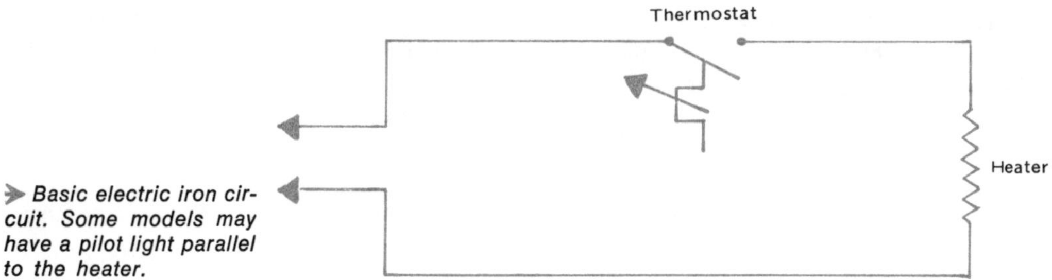

Basic electric iron circuit. Some models may have a pilot light parallel to the heater.

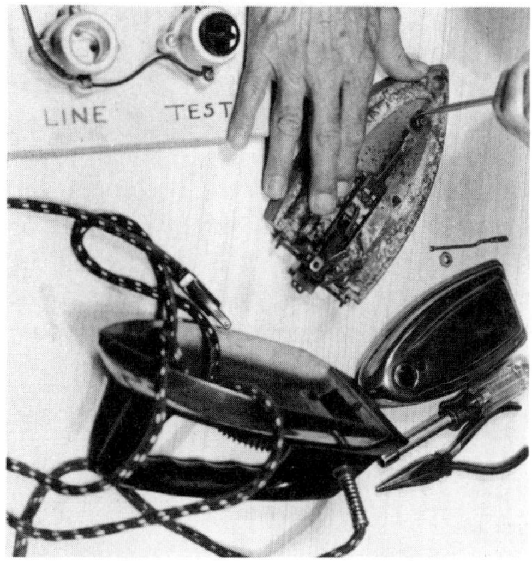

You can get to the thermostat by removing the water tank. The iron shown here is heavily corroded. Corrosion has disabled the thermostat, and the screws holding the steam chamber cover on are so locked in place by corrosion that they cannot be moved.

There are two types of steam iron; the boiler type and the flash steam type. In the boiler type, the tank holding the water is heated to generate steam in the tank. This steam is then released through holes in the soleplate to moisten the fabric being ironed. In the flash steam type, the tank holding the water is not heated. Water is allowed to drip from the tank to a heated steam chamber on the soleplate, from there the steam escapes through the vents in the soleplate.

General construction. The mechanical construction and parts location of a typical steam iron is shown in an accompanying drawing. The cord can be replaced by removing a screw, rear plate, circular cap and the decal. As these parts are removed observe their position to be able to reinstall them in their original location. For example, the indicating rib on the strain relief must be up and the circular cap should be inserted with the flat surface up.

Before proceeding any further with the dissassembly of a steam iron make certain that:

1. It's necessary.
2. You have all the correct tools, test equipment, spare gaskets and silicone sealer you need.
3. You have the manufacturer's service literature for the particular model iron you are working on.

Thermostat. The thermostat maintains the soleplate heat at the temperature desired by the user. It is mounted on the soleplate so that the bimetal (temperature sensitive) unit will operate a switch to turn off the electrical current when the soleplate is hot enough, and turn the current on again when it cools off. Usually the thermostat will operate from ON and OFF through a 10% temperature differential.

A good operating temperature with the control set in the beginning of the steam position would be about 325° F. With the control in the maximum ON position (high linen), the temperature should be about 500° F. Anything over 550° F. is too high and the thermostat should be checked and recalibrated. Many thermostats have a calibration screw recessed in the control stem.

A ⅛th of a turn of this screw could make a 20° F. temperature difference. Turning it clockwise would lower the temperature. Its usually best to follow the manufacturer's instructions for each specific model.

Heating element. This is an insulated resistance wire cast into the soleplate. Three things can happen to it.

1. It can burn out (go open, no heat).
2. It can develop shorted turns (overheat in one spot).
3. It can ground to the frame (shock the user).

Heater elements are not repairable. The entire soleplate assembly will have to be changed.

The heating element can be tested with a test light or an ohmmeter. When testing from terminal to terminal of a 1200-watt at 120-volt iron, the test light will light and the ohmmeter should read about 12 OHMS. No light or no reading would indicate a burned out element. Any light or resistance reading from one terminal to the soleplate would indicate a grounded element.

Electrical circuit. The wiring diagram shows the circuit to be a thermostat in series with the heater. Usually all wiring in the iron is uninsulated bus, spot welded or silver soldered to the parts being connected.

Electrical testing. In all electrical testing, we must assume that voltage is available at the outlet and the house wiring is O.K.

The first test to make is at the prongs of the attachment cap with the thermostat turned on. A test light should light; an ohmmeter should read between 12-15 OHMS, if all is well. If the circuit is open, the next place to test is at the terminals in the iron where the cord is attached. A correct reading here would indicate the thermostat and heating element to be good, thus the trouble must be in the cord.

See also: ELECTRICAL, HOME; INDIVIDUAL APPLIANCE LISTINGS.

IRON PROBLEMS AND THEIR CAUSES

PROBLEM / POSSIBLE CAUSE	BREAK IN CORD	DEFECTIVE THERMOSTAT	CARELESS FILLING	DEFECTIVE GASKET	LEAKY TANK	CONTROL LINKAGE DAMAGED	VALVE CLOGGED	LIME DEPOSIT
DOES NOT HEAT	√	√				√		
OVERHEATS		√				√		
LEAKS WATER			√	√	√			
WON'T STEAM							√	√
STEAMS ALL THE TIME						√		
SPITS WATER		√	√					√
DOES NOT SPRAY							√	

➤ *Graphite for loosening and lubricating locks is handily packaged in plastic squeeze containers and available at most hardware stores.*

Repairing Door Locks

Locks will only provide privacy and security if they are working properly. If you put your key in the door and it does not open, knowing how the lock works will save you in locksmith bills

COMMON LOCKS on your doors provide privacy and security—when they're working right. But suppose you insert the correct key into a cylinder (pin-tumbler) lock and it will not turn. After jiggling with it unsuccessfully for a while, you could call in a locksmith or get in through another door, remove the lock assembly and take it to a lock shop. Either solution can be very expensive and may leave your house unprotected while the lock is gone. A better idea is to learn about locks and fix them yourself.

Except for the combination type, all locks have two things in common—a key of special and individual size and shape and a bolt that fits into the casing. Turning the key withdraws the bolt and the door is open. But locks vary in the security they provide. A simple "warded" lock that requires the key only to pass some obstruction is common on furniture, "just to keep the honest people out." Interior door locks include wards plus a lever tumble that must be raised to a certain height by the key before the lock will release. These locks offer security against young children, but dime stores sell "skeleton" keys, one of which will almost surely open any one-lever lock.

For maximum security on exterior doors, you will use the 5-lever, bit-key locks and the pin tumbler lock operated by a wavy-type or paracentric key. The wavy effect of the key shape acts similar to a ward and offers additional key change possibilities. There are no "skeleton" key possibilities for either of these locks. Regardless of how the lock is mounted—mortised into face of door, mounted on inside or through the door, the lock must secure the door and yet be easy and quick to operate. Many people have been burned to death struggling with a reluctant lock.

What kinds of problems with these locks are you likely to run into? Most common is refusal of the lock to turn when you insert the right key. It can be due to sticky pins which may be cured by blowing powdered graphite into the keyhole. Never use oil in a cylinder lock. If the graphite treatment does not work, then the cause is probably wear on the key, a poor duplicate key or worn pins. To get at the trouble, remove the locking mechanism by loosening the two screws in the lock plate that holds the cylinder in place, then unscrew the shell with the key. Remove the screw that holds the cam to the cylinder or plug and remove the cam. Be careful not to let the cylinder slip out of the shell.

Push out the cylinder from the shell with a short length of tubing or dowel to keep driver pins and springs in place. With the key in place, check the cylinder to see if the pins are all flush with the surface. If any pins are either too long or fail to meet flush with the surface, that is the cause of the trouble. Pins that are too long can be filed flush, but short pins must be replaced. You can buy new pins from your local locksmith.

Remove short pins with tweezers. File off the new pins flush, with the right key in position. Remove any burrs left from the filing by lifting it out of the socket and filing the edges. Apply graphite to all pins before slipping shell back onto cylinder. Graphite for locks is handily packaged in plastic squeeze containers and available at most hardware stores.

Driver pins rarely cause trouble except when a spring breaks. Most lock shells are built with a cover that can be tapped off to expose springs and driver pins. If your lock does not include a cover, there is nothing to do but empty the driver pins and springs out through the cylinder hole. When replacing them, start at the back of the cylinder and work through the hole, one pin at a time. As they slip into place, work a dowel or tube from the back to keep them in place. New drivers and springs are available at locksmiths and also at many hardware stores.

When putting the locking mechanism back in the door, the cam should be in its locked vertical position and the shell screwed tightly against the spacing collar at the back. Line up the cam to engage the arm or lever in the lock case. Sometimes a collar of a different thickness or an adjustable spring collar can be obtained to locate the assembly in a different position so it will work better.

Another problem is to have a key break off in the cylinder. It may be possible to remove the broken key end with a long crochet hook or thin wire with a tiny hook on the end pushed in along the top of the keyhole (this pushes the pins up). Hook the end over the key and work it out of the lock. If this does not work, remove the locking mechanism and the cam from the back side which will allow you to push the key out with a wire.

The second type of door lock is the mortise lock. Most sluggish mortise locks are caused from gummed or sticky parts. Try blowing graphite into the lock with the latch bolt retracted. If this does not correct the trouble, remove the lock from the door by first unscrewing the set-screws holding one of the knobs to the spindle. Some knobs are threaded on the spindle; others slip on. With one knob off, pull the spindle

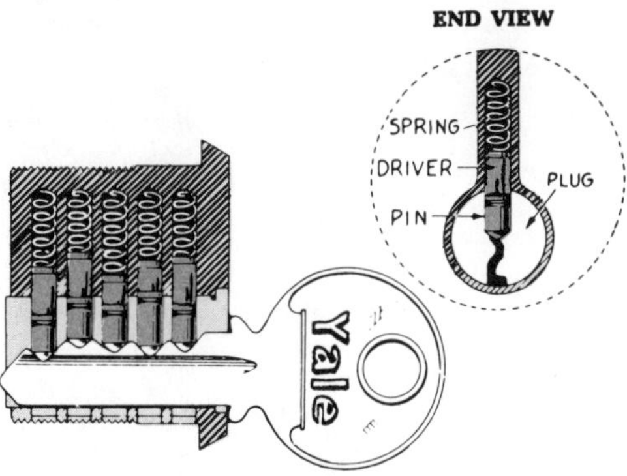

In case of a wrong key being used, pins and drivers are in irregular positions, forming obstructions which prevent rotation of the plug.

The right key will line up the pins and drivers at their intersections so that the plug may be turned to operate the lock.

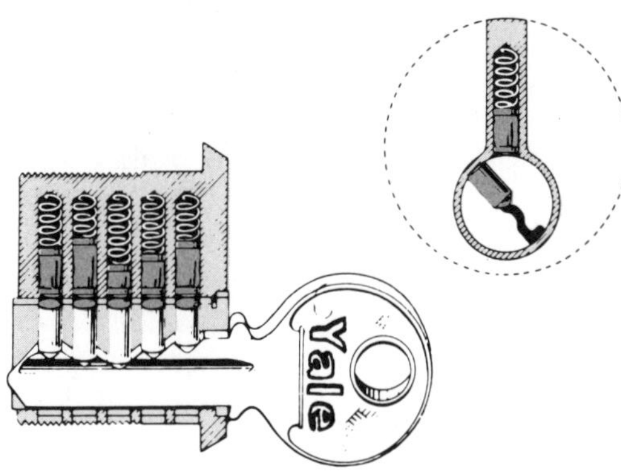

This key (for a warded lock) must pass an end ward in order to rotate.

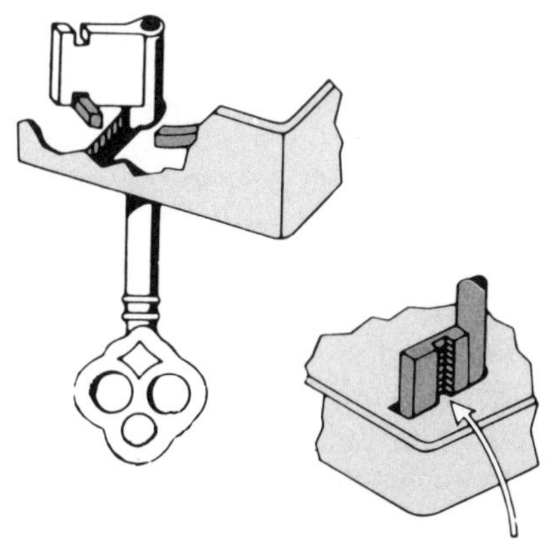

through from the opposite side and remove the screws from the face of the lock. Pry the lock out with a screwdriver.

Disassemble the lock by removing the screws in the side of the case, and soak the assembly in paint thinner or mineral spirits. For particularly dirty locks, scrub and brush the individual parts to remove grime. Wipe parts dry with a cloth, reassemble and dust with graphite until lock works smoothly.

Where the tumbler fails to operate the latch, you may have a broken tumbler spring. Flat spring stock suitable for cutting a new spring is available at most hardware stores. Common pliers are all you need to cut and bend a new spring to fit. If you should cut the spring short, you can enlarge it slightly by peening it with a hammer. File down a long spring to get a tight fit.

The catch-bolt spring may be broken if the bolt fails to extend properly. Most hardware stores carry lengths of compression coil-spring stock in a variety of diameters, so one should fit your lock.

For maximum security, exterior locks should be of the dead-bolt type. Once the bolt is in the keeper and the door locked, it is impossible to force the bolt back without using the key. To keep a burglar from forcing back a beveled bolt with a knife, drive several brass screws through the stop mold in line with the lock bolt, then fill the countersunk holes with putty.

After passing the respective wards on this lock, key rotates so as to lock the bolt.

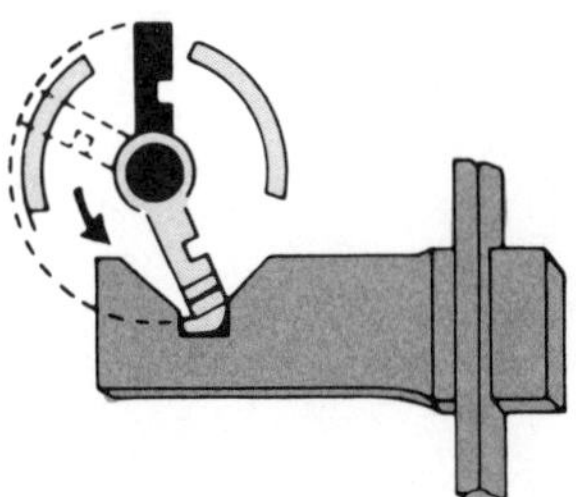

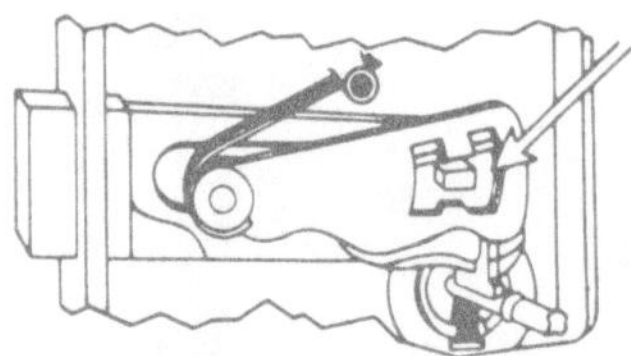

On this lever tumble lock, the key has aligne the lever tumblers s that the "fence pin" i passing through th "gate," and the bolt i thus turned.

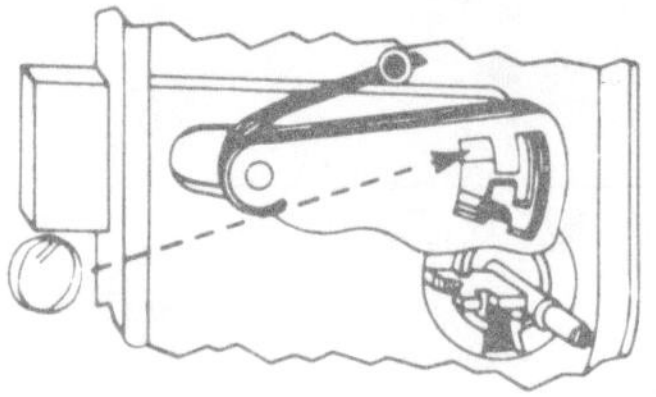

The bolt is in locke position and deadlocke against end pressure b the "fence pin," as th lever tumblers fall bac into place.

Settlement of the house structure or shrinking of partitions may move lock or strike plate enough that the bolt no longer enters the hole in the plate. If the bolt is only slightly off, you may be able to file out the opening in the strike plate. However, the best cure is to shim out the door hinge causing the door to hang improperly.

Loose door knobs are often troublesome. One cure is to loosen the set-screw and remove the knob from the spindle. Drop a pea-sized pellet of putty inside the knob and force it on the spindle. The putty forms a cushion to take up the excess space.

Keys can be so easily duplicated by a locksmith or your local hardware store that it hardly pays for you to file the blanks down yourself. If no master key is available from which to make duplicates, remove the lock or cylinder shell from the door and take it to a locksmith. He can make a new key in minutes. If the key cannot be duplicated or made from the lock immediately, be careful of the person you're dealing with. Members of the Locksmith Guild or locksmiths who represent a reliable safe manufacturer are checked and certified. There are cases where so-called locksmiths repair locks and keys only to gain access to your home. It is not a good idea either to carry your keys on a tag with name and address or car license number.

If your youngster locks himself in the bathroom or other room, you can try the old trick of slipping a newspaper under the door and pushing the key out so it drops on the paper. Then pull the paper and key under the door. Keep talking to the child to keep him from swallowing liquids from the medicine chest. But most interior doors lock with a turned bolt rather than keys. If there is no slot for opening the door from the outside and there's no outside window you can crawl through, rig up an auto jack with some scrap lumber. By working the jack, even the tightest door jamb will spring enough to let the bolt out of the keeper.

See also: ALARMS, BURGLAR; DOORS.

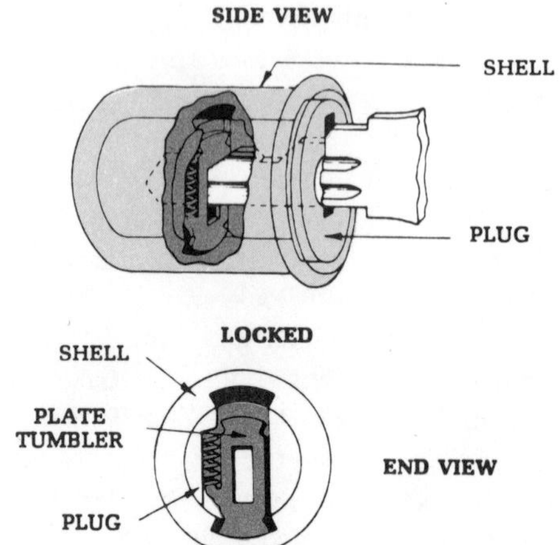

On disc or tumbler locks, until the proper key is inserted, the plates extend into the shell, thus preventing the plug from turning.

Proper key aligns plates, bringing them out of the shell and within the diameter of the plug. Plug is turned to operate the bolt.

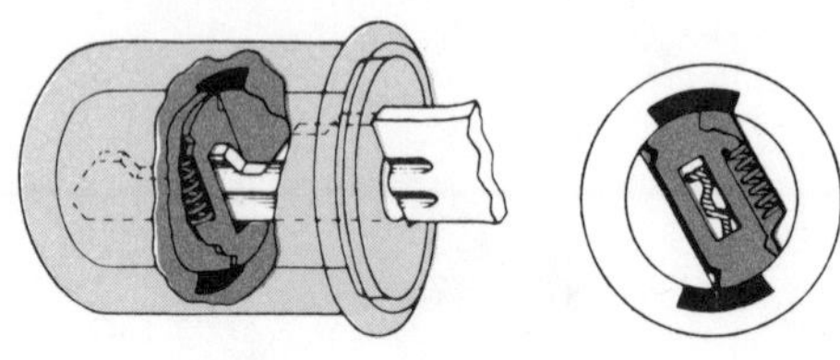

How to Repair Masonry

New materials have improved ability to bond with existing concrete or brick and resist cracking, chipping, spalling

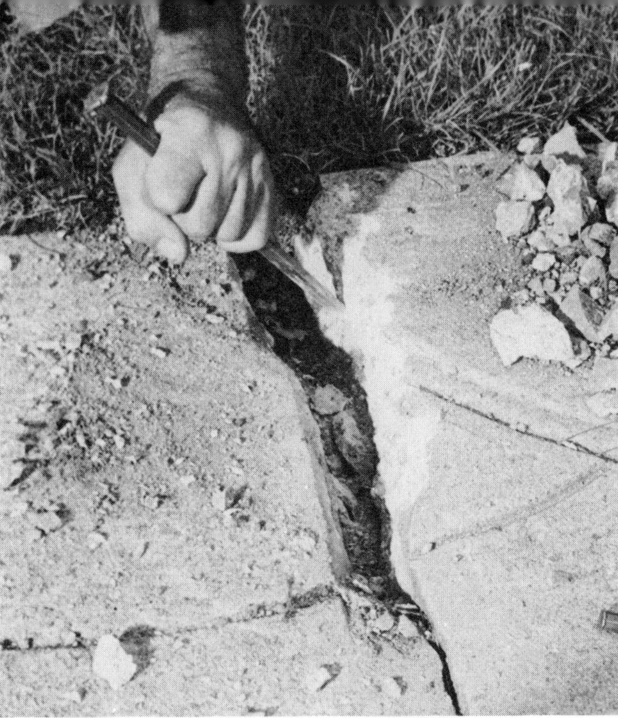

▲ *Widen and roughen area to be patched with a chisel, removing all loose and crumbling concrete. Undercut the sides, if possible, and remove some of the earth in the opening so that concrete will pack into the space beneath the slab and become locked in.*

REPAIRS OF CRACKED and broken concrete around the home have long been a frustrating task for many homeowners. However carefully they did the job, the repair would seldom stand up under heavy rains and winter frost. The problem of bonding the patch to old concrete now has been solved, providing assured success when done properly with the improved materials.

The breakthrough results from additives that provide better bonding to the existing concrete. One form consists of vinyl liquid that is mixed to a uniform consistency with cement, sand, and asbestos fibers. The mixture can be troweled down to ¼-inch thickness and works well also for smoothing rough surfaces and repairing hairline cracks. It has greater strength than standard concrete mixes, resists cracking and chipping, and is not affected by freezing.

The toughest and most expensive masonry patcher is epoxy cement, which is a two-part mixture of emulsion and hardener, mixed in equal parts just before using because it sets very quickly. The epoxy mixture may be combined with regular cement as an additive for greater adhesion, and is often used to seal leaks in foundation walls.

Another useful form of patching cement comes in cartridges, similar to those for caulking. It is used in a regular caulking gun. This form is useful for repairing fine cracks and for replacement of crumbling mortar in brick and stonework.

In addition, these patching materials can be purchased in small sacks of various mixtures for specific purposes, such as mortar, sand, and gravel mixes. There is, of course, a considerable reduction in waste when a 10-pound sack can be opened for a small repair job, and, perhaps homeowners are grateful they need not carry 80-pound standard sacks, plus the extra sand and gravel, and worry about disposing of the excess.

Generally, patching cement is mixed to a thick consistency with only enough water to moisten the ingredients. Some situations may require a thinner mix, sufficiently fluid for pouring into a crevice that cannot be reached for troweling.

Tools needed. A hammer and chisel to widen the concrete crack, a pointed trowel, and a pail for mixing the cement are all you need to make most patches. If the area of broken concrete is fairly large and you will need a considerable amount of cement, do the mixing in a wheelbarrow. For brick mortar repairs, a jointing tool will be useful to strike the mortar joints so that they match the rest of the wall.

Preparing the mix. Small amounts may be mixed in any clean container of glass, pottery, plastic, even paper. For mixing latex cement, place some of the powder into a bowl and add just enough water to form a thick paste. If the cement will be used for a thin hairline crack, start with a thick paste, let it stand for a minute, then stir thoroughly to obtain a consistency of heavy batter, which will be just fluid enough to pour, but not watery. If it is necessary to add water, do it very sparingly; the thicker mixture makes a stronger cement.

A plastic consistency, almost like putty, is better for larger patches. Add just enough water to the powder to moisten all the ingredients, turning frequently with the trowel so that no dry materials remain on the bottom. The resulting mix will be smooth and dry when compressed with the flat blade of the trowel, without free water rising to the top.

Mix just enough for no more than 10 minutes of work. The cement will begin to set in that time and no longer be workable. Use ordinary portland cement and sand, with a vinyl additive as a bonding agent for the average repair of broken concrete; use vinyl latex emulsion mixture for repairs of small cracks and for leveling and smoothing uneven concrete; use latex cement for coating coarse cement when a thin layer is desired, and for patches that will be under some pressure, as in foundation wall repairs, also for replacing broken corners of slabs and other concrete forms.

Filling sidewalk cracks. Use a chisel to clean away all loose and crumbling segments, then chip away as much material as you can to widen the crack, undercutting the sides so that they slope inward from the surface to provide a better joint. With a stiff wire brush, clean the old concrete surface to remove all dirt and mud. If the opening is muddy, use the exhaust end of the vacuum cleaner to blow out the water. Use the concrete mix with vinyl additive to pack the opening, then smooth it flush with the adjacent surface. If the space underneath the opening is muddy, fill to the level of the original concrete with sand or gravel, then pack in the repair cement.

Broken corners of concrete slabs—including the edges of driveway runways, sidewalk slabs, and patios—formerly were impossible to repair because the added patch was easily broken. Latex binder additives will provide a good bond. The repair requires installation of a form around the corner—this may be a couple of pieces of hardboard tapped into place and held

Clean sides of the break with a stiff brush to remove dirt and mud that would prevent bonding of the patching cement.

Base of opening receives stones or sand that form aggregates which become part of the newly-poured concrete patching material.

After cement has been troweled in place, allow it to set, then use a jointing tool to form the groove of the expansion joint.

To repair brickwork, chisel out the split segments. Then work vinyl cement into the area to be patched.

Vinyl cement additives assure a permanent bond in the repair of brickwork and other masonry.

◄ *Mixing concrete on driveway apron or other surface will cause staining. Use any convenient container, such as a wheelbarrow, or make a box which can be discarded after use.*

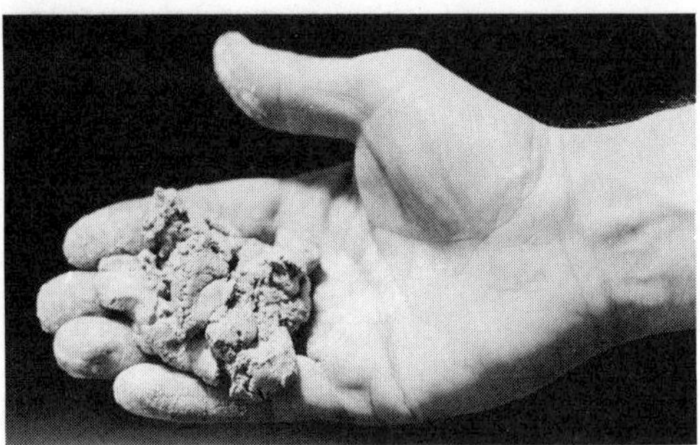

▲ *To form a putty-like anchoring compound for application in vertical walls, use very little water. Even if the mixture seems dry and crumbly, hesitate about adding liquid.* ▼

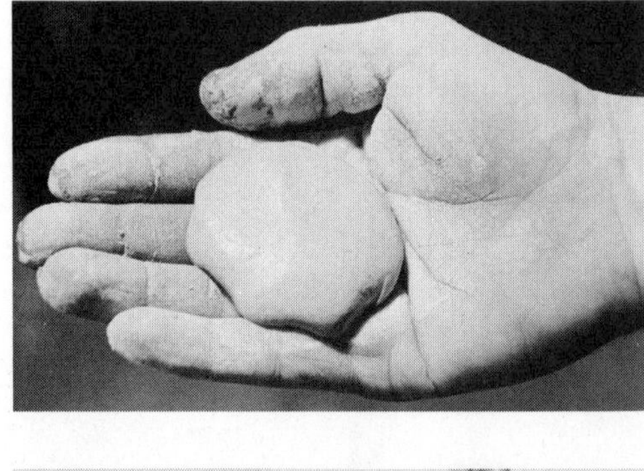

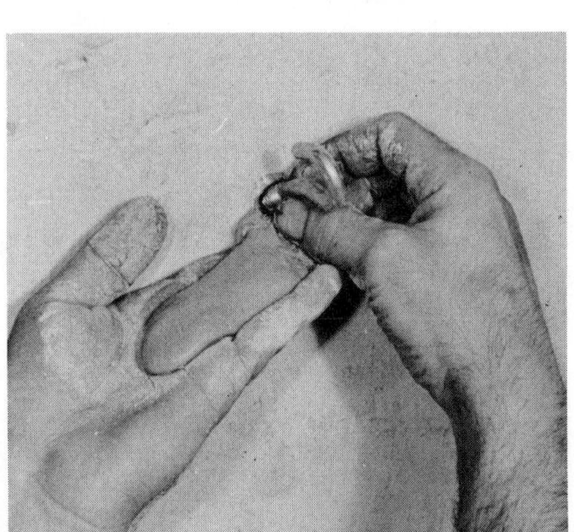

▲ *When the anchoring compound is mixed, force a little into the hole with the fixture to be mounted so that the hole is about half filled. Tap the fixture lightly with a hammer several times to make the compound flow around it.*

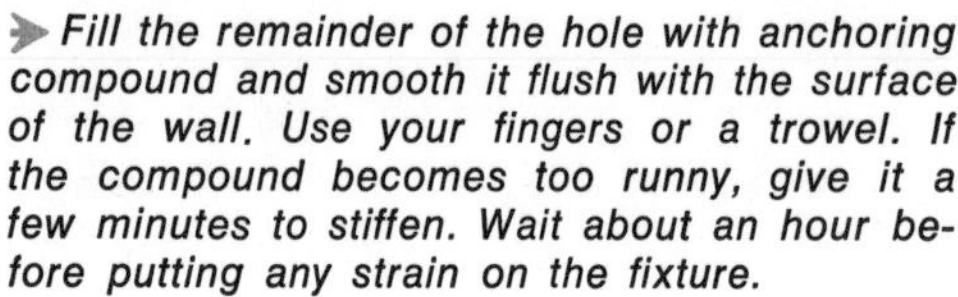

► *Fill the remainder of the hole with anchoring compound and smooth it flush with the surface of the wall. Use your fingers or a trowel. If the compound becomes too runny, give it a few minutes to stiffen. Wait about an hour before putting any strain on the fixture.*

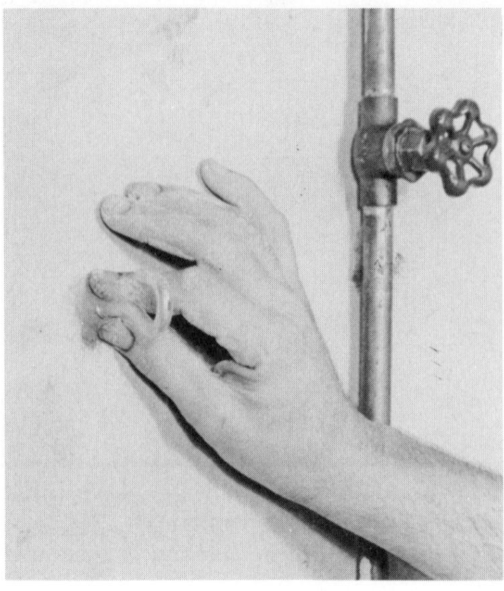

with stakes driven into the ground to be removed after the cement hardens.

Restoring roughened slab. Heavy rains, plus the expansion and contraction of temperature changes, will sometimes cause the top of a sidewalk to chip and spall, resulting in a rough and untidy appearance. A smooth new topping can be applied with epoxy cement, spread in a layer of only ⅛- or ¼-inch. This method also can be used for correcting the pitch of a patio or other concrete surface to assure proper rainwater drainage. Make sure the surface is perfectly clean. If there is paint on the surface, it will be necessary to use a solution of muriatic acid. Two 1/16-inch layers, almost as thin as a coating of paint, will provide a smoother and more durable result.

Match the color. While your patching effort will be successful, you may regret it if the color is so different from the original slab that the patch stands out and seemingly dominates everything in sight. The usual portland cement is quite light in color, while your sidewalk probably is much darker, or the brick mortar will be much different from the mortar used in brick pointing.

▲ Anchoring compound used to embed the post in concrete was mixed to a flowing consistency, then poured in place. After pouring, the post was tapped lightly with a hammer and mixture was troweled smooth.

The best way to handle this is to color the concrete when you use it, adding the necessary dye or pigments right in the mixture. Ordinarily, lampblack is used to darken portland cement, while various pigments may be used if necessary to match a colored patio or terrace. The problem is that you will find it difficult to predict the true color of the cement when it dries. The only real way to do this is to mix a batch and let it dry for a couple of days, but this can run into an extended project if you keep changing the amount of pigment and must wait a few days between each change. The best that you can do, if it is necessary to get on with the job, is to make a fair estimate of the degree of color tinting desired, keeping in mind that it usually dries lighter. You still have the satisfaction of knowing that you made a reasonable effort to obtain a match.

Another use for patching compound is to anchor posts, bolts, hooks and other fixtures in masonry floors and walls. The more specialized of these compounds expand slightly as they harden and form extremely strong beds for hardware. They also make strong patches for cracks and holes, although they cannot be spread as thinly as other patching compounds.

Anchoring compounds can be mixed in either a pouring consistency for work on horizontal surfaces, as in anchoring posts for railings, and in a thicker putty-like mixture for mounting hooks or bolts or the like in vertical walls. Study the directions carefully and always use as little water as possible.

Also, make sure the mounting hole or crack to be filled has a clean, dust-free surface. Some anchoring compounds require that the surface be moist, but not wet.

See also: BRICKWORK; CONCRETE.

How to Repair Electric Mixers

Most things that can go wrong with an electric mixer are easy to repair. Here's how to do it

YOUR FOOD MIXER is the secret of those light, fluffy cakes your wife has been making. Its range of speeds allows her to use just the right touch for whatever is cooking. So, if you want to continue eating cake, you had better know how to help care for the mixer.

Normally, not too much goes wrong with a mixer. Accidents can happen—a spoon might get caught in the beaters or the mixer might fall off the counter resulting in damaged beaters. Sometimes the damage is stripped beater gears, cracked housing or a broken handle. These are easy parts to replace; as is a damaged cord.

Basic construction and operation. Most mixers are powered by a small high-speed series motor that is geared down to the slow beater speed through a worm gear on the end of the armature shaft. This worm gear meshes with the beater gears which drive the beaters. Speed control is obtained by either a tapped field coil winding or by a governor and resistor circuit.

All of this is enclosed in a plastic case. Often the most difficult part in servicing a mixer is determining how to open the case. Some manufacturers hide the assem-

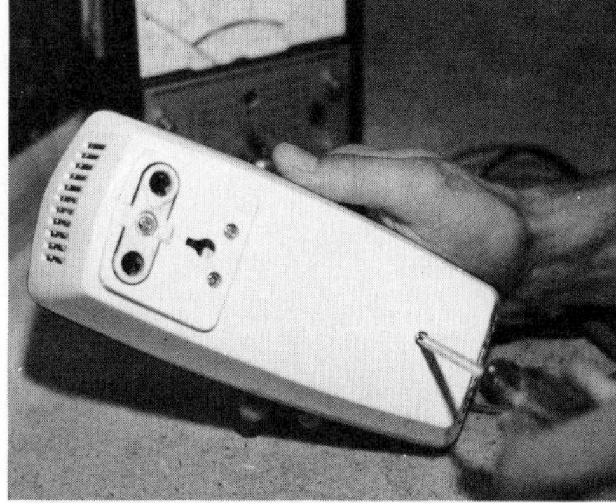

Removal of three screws—one at the back and two side by side near the front—allows the case to be opened to expose the motor.

bly screws under a nameplate. Some mixers come apart fore and aft. Others will open top from bottom. A careful examination of the case will usually determine which approach to use.

Replacing damaged beater gears. When the motor runs and the beaters fail to turn, you must suspect damaged beater gears. Each beater has its own drive gear and even though only one is damaged, both should be examined and if there is any question, both should be changed. Note that in many models there will be a left hand and a right hand gear. Each is different.

When reassembling the beater gears make certain that they are timed to allow the beaters to be offset from each other by 45°. This will prevent the beater blades from hitting each other. Also repack the beater area with a clean light grease. Do not use oil as it will seep down along the beater shaft into the food being mixed.

Speed control and operation. Any defect, either in the switch or the governor control, will affect the speed of operation. A defect in the field coil winding will prevent the mixer from operating at any speed setting, except in models which have a tapped field winding. Here, a break in coil B will prevent operation in the low-speed position and a break in coil A will allow operation at high-speed only.

A break or open circuit in the armature winding will cause excessive sparking or overheating. It may also cause low power or no operation at any switch position for any type of speed control system.

Brushes make the connection from the armature to the rest of the motor and

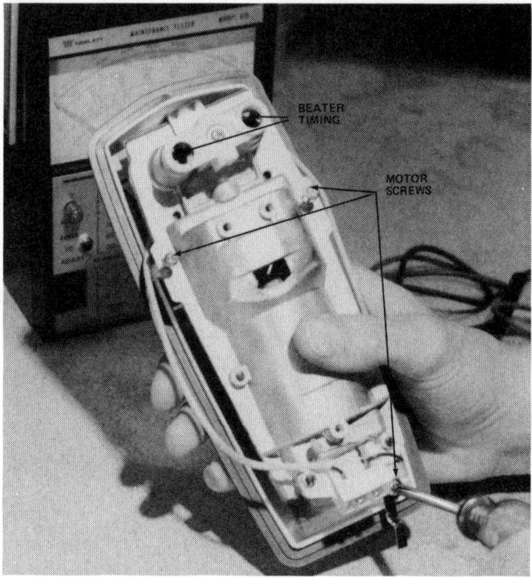

The mixer motor assembly is held in the top half of the case by three screws. Note the position of the beater sockets. They are offset 45 degrees so the blades of the beaters will mesh.

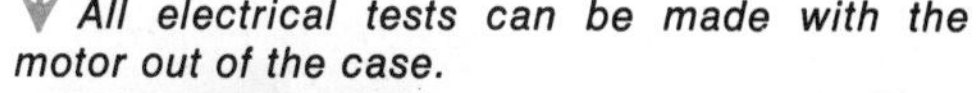

All electrical tests can be made with the motor out of the case.

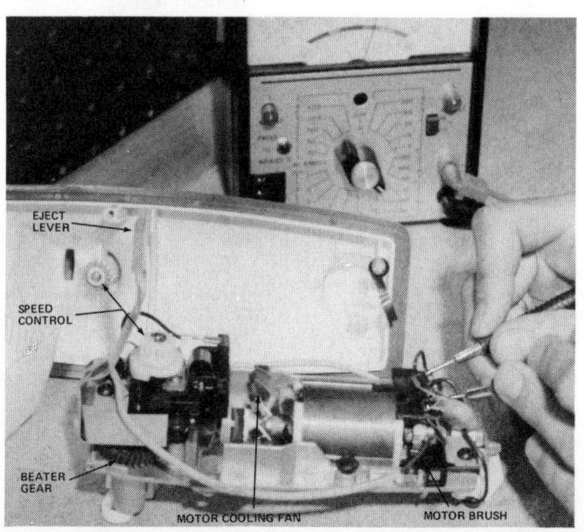

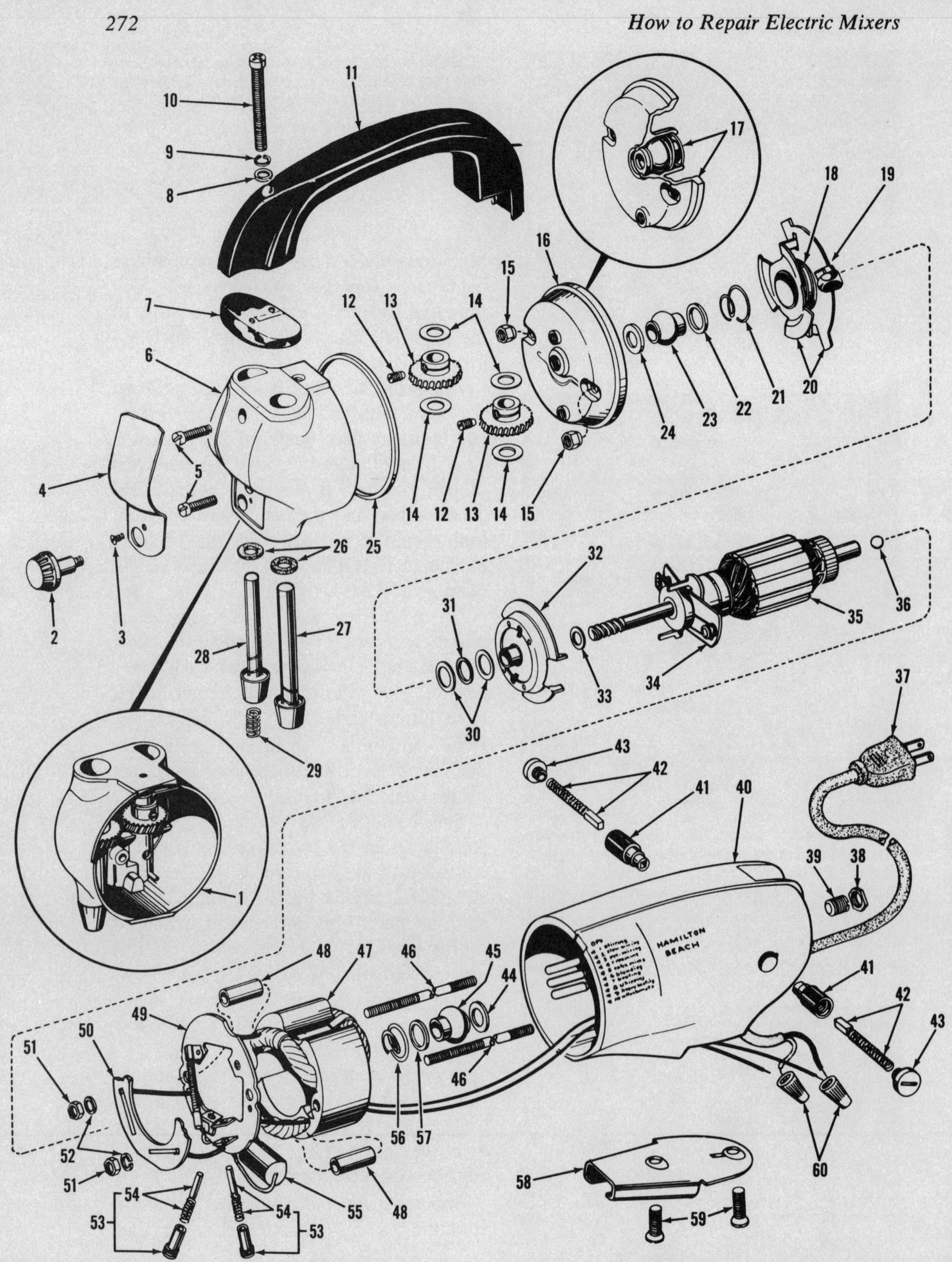
1
2
3
4
5
6
7
8
9
10
11
12
13
14
15
16
17
18
19
20
21
22
23
24
25
26
27
28
29
30
31
32
33
34
35
36
37
38
39
40
41
42
43
44
45
46
47
48
49
50
51
52
53
54
55
56
57
58
59
60
HAMILTON
BEACH

REF. NO.	PART NAME	QTY.
1	Gear housing complete with gears, shafts, set screws and felt packers	1
2	Mixing unit retaining screw	1
3	Front plate retaining screw	1
4	Gear housing front plate	1
5	Gear housing to motor screw	2
6	Gear housing only	1
7	Gear housing top plate	1
8	Handle screw washer	1
9	Handle screw lockwasher	1
10	Handle screw	1
11	Handle	1
12	Worm wheel set screw	1
13	Worm wheel with set screws	2
14	Worm wheel washer .027″-.030″	3
14	Worm wheel washer .023″-.026″	As Required
14	Worm wheel washer	As Required
15	Motor cover retaining nut	2
16	Motor cover only	1
17	Motor cover complete with bearing, felt washer & spring	1
18	Control cam spring	1
19	Regulating ring complete	1
20	Regulating ring and cam complete	1
21	Bearing spring	1
22	Bearing spring felt	1
23	Bearing	1
24	Bearing felt oil retainer	1
25	Gear housing gasket	1
26	Packing	2
27	Long gear shaft with coupling	1
28	Short gear shaft with coupling	1
29	Agitator tension spring	1
30	Fibre thrust washer	2
31	Steel thrust washer	1
32	Speed control plate	1
33	Retaining disc insulating washer	1
34	Governor complete	1
35	Armature with governor and thrust ball	1
36	Thrust ball	1
37	Cord complete	1
38	Thrust screw lock nut	1
39	Thrust screw	1
40	Motor case with bearing, spring brush holders and studs, and mixguide plate	1
41	Brush holders	2
42	Carbon brush and spring	2
43	Carbon brush screw	2
44	Bearing felt oil retainer	1
45	Bearing	1
46	Field studs	2
47	Field core, coils, slip ring brush holder plate and contact plate	1
48	Brush holder plate spacer	2
49	Resistor plate w/condenser comp. 90-130V	1
50	Contact plate complete	1
51	Field core retaining nut	2
52	Retaining nut lockwasher	2
53	Governor slip ring brush holder, brush and spring	2
54	Governor brush and spring	2
55	Condenser 76-130V	1
56	Bearing spring	1
57	Bearing spring felt	1
58	Motor bracket	1
59	Motor bracket screws	2
60	Wire nut	2

should be replaced when they are worn to ⅓ of their original length. Worn brushes will cause excessive sparking at the commutator and may cause a loss of power. Do not oil brushes! It will make them sticky in their holders causing poor contact to the commutator and excessive sparking. Oiling brushes will also shorten their life. They must slide freely in their holders.

A defective cord can cause erratic operation when it is wiggled while plugged in. Voltage must be available at the machine end of the cord when it is plugged in. It is usually best to replace a cord rather than to repair it.

Replacement parts. Beaters, handles, cases and switches are designed for specific brands and models. They are usually available only at the store from which the

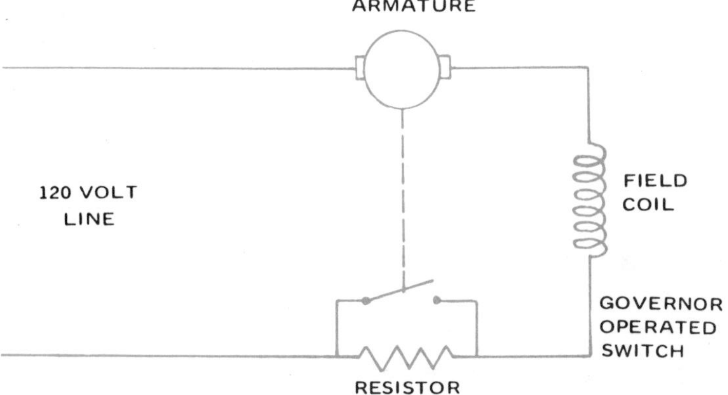

◀ This mixer is typical of those with governor speed controls. The governor (34) operates with the speed control plate (32), regulating ring (20), contact plate (50), and resistor plate (49) to switch the resistor in and out of the circuit. The resistor is wired in series across it, as shown in the schematic drawing. ▶

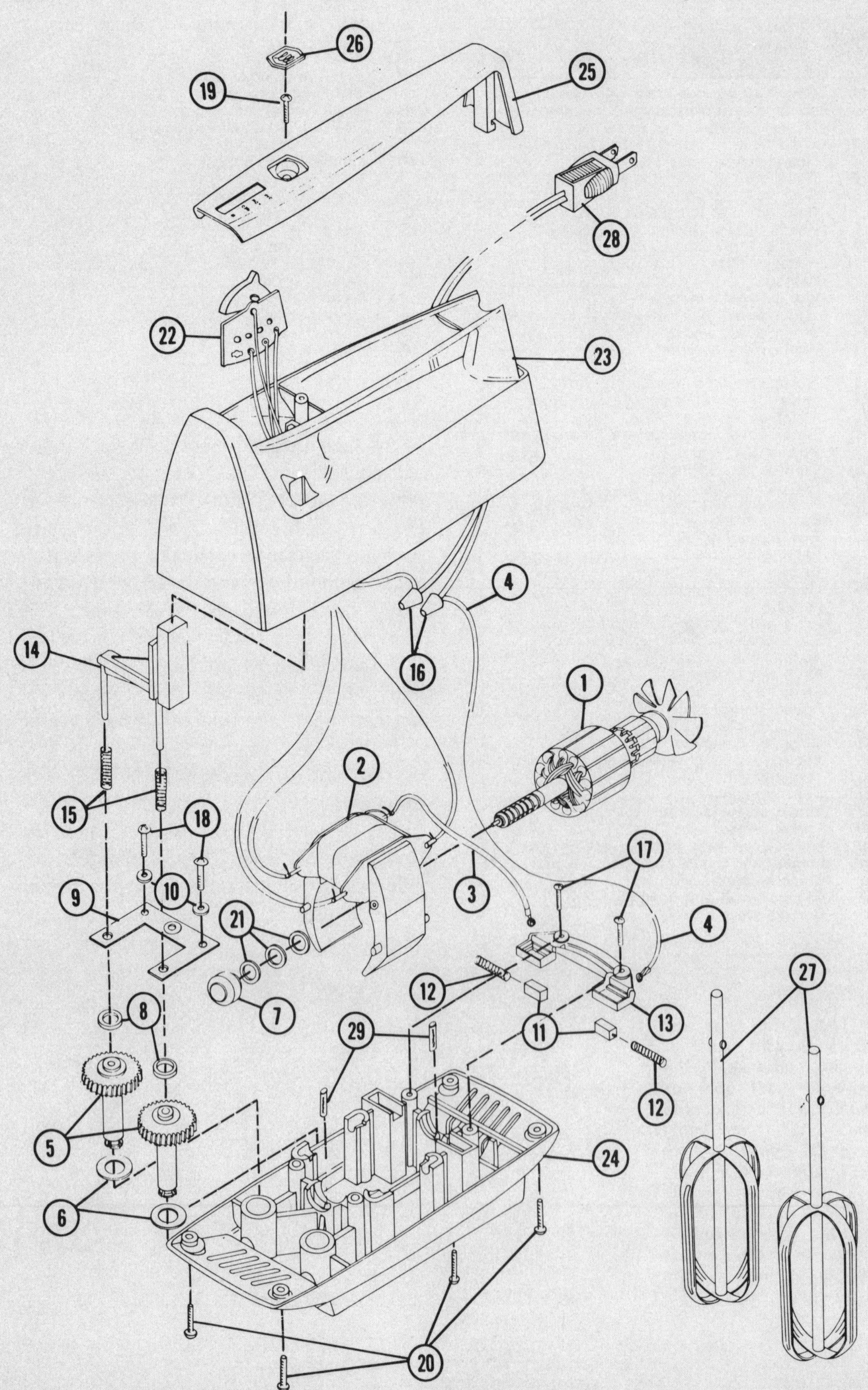
26
25
19
28
22
23
4
14
16
1
2
15
18
17
3
9
10
21
4
12
13
7
8
11
29
27
12
5
24
6
20

A simple four-position switch regulates the speed of this mixer which is equipped with a tapped-field-coil speed control.

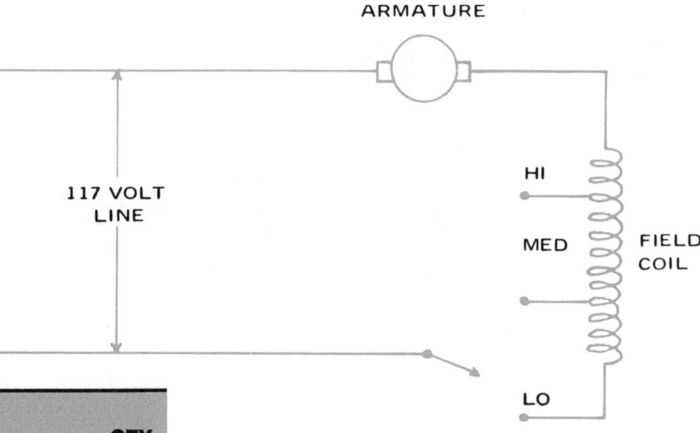

REF. NO.	PART NAME	QTY.
1	Armature	1
2	Field Coil Assembly	1
3	Lead Assembly 3″	1
4	Lead Assembly 5″	1
5	Gear and Sleeve Assembly	2
6	Washer, Beater Sleeve	2
7	Bearing	1
8	Felt Washer	2
9	Retainer, Bearing	1
10	Washer 3/8″ ODX 1/32	2
11	Brush, Commutator	2
12	Spring, Brush	2
13	Retainer, Bearing and Brush	1
14	Beater, Ejector	1
15	Spring, Beater Ejector	2
16	Wire Connector	2
17	Screw 6-20x1/2	2
18	Screw 6-20x3/8	2
19	Screw 6-20x9/16	1
20	Screw 6-20x3/5	4
21	Washer, Spacer	3
22	Switch	1
23	Upper Housing	1
24	Lower Housing	1
25	Handle Cover Assembly	1
26	Cartouch Plug	1
27	Beater	2
28	Cord Assembly	1
29	Oiler Felt, Bearing	2

product was purchased, or from the manufacturer who made the machine. These parts can be replaced without too much difficulty or cost.

If either the armature or the field coil is open (burned out), it will have to be replaced. Generally, replacement parts will have to be obtained from the manufacturer or an authorized dealer for that particular brand. At this point you should check costs because it may be more economical to buy a new mixer.

By using the exploded views shown here and the accompanying trouble-shooting chart, you should be able to handle any service problem on your mixer.

See also: ELECTRICAL, HOME; INDIVIDUAL APPLIANCE LISTINGS.

TROUBLE-SHOOTING
ELECTRIC MIXERS

PROBLEM / POSSIBLE CAUSE	DEFECTIVE CORD	DEFECTIVE SWITCH	OPEN MOTOR WINDING	FROZEN BEARING	JAMMED BEATER	STRIPPED BEATER GEARS	INCORRECT SPEED SETTING	MIX TOO HEAVY	SHORTED WINDING
MOTOR DOES NOT RUN	√	√	√	√	√				√
BLOWS FUSES	√								√
MOTOR RUNS, BEATERS DO NOT						√			
ERRATIC OPERATION	√	√							
SLOW SPEED							√	√	
MOTOR RUNS HOT								√	√

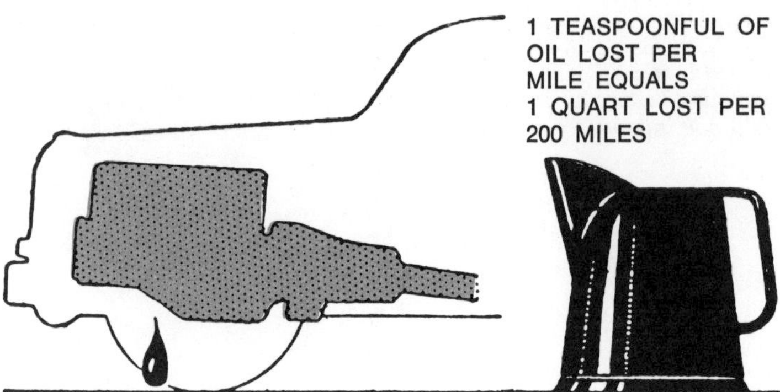
1 TEASPOONFUL OF
OIL LOST PER
MILE EQUALS
1 QUART LOST PER
200 MILES

How a comparatively small amount of leakage will add up on a trip of several hundred miles.

How to Stop Engine Oil Loss

Before you start thinking about an expensive replacement of piston rings, take a look at the many other factors that cause your car's engine to lose oil

YOU'VE HEARD THE SUMMER month vacationist say the trip was fine but that he "used a lot of oil," but, did he? Perhaps instead of using he was losing oil; there is a difference. You've seen those familiar dark streaks stretching endlessly along both sides of concrete highways—they are mute evidence of precious engine oil relentlessly dropped from motor vehicles.

How much can plain everyday oil leakage amount to? If your engine has an external leak which lets a teaspoonful of oil drip from the engine every mile, you'll lose nearly a quart of oil every 200 miles of travel. Of course, every normal engine uses oil when operating because some oil naturally is consumed in the combustion process. If this were not so, you wouldn't have to add a quart now and then to bring the crankcase oil level to normal. And, like excessive fuel consumption that goes along with sustained high speed driving, oil consumption, too, goes up with high speeds.

But there is such a thing as excessive oil consumption at normal driving speeds. Sometimes the cause may be hard to diagnose, but like a headache, excessive engine oil consumption tells you something is wrong somewhere.

If your engine has a lot of miles on it and the oil burning has been gradually becoming worse, the only cure is to go inside the engine.

Interestingly enough, worn rings are not the most common cause of high-mileage oil consumption. The ring manufacturers have done an excellent job of making rings that last, and their oil control rings are singularly good.

A more likely cause of high mileage oil burning is worn valve guides or damaged valve stem seals. The seals can be replaced with special tools without even pulling the cylinder head. Valve guide replacement requires pulling the head, but even that is not an extremely difficult job.

If you suspect your engine may be leaking oil, start your investigation by taking a look at your garage floor or wherever you normally park the car. The familiar "gooey" spot on the floor under the engine is a dead give-away of dripping oil. A good test is to spread some clean newspapers on the floor under the engine. Then run the engine at a speed substantially above idling. Allow the engine to run long enough to bring it up to idling temperature and for 5 or 10 minutes thereafter. If oil drips on the paper, get under the car and check where it is coming from. Remember that though the oil drops straight downwards with the car at rest, the source of leakage actually may be farther away with the oil creeping along inside the engine until it finds a convenient spot from which to drip. Also remember that the car's forward motion often makes excess oil show up where a leak is actually not occurring. If you suspect external oil leakage, look for "oil washed" areas on the engine; such areas are evidence of leakage ahead of the washed areas. While excessive oil consumption also may take place inside the engine, let's first trouble-shoot and correct the external leaks.

Very often just tightening a joint, installing a new gasket or tightening the oil pan drain plug, stops external leaks.

Oil loss can also be caused by too much pressure in the engine crankcase.

On older cars (1962 and earlier), crankcase pressure and turbulence (caused by wear of the piston rings, which allow exhaust and unburned gases to leak into the crankcase), would break the oil up into droplets, and these droplets would blow out the crankcase ventilating tube.

Since the introduction of positive crankcase ventilation, the oil droplets-laden gases now are pulled out of the crankcase and dumped into the intake manifold, where they go into the combustion chamber for burning. In high-speed driving, the engine will suddenly start to burn oil.

The positive crankcase ventilation system also can cause oil leaks. If the PCV valve is partly or fully clogged, the gases cannot escape. Crankcase pressure builds up and when it is very high, it can create leaks through any weak spots in the oil pan and other engine gaskets, including fuel pump, rocker cover, tappet cover, intake manifold (on some cars), and timing chain.

An increasingly common cause of oil burning on GM and Ford products creates an unusual mystery. The smoke is pouring out the tailpipe, but the engine dipstick doesn't seem to be showing any oil loss. In this case, check the transmission oil level, you will find it down. How can transmission oil burn in the engine? Very simple, on automatic transmissions with vacuum modulators.

The vacuum modulator is a transmission device that is connected by a hose to the engine's intake manifold. It contains a diaphragm that helps regulate transmission shifting according to changes in engine manifold vacuum. If the modulator diaphragm cracks or becomes porous, the intake manifold vacuum draws transmission oil up through the hose into the engine.

The switch to electric windshield wipers eliminated the combination fuel-vacuum booster pump that was used on most cars

If you suspect your engine of leaking oil externally, spread clean paper under the engine and allow it to run awhile. Then watch where the oil is dripping to localize leakage source.

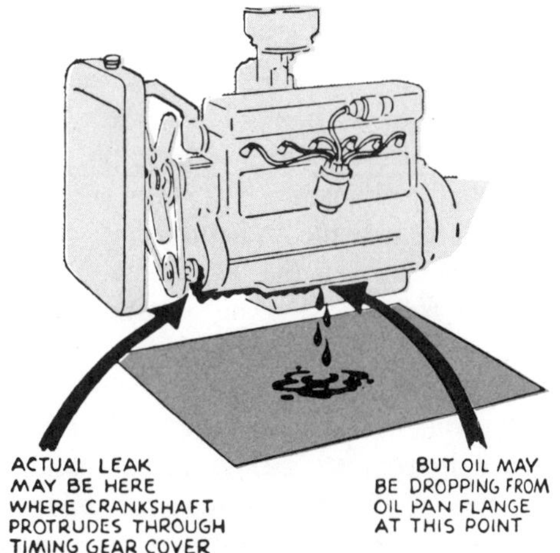
ACTUAL LEAK
MAY BE HERE
WHERE CRANKSHAFT
PROTRUDES THROUGH
TIMING GEAR COVER
BUT OIL MAY
BE DROPPING FROM
OIL PAN FLANGE
AT THIS POINT

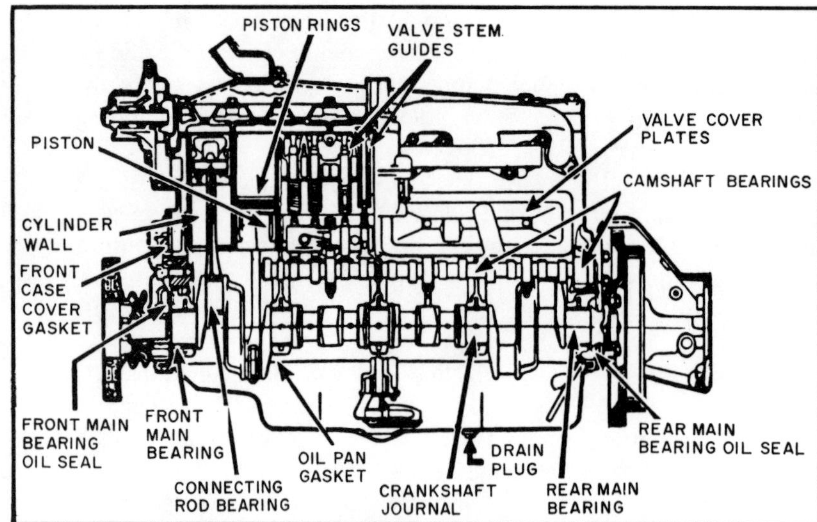

This illustration shows the engine parts involved in both internal and external oil leaks. Loose joints on such parts as the oil pan and front end timing gear cover do not allow gaskets to seal tightly. Internally, such worn parts as cylinders, rings and bearings, can cause excessive oil consumption.

with vacuum windshield wipers. And this booster pump was responsible for many cases of sudden high oil consumption. The pump was operated by intake manifold vacuum, and if its diaphragm leaked, the vacuum would draw oil from the engine block, into which the pump was bolted, up into the manifold. Only a few cars use vacuum wipers today, but you may have an older car that also has them, and you should not forget this possibility.

Checking for leakage. To check vacuum pump diaphragm leakage (indicated by sluggish windshield wiper action when the engine is accelerated), have the wiper in operation and disconnect the vacuum pipe at the manifold. Then hold a piece of clean paper near the open end of the pipe. If you get an oily discharge, it shows that oil is passing through the vacuum pump requiring replacement of the diaphragm.

Other reasons why your engine may be using or losing too much oil are: piston rings with too little "end" or "gap" clearance; rings installed upside down in grooves; wrong type rings for the engine; distorted cylinders caused by unequal tightening of cylinder head stud nuts; connecting rods bent or twisted; late valve timing; too much oil pump pressure (can be corrected on some engines by regulating oil pressure relief valve where such a valve is fitted); dirty oil; clogged oil passages; air-fuel mixture too lean (engine may overheat causing rings to stick or break); dirty cooling system, causing local hot spots, distortion and overheating of the engine. In some cases the remedies are obvious; in others, it means a tear-down and rebuild job which should be done by a well-equipped shop.

The more mileage on the engine, the more likely it is to use more and more oil. It usually will take more than just a "ring job" to bring back normal conditions with normal oil consumption. Wear is usually distributed over the entire engine so that when cylinders have to be reconditioned it's safe to say the valves, bearings, timing chain or gear, camshaft and crankshaft need reconditioning or replacement. The popularity in recent years of "rebuilt" or "exchange" engines testifies to the fact that fixing only part of the job certainly won't overcome high oil consumption in a worn engine. Oil consumption also goes up with

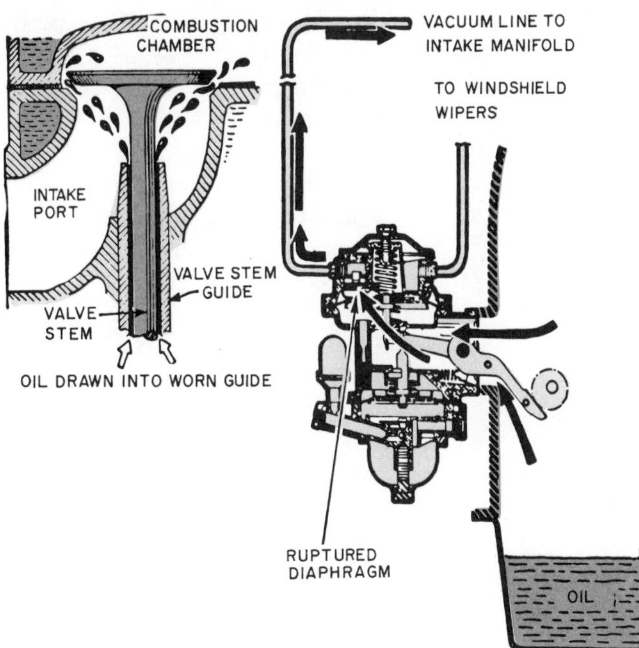

Excessive wear of valve stems and their guides causes oil to be drawn into combustion chambers where it is burned with the air-fuel mixture, causing the blue smoke from the exhaust. Worn piston rings also cause smoke.

high road speeds; as is true with gasoline, moderate speeds will save you money by using less oil.

Although rings have dropped to near the bottom of the list as a cause of engine oil burning, they still must not be ignored. Rings have a tough job to do in any engine. They must act as a guide for the piston, must conform to the cylinder walls, and seal against compression and combustion pressures, besides keeping the correct amount of oil on the cylinder walls. They have to constantly battle other hardships like oil dilution, cold weather starting, gum and foreign matter, all of which induce wear or cause sticking and breakage. Worn, broken, or sticking rings (rings that stick in the grooves of the pistons, because of gum, carbon, etc.), when removed and replaced with a new set of rings, often bring oil consumption back to normal.

But here is a point to watch. Blue smoke blowing from the exhaust pipe doesn't always mean the rings are to blame. Perhaps the rings are in fairly good shape but not able to handle the excessive oil "throw-off" from the bearings. Remember that bearings, too, have a lot to do with high oil consumption. Engines are fitted with piston rings, known as "oil rings," which are there to control the amount of oil for the cylinder walls. The oil rings scrape excess oil back to the crankcase, but when excessive bearing clearance allows too much oil to be thrown on the cylinder walls, the oil rings just can't handle the great volume of oil.

Therefore, when your engine uses a lot of oil and the trouble is traced to "rings," you are in for a job of (a) replacing the old rings with new, or (b) reconditioning the cylinders, fitting new pistons, pins, rings, main and connecting rod bearings. Along with this a "valve job" will be done because when an engine is "down" for major work on cylinders, pistons and bearings, the valves are sure to need replacement or reconditioning.

Many times, the effect of worn rings will be exaggerated. Worn compression rings and low compression readings do not mean that oil consumption must be high, or that

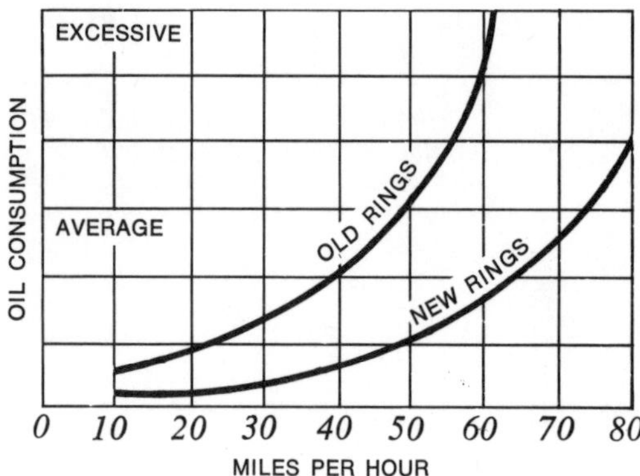

Curves showing how oil consumption goes up with high road speeds. Consumption is greater with old or worn piston rings.

Because modern engines breathe so deeply, the intake valve guide, when worn, is a major cause of oil consumption. Improved seals, such as the spring-loaded teflon type illustrated, can be installed to prevent oil loss from this problem.

the rings are the major cause of the problem.

Often, repairing a few minor leaks, replacing valve stem seals with new, improved seals, and servicing the positive crankcase ventilation system will restore oil mileage to an acceptable level.

Oil additives. Engine oil additives have become very popular in recent years as a performance improver. These very thick lubricants actually increase the oil's ability to resist thinning out as the engine warms up. As such, they can be helpful in reducing oil burning by preventing the oil from becoming thin enough to slip past worn rings and through worn valve guides. In conjunction with other measures, they can help keep oil mileage at reasonable levels without the expense of an overhaul, which on an older car may not be economically justifiable. P.W.

See also: BEARINGS; ENGINE; TRANSMISSION, AUTO; TUNE-UP, ENGINE; VALVES.

All about Painting Your Home's Interior

You can brighten up a dull room with a crisp new coat of paint. Here's how to do the job quickly and easily

THE INTERIOR of any home reflects the taste and personality of the owner. Freshly painted walls and crisply contrasting trim help to create the overall effect. As with any painting project, there are a few basic rules.

Never attempt to paint over a wall that is covered with an accumulation of oil or grease from cooking or heating. A clean surface is a must for maximum adhesion of the new paint. A sound practice is to wash walls from the floor up. This method prevents drips of dirty water from streaking the walls with a residue that is difficult to remove.

There are several products on the market which make this pre-paint cleaning easy. Some do not even require a rinse, others do. Read the label and follow directions. Your paint dealer will be glad to help you by recommending the right product for your purpose. After all, his paint needs a good foundation.

When painting rooms, remove any fixtures you can, such as face plates of electrical outlets, chandeliers and the like. This

▲ *Before starting a painting project remove as many things from the room as possible. Heavy furniture can be pushed to the middle of the room to form an island and covered with drop cloths.*

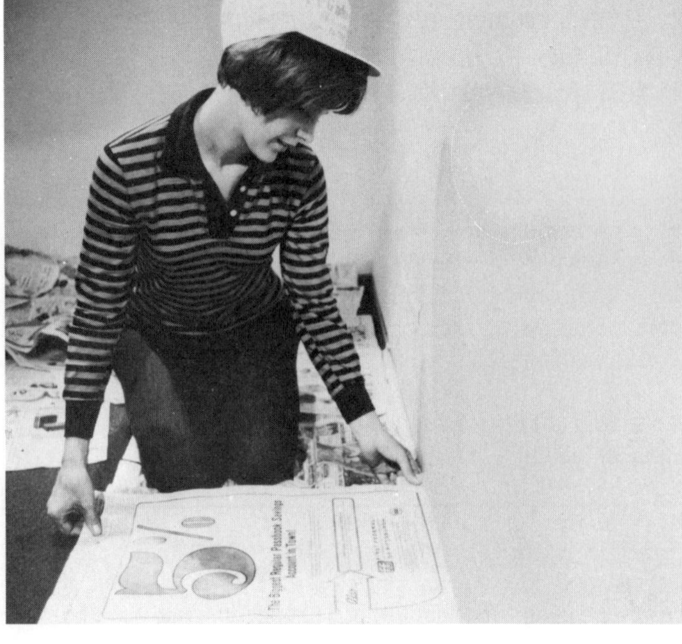

◄ *Use newspapers or drop cloths to protect floors. Mask baseboards, switches, door hardware and any other fixtures that cannot be removed. Remove as many fixtures as possible, such as lights, face plates, etc.*

Prime bare metal to prevent discoloration or rust from bleeding through and staining the new paint.

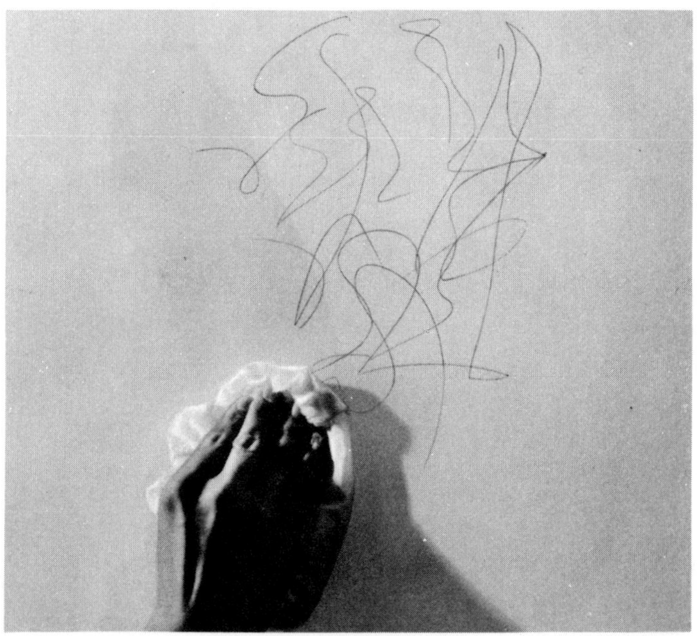

Wipe off grease and pencil marks, preferably with a liquid spray cleaner.

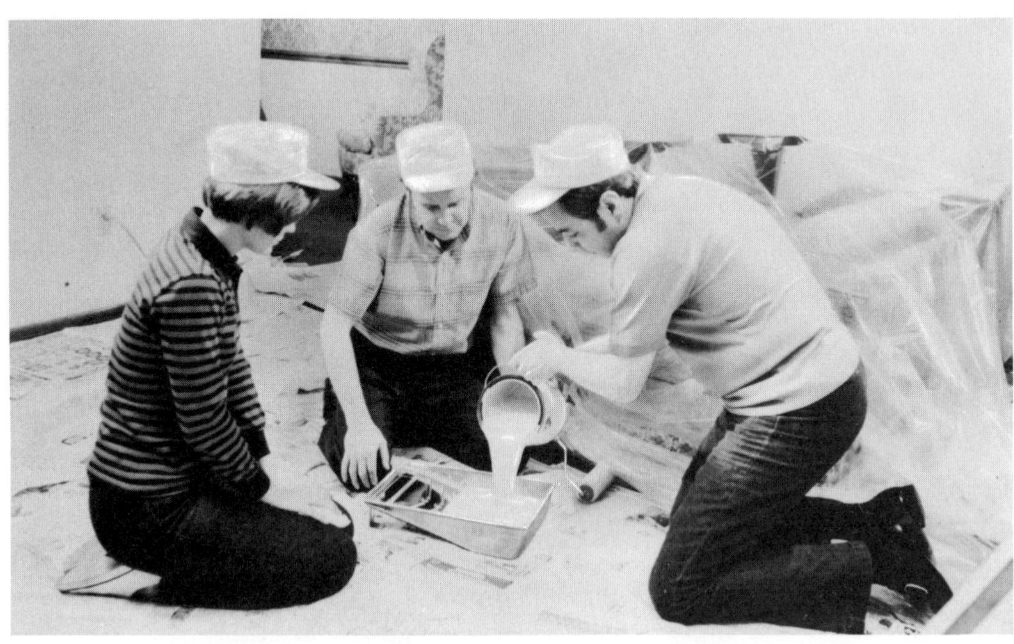

▲Fill the roller tray one third full of paint.

▼ Wet the roller with water and roll it out on newspapers. Wetting the roller before painting conditions the fibers and eliminates any possible bubbles. It only needs to be done once.

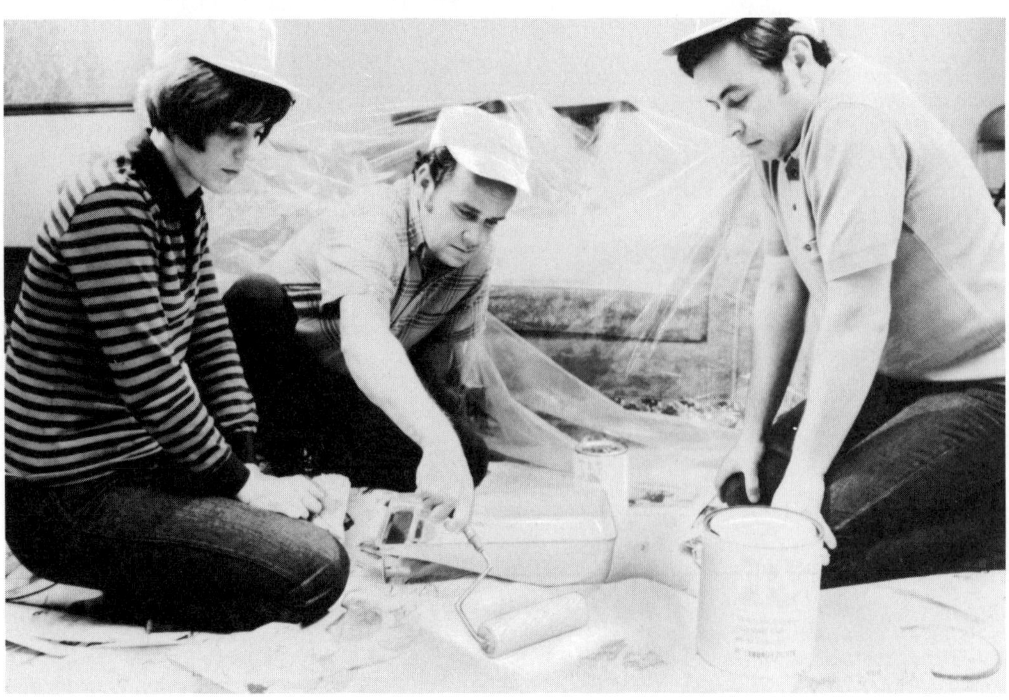

➤ *Paint the ceiling first. Start by applying a strip of paint around the edge next to the walls.*

▼ *On the ceiling, use roller across its full width for maximum color uniformity.*

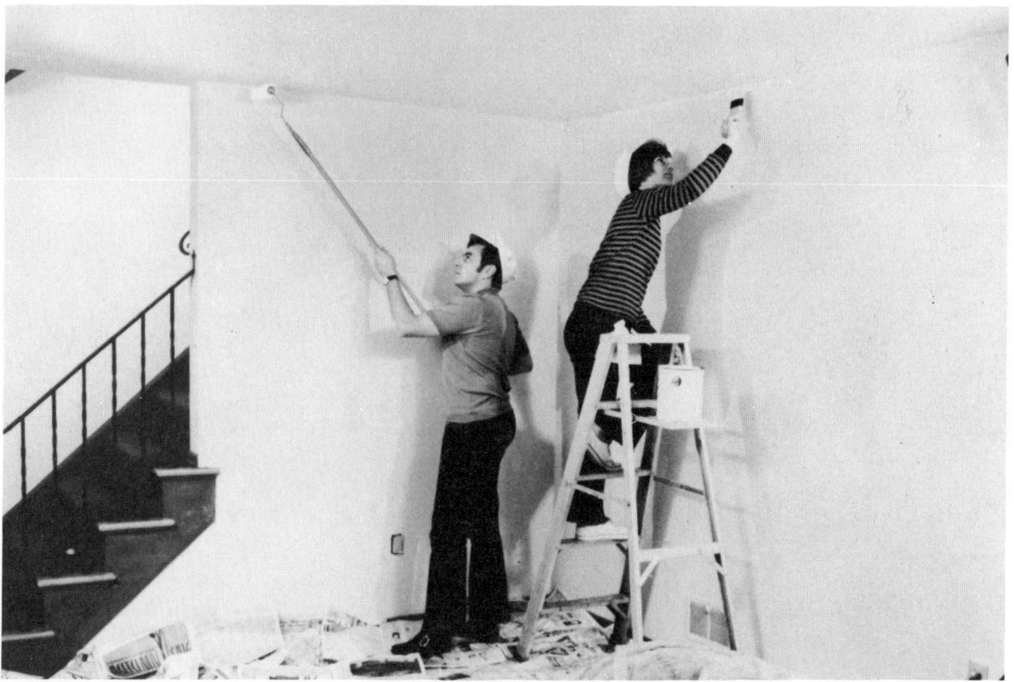

On walls, apply paint in a W (or an M) pattern, then fill it in.

Pad paint applicator is good for painting edges. Roller on either side serves as guide.

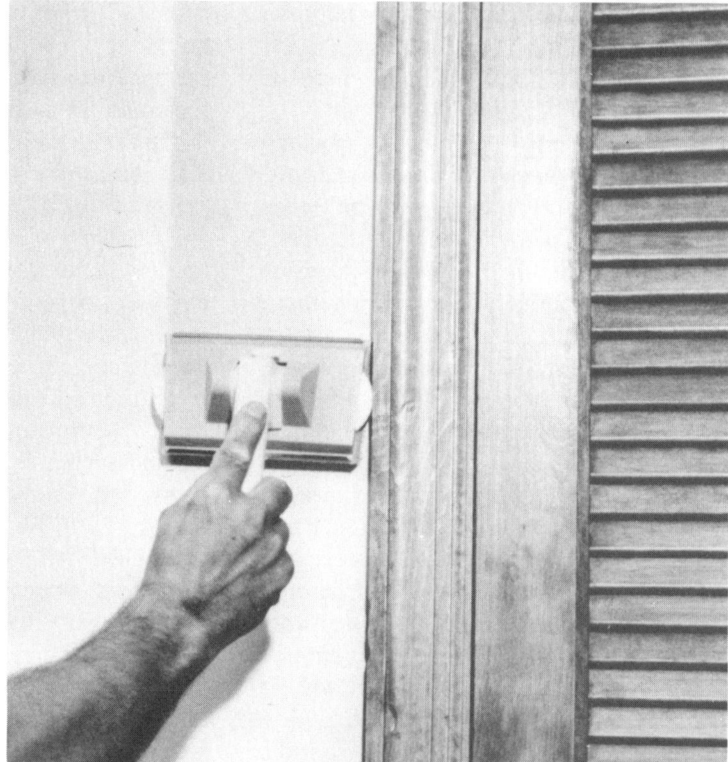

Using a pad applicator to paint next to a door frame.

Use a paint shield to protect wall-to-wall carpet while painting baseboard. Be sure to wipe the shield clean each time you move it.

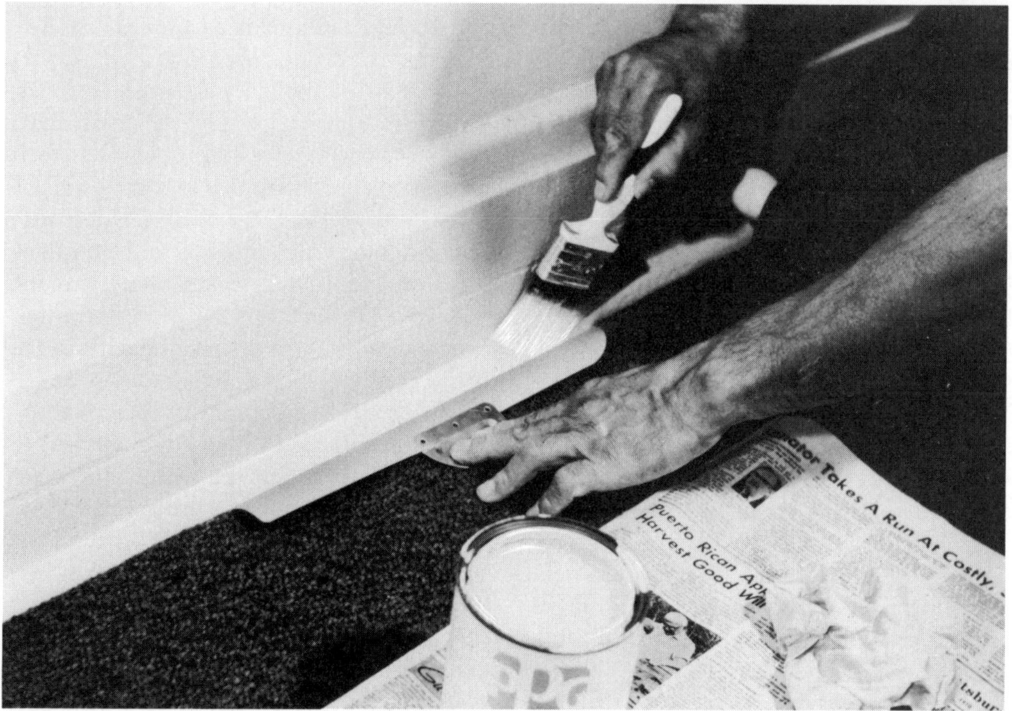

enables you to paint under the plates for maximum coverage, while keeping the fixtures paint free. You might also check on your wiring while you are at it.

Drop cloths. These may be the cheapest you can get. Chances are, if you do a good job all around the house, you won't need these again for many a year. Newspapers, fastened with masking tape, do a good job protecting furniture too bulky to remove from the room being repainted. However, if you have wall-to-wall carpeting, by all means cover it entirely with plastic sheeting because replacing this item would be a costly proposition.

Cracks. Many a beautiful old house or apartment has the original plaster walls, which have, owing to settling over the years, opened minute cracks and fissures. These tend to show up after the walls are washed. This is the time to take care of them, or else your new paint job will be love's labor lost. Widen the crack with a beer-can opener, and fill with spackle. Let spackle dry overnight, then sand lightly and seal if this is recommended for the paint you are to use. For a hurry-up job, patching plaster will speed the work.

Choosing the paint. For living rooms, bedrooms and dining areas, most people prefer a matte finish. Matte finish paints today are mostly water-thinned and dry so fast that the room being redecorated can be in use the same day it is painted. Generally odorless, they are not only easy to apply, but many persons who heretofore disliked painting, and put off the job, now enjoy putting fresh colors into their homes.

Since most interior paints can be applied with brush on roller, according to your choice, a speedy job can be accomplished by teamwork: cutting in with brush can be done by the wife while large areas are rollered by the husband. As cutting in is more tedious, a change half-way is a good idea.

As a rule, no room has all walls without a spot of sunlight, but if your room seems on the gloomy side, paint the wall that catches that patch of sunlight in a light tone, and for a change of pace, use enamel in the same color as the other matte walls. The reflective effect of the gloss will be most rewarding.

The nursery. Here, be sure to use paint that is not toxic. Children like to chew on anything at hand, and to protect them, manufacturers have perfected paints that do not contain lead. Available in a wide color range, these paints are a boon for rooms where small children play. Toys painted with this product can be washed and washed and washed again, so baby can chew away to his heart's content.

The kitchen. A great deal of time is spent in this room, so its colors should be light and gay. If your kitchen is small and cramped, the lighter the color, the better. The overall effect of the light tone will tend to push the walls away, and give you a feeling of spaciousness you never had before. For an easy-to-clean surface on walls and cabinets, enamel is a happy choice. Impervious to most kitchen films from cooking, it may be applied with brush or roller.

If your appliances are in good working condition but look a little shabby, there is a paint to rejuvenate them. It may well be that changing the color to match your new kitchen color scheme will give them a new lease on life, and save you many dollars.

Living areas. Over the years there has been a trend toward designating parts of the home as family rooms, living rooms, dining rooms or areas, based on the various activities indulged therein. The kids may want to set up darts in one place, parents may want to enjoy a quiet game of bridge over a leisurely cup of coffee. The background for these various activities is an important factor.

You can transform a room that has become boring by varying the texture as you paint. There are several ways to do this.

One is to use a sand paint. These paints are heavy bodied, and actually contain sand in the mix. Frequent stirring is advised so that the sand remains evenly distributed. When used over an old wall that has lots of small cracks in the plaster, or over badly taped seams in wallboard, it conceals these imperfections so well that it is almost as if the old wall had been replaced—but at a fraction of replacement cost.

Another trick for texturing is to apply the regular wall paint in a slightly heavier coat than usual, then use a sponge or stippling brush to achieve the effect you want. You can even use a wad of crumpled wrapping paper (don't use newspaper, as a water-thinned paint could allow the print to run and ruin the work). Apply light pressure, and with a slight twist of the wrist as you raise the wad, an almost flower-like pattern is achieved.

The texture from the sand paint is there to stay. Even after many successive paint jobs, you still have the effect. One advantage of the paper-wad or sponge method is that the texture is achieved with paint only, and if you desire to have a smooth wall when redecorating at a later time, sanding can remove the paint deposit in short order. If you are in doubt about how texturing will go with your type of decor, use the sponge or paper-wad method.

Fun with trim. For years and years, trim was always white or a match to the wall color. Many people have become so accustomed to this general scheme of things, they don't realize the effects that can be achieved by giving trimwork a decorative treatment. Sometimes the simple change from the matte finish on the walls to a high gloss on trim can transform a room, give it sparkle and life.

Doors. When you have paneled doors, they can often provide an accent if the panels are finished in a glossy paint and the rails flat, or vice versa. Many decorators advocate the use of contrasting colors for this type of door. The panels can be done in a color that picks out a flower tone from drapery or upholstery fabric, or if you want to add a really distinctive note, glue panels of fabric to the door, seal with clear lacquer and use solid color around the rim. G.D.

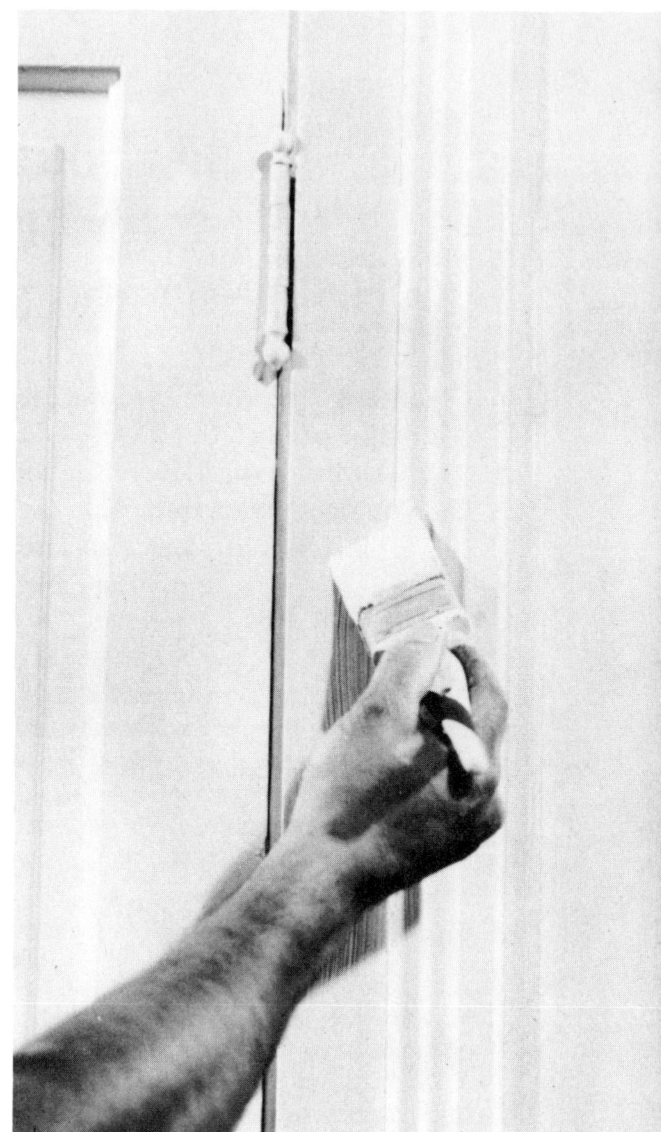

▲ *When paint is dry, check for spots you may have missed and touch-up with a brush.*

See also: ADDITIONS, HOME; DOORS; PATCHING; WALLBOARD; WALL COVERINGS.

All about Exterior House Painting

Painting your house yourself is a major project, but it can yield substantial savings. Here's what you need to know to plan the job, buy the materials and apply the paint

THE EXTERIOR OF ANY HOME, whether it be clapboard, shingle, board and batten, brick, masonry or cement block, needs a proper finish to preserve its inherent beauty. When the time comes to redo, observing a few simple rules will save many a headache.

On clapboard, make sure that all loose boards are firmly refastened. When you find a loose nail, replace it with a galvanized or stainless steel one in the next size larger to be sure of a tight fit with its neighbor. Don't attempt to drive it in all the way with a hammer; use a nail set for the final blow. It is much easier to fill a nail-head recess than a full hammer-head hollow. A spot of sealer, followed by filter or putty, spot-primed, will be covered when you paint.

Prepare the surface. Flaking, scaling old paint should be wire-brushed and feathered out for a smooth surface. Blisters, often caused by a previous coating having been applied over a damp surface, should be broken, sanded and allowed to dry out before refinishing. A putty knife is good for this, as it lifts any loose paint surrounding the blister.

Dried putty around windows should be removed and replaced before repainting. Painting over loose putty merely compounds the crime; it will crumble worse than ever, and make all your effort in vain. Trim that is sparkling clean and really *trim* accents the fenestration, so much a part of the design of houses.

Windows. If window sash is in good condition it is only necessary to make certain that the surface is clean and that any loose or blistered paint has been removed before starting the repaint job. Windows are particularly prone to moisture problems because of the large glass area that acts as a condenser in cold weather, bringing a flow of water down over the bottom of the frame whenever the condensation reaches the extreme. The melting of ice on storm sash does much the same thing.

If the sash is one that has been unpainted

for some years it is likely to be in such condition that mere scraping of local areas won't do the trick, because of the likelihood of trapped moisture beneath the aging paint. Rain beating against the glass flows off swiftly, and finds a way to seep between wood and glass no matter how well it is sealed. This causes unsightly crackling or alligatoring which cannot be concealed by additional coats.

There is a ready answer to this situation available at your paint store. Buy a good grade of paint remover, spread generously on the sash and allow to work for about 15 minutes. If the old finish is still stubborn, apply another coat of the remover before attempting to clean away the already "bubbled" first application. This way, all old coats can usually be removed at one time with brush, putty knife or spatula.

Some removers can be rinsed from the surface by simply hosing down; others require a specific wash. Be sure to follow directions here; any left-over remover may tend to lift your new paint or stain job. Proper drying times should also be followed. For instance, an alcohol wash, though it costs more, dries quickly. On the other hand, a water hose-down, although cheap, may take as long as two days to dry completely enough to enable you to start your painting, especailly in humid weather. A wire brush or a good old-fashioned scrub brush is a good bet for close corners and carved work, where little leftovers of remover tend to settle.

At this point, it is a good idea to replace old putty to stop annoying rattles as well as air leaks that make your home drafty in winter. Caulking around window and door frames should also be done now. Hardware that can be removed temporarily (so that it does not get spattered by brush, spray or roller) can be cleaned of old paint or, if brass, chrome, etc., repolished and lac-

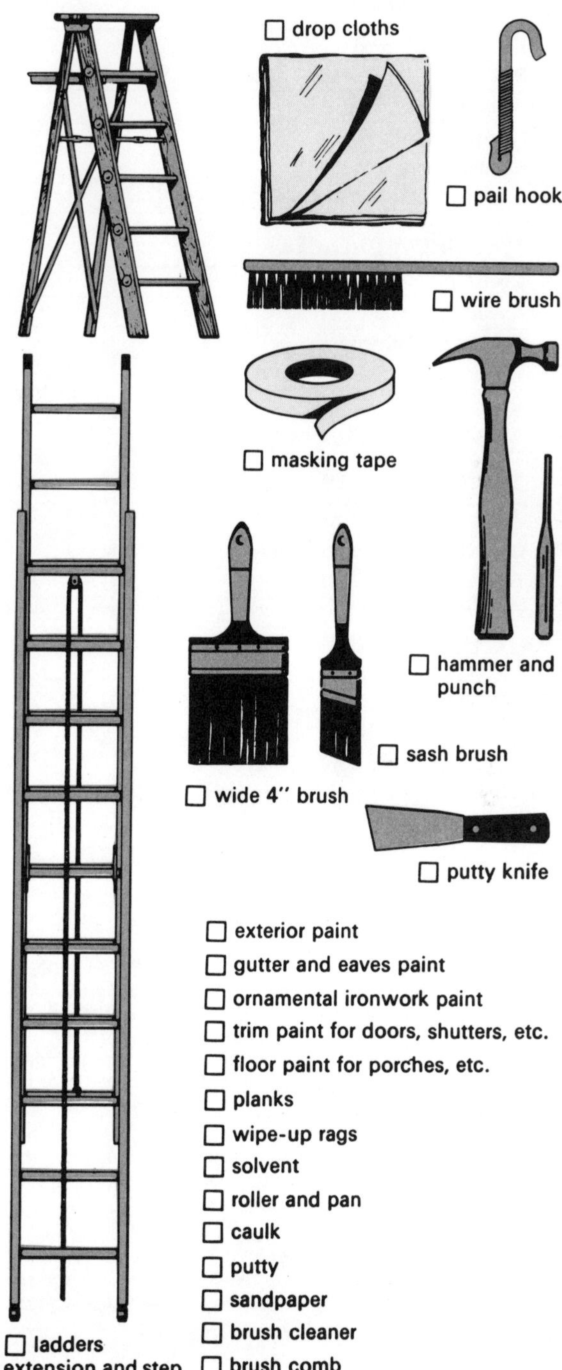

➤ *Use this equipment and materials check list to help plan your job.*

Use These Products For	LATEX HOUSE PAINT	GLOSS HOUSE PAINT	EXTERIOR STAIN	EXTERIOR MASONRY PAINT	OIL BASE FLOOR ENAMEL	LATEX FLOOR ENAMEL	ENAMEL	HI-GLOSS ENAMEL
WOOD SURFACES								
Clapboard	•	•						
Shingles	•		•					
Shakes	•		•					
Rough Lumber	•		•					
Exterior Plywood	•	•	•					
Shutters, Doors & Trim	•	•					•	•
MASONRY SURFACES								
Concrete	•			•				
Cement Block	•			•				
Asbestos Shingle	•			•				
Brick	•			•				
Stucco	•			•				
Asbestos Cement Board	•			•				
METAL SURFACES								
Aluminum Siding	•	•						
Gutters & Downspouts	•	•						
Flashings	•	•						
Railings		•			•		•	•
FLOORS								
Wood					•	•		
Concrete & Stone					•	•		

SAVE TIME AND MONEY

• Read label instructions thoroughly • Prepare the surface properly • Use recommended primers

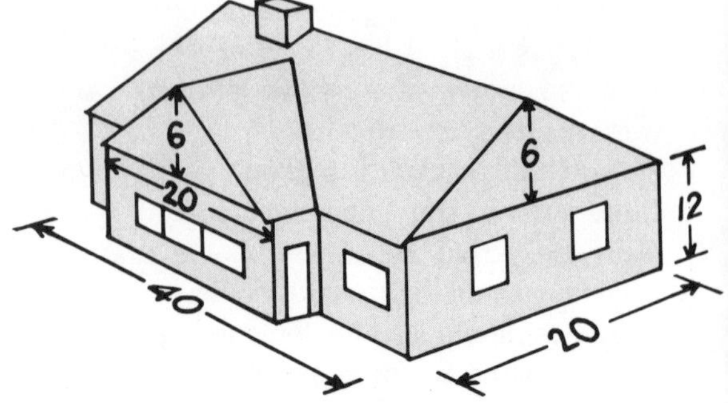

➤ Here is how to estimate the number of square feet you will need to cover. First estimate the area from the ground to the height of the eaves. To do this add the width and length of the house, multiply this total by the height and double the figure. In the example, 20 plus 40 equals 60. 12 times 60 equals 720. Two times 720 equals 1,440 square feet, the area from the ground to the height of the eaves. To find the area of gables, multiply the vertical distance from eave to peak and multiply the total by half the width of the gable. In the example, six times 10 equals 60 square feet, the area of each of three gables. Three times 60 equals 180 square feet. This is the total gable area. Add gable area to the area to eave height (180 plus 1,440) and the result is 1,620 square feet, the total area that will have to be covered.

quered, then replaced on the newly painted doors and windows.

Protect against spatters. When doing any outside painting, protect your foundation

If the roof of your house is	You can paint the body	. . . and the trim or shutters and doors															
		Pink	Bright red	Red-orange	Tile red	Cream	Bright yellow	Light green	Dark green	Gray-green	Blue-green	Light blue	Dark blue	Blue-gray	Violet	Brown	White
GRAY	White	\	\	\	\	\	\	\	\	\	\	\	\	\	\		
	Gray	\		\	\		\	\	\	\	\	\	\	\	\		\
	Cream-yellow		\		\		\		\	\							\
	Pale green				\		\		\	\							\
	Dark green	\				\	\	\									\
	Putty			\	\				\	\			\			\	
	Dull red	\				\		\						\			\
GREEN	White	\	\	\	\	\	\	\	\	\	\	\	\	\	\	\	
	Gray					\	\	\									\
	Cream-yellow		\		\			\	\	\						\	\
	Pale green			\	\		\		\								\
	Dark green	\		\		\	\	\									\
	Beige				\				\	\	\		\	\			
	Brown	\				\	\	\									\
	Dull red					\		\		\							\
RED	White		\		\				\		\			\			
	Light Gray		\		\				\								\
	Cream-yellow		\		\						\		\	\			
	Pale green		\		\												\
	Dull red					\		\		\	\						\
BROWN	White			\	\		\	\	\	\	\		\	\	\	\	
	Buff				\				\	\	\					\	
	Pink-beige				\				\	\						\	\
	Cream-yellow				\				\	\	\					\	
	Pale green								\	\						\	
	Brown			\		\	\										\
BLUE	White			\	\		\					\	\				
	Gray			\		\						\	\				\
	Cream-yellow			\	\								\	\			
	Blue			\		\	\					\					\

plantings and nearby shrubbery with drop cloths, as a paint film on leaves and blossoms can keep them from breathing and may cause irreparable damage. Old cloths or even paper, anchored with weights such as stones or bricks, should be placed on paved walks, patios, driveways, etc. Masking of windows with newspaper and masking tape minimizes clean-up, speeds the work and makes trim painting easier to do.

Where to start. It is not always necessary to paint an entire house at one time. The north side, or that which is exposed to the prevailing wind, is often the first to show signs of deterioration, especially in areas of severe winter weather. Give consideration to the possibility of rotating the job so that a portion of the work can be done at one time, the remainder at another. The complete job can be finished in a single summer season, but with a little time out to make it less of a chore.

On a complete house painting job it is likely that you may well wonder where to start. Most professionals start at the highest point—at the peak, if you have that type of roof line; in any case, under the eaves. In many instances, a ladder is necessary for this part of the work, and care must be taken for safety's sake. A general rule for using straight ladders: keep a base distance one quarter the length of the ladder. Thus, if your ladder is 12 feet long, it should be three feet from the house foundation. When using a step-ladder, it is bad practice to go higher than the second step from the top.

A wise precaution is to always have a second person on the spot. Never mount a ladder with shoes that are wet with mud, oil or anything that can cause a misstep. Non-skid pads, such as pieces of old inner-tube, fastened to the tops of the side rails of straight ladders add to the safety factor. Try the first few steps to see if you have a firm foothold below. After taking these precautions, you can proceed with the paint pots with speed and confidence.

When brush painting, the average man can cover a five-foot swath without leaning too far to either side. This means that in the course of doing a 20-foot wall, the ladder has to move only four times. When using one of the new rollers with an extension handle, two moves may well do the trick.

For a neat, clean job, most pros do all the walls and allow a good drying time before doing the trim. Some of the new latex exterior paints dry in half an hour, and it is tempting to see at least one wall completed. However, patience is still a virtue, and in painting it is almost always a must. For instance, although your wall paint seems dry and hard, a spot of dribbled trim white on a beautiful main color may mean another ladder-raising, and an uneven tone, unless the base color has really set. Don't take chances.

Paint application. The method of paint

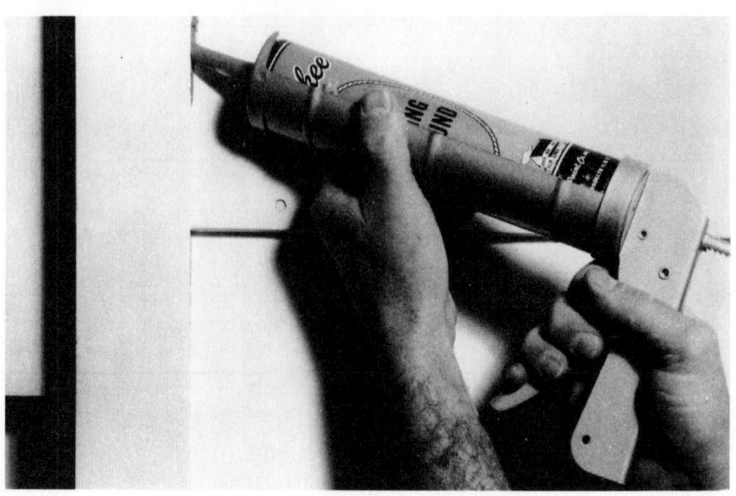

➤ *Caulk and make all the necessary repairs before painting.*

When filling brush, dip the bristles about one third to one half the way into the paint. Tap the brush gently against the side of the can to knock off excess paint. Do not wipe the brush on the lip.

When painting clapboard siding, paint bottom edge first, then flat side.

A roller can speed the work on flat surfaces, such as masonry or floors.

application you use for a big job, such as the exterior of your home, is a matter of individual preference. Spraying, when the tank sits on the ground and all you have to carry is the gun, is quick and easy. Here, masking windows, doors, etc. is a must, but don't worry about a little overspray; a trimming knife with an angled blade makes removal a cinch.

To get the under edges of shingles or clapboard, a cut-in roller is ideal. It puts the paint where you want it, instead of letting it dribble away. A follow-up with a long-fibered regular roller completes the job. A seven-inch roller is recommended for clapboard, as it covers the area exposed to the weather after the under edges are done. With the aid of an extension handle, the roller, long familiar for interior work, becomes a most handy tool for outside jobs, often eliminating the need for ladders and such in painting a one-story house garage.

Brushes and rollers are relatively cheap; spray equipment is more costly, although it does a faster job, and when time is a prime consideration, as when doing a whole building in a weekend, or beating threatening weather, it can save the day.

If you do not expect to have too much use for a sprayer, a good bet is a rental. In most areas they rent for about $8 a day with a 2½-gallon container for your paint. Rental services estimate that a one-story house, unless it is unusually large, can be completed (one coat) in one day. Two-story houses, of course, take longer, but still, renting is a good bet unless you plan

To paint windows, first, sand as necessary, dust and replace loose putty. Then, lower the outside sash, raise inside sash and paint exposed checkrail on each side.

Step two for windows is to paint the cross bars and frames wherever you can reach them with the windows in the same position as in step one. Use masking tape to keep paint off glass. When the upper checkrails are dry, return the windows to their normal position and paint the lower portions of the checkrails and the remaining crossbar and frame areas.

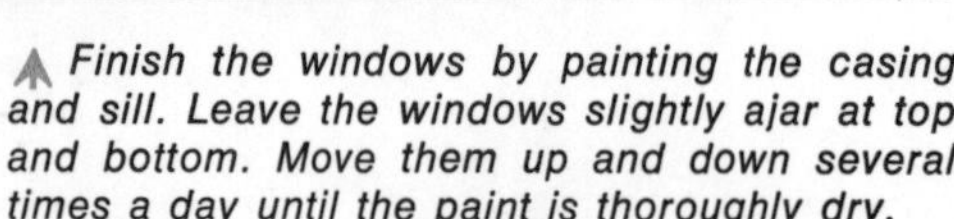

Finish the windows by painting the casing and sill. Leave the windows slightly ajar at top and bottom. Move them up and down several times a day until the paint is thoroughly dry.

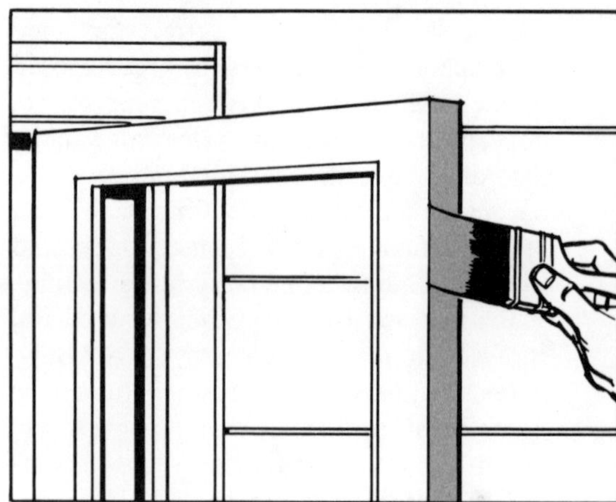

Open casement window and paint the top, side and bottom edges first. Next, paint the rails, frames, casing and sill.

extensive use of this type of equipment, as on your boat, car, etc.

No matter what method you employ, the tools you use will serve you in good stead for years and jobs to come, so do take care of them. Most manufacturers tell on their labels what to do: rinse in the appropriate thinner or solvent, and never use an incompatible type, such as turpentine for a shellac brush, or alcohol on a brush used in oil paint. As mentioned previously, many of the newer types of paint are thinned with water, thus making clean-up a cinch.

Stain, especially the heavy-bodied type, is a happy choice for rough siding and shingles. It penetrates deeply into the pores of the wood; covers, colors and preserves in one coat. A flat, velvety finish, reminiscent of old New England homes and barns, is most pleasing. Many stains are now available in lighter colors than the familiar barn red or deep green. When used with a contrasting trim of sparkling white, they are most attractive.

Thinner in consistency than most house paints, stain can be applied with brush, roller or spray gun. When using brush or roller, it is advisable to wear rubber gloves with inverted cuffs to catch runs.

Natural wood finishes. If your home has redwood or cedar siding, and you want to preserve the tone the wood was given by nature, shop around for the type of finish that will not discolor but rather will accent the natural grain, color and characteristics of your basic material. This also applies in some cases where the effect of weathered wood is desirable on a barn or shed used as a studio, where atmosphere is an integral part of the overall effect when used as a backdrop for art works, sculpture or handcrafts.

Special finishes are available for redwood siding which preserve the original tone of the wood. Sometimes people prefer to leave this wood without any finish. In this case, it weathers to a silvery grey, but loses the warm tone usually associated with this rare and wonderful building wood.

On the other hand, if the natural wood used around your house lends itself to a finish (carved or beautifully grained doors, for example), spar varnish is an ideal solution. More flexible than floor varnish, because it does not need the hardeners necessary for resistance to abrasion, it can stretch and shrink with the wood. If you prefer a natural wood finish to paint over large areas, as is sometimes the case in modern houses, here again, spar varnish is a good bet. Ask your paint dealer about varnishes

Begin painting doors by doing the panel moldings first. Then, paint each panel, starting from the top, brushing the paint first across and then up and down. Paint the remaining area and the door edges. If the door swings out, paint the latch edge with exterior paint. If the door swings in, paint the hinge edge.

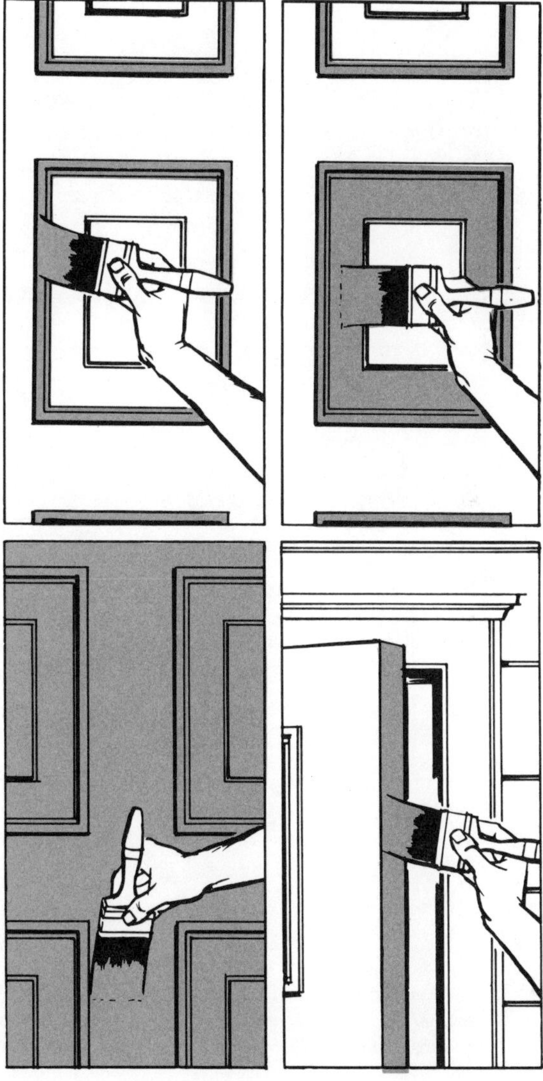

that have been perfected for boats. They are made to withstand wind and weather.

Trim. The trim around windows and doors may match or contrast with the basic house color. This is, of course, a matter of personal preference. If you have an exceptionally impressive and beautiful front door, accent it by all means. It will add a note of distinction to the appearance of the house. If you have an unattractive but useful louver tucked under an eave or in a corner, the unit may be painted or stained to match the main color; this way it will hardly be noticed from outside.

When doing the trim, use brushes or rollers sized and shaped for the job at hand. Trying to do muntins and mullions with a brush designed to paint siding is frustrating and wasteful of time, temper and paint, and is almost certain to ruin the brush as you attempt to flex it in and out of tight spots. A small investment in the right tool will pay off handsomely in a good job, and, properly cleaned and stored, the brush or roller will give years of service.

For porch columns, a pipe painter is very handy. Comprising five sections on a spring that makes it possible to do half of a post in one pass, it saves time and effort. It literally wraps itself around posts, pipes and other hard-to-do items. As the handles on these rollers are adjustable to almost any position, even hard-to-reach spots, such as the back of a post close to a wall, can be done with ease.

Roofing paint. For most modern roofing, aluminum is one of the most popular paints —sometimes in a formula of asphalt aluminum, sometimes an alkyd-base aluminum paint that may be had in white and soft pastels. The reflective properties of the aluminum flakes can keep the interior of your home as much as 15° cooler in summer and reduce heat loss in winter.

The asphalt aluminum used on built-up roll roofing can be spread by roller or long-handled brush. The alkyd type, usually containing asbestos fibers, is best applied with a brush. It seals the edges of asphalt shingles against wind and water. Both types seal pinholes and surface cracks, preventing leaks. The shinier the finish, the more reflective effect. Select your paint according to the result you desire.

The foundation. The exposed foundation walls may be painted to match or contrast with the side walls. If you are painting the

Scrape or wire-brush away any loosened paint, rust or other material before painting railings or other iron work.

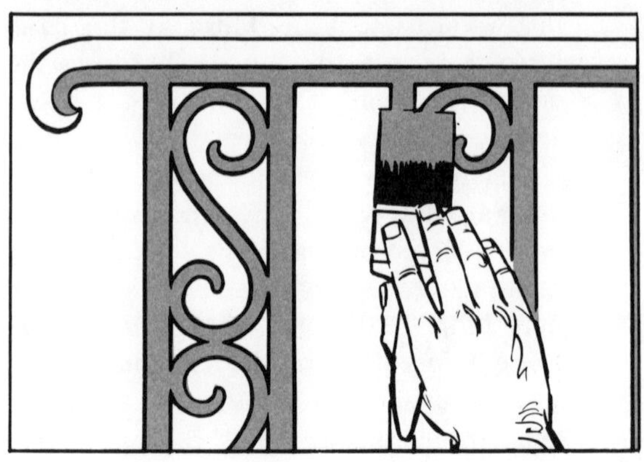

Give the work a coat of rust preventive primer, and finish with exterior paint. Do the interior and undersurfaces first, the top and exterior surfaces last.

➤*It is best to remove items you do not want spattered with paint, such as the globes on ornamental iron work.*

house with one of the new latex or vinyl paints, chances are you can use the same material on all the surfaces, be they wood, brick, masonry block or poured concrete.

If the masonry has been previously painted, brush off all loose, powdery paint. Glossy coatings should be dulled by sanding so that the new paint will bond firmly. Fill all holes and cracks for a smooth appearance. If the paint you select is a vinyl, be sure the temperature is at least 50° F. Brushes or rollers can be cleaned with soap and water, stored to use another day.

Shutters. If your home has shutters, be sure to remove them so that the areas behind can be painted easily. Even if you plan to do them in the same color as the walls, don't attempt to swing them out of the way, as a really complete job cannot be done this way. Moreover, if this maneuver is tackled from a ladder, it can be extremely dangerous.

For good coverage on the classic louvered types, lay the shutters across two sawhorses on the ground. A good idea is to do all of them on one side, then go back to the first one, flip it over for the second side, and so on. Working in this order, you will minimize the possibility of missed areas and wind up with a crisp, clean job. This is especially important if you use a contrasting accent color.

Doorways. As mentioned earlier, if you have a handsome front door, accent it by all means. But, if, after you have finished the whole job and your particular doorway looks unimpressive (in most cases of this kind, presenting a narrow, skimpy appearance, instead of a wide, welcoming entrance to your home), a simple, relatively inexpensive panacea is to buy a pair of full-length shutters and mount them beside the doorway. When they are the louvered type, the horizontal lines carry the eye outward, and give the impression of a wide, gracious entrance.

Another problem may be your aluminum combination storm and screen doors and windows. Although a great boon in draft-proofing the house, they may not be compatible in appearance with the style of the building. In some parts of the country, especially near the shore, they may also become pitted from exposure to salt air. In these instances, use the proper primer, and paint for the effect you want just as if they were wood.

Exterior fixtures. Usually made of metal,

Before painting the gutters, remove leaves and other debris and clean the gutters with a wire brush.

Coat the inside of the gutters generously with an asphaltum paint.

fixtures such as porch or entry lighting equipment need attention, too. And loose, scaling old finish or rust should be wire-brushed and sanded. A good prime coat is a must for proper paint adhesion. Any good exterior paint in the color of your choice can be used over this base. If your house is painted in a light color, black will accent the form of the fixture. If, on the other hand, your house is a fairly dark tone, such as New England barn red or green, snowy white is most effective.

Railings. Nothing is more attractive than a wrought-iron railing beside your steps—and it's an important safety factor in icy weather as well. If taken care of regularly, such a railing will stay beautiful for years.

With modern products, wrought-iron railings can be any color of the spectrum. Where a stairway is poorly lighted, fluorescent paint can spare you many a stumble, not to mention broken bones.

Wooden railings, found on many a comfortable porch, may be painted with regular house paint, provided it is not the chalking type. Kids love to sit on them on a summer night, and this type could be ruinous to clothes. The best bet here is to use a hard paint such as trim. Keep this in mind too, when painting porch posts and columns.

Porches. A porch can be a blessing or a curse, depending on how you paint it. If the ceiling is finished with glossy enamel in a light color, such as a sunny yellow or white, it will reflect light into the rooms behind it, while still providing shade in hot summer weather. If excessive heat from the sun is a problem in your part of the country, a cool blue will reduce glare and provide a light, airy atmosphere to the interior. If, however, you are located in the colder regions, where sunlight is not a problem but rather something to be desired, a warm

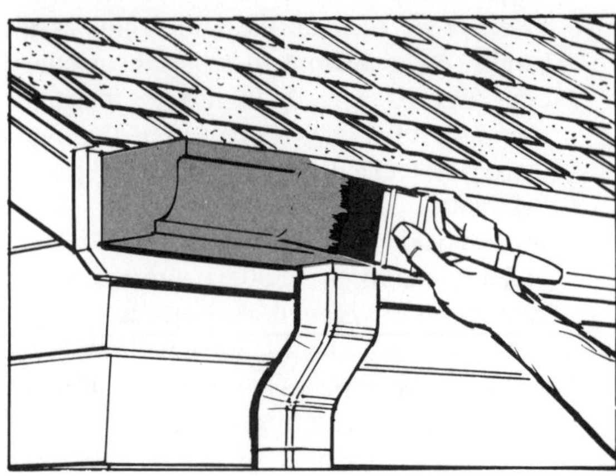

Give metal gutters and downspouts a coat of suitable primer, finish with exterior paint.

◀ Taking a chance. Shutters can be painted while they are on the house, but the job is easier if you remove them, and you don't risk spattering trim color over your house's new coat of paint.

▼ When painting porches or patios, start with the railings.

orange-red tone on the ceiling will provide a glow on the grayest of wintry days.

Downspouts and gutters. If you have wooden gutters on your home, treat them to the best of care. They can appear as lovely as a fascia board, and will last for years. Usually made of cedar or cypress, they are similar to the woods used in fine boats. A superior paint for these is, as you might expect, a product made for boats.

After cleaning out any dried leaves and twigs from gutters, allow to dry thoroughly. The leaves removed may seem crackly dry, but there is always a chance of residual moisture in the wood. To prevent more leaves and debris from landing in the cleaned gutters, a strip of screening laid along the length will be a great aid, during the drying period. When the wood is dry, lightly sand, wipe out the sanding dust and you are ready to paint.

An excellent product for this is a two-part epoxy that flows smoothly and gives an exceptionally high gloss. This is an advantage as further accumulations of leaves and debris can readily be removed.

If you have gutters and downspouts of galvanized metal or aluminum, time will take its toll. Aluminum is in a broad sense impervious to the weather, as are the aluminum paints. The galvanized gutters and downspouts most of us are familiar with, however, deserve care. They will stand up under adverse conditions and last for years. They can be painted to match, or contrast with, the siding, as you desire. If a downspout is near a porch post, paint it the same color as the post: if it seems to you an eyesore, color it the same as the background. Let your artistic self dictate here.

Fences. Many of us have our property fenced to protect small-fry from wandering into heavily trafficked roads, or merely to indicate the boundary lines or to set off a garden. Painting a fence need no longer be the chore Tom Sawyer found himself stuck with. Free-flowing, fast-drying paints of today take much of the laborious work out of this most necessary job. Instead of tedious brush-work on close pickets, spray equipment makes it a breeze. Cheap plastic dropcloths to protect lawn and flowers are a must, but there is a bonus here: re-use them in the fall and winter to protect the same shrubs from cold winds and ice storms.

With a spray-gun you can paint almost completely around the pickets. Another pass from the opposite side of the fence will finish the job. If you find a few missed spots later, a quick brush touch-up is all that is needed.

A pipe roller is another labor saving device for this kind of job. Since the roller flexes on springs to wrap itself around the palings, it is almost impossible to miss any area of the fence. Also, here you have no overspray problem—a minor drip or two can do no serious harm to lawn or garden.

General tips for exterior painting. Learn how to make your house blend with your neighbor's, while still following your own ideas of color, etc. A harmonious appearance all along the street where you live makes for happy living.

When there is a sale of house paint, and one homeowner does not see how he can take advantage of it because it would entail a larger purchase than he can use on his home, often a community get-together will ante up the money for a fresh paint job all along the road. This kind of overall planning and cooperation can transform a small street of similar houses into an impressive vista, even adding to the resale value if you have to move.

When painting large areas, plan to stop work for the day at a doorway, window or, if possible, a corner if you cannot finish the entire section. This prevents laps from showing. Fortunately, modern paints seldom present much of a problem on this score. **G.D.**

See also: ADDITIONS, HOME; BRICKWORK; CONCRETE; FENCES; HOME IMPROVEMENT; MASONRY; ROOFS; SIDING; STUCCO.

Leave porches, steps and patios until last. Paint steps this way: do underside step extension first, then back panel and, finally, the horizontal surface.

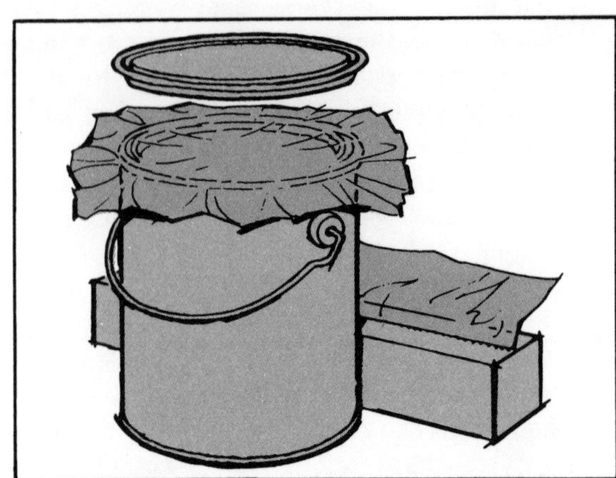

To preserve leftover paint, place a sheet of plastic wrap or other light plastic over the opening before replacing the lid. Be sure to pound the lid down tightly.

How to Repair Holes in Wallboard

Plasterboard has no lath to provide a backing for the patch, but you can use this trick to provide one

UNLIKE A PLASTER WALL which has a base of wire, wood or gypsum lath under the plaster, plasterboard stands alone, which poses a problem. Some backing material must be found before patching plaster can be used to fill the gap.

The accompanying photos show how easy it is to attach a length of wire to a piece of screen mesh, force it through the hole in the wall to provide a solid backing for the patching substance. Hardware stores and building supply houses carry several brands of patch plaster for this duty. Avoid wetting the adjacent plasterboard walls any more than necessary. They have a paper surface which is easily scarred. For this reason, a final coat of shellac over the hardened patch is recommended as a basecoat for finish paint. Holes up to three or four inches in diameter can be repaired in this way. If the work is done correctly, no visible spot will reveal the presence of the patch.

See also: BASEMENTS; PAINTING, HOUSE; WALLBOARD; WALL COVERINGS.

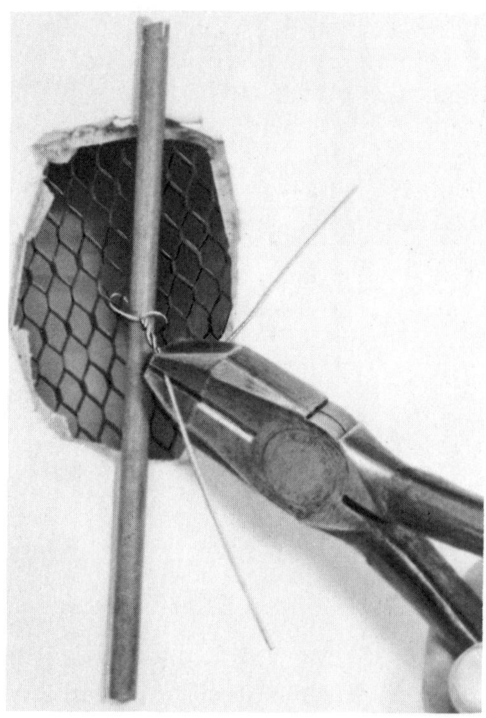

▲ To fill a hole in plasterboard, first cut a piece of wire mesh slightly larger than the hole, tie a piece of wire to it and force it into the hole. Then bend the wire around a nail or larger stiff piece of wire to hold the mesh in place.

▼ Apply spackling compound to the hole, using the wire mesh as a support behind the patch. When the patch is hard, snip off the end of the wire. The buried mesh and wire stay in place. The exposed wire is removed. After the wire is removed, sand the patch flush with the wall, but do it gently. Pressing too hard will form a depression in the patch.

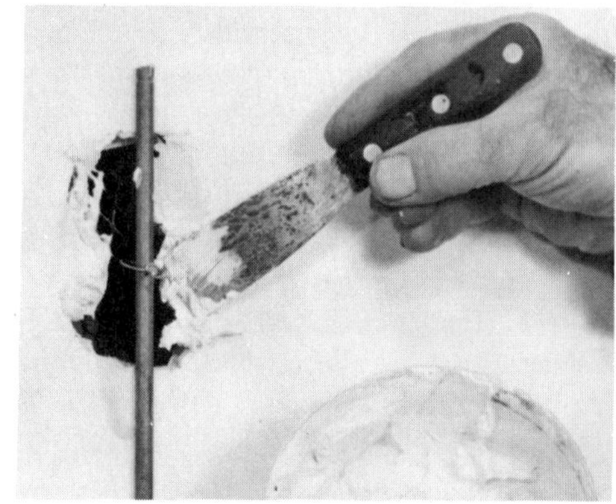

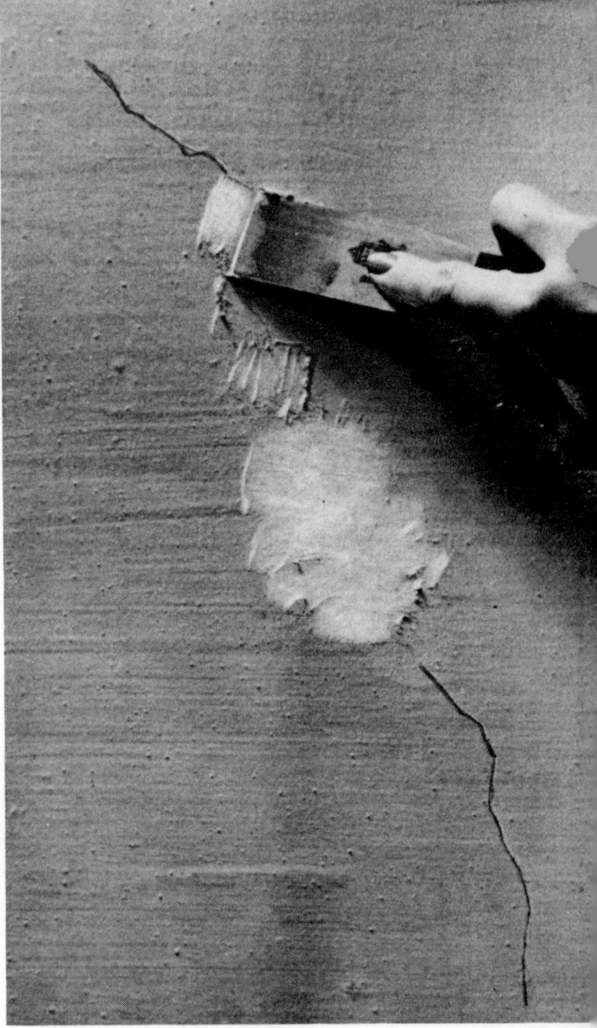

How to Patch Plaster Walls

Plastering a whole wall is a job for a professional, but any householder can make repairs, from hairline cracks to fairly large sections

PLASTERING AN EXTRA ROOM added onto the house, or an extensive remodeling job, is something few non-professionals will master, but the same cannot be said of plaster patching. Repair of plastered walls requires few tools: a trowel, putty knife, water brush, bucket, chisel, sanding block and drop cloth. The methods are so standard that it's hard to imagine anyone having difficulty if he follows directions.

Few people appreciate the inherent quality of a plastered home. Most ordinary plaster cracks are only surface deep and pose about as much threat to your home as a scratched fender is to your car. A crack is unsightly and it collects dust, but beyond that it's no cause for worry. Plastered walls are seamless. There are no nails to pop out, no paper surfaces to deteriorate and no joints to pull apart with age. It's fireproof to an amazing degree, and it's a durable wall that you aren't likely to penetrate with a bump of your elbow.

The important point is that plastered walls are well worth repairing, and even a battle-scarred home 30 years old can be made to look like new after a couple of hours of patching. Rest assured that a few cracks, and perhaps a hole here and there, have little (if any) effect on the total strength of your plastered walls.

The right materials. You can avoid a great deal of trouble right at the outset by ignoring special "blends" or "additives" that can be mixed with plaster to make it set slower or faster. These are handy devices for the professional who has the experience to use them to advantage, but generally the handyman will only be confused, delayed, excited and angered if he tries to whip up complicated concoctions.

Just about any building supply store carries plaster materials. In large cities, you may find a specialized plaster building supply store, which is the best place to obtain patching products. Here are the patching materials to use for the basic plaster problems.

For surface cracks, commercially packaged patching plasters work best. Sometimes the buyer has a choice of slow-set or fast-set products. The inexperienced user will do best with slow-set materials. The fast-set label means just that, and such a product may become hard in less than three minutes after mixing. This is not enough time for the amateur to mix, fill and smooth the repair.

Professional plasterers use ordinary casting plaster for patching duty. This material is packaged, with very slight differences, for sale in drug stores under the name of Plaster of Paris. The price in a plaster supply house is a few cents a pound. At the drug store, the price may be from 10 to 30 cents per pound. This comparison obviously indicates that plaster repair materials should be purchased at the right source: the supply house.

All pre-mixed packaged patch materials need only water to make them effective and ready for use. So why get involved in additives or use secret formulas?

Light surface cracks, screw and nail holes, dents in the wall, holes where pipes have been removed and areas that have succumbed to dry rot are all easily repaired with ordinary patching plasters.

Extensive repairs. Wall openings more than a few inches in diameter should be filled with gypsum-base plaster. The materials for this are more adaptable and less expensive than patching plasters, more elastic and easier to handle, and slower setting for better workability. Use gypsum-base (or fibered) plaster when covering areas where windows or heaters, etc., have been removed for filling large areas that

Use a beer can opener to widen cracks for patching. Undercutting the edges is unnecessary. After the crack is widened and all loose plaster brushed out, wet the crack before filling it with plaster.

have been afflicted with dry rot and for filling areas where the plaster has been knocked out down to the exposed lath (lath is the material—wood, metal or gypsum board—on which plaster is applied).

Ratios for mixing gypsum plaster vary from about 10 to 20 shovelfuls of sand per 100-lb. sack, according to the directions of the manufacturer, so be sure to read these directions on the bag when buying gypsum plasters. For mixing smaller amounts, figure it percentage-wise.

Lime-base finish plasters are necessary only when very large areas (say, over 2 feet square) are covered. In such cases, purchase colored interior stucco. This material is spread over the gypsum basecoat which has filled and leveled the surface, and been fully cured. It is not an expensive material, and it is easy to handle if you spread it with a plasterer's trowel.

If the repair will be covered with wallpaper or wood paneling, there is no need for this finish coat of interior stucco. The application of gypsum plaster alone is then sufficient. The finish coat merely gives a smoother appearance.

Patching methods. Cracks in plaster should be opened slightly so that a sufficient amount of patching plaster can be forced in. In the opinion of most professional plasterers, undercutting a surface crack is not necessary. The cracks are so tiny to start with and the repair so simple to handle that it's simply wasted motion to meticulously go down the length of a long crack, tediously digging away under every edge. The theory has been that undercutting allows a stronger bond of the patch to the original material and that undercutting the edges tends to seal in the filler agent. Actually, undercutting a crack often weakens the edges severely (the spot where most strength is needed!) and thus leads to future problems.

The easiest way to open the crack is with a beer can opener held at an angle to the crack. Run the opener vigorously down the crack, making sure that loose particles are brushed out. (You may also use a chisel or a screwdriver.)

Far more important to a good bond than anything else is getting a firm surface-edge and wetting it carefully before repair. Patching plaster does not adhere well to dry surfaces. It is best to wet it with a saturated brush run through the crack. On larger patches, wet the edges all around,

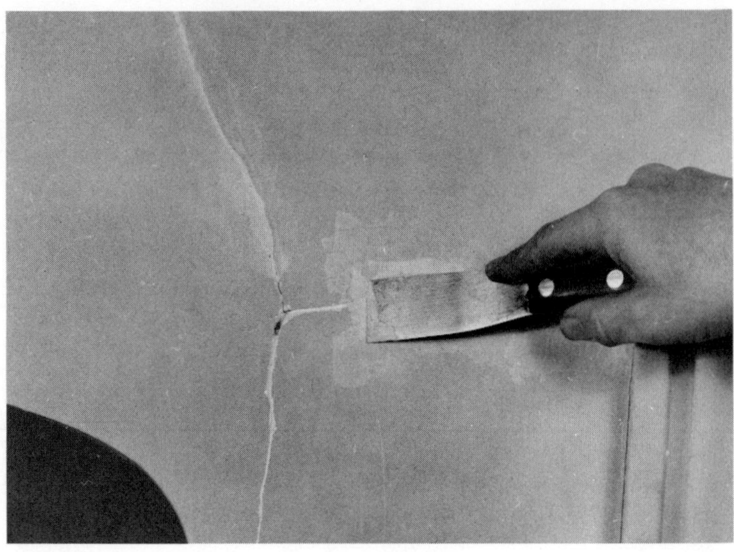

Force plaster into the crack with a putty knife.

then immediately proceed with the filling operation.

Mixing materials. Add water to the plaster in small amounts—don't fill a bucket with water and pour in the plaster. Adding water to the plaster allows the user to get the consistency he desires. The ideal mix is about as viscous as cooked oatmeal. Too thin, and it will slide out of the repair. Too thick, and it will prematurely harden and be difficult to spread.

Use a flat board about 12 inches square to carry small amounts of patching plaster from room to room. Keep a bucket of water handy for softening the plaster when it gets too hard.

Filling cracks. With the crack widened and edges wetted as previously described, force in your patching plaster the full length of the crack, making no attempt to level the surface; overfill the crack slightly. After filling, wet the edge of your putty knife and run it with the flat side of the blade over the top of the crack. This removes excess material. Allow the patch to dry hard, then sand it smooth. That's all there is to it.

Ceiling patches. Pull away loose finish plaster until a firm surface is encountered, mix patching plaster and wet the surface. Apply plaster in thin layers until the right depth is achieved; then run a wet trowel repeatedly over the repair. The more you trowel it, the smoother it will get. This technique can be used on any interior patch with a diameter of less than about 12 inches.

Large repairs. As suggested, use gypsum plaster to fill large wall areas. Some method must be found to level the surface, since the area may be wider than the trowel used to spread the material. Any straight, smooth board can be utilized. Let each end of the board ride firmly on the adjacent walls while you "saw" the board back and forth up the wall, carving off excess plaster. If depressions remain in the surface, spread more gypsum plaster over the low areas and board it off again. Repeat this process until the surface is true and flush with the original wall.

Use a putty knife to fill small holes.

You can smooth gypsum plaster while it is still soft by sprinkling the surface lightly with water and running a trowel, held nearly flat, over it. Keep the trowel clean and wet while slicking the surface. Plasterers use a "darby" but, unless the area being repaired is quite large, avoid it —it only leads to difficulty for the novice. But almost anyone can handle a trowel.

Wallpaper or wood paneling can be applied right over the gypsum basecoat after it has cured hard (a matter of days). If the surface is to be painted, apply a finish coat of interior stucco over the gypsum plaster after it has hardened. This is applied with overlapping strokes in a thin ⅛-inch layer and troweled smooth with a wet brush and trowel.

See also: PAINTING, HOUSE.

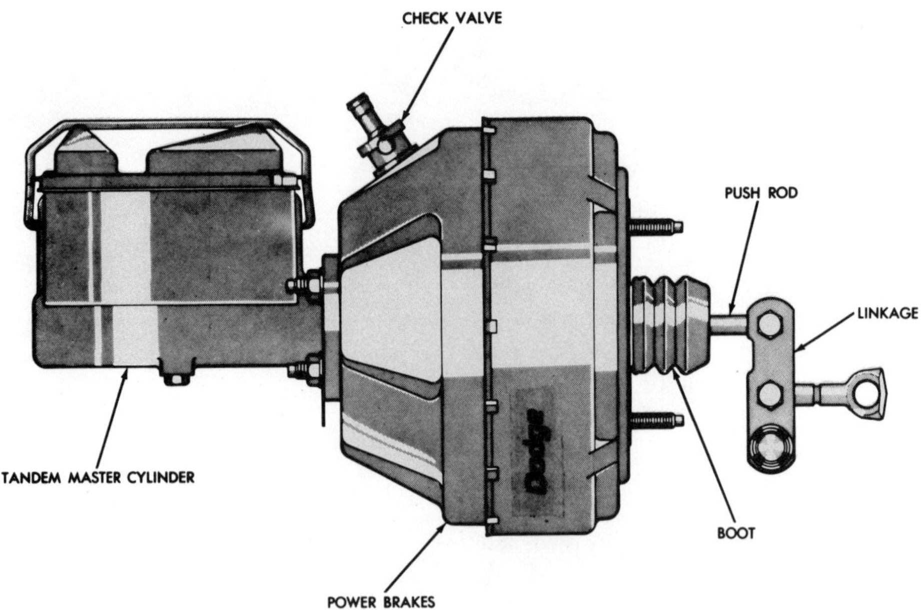

Typical power brake arrangement on car with dual master cylinder. Adjustment of pedal height is on the link (extreme right), which is threaded.

Trouble-shooting Power Brakes

You can make simple tests on your brakes to avoid costly replacement of linings and excessive fuel consumption

So-called power brakes are not really power brakes at all. Power assist from engine vacuum helps you push down the brake pedal of an otherwise ordinary hydraulic brake system. All makes of power brakes, or more exactly power boosters used on American cars, are similar and fairly simple in operation, maintenance and trouble-shooting.

Basically, the power booster is a vacuum operated cylinder added between the brake pedal and the hydraulic master cylinder. When you touch the brake pedal lightly, vacuum sucks a piston forward to push hydraulic fluid from the master cylinder into the brake lines and out to each wheel cylinder. Without power assist, your foot pedal linkage pushes directly on the piston in the master cylinder. (This is what gives non-power brakes a better feel and controlability than power brakes even though it takes more leg power to operate them.)

Most vacuum brake booster units have three major parts: vacuum cylinder, vacuum piston with built-in control valve,

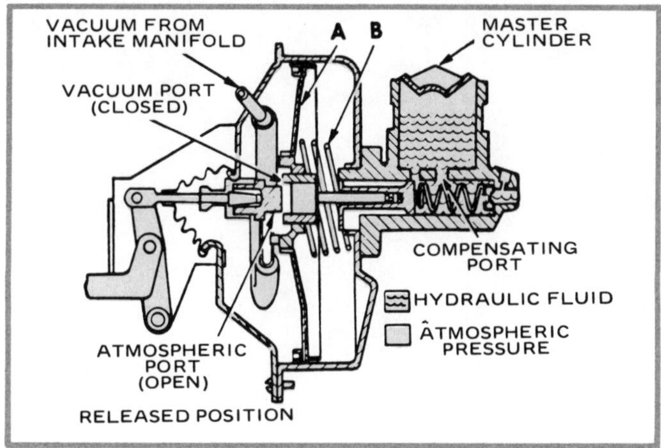

Vacuum power cylinder in released position with air pressure equal on both sides of power piston (A), located by return spring (B).

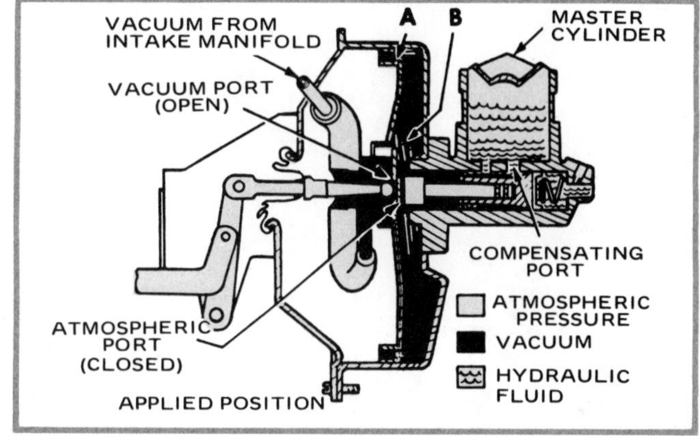

Power cylinder with brakes fully applied. Piston (A) has been sucked forward by engine vacuum, through vacuum valve, compressing spring (B) and forcing piston in brake master cylinder to apply the brakes.

and end plate with bracket and lever assembly. Vacuum to power the unit comes from a tube attached to the intake manifold of the engine.

When your foot is off the brake pedal, the vacuum unit is in the released position. The vacuum port to the engine remains closed, but the atmospheric port is open. Air can pass freely from one side of the piston to the other. With equal pressure on both sides, the return spring holds the piston in the off position. Another port, the compensating port, between the vacuum cylinder and the hydraulic master cylinder is also open. This lets hydraulic fluid from the brake lines return to the master cylinder.

When you touch the brake pedal, the atmospheric port closes and the vacuum port opens. Vacuum from the intake manifold then sucks the piston forward against the pressure of the return spring. This motion pushes the operating rod in the hydraulic master cylinder to apply the brakes.

Should the power booster fail, then the operating rod for the power system would move forward to push directly on the operating rod for the master cylinder hydraulic piston. Thus, when you stepped on the brake pedal, you would notice slightly longer pedal travel and increased braking effort, but you could still stop the car.

Trouble-shooting power brakes calls for some simple tests you can make yourself. You can repair leaks in connections

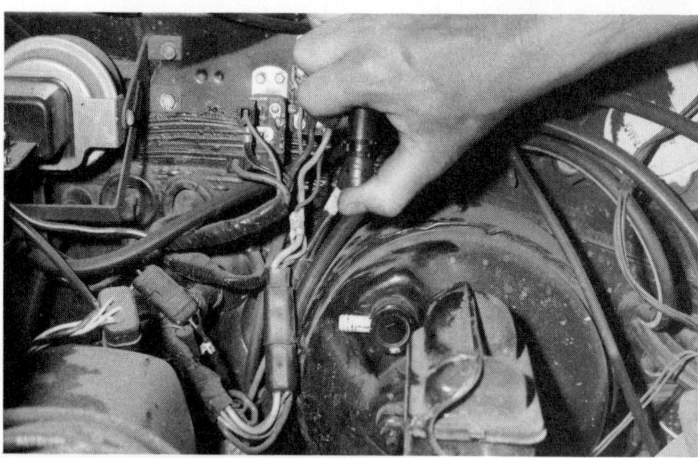

Vacuum hose to power brake unit is shown disconnected and with engine running you should feel vacuum at end of hose.

If vacuum valve is defective, it can simply be pulled out of the rubber grommet in which it sits in the power brake unit.

and hoses, or replace the whole vacuum unit with a rebuilt; but very possibly, repairs to this unit may require special tools and skills as well.

Start by testing booster operation. Shut off the engine and pump the brake pedal several times to exhaust all vacuum in the system. Older model power brake systems often incorporate a vacuum reservoir tank, so these may take a few more pumps on the pedal to clear them of vacuum.

Now step on the brake pedal and hold it down firmly while you restart the engine. If the vacuum system is working right, the brake pedal will move forward slightly when the engine starts. If there is no movement and the pedal feels hard, the vacuum unit is not working.

The fault may lie in the unit, or it may not be getting any vacuum. Check by removing the vacuum hose from the power cylinder. Hold your thumb over the open end of the hose. You should be able to feel the suction.

No vacuum at the hose means there is a leak in the system, or the engine is not in good shape. Check the hose for kinks, collapsed areas, or tears. Replace the hose if defective.

If the hose is working properly and you still get no suction, check for vacuum at the intake manifold. A vacuum gauge should show 17 to 21 inches with the engine idling. If it does not, check first for manifold leaks. A quick way is to idle the engine after putting oil on the joints at carburetor flange to intake manifold and intake manifold to cylinder block. If there is a leak, vacuum will suck in the oil to seal it temporarily. With proper vacuum, the engine will speed up. Fix the leaky joint by tightening the attachment bolts, or if this does not work, by replacing the gasket.

If you find no leaks, lack of manifold vacuum points to the need for an engine tune-up or possibly even an overhaul.

If there is vacuum at the hose, but the booster unit does not work, the vacuum booster itself is at fault. Before removing the unit from the car, test the vacuum check valve, a common cause of trouble.

The vacuum check valve is a one-way affair which lets air be sucked out of the vacuum booster into the intake manifold but does not let the vacuum out of the unit when the engine is shut off. To remove it from the cylinder, disconnect the vacuum hose and simply unscrew the valve. In most systems you can do this without removing the vacuum cylinder from the car.

Check the valve by blowing through it; first one way and then the other. No air should come out the end to which the vacuum hose is attached, but you should be able to blow through other end. If the valve is faulty, replace it.

If the valve is in good condition but the unit still does not operate, you must remove unit from the car. Further disassembly and inspection should be performed by a serviceman experienced in vacuum unit repair who has the proper tools for the job. He can repair the unit for you, or you can exchange it for a new or rebuilt unit.

You can, however, test your vacuum unit to see if it is causing the brakes to drag. This can wear out one set of linings after another in addition to cutting deeply into your fuel mileage.

First make sure shoes are properly adjusted and that wheels turn freely. Raise the front end of the car and start both front wheels spinning. Immediately start the engine and let it idle. Keep your foot off the brake pedal. Each front wheel should coast to a stop and still turn freely. If one or both stops more quickly than it should, or if you can feel a noticeable drag, there is trouble in the vacuum unit. You may find it necessary to have it repaired, or even replaced.

All power booster units have a filter to clean the air drawn into the system. On some boosters this filter is external and can be removed for cleaning. Check the workshop manual for your car to see if it has this type of filter and how often it should be serviced. Many makes have an internal filter which only needs servicing when the booster cylinder is removed from the car.

To clean either type of filter, wash it in alcohol or some other non-oil base solvent. Gasoline or similar solvents should be avoided because they can damage rubber parts in the braking system.

One last check completes the work you can do on your power brake system. Make sure no brake fluid is being sucked through the vacuum line into the intake manifold. To do this, remove the vacuum hose from the intake manifold and run a screwdriver or pencil around the inside of the open end. If it comes out wet with brake fluid, there is a serious leak past the vacuum cylinder piston. The whole unit will have to be rebuilt or replaced to cure this leakage. If it continues, the engine will idle roughly, perform poorly, and hydraulic fluid can form gums which cause sticking valves and may create a variety of other problems.

These simple checks will enable you to tell when your power brake booster is working properly. When it is not, they will help you pinpoint the trouble, and in many cases you can cure it yourself.

See also: DISC BRAKES.

Understanding Your Car's Power Steering

You can make some of the repairs yourself. The others must be done by a mechanic, but if you know your car's steering system, you will get a cheaper, more reliable job

UNDERSTANDING YOUR POWER steering is easy and important when pinpointing trouble. Fixing it though, may be another matter. You can easily make some repairs, but if the trouble is in the power steering unit itself, most repairs are best left to an expert who knows what he is doing and has the special tools and gauges. However, if you watch the repair being done and know your power steering, you should get a more careful and less expensive job.

All power steering systems have these three components: 1) a pump which supplies oil under pressure to provide the power and 2) a control valve assembly to meter the amount of fluid delivered to 3) the cylinder and piston assembly that does the work.

Systems differ in design and location of control valves and cylinder and piston assemblies. The two basic categories are those where the power is applied to the steering gear and those where it is applied to the linkage. Gear-type units are built into the steering gear box with opposed power pistons working on a crank attached to the pitman arm shaft. Some use a single power piston working on the pitman arm shaft through a power rack. Both of these gear-type units have the shaft from the steering wheel passing through the control valve assembly.

Linkage-type power steering mounts the cylinder and piston assembly between one of the steering rods and the vehicle chassis or frame.

Here is what happens when you turn the wheel on a power steering equipped car. The pump, belt driven by the engine, draws hydraulic fluid from a reservoir and sends it out under pressure. Inside the pump, flow-control and pressure relief valves govern the amount of pressure in the system. The harder you turn the steering wheel, the more hydraulic pressure is applied to help you turn it.

Two hydraulic lines connect the pump to the control valve. One is a flow line, the other a return line, or both may be flow lines depending on front wheel position. The control valve, like a traffic cop, directs fluid under pressure to the power cylinder.

With the wheels straight ahead, a centering spring holds the control valve spool in the neutral position. Fluid from the pump bypasses the valve, enters the power cylinder and returns to the reservoir. Pressure is equal on both sides of the piston.

When you turn left, twisting the steering wheel makes the valve spool move to the right, overcoming the control valve centering spring. Hydraulic fluid, under pressure from the pump, flows through the line to the right side of the power cylinder. Fluid on the left side of the cylinder is forced back through the return line as the piston moves to the left to assist your turn. On a right turn the process is reversed.

Spotting power steering troubles. Leaking fluid, hard steering, binding or poor recovery, excessive free play, noise, steering chatter, rattles and complete loss of power assist are all trouble symptoms. Fluid loss and hard steering are the most common.

When you notice one of these symptoms, there is usually no need to replace any of the complete power steering assemblies, let alone the entire system. Never let yourself be talked into such replacement until you are absolutely certain you need it.

Fluid leaks show up as a few drops or even a puddle on the garage floor. Ignore this warning and you're in for hard steering and the expense of replacing fluid.

To find the leak, get under the car. If you can get it up on a hoist, it is much easier. Clean off the pump, control valve, power cylinder, and all the flexible lines and fittings. Drain the pump reservoir, catching the fluid in a clean container. Add ½-teaspoon of premixed red oil-soluble aniline dye to each pint of fluid. Some auto supply stores carry this dye. Then refill the pump reservoir with dyed fluid. Start the engine and turn the steering wheel from one side stop to the other at least ten times to circulate the dye through the system. Get an assistant to turn the wheel from one stop to the other and hold it at each stop for 10-15 seconds while you look for leaks in the system.

If a tubing fitting leaks, try tightening it. Use special tubing fitting wrench in preference to an open-end wrench. (If you don't have a tubing wrench, go ahead and use an open-end. Just be careful.) If this does not help, replace it with a new fitting of the same size and type. If the leak is in one of the fluid lines, replace the line.

Leaks can occur at six places on the power steering pump and reservoir unit: cover joint, cover center stud, reservoir

Sectional view of a Dodge power steering gear which consists of a gear housing containing a gear shaft with a sector gear, a power piston with gear teeth milled into the side of the piston (which is in constant mesh with the sector gear), and a worm shaft connecting the steering wheel to the power piston (through a U-joint). The worm shaft is "geared" to the piston by recirculating balls. The steering valve, a spool type, is mounted on top of the steering gear and directs flow of fluid into the system.

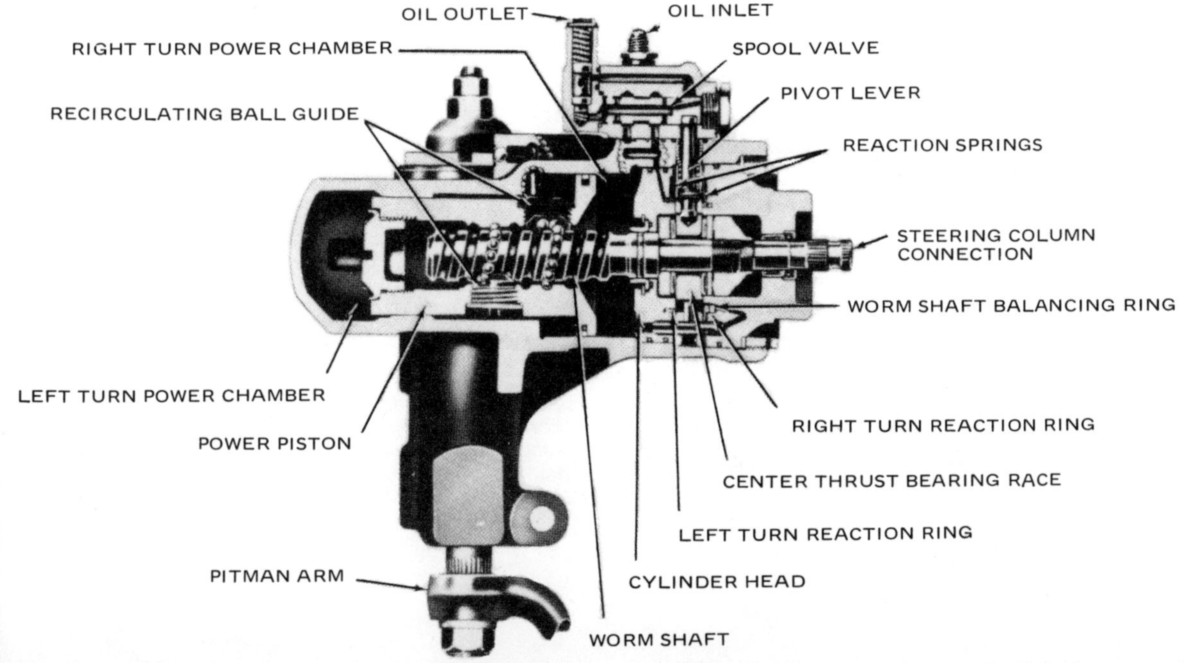

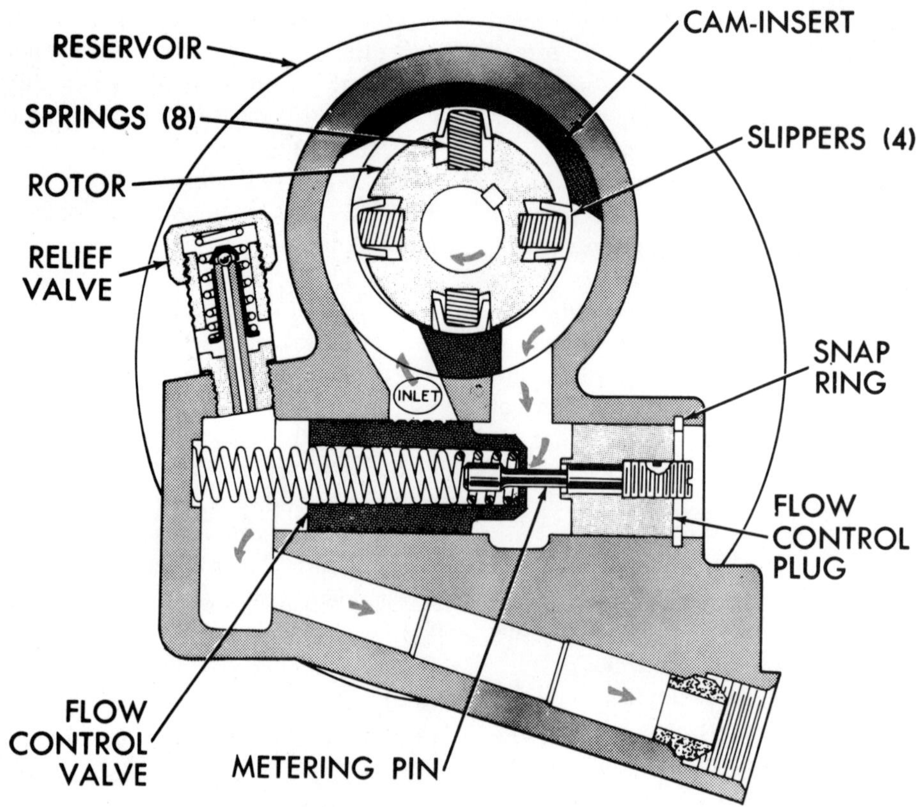

This is a typical power steering pump, designed to deliver most of its pressure at low speeds for easier parking. At low speeds, the flow control valve is so positioned that additional oil flows through the valve orifice to the power steering gear. At higher pump speeds, the increased oil flow moves the flow control valve against the spring pressure, diverting much of it back into the pump inlet. At the same time, the metering pin reduces oil flow to the power steering gear.

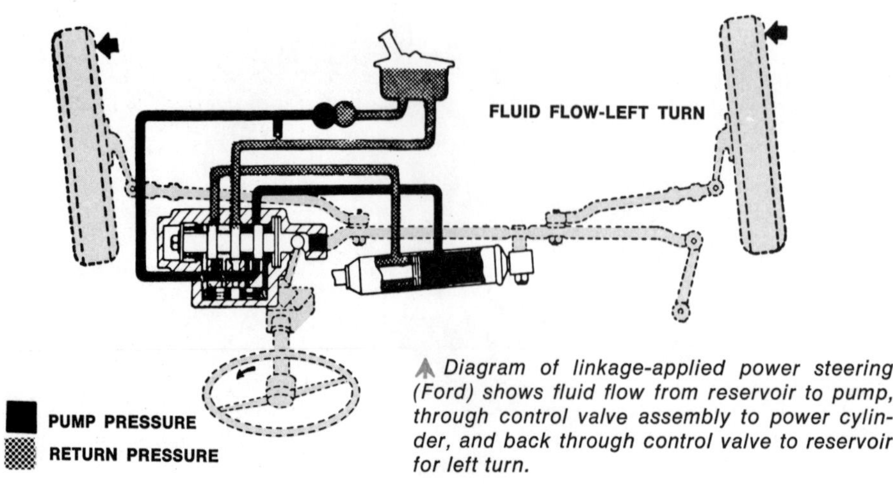

Diagram of linkage-applied power steering (Ford) shows fluid flow from reservoir to pump, through control valve assembly to power cylinder, and back through control valve to reservoir for left turn.

Dipstick permits easy checking of power steering pump reservoir.

body to pump housing joint, between pump body valves, carrier shaft, and relief valve retainer. Fix any of these leaks by removing the pump and reservoir units from the car and replacing the leaking gasket or seal. Individual gaskets and rebuild kits are available from auto supply stores and mail order houses.

Bleed air out of the system whenever a line has been disconnected, a component replaced, or the reservoir has been emptied to change the fluid. Make sure the reservoir is full. Jack up the car so the front wheels clear the ground. With the transmission in neutral, the rear wheels blocked, and the engine running, depress the accelerator until the engine races at a speed equal to about 35 mph. Slowly turn the steering wheel all the way left, then all the way right. Lower the car to the ground and again turn the wheels slowly all the way left, then right. Recheck the reservoir, add fluid if needed and the job is done.

Hard steering can be caused by a slipping power steering drive belt. All belts squeal to some extent when you have the steering wheel cranked all the way during a parking maneuver, but the belt should not squeal during normal low-speed or high-speed driving. If it does, adjustment or replacement is indicated.

Two bolts hold the typical power steering pump. Slacken both and tension the pump with a pry bar.

Any further service on power steering requires special test gauges, and should be left to the professional mechanic. P.W.

See also: BALL JOINTS; BEARINGS; DISC BRAKES; DRUM BRAKE SERVICE; POWER BRAKES.

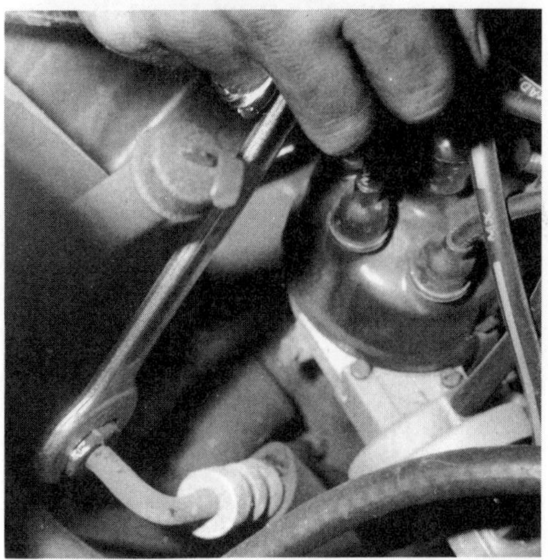

Although tubing wrench is best, open-end wrench can be used on power steering hoses.

Two bolts hold the typical power steering pump. Slacken both for pump belt adjustment. (Finger points to bolt on elongated hole adjusting brace; arrow points to the other bolt.)

Maintaining and Repairing Your Refrigerator

By operating and maintaining your refrigerator carefully, you significantly postpone the day when it just stops running. And, when the breakdown does occur, you can make the repair yourself 98 percent of the time

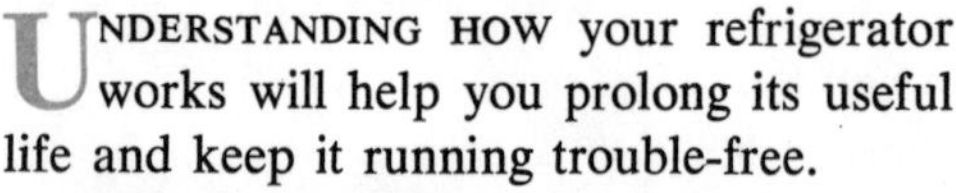

UNDERSTANDING HOW your refrigerator works will help you prolong its useful life and keep it running trouble-free.

Basically, the refrigerator is an insulated cabinet with a refrigeration unit that absorbs heat inside the box and releases it outside.

The word "heat" in discussions about refrigeration is used in a slightly different way than in ordinary conversation. For example, if you picked up an ice cube in your freezer compartment, you wouldn't call it "hot." But it has heat, even though its temperature is fairly close to 0 degrees. It has a lot less heat than a freshly poured cup of tea, but it also has much more heat than an ice cube frozen down to −100 degrees. Think of it as a difference in temperature. If two similar objects have different temperatures, one has less heat than the other and one has more, even if both feel cold to the touch.

Three systems comprise the refrigeration unit—a compressor, a condenser and an evaporater. It works this way. The compresser compresses a refrigerant gas. As the gas is compressed its temperature rises to about 120 degrees and it passes into the condenser. The condenser is a heat exchanger, like the radiator in an automobile. The gas loses heat through the walls of the condenser to the outside atmosphere. The compression and loss of heat change the gas into a liquid.

The liquid refrigerant passes from the condenser through a filter-dryer that removes impurities and then through a capillary tube (about 0.036 inches inside diameter) that meters the flow of liquid into the evaporator inside the cabinet.

The evaporator is also a heat exchanger. Heat in the refrigerator cabinet (even though the inside of the refrigerator feels cold, it has heat that it will transmit to something of lower temperature) is passed through the walls of the evaporator to the liquid refrigerant. The heat changes the liquid to gas. The gas is drawn to the suction side of the pump and begins the cycle again.

In addition to the refrigeration system, the refrigerator has other equipment that makes the system more effective or more convenient to use—a thermostat to control the temperature, for example, or an overload switch to protect the motor, or the circuit that turns on the light when the door is open.

The refrigerants in common use are Freon gases especially compounded for refrigeration. One of these, R-12, has a boiling point of −21.6 degrees F at normal atmospheric pressure. At 120 degrees F its pressure is 157 pounds per square inch. This refrigerant is contained within the completely sealed refrigeration system.

There is nothing that you can do to service a sealed system without an expensive set of tools and test equipment designed for refrigeration service work. Our advice on sealed system service, if needed, is to turn it over to a professional.

Since less than two per cent of the service calls on refrigerators involve a sealed system failure, there is much you can do to keep your unit running at its normal efficiency.

Refrigerator use. The use and care a refrigerator gets will affect its life and efficiency of operation. Some detrimental factors are:

1. An abnormal ice cube demand.
2. Excessive door opening and closing.
3. Leaving the door open for long periods of time.
4. Not completely closing the door.
5. Overcrowding that hampers normal air circulation.
6. Careless loading that damages shelves, chips the porcelain liner, cracks breaker strips, etc.

All of these conditions will cause a unit to run more than it normally would. It could be running continuously and yet not remain cold enough to preserve the foods.

Location. The refrigerator should be located on a secure, level floor. There should be enough clearance to allow adequate air circulation to carry off the condenser heat. There should be at least a three-inch clearance around the sides and top of a machine without a forced-air condenser.

A machine with a forced air condenser

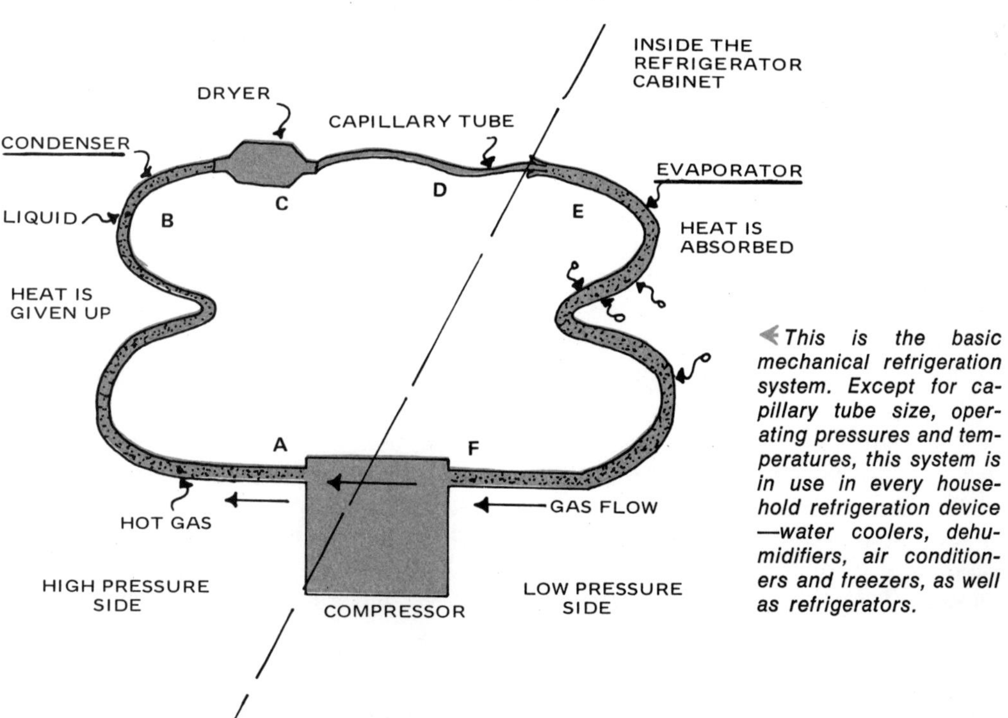

This is the basic mechanical refrigeration system. Except for capillary tube size, operating pressures and temperatures, this system is in use in every household refrigeration device—water coolers, dehumidifiers, air conditioners and freezers, as well as refrigerators.

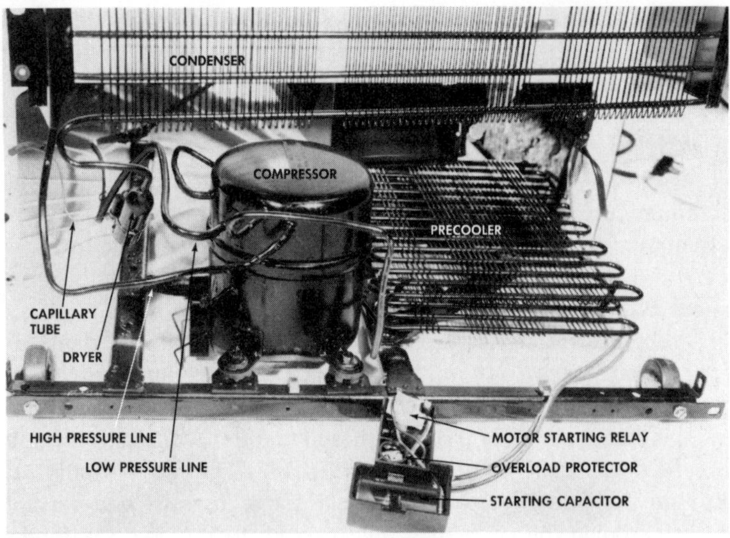

These components are those that are normally outside the refrigerator cabinet. They are all high-pressure parts of the system, except for the low-pressure line.

should have enough space for installation and moving. Make certain the front of the machine, under the door, is clear to allow air flow. The door should swing freely without bumping into furniture or other cabinets.

Your refrigerator should also be out of direct sunlight and away from the stove, radiator or other heat sources. It should be dry because a damp location can cause abnormal cabinet rusting and corrosion of the electrical controls. The electrical supply should be within 10 per cent of the nameplate rating, while the unit is running.

Cabinet care. Dust, animal hair, newspapers, etc. that collect on the condenser should be removed at least twice a year. This will maintain maximum heat transfer from condenser to air. A vacuum cleaner does this job well.

Scratches on the cabinet and rust spots anywhere should be sanded and touched up as they appear. Door hinges that get stiff or squeaky should be lubricated with a little light oil. Door latches on older refrigerators should operate freely and hold the door securely closed. If they do not, the door gasket or seal will not seat properly around the door. This allows cool air to escape and warm air to enter the cabinet causing a frost or ice build-up around the door. Also, the compressor has to work harder to keep the unit cool. Door gaskets that have become torn or have hardened with age will do the same thing. They must be replaced.

Condensation on the outside of the cabinet occurs because the door gasket is leaking cold air at that point or because insulation within the cabinet has shifted out of place.

Magnetic gaskets being used on the newer refrigerators have eliminated the

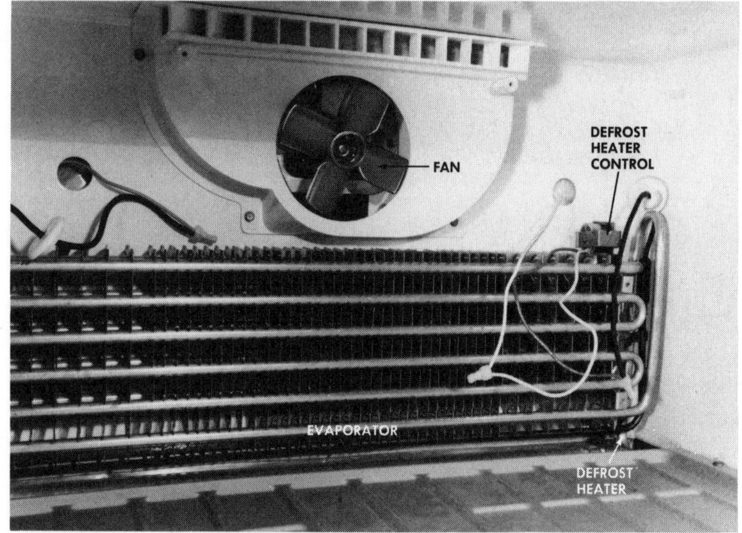

The evaporator, the part of the refrigeration system that absorbs heat inside the cabinet, is often located behind a panel on the rear wall of the freezer compartment, as is this one. Another common location is between the freezer compartment and the refrigeration compartment.

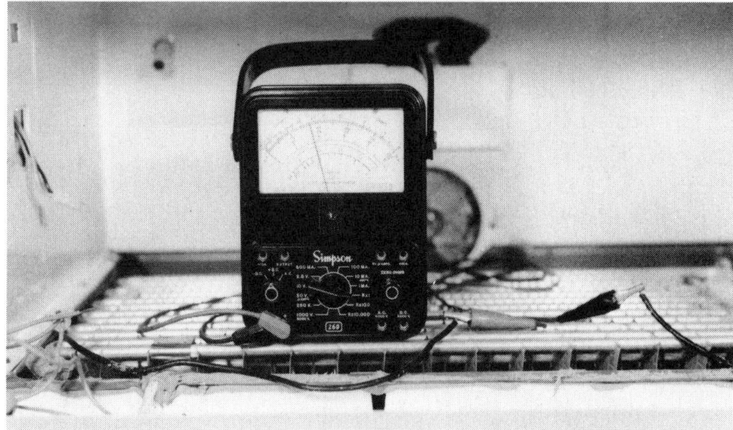

Once the evaporator cover has been removed, the defrost heater can be tested for continuity.

The defrost timer is often located behind the plate under the door. It should be set to the correct time of day when it is installed and reset after any power failure.

It is necessary to remove the breaker strips to get at some of the wiring between the controls and the compressor. The breaker strips are the plastic strips that form the frame around the refrigerator opening. Usually they are snapped in place and can be removed by using a putty knife to push the strip away from the metal shell and prying outward. They break easily, so be very careful when prying them out or when snapping them back into place.

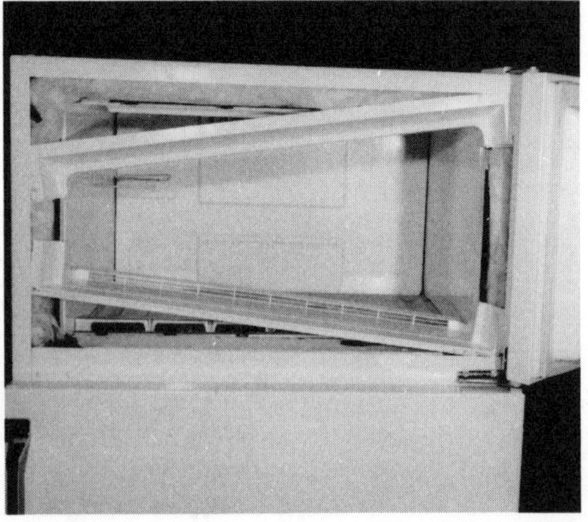

door latch problem and allow a certain amount of door misalignment without cold air leakage from the cabinet. Make certain this seal is not cut or torn. The simplest test for proper door seal fit is to close the door on a piece of paper; then draw the paper out from the seal. There must be an appreciable drag as you pull. A piece of paper the size of a dollar bill would do very nicely.

Inside the cabinet there must be room for the air to circulate, to allow all of the interior to attain the same temperature. The acceptable temperature range in a refrigerator is from 35 to 45 degrees F. In the freezer compartment, temperature should range from 0 to 10 degrees F.

Many of the combination refrigerator-freezers have a fan that circulates cold air from the freezer area through the refrigerator section. Thus, if the freezer section is cold but the refrigerator section is not, make certain the fan is operating and that the air ducts have not clogged with ice. If the fan is defective, it must be replaced. If the duct is clogged with ice, the machine will have to be unplugged to allow the ice to melt.

A defective defrost heater or defrost timer, in refrigerators that have such parts, could cause an ice build-up on the evaporator or in the air duct. The defective parts would have to be replaced.

Electrical. The key to understanding the electrical system is being able to interpret the wiring diagram that is attached to the back of the appliance before it leaves the factory. Every refrigerator having a compressor must have a motor to drive the compressor and a thermostat to stop and start the motor at the proper temperatures. Also necessary are a relay in the motor circuit that automatically disconnects the start winding when the motor attains its proper operating speed and an overload switch that shuts off the electrical power when the motor overheats. This could happen if the line voltage were low, or the condenser were covered with dust and not doing its job, or if a defect occurred in the compressor that would make the motor work harder than it is supposed to. This is the basic circuit that operates the compres-

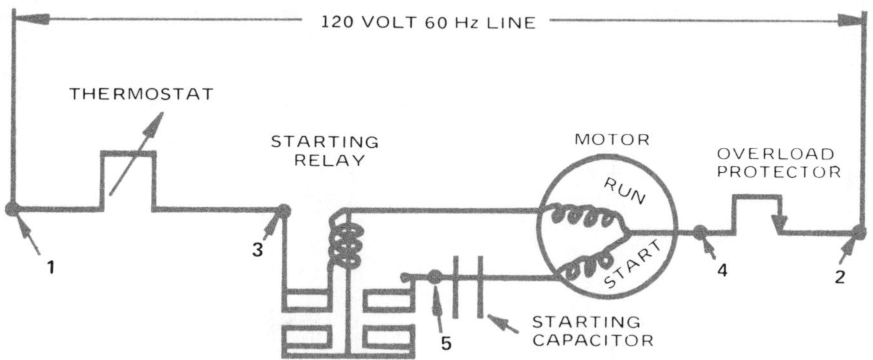

Basic refrigeration compressor motor circuit.

Use an AC voltmeter to test the basic compressor motor circuit from point to point as indicated in the chart. The motor run and start windings can be tested with an ohmmeter. Each must show a low resistance reading. An open circuit will read ∞ (infinity) and means the winding is defective. The capacitor should show a momentary reading, then drop to ∞ (infinity). No reading, or a stable resistance reading, indicates a defect.

BASIC CIRCUIT CHART

Test Points	Reading 120 Volts	Reading 0 Volts
1 and 2	Power is available	No power to circuit
3 and 2	Thermostat is on	Thermostat is off or open
3 and 4	Overload is closed (has not shut off motor)	Overload is open (has shut off motor)
5 and 4	Start relay and run winding are functioning	Defect in start relay or run winding

sor. Whenever the refrigerator fails to operate, check this part of the circuit first.

With your voltmeter or test light follow the test sequence shown on the Basic Circuit Chart. This should allow you to locate the defective part. All parts are relatively easy to replace except the compressor motor. Servicing this requires special tools and replacing it is expensive. A request for a quote on compressor replacement to the local dealer for your make and model refrigerator would be in order. This may also be the time to consider the age of your unit, the repair costs and the price of a new refrigerator.

While the compressor circuit is the electrical heart of a refrigerator, many other electrical parts, controls and improvements have been added to make the refrigerator more convenient to use.

Use your voltmeter or test light to determine whether a part such as a light, heater or motor is getting voltage. If it is and still does not work, use the ohmmeter to test the part for continuity. CAUTION—before using an ohmmeter make certain that the machine is disconnected from the power line. The ohmmeter can also be used to determine if a switch or thermostat is making contact or if the defrost timer switch is in the defrost position.

Always make certain you know what position the defrost timer is in while testing the refrigerator. Some defrost timers are in the defrost position twice a day for 20 minutes, others three times a day. A timer that remains in the defrost position too long raises the temperature inside the refrigerator too much and could cause melted ice

WHERE TO LOOK WHEN THINGS GO WRONG

PROBLEM / POSSIBLE CAUSE	BLOWN FUSE	LOOSE CONNECTION	THERMOSTAT "OFF"	DEFECTIVE THERMOSTAT	DEFECTIVE MOTOR	DEFECTIVE START RELAY	DEFECTIVE COMPRESSOR	REFRIGERANT LEAK	REFRIGERANT STOPPAGE	THERMOSTAT STUCK "ON"	INCORRECT THERMOSTAT SET	DEFECTIVE DOOR SEAL	DIRTY CONDENSER	HOT LOCATION	LOW LINE VOLTAGE	DEFROST TIMER	DEFROST HEATER
DOES NOT RUN	√	√	√	√	√	√	√				√				√	√	
DOES NOT GET COLD			√	√				√	√		√	√	√	√	√	√	√
GETS TOO COLD				√						√							
EXCESSIVE FROSTING UP												√					√
MOTOR RUNS TOO LONG										√		√	√	√	√		

cream and ice cubes in the freezer compartment.

The accompanying trouble diagnosis chart can serve as a guide to where to start looking for the trouble indicated by the listed symptoms. G.M.

See also: ELECTRICAL, HOME; INDIVIDUAL APPLIANCE LISTINGS.

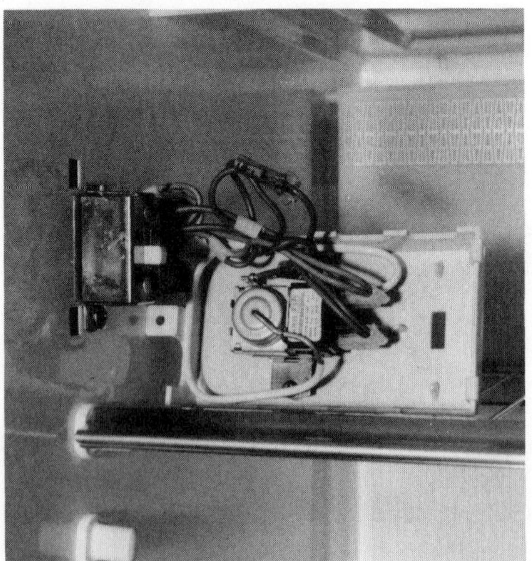

The thermostat is often mounted in a plastic housing held in position by two screws or a snap-in type fastener. Unfastening the housing from the cabinet will expose the wiring and sensing element.

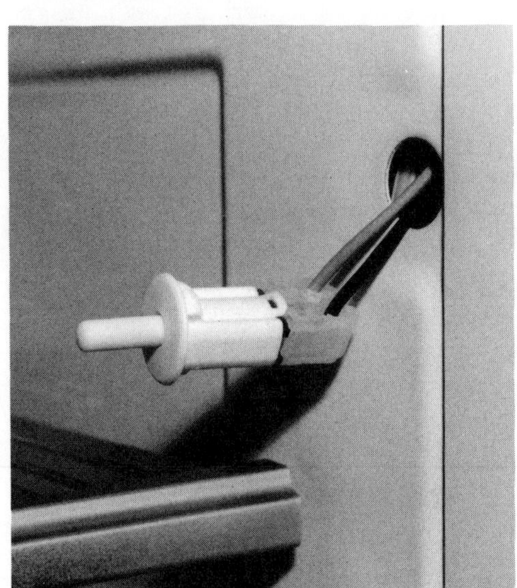

The door switch controls the cabinet light and fan system. It usually is snapped into place and can be pried out with a screw driver or putty knife.

Repairing Roofs and Gutters

Periodic inspections and prompt attention to small flaws will stave off the professional repairman's visit for many years

TAKE AN HOUR and get to know your house. Climb a ladder and take a look at the roof. Examine the siding. Get to know the house around you. It can and should be kept tight and sound with regular, minimum upkeep, at little cost. The average homeowner can do these minor things, prolonging the life of the house and avoiding the higher costs of professional help.

Roof shingles. In all but faulty installations, shingles will last for years requiring little or no maintenance. As they begin to age, however, individual shingles will curl and strong winds will lift them. Sometimes they break or stay curled up. They must be either flattened or replaced, as rain driven by winds will shortly get under the other shingles and begin to deteriorate the sheathing or sub-roof.

All the material this requires is a can of black roofing cement, a box of annular roofing nails, a putty knife, and a hammer. Plus, the replacement shingle, if any, available at the building materials supplier.

For lifted shingles, dab the underside with roofing cement and press it down. If the shingle is torn but in one piece, do the same thing—then apply more cement to the crack line. If the shingle is in two pieces and the separated piece is available, dab it back in place, drive two or three roofing nails along the tear line, and add more cement to both the tear line and the nail heads. Always cover exposed roofing nail heads with cement.

If a torn shingle has to be replaced, the process is simple, if a little awkward at first.

The remaining half of the shingle has to

be removed. It can probably be pulled free, leaving only the nail heads. The nail heads, up and under the overlap of the neighboring shingle, can be removed with a long-shaft screwdriver—or, simply, drive them all the way into the roof, hitting the shingle overlap.

Now the replacement shingle can be slipped into place and correctly positioned (align it with the adjoining shingles). Ideally, new roofing nails should be driven in at a point as far up the new shingle as possible—but this necessitates bending the overlapping shingle to a degree that may crack it. There are three options. Drive the nails at a lower point, but still under the overlap. Use the shaft of a heavy screwdriver as an extension (clumsy, but it will work). Drive the nails through the top of the overlapping shingle, into the new one under it (dab the heads with cement).

For the next maintenance step, examine all the flashings—the seals that wrap around the chimney and vent pipes, and the seals in the roof valleys (where two sections of roof adjoin). This is usually sheet metal cut and shaped to bridge the gap created by the protruding vent of chimney and the cut or notched portion of the roof. The flashings or metal is also overcoated at the edges with roofing cement. Ordinarily, the flashings will hold firm but the cement in time dries and flakes away, and the exposed edges catch rainwater. Therefore. all suspect flashings should be periodically coated with roofing cement to assure a good seal. If the flashings themselves appear loose, they should first be nailed, then coated.

Flashings in roof valleys are for the most part concealed by the valley shingles. Only when a shingle curls or is torn should you poke under it to determine if the flashing is sound. Repair with roofing cement and, if necessary, roofing nails. Hip shingles (the reverse of valley shingles) may tend to crack or separate as the years go by; they, too, can be dabbed at all the crack lines with roofing cement. If the deterioration is severe, it is a simple matter to cap the area with a new, replacement, hip shingle.

Inspect every foot of the roof gutters. The gutters themselves should be clear of accumulated debris, especially at the drain that feeds the downspout. It's a good idea, too, to clear out the scattered leaves and twigs, as the next rain is sure to carry it all to the drain, where it will probably clog. Cap the drain with wire mesh screening—or, better still, install wire mesh strips over the gutter troughs. This allows the water to flow and drain freely; leaves on top of the screening will eventually blow away.

Examine the firmness of the gutters. Where they are wobbly or unsound, use roofing nails to re-anchor them. Coat the

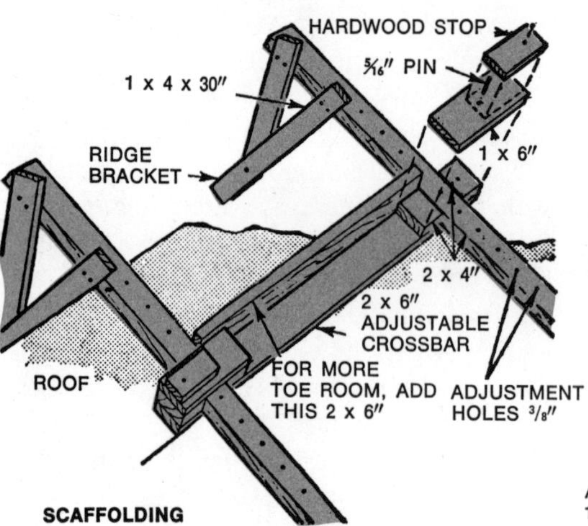

This roof creeper, for use on all but extreme-pitched roofs, makes a good working platform. Calculate the angle of the roof and allow 1 inch for hanger brace. Nail hangers in place, then slide brace for snug fit and nail in place.

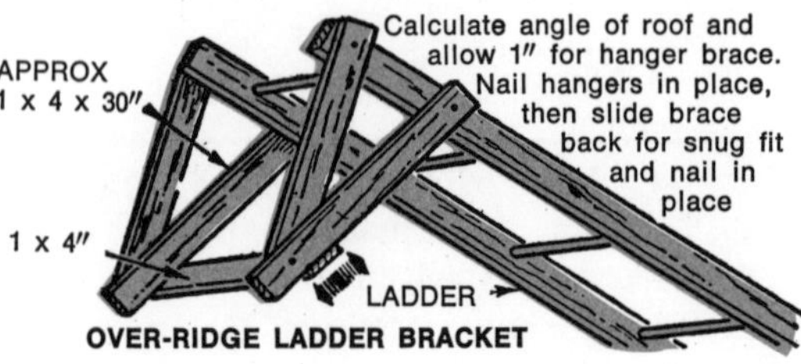

➤Faulty flashings, the seals that wrap around the chimney and vent pipes, can be resealed with roofing cement and if necessary, repaired with roofing nails.

exposed nail heads. Just be sure in repairing loose gutters that the pitch (downward, about 5 degrees) is maintained in order to drain the water.

Next, the downspouts. These should be clear of matter. If not, they back up (a stoppage at a low point could back up enough water weight to cause the downspout to come loose or fall), causing gutters to overflow, battering plantings below with sheets of roof water.

The hangers should also be tested for soundness. These hold the downspouts firmly to the siding; they also hold the downspout firmly against the gutter outlet (loose downspouts usually separate from gutter drains and the water just sprays downward). Loose hangers or straps can be re-nailed, or they can be replaced as easily with a new one.

The troughs of old gutters can be coated with roofing cement in order to extend their life.

Siding. The key to well maintained house siding is a good paint or stain finish. If the finish is in good repair, the siding materal —shingles, shakes, clapboard, whatever— will be well protected and relatively free of problems.

A thorough siding inspection begins at the roof line. Look for staining (signs of water being driven into any roof-siding separations by wind), warping, shingle or board separations, paint cracks or flaking, and rusty nail heads. These could be early signs of future damage.

Wherever there is staining, test the area

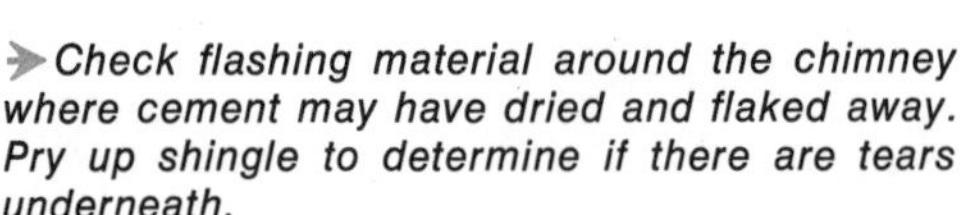

➤Check flashing material around the chimney where cement may have dried and flaked away. Pry up shingle to determine if there are tears underneath.

◀ Deteriorated roof trim should be replaced or at least strengthened with roofing nails and repainted with the proper paint for the job.

▲ Examine the firmness of the gutters. Where they are wobbly or unsound, use roofing nails to reanchor them.

▶ Gutters should be clear of accumulated debris, especially at the drain that feeds the downspout.

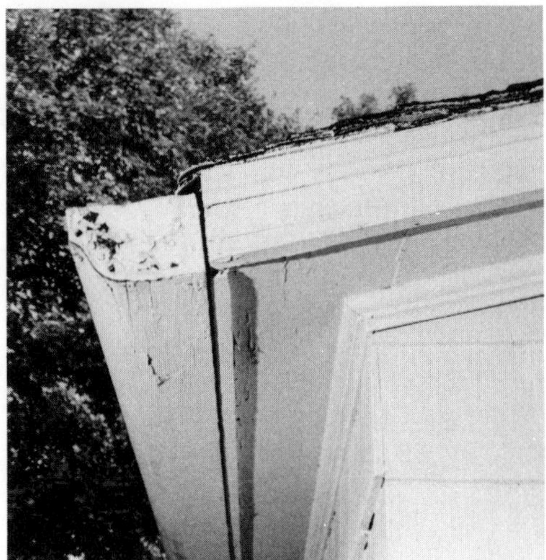

Corroded gutters can be temporarily repaired by coating the interior with paint or roofing cement. Be sure to maintain pitch for good drainage.

with a nail or ice pick to determine if the wood is soft or deteriorated. It would pay to scrape away some of the finish in order to see how severe it may be. If it is local only, let it dry thoroughly, add an extra nail for firmness, then re-seal and touch up with paint. If it is a bad section that is far gone, a carpenter may have to be called.

To remove and replace a shake, shingle, or section of clapboard requires some dexterity.

Shakes and shingles are handled in approximately the same way as roof shingles. Pull the nails or shear the heads of nails. Position the new shingle and nail. In the case of asbestos shingles, there will be a pre-drilled nail hole to serve as a guide; if not, drill one—do not attempt to hammer a nail directly through asbestos.

Sections of clapboard can be cut with a backsaw. It doesn't matter at what point along the line. It will be awkward, but the idea is to saw on the flat of the board in short strokes, up to the next overlapping board. When the board is cut through at the two end points, snap out the soft section up to the overlap. The portion of old board left under the overlap has to be chiseled out, a job which will take some patience. The old nails will have to be sheared after all of the old board is out. After that, cut and position a new board section, nailing it through the new board section. Countersink these heads and putty the holes. Re-paint or re-stain the new section.

Whenever removing a shingle, shake, or section of clapboard, it's a good idea to examine the interleafing black (builder's) paper to be found underneath. If it, too, has deteriorated, peel it off and examine the wood sheathing. If the wood sheathing is water damaged, then this is the time to call in a carpenter for a professional repair. If the sheathing is dampened in a minor way only, allow the exposed section to dry thoroughly (rip out as much as you have to in order to confirm the extent of the dampness), then install new paper and new siding.

See also: ADDITIONS, HOME; CHIMNEYS; HOME IMPROVEMENT; PAINTING, HOUSE; SIDING.

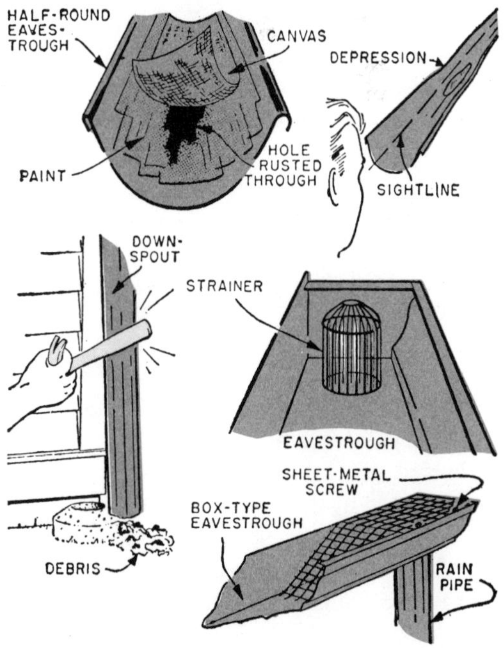

Resurfacing a Flat Roof

Flat roofs require more care than sloped ones, but any householder is capable of patching or resurfacing one himself

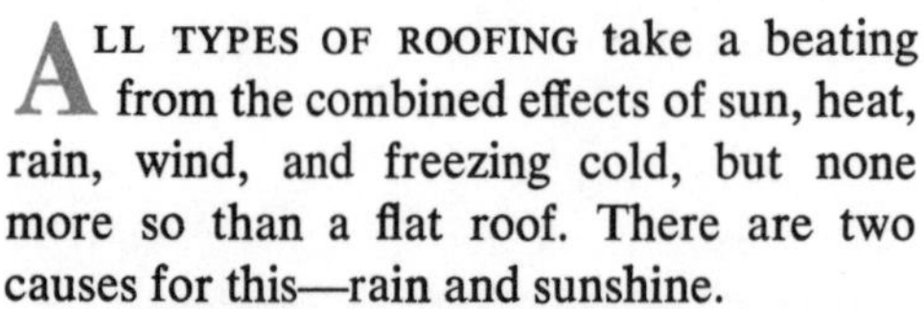

ALL TYPES OF ROOFING take a beating from the combined effects of sun, heat, rain, wind, and freezing cold, but none more so than a flat roof. There are two causes for this—rain and sunshine.

A flat roof cannot shed water as easily as a pitched roof does (a flat roof is any roof with a pitch of less than 23 degrees). It cannot be covered with shingles for this reason—that is why flat roofs are relatively unattractive black surfaces of tar. The sun bakes this roof coating. Depressions form and water collects. Bubbles form and the skin splits. In time, these weak points erode and water enters. After that, the roof problem also becomes a ceiling problem in the room below. Unattended, the flat roof will continue to worsen progressively. At the very least, it needs a quick patch job. But the best bet by far is to re-cover the troubled roof, a job which may be easily undertaken by the average homeowner.

The basic materials include rolls of heavy roofing felt, roofing tar, roofing nails, and a roll of aluminum stripping about 9 inches wide. For tools, you'll need a ladder, a hammer, an applicator brush with a long handle, a wallboard knife (for cutting the roofing felt), and a heavy pair of scissors (metal shears are not necessary) for cutting the very lightweight aluminum. When you go to the hardware store or building supply dealer, make a note of the area to be covered, as this will be a guide to the quantity of felt and tar needed for the job.

The project shown here is a typical flat roof, pitched to about 10 degrees. In addition to having developed a break in two places, there were two other signs of trouble. Water stains at the joint where the roof and the shingle siding met indicated that wind-driven rain was settling in the unprotected joint. One edge of the roof also showed signs of deterioration through lifting and edge-curling of the old covering.

One of the first steps in the repair was to install a strip of flashing (the aluminum) along the deteriorated edge using the roofing nails. This strengthened an otherwise weakened edge. Working from the outside limits inward, the first coat of tar was applied to one roll-width of the roof, includ-

▲ The weakened edge of the roof is strengthened with a nine-inch wide strip of aluminum flashing, using even-spaced roofing nails.

▲ New roofing felt is applied along the front edge of the roof. It is then nailed every three or four inches lengthwise along edge.

▲ A wallboard knife is used to trim the edge of the roofing felt to be flush with the aluminum flashing edge, for a professional look.

▲ Tar is applied for the second strip of felt, both on the old roof and overlapping the first strip of felt about one-third width.

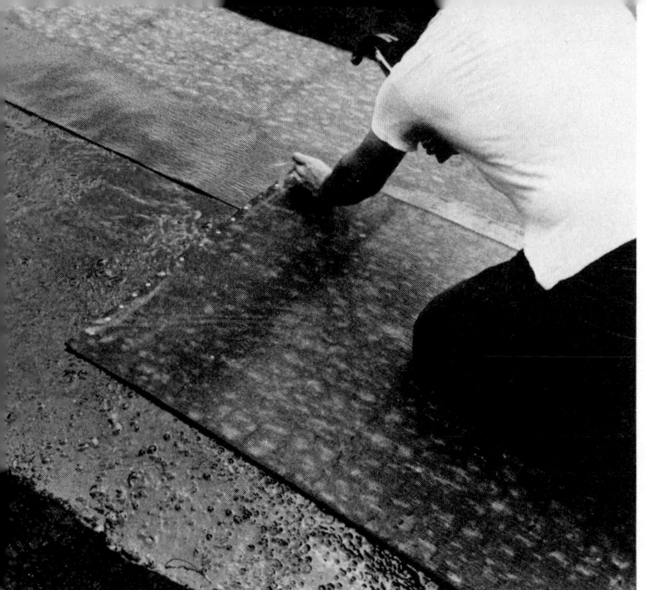

▲ *When the end of the first roll of felt is reached, midway during the job, the edge is secured with roofing nails evenly spaced.*

▲ *After tarring the secured end, tar is applied and the new roll is overlapped. The leading edge is secured with nails, as in last step.*

▲ *The third roll of roofing felt is unrolled. Note that each roll is generously overlapped and a margin has been left at edge for trim.*

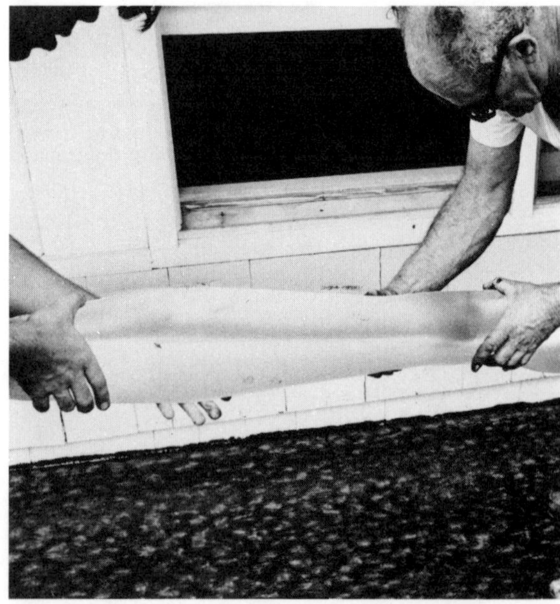

▲ *To thoroughly seal the joint, the aluminum stripping is shaped into a cove molding and slipped under the bottom course of shingles.*

in a good smear on the newly installed flashing. This done, the first new roll of felt was unrolled and nailed every three or four inches along both sides. The end was trimmed flush with the edge of the roof, using the wallboard knife.

Thereafter, tar was applied for the second strip of felt, both on the old roof and overlapping the first strip of felt. When the first roll of felt came to an end midway in the repair, the end was well secured with roofing nails. More tar was applied to this

▲ *The bottom edge of the aluminum flashing is nailed directly into the new roof covering, and the edges are given a first seal of tar.*

secured end, and when the new roll was started, it overlapped the end of the old roll. More roofing nails secured the leading edge of the new roll.

Subsequent rolls of felt over fresh tar followed until the last roll was laid, flush in the joint where the new covering and the shingle siding met. In order to thoroughly seal this joint, the aluminum stripping was shaped into a cove molding and installed in the joint with the top edge slipped under the bottom course of shingles. The bottom edge of flashing was nailed directly into the new roof covering, and the edges given a first seal of tar.

After the installation was complete, a final, overall topping of tar was applied, with particular attention to exposed nail heads. This finished the job.

Although the pitch on this roof was only 10 degrees, it was and is necessary to recover all flat roofs, regardless of pitch, in overlap fashion—as you would overlap pitch-roof shingles. This arrangement does not give water any edge to collect against, however slight the pitch may be.

After a short period of time, perhaps a month or two, a few nail heads may pop up. This will not be due to any fault in the

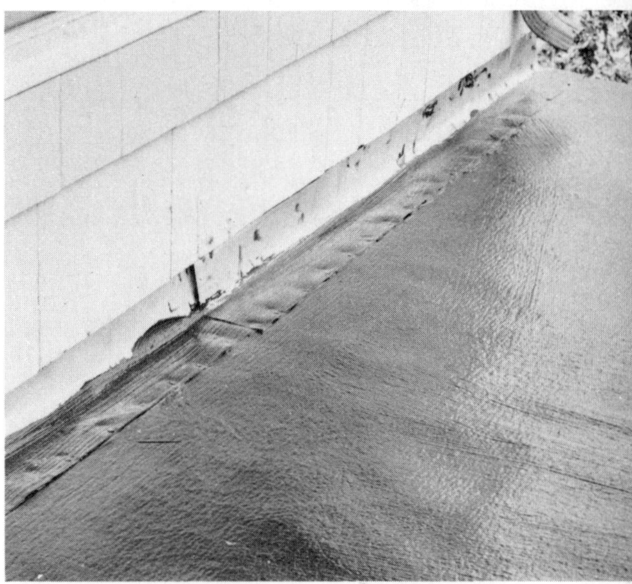

▲ *A final overall topping of tar is applied, giving particular attention to any exposed nail heads and to areas that need extra tar.*

re-covering process—it is because these nails happen to have been driven between two boards and have no purchase. Simply tap them back into place and dab the broken skin with more tar. Better still, use a roof patching compound that contains some asbestos particles. This sealer will ooze into whatever breaks the popped nail caused and will be stronger in the long run.

It wouldn't hurt to re-coat the new roof job seasonally. Once a year will do, in the fall or spring. This will extend the life of the basic repair and add a neat appearance.

If accidental breaks occur (a tear from a heavy tree limb or the feet of a sharp metal ladder), a good patch may be made with materials left over from the big job. Following the same basic plan, coat the tear and the surrounding area with tar, place a patch over it, nail the edges all around, and add a final top coat of tar. This kind of repair is every bit as good in technique as the basic re-covering. B.M.

See also: CHIMNEYS; PAINTING, HOUSE.

How to Make Screens and Storm Windows

Do the job yourself with inexpensive aluminum components and a few simple tools

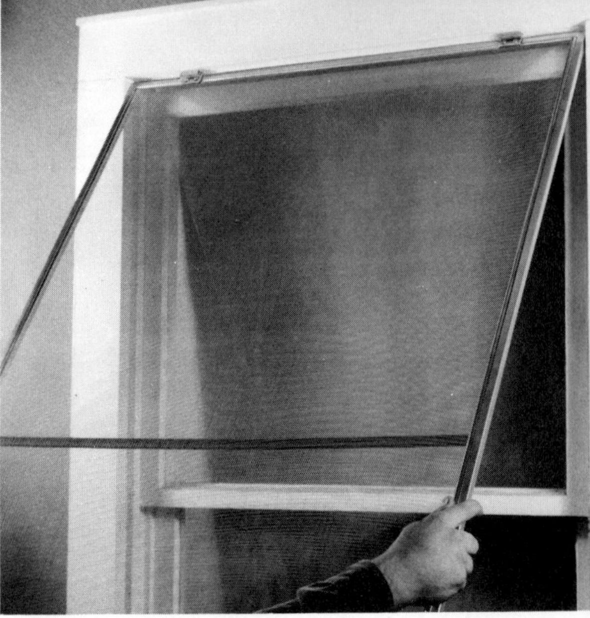

▲ *Completed screen is hung from brackets at top and held by hook and eye fasteners at the bottom.*

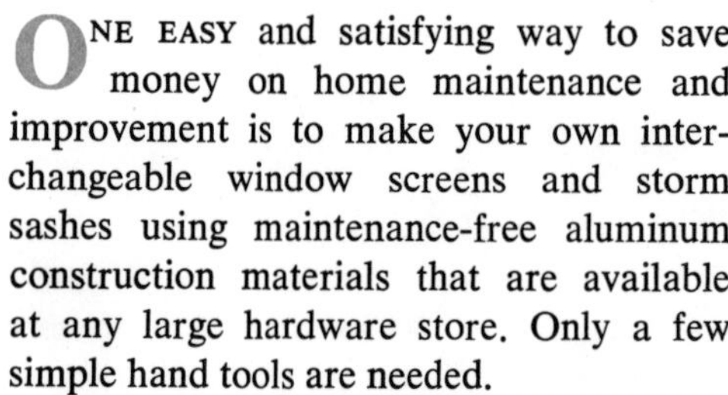

ONE EASY and satisfying way to save money on home maintenance and improvement is to make your own interchangeable window screens and storm sashes using maintenance-free aluminum construction materials that are available at any large hardware store. Only a few simple hand tools are needed.

The following discussion applies primarily to the making of full-size screens for installation on conventional double-hung windows. But screens for any other type of window can be made as easily, following the additional tips provided at the end of this article. Surprisingly, constructing storm sashes is even more of a breeze than making the screens. The only important point to bear in mind is that you need one type of framing material to hold screening, and a different type for glass (see diagram). The corner locking pieces and hanger units are identical in each case.

To avoid wasting material, rough-measure your window height and width to determine whether the six- or eight-foot lengths of framing material will be more economical. Re-measure the windows just outside the blind stops more carefully when you are ready to cut the framing to proper size. Make the vertical and horizontal sections all ⅛-inch shorter than the actual window measurements to avoid an over-tight fit. After removing the U-shaped spline that locks in the screening, mark 45-degree angles at the measured points so that the edge forming the channel accepting the spline becomes the shorter of the two sides. Cut accurately along the 45-degree lines using a hacksaw. If you plan to make many screens and/or storm sashes, the construction of a simple miter box (see photo) will save much time and ensure precise cuts. De-burr the cut ends with a file or sandpaper.

To assemble the frame, push a corner lock into each end of one short side, add vertical members to the exposed portions of the corner locks, and finish off by pushing on the other end piece to which corner locks have been added. Check all corners to make sure they form good right angles. The frame is now ready for addition of the screening if the screen area is six square feet or less. A cross brace should be added to larger screens, as shown. Just notch back two ends of a length of framing material to form ⅝-inch lips to overlap the basic frame. Drill a hole in each lip to accept a #6 3/8-inch aluminum sheet metal screw, and smaller pilot holes in appropriate positions on the frame. Note that the screening is *not* attached to this brace.

During the following operations, make certain that the weave of the screening runs parallel to the frame channels, and try to cut carefully between two adjacent screen wires to help keep the screening square. Ordinary household shears can be used to cut the screening.

Start by aligning the selvedge edge, or a pre-cut straight edge, along one long channel so that the screening just covers the channel opening. When this edge is pressed into the channel later, it will fit down against the inside edge of the groove *only*; do not allow it to run across the bottom of the channel. While holding the screen in place, cut about two inches up an adjacent side, then snip a small triangular bit of screening off the corner to avoid bunching inside the channel.

Use an ordinary putty knife to press the selvedge or pre-cut edge into the groove. This is easier if you lay a strip of 1/4-inch thick plywood above and below the screen as shown. Try to obtain a neat right-angle bend. Lock this edge of screening in place by inserting the proper length of spline which has been square-cut to run the full length of the channel. Tighten the spline by tapping a length of 1/4-inch thick plywood laid atop the spline. To avoid dents, slightly round the edges and ends of the plywood.

Before cutting and locking in the other edges in the same manner, place some scraps of aluminum framing, or wood scraps of the same thickness, under the screening to keep it from sagging during the finishing operations. Cut the screening along the two short edges so that the edges can be shaped neatly along the inside walls of the channels. Lock in place with splines, and then complete assembly of the fourth side in the same manner.

MATERIALS FOR SCREENS

	Reynolds No.
Aluminum screen framing complete with spline:	
6 ft. lengths	6020
8 ft. lengths	6021
Corner locks (4 per frame)	7210
Hangers (2 units per frame)	7215
Aluminum screen cloth	
Small hooks with screw-eyes (2 each per frame)	

Aluminum screens and storm windows are assembled in about the same way, but screen uses a different frame member (left) than the storm window (right).

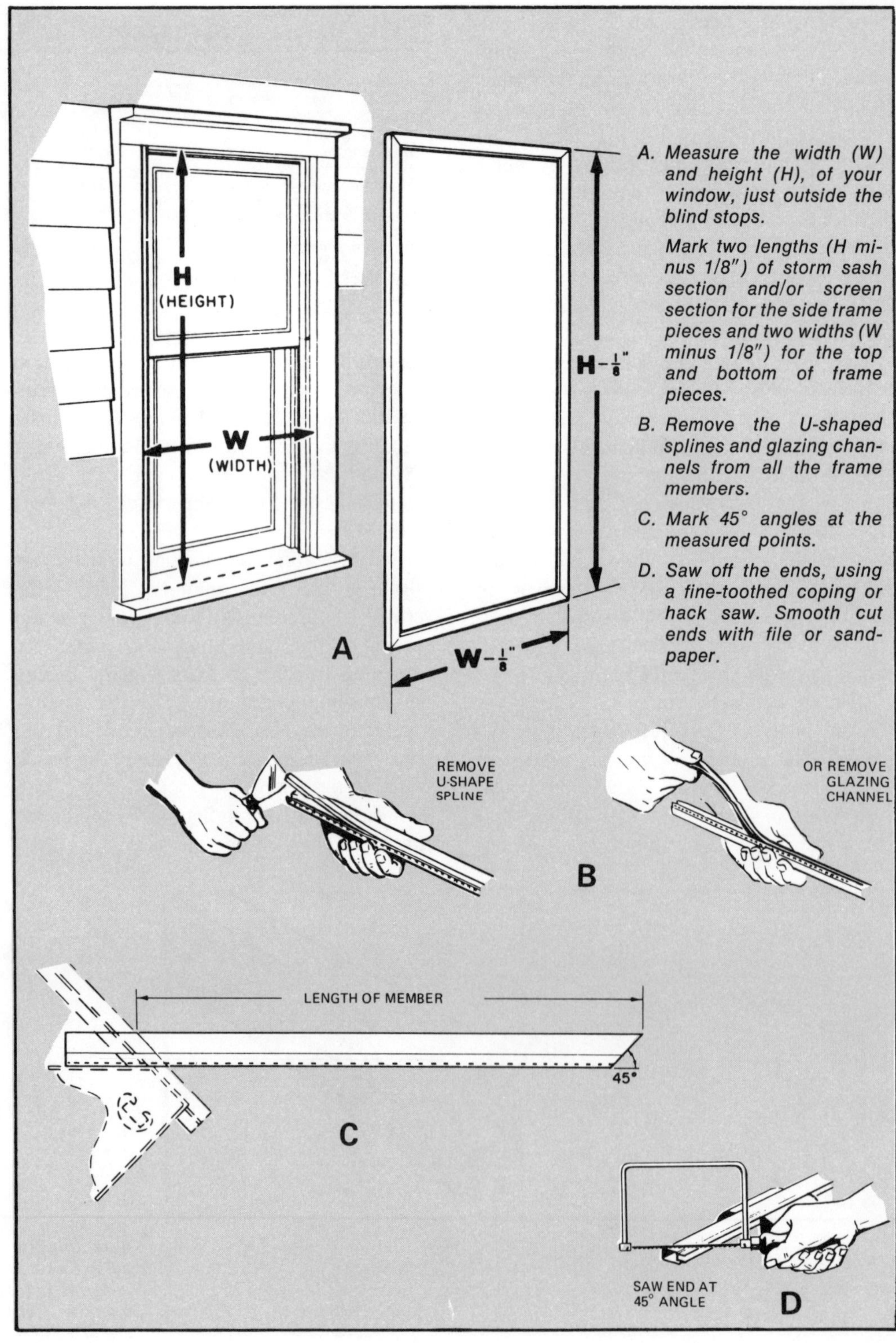
H
(HEIGHT)
W
(WIDTH)
H-1/8"
W-1/8"
A
A. Measure the width (W) and height (H), of your window, just outside the blind stops.
Mark two lengths (H minus 1/8") of storm sash section and/or screen section for the side frame pieces and two widths (W minus 1/8") for the top and bottom of frame pieces.
B. Remove the U-shaped splines and glazing channels from all the frame members.
C. Mark 45° angles at the measured points.
D. Saw off the ends, using a fine-toothed coping or hack saw. Smooth cut ends with file or sandpaper.
REMOVE
U-SHAPE
SPLINE
OR REMOVE
GLAZING
CHANNEL
B
LENGTH OF MEMBER
45°
C
SAW END AT
45° ANGLE
D

ASSEMBLING STORM SASH:

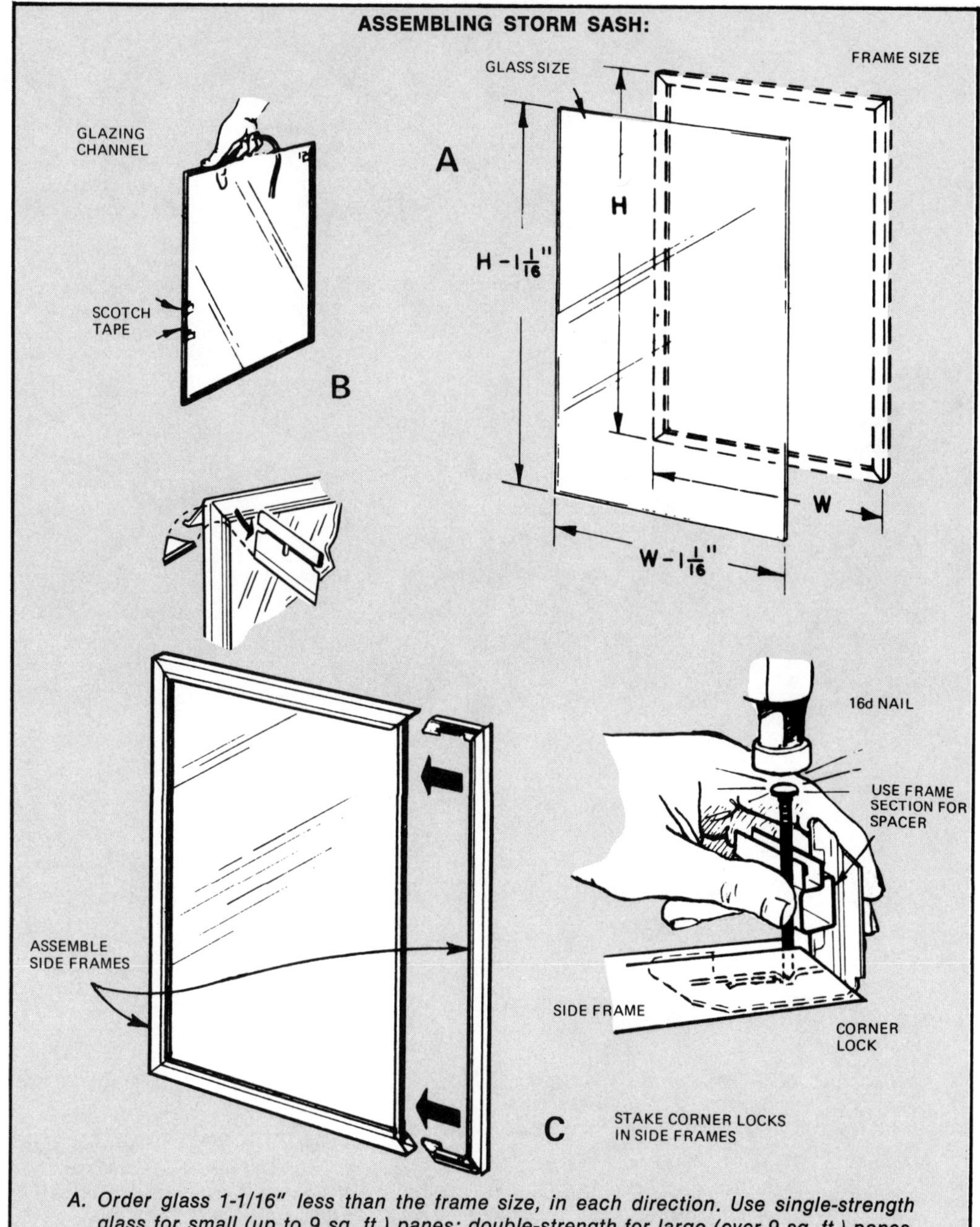

A. *Order glass 1-1/16" less than the frame size, in each direction. Use single-strength glass for small (up to 9 sq. ft.) panes; double-strength for large (over 9 sq. ft.) panes.*

B. *Starting at one corner, fit glazing channel around edges of glass. Make pie cuts at corners.*

C. *Insert the corner locks into the two side frames. Stake corner lock in place with nail mark—just behind the edge of the corner lock web.*

Center end frame members over top and bottom edges of the glass, so they will match with side members.

Add side frame members (with corner locks already in place) to complete assembly.

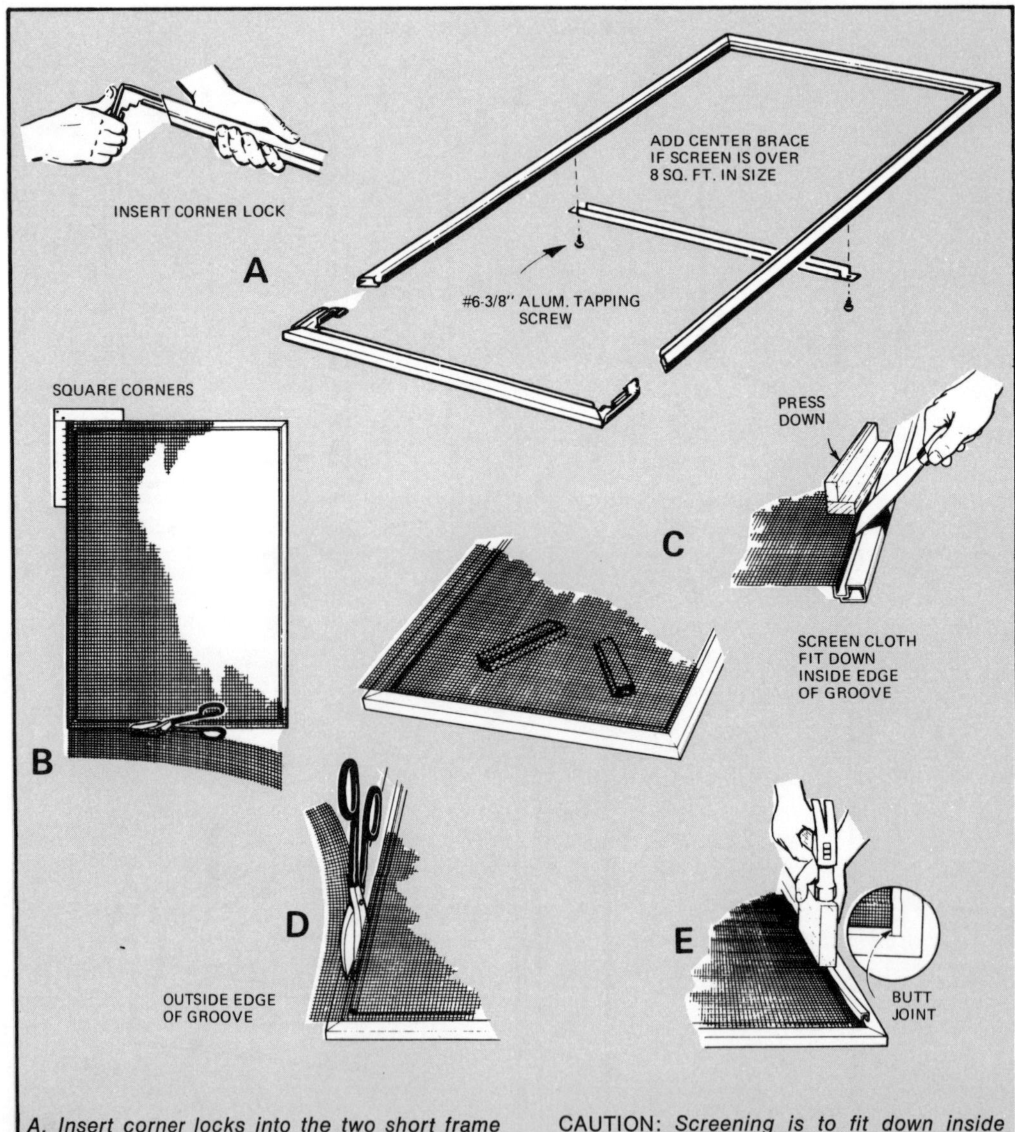

A. *Insert corner locks into the two short frame pieces. Slip the two long frame pieces onto one of the end pieces. Finally add the other end as shown to complete the frame.*

B. *Cut screening to outside dimensions of frame. Cut carefully between two screen wires to keep screening square.*

Place frame on table and scatter scraps of frame section in the center area to hold screening level with top of frame.

C. *Line up screening with the outside edge of the screen groove, at the side and end of the frame shown. Bend the screening into the side and end grooves.*

CAUTION: *Screening is to fit down inside edge of groove only.*

D. *After completing operation along one side (as in step above), cut off excess screen cloth along line even with outside edge of groove in other adjacent leg.*

E. *Cut U-shaped splines to length of spline groove; make butt joints at the corners.*

Next, tap spline into groove (on one long frame piece) to hold screening securely.

In the same manner, form screen cloth on the two short sides, cut off excess screen cloth and insert spline. Then, complete fourth side.

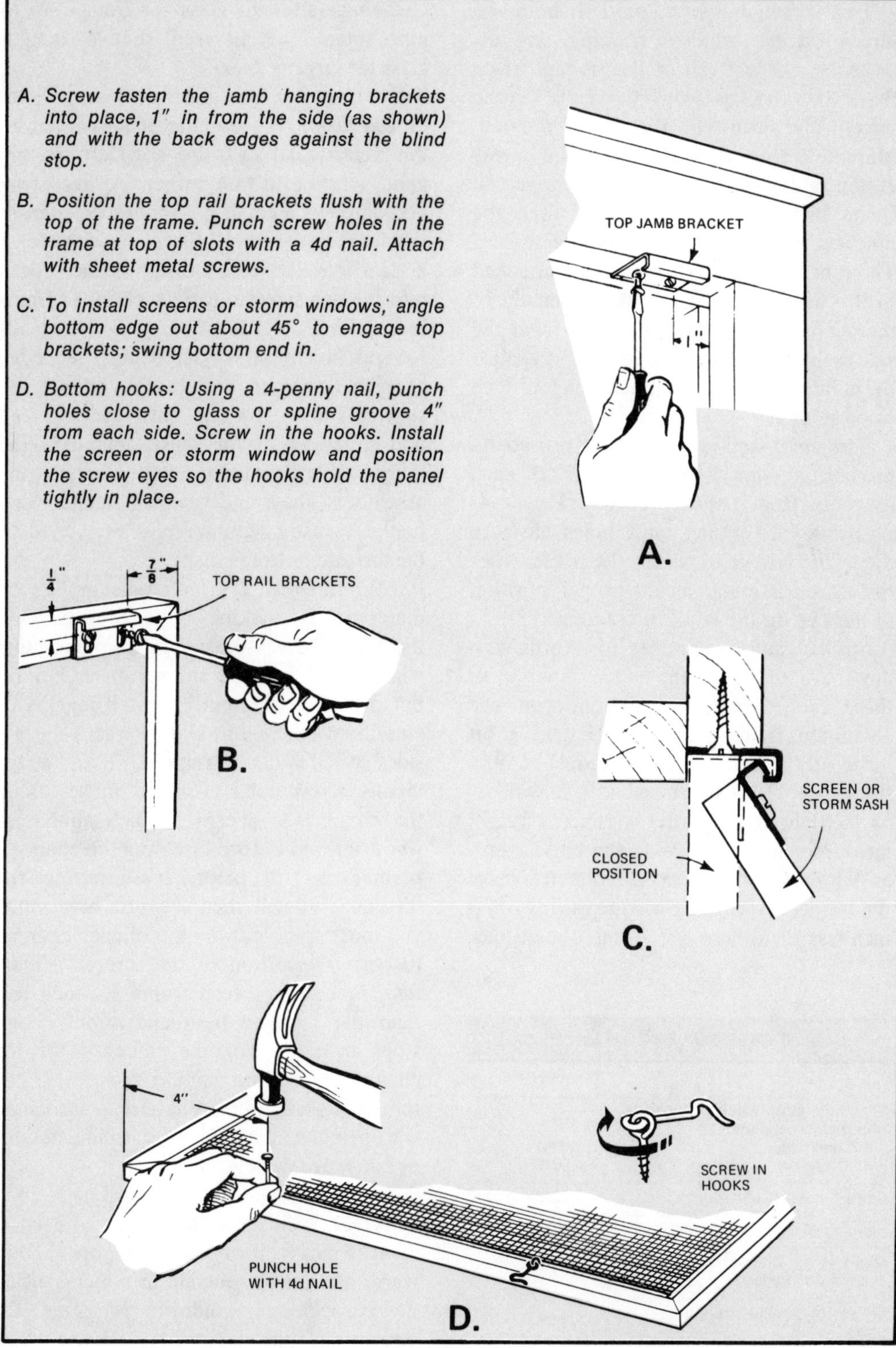
A. Screw fasten the jamb hanging brackets into place, 1" in from the side (as shown) and with the back edges against the blind stop.
B. Position the top rail brackets flush with the top of the frame. Punch screw holes in the frame at top of slots with a 4d nail. Attach with sheet metal screws.
C. To install screens or storm windows, angle bottom edge out about 45° to engage top brackets; swing bottom end in.
D. Bottom hooks: Using a 4-penny nail, punch holes close to glass or spline groove 4" from each side. Screw in the hooks. Install the screen or storm window and position the screw eyes so the hooks hold the panel tightly in place.
TOP JAMB BRACKET
1"
A.
1/4"
7/8"
TOP RAIL BRACKETS
B.
SCREEN OR
STORM SASH
CLOSED
POSITION
C.
4"
SCREW IN
HOOKS
PUNCH HOLE
WITH 4d NAIL
D.

Two screen brackets, used to hold the screen on the window framing, are attached to the top rail of the screen. Place these $3^{15}/_{16}$-inches from the ends of the screen, and flush with the top of the rail. Mark hole positions at the top of the bracket slots, and punch screw holes in the screen frame using a 4-penny nail. Attach the brackets with ⅜-inch self tapping screws. The other half of each bracket is attached to the window jamb, on the underside of the window casing and 4 inches from the side casings. Put the back edge tight against the blind stop. Fasten in place using ¾-inch wood screws.

Two hook-and-eye catches are used on the bottom edge of the screen. Place each 4 inches from a lower corner. Use a 4-penny nail to punch pilot holes close to the spline groove to accept the hook. After the screen is hung, locate proper position of the eye on the window framing.

Storm windows. Frames for storm windows are made in the same manner as those for screens, except that you use aluminum framing material shaped a bit differently; it has a glazing channel to hold the glass. Make the frame for a window ⅛-inch shorter than the width and height measurements just outside the blind stops, as before. Check the *outside* dimensions of the frame, and order glass measuring $1^{1}/_{16}$-inch less than these two frame dimensions.

MATERIALS FOR STORM SASHES	
	Reynolds No.
Aluminum storm sash framing with glazing channel:	
6 ft. lengths	6041
8 ft. lengths	6042
Corner locks (4 per frame)	7210
Hangers (2 units per frame)	7215
Small hooks with screw-eyes (2 each per frame)	
Single- or double-strength glass	

Use single-strength glass for frames up to nine square feet in area, double-strength glass for larger panes.

Fit the flexible glazing channel (removed from the framing material before the metal is cut to frame size) around the glass, starting at one corner. At each corner, snip out a small pie-shaped piece from the front and rear of the channel to form a neat beveled turn. Insert corner locks into the two side (longer) sections of framing, staking them firmly in place with nail-formed indentations just behind the edge of each corner lock web. Now center the shorter frame sections onto the top and bottom edges of the glass, then add the longer side members to complete the assembly. The same types of hangers and hooks as used with screens are added to the top and bottom edges.

Half screens. You can save money on materials by making screens to fit only the lower halves of standard double-hung windows. You make the screen as before, but mount it differently. Install lengths of aluminum *channel* as sliding tracks on two sides of the window frame. Drill and countersink screw holes every six inches along the channel to accept ¾-inch aluminum wood screws. Before fastening the channels permanently in place, try inserting the screen. You will then see just how much you must notch out the top of each channel to permit insertion of the screen. *Important:* make the screen frame $^{3}/_{16}$-inch less than the opening between window blind stops to allow for the thickness of the channel. Insertion and removal of the screen is easier if the channel is lubricated with products available at gasoline stations or hardware dealers.

Basement windows. A storm sash and/or screen is fitted on the inside of a basement window if the window opens outward, and on the outside in the case of an inward-opening window. Measure the opening inside the window frame, then

How to Make Screens and Storm Windows

➤ *Join adjacent screen frame members by simply pushing them on angular corner locks. Deburr the cut ends before joining them.*

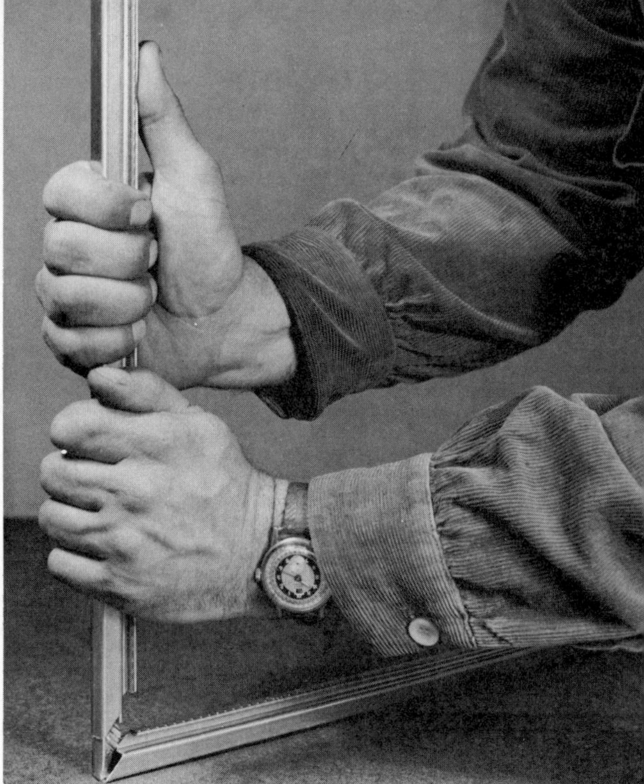

▲ *Make a 90-degree corner jig by nailing two strips of 1/4-inch thick plywood on working surface. This will improve accuracy and lighten your work load.*

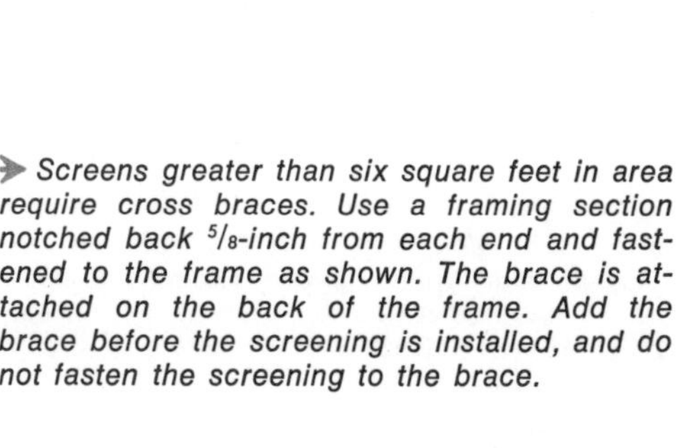

➤ *Screens greater than six square feet in area require cross braces. Use a framing section notched back 5/8-inch from each end and fastened to the frame as shown. The brace is attached on the back of the frame. Add the brace before the screening is installed, and do not fasten the screening to the brace.*

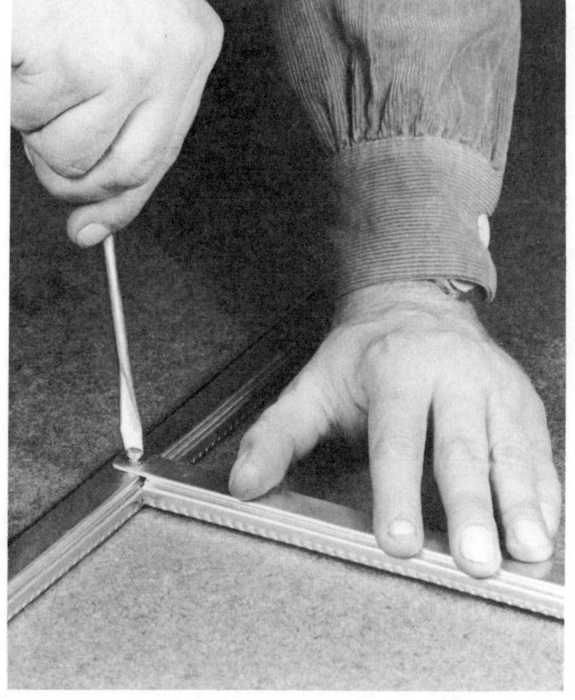

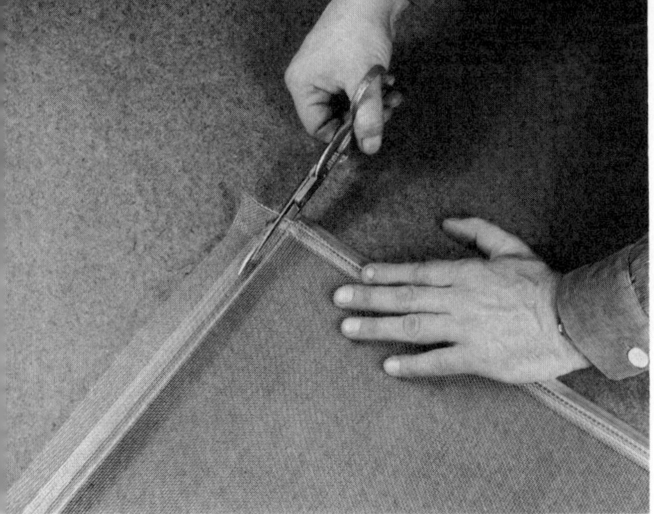

Align selvedged side of screening so that it just covers one long groove. Cut about two inches along the adjacent side and snip off a little of the corner so the screening will fold into the grooves without bunching. Cutting can be done with kitchen shears.

Press screening into groove with a putty knife so that it runs close to the bottom of the groove, but no further. Strips of wood 1/4-inch thick laid under and on top of the screening make it easy to fold neat 90-degree bends in the screening.

Spline locks screening into groove. Hammer a 1/4-inch thick length of plywood laid over the spline to drive it home. Round the edges of the plywood slightly to prevent it from marring the spline. Note that the spline is straight cut, not beveled.

How to Make Screens and Storm Windows

➤ *Punch screw holes for screen brackets with a 4-penny nail, then attach the bracket with 3/8-inch self-tapping screws.*

▲ *Small hooks on bottom rail of screen engage with screw eyes fastened to window frame to hold screen in place. Screw the hooks into pilot holes made with a 4-penny nail.*

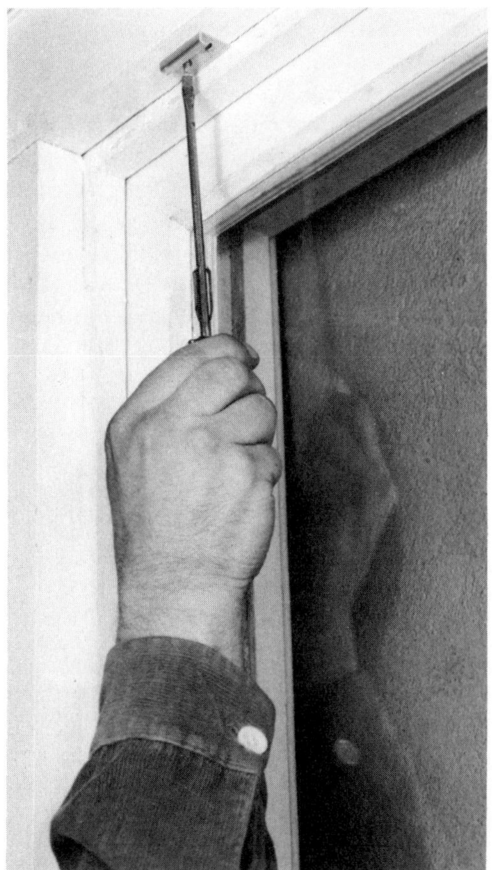

◄ *Jamb brackets on underside of window casing engage screen brackets. They are attached with 3/4-inch wood screws.*

add ¾-inch to each dimension to provide a ⅜-inch overlap on all four sides of a *wooden* basement window frame. If you have metal window frames, they probably have holes for attaching screens or storm sash. Use self-tapping screws and clips made from 1 x 1 x 1/16-inch aluminum angle iron to install the storm sash on metal frames. Use round-head wood screws on wood window frames. Attach a strip of felt or rubber tape weather stripping around the edge of the storm sash between the sash and metal window frame. Frames for metal basement windows are made in the same manner as those used for casement windows.

Casement windows. Determine the width of a casement window storm sash by measuring between screw holes you will probably find on the sides of the window frame. For height, measure from top of the crank mechanism to the top of the window frame, then add ¼-inch for overlap at the top. The completed storm sash, or screen, is held in place with angle clips made from 1 x 1 x 1/6-inch aluminum angles. Use self-tapping screws to fasten these to the edges of the frame. Be sure to use felt or rubber stripping between the screen or storm sash frame and a *metal* window frame to prevent acceleration of corrosion that occurs when dissimilar metals are in contact.

Awning windows. If your awning window opens outward, fit the storm sash or screen around the blind stop on the inside. It may be necessary to fit a wood filler strip on the window sill to clear the crank. Drill a hole through the wood for the crank.

Measure the width of the window opening just inside the blind stop and cut the top and bottom sections of the frame ⅛-inch shorter than this dimension. Measure the height from the top of the wood filler strip to the top of the window opening, just inside the blind stop. Make the side pieces of the frame ⅛-inch shorter than this measurement. Attach a strip of felt or rubber weather stripping along the bottom of the sash. Attach the sash or screen with screws passing through the side sections of the frame into the blind stop.

One final tip: measure the width of your window opening at three different positions (top, middle and bottom) and use the shortest dimension if there are differences. Also measure the vertical distance on both sides of the window to be sure that they are the same. J.H.

See also: ADDITIONS, HOME; GLAZING; HOME IMPROVEMENT.

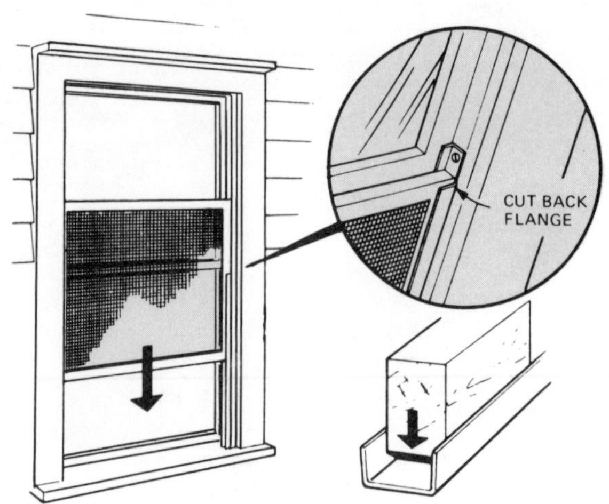

◄Half screens for standard double hung windows may be installed using aluminum channel (Item #6010) as a sliding track. Drill and countersink screw holes every 6" along channel on 3/4" aluminum wood screws. Cut back flange on one side to insert screen. Spread track slightly if necessary. Attach channel to blind stop flush with the inner edge. Make screen frame 3/16" less than opening between blind stops. Lubricate channel with products available at gasoline stations or hardware dealers.

How to Make Screens and Storm Windows

➤ Casement windows usually have screw holes drilled along sides of frame for installing screens or storm sash on the inside. Measure for width of storm sash between inside edges of holes at sides. For height, measure from top of crank mechanism to frame at top (see sketch). Add 1/4" for overlap at top. Hold completed sash in place with angle clips (made from 1"x1"x1/16" aluminum angle) and self-tapping screws. Whenever aluminum storm sash is installed on a metal frame, be sure to use a felt or rubber strip between them.

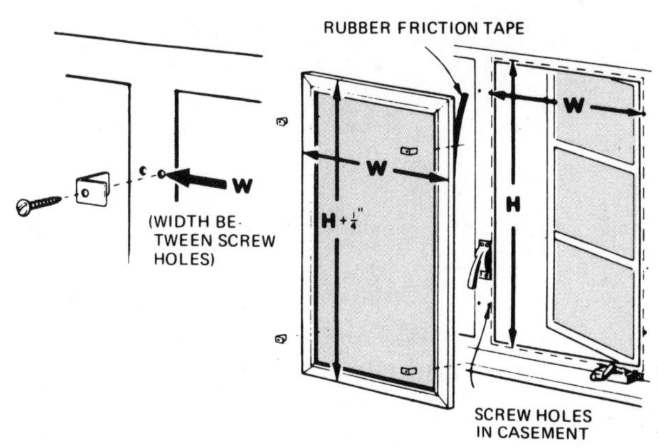

➤ Awning windows which open out are fitted with storm sash or screens around the blind stop on the inside of the house. Usually it is necessary to fit a wood filler strip on window sill to clear the crank. Drill a hole through the wood for the crank.

Measure width (W) of opening just inside of the blind stop and cut the top and bottom sections 1/8" less than W. Measure height (H) from top of wood strip to top of opening just inside blind stop. Length of side pieces equal H minus 1/8". Attach a strip of felt or rubber along the bottom of sash. Attach sash or screens with screws through the side sections into blind stop.

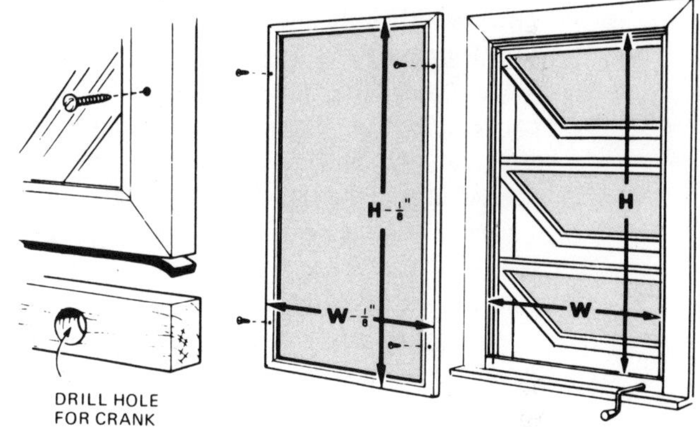

➤ Basement windows are fitted with storm sash outside if they open inward or inside if they open outward. Measure the opening inside the window frame. Add 3/4" to height and width for a 3/8" overlap on all four sides of wood frames. For metal frames follow instructions on casement windows. Holes are usually provided in metal window frames for attaching screens or storm sash. Use self-tapping screws and clips made from 1"x1"x1/16" aluminum angle to install the storm sash on metal frames or round head wood screws on wood window frames. Attach a strip of weather stripping, felt or rubber tape, around the edge of the storm sash between the sash and metal window frames.

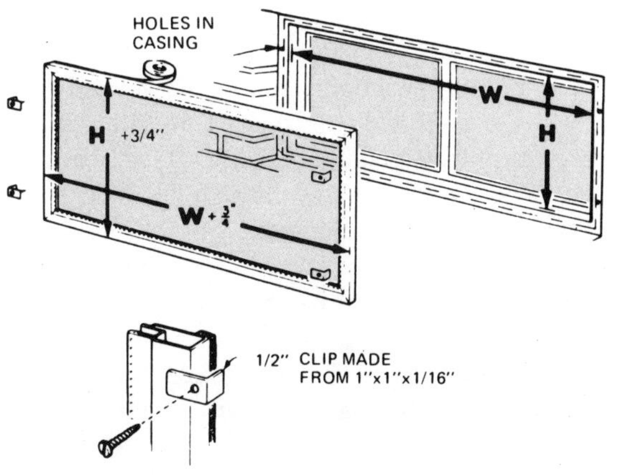

Stopping Leaks in Wood Siding

Moisture penetrating your house's siding can lead to decay and plaster damage. The place to stop it is at the walls

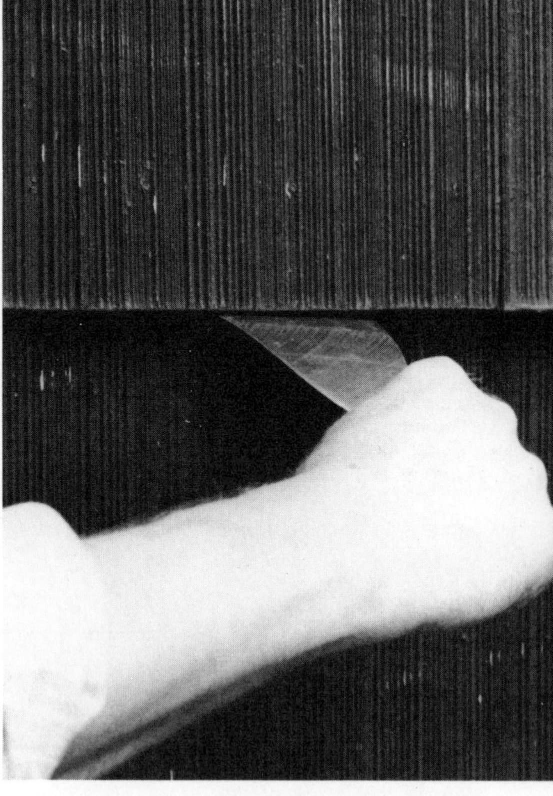

▲ *Check your wood siding for leaks and scrape away loose paint. Small splits and knots can be patched. Large cracks may require replacing section of siding.*

SPLITS IN WOOD SIDING, loose knots, leaks in flashing, all invite moisture to enter wood walls and start costly decay in your home. Fungi, which feed on damp wood, hasten the progress. And, if water can continue to enter, you may also get water-stained and weakened plaster walls and ceilings in the interior.

The best attack on the moisture problem is to give the house a complete inspection. Be sure gutters and drains are clear, and check around edges of roof and near chimneys and windows for leaks in flashing, or other materials. Then check the siding for looseness, splits or breaks.

Nail down any loose siding you find. If the siding is badly split or decayed, replace it. Bore a hole near a stud, so you can cut along the stud with a compass saw or an electric saber saw. Split out the damaged wood and use an old chisel or tire iron to pry up the lower edge of the siding board above. If there is danger of splitting this next board, slide a hacksaw blade between the boards and saw through the nails. Work the heads of the nails out of the board above. Use a nail set to drive the nail stubs in, and you can remove the board.

The new siding board should be face-primed and back-primed first. Where there is no sheathing, nail 1 x 3-inch strips to the sides of the 2 x 4 studs to catch the ends of the new piece. Over sheathing, use a circular saw (set to shallow depth), or a chisel, to cut the edge of the board at the joint.

If a board is sound and free of decay, but has a loose knot, or a small split, you can make a neat patch repair. Clean the area removing scaling paint and dirt with a wire brush. For a knothole, use a disc larger than the resinous rim of the knot; for a

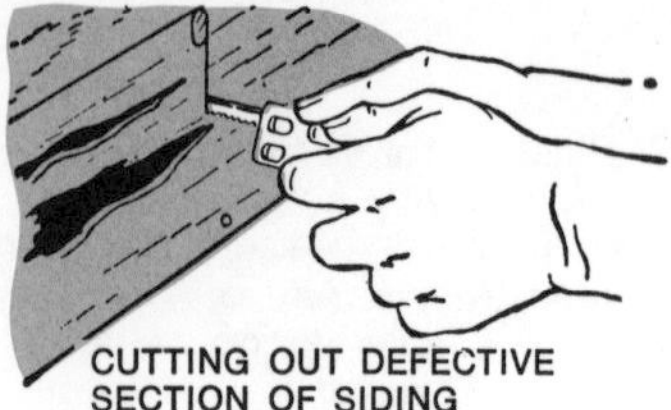

CUTTING OUT DEFECTIVE SECTION OF SIDING

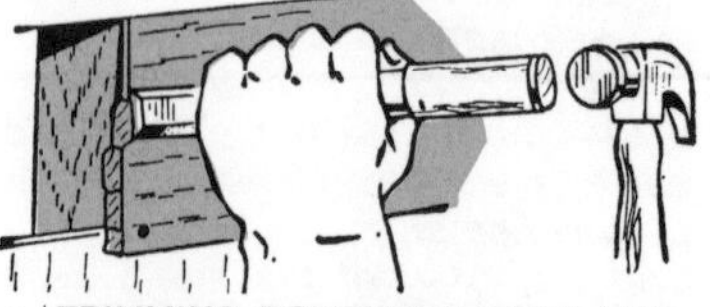

TRIMMING ROUGH-CHISELED END

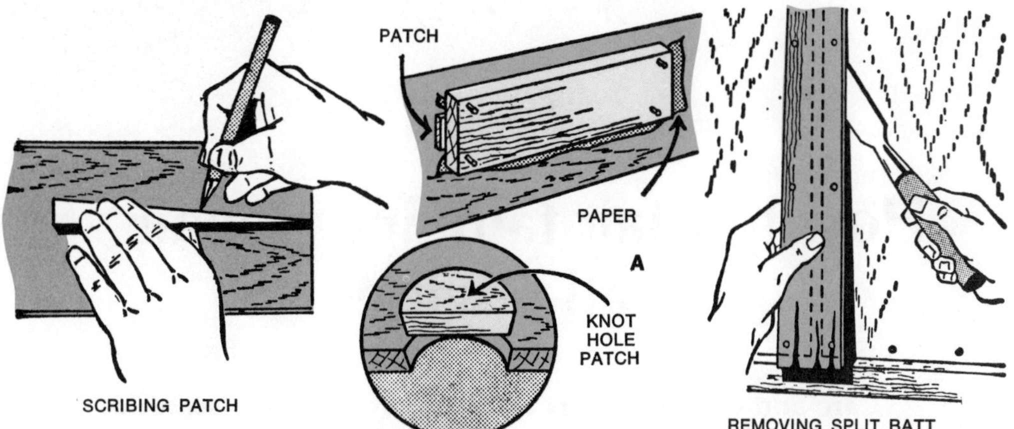

SCRIBING PATCH

REMOVING SPLIT BATT

split, cut a wedge of wood larger than the crack and slightly thicker than the siding. Bevel the edges toward the back. Hold the patch in position over the fault, and trace around with a sharp pencil. Saw along the line with a compass saw, and then true and bevel the edges with a file. Coat all joining edges with resorcinol waterproof glue, and push the plug into place. Cover with a strip of paper, and clamp by temporarily tack-nailing a board over it. When the glue dries, remove the clamping board and plane the plug flush, filling any cracks with plastic wood. Sand, prime and paint.

Split batts over joints due to shrinkage in vertical boards may cause leaks. Pry off the faulty batt, remove any nails remaining in the boards and clean the edges beneath. Paint the edges and backs of the new batts before nailing in place.

Sometimes decorative extra wide siding boards such as redwood will shrink so much the rabbets lift entirely off the boards beneath. If removing and renailing is not enough to bring them together again, metal inserts are the answer. The boards are usually badly stained because water has leached black matter from the asphalted felt behind them. You can resurface without a lot of labor by renting a portable belt sander. Use the coarsest grit belt for roughing and finer belts for finishing. Take the first cuts across grain along window or door trim. Then sand with grain until the main surface is cleaned. A small vibration sander is handy for touchup work around corners.

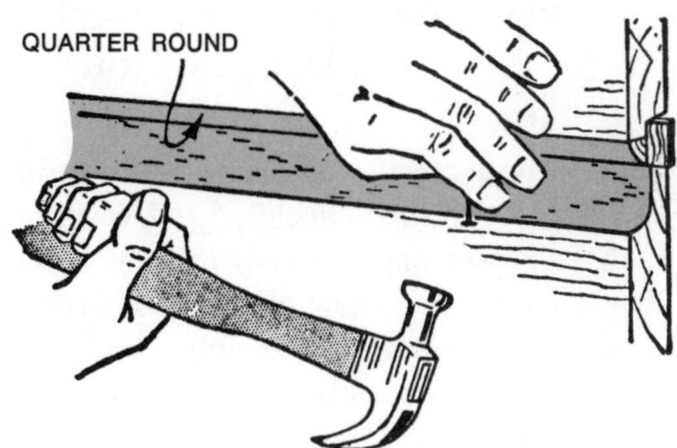

HIDING FLASHING WITH QUARTER ROUND

Close the rabbets with strips of sheet aluminum or galvanized iron. For easy handling, have your local tin shop shear them 3 feet long by ¾-inch wide. Slip these strips up into the rabbets of the boards and lap over the boards below, prying the upper boards out slightly with a chisel, if necessary. Drive the strips up with a strip of flat metal and hammer. If the strips tend to project outward, drive in brads. Then hide the metal with ⅜-inch quarter rounds primed with finishing material to match, and nailed into the lower edges of the siding. E.M.L.

See also: ADDITIONS, HOME; HOME IMPROVEMENT; PAINTING, HOUSE; ROOFS; STUCCO.

How to Maintain and Repair Small Engines

Care and simple repairs can make your small engine machines run economically and last years longer

TALK to an engine repairman and he will tell you that the typical 2, 5, 10, or even 12 horsepower engined snowmobile, lawn mower, mini-bike, snow blower, go-cart or out-board motor owner gets only about one trouble-free year for his investment. By the second year he's having trouble starting or trouble handling heavy loads. At the end of a bothersome year, many are willing to unload what they consider a lemon and buy a new one next season. But, with a little care, you can have better luck.

Gasoline selection is a good place to start. Regular is the proper choice, not high test and not white gasoline. Unless you have a two-cycle engine—such as on an outboard motor, most chain saws and a few lawn mowers—do not add oil to the gasoline. If a mixture of oil and gasoline is required, your user manual will tell you. Take note of the fact that more oil is mixed with gasoline during the break-in period than is normally required in two-cycle engines.

Lead is as harmful to your small engine's valves and piston rings as it is to your lungs. Try to buy either the lead-free or the low-lead fuels. Those lead-packed deposits around the valves and rings in your car can go just about unnoticed because you have half a dozen cylinders pulling the load. The small engine has only one set of valves so a chunk of leaded carbon on a valve seat can be a major calamity.

Gasoline companies change the blend of their gasoline according to the season. They add light, volatile chemicals in the winter to assist starting. And in the summer they put in additives to cut back on "boiling" and vapor locks. Take advantage of the best blend for the season by buying your winter sports gasoline in the winter and your lawn mowing gasoline in the summer.

Do not store gasoline very long. One year is the absolute maximum length of time you should keep a supply on hand because it oxidizes. A tank or can of gasoline exposed to even a little air gradually builds up deposits of varnish and gum, and you can imagine what that will do to carburetor openings, fuel pump diaphragms and valves.

Oil comes in several different grades. Oil quality ratings are actually expressed in letter codes such as DM, DG, ML, MM and MS. The DG and DM are high detergent oils intended for diesel engines and will not do well in a small gasoline engine. ML is for light service in a gasoline engine and should also be avoided. MM is the minimum recommended grade for small gasoline engines. And MS, which is intended for severe operating conditions, is preferred. If you have an additional choice

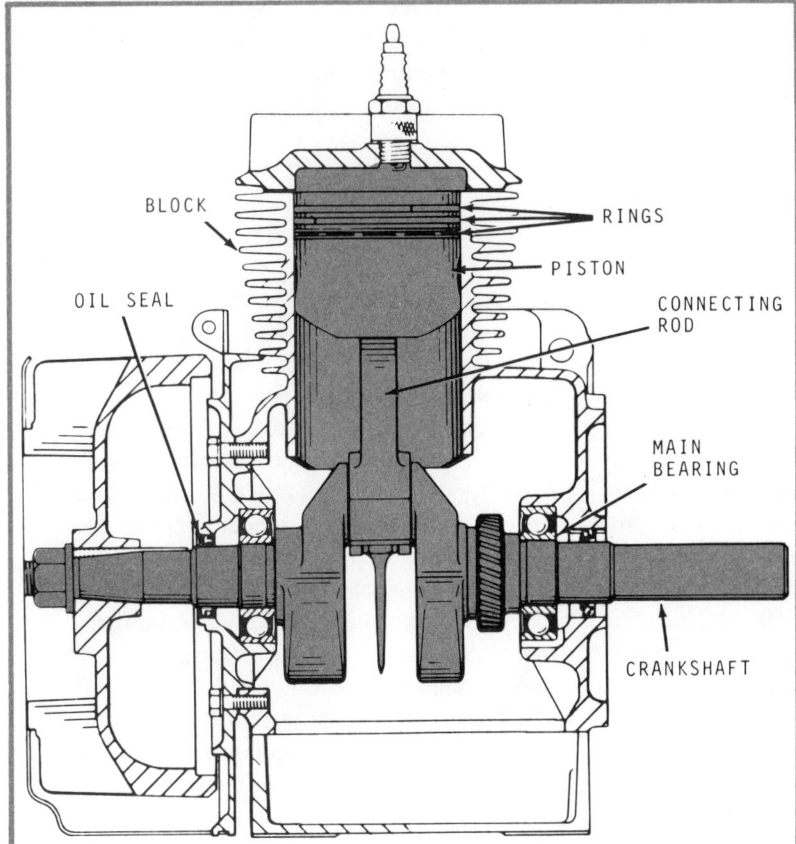

Cutaway view of a typical 4-cycle engine. They are easy for the home mechanic to repair.

Oil foam air cleaner is cleaned by washing in water, wiping with clean cloth, adding enough clean motor oil to soak the foam, then squeezing out the excess.

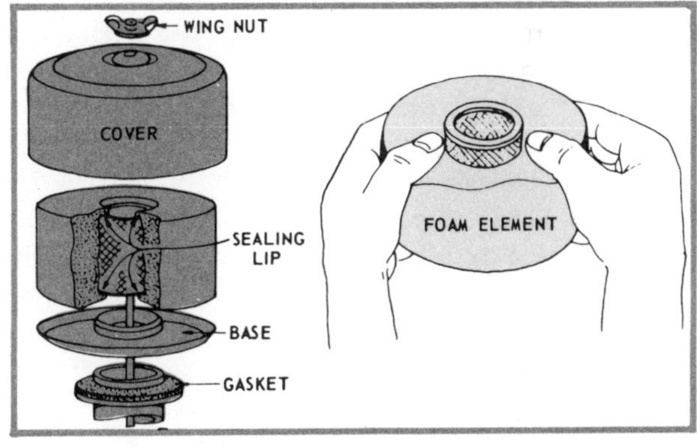

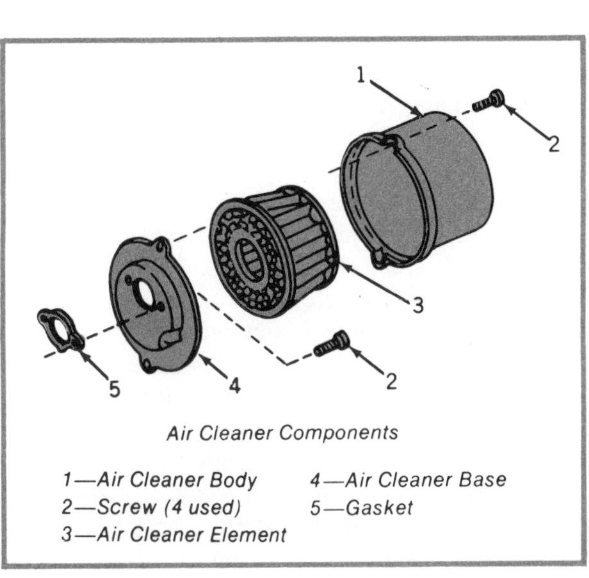

Air Cleaner Components

1—Air Cleaner Body
2—Screw (4 used)
3—Air Cleaner Element
4—Air Cleaner Base
5—Gasket

Paper air cleaner elements can be cleaned by knocking on soft surface and brushing with a soft brush.

of detergent or non-detergent, pick the detergent. (Oil companies are in the process of changing over to new codes; under the new system, SC or SD are the grades to look for.)

Outboard motor oil, used for mixing with gasoline in two-cycle engines, is also rated by quality codes. The MM and MS (or SC and SD) grades are proper here.

The end of the season, unfortunately, is one of the most important times in the life of any gasoline engine. The rust, varnish, moisture and gunk which accumulates because of inactivity can be as damaging as rough and steady use of an engine. Drain the gas tank and fuel line thoroughly. Then add fresh gasoline and flush the tank, carburetor and fuel line again. Unless the carburetor and fuel lines are ideally suited to being drained, you will probably have to run the engine awhile to consume the last drop of fuel. A tank and carburetor left with gasoline in it over a winter or summer will be seriously hampered by deposits of gum and varnish—if not after the first year, then after two or three years.

Change the oil as part of your end-of-season ritual. And flush out the oil pan with thin oil before filling with fresh oil for the rest period. The moisture and acids which build up inside the oil and oil pan after a few hours of use can be doubly damaging when given six months of free access to metal parts. While you are changing the oil, apply some to all of the moving parts which benefit by oil. However, do not squirt grease into fittings at the end of a season. Left untouched for several months, grease gets very stiff. You will be much better off by adding fresh, unstiffened grease to fittings at the start of your next season.

Also at the end of a season, remove the spark plug and add a tablespoon of your normal oil through the spark plug hole. Then move the piston up and down several times by spinning the flywheel or starter. This extra oil will smoke like the devil when you start the engine next season but, in the meantime, the oil will protect the cylinder, piston and piston rings from moisture.

Oil is helpful for all non-moving parts to prevent rust over a winter or summer of rest. An aerosol can of light oil makes for an easy oil treatment of all metal parts like lawn mower handles and blades, the inside of metal bodies and frames, chain saw blades, snow blower blades, plus miscellaneous chains and controls.

If you are leaving a storage battery in a cold garage or basement over the winter, make sure it is fully charged. A discharged storage battery can freeze and crack the cells wide open. The nickel-cadmium batteries are unaffected by cold temperatures but they cannot be charged when the thermometer rests below 40 degrees without serious damage.

Two of the simplest, yet most important, routine maintenance requirements are ignored by many people pushing equipment with small engines. Change the oil. In dusty parts of the country, or during dry spells, change the oil every week or every month if your engine gets much use such as on go-carts and scooters. Unless you put them to professional use, you should change the oil in mid-season, at the end of a season and at the start of every season on lawn mowers and snow blowers. Pros must change the oil weekly.

Clean the air cleaner. It is believed that only one out of every thousand lawn mower owners bothers to even check the air cleaner, a fact which results in the typical rotary power mower lasting only two years when it should last for five. Shortened life span hits every engine with a neglected air cleaner. Air cleaners are especially vital on those appliances which get into more dust than the rest—chain saws, roto-tillers and rotary lawn mowers. Many engines on snowmobiles do not have an air cleaner;

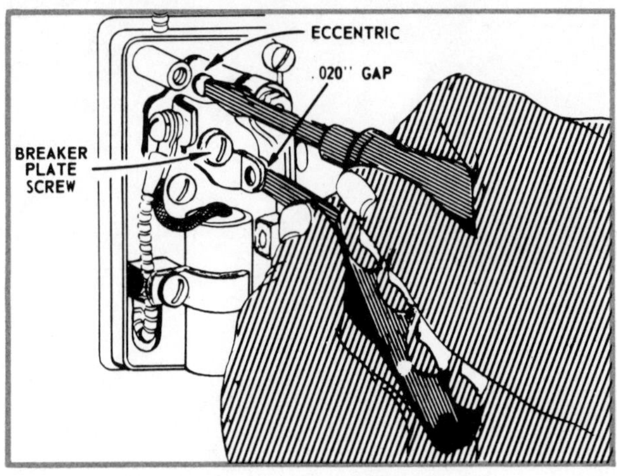

Correct gapping of plugs and points is important. Points are almost universally set at .020-inch.

as a result they should not be adapted to any summer-time pleasures. The user manual should give detailed instructions on how to clean the particular air cleaner included with your engine.

Air is one of two vital ingredients for every gasoline engine. If it weren't for an effective air cleaner, the pistons and valves would soon be scratched by sand and dust and bird feathers. If you have any doubt about how well yours is functioning, replace it.

Oil helps small gasoline engines keep their cool. But air does the rest. Consequently, the cooling fins on your engine have to be kept clean. Some go-cart and scooter owners happily bolt on shroulds, cowlings, decorations, windbreakers, fenders and bodies, forgetting all the while that if a steady stream of cool air is not available for the engine, it's going to run hot, which means it will run for fewer years. Some outboard motors are air cooled and the cooling fins on those models have to be kept free of seaweed, fish scales and other nautical debris. Wood chips and saw dust plague the chain saw cooling fins; grass and leaves clog the fins on lawn equipment. Fortunately snow isn't much of a problem on the well heated cooling fins of snowmobiles.

Engines which run for long stretches at high speeds build up a lot of carbon which becomes especially harmful around the valves first. Four cycle engines given heavy use, such as professional lawn mowers and garden plows, or rental and resort-based go-carts, scooters and snowmobiles, should have carbon removed from the valves and cylinders about once a month. This means, of course, that you'll have to pull off the cylinder head which is only a five minute job on tiny gasoline engines. Engines used only occasionally should have the carbon cleaned off the valves and pistons every year or two. Either learn to do it yourself or take it to a competent repair shop.

Two-cycle engines, the type common on outboards, chainsaws and even some lawn mowers now, have no metal valves. Instead the usual maintenance procedure calls for removing the muffler and using a wooden dowel to gently ream away carbon which has accumulated at the open exhaust port.

One of the best investments you can make when you buy a fun-mobile or a draggy lawn mower, is the official repair manual put out by the engine manufacturer. You may not be equipped to handle *all* of the repairs covered by the manuals, but the maintenance tips and minor repair instructions you will pick up are worth the investment. F.P.

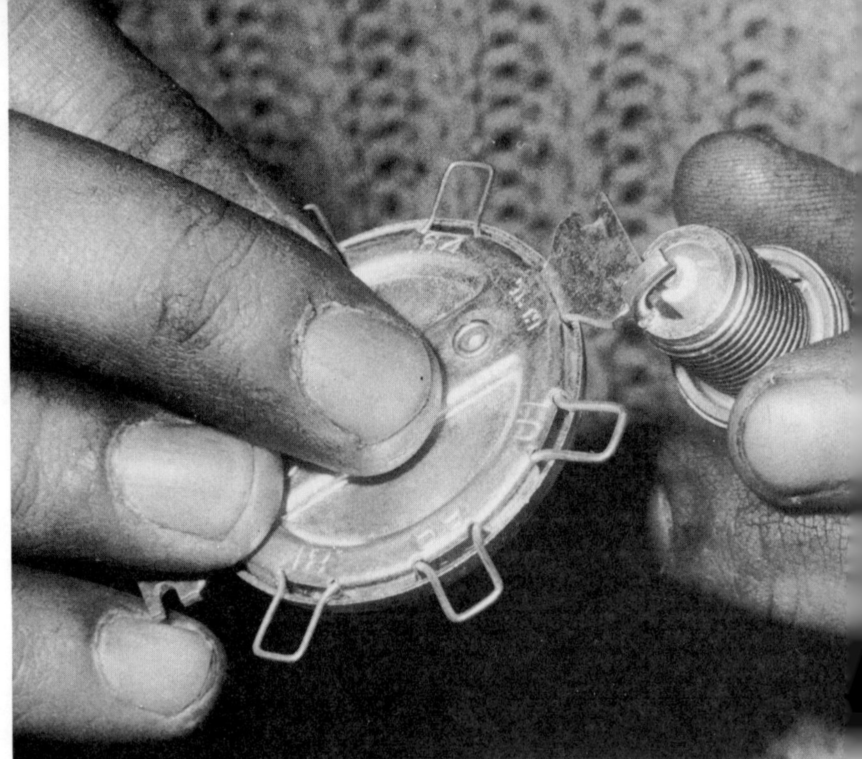

➤ *Regapping spark plugs. Only bend the side electrode. Always measure with a wire gauge. (A flat gauge gives a false reading in many cases.) Wire gauge fits in and is withdrawn with moderate drag.*

Trouble-shooting Your Engine's Spark Plugs

The attention you give your car's spark plugs can improve its performance and, if you know how to read the signs, help you diagnose other engine problems

YOU CAN LEARN A LOT about a car by inspecting its spark plugs.

For example, the type of deposit on the firing end of the plug can reveal how the car has been operating.

If the deposit is wet, black and oily, the car probably pumps oil, due to worn rings, pistons or cylinder walls, or worn or sticky valves. Or the ignition system may not be supplying enough power to the plug.

The plug itself may be faulty—with a badly worn electrode, or even a cracked insulator. These, too, are clues to the condition of the car, and to the type of service attention it has been receiving. Once you learn how to read such clues, you can usually correct the trouble, and avoid some burdensome repair bills.

Before removing a spark plug for inspection, carefully blow any dirt out of the spark plug well. This will keep dirt from falling into the combustion chamber when the plug is taken out. Pull the wires from the spark plug terminals *gently* until the snap fitting comes free. If you jerk them, you may separate the wire from the terminal connection, and although a broken lead wire isn't visible, it will form a secondary spark gap and eventually burn through the ignition cable, causing electrical failure.

Always pull by the spark plug wire's terminal, not by the wire itself. On today's cars with resistance wire, careless removal almost always results in internal damage to the wire, and the engine misfires.

All plugs normal. If all plugs have light tan or gray colored deposits and a small amount of electrode wear (not more than about .005-inch gap growth), plugs probably can be cleaned, regapped and reinstalled.

All plugs fouled. These plugs may simply have been "drowned" with wet fuel during cranking. If choke is operating correctly, fouling may be engine oil. (Is car burning a lot of oil?) Fouling can be retarded by use of a hotter plug or a booster gap plug.

One plug fouled. If only one plug in a set is carbon fouled and the others appear normal, check the corresponding ignition cable for continuity. A compression check or cylinder leak test might also indicate mechanical trouble in the one cylinder.

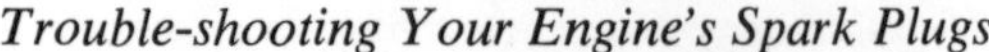

One plug badly burned. If one plug in a set has melted electrodes, preignition was likely encountered in that cylinder. Check for intake manifold air leaks and possible crossfire. Be sure the one plug is not the wrong heat range.

One or two plugs "splashed" fouled. Some plugs in a relatively new set may have splashed deposits. This may occur after a long-delayed tune-up when accumulated cylinder deposits are thrown against the plugs at high engine rpm. Clean and reinstall these plugs.

Chipped insulator. If one or two plugs in a set have chipped insulator tips, severe detonation was likely cause. Bending center electrode during gapping can also crack insulator. Replace with new plugs of correct gap and heat range. Check for over-advanced timing.

As you remove the plugs, first check each gasket washer. The surfaces of the washer which contact the plug and cylinder head should be bright, clean, uniform and unbroken. And the washer itself should not be completely flattened.

If the gasket washer is discolored, corroded, or irregularly marked, the plug was not tightened enough during installation. This produces an incomplete seal which allows gases to leak by, and the plug to overheat. And such overheating will cause rapid wear of the electrodes and preignition.

On the other hand, an entirely flattened washer means that the plug was tightened too much, and this will often cause a fracture in the plug shell, stretched threads, or a cracked insulator.

Flash over. When an insulator has been cracked during installation and this crack fills up with a film of dirt and oil, you will have a condition known as "flash over." Electricity flows directly from the top terminal to the grounded plug shell, completely bypassing the electrodes and spark gap. The plug is thus short circuited, and the only remedy is to replace the plug.

You can also have a flash over condition when an accumulation of dirt and oil coats the top insulator enough to allow current to pass through it. The cure here is to wipe the insulator with a cloth moistened with a gasoline or alcohol solvent which will cut the oil film.

When flash over occurs at the upper insulator, it may be visible in the form of a dim blue spark discharge around the plugs. This is sometimes confused with corona—the steady blue light that will appear around the base of the upper insulator, indicating a high tension field.

Inspecting the electrodes. Electrode inspection is your next step. Here you may encounter the examples of fouling or deposit accumulation, as mentioned earlier. If the electrodes are covered with a wet oily deposit, the plugs will probably give you good service after they have been cleaned and regapped. Such deposits are tell-tale signs of oil pumping in the engine, however, and you should check for worn valves or valve guides, rings, piston and cylinder walls. New rings might cut down the pumping. Or the battery or generator might be ailing to the point where not enough power is being delivered to the plug for proper ignition.

When the electrodes are coated with a hard, baked-on deposit, it's a sign that too cold a plug is being used in an oil-burning engine. You should change to a hotter plug. If such oil fouling then continues, you'll need an engine overhaul to correct the trouble at its source.

What is meant by cold or hot plugs? To function properly, a spark plug must operate within a specific temperature or heat range. So all plugs are classified by heat ranges as well as by size, thread and reach.

The heat range of a plug is primarily

Mechanical damage. A broken insulator and bent electrodes result from some foreign object falling into the combustion chamber. Because of valve overlap, objects can travel from one cylinder to another. Always clean out cylinders to prevent recurrence.

All plugs overheated. When entire set has dead white insulators and badly eroded electrodes (more than .001-inch gap per 1000 miles), next colder heat range plug should be installed. Be sure ignition timing is not over-advanced.

"Question mark" side electrodes. Improper use of pliers-type gap tools will bend the side electrode and push the center electrode into the insulator assembly. Because of the force multiplication exerted by these tools, use them with care.

All plugs worn. If all plugs have tan or gray colored deposits and excessive electrode wear (about .008 to .010-inch more than original gap), they probably have over 10,000 miles. Replace entire set with new plugs of same heat range.

controlled by internal exposed length of the center insulator, and is, basically, the speed with which the electrodes will cool after the cylinder fires. The electrodes must remain hot enough to prevent fouling, but must not get so hot that they will ignite the fuel mixture without an electrical spark (preignition).

The problem is that combustion chamber temperatures vary greatly with the type and condition of the engine, how fast it is run and the load it is pulling. For example, when an engine fitted with spark plugs of intermediate heat range is run at slow (city traffic) speeds for a long time, the electrodes will stay cool enough to allow deposits to form rapidly.

This electrode fouling causes the plugs to misfire, and you get hard starting, poor gas mileage and a loss of power. But when the same plugs are given a high-speed workout on the open road, many of the deposits may be burned away, in effect cleaning the plug. So, if you are getting spark plug miss from city driving, take your car out on the open highway and run it hard for an hour or so. Really run it up to peak engine speed and hold it there for a few seconds before you change gears. Such a "hard run" treatment may be the cheapest tune-up you can get.

It helps to clean away the type of fluffy dry carbon deposits in the electrode and inner insulator which are caused by gas-fouling. To prevent a recurrence of such rapid fouling, you might—in addition to regular high-speed workouts—lean down the fuel mixture by adjusting the carburetor. Then, if you still get rapid fouling, even after a carburetor adjustment, it might be wise to change to a hotter range of spark plug.

White, yellow, brown deposits. The most common form of deposit fouling results in white, yellow, brown or red coatings on the electrodes. These are normal by-products of combustion which result from the many additives in today's fuels and lubricants. In their original powdery form, they usually have little effect on spark plug operation. But when high speeds or heavy loads raise the engine temperature enough, such deposits melt and form a glaze coating on the inner insulator. When hot, this glaze is an excellent conductor, and allows the current to follow the glaze instead of jumping the spark gap.

Periodic sandblast cleaning usually removes these coatings and restores the plugs to proper operation. If the deposits are compacted between the plug shell and the inner insulator, however, replace the plug. It is almost impossible to remove such compacted deposits without damaging the insulator.

The sandblast treatment, available at some service stations, is the most effective way to clean the face of the plug and the inner insulator. It won't always remove all the scale and oxide deposits from the center electrode and from the underside of the ground electrode. So, to ensure clean firing surfaces, try bending the ground electrode up slightly and cleaning both surfaces thoroughly with a flat distributor-point file.

After a cleaning, you frequently discover other faults, such as a broken inner insulator. This may be caused by carelessness in regapping, or sustained operation with heavy detonation and preignition.

If the lower insulator is cracked and the center electrode worn to a fine point, while the ground electrode shows no sign of wear, the plug is operating too hot. The solution is to discard the damaged plug and replace it with one of a lower heat range.

Damaged plug shells are unusual. They are always the result of such mishandling as overtightening during installation. The damage generally shows up as a crack in the threads near the gasket seat, and such a plug should be promptly replaced.

Electrode wear. Once the fouling deposits have been cleaned off the electrodes,

TO START THE FIRE

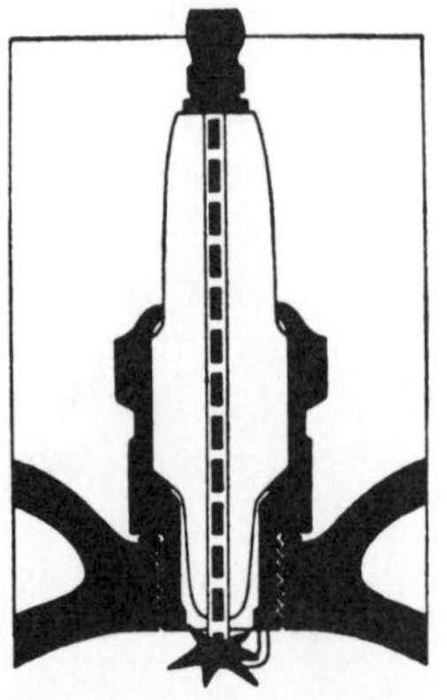

NORMAL IGNITION

When a spark occurs at the proper instant across the spark plug gap, we can say that ignition is normal. This requires an ignition system properly timed, and delivering adequate voltage to plugs in good condition.

SURFACE IGNITION

Sometimes a surface in the combustion chamber becomes hot enough to fire the fuel charge. Usually this type of ignition occurs before the timed spark and is called preignition. Deposits, overheated spark plugs, valves and sharp edges in the combustion chamber are all good sources of "hot spots." The driver may not be aware of the condition, but besides losing power, extensive engine damage could occur.

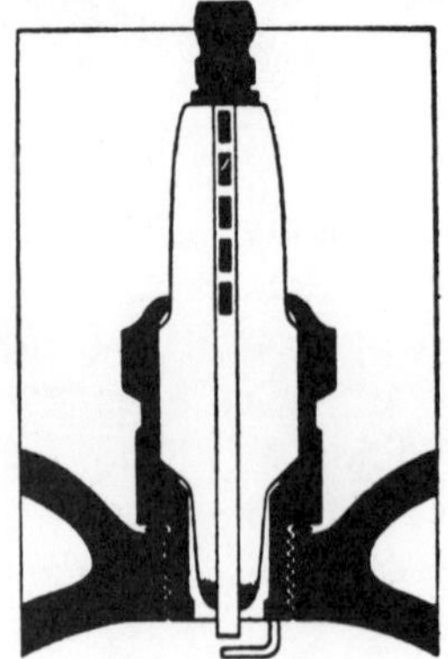

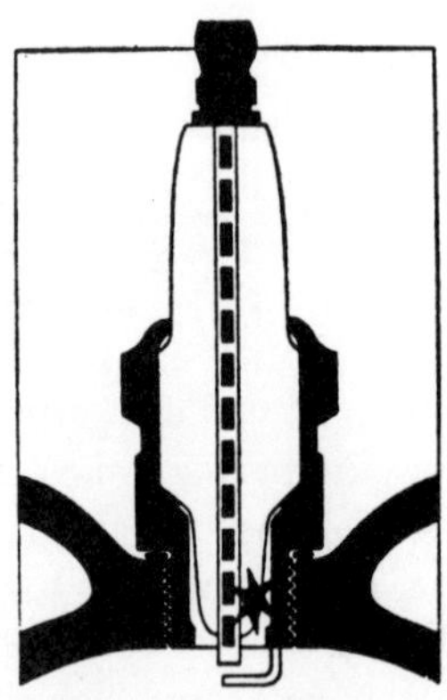

TRACKING IGNITION

Instead of jumping the electrode gap, the spark may jump from one deposit "island" to another along the insulator nose. The fuel charge may be ignited, but the effect is to retard timing. Performance and economy are lost and the driver is unaware of the problem.

you can check them for wear. As a rough guide, remember that a set of spark plugs, properly cared for and regularly cleaned and regapped, should give you good service for about 12,000 miles. Considering that the spark plug must give off from 1,000 to 3,000 sparks per minute while operating in gas temperatures as high as 4,000° F.—and

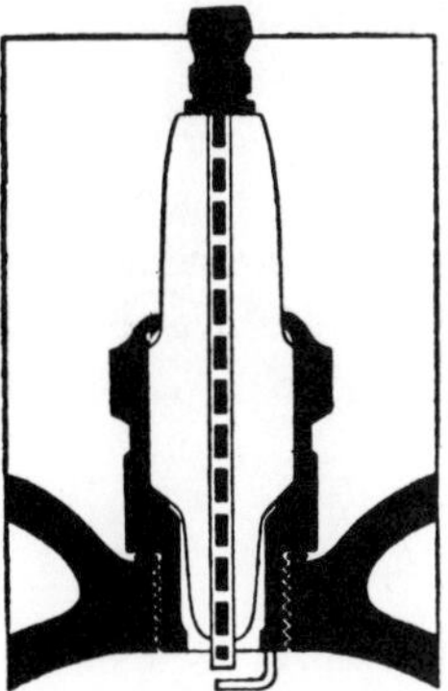

◄ *WIDE ELECTRODE GAP*
When spark plug electrode gaps become worn, the ignition system may not be able to supply enough voltage to jump the gap.

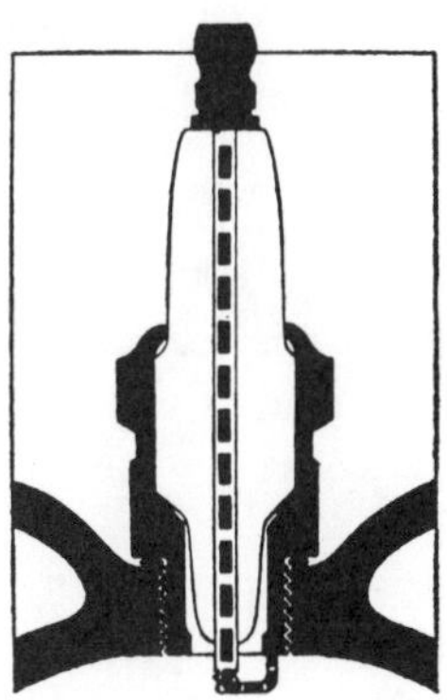

► *BRIDGED GAP*
If deposits bridge the electrode gap, coil voltage is shorted to ground. Under this condition no spark occurs to "start the fire."

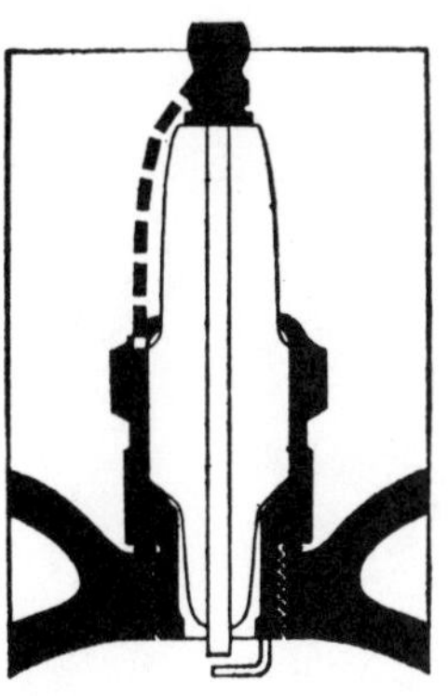

▼ *FOULED PLUGS*
Some deposits that form on the insulator nose will conduct electricity. The coil, "seeing" this easier path to ground, will not build up enough voltage to jump the electrode gap.

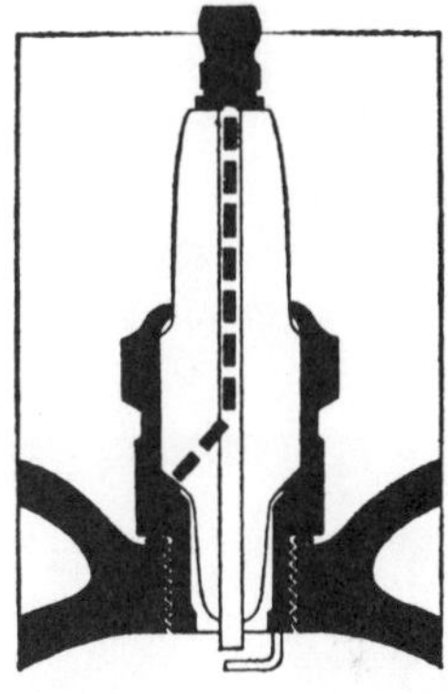

▲ *FLASH OVER*
When dirt, grease and moisture are allowed to accumulate on the spark plug insulator, high voltage may short over the outside of the insulator. Hard, brittle plug boots can encourage flash over. (Champion five-rib insulators help guard against flash over.)

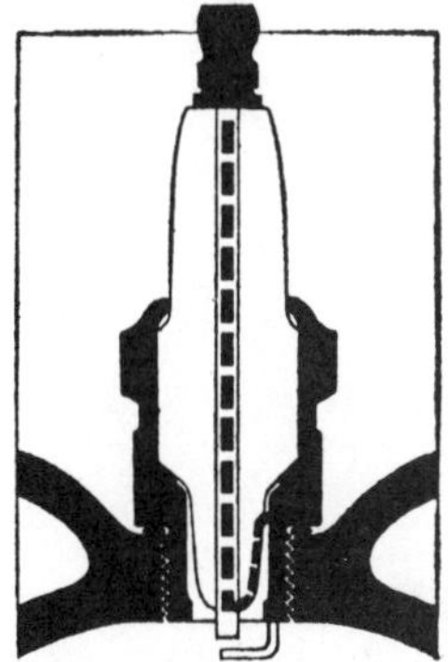

▲ *CRACKED INSULATOR*
A cracked insulator may allow high voltage to leak to ground. (Be careful not to damage the insulator with your gap tool.)

also withstand explosive pressures of up to 800 pounds/psi—this is a remarkable life expectancy.

These intense pressures and temperatures, when combined with the corrosive gases in the combustion chamber, gradually wear the electrodes down to the point where the gap can't be effectively reset.

Replace such plugs. Deposits may become too embedded to clean. Replace plugs once a year or every 12,000 miles, whichever comes first.

When the plug is fairly new, and shows substantial wear, the trouble may be faulty installation, too lean a carburetor mixture, an over-advanced spark, dirty or damaged gasket seats, or a plug which has too hot a heat range.

Cleaning and regapping. A good rule of thumb for spark plug servicing is to remove, clean and regap plugs at least once every 5,000 miles.

Always regap an old plug to the exact specifications set by the engine manufacturer. If you use a new plug, check it before installing to make sure it also meets the engine specifications. Make the gap adjustment by bending the ground electrode. If you bend the center electrode, you'll fracture the inner insulator tip.

Always use a round wire gauge (from an automobile supply store) when setting the plug gap. Because the wearing away of the electrode tends to form a concave hollow on the underside, a flat feeler gauge cannot give an accurate gap measurement.

Seating the plug. The ideal way to ensure a correct seating of the plug is to use a

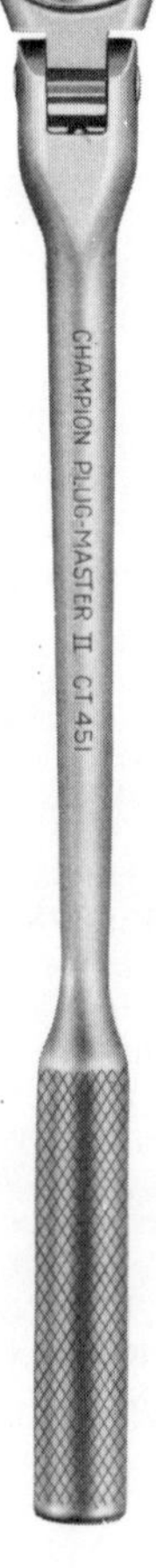

This is a Champion Plug-Master wrench, ideal for those inaccessible V-8 plugs. Handle is curved, ratchet head has universal joint.

Notice how Plug-Master wrench fits in without the need for disconnecting or pulling out anything.

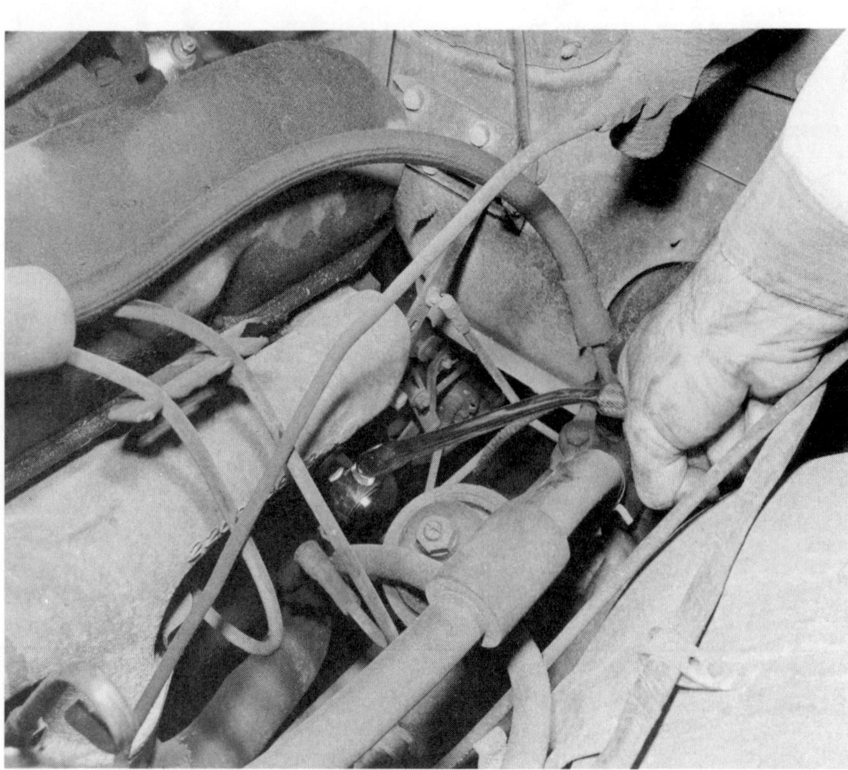

torque wrench for tightening down the plugs. If you own one, and put in your own plugs, follow what the manufacturers recommend.

If you can't torque in your plugs, hand turn the plug in until it seats finger tight on the gasket. Then, using a proper fitting spark plug socket wrench, give it an additional half turn. This will produce the proper seal between the plug and the cylinder head.

When you go to buy a new set of plugs, remember that the manufacturer's chart gives the recommendations for average driving (about 40% city and 60% highway). If you are on the highway a lot, covering most of your distance at fairly high-speed, you may need a plug that is a little cooler than average. If you're a "stop and go" driver, putting on most of your miles in the city at slow speeds with lots of waits at traffic lights, maybe a hotter plug will keep you going longer between tune-ups. P.W.

See also: BATTERIES; ENGINE; STARTER; TRANSMISSION, AUTO; TUNE-UP, ENGINE.

Use a torque wrench to tighten anything you can fit it on, including spark plugs.

How to Remove Spots from Rugs and Carpets

The sooner you act when something spills on the carpet, the greater the chances of removing the spot. Use this handy guide to match the cleaning method to the type of stain

SPOT REMOVAL CHART	
OILY AND CREAMY SUBSTANCES	Use dry-cleaning fluid or absorbent powder cleaner.
SUGAR AND STARCH	Wipe spot with cloth wrung out of clear water.
MILK	Sponge with detergent solution, then clear water.
BEVERAGES	Use clear water or detergent solution.
ACID SUBSTANCES (FRUIT JUICES, ETC.)	Blot up liquid as soon as possible with damp cloth; sponge several times with clear water. If spot remains, sponge lightly with solution of 1 tablespoon of ammonia or baking soda in quart of water.
BLOOD STAINS	Sponge with cold water. If spot remains, use small amount of detergent and water.
NAIL ENAMEL	Quickly blot up as much as possible, taking care not to spread the spot. Lacquer thinner or nail polish remover may remove spot. (Do not use on rayon or rayon-and-wool blends—it will dissolve the fibers.) Apply liquid to small area, then blot up excess.
PET SPOTS	Sponge urine spot thoroughly with clear water and blot quickly. Go over spot with detergent solution, then wipe off with cloth dampened with clear water, blotting up excess. If spot has dried, saturate with solution of 1/2 cup white vinegar to a cup of warm water and let stand for a few minutes. Blot and repeat treatment until discoloration disappears. Then dry carpet as quickly as possible. For regurgitated food, scrape up solid materials. Sponge with clear water and blot up liquid. Follow with neutralizing given under Acid Substances.
INK	Washable—use damp, absorbent cloth. Ballpoint—use dry-cleaning fluid. Permanent—consult a professional.
RUST	Try clear water. If unsuccessful, consult a professional.
CIGARETTE BURNS	If burn chars only surface of rug, use sharp shears to snip away blackened ends of tufts. Sponge with detergent solution, then clear water.
WAX	If wax has dried, use stiff bristle brush to remove solid matter. On spots caused by paste or liquid polishing wax or no-rubbing furniture wax, use dry-cleaning fluid. If stain remains, rub with warm soapy water or foam-type rug cleaner. Spots from self-polishing floor wax and cream-type waxes should be cleaned with warm water and detergent. If necessary, follow with foam-type cleaner.
UNKNOWN	If fresh; absorb all liquid possible with clean, slightly damp cloth. Scrape off solid material carefully with spatula or spoon and pick up with cloth. Sponge with cloth wrung out of clear water. If spot remains after drying, use solution of detergent and water, followed by sponging with cloth dampened with clear water. If possible, raise rug to let back dry.

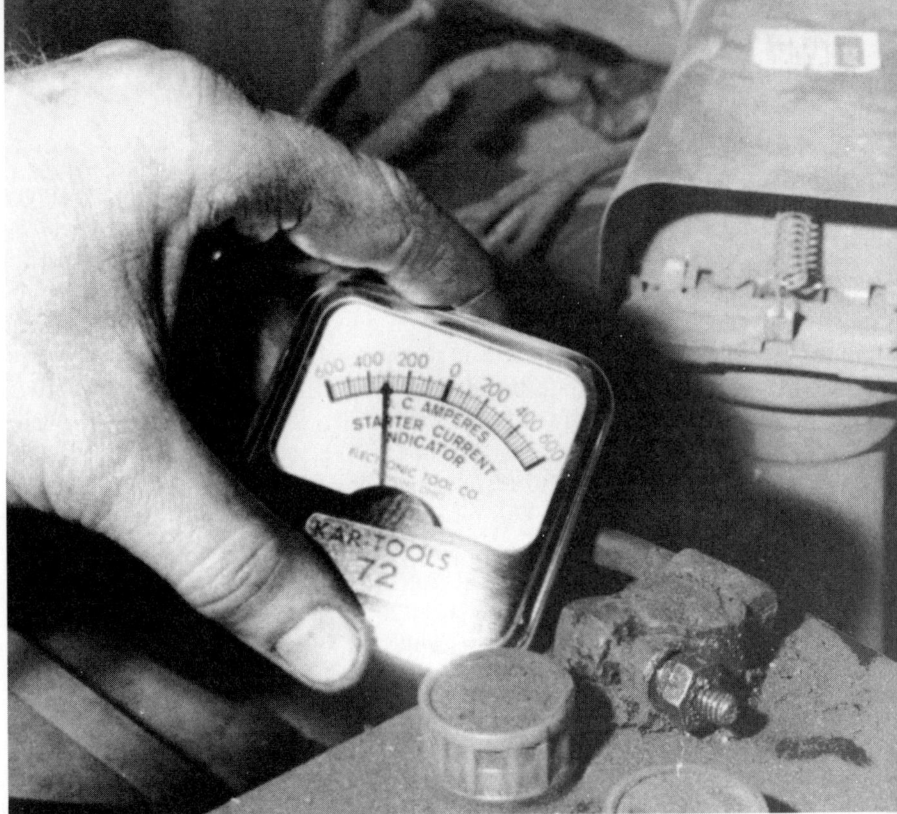

This little induction ammeter measures starter current draw when clamped onto battery cable while engine is cranking. Note reading of 350 amps, which is excessive.

How to Revive a Faltering Starter

Despite their reliable reputation, millions of starters require servicing each year, but most of this repair can be done in your own garage at a real savings

EVEN THOUGH THE STARTER motor seems to be the most reliable part in an automobile, and many car owners have found it to last the life of the car, statistics reveal that millions of starters are replaced each year.

Also, there are many possibilities of failure within the entire starting circuit, so when all starting problems are totaled they run into the tens of millions. A significant percentage of these are characterized by complaints like "the engine is not cranking" or "it is turning over too slowly."

The no crank solution is usually found in the electrical feed to the starter—a weak battery, loose or corroded cables. A simple test is made with a hydrometer, an inexpensive and easy to use instrument.

If you are a reasonably careful weekend mechanic, the problems associated with a weak battery or bad cable connections will probably be part of routine maintenance.

A common cause of slow cranking is the use of heavy engine oil in the winter. This creates so much drag that the starter cannot overcome it. Many people start out with a light oil, such as 5W-20 or 10W-30, but they add a can or two of oil additive, which is a thickener. A couple of cans of oil additive in a normal crankcase can turn a 10 weight oil into a 30 or 40 weight.

The remaining possible problems are with the starter itself or with some special switches. The most common difficulties are well within the ability of the weekend mechanic to trouble-shoot and correct.

The parts most likely to give trouble in the area of starter and special switches are:

Starter solenoid. This is an electromagnetic switch built into a hump on top of the starter. When energized, it permits battery current to flow into the starter to motorize it, and it actuates a fork that pushes the starter's little drive gear into mesh with the flywheel ring gear to crank the engine.

Starter brushes. The typical starter has four brushes which are soft metal contacts with the armature, a wired shaft that spins to impart power to the starter drive gear. Each brush is part of the circuit that keeps the armature spinning. When the brushes wear down, the springs that maintain tension against the armature are fully extended. The brushes may make irregular contact thus impeding current transfer.

▲ Solenoid is easily removed from top of starter. Just take out the screws or bolts, then lift it up and out.

Starter drive gear assembly. The drive gear is subject to damage to gear teeth, to the clutch mechanism that disengages it when the engine starts, and with the splines along which it rides to engagement, to rusting.

Neutral safety switch or clutch switch. The reason you can only start an automatic transmission car with the shift lever in certain positions, and some clutch cars with the pedal depressed, is that a special switch is incorporated into the starting circuit. This switch only completes the starting circuit when the shift lever or clutch pedal, is properly positioned. If the switch fails, the car will not start regardless of positioning.

Starter relay. On most Ford products and some Chrysler cars, the starter relay is a switch mounted on the body sheet metal in the engine compartment. It is a convenient gathering point for the action of the special switches, and as an example, it can be triggered by the automatic transmission switch, or by turning the ignition key on. When the relay is actuated, it permits current to flow to the starter solenoid.

Normally these special switches and relays are reliable. When they fail, the lo-

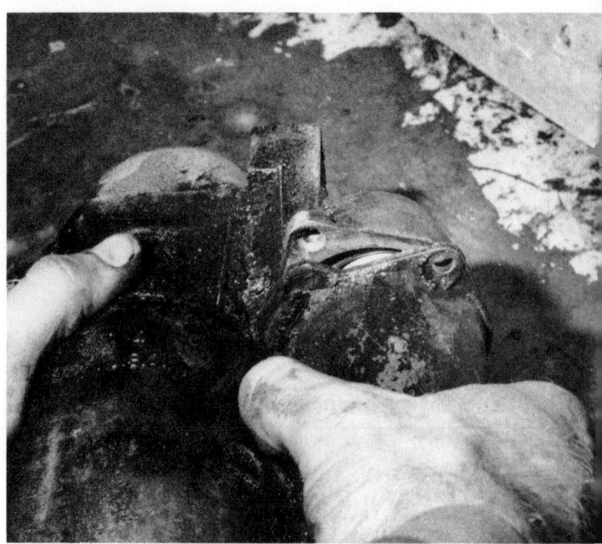

➤ On some starters, solenoid must be twisted before it can be removed. Twisting unlocks flat tang (to left of screw hole on solenoid).

◄ *To get to brushes, remove the through bolts (two through the starter end plate).*

▼ *Starter brushes are held in various ways. In this starter, a pin is used. To get brushes out, pull pin, then remove leaf spring that tensions them against armature; brushes can then be lifted up.*

cating and trouble-shooting of them should be left to a professional mechanic.

The weekend mechanic is safest limiting himself to troubles in the starter. The quickest way to determine if the problems are in the starter is to listen for a click at the starter solenoid. If you hear it, the problem is in the starter. If you do not, disconnect the wire to the solenoid "S" terminal and run a 14 or 16 gauge jumper wire from the battery cable to that terminal. If you now hear a click (perhaps the starter will even work), there is a problem in the wiring up to the starter. If the solenoid merely clicks, there is a problem in the starter, too, but fixing it will not solve the whole problem.

The most common symptoms of starter trouble are:

1. Very slow cranking.
2. Failure to crank at all.
3. Starter spins, but the engine does not crank.
4. Starter cranks but does not disengage readily when the engine starts.

Very slow cranking, when not caused by poor battery connections or heavy oil, may be caused by high resistance in the solenoid, badly worn brushes, binding of the armature and a defect in the armature.

A simple check you can make is to test starter current draw during engine cranking, using an induction ammeter. This little device clamps onto the battery cable to the starter and gives an approximate reading of current flowing to the starter. It is not the most accurate gadget in the world, but it is inexpensive and it can usually pinpoint excessive current draw. If current draw is in the under 200-amp range, it is normal; if it is in the 300- to 400-amp range, it's entirely too high and something is wrong. Heavy oil or a rebuilt engine that was set up with clearances too tight are the common causes of this. However, there are internal starter causes too.

If the current available to the battery is adequate (charged battery, good connections), and current draw is within limits, then slow cranking is most likely caused by one of these: a defective engine ground (the ground strap from engine to body); high solenoid resistance; worn brushes or an armature defect, such as a wiring break.

Failure of the starter to crank has many causes. If the solenoid does not click, even with the jumper wire procedure outlined earlier, it is apparently defective. If the solenoid clicks, but the engine does not crank, the starter should be disassembled and inspected.

If brushes are badly worn, just unscrew the old and install the new.

Removal of starter drive depends on design. In this particular unit (a Delco), a 9/16-inch deep socket must be used (with a soft-face hammer) to drive a bushing over the snap ring. Then the snap ring is removed and the entire starter drive assembly just slides off.

Starter drive, shown being slid off, is replaced as a complete assembly.

When the starter spins, but the engine does not, there is one likely possibility and some remote ones. The odds are that the drive gear is not engaging the flywheel ring gear, and the exact reason must be determined by starter disassembly and inspection. Also possible are broken teeth on the drive gear or flywheel ring gear, failure of either starter gear to hold on the armature or ring gear to hold on the flywheel.

If the starter will not disengage normally, it is probably a defective solenoid or defective starter drive gear clutch. A defective key switch is also possible. On cars with a relay, the relay is the first thing to suspect.

Removing the starter motor is usually uncomplicated, although in most cases the job requires jacking up the car and working from underneath.

Before you begin, make a simple sketch of all the wires that connect to the starter and solenoid. If terminals have letters adjoining, note the letters (you may have to brush off road film to find them, but they're usually there).

Always support the car on safety stands, unless it is being raised on ramps.

Do not disconnect anything at the starter until you have removed the ground cable from the battery. Now you can get to the starter itself.

A starter is normally held by two bolts through the bellhousing and into the engine block. (Many GM cars have two bolts from the bottom of the starter up into the engine block, and a third on top into an engine block bracket.)

On some cars, it is necessary to take off some part, frequently the oil filter, to gain enough clearance to remove the starter. If you see this problem, drain the engine oil, then remove the oil filter so that you do not get doused with oil when you are under the car.

Pull the starter forward, then tilt down or up to clear nearby components.

Before dismantling, check the starter with jumper cables and a good battery. Connect one cable to a starter body bolt or flange, and to the battery ground terminal (usually the negative post). Connect the other cable from the battery to the thick cable post on the starter. Also run a thin (14 or 16 gauge) jumper wire from the starter "S" terminal to the battery cable post on the starter (note: the starter should be held firmly, preferably in a vise). If the starter now works, the problem is in the car wiring.

If the solenoid does not click, replace the solenoid. Two or three screws hold it in place, and once they are out, the solenoid can be lifted up and out, as shown in the illustrations.

If a worn brush problem was indicated, remove the through-screws from the end plate and pull it off. This will expose the brushes bearing against the commutator section of the armature. The commutator consists of many copper segments separated by insulation. If the commutator is not smooth, it should be removed and resurfaced at a machine shop. Minor burrs can be smoothed out with fine crocus cloth.

Try to turn the armature. It should turn easily and with no signs of binding. If you encounter binding or looseness of the commutator in its guide bushings, get a rebuilt starter.

If the brushes are badly worn, replacing them is not complex. A typical brush mounting and its removal are shown in the illustrations. If you are unsure about the condition of the brushes, and no other problem is obvious, take a look at new brushes, and if the old ones do not seem to be worn to the nub by comparison, get a rebuilt starter.

Go to the front end of the starter and check the drive mechanism. It should move easily on its splines, hold when it gets to the end and turn the armature when you turn it.

Replacement of a defective starter drive varies according to the make of starter. In the Delco unit illustrated, you have to drive an end bushing over a snap ring, using either a special tool or a $\frac{9}{16}$-inch deep socket. Then pull the snap ring and take off the drive gear assembly.

If the starter cannot be motorized out of the car, it will not work in the car either, so do not try this and then put the starter back in and hope. Always connect a battery to it, as described earlier, to check it out.

Unless a problem is limited to a solenoid, brushes or starter drive, buy a rebuilt starter. This is usually the cheapest way out when anything major is wrong, and very time-saving when the problem is not obvious.

There is no perfection in this world, particularly in the rebuilding of starters. Always ask the parts house from which you are buying the unit to check it out with a battery before you leave. P.W.

See also: ELECTRICAL, AUTO; ENGINE; TUNE-UP, ENGINE.

How to Install Curbs, Edging and Ground Cover

Use these easy, inexpensive methods to beautify your garden, patio and lawn

STONE CURBING, EDGING AND ground cover can beautify your garden, lawn or patio as well as mark off one zone or area from another.

Many shapes, colors and textures of stone are available for these uses at a variety of prices. Consult your dealer to find out what's available in your part of the country and the cost.

Stone curbing or edging can be set in dry soil or it can be set in concrete.

The simplest, but least sturdy method is to set it dry. Just set the stone in a slightly excavated trench and pack dirt around it, keeping the stone level and erect.

The wet method using concrete requires a larger trench, into which is poured a mixture of one part cement, two parts sand and four parts gravel. The curbing is set in the wet concrete mixture so that no concrete is allowed to show. If there are visible joints, fill them with a mortar made of one part cement, three parts sand and sufficient water to make the mixture workable.

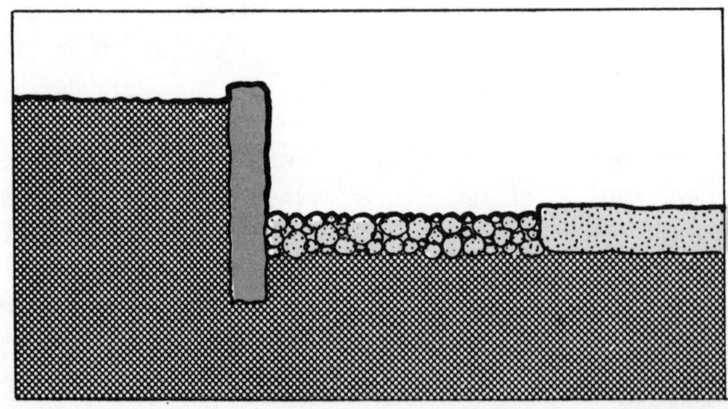

Linear strip curbs can be simply set in the ground, as shown here.

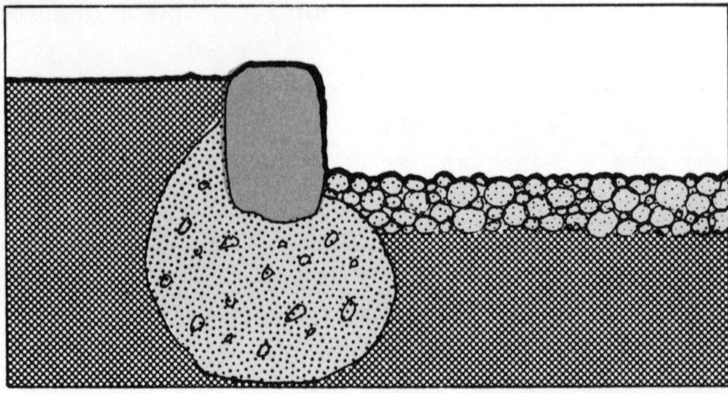

This method can be used to set curbing in concrete. The concrete is poured and shaped so it doesn't show.

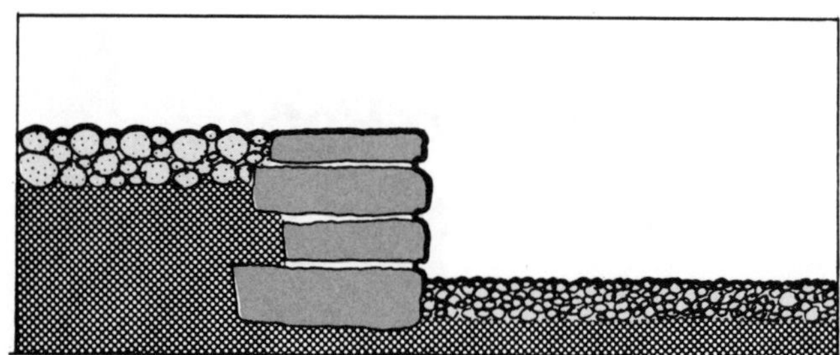

Layer type curbing can be set with or without mortar.

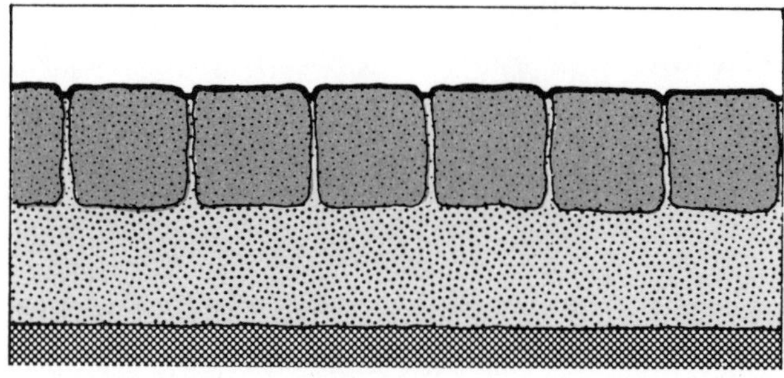

Set paving blocks for walks or patios on a four-inch thick bed of sand. Fill joints between blocks with sand.

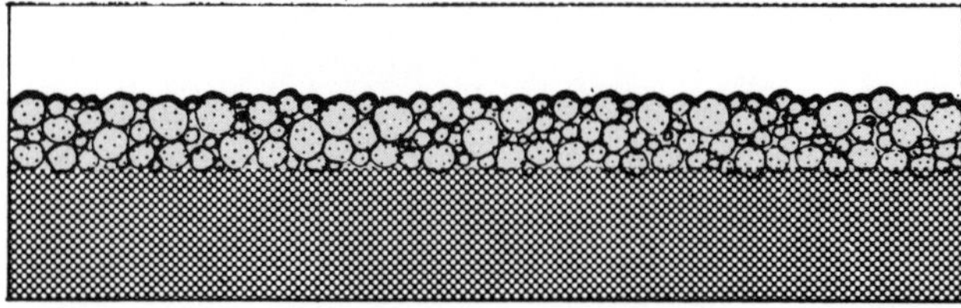

For a soft surface, just spread an aggregate of pebbles or stone chips over a surface with a rake. Aggregate can be bought by the 100-pound bag or by the ton.

A layer type curb, built up of long, flat stones, is like a mini-retaining wall. These require no mortar, but if you wish, you can set the stones in a mortar mix.

Stone ground cover can be either paving blocks or aggregates of pebbles or chips.

Use blocks where there will be heavy foot traffic, such as a patio or walk. Simply set the blocks on a 4-inch-thick bed of sand, keeping the blocks as closely spaced and level at the tops as possible. Fill the joints with sand.

An aggregate of pebbles or chips forms a softer surface. It can not stand a great deal of foot traffic. It is used widely in garden areas where a decorative effect is required, but the firmness of a walk or patio surface is not needed.

Generally, these materials are simply poured over a hard dirt surface and spread with a rake. Sometimes, plastic sheeting is put down beneath the aggregate to keep weeds from growing through it.

Aggregates are sold in 100-pound bags or by the ton. See the accompanying chart to determine what quantity of pebbles or chips is required to fill an area.

See also: BRICKWORK; CONCRETE; HOME IMPROVEMENT; MASONRY.

AGGREGATE COVERAGE

Thickness	Square Feet Per 100 Pounds	Square Feet Per Ton
1 in.	8-10	160-200
2 in.	4-5	80-100
3 in.	2-3	40-60

How to Repair Stucco Surfaces

Damaged stucco walls, even those with nothing more than hairline cracks, are vulnerable to moisture. Early attention can save you from costly repairs later on

▲ Damaged stucco should be repaired as soon as possible so weathering will not cause hairline cracks and larger openings to develop into major repair jobs.

EARLY REPAIR of damaged stucco walls is essential. Moisture can get between the coats of stucco, even through hairline cracks, and cause serious damage.

Although stucco makes a tough wall, a blow from a car bumper or rock can crack one or more of the three coats. Corners are especially vulnerable, particularly those near a driveway.

With tools as a hammer, cold chisel, screwdriver, whiskbroom, block of wood, finishing and pointing trowels, scratcher, and a wooden tray with a handle called a plasterer's hawk, you can be sure of getting a surface that will match the existing wall.

Materials needed to repair small hairline cracks are Portland cement and No. 1 torpedo or masons sand. Larger cracks and damaged areas can be repaired with premixed stucco cement or plastic cement. Don't add anything as fine as plaster sand to your mixture, because this would cause fine cracks to appear in the surface when it dries. Coarse sand used in concrete would make the finish too grainy.

Plastic cement consists of Portland cement with a plasticizing agent ground into it to make the mix more workable. If this is not available, you can add a plasticizing agent to regular cement. They include hydrated lime, diatomaceous earths, finely divided clays, asbestos flower or fibre, or lime putty. Use one part cement, three parts of sand, and not more than 10% by volume of plasticizer.

If any doubt exists about getting a good bond between the new work and the original surface, get a bonding agent. Brush this on the old surface and mix it with the new mortar.

All ingredients should be well mixed. Work the dry cement and sand together for at least 10 minutes, and for the same length of time when water is added. Use clear water, good enough to drink, and only enough to give you a stiff batter.

Fill small cracks with a mixture of one part Portland cement and two parts sand. All other work calls for one part Portland cement, or cement with a plasticizing agent and two and a half parts sand.

Pre-colored walls can be repaired with a factory colored stucco cement. If you can't get the right color, however, you can mix your own. For a white wall use white Portland cement and silica sand. Use high-grade mineral pigments for the other colors, such as burnt oxide or Germantown lampblack for gray, chromium oxide for green, red oxide of iron for rose, and yellow oxide of iron for cream.

Mix only a small amount of color pigment into the dry cement and sand until it matches the existing wall color before adding water. The mixture will turn darker when wet, but after the patch is cured and dried the color will blend with the surrounding surface.

Uniform suction is necessary to get a proper bond between succeeding coats of stucco, or when the first coat is applied to a masonry wall. Suction is caused by the base or underneath coat drawing water from the new coat.

This drawing process must be slow and uniform. If you apply the new coat over a dry surface the water will draw out so rapidly that it will be weak and crumbly. Get uniform suction by dampening the base surface until it absorbs all the water it can. Don't soak it until the surface gets spongy. Use a fine fogging spray and keep dampening the surface ahead of the work.

On masonry walls the base must be roughened and cleaned before dampening. On wood-sheathed walls there is no suction possible for the first coat so it is important to start the scratch coat with a wire mesh or metal lath base. After the first coat is cured and dried, you can get suction for the succeeding coats by dampening the base.

Careful curing is an important factor in making a good stucco wall or patching job. Keep each coat damp for at least two days after it's applied. Cover the repair with a damp burlap bag to hold moisture in on hot days when the humidity is low.

Let the surface dry for a week before redampening and applying the next coat. It is best to let the second coat dry for two or three weeks before applying the final coat. This way any cracks that show up can be covered with the finishing coat.

Repair hairline cracks by enlarging the crack with a screwdriver or chisel until you have an opening down to the solid surface of the existing wall. This gives the patching material a firm base to fasten to. Dampen the opening to build up suction.

Use a rich mixture of one part Portland cement and two parts of sand for crack repair. Add water until a stiff batter forms and fill the crack by pressing the mortar in with a trowel. When the patch begins to harden, use a whisk broom to remove excess mortar, and scratch the surface. Trowel the final ⅛-inch coat to match the existing wall surface. Let the surface dry and paint it if you haven't added a color pigment to the mixture.

Major damage that goes through to the base surface requires the full treatment of three coats of stucco. First remove the damaged stucco down to the base, then build up suction by dampening. Apply the first, or scratch coat to the wall about ⅜-inch thick. When the mortar begins to harden, scratch it horizontally and vertically to give the surface a waffle iron look.

You can use a garden rake as a scratcher, or make one by driving 8*d common* nails 1-inch apart through a block of wood. A single nail or a screwdriver can be used to roughen a small surface.

After the first coat is thoroughly cured, dampen it again to build up suction for the second coat. This second coat should be ⅜-inch deep, and come to within ⅛-inch of the finished surface.

Damage seldom goes beneath the second coat in stucco walls built over metal reinforcement. Remove the damaged stucco with a cold chisel down to the metal reinforcement and brush out loose mortar with the whisk broom. Prepare the base by building up suction, then work the filler between the metal reinforcement and against the base coat of stucco.

When the second coat begins to set up, float it with a block of wood. Work the surface with a circular motion to level and roughen it. This coat should not be worked more than is necessary to secure proper density. Over-troweling tends to bring the cementitious material to the surface and crazing and map-cracking are likely to result. Sometimes, instead of floating, the surface can be lightly scratched with a whisk broom to provide a bond for the finish coat.

Cure the second coat with a spray of water and let it dry for 7 to 10 days, then apply the ⅛-inch finishing coat. While the finish is still damp, texture it to blend with the type of finish that exists on the surrounding area.

A simple method of texturing is to brush the finish coat with a whisk broom while it is still damp. Another way is to work the repaired surface with the finishing trowel that is held flat.

Damaged corners can be repaired by cleaning out the opening with a screwdriver or cold chisel, then moisten the area to be repaired with a fine spray of water. Unless the damage goes through to the base, only two coats of mortar have to be applied. Use a small board to square off the corner when you force in the mortar. Keep this coat from ¼- to ⅜-inch below the finished surface.

▲ *Metal reinforcing mesh often prevents damage from going beneath second stucco coat.*

▲ *Hold finishing trowel flat when you blend the repaired area into surrounding surface.*

▲ *Before applying each coat of stucco, evenly dampen the base coat to control suction.*

◄ *Enlarge hairline cracks with a screwdriver or chisel, so the mortar can adhere to the solid surface of the existing wall.*

Scratch or roughen the mortar when it begins to harden. Let it cure for 7 to 10 days, then use a larger board held flush with the existing corner to true-up the finish.

Like brick veneer, stucco can be applied over a frame wall or any type of masonry surface. You must work from the base up when replacing a window or door with a stucco surface.

On masonry walls the stucco is applied directly to the surface. On wood frame walls the new surface must be covered with waterproof building paper and a metal reinforcement that is similar to that used on the existing wall. Make a 4-inch lap to join the two papers and seal it with waterproof paint.

Fasten the mesh with furring or stucco mesh nails. These fasteners have ⅜-inch fiber washers on them to hold the wire away from the paper so the mortar can get behind it to ensure a good grip. After you have applied the three coats of stucco, use a rubber base masonry paint to increase the weather seal of the new surface. P.A.C.

See also: BRICKWORK; CONCRETE; MASONRY.

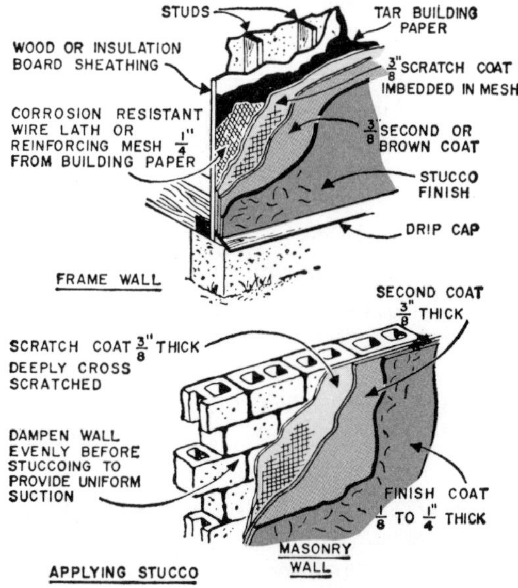

STUCCO FINISHES

Three simple finishes are: a troweled surface which is relatively slick; a floated finish which is grainy; and one made with a bonding cement paint. There are, however, seven standard finishes, and here are the ways to get them:

Spanish texture. Made by applying the finish coat in heavy layers, making strokes in all directions. Smooth out rough edges with a round-point trowel before the mortar hardens.

California texture. Put on in gobs with the trowel. Before the mortar hardens, rub the surface down with a wad of burlap to produce a wavy, irregular, coarse surface. To finish, trowel the surface creating highlights.

Italian texture. Over a thin final coat, dash on small quantities of mortar with quick strokes of a whisk broom. To finish, place your trowel flat against this dash coat and draw evenly across the wall from left to right. Smoothing return strokes erase possible trowel marks.

English Cottage texture. Over a ⅛-inch thick finish coat add small amounts of mortar, feathering the edges with a twisting motion. Apply in all directions to get the random rough effect.

Colonial texture. Apply a thin finish coat over the second coat. Allow to dry long enough so the grainy texture will not rub off when you go over it with a wood float or block of wood covered with a piece of carpet. Surface may have to be dampened.

Modern American. Let the finish coat be ¼-inch thick. Stroke the surface upward with the edge of a block of wood. Don't worry about trowel marks.

Italian Travertine. The troweled finish should be fairly smooth. Use a whisk broom to pull up an irregular texture, then trowel the surface while it is still workable.

Ceramic Tiling Your Bathroom

By doing-it-yourself and using new adhesive cements you can install real ceramic tiles in an average bathroom for a reasonable cost

ONE OF THE FIRST items a proud home owner is likely to mention about his house is the ceramic tile bath, because real ceramic tile in the bathroom or kitchen adds a touch of practical luxury. "Real" (meaning ceramic) tile has a rich, handsome look and, with proper care, it will last the life of a house because its glazed surface resists water, most cleaners and wear.

A new adhesive method makes setting ceramic tile as easy as applying many of the substitute materials that have become popular during the last few years. Of course, ceramic tile materials (Fig. 3C) cost more than some other materials, but the amateur can now obtain them easily, and doing his own setting will offset this higher cost. For comparison, let's consider the simple 5x6-foot bath shown in Fig. 3A. The 87 square feet of tile required to cover the walls only plus the bull nose cap, feature strip and bottom course would cost about $95. Covering a similar area with plastic tile along with a trim strip around the bottom would cost $51, but considerably more if you pay to have the work done. Making a sketch similar to the one in Fig. 3B will not only allow you to figure what the cost of tiling your bathroom will be, but will help to plan what kind and how many tiles to order.

Field tiles along with the trim pieces (Fig. 3C) are available in a variety of colors along with white and black. Most wall tile is glazed, while floor tile is unglazed to prevent slipping. Sizes of tile vary with the manufacturer, even though standards call for field tile to be 4¼x4¼ inches. So buy all of your tile from the same manufacturer and specify a cushion edge—the kind with a slight slope near each edge.

Tiles come in two grades too—standard

and seconds. Standard grade is graded uniformly for color and is free from defects or uneven glazing. The lower-cost seconds may vary in color shade and come with chipped corners or spotty glazing. If you use seconds, buy about 10% more than you need to allow for replacing poor tiles.

Each grade of tile carries three designations: color (specified by number), size (specified by a letter), and shade of color (again specified by number). Most manufacturers stamp these designations on the top of a tile carton, for example, 104-D-5. Make sure all cartons purchased bear identical designations for color match. Colored tiles usually do not cost any more than whites. Wall tiles are usually ⅜-inch thick and come packed in cartons that weigh about 55 pounds each and contain 120 tiles or enough to cover 15 square feet.

Telephoning local tile dealers or installers will usually turn up one who will sell you enough tile to cover a bathroom or kitchen. If you can't buy tile and adhesive locally, order them by low-cost freight from mail order companies.

The two types of adhesive for applying wall tiles are—(1) *buttering wall type,* a quick-setting adhesive that sets in about five minutes after placing on the back of the wall tile, and allows you to do all the starting courses on wall areas of less than 50 square feet without waiting for the adhesive to set up, and (2) *floating wall type* that sets in about one hour and is spread on the wall; you will need both the floating and buttering wall types for wall areas over 50 square feet. Each type covers about 50 square feet per gallon. Adhesives should bear the label "CS-181" to indicate that they meet specified performance requirements. For repairing tile, use the buttering type adhesive.

Making cutouts. The cutter (Figs. 4 and 5) not only cuts wall tile to width, but can also cut tiles on the bias, and split tiles to make cutouts for clearing pipes, and electrical switches. Nippers (Fig. 6) are used to cut off about ⅛-inch piece of tile at a time, working from each end toward the center gradually. Nip off only small pieces, since applying excessive

Spread floating type adhesive with notched trowel. This type of adhesive may be used after the starting course of tile has been set with buttering adhesive, applied with a putty knife.

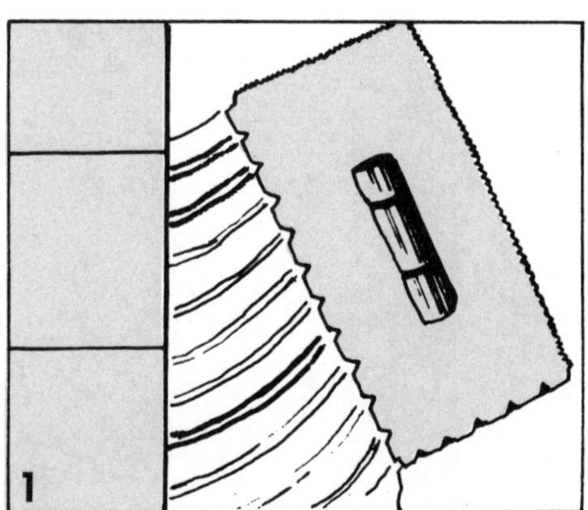

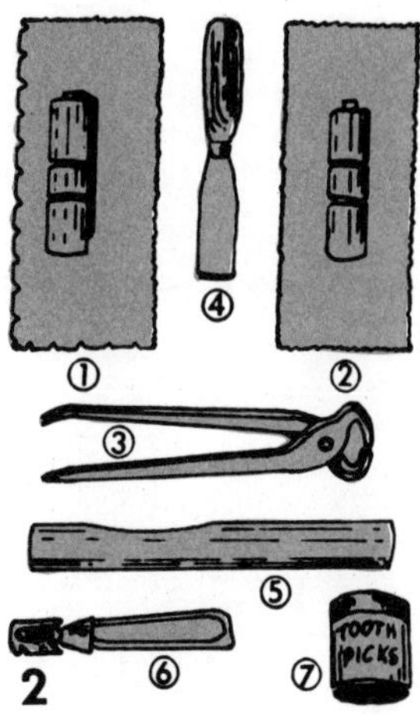

Tools you'll need for tiling: (1) Notched trowel for applying floating type of adhesive—large notches along one side and one edge are made with ¼-in. round file, cut ¼-in. deep on ⅞-in. centers. (2) Saw-tooth edges for floor tile made with triangular file; teeth are ⅛-in. deep on 3/16-in. centers. (3) 10-in. nippers for breaking out irregular cutouts in wall tile. (4) Small putty knife. (5) Medium grit scythe stone for finishing cut edges of tile. (6) Glass cutter. (7) Ordinary wood toothpicks.

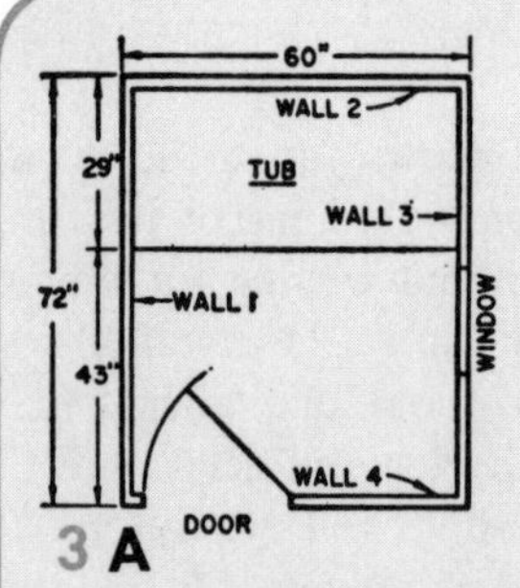

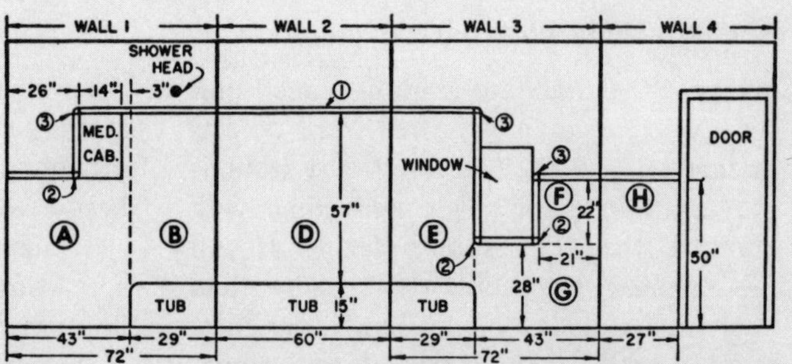

(A) Typical floor plan of bathroom. (B) Layout to scale of bathroom walls in clockwise direction to figure tile quantities and provide working drawings. (C) Types of tile—(1) surface type bull-nose cap; (2) inside corner; (3) creased outside corner; (4) wall field tile; and (5) decorative or feature strip.

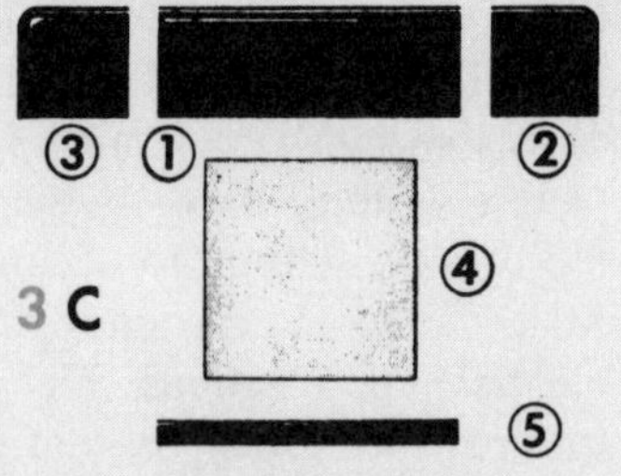

Estimating Tile Requirements

The amount of the wall tile required is determined by the height to which you want your wall tile to extend on the walls and the size of your bathroom or powder room walls. The normal height for wall tile in a bathroom is 52 in. except around the shower head area, where it should extend to just below the shower head, or about 72 in.

Let's use a typical 5 x 6-ft. bathroom (Fig. 3A) to show how you can figure the amounts of the wall tile and trim pieces you'll need. Fig. 3B shows the four walls of the bathroom in clockwise rotation with the wall areas divided into convenient rectangles for easy calculation. The corner letters on the cap course are the same as those listed under Fig. 3C. A convenient way to lay out your own plan to scale is to use graph paper.

Tables A and B show quantities required after making a 5% allowance for waste.

Making a similar sketch of your own bathroom or powder room not only helps to find the material required, but also gives you a working drawing. Heights of the wall tile are approximate because the final height will be determined by the actual size of the tile purchased plus the joint spaces. Measuring the distances along walls accurately to the nearest inch is all that is required for estimating purposes.

Table C allows you to easily find out the number of cartons of tile or the number of square feet of wall tile to order, once you have figured out the area of the walls to be tiled in square inches. Just find the wall space figure nearest to that of your own, using the next higher figure in Table C.

Buy your accessories (soap dish, towel bar, etc.) when ordering the ceramic tile so that it is possible to determine sizes of wall cutouts required and location of accessories.

TABLE A— WALL TILE REQUIRED

		Area	Sq. In.
Wall Tile	"A"	50 x 43	2150
	"B"	57 x 29	1653
	"C"	22 x 3	66
	"D"	57 x 60	3420
	"E"	57 x 29	1653
	"F"	22 x 21	462
	"G"	43 x 28	1204
	"H"	50 x 27	1350
		Total	11958 sq. in.
		add 5% allowance	600 sq. in.
			12558 sq. in.
		divided by 144	87 sq. ft.

If carton contains 15 sq. ft. of tile, this area requires six cartons of wall tile.

TABLE B—STRIP TILES REQUIRED

Bull Nose Cap 6" long (Buy S-4200 surface type of cap)	lengths starting at area "A" 24, 20, 46, 60, 29, 42, 18, 20, 21, 27 Total—307 in. divided by 6"—52 pieces allow for breakage— 4 pieces Total to order 56 pieces
Feature Strip 6" long	total length approximately the same as the bull nose cap, so 56 pieces will be required
Bottom Course Wall Tile (If desired in different color)	lengths starting at area "A" 43, 43, 27 Total—113" divided by 4"—29 pieces allow for breakage— 3 pieces Total to order 32 pieces

TABLE C—TILE ORDERING DATA

*Wall Space, Sq. In.	Boxes of Tile Required	Square Feet	Tiles
2050	1	15	120
3080	1½	22½	180
4100	2	30	240
5140	2½	37½	300
6170	3	45	360
7240	3½	52½	420
8220	4	60	480
9250	4½	67½	540
10280	5	75	600
11300	5½	82½	660
12340	6	90	720
13370	6½	97½	780
14400	7	105	840
15400	7½	112½	900
16450	8	120	960

*Allowance of 5% has been made for the waste and breakage. Find actual wall space as shown, and order next higher figure in column #1.

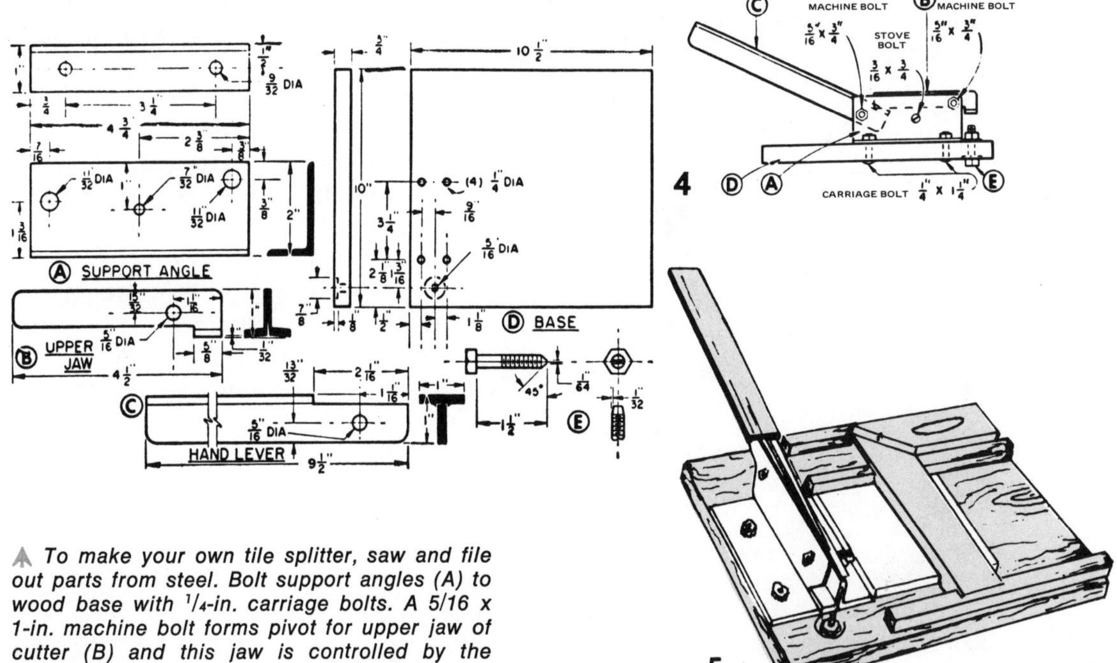

To make your own tile splitter, saw and file out parts from steel. Bolt support angles (A) to wood base with 1/4-in. carriage bolts. A 5/16 x 1-in. machine bolt forms pivot for upper jaw of cutter (B) and this jaw is controlled by the handle (C) also pivoted on a 5/16 x 3/4-in. machine bolt. A pointed 5/16 x 1 1/2-in. machine bolt is assembled in line with the center of the upper jaw with its height adjusted by inserting plain washers between its head and the counterbored hole in the base. Allow about 1/16-in. clearance between upper jaw and bolt point when wall tile is in position. The 3/16-in. bolt fastened through the support angles keeps the upper jaw from falling down too low between the angles.

Mount cutter on wood base large enough to fit a trysquare between two 1/2-in. strips. Edge of square guides glass cutter when scribing tile. A section of dime-store ruler under the square speeds cutting.

Cutting tile with the splitter is a 2-part operation. Slip tile in position and locate cut from ruler. Scribe tile with glass cutter, bearing down heavily, in one continuous line. Scribe line only once. Insert tile between upper jaw and pointed bolt with scribed line on top and in line with point. Applying pressure on hand lever forces tile apart on line. Minimum width that can be cut is about 3/4-in.

pressure will crack the tile. Practice this on scrap tiles first.

To make a cutout for a pipe, measure its diameter first. From the course of tile below the pipe measure to the bottom of the pipe and add one half of the pipe diameter. Lay out distance to pipe's center line on a tile. Repeat from the side tile next to the pipe. From pipe's center draw a circle about ¼-inch larger than the pipe diameter (Fig. 7B).

Using the cutter, split the tile vertically through the center of the circle. With the nippers, cut a semi-circular opening in each half of the split tile to fit around the pipe (Fig. 7A). Use the same procedure for making cutouts to clear electrical switches and receptacles (Fig. 8). In remodeling work, raise the switch or receptacle with spacers under its mounting ears to compensate for the added thickness of tile.

To fit a piece of tile to an irregular edge, such as around the curved edge of the tub (Fig. 9), first cut a cardboard template by trial and error. Then cut a tile to match the template using the cutter and end nippers. The scythe stone (Fig. 2) smooths the edge after the rough outline

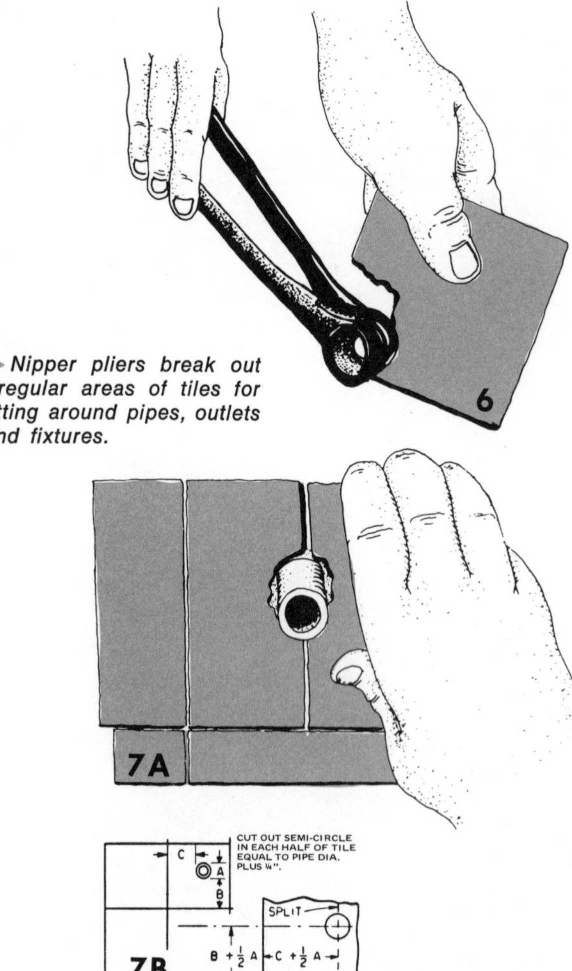

Nipper pliers break out irregular areas of tiles for fitting around pipes, outlets and fixtures.

Fig. 7A. Tile in pipe area. Split on center-line. Nippers break out tile in small pieces until it clears pipe. Fig. 7B. Measure from tiles around pipe area to locate cutout to clear pipe. Split tile vertically.

has been cut with the nippers. Caulk any space left between the tile and the tub.

Preparing the surface. Ceramic wall tile can be set over plaster, concrete and gypsum wall board at least ½ to ⅜-inch thick if all cracks are repaired and surface is level and free from loose or calcimine paint. If walls have sharp hollows or bumps, spread a coat of underlayment (sold by tile dealers) using a straight edge trowel, and check resulting surface with a straight edge. Cover walls with waterproof primer or shellac (don't prime floors with shellac).

In new work where plasterboard is used in the bathroom, install one of the four paper-bound edges of plasterboard at the intersection with the tub ledge. Heavily prime all edges of wallboard around the tub with the waterproof primer.

In fitting tile around the tub (Fig. 10), note that the vertical edge of the tub lip is set into notches cut into the studs, to present a level surface for the wallboard and the tile. You can leave plumbing fixtures in place and cut and fit the tile around them. However, it's better to remove the fixtures and lengthen all pipe nipples for the lavatory and closet by ½-inch to allow for the thickness of tile and adhesive.

Bathroom accessories. The tile dealer can supply the accessories you need in sets or singly, to match your tile. One type of accessory has a flange which mounts flush with the tile wall. Another type has a flange that overlaps adjoining tiles. If possible, select accessories that will mount in a 4¼x4¼-inch opening, so that you can skip one tile space for the accessory and keep on tiling. For the soap dish and grab bar, you may have to leave out two tiles. Towel bar brackets which require a smaller

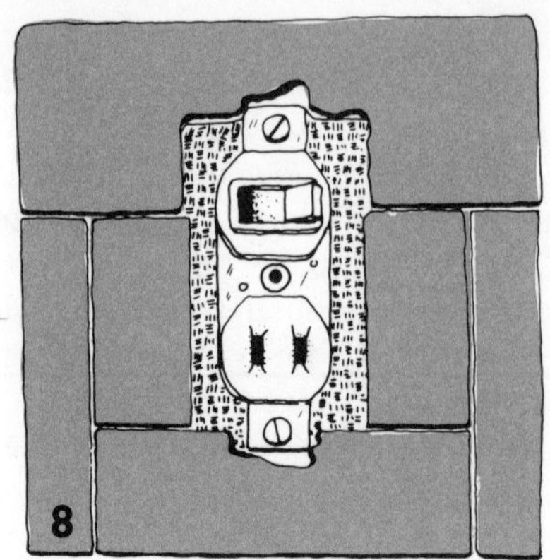

Tile can be split along bottom edge of cut-out for switch and side pieces split for quicker fitting. Nip out section from one edge of bull nose cap to leave top edge unbroken.

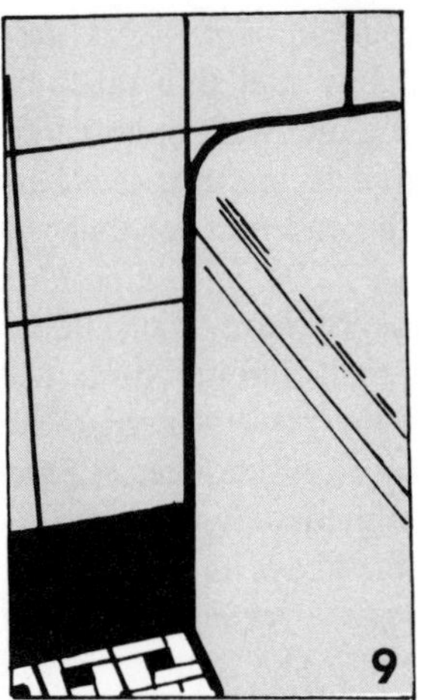

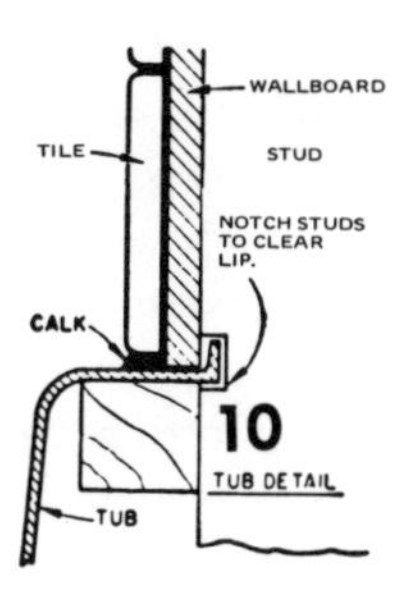

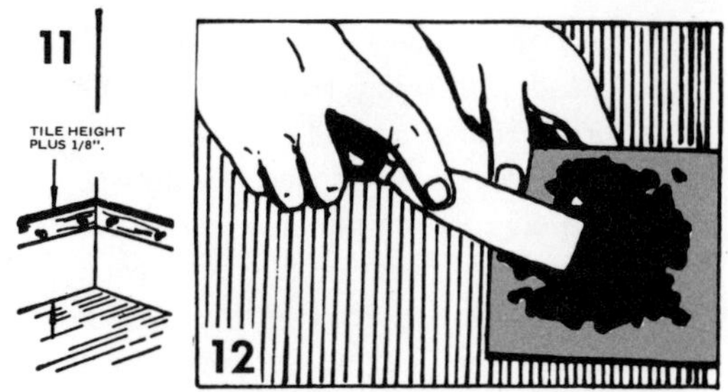

Fig. 11. Straightedged wood strip aligns second course where floor is not level. Lower course cut to fit floor. Fig. 12. Buttering type of adhesive is applied directly to tile to cover about half of area 1/16-in. thick.

Fig. 9. When fitting tiles around irregular areas, such as a bathtub, cut a cardboard template first, break out tile to rough outline with nippers, then smooth with stone. Fig. 10. Around tub's edge, notch studs for lip. Set wallboard and tile close to tub and caulk immediately.

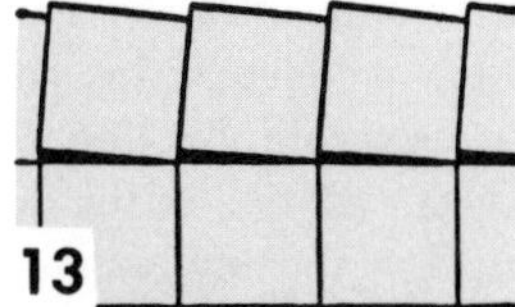

Fig. 13. How corners of tiles not set square project above adjacent tiles. Fig. 14. If you can't get the "lug" type tile (which spaces the tiles automatically) you will have to use toothpicks to space the tiles.

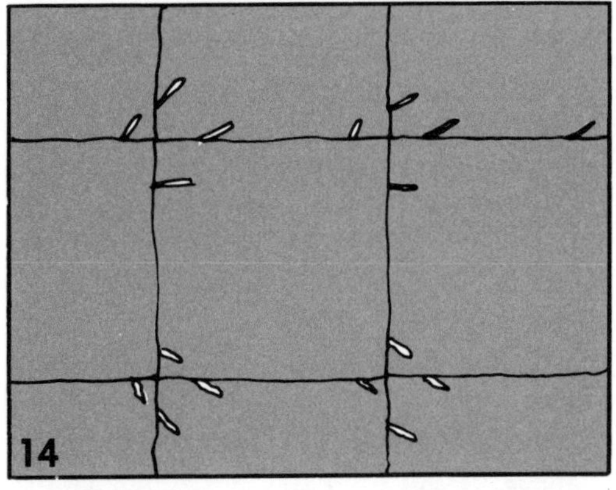

opening, should also have the tiles left off the wall where they are to be mounted. Plan the cutouts for the towel rack bar to come in the corner of the tiles, so the flange on the bracket covers the cutouts in the tile.

Cutouts in the wall itself for accessories are made after all of the tiles have been set in place. *Caution*—Mark the location of all wall studs on the wall above the top course of tile so that you don't select a place for your accessory on front of the stud.

Setting wall tile. Now let's get at the job of setting the wall tile. In a remodeling job, remove the baseboard. If you plan to tile the floor (we will explain how to do this after we finish the walls) the base you will need for the floor tile should be in place before starting the wall tiling. Ceramic floor tile can be set on either a concrete base or by covering existing sub-floor with ½-inch exterior grade plywood, nailed to the subfloor with 1¼-inch screw-type nails. Space nails not over 4 inches apart each way.

Make sure that the floor surface is level.

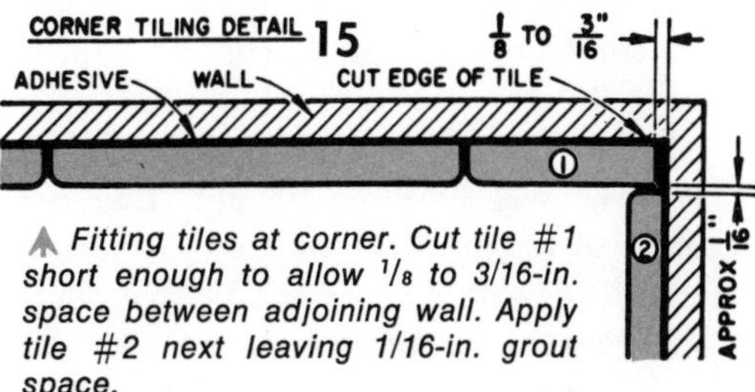

Fitting tiles at corner. Cut tile #1 short enough to allow 1/8 to 3/16-in. space between adjoining wall. Apply tile #2 next leaving 1/16-in. grout space.

If the floor is level within $\frac{3}{16}$-inch or less, go ahead with tiling, starting with the lowest or bottom course. The ¼-inch ceramic floor tile covers any space left between the bottom edge of the tile and the floor. Using a level, draw a line on the wall even with the top of a tile placed on the high side of the floor. This will be the top edge of the tile in the lowest course.

If the floor surface is off level by more than $\frac{3}{16}$-inch, nail a straight piece of ½ x 1-inch wood trim to each wall (Fig. 11). Starting at the low end of the lowest wall, measure up the distance equal to one tile plus ⅛-inch, and draw a line with the level. Nail the wooden strips so their top surfaces are even with this line. Don't drive the nails flush, as the strips will be removed later. The starting course of tile sits on top of these wooden strips. When the rest of the tiling is finished, remove these strips and cut each tile with the nippers or cutter to within ⅛-inch of the height along the floor course of tile. Use the buttering type of adhesive on the back of tiles set along the bottom, and set the tile with the cut edge down. *Provide good ventilation and avoid smoking when using the solvent-type adhesives.*

If you don't plan to use ceramic floor tile, cement a synthetic rubber cove strip over the joint between the wall tile and the floor covering.

If there is a bathtub in the room you're tiling, start a full course of tile directly over bathtub's ledge. Run one vertical course of tile from this horizontal course down to the base line, which is the top edge of the lowest course of tile. The second course of tile may be cut in height as in Fig. 9.

Before starting, find out how much the end tiles will have to be cut. Lay one course of tile on the floor next to the wall to be tiled, with a toothpick between each tile. Measure the amount of space left for the last tile; if it is ¾-inch or less, cut an inch off the starting tile. This short starting tile avoids narrow and difficult-to-cut last tiles. After tiling one wall, measure the tile space on it equal to the next wall, and thus determine if the end tiles for that wall need to be cut.

Starting with the buttering type of adhesive, spread a small amount of it with the putty knife on the back of each tile to cover about half of its surface $\frac{1}{16}$-inch thick (Fig. 12). Immediately press the tile in place on the wall. Draw horizontal lines on the wall surface, one for each course of tile. You must set the tiles square as well as level, or their corners will project as in Fig. 13.

As each tile is added in the horizontal course, place the toothpicks (unless you use the "lug" type tile) on four sides of each tile (Fig. 14) to automatically gage the separation between the tiles for the addition of grout later; the lug type tiles will space themselves automatically about $\frac{1}{16}$-inch apart. Press the tiles into place with a slight twisting motion, but don't force adhesive up between the tiles. After a row of tiles has been set up, use a solid piece of wood to exert pressure on the face of the tiles to level adjoining tiles.

The floating type of adhesive (which can be used after the starting course of tile has been set with the buttering adhesive) is spread on the wall surface with the slotted trowel (Fig. 1). Cover a large wall area with the floating type before starting to tile, since it doesn't set up for an hour.

If possible, start on the wall having the least number of breaks for pipes or accessories, and work clockwise around the room. At inside wall corners, set tiles according to Fig. 15. As you near the top limit of the wall area to be tiled, lay out a line ⅛-inch below the top edge of the last wall tile or cap. This line will be the top limit for the adhesive, and will prevent spreading hard-to-remove adhesive on the untiled portion.

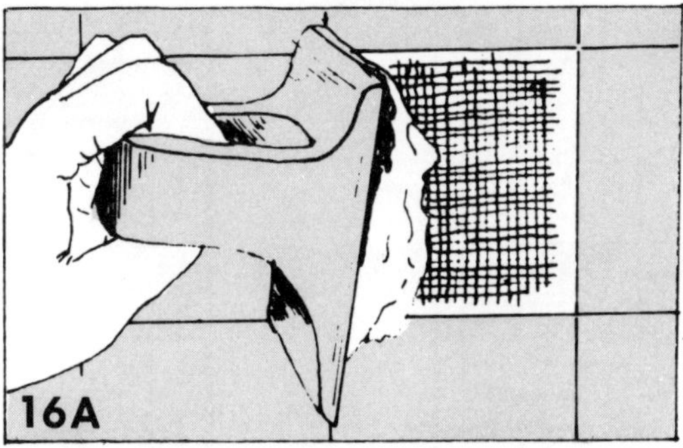

(A) Installing accessory in open space left when tiling and before grouting. Excess Keene's cement is forced around screen mesh in hole to hold accessories in place. (B) Wire basket keeps cement from falling into wall space, helps grip cement on lug.

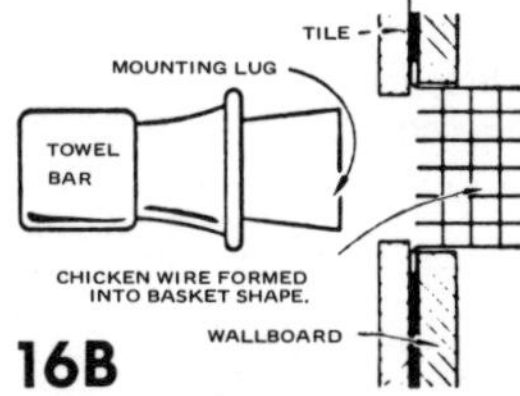

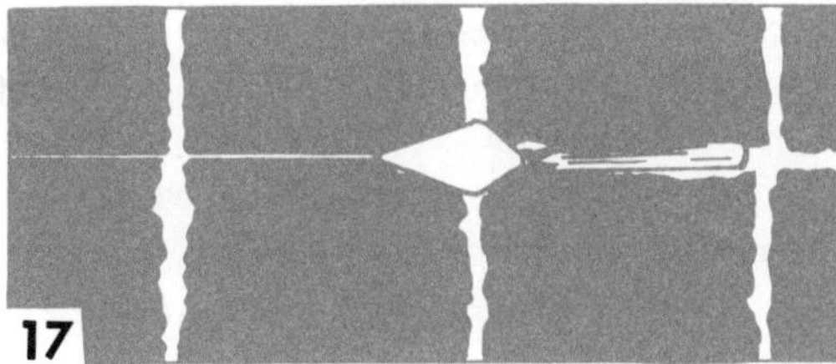

Pointing grout between joints with rounded end of seed marking stick.

Setting bathroom accessories. After completing the wall tile work, the accessories are set in place. Cut out the holes in the wall to clear their mounting lugs. Use finishing plaster cement (sold by building supply houses) for setting them, as it sets rapidly and is white in color. Fill the space in back of the wall cutouts with chicken or reinforcing mesh wire (formed into a cup shape) to keep the cement from falling off the accessory's mounting lug (Figs. 16A and B). Mix the cement with clean water to heavy cream consistency. Apply an excess amount of cement on the mounting lug and force it into the wall opening. Remove all excess cement on the accessory and adjoining tiles before it sets hard.

You may need to prop some heavy accessories with a wooden stick, from the opposite wall, until the cement has a chance to set. This cement becomes the grouting means around the accessories and should be finished flush with their sides.

Caulking. Some joints (such as those between the wall tile and the tub, medicine cabinet to wall tile, etc.) where there might be movement between the fixture and the wall, should be sealed with caulking compound to keep water out and the joint free from cracking, which would happen if conventional grout were used. Use the same compound wherever pipes emerge through cutouts in the tile, together with pipe rings or caps.

Grouting should not be done until at least one day after completing the tiling job. Clean up all joints of any adhesive that may have been forced up, and remove the toothpicks. Use a sharp knife or a razor blade.

For grout material use tile grout, made especially for this purpose. Use non-shrinking tile grout, mixed with clean water to a light cream consistency. Just before the grout is prepared, soak the tile joints with water to prevent the absorption of the water in the grout. Saturate a cellulose sponge or cloth with water and go over wall tile joints repeatedly. Then spread the grout mixture over the tiles with a whitewash brush. After going over the walls once, go back to the starting wall and brush it on again to fill the joints. After the grout has set a few minutes, remove excess grout with a small squeegee. Then, using a wooden stick (Fig. 17) finish the joints flush with the glazed surface of the tile. Don't forget to grout the top edge of the bull nose cap and the corners as well. Sponge off walls after grout has set.

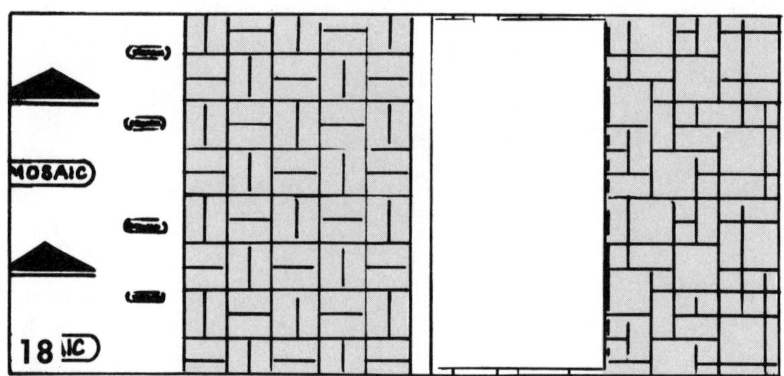

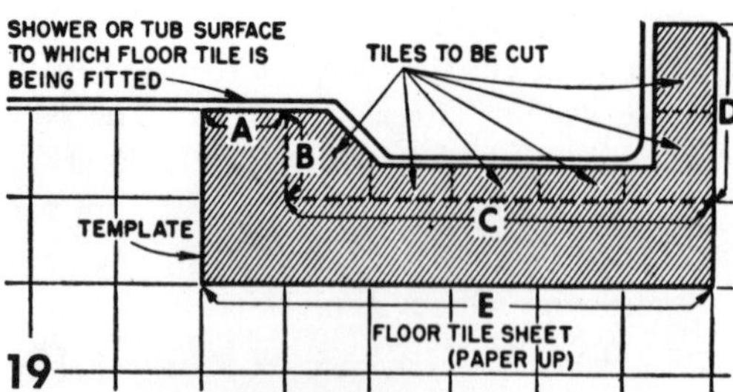

Fig. 18. Typical floor tile patterns come in sheets like this, the papered side being the top side of the tile. Fig. 19. When fitting floor tile around irregular surfaces, first cut Kraft paper holding tiles together along lines A, B, C, and D. Then make cardboard template (shaded area) to fit curvature with its lower edge even with tile division line B. Lay template even with line E, and lay tiles to be cut under template. Finally mark tiles, cut them, and attach them back to tile sheet with Scotch tape.

How floor tiles fit around and under door opening.

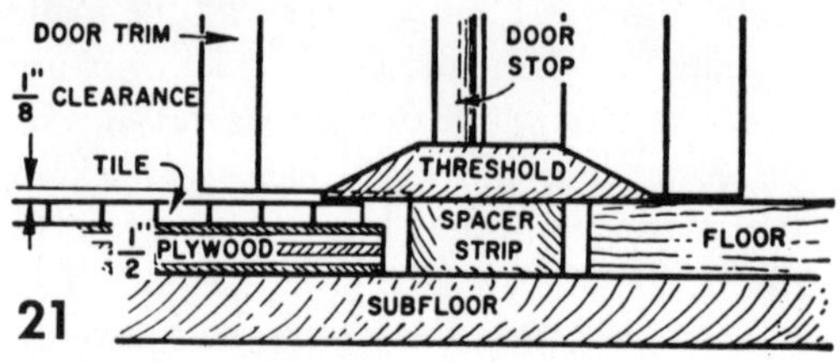

Setting floor tile. Floor tile is sold in sheets (Fig. 18). After selecting the pattern you want and determining the size of the sheet it comes in, you can calculate how many sheets you will need. Take several sheets of the floor tile pattern you select and try laying them lengthwise or crosswise on the floor area, to determine which arrangement gives you the least number of joints between the sheets. If your walls are square, then cutting the sheets to size should be easy.

Lay as many of the full tile sheets as you can around the floor area, with the paper side up. Then, starting in one corner measure the distance remaining from the edge of the sheet to the walls. Lay off this distance on top of the paper on a full floor tile sheet. Cut this sheet along the paper between the tiles nearest to the layout line. If the layout line comes part way on some of the tiles, cut the paper at the nearest full tile space and attach the tiles that will have to be cut, temporarily at their place on the sheet, with Scotch tape. They can be swung back on the sheet to get them out of the way. Repeat this procedure with all of the partial sheets around the room. Then cut the tiles that have to be cut as you did the wall tile, and attach back to the sheets.

You can leave a space of about ⅛-inch from the edge of the last floor tile to the wall tile.

If the closet bowl is to be left undisturbed then cut the tile out to fit around it. Otherwise, trim the tile to the closet flange after the bowl has been temporarily removed. In either case, make your cardboard template first.

Where the floor tile fits against an irregular edge (such as a tub or a shower) first make a cardboard template and from it mark up the tile sheet (Fig. 19). Figure 20 shows you how to fit tile around the door trim. Cut off the door trim so that its end is about ⅛-inch above the top of the floor tile. When the tile is being set, slip the edge of the tile sheet which fits under the door trim under first. Note, in Fig. 21, how the tile sheet ends, and a space is left before the floor in the hall starts. Over this space an oak threshold is placed, supported by a spacer strip, the threshold covering the ends of the tile and the hall flooring, and extending from one side of the door frame to the other.

Remember to mark the tile sheets so you'll know where they are to fit on the floor. Finish trimming all sheets before spreading adhesive on the floor.

After priming the floor and allowing the primer to set up hard, spread the floor type of adhesive over the floor area, using the saw tooth trowel previously described, leaving no bare spots, and working yourself toward the door. Don't forget to put adhesive on the floor under the door trim. After the adhesive has set up for 15 minutes, put down small boards to stand on while you put down the tile sheets. Apply the tile sheets within 30 minutes after spreading the adhesive, using a short sliding motion, and aligning the sheets carefully with each other. Don't slide too far, or the adhesive will be forced up between the tiles, making it difficult to grout properly.

Within a half hour after the sheets have been set, remove the heavy kraft paper on top of the tile sheets by wetting it with a sponge until the glue softens enough for you to peel the paper off. Do any adjusting of the individual tiles now and use a straight edge, if necessary, to level the top surface of the tile. Place boards on the tile while working, so you won't stand or kneel directly on them, forcing individual tiles lower than the rest into the adhesive.

Grouting floor tile. Grout floor tile as you did the wall tile. The grout mixture should fill spaces between individual tiles completely. After allowing it to set a while, go over the joints with the wooden stick to get the grout slightly below the surface of the tile.

In addition, you will need to "cure" the floor grout, after cleaning it off, by covering the finished floor with damp burlap bags for three days. Cover the burlap with building paper to prevent the evaporation of water. N.R.

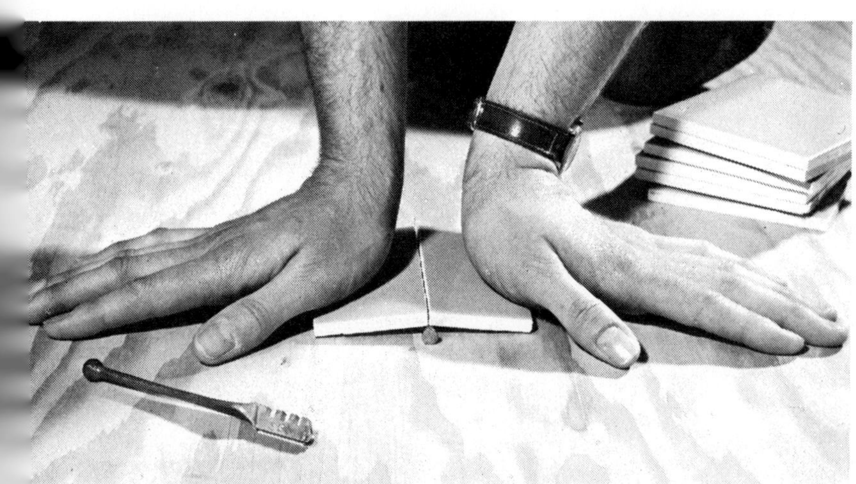

◀ A simpler alternative method of cutting tile calls for nothing more than a glass cutter, a rule and a finishing nail, but it is not recommended for big jobs. It works this way. Score the tile with the glass cutter. Place the tile on the floor over the finishing nail, so the nail is under the score. Press down each side of the tile and it will snap along the scored line.

How to Repair Your Toaster

Changing a damaged cord occasionally and cleaning the crumb tray regularly are usually the most maintenance this simple device will require. If it goes much beyond that, it may be cheaper to replace it rather than make repairs

With a little care in cleaning and handling, your toaster should lead a long and useful life. The three major reasons for toaster failure are: dropping, failure to clean out the crumb catcher periodically, and poking out small pieces of toast with a knife or other metal probe.

The two most common complaints about toaster operation are:

1. The toast will not pop up.
2. A heater does not work.

Most toasters operate in much the same way and change very little from year to year. An analysis of one should provide a background that can be applied to many.

Operation. A slice of bread is dropped in the slot and the toaster carriage handle is pressed down until it latches. This action: compresses a spring which later lifts the toast up partially out of the slot; closes a switch which allows electricity to flow through the heating elements; winds the clock mechanism for toasters with clockwork timers, or closes the switch to the bimetal heater for those toasters that have a bimetal or thermal timer. The thermal type timer is most commonly used.

The timer controls the toast color. That is, it controls the length of time the heater elements are on. When the timer turns off it releases the latch and the spring lifts up the carriage and holds it up until the next time it is depressed.

Electrical test and service. When a toaster fails to operate or heat up, the first thing to suspect is lack of power. This may be due to a blown fuse or a defective power cord. Always check the outlet first to make certain power is available. Either plug in a lamp, or use your AC voltmeter. The next item to test is the power cord. Be especially suspicious of this if the operation is erratic, because movement of the cord may cause a broken wire to make contact and the toaster will work for a while. Working the cord back and forth while the toaster is plugged in and turned on will not always show up a defect. The best method is to use an ohmmeter and test the circuit for continuity from point to point.

Most toasters have their heater elements connected in parallel. This type of connection allows one element to heat even if others are burned out. Most often these test points are accessible by removing the bottom of the toaster. The cord can be replaced readily. Fixing any of the other parts usually requires removal of the case.

Mechanical service. To disassemble the toaster, invert it on a soft surface to protect the finish. Remove the screws that hold the

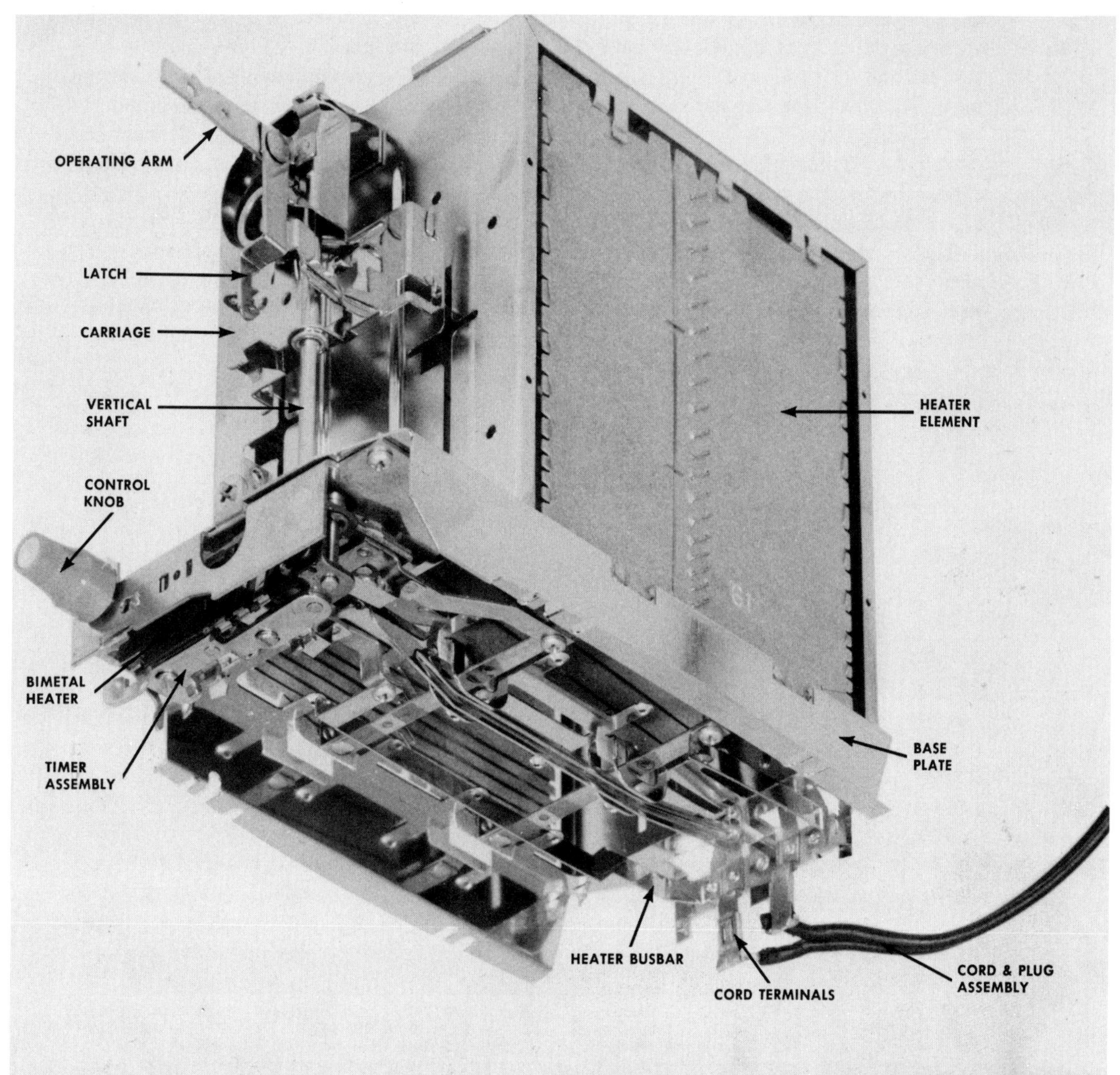

undercover in place. Next remove the handles—the plastic parts—at each end. Also remove the operating handle which is often held in place by a screw on its underside.

The timer knob—light-dark control—may have to be removed depending on the size of the hole in the case. Some have a small center screw which has to be removed

▲ *Once the outer shell of the toaster is removed, the working parts are exposed. Usually it is not necessary to remove the shell to change a cord or clean out accumulated crumbs.*

first. Remove the screws holding the case to the frame.

When the case has been completely loosened from the frame, hold the toaster together and set it in an upright position with the bread slots up. Gently raise the case up and over the operating lever to remove it. Next remove the bread guard wires before they fall out of place and damage a heater element. This should expose the heater elements, carriage mechanism and timer.

The toast carriage guide rod must be clean and straight or the carriage will stick part way, or be slow in lifting. Lighter fluid or dry cleaning fluid can be used to clean the gummy deposit from this rod. Lubricate the rod sparingly with a silicone grease.

Make certain the holding latches and the timer linkages are clean and smooth in operation. Here, too, a good cleanup and careful lubrication can do much to restore normal operation.

Switch contacts can become pitted and coated, causing them to make poor contact. Careful filing and burnishing of the contacts can add additional life, if the contacts are not too far gone.

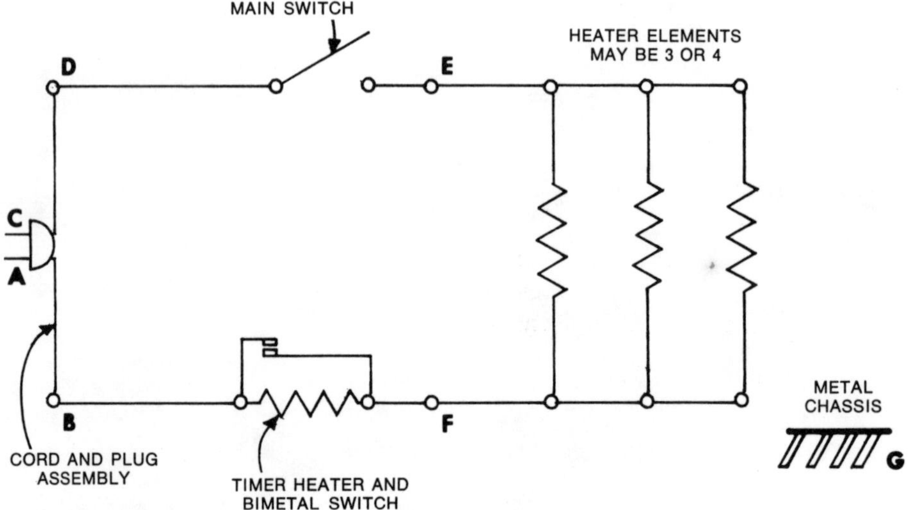

OHMMETER ANALYSIS OF CIRCUIT

Points	Correct Ohmmeter Reading	Possible Cause of Incorrect Reading
A to B	0 ohms	∞ = open cord
C to D	0 ohms	∞ = open cord
D to E	0 ohms[1]	∞ or any reading is defective switch
B to F	0 ohms ∞ ohms	Closed timer contacts Open timer heater
E to F	12-15 ohms[2]	Higher = open element Lower = shorted element
A-F to G	∞ ohms	Any reading is short to ground which may shock user

NOTES: [1] With switch closed.
[2] For 1000 to 1200 watt toasters.

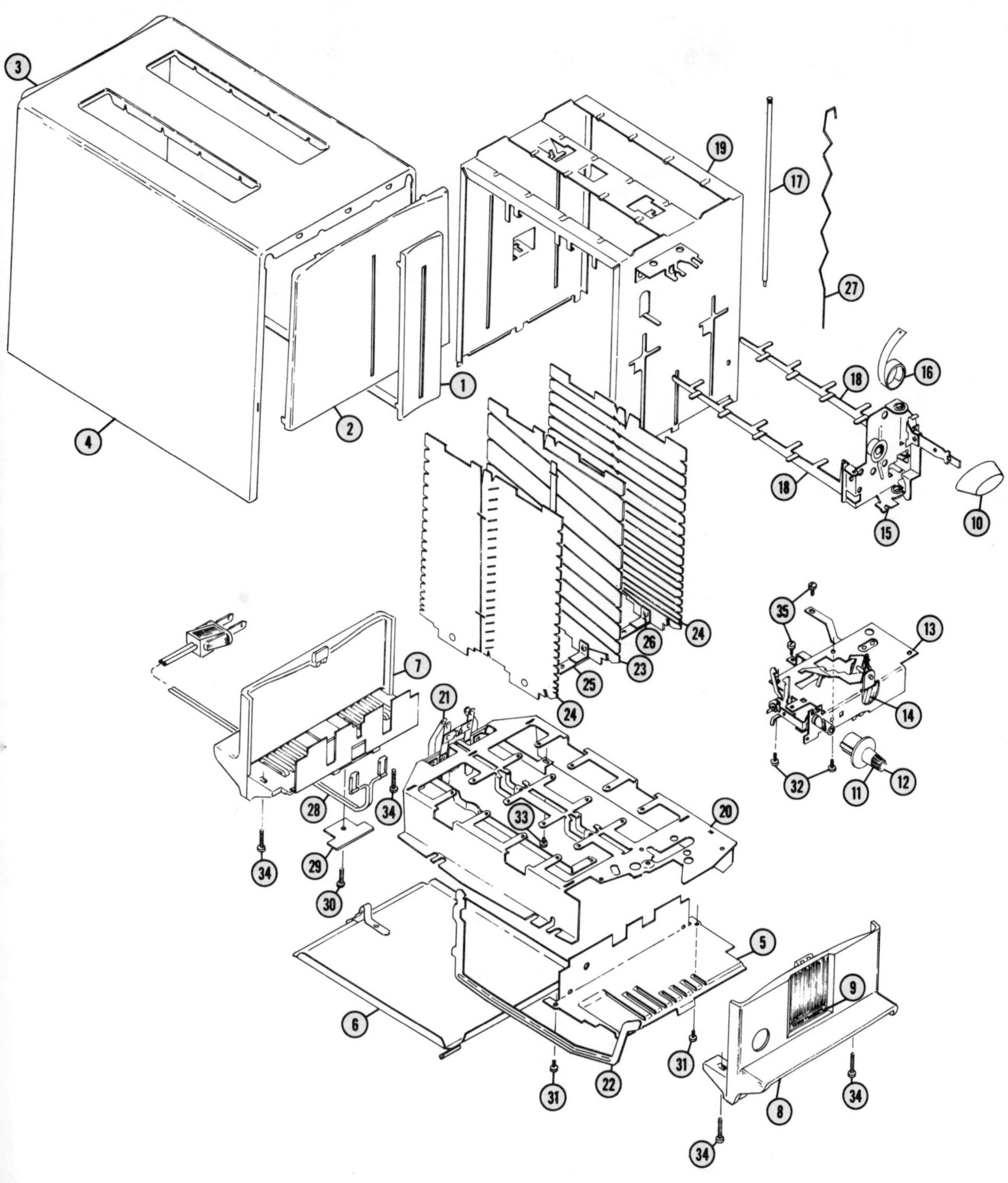

Typical toaster design is shown in the exploded drawing. Use the reference key to identify the parts.

REF. NO.	PART NAME	QTY.
1	Decor plate	1
2	Case, front	1
3	Case, end	1
4	Case, center	1
5	Front stat. under cover	1
6	Hinged crumb tray assembly	1
7	Rear handle and buffle assembly	1
8	Front handle	1
9	Nameplate decal	1
10	Operating handle	1
11	Control knob	1
12	Insert, control knob	1
13	Timer assembly	1
14	Bimetal arm assembly	1
15	Carriage assembly w/op. lever	1
16	Negator spring	1
17	Vertical shaft	1
18	Bread rack	2
19	Frame and vert. shaft brkt. assembly	1
20	Base plate	1
21	Main switch lever	1
22	Switch bus bar and ins. assembly	1
23	Element, center	1
24	Element, outside	2
25	Bus bar, element connection	1
26	Rivet	As Required
27	Guard wires	As Required
28	Cord and terminal assembly	1
29	Cord retainer cover	1
30	Screw, cord ret. cover	1
31	Screw, 3-48 x 3/16 front stat. to frame	2
32	Screw, 4-40 x 3/16 timer to frame	2
33	Screw, 5-40 x 7/16 bus bar to frame	1
34	Screw, 5-40 x 1/4 plastic handles to frame	4
35	Screw, 3-48 x 1/8 timer to frame	2

Some heater elements are attached to the power bus bars by screws, others by rivets. Those riveted in place should have the rivet drilled out and new elements installed with small screws.

Replace or repair? As a rule the best source of parts is the dealer who sold the toaster or a factory authorized service station. Some metropolitan areas have large well-stocked appliance parts suppliers. These can all be found in the yellow pages of your phone book.

When deciding whether to repair or replace your toaster, consider the cost of a new one against the cost of the part, acquiring it, and installing it. Generally speaking it is economical to replace only the cord or the plastic parts on a toaster and, of course, clean it internally.

In any case get the right part by number for the make and model toaster you are fixing. The accompanying trouble diagnosis chart will show you the area in which to look for specific problems G.M.

See also: ELECTRICAL, HOME; INDIVIDUAL APPLIANCE LISTINGS.

TOASTER TROUBLE-SHOOTING CHART

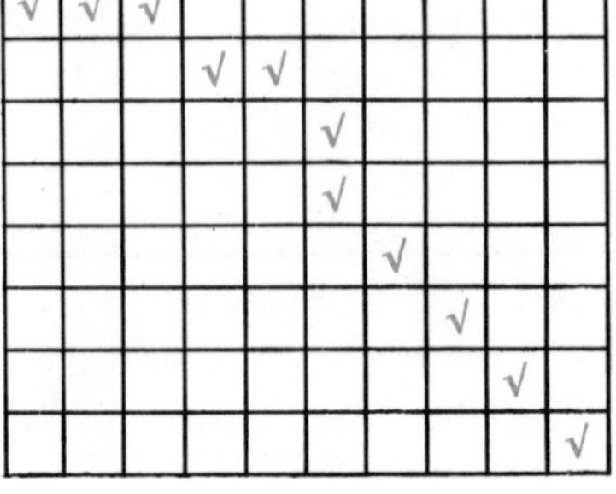

PROBLEM / POSSIBLE CAUSE	BREAK IN CORD	DEFECTIVE HOLDING CATCH	SWITCH DEFECTIVE	TOAST CARRIAGE BINDS	RELEASE LATCH BINDS	WEAK OR BROKEN SPRING	EXCESSIVE SPRING TENSION	INCORRECT TIMER ADJUSTMENT	DEFECTIVE HEATER ELEMENT	GROUNDED WIRE
DOES NOT HEAT	√	√	√							
TOAST WILL NOT STAY DOWN				√	√					
TOAST WILL NOT POP UP						√				
TOAST LIFTS TOO SLOWLY						√				
TOAST LIFTS TOO RAPIDLY							√			
TOAST TOO LIGHT OR TOO DARK								√		
ONE SIDE UNTOASTED									√	
SHOCKS USER										√

How to Repair a Faulty Flush Tank

Plugging a leak the size of a pinhole can save about 95,000 gallons of water a year

FLUSH TANK DIFFICULTIES are among the most annoying because they are so noisy and persistent. While these troubles can be corrected, easily and inexpensively, they often are neglected because the parts are not visible or readily accessible and the functioning of the mechanism seems a mystery.

Many water closets do not have a shut-off valve and the inexperienced homeowner tries to make repairs with the tank full or with cold water constantly rushing in, which definitely is a handicap.

An understanding of how the tank valves work, and some tips on curing any annoying troubles, will enable you to keep the water closet in good working order.

How it operates. The water closet tank operates by means of two finely balanced mechanisms which function automatically:

1. The flush valve, actuated by a handle on the tank, lifts a stopper plug over the water discharge tube.
2. The inlet valve is controlled by a float which fills the tank and shuts off the water at the correct level.

In addition, there is an overflow tube which bypasses the flush valve and empties any excess water into the bowl if the inlet valve fails to shut off. There also is a refill tube whose purpose is to pour water into the bowl for a period after flushing to maintain a waterlock in the drain trap so that sewer gas cannot come up.

There are differences in the shape and arrangement of these parts in various makes of water closets, but the system essentially is the same.

Flush valve. The handle on the tank trips a lever which pulls up a stopper at the bottom. The stopper ball floats to the top while all the water in the tank rushes out. When the tank is empty, the stopper ball, guided by its lift wire, drops back into position over a seal ring, closing the discharge opening. The weight of water entering the tank through the inlet valve holds the stopper in position.

It is this rubber ball that causes most of the trouble. The ball is attached to a copper stem that rides up and down inside a stem guide, and the stem in turn is connected to the trip lever with a lift wire. The flush ball, round or conical in shape, drops straight down to seat in a brass ring and closes the discharge outlet.

If the water continues to flow, or even to drip, it causes disturbing noises. The inlet valve also is affected and permits water to flow into the tank as well.

First see if pressing down on the stopper ball will end the water flow. If so, find what has prevented it from seating automatically. The chain of search for the trouble starts with the trip lever at the top. See that it is not stuck, thus holding the stopper ball above the valve seat. The lever can sometimes become bent or jammed.

The next point is the lift wire attached to the handle lever. There should be about ¼-inch play in the lift. If it is bent, the distance is shortened and the stopper can't drop all the way down, as it should. Disconnect the lift wire from the stopper stem. See if the stem moves freely up and down in its guide.

Also, and this is important, make sure

the stem guide is directly above the discharge opening. The guide is attached to the overflow pipe and its position can be adjusted by loosening a setscrew at the side with an offset screwdriver.

If all these check out OK, lift out the stopper ball after unscrewing the threaded stem, and see if it is spongy, out of round, or bloated—any of which may prevent complete seating and closure at the valve.

It's a good idea to replace the flush stopper ball at intervals, so do that while it is out. New ones don't cost very much and many can be purchased complete with new stem and wire.

These inspections and adjustments of the stem guide can be made more comfortably and efficiently when the tank is empty. If your water closet does not have a shut-off valve, you can stop the inflow of water by tying the float ball with a string, or placing a short stick under the intake valve bar.

Replacing seal. When the tank is empty examine the brass discharge seal at the bottom into which the stopper fits. See if it is pitted or corroded and whether the surface is rough to the touch. Any damage to the seat would prevent complete sealing of the valve. It is possible to sand it smooth with a piece of emery cloth, but a complete new assembly costs just a few dollars and can be installed quickly in the opening without special tools.

Use a monkey wrench to loosen that nut underneath the discharge pipe to break the connection with the bowl. Remove the short chrome pipe, then turn out the large nut on a threaded pipe extending under the tank. Loosen the flush valve gaskets by working the overflow pipe from side to side until the assembly comes free.

Remove the flush valve parts, unless you have purchased the complete assembly with overflow pipe and stem guide. The new unit comes complete with gaskets and washers, and is installed through the tank with just enough tightening of the bottom nut for a watertight fit.

Special devices. Many devices have been developed to overcome the persistent problems with the flush valve stopper. These still operate on the same principle (no practical substitute has yet been found for the hollow stopper ball) but aim primarily to keep the stopper always in line with the discharge opening seat.

A leading manufacturer of faucet washers and valve seals offers one product which depends on a group of prongs inside the discharge opening to line up the ball stopper.

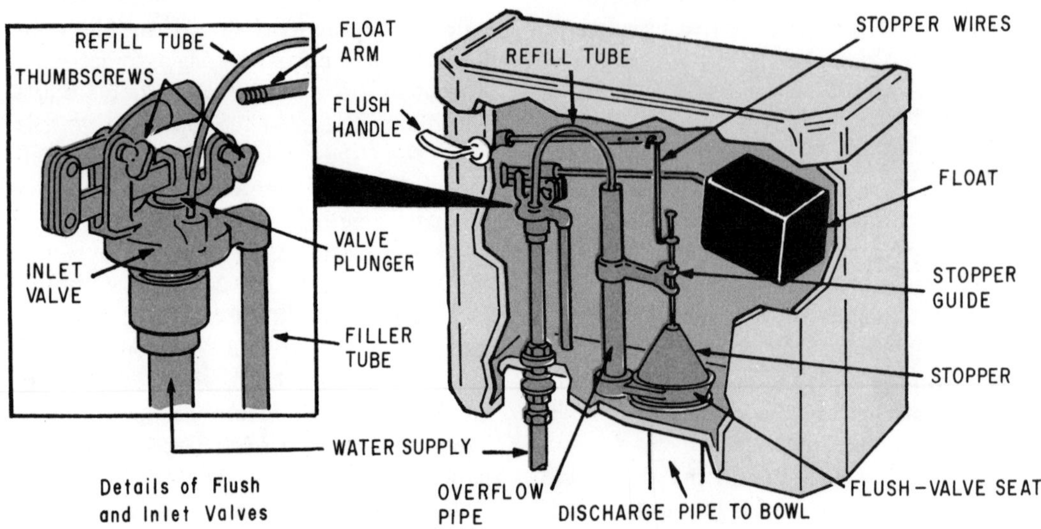

Details of Flush and Inlet Valves

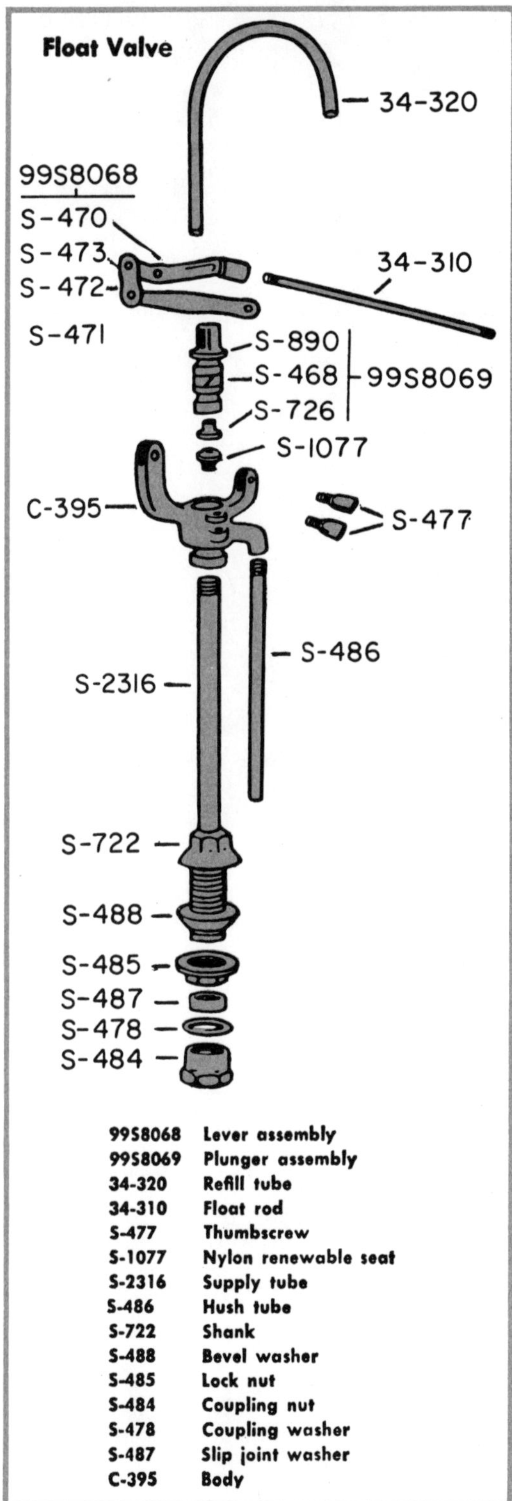

Another company offers a mechanism which depends on an exterior plastic guide tube to keep the stopper in line.

There are many others, and each will solve the trouble temporarily. Until the perfect solution is invented, keep your flush tank valves in good condition and correct adjustment, and the performance will be quite satisfactory.

Inlet valve. When water constantly drips down through the overflow pipe, the trouble is with the inlet valve and usually is due to improper functioning of the float ball. This may be the result of pinholes in the copper.

You can test the float by unscrewing it from the rod and shaking it to see if it has water inside. Soldering is not worthwhile, as a new foam rubber or copper float costs very little and is installed in just a few minutes without tools. Make sure the float is not hitting the side of the tank and the float rod is bent at the correct angle.

The float arm should be adjusted to maintain water level in the tank at about an inch below the top of the overflow tube.

The intake valve may require occasional replacement of its washer. To do this, after emptying the tank as described above, turn out the thumbscrews that act as shafts for the valve levers. Then lift out the piston assembly and slide it off the lever. The washer is at the bottom of the stem, and is usually held with a brass screw or a locking ring. If the thumbscrew pins or washer ring are corroded, replace them with new ones.

Another cause of ball cock leak is the split leather packing ring on the piston plunger at the top of the assembly. The ring slides off the groove for replacement.

A leak at the discharge tube into the water closet bowl is due to a worn spud washer. To replace, uncouple the chrome slip nuts, slide the tube out of the brass spud at the back of the bowl, unscrew the jam nut and pull the spud clear. Replace the washer with one of the correct size, and reassemble.

390

Flush valve cut away

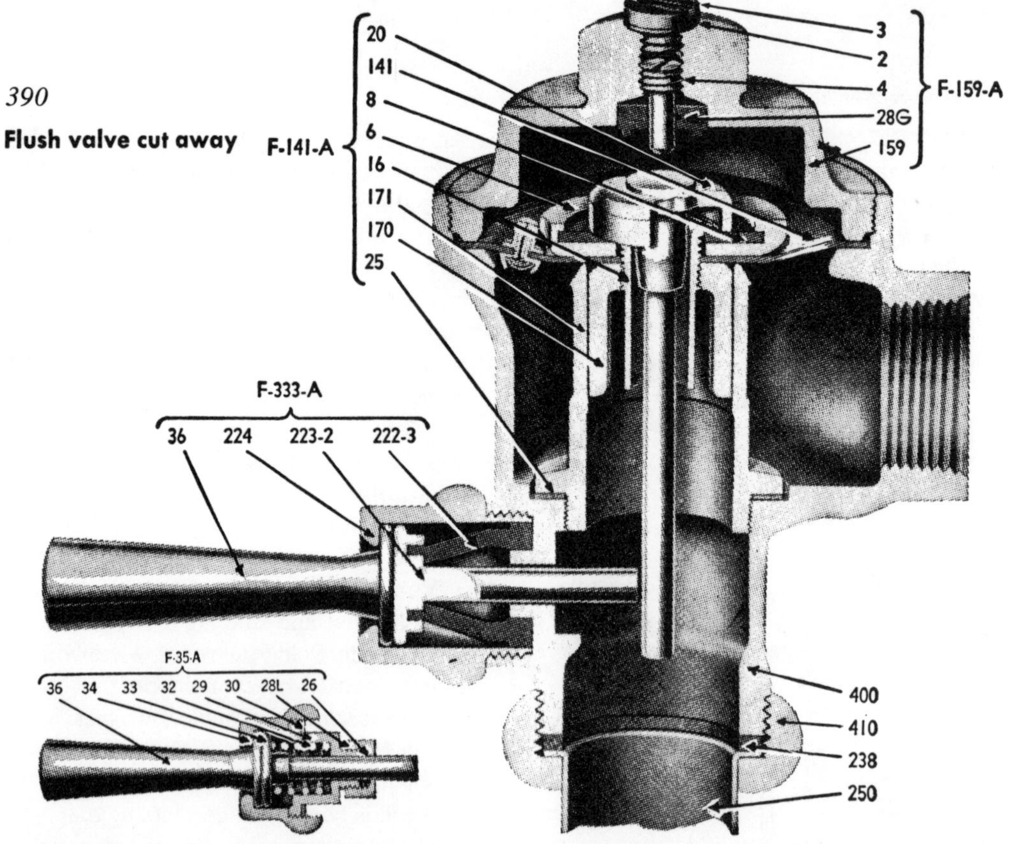

REF. NO.	PARTIAL ASSEMBLIES
F-141-A	Diaphragm operating assembly, complete
F-159-A	Cover assembly, complete
F-333-A	Handle assembly
F-35-A	Spring loaded handle

REF. NO.	INDIVIDUAL REPAIR PARTS
F2	Washer for cover screw
F3	Cover screw
F4	Regulating screw
F6	Auxiliary valve seat holder
F8	Auxiliary valve rubber seat
F16	Diaphragm bushing
F20	Bronze auxiliary valve assembly
F25	Fiber main valve seat washer
F26	Packing for handle packing nut
F28G	Packing for cover
F28L	Packing nut for handle
F29	Spring housing
F30	Fiber washer
F32	Spring for handle
F33	Operating stem
F34	Handle nut
F36	Metal handle
F141C	Diaphragm with by-pass (for closet valve)
F141U	Diaphragm with by-pass (for urinal valve)
F159	Cover assembly, complete
F170C	Seat guide (for closet valve)
F170U	Seat guide (for urinal valve)
F171	Main valve bronze seat
F223-2	Operating stem
F222-3	Rubber flexer
F224	Handle nut
F238	Fiber coupling washer
F250	1½-inch chrome plated tailpiece with collar
F400	Valve body only
F410	1½ x 1½-inch coupling nut

Condensation on tank. With a tank full of fresh cold water, it is to be expected that the room humidity will cause condensation on the tank. This unsightly condition can be extremely annoying because of constant dripping of water on the floor causing mildew of linens in the room, and is generally untidy.

Plastic drip pans can be purchased to fit under the tank for catching the condensate. A more expensive but practical correction is a tempering valve which feeds enough hot water into the tank to maintain room temperature.

Flushometers. Flush valves are coming into wider use in homes, wherever there is sufficient water pressure, and the pipe system is large enough for an ample flow of water.

These valves are highly efficient and can keep operating for long periods without any malfunction. But when they do go off the beam, they can play havoc with any well-ordered home. Water gushes forth at an alarming rate, hour after hour, and jiggling of the level handle just seems to call for more of the same.

Of course, the shut-off valve can be closed, but most members of the household don't even know about that, or where it is. Other difficulties with these valves are that they deliver either insufficient or excessive flow of water at each flushing, or water drips from the handle stem.

Inside the bell-like housing at the top there are two water chambers, separated by a leather diaphragm. A dish relief valve is in the center of the diaphragm. A slight touch of the level handle in any direction pushes in the plunger and tilts the relief valve, releasing the pressure in the upper chamber. The water supply pressure then pushes up the entire diaphragm and valve; the gush of water flushes the bowl.

Some water, however, seeps through the bypass and gradually fills the upper chamber to again close the valve.

Trouble-shooting. Here are the various troubles that might develop:

1. Water continues to run. Bypass screen may be clogged with grit or diaphragm badly worn. Clean bypass with fine wire. Sometimes the valve fails to close fully due to sediment on the rubber washer which serves as valve seat. Replace diaphragm or cup washer.
2. Water drips from release handle. Replace with handle coupling washer.
3. Water flow is inadequate or too long. Turn regulating screw at top of valve chamber to obtain best timing of valve.
4. Leak at tailpiece coupling under valve. This may be caused by deterioration of rubber vacuum breaker. Replace with new one if necessary. Do not seal off the air ports at the side, as they are necessary for proper functioning of the vacuum breaker to prevent siphonage.

To install the new valve washers, close the shutoff valve at the water inlet side, by turning clockwise. Use adjustable wrench to turn off valve cap. The valve plunger and diaphragm may now be lifted out.

Use a spanner wrench to remove the disk ring that holds the valve seat washer. Clean the disk carefully with a brush—do not scrape with knife or screwdriver. The diaphragm now can also be taken out and replaced with a new one of the same size.

When replacing the diaphragm, be sure that it is pushed down to bottom of thread and rests flat on the seat, to prevent wrinkling and curling. Don't use white lead. Restore relief valve over diaphragm and screw the housing cover back tightly.

The plunger washer may be replaced quickly by loosening the coupling, so that entire plunger arm may be pulled out. The small coupling washer is near the end and can be pushed out. Put on new handle packing washer before replacing the plunger.

If there is a vacuum breaker in the flush valve, the tailpiece pipe will have an air vent near the top, which will be hidden by the cowl nut. If there is leakage at this point, drop the cowl nut to loosen the pipe and take out the rubber sleeve and brass insert. If the rubber shows any signs of distortion or damage, replace with a new one.

If there is not sufficient flow at the flush valve, check the water pressure in the house. Any drop at the street main below the rating required for your house will affect the flow at the bowl. Your plumber or water department can easily check this with a gauge if you suspect a sharp drop in main pressure.

See also: DRAINS; FAUCETS.

How to Select Tools

Use this guide to equip yourself with the kind and quantity of tools you'll need for the jobs you want to do – whether you are an apartment dweller with little space or a homeowner setting up a workshop

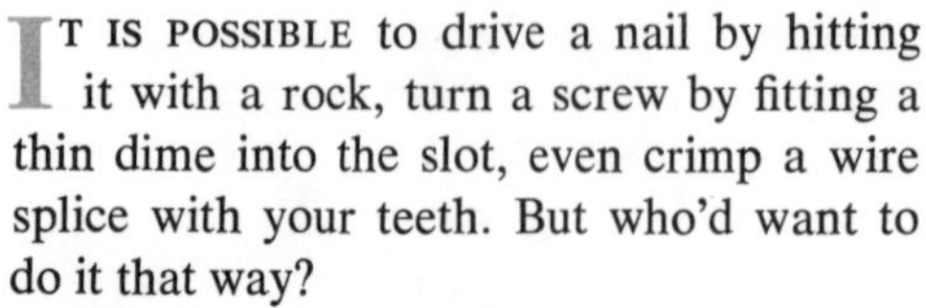

IT IS POSSIBLE to drive a nail by hitting it with a rock, turn a screw by fitting a thin dime into the slot, even crimp a wire splice with your teeth. But who'd want to do it that way?

Some people strangely manage to get along without any tools at all—not even a screwdriver or pair of pliers. Apparently they never break anything, fix anything, or make anything!

The facts probably are that they either shell out a lot of dough for handyman repairs, or just let everything go to pot—held together with string and chewing gum.

Then there's the other extreme, the collectors who buy and bring home every tool that strikes their fancy, even if they don't know what it's for, stashing it away in hope it will come in handy some day. When the time comes, it's unlikely they can dig out of the mess the one or two items to do the job.

In this many-sided game, the right place is in the middle. That means owning the tools that meet your own particular needs, whether it's a $5 assortment for the young apartment dweller or a well-fitted workshop for the homeowner who can tackle any woodworking or mechanical task.

You should, however, take advantage of the versatility of certain tools to serve additional purposes, and also remember you can rent special tools for one-time use.

But basic tools cost so little it's silly not to have the ones you'll need, even those that will be used only occasionally.

Prices are low. Many hand tools cost $2 or less, and last a lifetime. Examples are screwdrivers, pliers, chisels, awls, punches, hammers, wrenches, squares, rulers and levels. Portable electric tools like drills, sanders and jig saws run from $10 to $40 and are worth their weight in gold. Power tools of good quality (the only kind you should buy) are $75 to $300, the best investment you can make for that money. Prices of tools are actually lower than before because of greater production and intense competition.

When it costs anywhere from $8 to $20 for a simple home appliance repair, a minimum of $8 to get a small window pane replaced, $100 and more just to have some wood trim painted, the cost of tools and equipment that enable you to do these jobs yourself is insignificant and is repaid many, many times over. Besides freeing your household from reliance on undependable outside service, these chores give you an unmatched sense of satisfaction and stimulate further improvement projects around the house.

Save on repairs. The knowledge that tool prices have remained low while outside service charges are soaring, compels a resolve to equip yourself for home maintenance to the extent of your capabilities, an important economy for the hard-pressed homeowner and even a prosperous one.

There are actually hundreds of basic tools, each one in various sizes and types, and a considerable range of quality and prices. Then there are additional hundreds of ingenious tools that were developed to meet special problems, and also each trade field like masonry, electrical, plumbing, radio and TV, auto repair, metal working, etc. has its own catalogues of interesting tools.

Which tools should you own? How do you select them for quality and widest versatility? Where to keep them safe and available?

Basic selections. A practical approach to tool selection must consider the varied needs of the individual. Thus, we have devised classifications and worked out recommended tool assortments for each. These recommendations are not haphazard, but were compiled on the basis of actual experience plus extensive interviews with home-owners and others in widely separated areas.

Select your own category from the chart, then study the recommendations given. Also, look through the descriptions of other tools so that you become familiar with their functions and can add some of those to your collection when the need arises.

Workshop check lists. The following check lists will help you build your tool chest in an orderly way. Each category shows the basic essential requirements and you would do well to get them together at one time, but it could be done "as you go," adding the various items as the need arises. No doubt, you'll find that some tools not on the lists will be acquired because of your own special requirements or interests. Some people go in for appliance repair, others like jewelry repairs or model making, but the guide holds true for the average.

Judging quality. Any experienced mechanic or craftsman will confirm that quality is the buy-word for tools. A well-made tool enables you to get best results from your work, is safer to use, and lasts longer.

For example, a carpenter's saw should be made from steel having the desired flexibility and resilience, hardened and tempered to hold the set of the teeth and resist wear. The steel must be taper-ground, and sufficiently polished for both brightness and smoothness, the handle designed for comfortable grip and tightly secured. Any Disston saw will meet these requirements. Bargain saws are punched from blanks of indifferent steel, without any further tempering.

Chisel and plane blades must be forged and properly tempered to hold their cutting edge. Files made by Nicholson are engineered for efficient cutting, and carefully hardened to function long after cheaper files are consigned to the junk pile. Screwdrivers look simple enough, yet there are "built-in" qualities that separate the good and the bad products by miles.

You can buy a six-foot folding rule for 79 cents, 95 cents, $1.65 and up to $3. Which should you take? They all look pretty good when new, all of them may be quite accurate in dimensions. However, there are important differences. For one thing, the calibrations on some cheap rules are so poorly printed that they soon wear off. Another fault is poor design or construction of the folding joints, which fail to hold the rule straight when open, and break easily so that the rule becomes worthless.

Standard brands like Stanley and Evens assure readability, color contrast, and a plastic finish that protects the markings.

With rules, as with most other tools, there are "features" which may add to the cost. An example is the extension slide, which is a brass bar eight inches long, calibrated for measuring inside area where the folding ruler cannot be opened another stick. The slide shows the additional space which is added to the dimension of the open rule.

The essence of quality would be dramatically emphasized if you bought some of the packaged foreign tools at some discount and variety store—and unfortunately, now also coming on racks in some previously quality-stocked hardware stores. A set of eight highspeed drills from one foreign country is sold for $1 (some American-made drills are $1 each), but each drill will either bend or burn out in seconds. A couple of sets purchased for testing burned out immediately when used on a soft brass plate, while the smaller sizes bent under slight pressure while drilling a piece of oak.

This experience was repeated when testing tools from several other countries. Wood chisels easily nicked, a block plane could not hold its blade in position, the cutting edge broke on several auger bits.

Unless you're prepared to test out various tools in actual use to determine quality (and you would do that only if you planned to buy a large supply of each type), the safest way to select your home workshop tools is to stick to well-regarded brand products. Also, lean to the higher-grade or at least medium-price range, as some manufacturers now also put out lower-quality items to compete with the influx of foreign products.

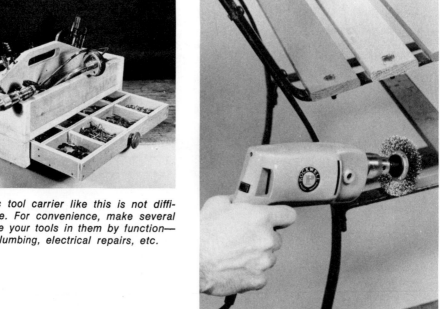

A classic tool carrier like this is not difficult to make. For convenience, make several and organize your tools in them by function—carpentry, plumbing, electrical repairs, etc.

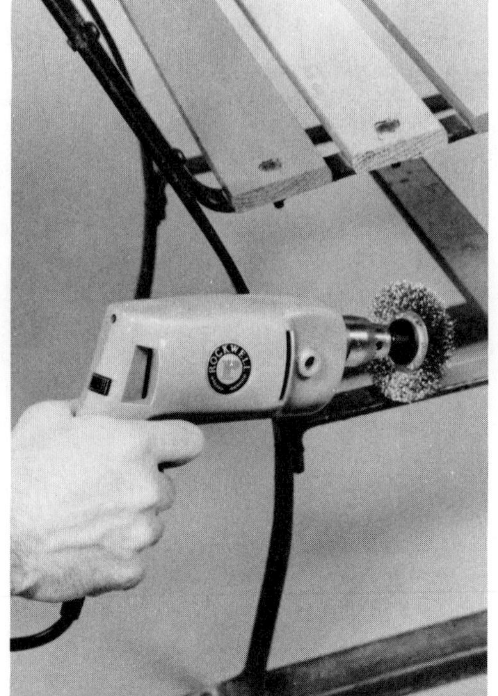

An electric drill can perform a variety of jobs. If you plan to acquire powered hand tools, this is the place to start.

◀ This combination workshop power tool combines a variety of functions—saw, lathe, bandsaw, drill press—within a limited space.

▼ If you are going to do a lot of sawing, a portable circular saw is a labor saver, and it can be carried from job to job.

Quality selection of power tools, whether portable or stationary, is even more critical. A cheap electric drill has limited capacity, will burn out quickly. Cost of repair, often the same as for an expensive tool, would not be justified and thus the entire tool becomes a total loss.

More than that, insufficient motor power can be hazardous, for example with a portable circular saw which balks and kicks back because it lacks power to go through the work. A good portable saw will have sufficient heft to keep the saw steady, a large enough shoe so it can be guided accurately, and a dependable switch.

In electric drills, the points to watch are motor ampere rating, size and type of chuck, and non-load speed. Actually, the more expensive drills are geared down for slower speed. A valuable new development is the variable-speed control on several types of tools.

Of stationary tools, the bench saw is the more frequent purchase. Generally, a large table is essential for safety, wider range of work, greater versatility. A self-aligning fence, an accurately milled, solidly cast table, vernier adjustment gauges, tilting mandrel and efficient power chain are essential details.

Renting tools. One of the things that makes possible a more selective home workshop assortment is that you can rent almost any kind of tool, whenever you need it, at a moderate fee.

Suppose you have to climb to the roof to batten down a chimney flashing. This might require a 40-foot ladder, something that is hardly worth owning because of its cost, large space needed for storage, difficulty of handling.

It's so much better to rent the ladder for a day, get the job over with, and send it back so it's off your hands. The rental for an aluminum 40-foot in most areas runs less than $5 a day—while the purchase price could be around $50 to $60 for something that you might use perhaps once a year. If you do need a ladder for occasional use like cleaning roof gutters or painting trim, it might be better to have a 16 or 18 footer, then rent the additional extension section whenever you might have to climb all the way to the peak.

Even a small tool like a $\frac{9}{16}$-inch staple tacker, which is much more costly than the ordinary stapling gun, can be rented by the day for the infrequent times it would be useful.

Other tools in common demand at rental shops are floor sanders and edgers, wheelbarrows, cement mixing troughs, pneumatic hammers, routers, conduit-bending hickeys, electric planes, ceramic tile cutters and various jigs.

You'll be doing yourself a favor by stopping in at a well-stocked rental dealer to look over the items—just to see what's available when you want it.

Storing tools. Keep tools always in the same place. They will then be found instantly when needed and any missing tool, perhaps loaned to a neighbor, will be spotted. Plan the arrangement to take up minimum space and to protect the tools from needless damage. The best place is on a wall over the workbench with individual holders or brackets for each tool. You can do this most easily with perforated Pegboard wall panel, for which there are dozens of special wire fittings, including brackets to hold small shelves for planes, which should be placed always on their side to protect the blade edge. The Pegboard hangers come in loops, and other shapes to receive screwdrivers, chisels, pliers, levels, hammers and other items.

Chisels and files should have individual hangers and not be kept in drawers where the hardened steel would be chipped when another tool is tossed on top.

Auger bits can be kept in a long wood block, with a series of drilled holes to hold the bits in a procession of sizes so you can pick the right one automatically. Add small holes for center punches, countersets, picks and drift pins. Similarly, a single wood block can hold all your Allen wrenches, another block a set of wing drills.

Pipe clamps often are troublesome in storage, taking up considerable space and becoming entangled when placed against the wall.

If you have the space, put two parallel lengths of 2x4s on a wall about 2 feet apart, with cup-like spring clips so that each pipe clamp is held separately, off the floor. If you lack extra space, and use these clamps only occasionally, the best way is to remove the clamp heads and slip off the caps, so the pipes can be tied into a bundle and the clamp parts stored in a box or drawer.

Small instruments and tools, like cal-

For a workshop installation, choose an ordinary circular table saw or a radial arm saw like this one.

ipers, triangles, glass cutters, etc. are best kept in their original boxes in a drawer.

Another storage problem for some workshops is dampness, which rusts and corrodes fine tools. Where the condition is mild, a dehumidifier or even just a sack of copper sulphate crystals will keep the place sufficiently dry. Extreme conditions may require extra attention to avoid damage. Hand saws can be protected by keeping them in special damp-proof wrappers.

Milled steel surfaces, such as bench saw and drill press tables, vises, shears, hatchets, some wrenches and squares, can be protected with a thin coating of machine oil. One caution, before feeding wood stock into the saw, wipe off the oil coating from the blade with a solvent to avoid staining the wood. When the job is completed, be sure to restore the protective coating.

Watch for clearance. Power tools in a shop should be arranged for sufficient clearance to handle the stock, and so that one machine does not stand in the way of another. For example, if you're running an 8-foot board through a bench saw, you'll need a minimum clearance of 17 feet at the saw—at least 8 feet in front of the blade, 8 feet at the rear when the work comes through, and the space occupied by the raised blade itself, plus, of course, enough room for you to stand while feeding the stock. This would be a close squeeze even with a narrow board, but if you were to rip a 4-foot wide plywood panel you would need at least another foot clearance to get behind the panel. A suggestion is to locate your workbench, or another tool such as the table of a radial saw or drill press, at the same height as the bench saw to act as a support for the long end of the work as it comes through.

For the workshop with limited space, a good suggestion is to equip tool bases with locking-type casters so they can be moved around for maximum space utilization. In the case of the bench saw, it can be turned to either side for needed clearance when ripping or cross-cutting long work.

Specialized kits. One of the most effective additions to a homeworkshop is a tool carrier, so that when you have to do a chore anywhere in the house you can carry along all the tools and materials at one time. The carrier might have a partitioned drawer or small box containing many sizes of nails, screws, nuts and other things you might need without going back and forth a dozen times.

Taking this a step further for greater efficiency, you might set up several carriers, or tool boxes, each containing the complete assortment needed for any particular type of job. For example, if you have to fix a faucet, take the plumbing box which will have open end and Stillson wrenches, slip-joint channel lock pliers with toothed and smooth jaws (the latter for turning cap nuts without damaging the chrome finish). Also, the carrier will have your assortment of faucet washers, graphite packing and other supplies all in one place.

Similarly, for electrical work, a separate toolbox can contain your linesman's pliers, hacksaw, wire stripper, assortment of

The versatile electric drill with a hole cutter mounted in its chuck.

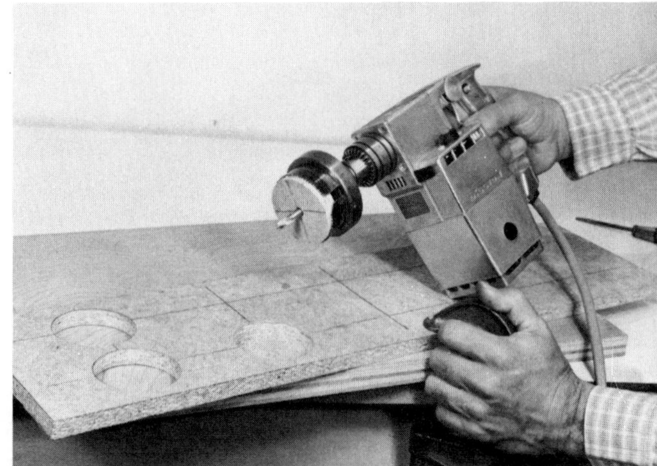

screwdrivers, threading and tapping dies, together with the supply of wire nuts, connectors, and splicing tapes.

This duplication of tools in boxes for different work won't add much to your basic workshop investment. All it really means is having some extra pliers and screwdrivers—the other items will be part of your regular assortment, only kept in special places for quick access.

Lending and borrowing. If you're in the habit of borrowing tools, or have neighbors who do the same, keep a little notebook handy and jot down whenever you let out a tool so you'll know where it is when you want it—and also know how long it's been away. It'll help prevent arguments on the block. Also, it's a good idea to punch your name or initials on all your tools so there's no chance of an argument as to whether it's yours.

▲ Two portable power tools that are important for many jobs, a saber saw (above), and a router. Shape, edge and trim with router. ▶

Combination tools. The trend towards combination tools has accelerated steadily. Not only does the combination tool mean less outlay, it also saves storage and allows the homeowner a wider range of work than he would have otherwise.

The Shopsmith is an outstanding example of versatility, performing satisfactorily as a bench saw with exceptional size capacity, a drill press, wood lathe, borer. Setup changes are made quickly with a minimum of effort.

The most recent, and remarkable development in combination tools is General Electric's triple play. This consists of a separate power unit that runs a ¼-inch or ⅜-inch drill, a saber saw, and a sander.

The tools may be purchased one at a time to build up the complete set. Start with the power unit and any one of the units you need at once, then add the two others as you go, together with the practical metal carrying case.

The biggest point to watch in any combination tool offer is that the changeover from one unit to another can be done quickly, without tiresome preparations and assembly. General Electric hit the jackpot with this one, as changeover takes less than a minute—all you do is loosen three screws

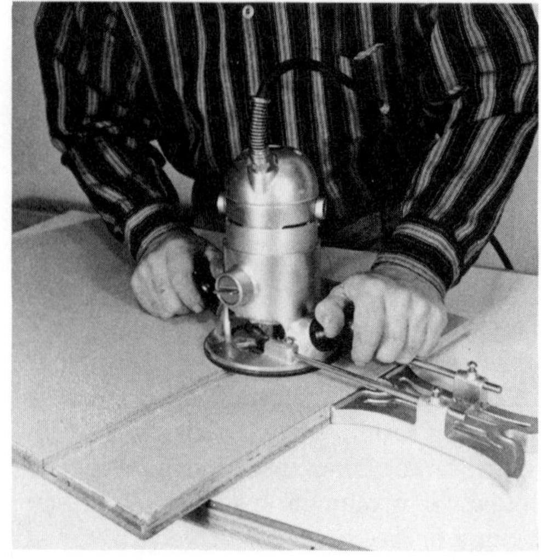

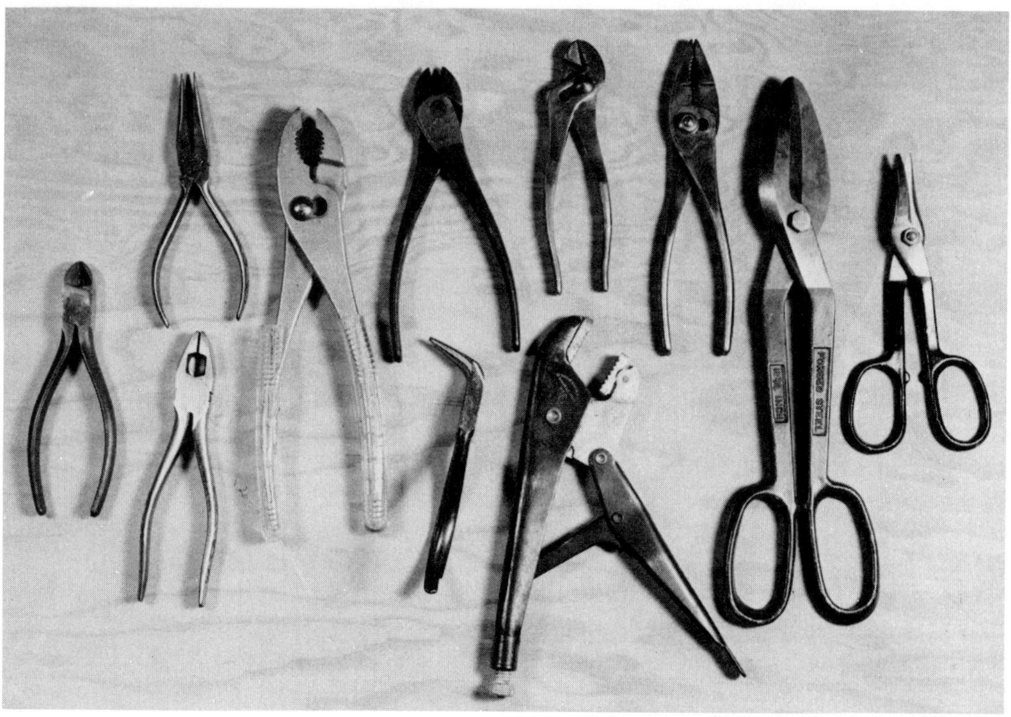

A sample of the variety of tools available to the home craftsman to snip or grip with.

in the power head (the screws remain there, can't be lost) separate the ⅓ h.p. power head and slip the splined drive onto the new unit. Tighten the three specially hardened screws and you're ready to go. It's that simple.

Both drill sizes come with Jacobs geared chuck. The ¼-inch drill has a no-load speed of 800 rpm, the ⅜-inch drill is geared down to 900 rpm, making it perfect for drilling masonry with carbide bits and for drilling heavier metal, which requires slower speeds to save the bits.

The saber saw has interesting features. Blades are easily attached by tightening a single set screw, and can be put in either of three positions, facing front or to either side which permits cutting to within ¼-inch of a wall. Tilt table in either direction permits angle cuts up to 45 degrees. Ripping and circle guide included.

The orbital sander, as with the saber saw, has permanently lubricated bronze bearings. The sand pad covers a 33-square-inch area.

In addition to the 3-unit power workshop, General Electric is producing a 7-inch circular saw powered by a 1⅓ h.p. motor, which can cut 2x4s at a 45-degree angle in less than a minute. Total saw weighs a comfortable 10 pounds. A slip-clutch provides a safety factor.

Other tool manufacturers also offer interesting and practical tool combinations with similar separate power units.

Don't pinch on pliers. Any pliers will do in a pinch, but having the right one for the job is smarter.

Many homeowners haven't gotten beyond that old standby—the dime store gas pliers. And it should be said right here that there's nothing wrong with it. In fact, the old slip-joint gas pliers still handles most of the ordinary everyday work, and does it fine. But we're not living in an ordinary everyday world. Just try reaching into an audio chassis with it to hold a wire for soldering, and see what happens. Or try repairing the catch on a string of pearls. The point is—a gas pliers has no point.

Pliers really boil down to a few family types, with some interesting individual variations. There's the long-nose, with side cutters, and an important variant here is the "bent-nose" very helpful in certain quarters! There's the diagonal cutter that's ideal for clipping cotter pins, baling wire and such jobs. The linesman's pliers is a standard for all electrical work, and the parallel head slip-joint (with both toothed and smooth jaws as mentioned previously) like the channellock, with long handles for a powerful grip that functions like an adjustable wrench.

Prices are low enough for you to assemble a basic assortment consisting of a pair each of gas pliers, needlenose, diagonals, linesman's or insulation skinner type, and the parallel slip-joint.

Choosing hand saws. One good carpenter's saw, a back saw, a hacksaw, and a coping saw should set you up for almost anything you might have to do. A small dovetail saw and a keyhole saw will round out a full complement for the real craftsman.

The carpenter's saw should be the crosscut type, unless you're likely to do considerable sawing and have no power tools, in which case a rip saw also would be helpful. What's the difference between them?

Rip saws have 5½ teeth to the inch, the teeth set closely and only 8 degrees from the perpendicular on the front, 52 degrees at the back, so that the teeth are faced almost square ahead like rows of chisels, each one chipping off a bit of wood as the saw moves along the grain.

In the cross-cut saw, there are from 8 to 12 teeth per inch, set more sharply and pointed so that rows of the teeth cut the grain fibers like knives, while the wide set forms a kerf to let the saw bite deeper. For ordinary work a 7- or 8-point cross-cut saw is recommended, though cutting of dry, well-seasoned lumber will go quicker with a 10- or 11-tooth saw.

Both cross-cut and rip saws are usually purchased in the 26-inch length. For some work, a short 20-inch saw would be more convenient. Saws should be wiped with a light oil for rust protection unless stored in a moisture-proof cabinet. Avoid finger marks which also tend to cause rust spots.

Back saws have a channel plate across the top for stiffening, come in 10- to 16-inch lengths, 13 points to the inch. Miter box saws are similar but longer, 26 or 28 inches, and have 11 points to the inch.

Keyhole saws are tapered almost to a point, often come in sets of three sizes. They are tempered for cutting thin metals and lead pipe, fretwork and similar inside cuts. They should not be used on gypsum board which requires the harder steel of hacksaw blades.

Coping saws are used for curves, shaping the ends of moldings to fit into corners, and making inside cuts for which the blade end can be inserted first into a drilled hole, then fastened into the handle to make the cut.

Saws must be kept "sharp" to work properly. Some meticulous craftsmen like to set and file saws themselves, and for this they need a jointer (which files down uneven teeth to uniform level), a plunger-type tooth setter, and a filing clamp for sharpening.

Hacksaw frames take blades of 8, 10 and 12-inch lengths. A sturdy, easily opened and tensioned frame is required. Most have a wing nut to tension the frame; others have tension levels that work very well and are more convenient.

The essential point is to select the proper blade for the job. Use 14-teeth-per-inch blades for cutting material one inch thick,

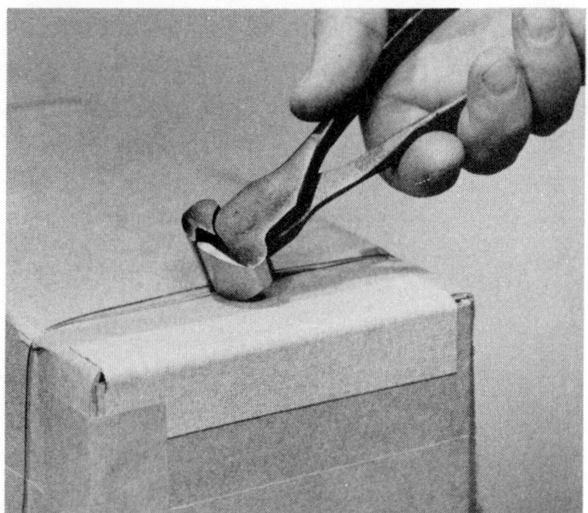

▲ *Nippers can be used to snip wire, pull nails and chip edges of ceramic tile for shaping.*

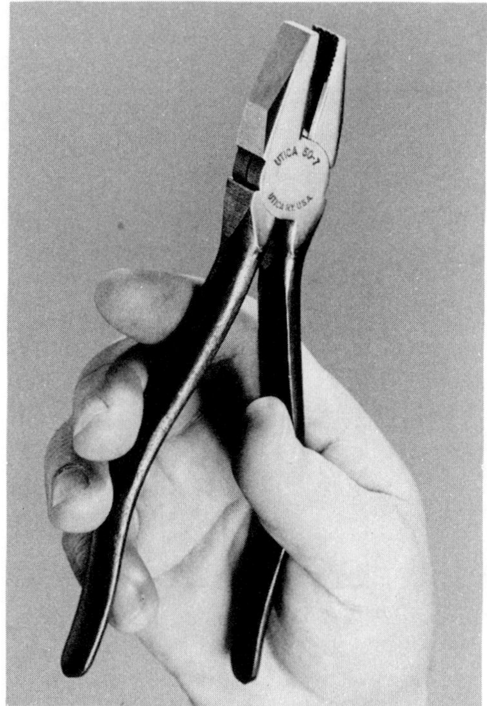

▲ *Linesman's pliers have wide jaw faces, wire-cutting slots, long handles.*

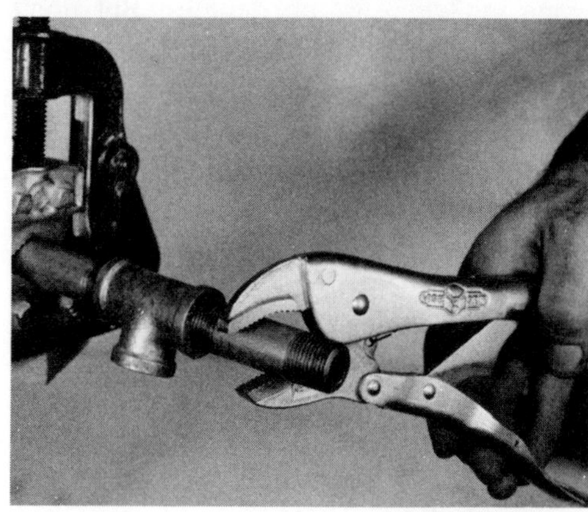

◀ *Lock-jaw pliers grip pipe or other round objects. On flat-sided objects, as bolt heads, jaws can be tightened and locked in position.*

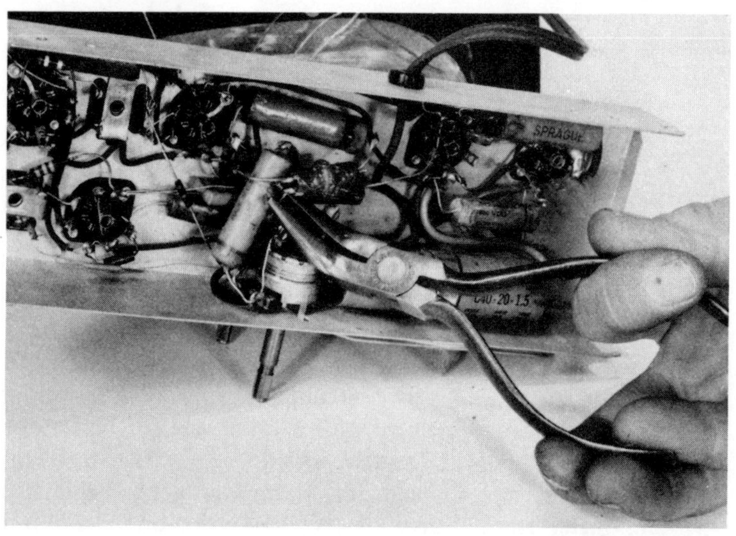

▶ *Bent-nose pliers have long jaws designed to get into hard-to-reach places.*

Use backsaw and miter box to make accurate angled cuts.

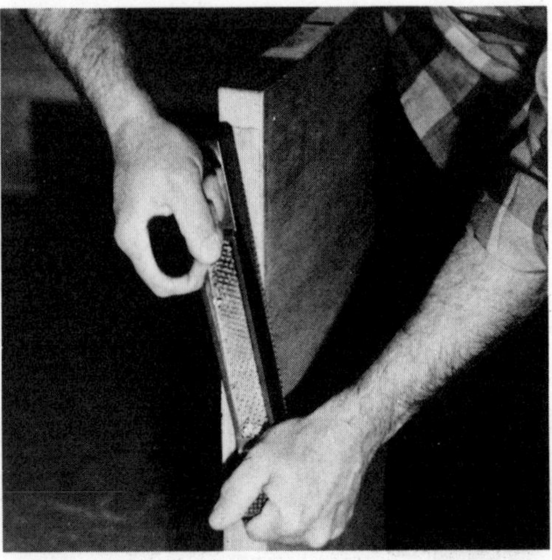

This versatile rasp has a sheet of steel grater-like material mounted on a holder. With other holders it can be formed into curves to work curved surfaces.

18 teeth for high-speed steel, aluminum, bronze, 1/4-inch to one inch thick. Use 24 teeth for steel and copper from 1/8-inch to 1/4-inch thickness; use 32 teeth for cutting any thin metal stock below 1/8-inch. In other words, the thicker the material, the fewer teeth per inch.

Two-man saws. And let's not forget those old buck saws that hung in the woodsheds when homes had a lot more land, fore and aft, than any development house today. Though largely replaced now by the gasoline-driven or electric-powered chain saw, there's many an occasion when a 6-foot cross-cut would come in handy. These saws, lightly arched in shape along the toothed edge, were the pride of Disston's saw works way back when. They're still available in 4 to 6-foot lengths, taper-ground so the back is 2 or 3 gauges thinner than the rest to slide clear in the kerf. One-man models come in 3 to 4½-foot lengths. But don't get one if you're not likely to use it often!

Files and rasps. The most amazing thing about files is their low price, after the painstaking shaping, cutting, annealing, sizing and hardening involved in their production. The two or three files you should own make a very small dent in the budget at a cost of 50 cents to $1 each. An 8-inch mill file and 6-inch round (or rattail) file will service most jobs around the house. If you want to round out the assortment, get a slim taper of 6-inch or 7-inch length, and also a half round which is available from 4- to 16-inch lengths, and in smooth, medium and bastard (coarse) cuts. For very delicate work there are fine, tiny jewelers' files in a dozen shapes. Get a file card and brush, too, to clean clogged gullets and keep the files in perfect cutting order. Be careful not to drop other tools or metals on a file, as it is quite brittle.

Wood and cabinet rasps come in flat, half-round and round shapes, with coarse or smooth cuts. The precision-cutting of power tools make for less reliance on the use of a rasp for fitting joints, but they do come in handy on occasion.

Scrapers. A cabinet scraper is a simple oblong of thin steel, usually 3x5 inches. An important tool in cabinet and veneer work, it gives a smoother finish than can be obtained by planing or even sanding. The scraper is honed for a perfectly square edge so that when drawn across a wood surface it trims off fine slivers, cleans off fibers. If you do any furniture building and refinishing, a cabinet scraper will help obtain a better job.

Numerous types of scrapers are made for other specific purposes. Wall scrapers, 3 to 4 inches wide, are used for removing old wallpaper and for spackling plaster surfaces. Similar are putty knives (narrower and much more flexible), and very wide wallboard blades that are excellent for taping gypsum wallboard joints.

Paint scrapers come in every possible form, from razor holders to carbide-edged bars, for that tedious chore of cleaning old surfaces. There's no recommendation here, you'll no doubt try several to find one that comes closest to suiting you.

Drills. Somehow, the nomenclature on drills left something out. The word drill means both the cutting instrument that forms the hole, and also the tool that provides the power.

Thus, you have the hand drills (often referred to as eggbeaters) and the electric drills. Also the drills themselves which may be twist drills, or wing drills with a pointed screw that starts the hole. In a separate category, but serving the same purpose, are the old-time brace and auger bits.

The hand drill has largely been replaced by the electric drill except for the very small-diameter holes in jewelry and model work. But the brace is still a standby because it can handle auger bits up to 1¼-inch size and make even larger holes with expansive cutters.

With either the hand or electric drill, you should have an assortment of twist drills. For woodworking, a set of carbon steel drills from ⅛- to ¼-inch will suffice. For more exacting work, particularly if you have a drill press, a more complete assort-

A variety of files. In the center is a wood rasp. Flat files are at left, round and triangular files at right.

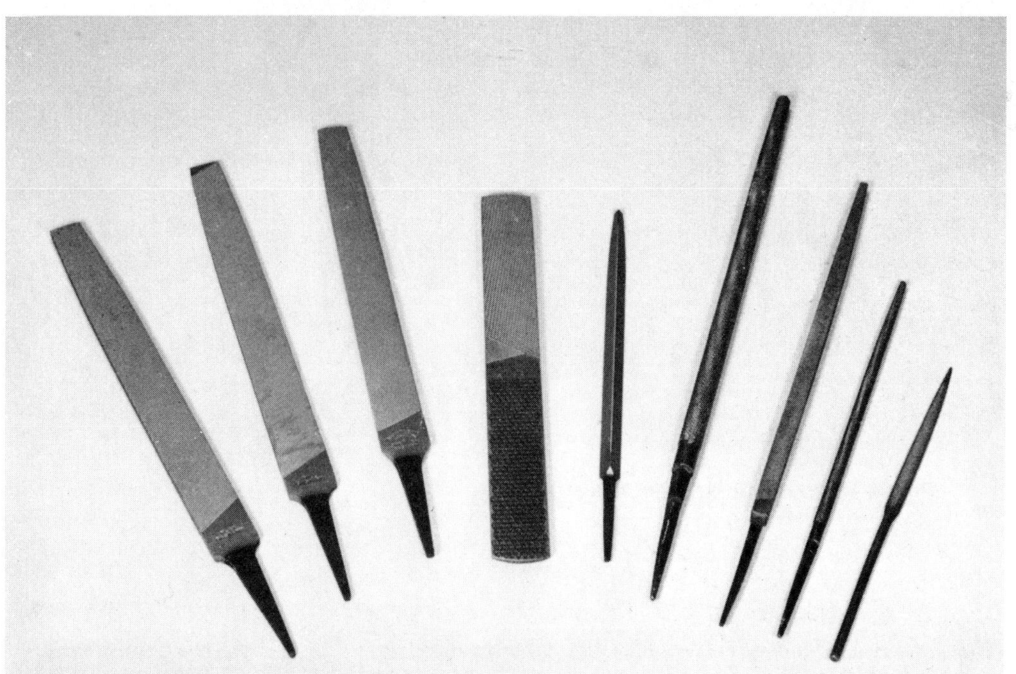

ment of high-speed drill sizes to ½-inch will be desirable. A drill box, of the size equal to your assortment, is necessary to keep the drills in order of their sizes and protect them from damage.

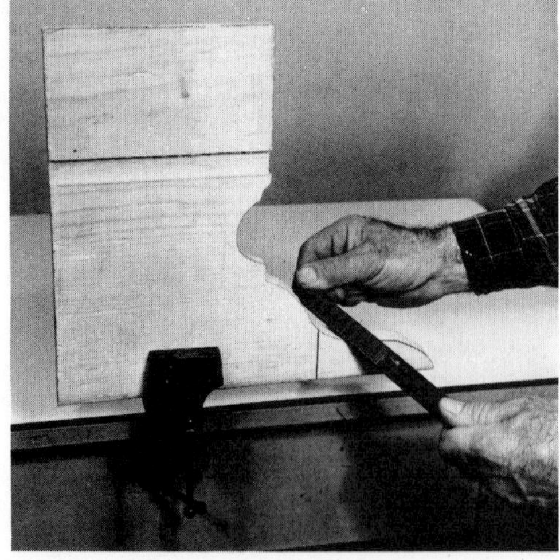

Shaping irregular work with a rasp.

Removing burrs and smoothing edges of cutouts in a brass plate.

A brace with the basic six sizes of bits is a standard item for any shop from the most elementary to the craftsman's den. Be sure the brace has an efficient alligator-type chuck, and reversible ratchet. A ball-bearing head is useful only when extensive work may be undertaken.

There are extra-long drills, 10- and 12-inch length for drilling right through a wall or floor, and extension rods to go even deeper, excellent for stringing bell and annunciator wires, or for connecting audio speakers around the house. A push drill is a handy small unit that stores its bit inside the head cap, for small work like drilling pilot holes in cabinets for hinges and locks. There is also a screwdriver blade that can be used with the drill and don't miss the great pilot hole drills that form a countersink recess in one operation.

Masonry drills. Percussion and rotary tools are the two means of drilling brick, plaster or concrete for masonry fasteners.

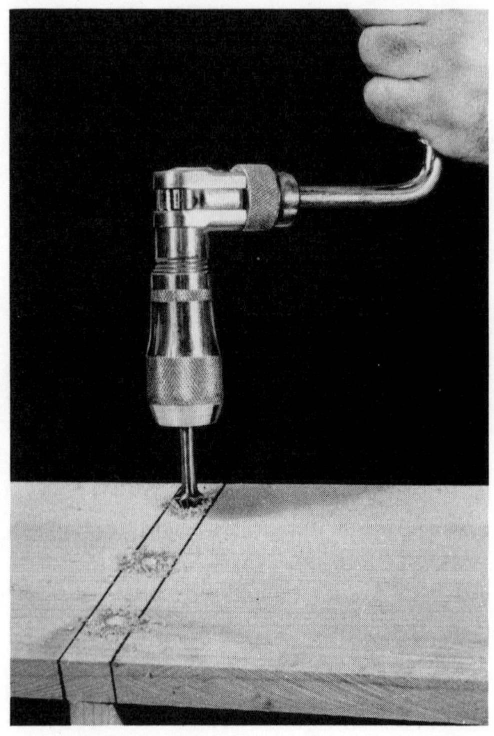

Using a countersink bit with a brace to cut recesses for screw heads.

Percussion tools consist of the star drill and the spiral drill. These are shaped and hardened, used with a rubber-capped handle. Repeated sharp taps with a heavy hammer will quickly bore into even hard concrete.

A helpful improvement on this system is Rawl's drill-hammer attachment, used in an ordinary ¼-inch electric drill. The spring-actuated action sounds like a muted machine-gun, but does the job in seconds without effort and permits better control of drilling.

With an electric drill, use carbide-tipped drills of the exact sizes specified with the various masonry anchors.

Levels and plumb bobs. A good many jobs you do around the house will call for the use of a level. Examples are putting up shelves, attaching any kind of wall brackets, setting up a washing machine or dryer, wall framing and masonry work. Less often used, but just as necessary is the primitive plumb bob.

What makes a level function? A short glass tube or vial filled with a non-freezing fluid is sealed at both ends, leaving just a small air bubble inside. The tube is set into a perfectly straight holder of either wood or aluminum. The glass tubing is marked with cross lines; when the bubble is exactly between these lines, the work is level.

A "proved glass" level has a tubing that is slightly curved for a high center position for the bubble. A "ground" glass is straight, but the inside barrel is shaped to form a high point at the center.

Levels are made of seasoned wood, aluminum, or steel. Some types have two and as many as six vials, so they may be viewed accurately from any position, and will continue to function even if one or two vials are broken. Vials placed across the ends serve for plumbing a wall, making two tools in one.

Some professional-type multi-vial levels are adjustable to any angle or degree of

▲ *Spirit level (see text) and plumb bob are essential for keeping work straight and true.* ▼

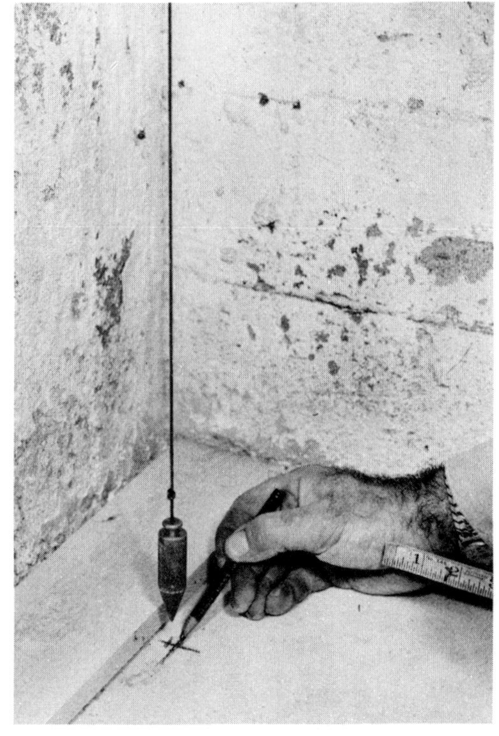

pitch per foot, very handy for masonry work and other jobs.

Levels come in many lengths, 4 inches to 6 feet. Use the longest level convenient on any work for accuracy and easy sighting.

Line levels are small metal tubes with catches that grip a string or line which is held taut, to determine grades and pitch in foundation, slab and brick work. Other interesting types are camera levels, pocket-size torpedo levels, and level-sights to obtain a straight run of fencing and walls.

The average home shop should have a wood or aluminum carpenter's level 18-inches long, and perhaps a pocket-size one.

Any simple plumb bob will serve average needs. A 5- or 8-ounce pointed bob costs very little.

Screwdrivers. Probably no other tool is as simple in its concept, yet so important, as a screwdriver. Just a metal shaft, flattened and filed square at one end, a handle on the other end.

Yet a lot goes into making the screwdriver as dependable and long-lasting as it is. The bar must be strong enough to withstand strains and remain perfectly straight —a bent screwdriver is worthless. The blade must be correctly tapered, forged and tempered so it won't chip at the corners, the tip ground square to hold in the screw slot. Handles may be wood, rubber or plastic, shaped for a good and comfortable grip and securely fastened to the bar. A screwdriver with a loose handle should be discarded before it causes a painful injury.

Simple as it is in design, there are probably as many varieties of screwdrivers as any other tool. First comes the range of sizes, from the tiniest jewelers precision drivers to massive square bars that can be given extra torque with an open end wrench.

There are long and thin drivers for radio work, short and thin drivers for accurate turning of the oval screws in cabinet hinges.

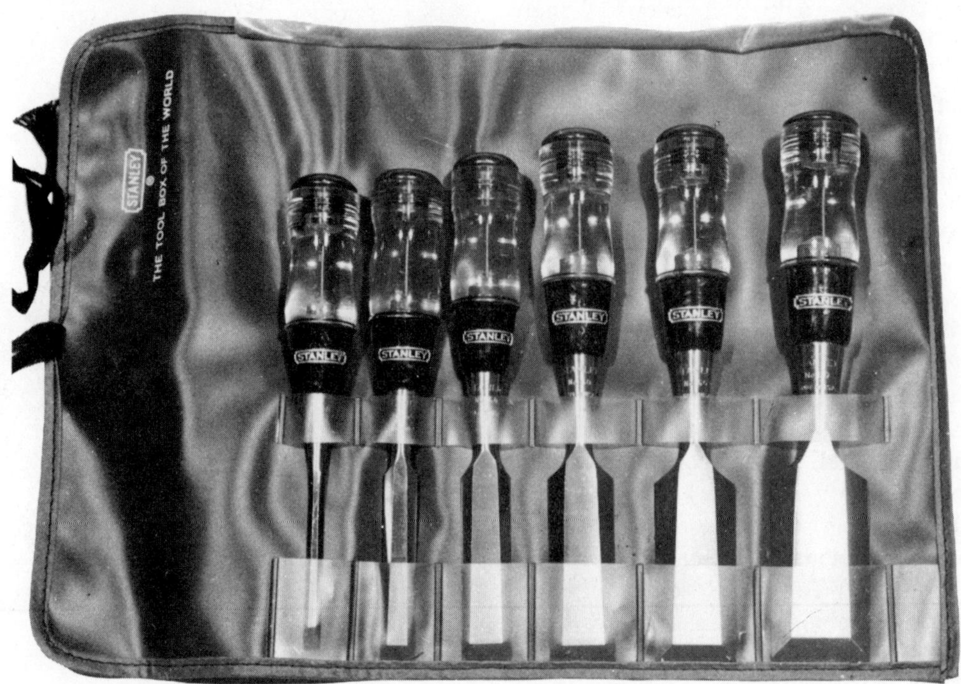

▲ *Wood chisels come in widths up to 1-1/2 inches in 1/4-inch steps.*

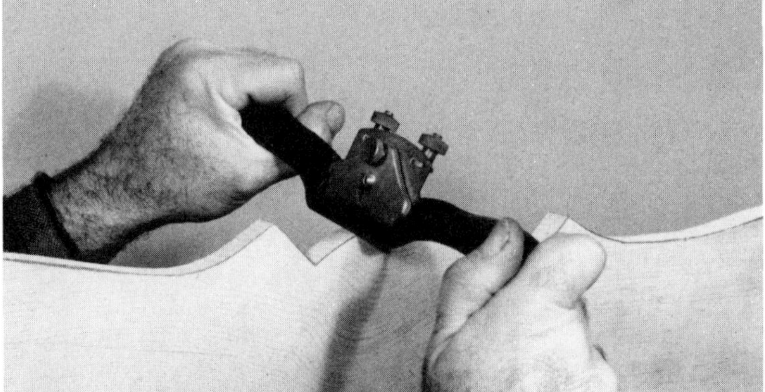

Smoothing and trimming an irregular shape with a spoke shave.

"Stubby" screwdrivers come less than three inches overall to fit close quarters, while offset screwdrivers work in even more difficult locations.

There are ratchet drivers of many types including a spring-action, push-type driver. If you're looking for speed when there are a lot of screws to turn (building a small boat takes hundreds of screws), you can use a clutch-type driver as an accessory with your electric drill.

There are also screwdriver bits that fit into a drill brace, and into offset ratchet drivers that need only an inch or so of clearance. A popular novelty item is a "combination" hollow tool holding a half-dozen and more screwdrivers of progressively smaller sizes, each fitting into the other.

In recent years, the Phillips cross-slot screws have become more widely used, requiring that you have at least two of these drivers.

Screwdrivers are used so frequently around the home that a goodly supply is needed so they can be kept in several places, in addition to the workbench supply.

Chisels. Chisels are an essential component of every toolbox. They are used for

Spoon chisel lifts splinter for invisible nailing. Nail is driven through molding beneath splinter. Then, splinter is glued back in place over nailhead.

Leveling a board with a smoothing plane.

cutting mortises, squaring drilled sections, scraping dado grooves, tapering and fitting cabinet joints, recessing door latch plates and other jobs.

In addition to the standard flat type, which comes in blade widths up to 1½ inches in ¼-inch steps, there are wood-

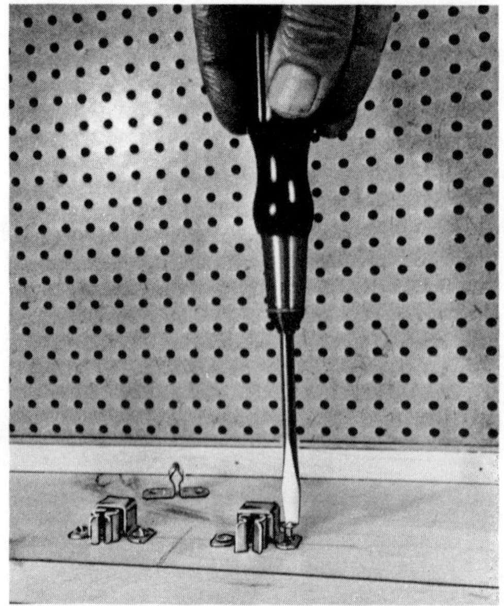

To prevent burring of the screw slot, always choose a screw driver the correct size for the screw—whether using an ordinary screw driver (left), a hefty one with a square shank . . .

. . . or one with a screw holding spring clip.

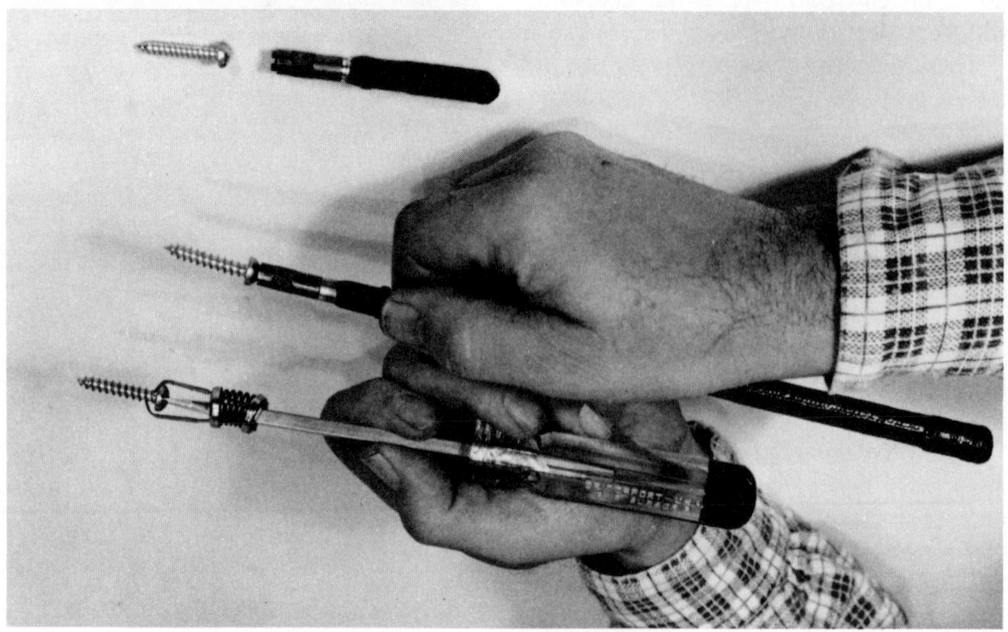

carving chisels of many shapes, wide-blade glazier's chisels that make quicker work of cleaning out old putty (and are strong enough for use to ease up stuck windows) and even wider floor chisels beveled on both sides of the tip to cut through the tongues in flooring boards. Another group is known as turning chisels for use with a wood lathe to cut roundwork.

Cold chisels are specially tempered for cutting brick, cement blocks, other hard surfaces, come in a wide assortment of lengths and blade widths. Machinists chisels come in handy on many metal-working and auto repair jobs—an example is splitting a rusted stud nut that can't be turned. Available in many sizes.

Planes. The main types of planes are:

Block plane, for cutting across the grain; blade adjusts at ends, sides, throat. About 7 inches long.

Smooth plane cuts along the grain, obtains a very smooth surface, runs about 7 to 10 inches long.

Jointer or fore plane, 18 to 24 inches, for long work such as the edge of a board. Length aids obtaining level surface.

Modelmaker's plane is short, about 3½ inches, has 1-inch wide blade.

Rabbet plane has open sides, so blade cuts right up to the edge for weatherstripping work, and to cut notches, rabbets, grooves. Plane has adjustable fence for controlling width of cut.

Circular plane has rounded bottom, adjustable to cut concave and convex surfaces. Blades can be tilted in either direction.

Scrub plane cuts fast to remove quantity of wood, for leveling surfaces, trimming boards to size. Not for smoothing.

Beading plane takes a large assortment of shaped cutters to form picture frame and decorative moldings and similar purposes.

For the average workshop, a pair of bench planes consisting of a block and smoother plane will do for around-the-house purposes. Any of the other types are worth getting when needed for a particular job.

Spoke shaves are in the category of planes. They are held in both hands by the side handles, and pulled along the work, rather than pushed as is a plane.

Wrenches. There are so many types of wrenches they've almost run out of terms for describing them—and no doubt new ones will come along to cope with old problems and handle the new types of hardware.

Following are the most commonly used types with suggestions for your personal assortment.

Adjustable (including monkey wrenches), from light to heavy weights, with side, end and offset jaws. Can be fitted to any size nut or cap up to 2 inches. Because the fit is not exact, adjustable wrenches may slip and round off the nut. Better-quality adjustables with closely-matched gears do the better job.

Open-end wrenches with a different size at each end, in every possible size for exact match. The ⅜-, ½-, 9⁄16- and ¾-inch are basic sizes, should be in every tool chest.

Socket wrenches and box wrenches give assured grip, are essential for auto and machinist work. Sets available for various purposes. Some socket wrenches are fitted with handles; others are used with separate ratchet handles, cross-bars, speedy brace, and other devices for meeting difficult conditions.

Deep sockets, used for certain in-the-wall faucets and for auto spark plugs.

Stillson (pipe) wrenches have spring-tension jaw, deep notches to grip rounded surfaces. Essential for plumbing work. Own a large (14-inch) and small (8-inch) one.

Basin wrench has long bar to fit up behind wall basins, with swivel jaw, cross-bar at bottom for turning.

Wide-mouth locknut wrench opens to 3 inches, for slip nuts on sink, traps, etc.

Socket chain wrench grips hex nuts and round surfaces, self-adjusting to any opening. Has long pull handle. Snap wrench serves the same purpose, but has smooth surface to avoid damaging chromed fixtures.

Allen wrench fits internal hex openings as in set screws. All sizes to ¾-inch available.

Pipe and tube cutters. Pipe and conduit cutters have alloy steel cutting wheel which revolves around the pipe, cutting gradually as threaded handle is tightened. Does neat job, quickly, though cutter burrs inside of pipe.

The smaller copper tubing cutter clamps around the work, has a thin cutting wheel that goes through without distorting the tubing.

Pipe also can be cut with a hacksaw, but the ends will not be square across.

Hammers. A good-quality carpenter's claw hammer is so versatile that it will do 95% of the hammer work around the house. However, for easier and more efficient work, you might want to get several special-purpose hammers.

Claw hammer, the basic type, recommended size, 16 ounce head, 13-inch length, and of good standard make which is properly tempered, perfectly balanced, with selected and well-fitted hickory handle.

Machinist hammer in the 8- or 12-ounce weight, has round peen head.

Plastic, wood or rubber mallets for caulking boats, forming soft metals, jointing cabinets and similar work where a resilient head is desirable to avoid marring surfaces.

Bricklayer's hammer for aligning brickwork, slate, stones. Has long, tapered head that serves as a lever.

Stone hammers have one beveled and sharpened edge for chipping stone, the other square for tamping.

Sledge with 4-pound head is handy for all kinds of heavy work. Long-handle sledge is fine for breaking sidewalk slabs, splitting logs (with wedges) and similar work.

Tack hammers, also for upholstery work, long and narrow heads, some of magnetic steel for holding tacks.

Auto fender hammers, in dozens of shapes, used with forged backing blocks, or dollies, curved or rounded surface.

Hatchets. Hatchets and axes are in this group too. A small half-hatchet (one cutting edge) will be valuable to homeowners for many tasks, both in the workshop and grounds, to shape stakes, clear small trees, trim framing studs, split fireplace wood. For the camper and hunter, there's a special type. Hatchets are sharp, can be dangerous if left lying around. Set up a special place with a leather holster to protect it. For the rural and suburban dweller, a good axe is still handy around the house.

Squares. A carpenters square is a simple tool with the "built-in" knowledge of a slide rule. Mostly it's used for checking the alignment of work, whether it's a small cabinet or bookshelves, but the square also gives information needed for cutting rafter angles, lengths of braces, board measures, etc. A simple but practical square two-feet long with a one-foot tongue will serve your purpose unless you go in for building a den and other construction jobs, in which case you'd want a carpenter's square.

Trysquares and miter squares are smaller, easier to handle. Some have a true 45-degree fitting at the handle for testing miter joints.

Combination squares have sliding steel blades, plus miter gauge and spirit level. They can be used readily as a depth gauge, marking gauge, miter square, plumb and level, and as a straight edge (by removing the blade).

In the category also are various angle dividers, used mostly by carpenters on building jobs and by cabinetmakers for marking precise angles in fitted work.

Marking gauges are of wood or metal,

have a block-mounted marking pin that slides on a calibrated bar to measure off desired distance. A thumb screw in the block locks it at any position.

A special tool is a butt gauge used for laying out the hinge mortises on doors and their castings, also positions of latch plates. Assures accurate alignment of hinges, saves time.

A companion tool is the butt marker, like a rectangular chisel. Place the marker on the hinge position and strike it with a hammer. The chisel-like edges cut the outline of the mortise which then can be neatly cleaned out with a chisel.

Awls, punches, nailsets. A good-quality scratch awl, similar to an ice pick, is essential in every tool collection from the most elementary to advanced craftsman. It is used to start screw holes, especially for hinge screws (failure to get exact center can force the hinge out of alignment), cup hooks, and similar work. It can mark guide lines on metal for sawing, and is used to spread the center of Rawl fiber masonry plugs before the anchor screw is turned in, and any other work requiring a sharp point.

The awl should be of top quality, properly tapered and tempered.

A center-finder combines the principle of a punch and an awl. It is a metal rod, beveled on one end to fit the countersink of a hinge leaf. The center has a pointed blade, retracted by a spring. When tapped, the blade point enters the center, starting the screw hole in the wood.

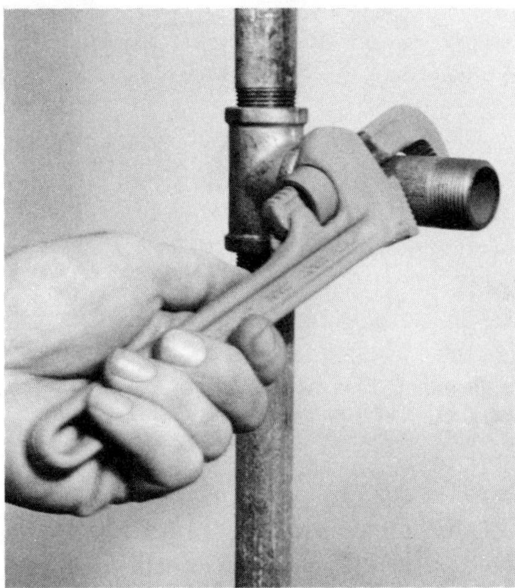

Both the Stillson wrench (above) and the chain wrench (left) tighten their grips around pipe, or round or irregular shapes, as pressure is increased.

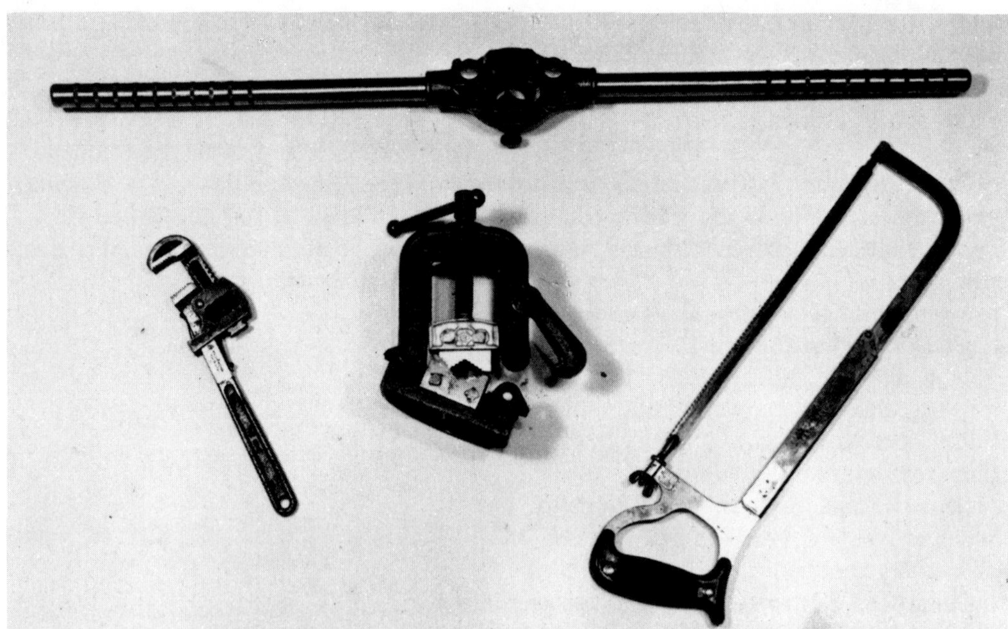

▲ *Plumbing tools include holder for pipe thread die (top) and (bottom left to right), a Stillson wrench, pipe vise and hacksaw.*

Other center punches are used to locate the precise drill point in metal. Sizes are based on the diameter of the tip. Nailsets range in size from $\frac{1}{32}$ to $\frac{1}{8}$-inch. Use the size roughly equal to that of the brad head.

Soldering irons and torches. An instantaneous soldering gun is perfect for all radio, electronic, jewelry, electric wiring, and other light work. The Weller gun is justly famous for its dependability, high capacity. Comes with several tips in different shapes for special purposes. The bigger models also have tiny "headlights," an invaluable feature.

For heavy soldering, like copper roof gutters and for brazing, the old-type soldering "iron" that is heated on a gas stove, or a heavy-duty electric iron of over 250 watts is still needed. Small soldering irons with variable tips are used for continuous assembly work.

Propane torches are the thing for plumbing, electrical and dozens of other purposes like thawing frozen pipe. Easy to use, lights up in a second. Flame is adjustable. Complete torch sets include flame spreader, soldering tips, burner hood, paint scraper attachment. Replacement gas cylinders are available.

Gasoline blow torches are used now mostly by professional plumbers and other trades that need a continuous flame. Small alcohol torches are used in many crafts, such as cabinet finishers. Alcohol lamps also are still common, used for melting shellac sticks in furniture repair work, and for hobbyists interested in chemistry, plastic modeling, etc.

Clamps and vises. A decent supply of both pipe and C clamps is a must for your workshop. You can't have too many, for cabinet making, chair repair and other work.

Pipe clamps are vital for gluing. They come with separate cap and jaw faces, are used with a length of $\frac{3}{4}$-inch pipe threaded at one end. Old iron pipe, provided it is straight, can be used. The cap is threaded inside, turns on the pipe threads; the jaw face slips on the other end of the pipe, has a ratchet clutch that slides for quick closing of the clamp. A screw handle in the cap applies pressure.

Bar clamps are complete units, easier to use, dependable. The tail jaw is gripped at notches along the bar. Lengths run to six feet.

C clamp (or carriage clamps) of malleable iron are measured by the throat depth, from 1 to 8 inches.

Handscrews with maple jaws are splendid on wood cabinet jobs, favored by professionals. Sizes to 10-inch jaws, but quite expensive.

Bench clamps attach to a straight and rigid surface such as a workbench top, handle long work conveniently.

Hinged clamps by Jorgensen are for permanent mounting on workbenches, swing down out of the way when not in use, but always available for setups.

The Jorgensen line also includes special-purpose types like rounded body clamps for clearance around the work, strap clamps that fit any irregularly shaped surface, spring clamps, miter clamps.

If you need any special kind or shape of clamp for a chore, just look around the stores and you're bound to spot one that will do the trick.

Bench vises vary in size and strength. A solidly-built vise with a 3½-inch jaw will do for average use, though a 4¼-inch or even 5-inch opening may be desirable if heavy work is done. Look for features like

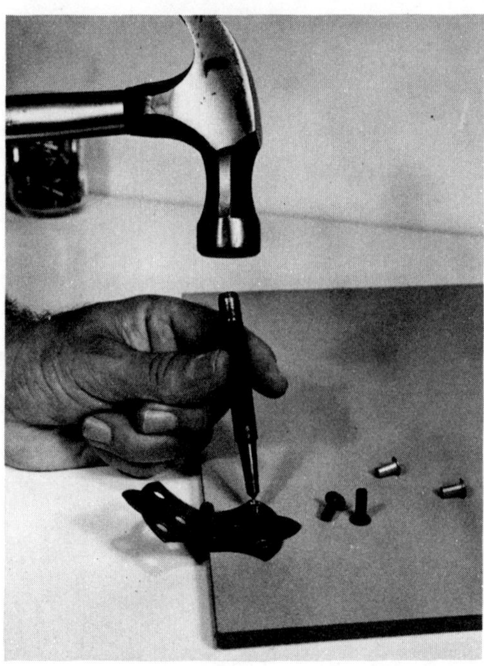

Use a punch to peen hollow rivets.

Few woodworking jobs can be completed without the use of a try-square to align, mark and measure.

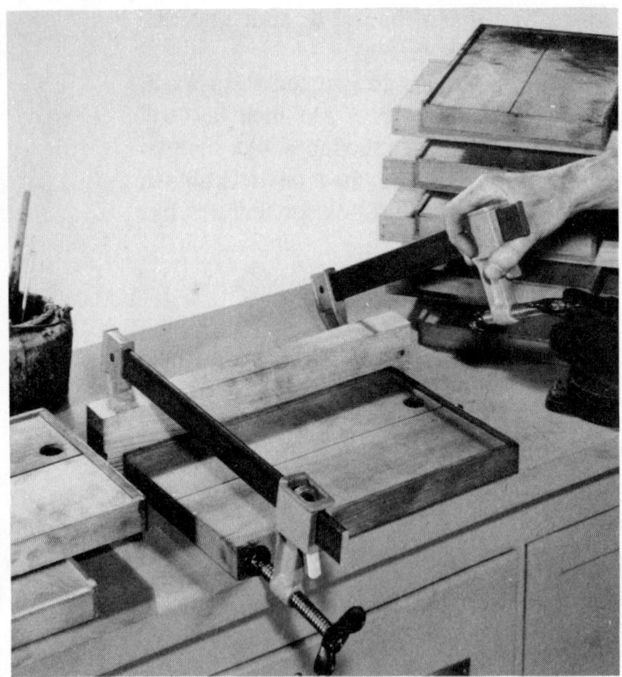

Bar clamps come in a variety of lengths.

a swivel base, enabling you to turn the vise to any direction for work clearance or easier access, replaceable steel jaw faces, a pair of pipe jaws under the regular jaws to hold round objects, an anvil and horn for hammering and shaping metals, and a hefty handle.

A woodworker's vise is a worthwhile addition to any bench, has large flat jaws that hold boards for planing, sawing, etc.

A portable vise, with attachment clamp, is useful when doing work away from the workshop. Fastens easily to doors, etc.

Drill-press vises come in many types, such as angle vise adjustable to 90 degrees, squared vise, and various work holders with jaws for tapered and irregular shapes. In this category, too, are adjustable hold-downs for locking work in position on the drill-press table.

A small scissors clamp, with finger grips and serrated jaws, holds small parts securely while doing precision assembling, soldering, etc. Tweezers also are in this group, often are of great help when working with small items.

Staplers. A stapling gun is useful for light upholstery work—such as recovering kitchen chairs and attaching slipcovers—and generally outmodes the use of tacks.

The popular-priced models handle staples of 5⁄16-inch leg length. More powerful compression models, needed for such work as installing ceiling tiles and other jobs requiring staples of ½-inch to 9⁄16-inch leg length, are more expensive.

Masonry tools. Sidewalk repairs, brickwork pointing, concrete patio slabs, flagstone laying, and other masonry jobs are quite routine in the modern home. The tools listed are used for various types of work, but only a few may be necessary for your particular needs.

Brick trowel pointed, is one of the basic masonry tools, used not only for laying bricks but also to apply and fill cement into forms and repair openings.

Patching trowel has 1¾-inch blade, used for plaster as well as cement, has blunt front edge.

Hawk is a sort of tray with handle underneath to hold mortar and plaster for application.

Square trowel of spring steel blade, for

leveling and smoothing concrete or plaster.

Groover cuts ⅜-inch wide groove in sidewalk, panels, stucco walls, etc.

Wood float is used for "working out" and smoothing concrete surface.

Rub brick dresses and smooths tile, marble, concrete. Selection of 60, 80, 120 and 150-grit.

Outside and inside corner tools with handles, for clean squaring of concrete corners.

Brick jointer is a narrower bent steel bar for packing mortar between brick and finishing off the joint.

Tuck pointing trowel, narrow with handle, for brick mortar repairs.

Plumbing tools. Plumbing work ranges all the way from changing a faucet washer —about as simple a little job as you'll have to do around the house—to complex projects like extending a new water line or drain. So the tools you'll keep on hand certainly won't attempt to cover more than the few that let you handle properly the everyday chores plus handling any emergency.

Stillson wrenches. A small Stillson will serve most purposes, but for any pipe work you'll need two wrenches to ease the strain on the lines. Make the second Stillson a really large one that can be used to "break" tight pipe joints. A sprocket chain wrench will do as a substitute.

Gas pliers, large slip-joint channellock without teeth.

Adjustable wrench, side of offset jaws. Also, open end or box wrenches, sizes ½, 5⁄16, ⅝, 11⁄16 and ¾ inches.

Pipe cutter and reamer, for ½- or ¾-inch pipe (depending on the size in your home).

Pipe threader of required size.

Copper tubing cutter and flaring tool.

Propane torch for sweat soldering of copper tubing.

Special-purpose tools. Hose clamp pliers

Drill press angle vise is designed to hold almost any stock at any angle for drilling.

One of many uses of the blow torch: softening old paint for scraping.

opens the high-tension spring wire used as hose clamps on cars, washing machines and dishwashers.

Eyelet pliers punches holes in cloth, plastic sheeting, canvas, then crimps grommets or eyelets for tear-proof lacings.

Pop rivet tool, for "blind" riveting when you can't get back up with ordinary peen

TOOLS TO FILL A TOOLBOX OR BASEMENT SHOP

Group 1. Minimum Assortment		
Claw Hammer	6-foot rule or tape	Putty knife
Screwdrivers—small and medium	Small block plane	Scratch awl
Slip pliers		
Group 2. Handy Apartment Tenant		
Screwdrivers—large, small, Phillips	Spirit level and plumb bob	6-foot rule or tape measure
Claw hammer	Wood chisel	Scratch awl
Hand or 1/4" electric drill	Pliers—slip-joint, needle-nose, wire stripper	Putty knife
Coping saw		
Group 3. Homeowner Doing Minimum Maintenance		
All the tools in Group 2	Caulking gun with cartridges	Trysquare
Carpenter's saw	Set of 6 wood chisels	Scraper
Stillson and monkey wrench	Brace and bits	Wall knife
Crowbar or pinch bar		
Group 4. The Ship-Shape Homeowner		
Screwdrivers—full sets including Phillips	Paint brushes	Crowbar or pinch bar
Hammers—claw and tack	Electric sander	Putty knife, wall knife, scrapers
Pliers—slip-joint, needle-nose and wire stripper	Miter box and back saw	Set of deep socket wrenches (spark plug type)
Wrenches—2 Stillsons, adjustable, open end	Trysquare; large square	Stapling gun
Wood chisels—full set	2 Pipe clamps	Caulking gun
Block plane	2 C-clamps	A good workbench with vise
Electric 1/4" drill, set of bits and carbide #10 size	Folding rule and tape	2 Nailsets, center punch
Carpenter's saw, hacksaw, keyhole saw	Plumb bob and spirit level	Ladder
Electric jig saw	Soldering gun	Propane torch
Group 5. The Project Builder		
All the tools in Group 4	Spoke shave	Masonry drills or pneumatic hammer
Bench saw or radial saw	Carpenter's level and line level	Wood vise and machinist's vise
Drill press	Oil stone	Coping saw
6 or 8 pipe clamps and C-clamps	Grindstone and buffing wheel	Ladder
Router	Block plane and jack plane	Cement trowel
Doweling jig	Sledge hammer, hatchet	

Group 6. Craftsman and Hobbyist

Screwdrivers (full sets)	Scratch awl	Band saw or jig saw
Hammers—claw, machinist's, tack and sledge	Center punches, nailsets	Jointer
Carpenter's saw, keyhole saw, hacksaw, dovetail saw	Levels, plumb bob	Portable saber saw
Set of files	Block and jack planes	Electric ⅜″ drill
Set of wood chisels	Assortment of clamps	Portable circular saw
2 cold chisels	Doweling jig	Router
Shovels, wheelbarrow	Miter box and back saw	Belt and disc sander
Masonry drills	Scrapers, paint brushes	Portable orbital sander
Trysquare and large square	Wallboard and hooked knives	Router with edge trimmer
Rulers, tapes, calipers	Tinsmith shears	Lathe
Soldering gun	Oil stone	Electric planer
Stapling gun	Grindstone	A good workbench with machinist's vise, plane stops, wood vise
Caulking gun	Bench saw	Ladders
Wrenches—box, open, socket	Radial saw	Propane torch
Pliers—slip, linesman's, needle, diagonal, wire stripper	Drill press	

rivets. Pop tool pulls a hardened, specially shaped pin through the back of the rivet until it is squeezed tight, then snaps off the pin.

Copper tubing benders. Coil springs of exact size slip over tubing, prevent kinking when tube is bent.

Retriever tool. Ever drop a small part deep down in an appliance or car and can't reach it? The pickup tool is a long tube with spring steel fingers that are pushed out and allowed to grasp the part, then retracted to hold it tightly.

Edger for plastic laminates. Adjustable jig with carbide cutter, used with a router, trims overlap edge for perfect corner joint. Used to make self-edged plastic tabletops and kitchen counters. Forms clean, uniform line when two sides join.

Cornering tool is curved metal bar, with beveled, elliptical-shaped holes at each end, used for rounding sharp edges on shelves, furniture, patterns.

Doweling jig clamps on both parts of work, has collars for drilling guide. Single adjustment assures dowel holes will match.

Stencil paint roller made of rubber or plastic with embossed design, gives interesting wallpaper effect right on painted walls. Used with contrasting colors.

Asphalt tile cutter has platform with long bar, cuts tile to exact size like a paper cutter.

Flaring tool shapes end of copper tubing for tight seal in flare-type fitting.

Plank rods for reinforcing timbers, wood planks. Steel rod 10 or 12 inches long has a drill point, is used with centering guide and ordinary electric drill, into side of plank. Projecting end of rod is bent and hammered into the wood. R.T.

See also: BICYCLES; BRICKWORK; CONCRETE; DOORS; DRAINS; ELECTRICAL, HOME; ENGINE; FAUCETS; GLAZING; HOME IMPROVEMENT; LOCKS; PAINTING, HOUSE; ROOFS; SCREENS AND STORM WINDOWS; TILE, CERAMIC; TOILET; VALVES.

Servicing Your Car's Automatic Transmission

A trip to an automatic transmission shop is always expensive. You can avoid one by servicing two simple parts with inexpensive tools. All it takes is about an hour's work every 12,000 miles

THERE ARE THOUSANDS of automatic transmission specialty shops throughout the country, very busily rebuilding automatics at about $300 each. By giving your automatic some very simple care—a form of tune-up—you can greatly extend the life of your unit and hopefully avoid an overhaul for the life of the car.

Nearly 80 percent of the automatic transmissions on late-model cars have replaceable oil filters. More than 75 percent have vacuum devices—called modulators—that play a major part in the shift quality of the transmission. These two items, along with transmission oil, are the things that you can attend to, to keep your automatic in good condition.

The transmission tuneup should be performed at 24,000 miles, and once a year thereafter or 12,000 miles, whichever comes first.

The only tools you will need are ordinary hand tools, a good jack, a pair of safety stands and on Ford products, an inexpensive special wrench for the vacuum modulator.

You can buy a transmission oil filter from most parts houses, as independent filter manufacturers market them. The same is true for vacuum modulators.

General Motors automatics have replaceable filters and vacuum modulators. Ford products have replaceable vacuum modulators and one transmission has a replaceable filter (the C-4 unit). Others have cleanable screens. Chrysler products have replaceable filters, but use mechanical linkage instead of vacuum modulators. American Motors cars have modulators and cleanable screens.

Start the job by dropping the transmission oil pan, which is held by screws. If the transmission has a replaceable filter, the filter container also will have a pan gasket. If the transmission merely has a cleanable screen, you should buy a replacement gasket before you start the job. (One cautionary note: because there is no drain plug in the oil pan, some care is necessary to avoid

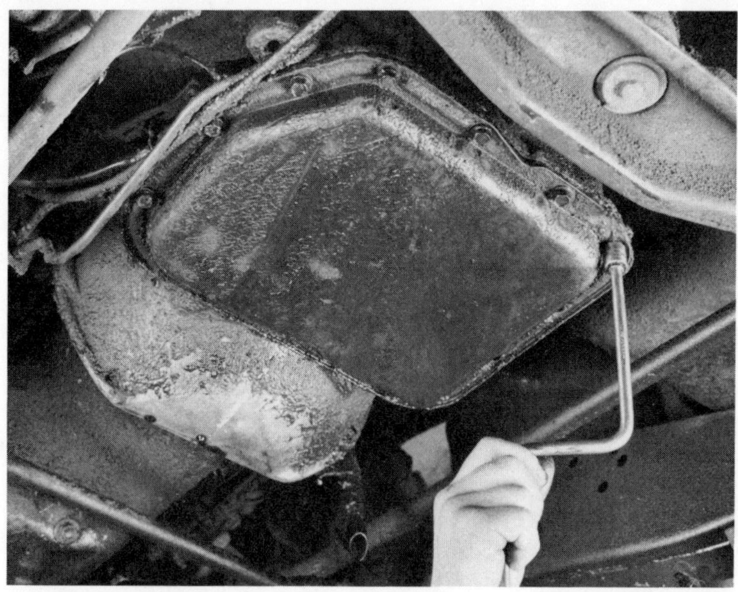

Job of installing a replacement transmission filter starts with removal of oil pan bolts. Remove rear bolts and work crisscross toward front, so pan will tilt down from the back and drain into the drain pan.

Pan will contain bits and pieces of gasket, sludge and metal shavings. Clean pan thoroughly with solvent. Scrape old gasket off.

Old filter sits just under transmission valve body. It will be held by screws (as shown), or perhaps by clips.

Once screws or clips are disengaged, pull old filter straight down. If there is a connecting pipe, it will come too. If an O-ring is used on pipe, make sure that it comes out with it.

Install new filter. If there is a connecting pipe with O-ring, the new assembly will have it.

If any parts of old oil pan gasket stuck to transmission, scrape off with gasket scraper or putty knife. Do not use screwdriver as it could damage the gasket surface of transmission, which probably is aluminum and easily scored.

spilling oil all over the place when you drop the pan.)

Get the largest pan you can find and put it directly under the transmission oil pan. Undo the rear pan bolts first and then work evenly toward the front so the pan will tilt slightly down from the rear, allowing much of the oil to spill out from there, into your drain pan. (If the transmission oil pan gasket sticks to both pan and transmission, you'll have to free it.) About three quarts of oil will come out.

Remove old filter. With the pan off, the filter is readily accessible. On most cars, it is retained by a few screws. Remove them and pull the filter straight down.

On a few cars, the filter is held by a clip, which either must be removed or twisted aside for filter removal.

Many filter assemblies have an O-ring on the neck that connects the filter to an oil tube or gallery. If the O-ring sticks when you pull the filter down, be sure to remove it. The replacement filter has a new O-ring already fitted to the neck.

If the old transmission pan gasket sticks to the bottom of the transmission, scrape it off. (Caution: many transmissions are made of aluminum and care should be exercised to avoid scoring the transmission's gasket surface.) A gasket scraper or putty knife should be used, not a screwdriver or chisel.

If there are grooves in the pan's gasket mating surface, they should be cleaned with a wire brush. Don't use a screwdriver or chisel, and don't use that wire brush to buff the transmission's mating surface.

Always clean the interior of the transmission oil pan with a general duty automotive solvent and wipe it dry before installing the new filter.

New filter. Installing a new filter is a simple matter of slipping it into place, screwing it down and/or attaching the clip and making sure the O-ring is seated (no real problem).

If you have a 1967 GM car, you should be very careful to obtain and install the

Apply light coating of white grease to oil pan gasket surface to hold new gasket, which comes with filter. You may use a flexible sealant instead of grease. Never apply grease or sealant to the transmission gasket surface, only to the pan surface.

Fit gasket onto oil pan surface. If gasket has dried out, it may have shrunk. The only way to save it is to soak it in warm water. Never try to stretch a dried-out gasket or it will probably break.

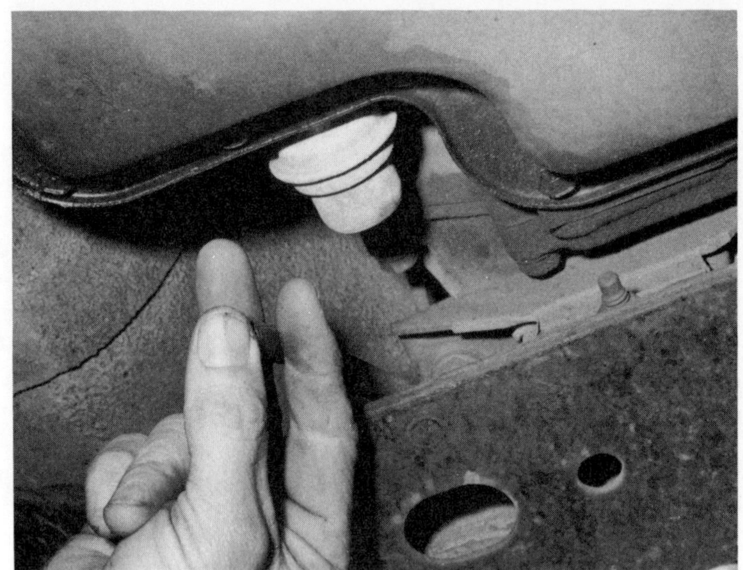

➤ Replacing a transmission modulator is easy, once you find it. You can identify it by vacuum hose on its neck and cylindrical shape. To replace, first take off vacuum hose. Check inside of hose with pipe cleaner and if you find oil, replace hose.

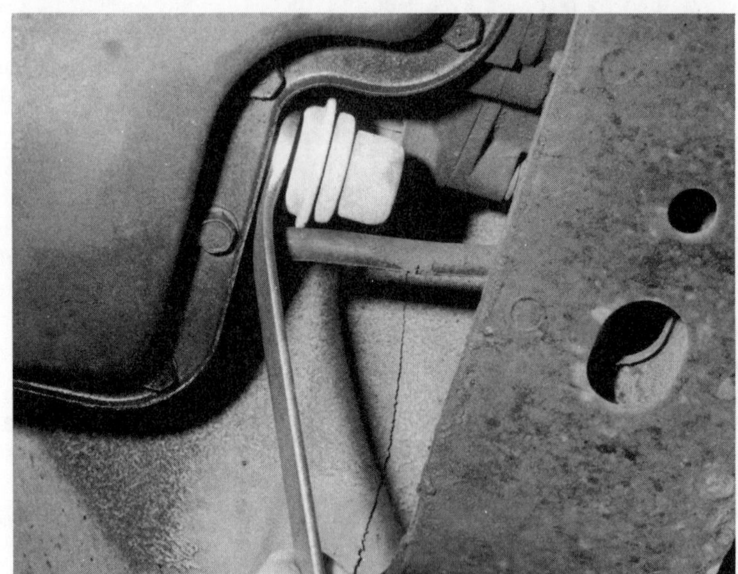

➤ To remove old modulator or install new one, you need a thin wrench on most Ford products. On larger Ford products, a very thin wrench, bent slightly as shown, will get in on the nut.

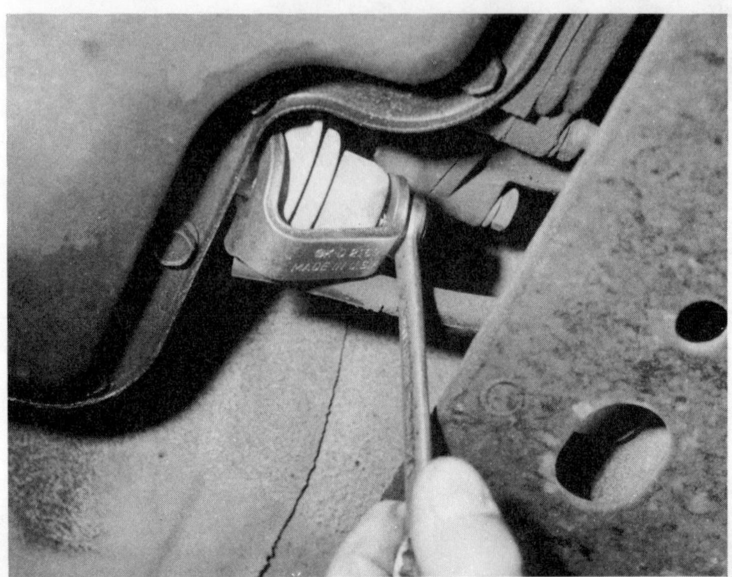

➤ On smaller Fords, you may not be able to get to modulator even with thin wrench. In this case, you can buy inexpensive crowfoot-style wrench designed specifically for the job.

correct filter, as two different types were used this year, on the following models:

Buick (full-size) with Super Turbine 400
Chevrolet with Turbo Hydra-Matic
Cadillac except El Dorado
Oldsmobile (full-size) except Toronado
Pontiac (full-size) with Turbo Hydra-Matic
Pontiac GTO with Turbo Hydra-Matic

The early filter had a bypass valve and carries original equipment part No. 557-9822. The late filter has no bypass valve and carries part No. 6437741. (Note: the bypass valve was eliminated from the late-1967 filter to force replacement when it is completely clogged. If completely stopped up, the filter can be responsible for transmission growling, slipping and even a no-drive condition.)

The two filters are physically interchangeable, but the replacement must be the same type as the original or the filter may be crushed by the pan or cause transmission damage.

On cars with cleanable screens dunk the screen in solvent, agitate for a few minutes, then remove, shake out excess solvent and allow to air-dry for half an hour.

Refit the transmission oil pan with a new gasket. To simplify installation, a flexible sealant can be sparingly applied to the oil pan's gasket surface (never to the transmission itself).

Modulator. Tighten the pan screws evenly in a crisscross pattern.

Next, while the car still is up on safety stands, replace the vacuum modulator on cars so equipped. A new modulator will smooth the shifting.

You can identify the modulator by ordering a new one for your car and finding the equivalent on the transmission body somewhere underneath. It will have a vacuum hose attached to it.

To replace the modulator, simply pull off the hose and unscrew the unit. This is a simple and obvious job, but you can run into a wrench clearance problem on Ford products.

The modulator screws directly into the transmission, and on Ford products the hexagonal nut that permits removing and installing the modulator is flush with the transmission. An ordinary wrench is too thick to fit in.

The solution is to use a very thin wrench (the wrench size is ¾-inch) if you have one, or buy a special wrench made for the purpose. It is thin, C-shaped, and costs just a few dollars at auto parts stores.

Add oil. Now you are through underneath. The job is finished by topping up the transmission with oil and adding a can of "sealer" through the dipstick hole.

Make sure you use the correct oil for your transmission. The wrong oil can severely damage a transmission. All Ford products should be topped up with a fluid that is labeled "F-M2C33F, suffix 2P." All GM, Chrysler and American Motors cars should use fluid labeled "Dexron."

The topping up should be done on a level floor. The engine should be running and the shift lever should be in neutral on Chrysler and American Motors cars, and park on Ford and GM cars.

Check level. After the engine has been running for five minutes, cycle the transmission. That is, apply the brakes and move the shift lever into all positions, ending up in the position necessary to check fluid level. Then recheck the fluid level.

The "transmission sealer" is not really a sealer. It is a chemical designed to keep the seals supple, preventing them from shrinking and allowing oil to leak out.

When you reinsert a transmission dipstick to check level, be sure it is seated fully. Many dipsticks require twisting to seat, and will give false reading if not fully installed.

See also: ENGINE; FILTERS; GASKETS; OIL, ENGINE; TUNE-UP, ENGINE.

How to Repair a Trash Compactor

Compacted trash is easier and cheaper to dispose of than loose trash. These simple machines do the compressing job with a one-ton squeeze

THE COMPACTOR is an appliance designed to reduce the volume of trash and prepare it for refuse pickup. It will accept cans, bottles, cartons, paper and garbage, although garbage is better handled by a disposer.

Installation. The compactor can be located where convenient, provided the floor is secure and the leveling legs have been adjusted to insure that the compactor is level and set firmly on the floor.

It requires a 120 volt, 60 Hz AC electrical outlet with a provision for a grounding terminal.

Operation. Trash is thrown into the machine through an access door. Compacting action commences when the start button is activated. A motor screw drives the ram about 2/3 the way into the container drawer or basket to compress the waste. It then moves upward to its original position. As the container fills, the ram will travel until it exerts about 2,000 pounds of pressure. Then the motor automatically reverses to retract the ram.

If the ram should jam on the downstroke, owing to some object being wedged between the ram and the container, momentarily depress the stop button. Then push the start button again. This reverses the motor to pull the ram up and allow for repositioning or removal of the offending article.

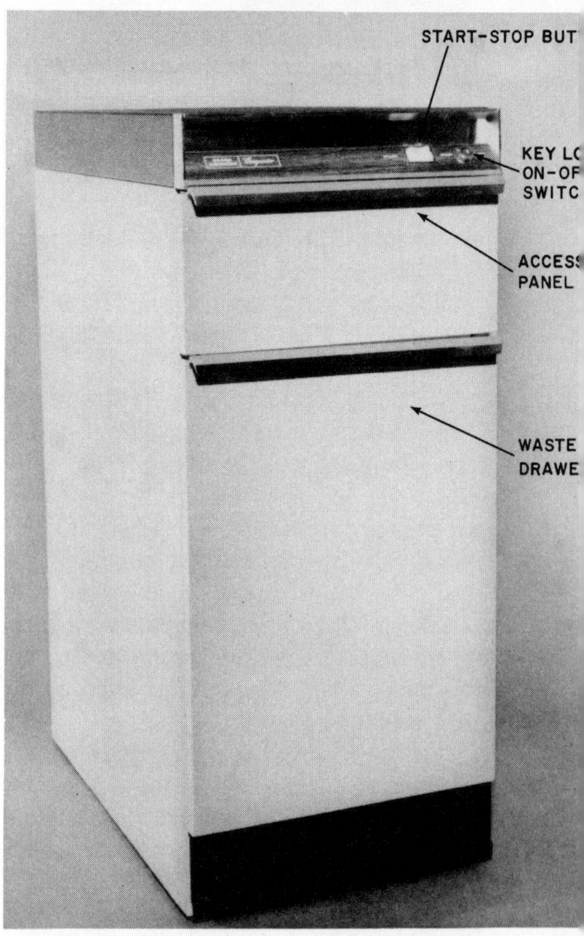

To open the waste drawer of this trash compactor, lift up slightly on the handle and pull it out to its stop position. The waste drawer must be halfway open before the access panel is opened.

Cleaning. Cleanliness is important. The outside of the compactor can be cleaned as you would any other appliance. The inside can be cleaned after removing the trash container. For one typical unit, simply removing the refuse container will provide room enough to clean. For other units, the drawer can be removed by pulling it all the way out to its stop position. Then push down on the drawer release tabs which are located on each side of the drawer near the cabinet bottom.

The ram and other inside areas that have been exposed to trash can now be cleaned with detergent and water. Then they can be

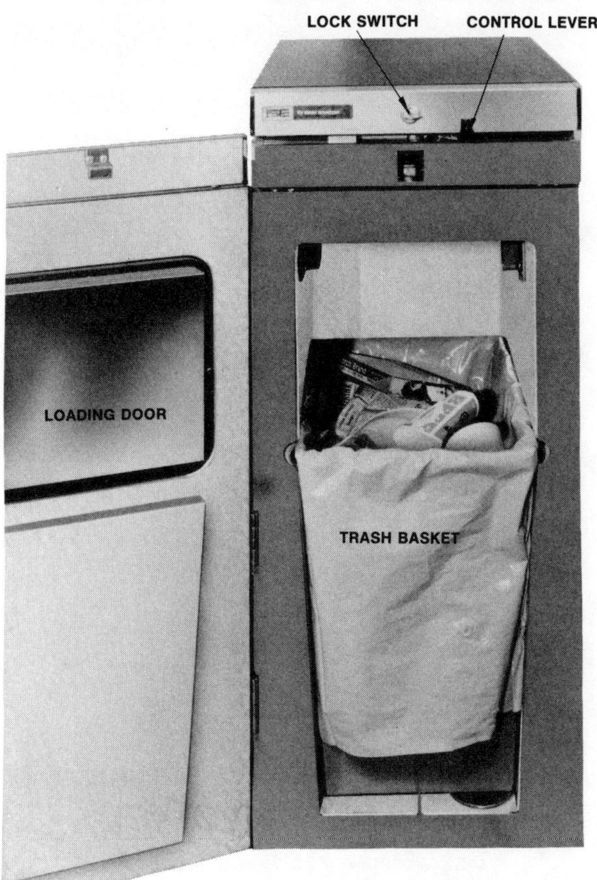

In this trash compactor, the access door is opened to remove compacted trash. The device is loaded through a smaller tilt-down loading panel in the access door.

The motor, jack and ram assembly of an In Sink Erator trash compactor in the retracted position.

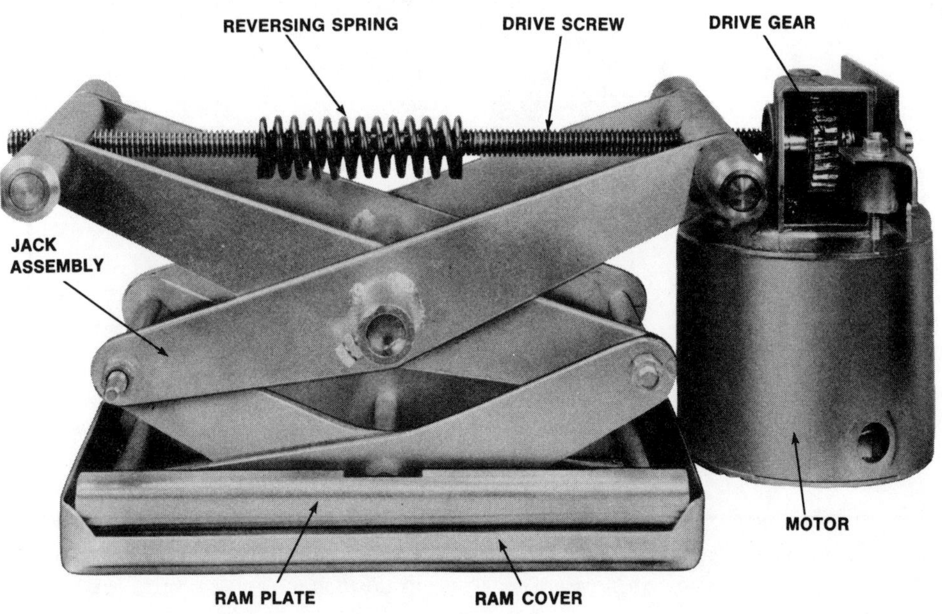

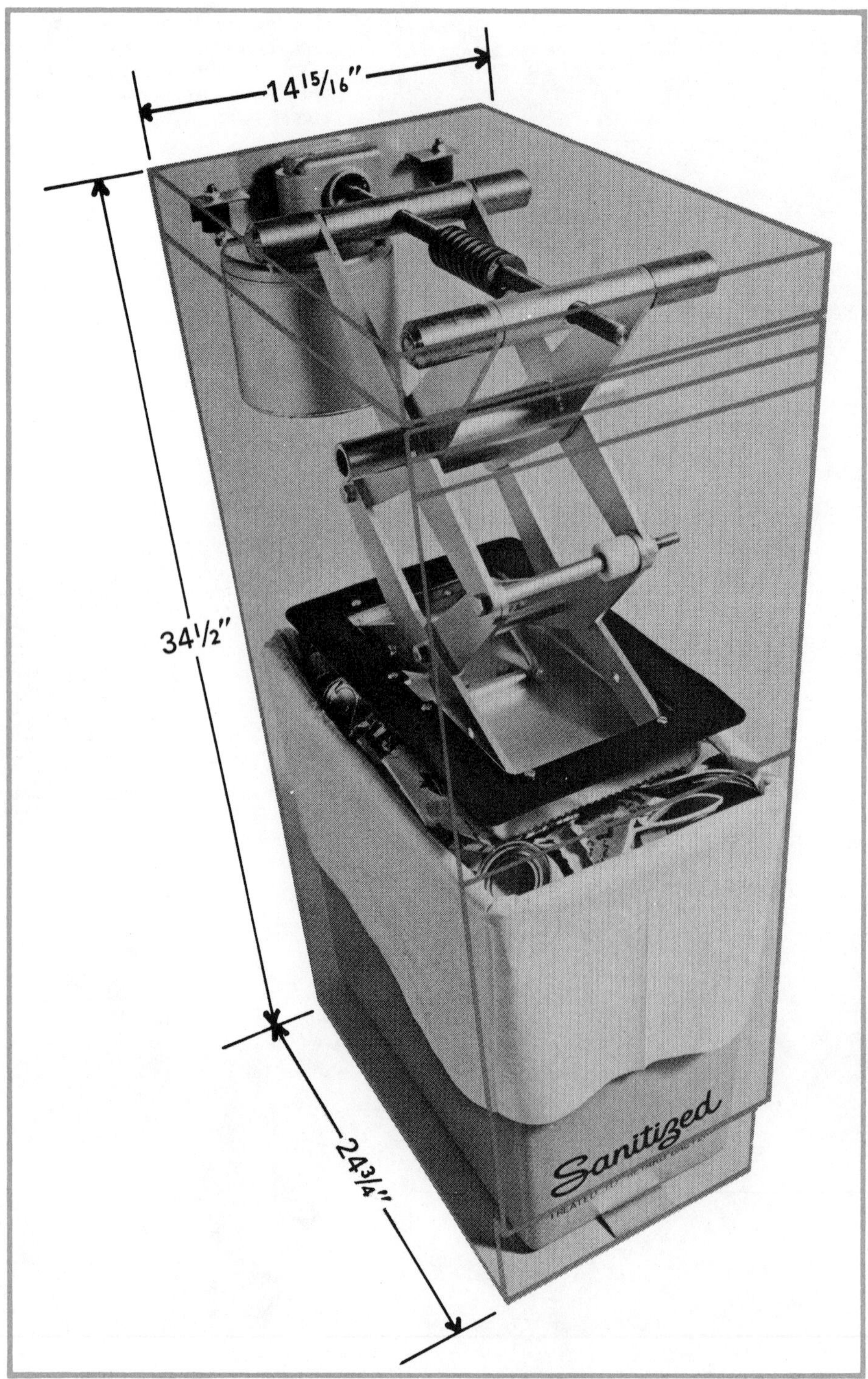

Scissors jack action transforms motor power into ram pressure for trash compaction.

This Whirlpool trash compactor uses two screw jacks, one on each side, to move ramp up and down. The screw jack and its mate on the opposite side are turned by a chain drive. The chain and sprockets are accessible from the bottom of the machine.

The top limit switch and directional switch of this compactor are mounted above the ram. The top limit switch shuts the unit off when the ram returns to the top of its stroke. The directional switch changes the direction of ram travel at the bottom of its stroke.

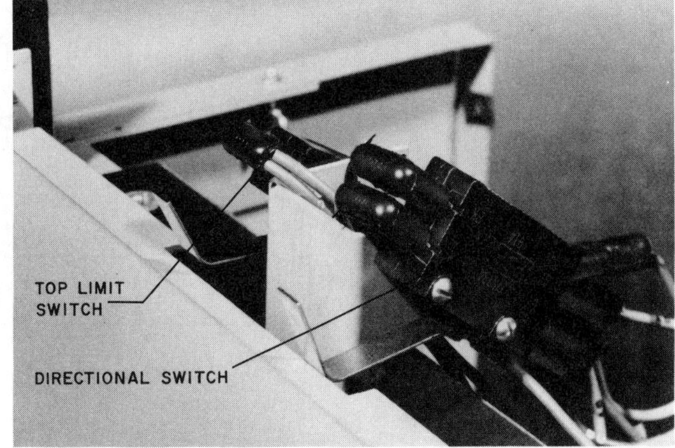

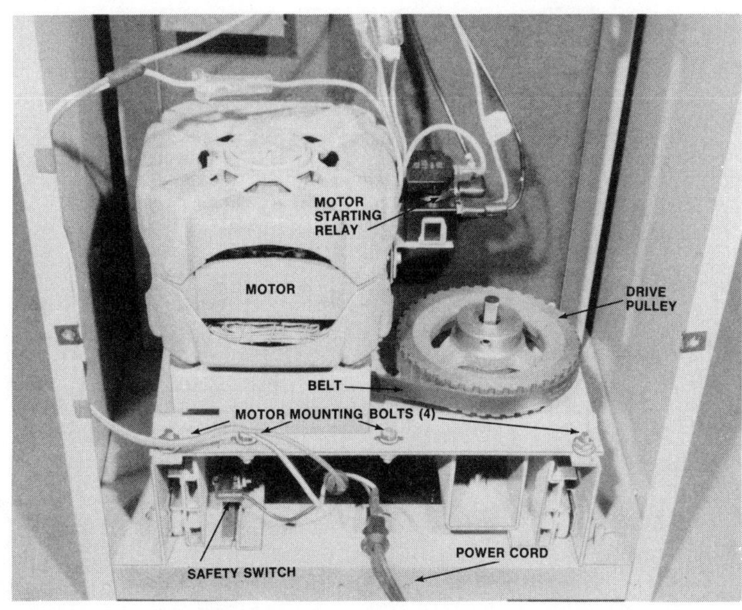

Whirlpool trash compactor motor and drive assembly are reached by removing the rear panel. Adjust belt tension by loosening the motor mounting bolts and sliding the motor to achieve 1/8-inch belt deflection.

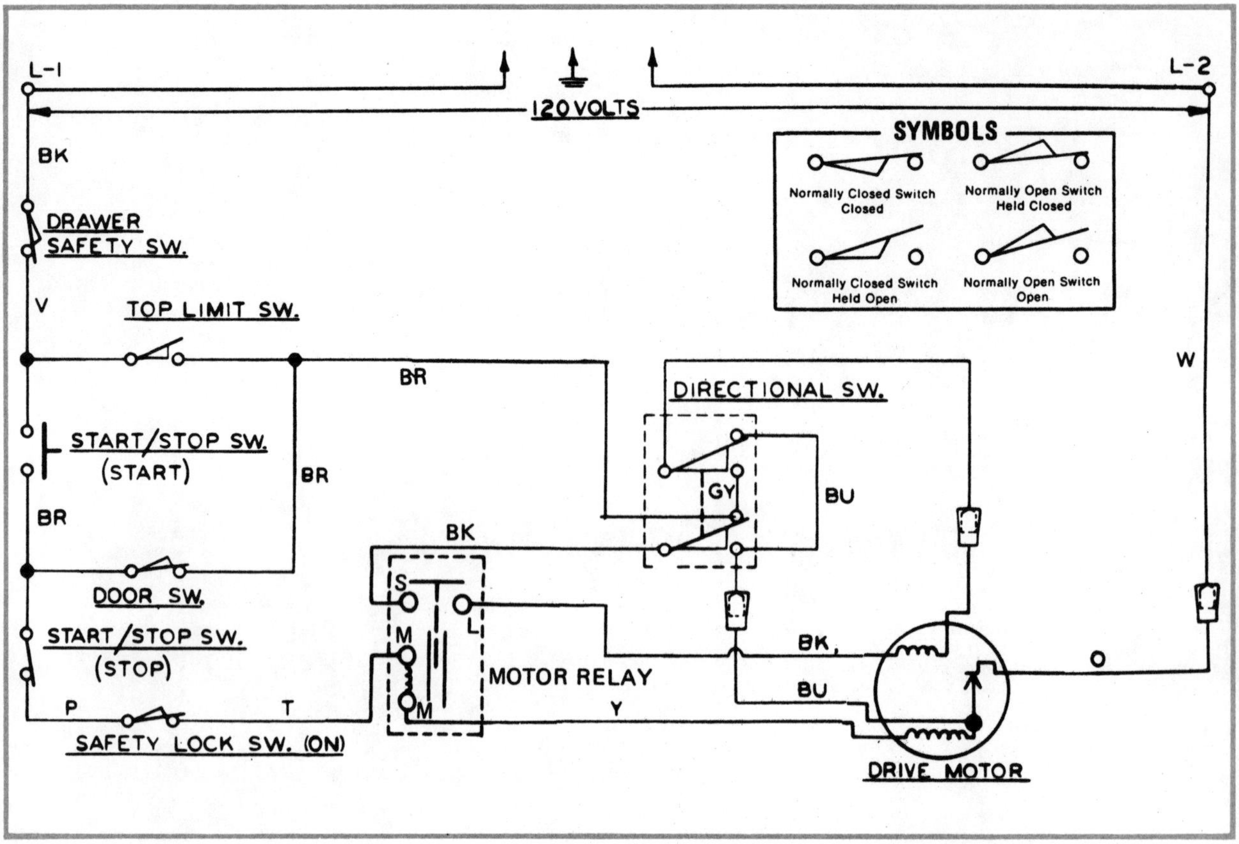

L-1
L-2
120 VOLTS
BK
DRAWER SAFETY SW.
V
TOP LIMIT SW.
BR
START/STOP SW. (START)
BR
BR
DOOR SW.
START/STOP SW. (STOP)
P
T
SAFETY LOCK SW. (ON)
SYMBOLS
Normally Closed Switch Closed
Normally Open Switch Held Closed
Normally Closed Switch Held Open
Normally Open Switch Open
W
DIRECTIONAL SW.
GY
BU
BK
S
L
M
M
MOTOR RELAY
Y
BK
BU
O
DRIVE MOTOR

Typical trash compactor wiring diagrams.

ON-OFF RAM SWITCH
N.O.
N.C.
COM.
COM.
COM.
REV. SW.
MOTOR ASS'Y.
BROWN
BLUE
ORANGE
RED
WHITE
BLACK
BLACK
BASKET SWITCH
INTERNAL MOTOR CONNECTIONS
AUTO-RESET O.L.
MAIN WINDING
WHITE
RED
MOTOR ST. SW.
CAP.
START WINDING
BL.
BL.
ORANGE
BLACK
N.O.
BASKET SWITCH
COM.
BLACK
N.C.
RAM SW.
COM.
BROWN
RED
BL.
N.C.
N.C.
COM.
REV. SW.
COM.
N.O.
N.O.
WHITE
MOTOR TERM. BOX
BLACK
GREEN
WHITE

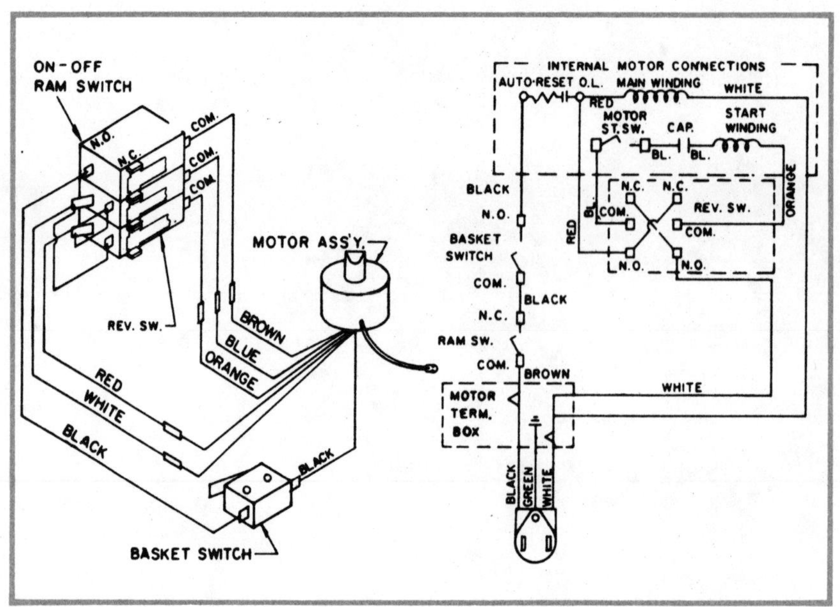

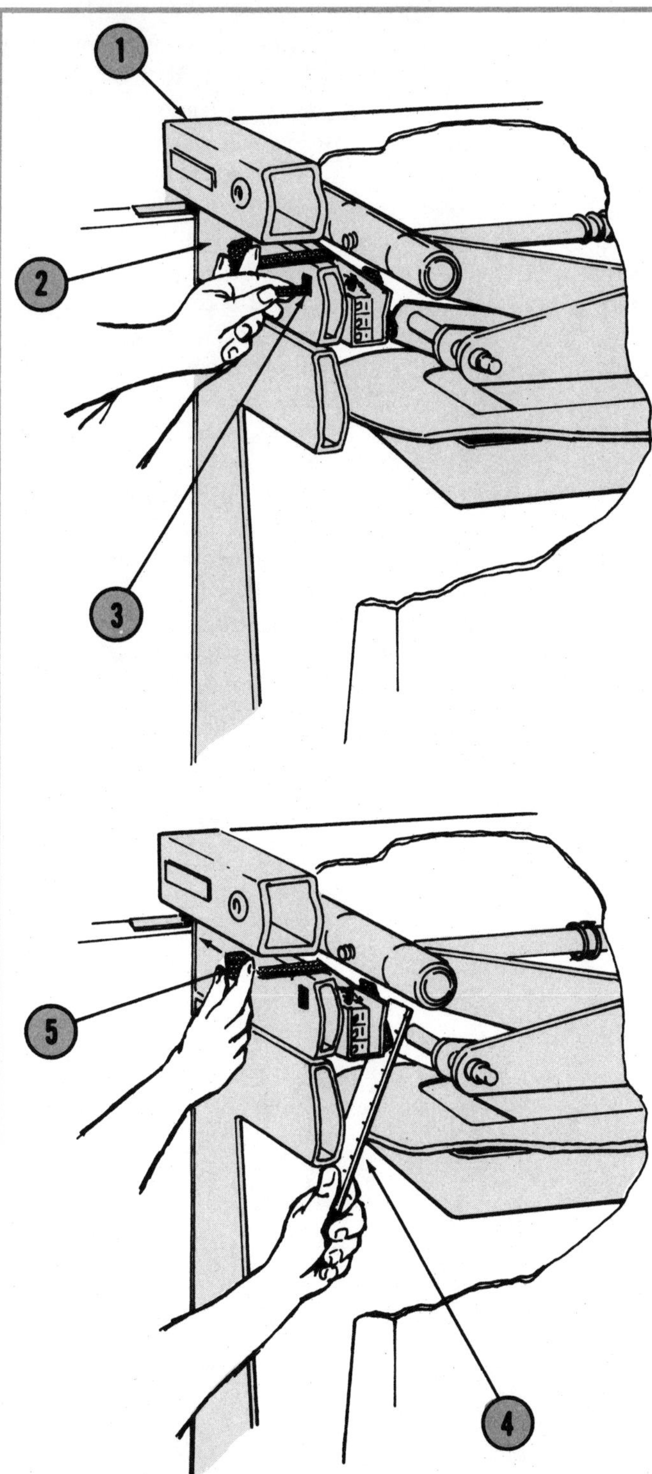

The necessity of manually pressing the ram lever switch is brought about by the ram having traveled down far enough to open the "down" cycle switch, but not far enough to close the "up" cycle switch. When this condition occurs, the latch lever can be moved to the extreme left position to close the on-off switch, but the unit will hum only and will not run because only the run winding is being energized. To activate the unit, it is necessary to manually press the ram lever switch to close the start winding circuit, at the same time moving the latch lever to the far left position to activate the on-off switch. The motor will then run and the ram will start downward. To accomplish pressing the ram lever switch, proceed as follows.

Remove electrical plug.

Open both doors.

Leave basket in compactor.

Insert an object such as a 12" wooden ruler into the opening between the rubber ram wiper and the front of the cabinet at the area marked (4). Press towards yourself and listen for the switch to "click" to assure that you have the ruler located properly. After you have located the switch properly, proceed as follows.

Install electrical plug.

Directly below the control panel (1) is a trim panel (2) retained by two screws, one at each end. On the right side of this trim panel is a vertical slotted opening (3) approximately 1/4-inch wide by approximately 3/4-inch long. Insert a wooden pencil, or other non-conductor of the same size, into opening and press in. This will activate the loading door safety lever and will then allow you to move the latch lever to the center position.

Again insert the ruler into the opening between the rubber ram wiper and the front of the cabinet (4). Press the ruler towards yourself, at the same time moving the latch lever (5) to the far left position. The unit will start and the ram will proceed to travel down. As soon as the unit starts, remove your hand and the ruler quickly. The ram will make a complete cycle, return to the retracted position, and then shut off. Move the latch lever to the far right position, close the doors and the unit can then be operated normally.

disinfected. The cleaning process will have to be done more frequently if any amounts of unwrapped garbage are added to the trash.

For your safety it is advisable to disconnect the compactor from its electrical outlet while you are working on the unit.

Service. Most service work can be performed by either removing the drawer or container, or by removing the rear service panel.

The wiring diagrams show the interlocking safety switches, reversing switches and the motor connections. These diagrams may be used for reference but, as with other major appliances, there should be a wiring diagram for your model attached to the back panel. Use that diagram.

As with all electrical appliances, make certain that voltage is available to the machine. This test should be made with a voltmeter at the machine end of the power cord. If voltage is available there, the safest thing to do is to disconnect the power cord from the wall outlet and test each part with your ohmmeter for proper operation. Follow each circuit and test it from point to point. The motor windings should show continuity and a switch will change from 0 (zero) to ∞ (infinity) reading as it is turned on and off.

Pay particular attention to the limit switches. These switches only operate when all moving parts, drawer, basket, ram, etc., are in their correct position. That is, when all switches are making firm contact to the switch actuating lever. Either the switch or the part may be out of position. Check the moving part first.

Most of the electrical parts on some compactors are accessible from the rear. The door switch is located above the drawer opening behind the front frame.

Service parts for the compactors are available through the local dealer for the particular make and model you have. G.M.

See also: ELECTRICAL, HOME; INDIVIDUAL APPLIANCE LISTINGS.

TRASH COMPACTOR TROUBLE-SHOOTING CHART

PROBLEM / POSSIBLE CAUSE	NO POWER	SAFETY SWITCH OPEN	DEFECTIVE SWITCH	LOOSE CONNECTION	MOTOR OVERLOAD TRIPPED	BLOWN FUSE	LATCH HANDLE STUCK	LOOSE PART VIBRATION	DRIVE GEAR, CHAIN, BELT	DRIVE SCREW DRY	RAM STUCK PART WAY	TOO FULL	SPOILED FOOD IN CONTAINER	INSUFFICIENT DEODORIZER
WILL NOT RUN	√	√	√	√	√	√								
STARTS, THEN STOPS		√	√	√	√	√								
RAM RECYCLES			√				√							
NOISY OPERATION								√	√	√				
CONTAINER STUCK		√	√	√	√	√					√	√		
BAD ODOR													√	√

How to Tune a Wankel Engine

Don't be overwhelmed by the rotary engine just because it's new and different. Except for the rotor orbiting in the chamber, every part is the same as it is on a standard piston engine

THE WANKEL IS AN ENGINE that could make weekend mechanics fun again, although it probably has most Saturday wrench twirlers petrified at the thought of servicing it.

Yes, the Wankel is different in that it has no pistons, rings or valve train. Instead, a rotor takes an eccentric path through a chamber, relying on seals as its three tips to form areas in which fuel and air are admitted, compressed, burned and expelled as exhaust.

Don't be overly concerned about the engine's innards. If you're a typical weekend mechanic, you're doing tune-ups, cooling system work, oil changes, filter replacement, brake jobs and the like. You probably haven't done an engine overhaul on a piston power-plant, so why worry if you can do one on a Wankel? The Japanese Mazda is the only production car with a Wankel engine at this time, and its engine is doubtlessly typical of what to expect for the most part. It has a double chamber and two rotors—sort of two Wankels joined together.

Lift the hood of a Mazda and the first thing you'll see is lots of room. The Wankel is about half the size of a comparable-performance piston engine, so you'll find that there's plenty of room for even oversize hands and arms, and the physically larger, conventionally-shaped wrenches and other tools that the weekend mechanic is most likely to have. In short, few special tools are needed.

Actual maintenance work on the Wankel is not much different from the piston engine. The air filter sits in a housing under a cover held by a few spring clips. The filter is a standard pleated paper element and replacing it is exactly the same as on a piston engine.

The Mazda Wankel may be a bit more sensitive to a clogged air filter element, however. The carburetor used in the Mazda has secondary throttles controlled by vacuum demand (somewhat similar to the GM Quadra-Jet carburetor). That is, the secondary throttles are linked to a vacuum diaphragm, and when there is high vacuum in the venturi of the primary throttles, and

At their first glance under the hood, most people won't even notice that the Mazda has anything unusual for an engine. Air cleaner, generator, oil filter and both distributors are right up top with room to spare.

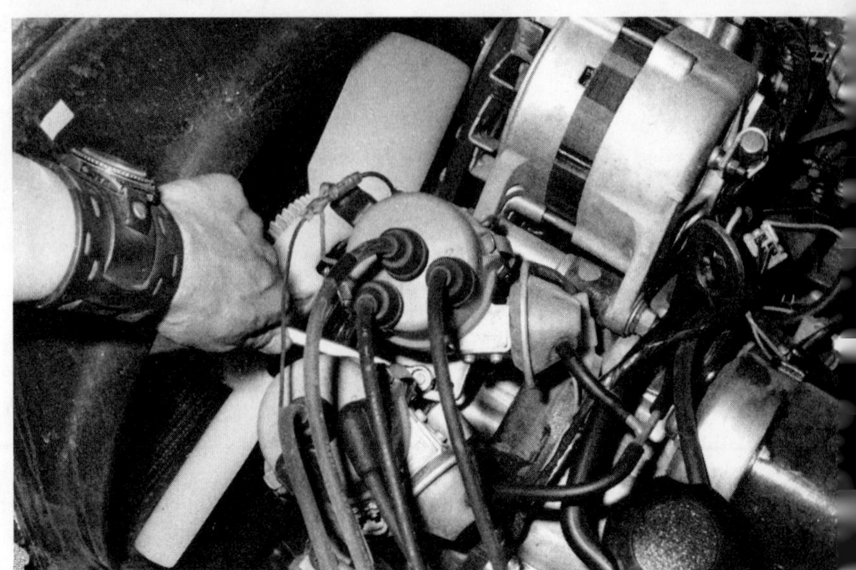

The lock nuts for the distributors are easily reached with a box-end wrench. When nut is slackened, timing can be adjusted by rotating the distributor in usual way.

when the primaries are opened 50 degrees or more (which releases a lockout), the secondaries pop open.

Normally, this occurs only under heavy load, which is when you need the secondaries. However, a plugged filter also creates high vacuum, and the primary throttles must be opened past the lockout position to overcome the restriction posed by the clogged filter. Result: the secondaries pop open and the engine suddenly speeds up—a condition called runaway. This uncontrolled speedup may occur during normal operation at medium road speeds, or when starting with the throttle cracked open sufficiently. It takes a really plugged filter to cause runaway, and the careful weekend mechanic who changes his filter once a year should never encounter it.

The Mazda air filter housing cover is different in that it holds the charcoal canister for the gasoline evaporative emission control system used on most cars. The charcoal canister is affixed to the underside of the cover, and it removes easily for replacement.

The Mazda oil filter is a conventional design spin-on, and it's so completely accessible on top of the engine that even an absolute beginner should have no difficulty in replacing it.

Most other external engine components are quite similar to those on a piston engine.

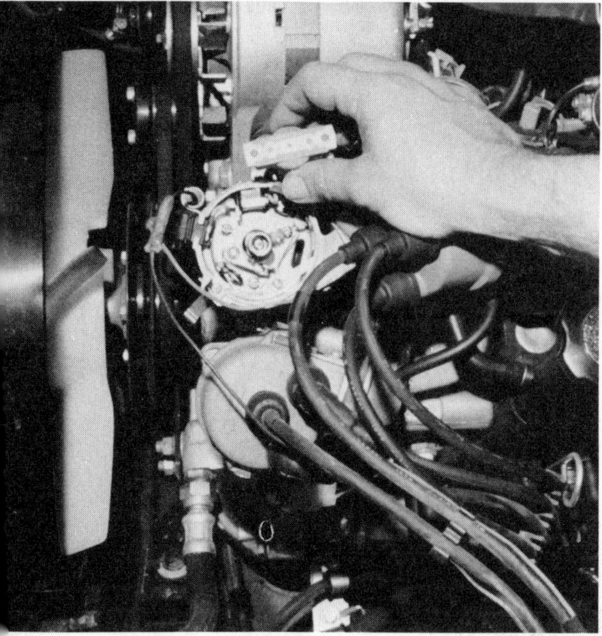

Points, condenser and rotor are replaced and/or adjusted as on any other car. On the Mazda, of course, you simply have to do the job twice. Remember that there are two sets of timing marks, one for each distributor. Make sure you're working with the right set before you make any changes in the timing.

Alternator bracket is within easy reach for belt adjustment.

Changing the air filter remains the simple task that it is on most cars. Release four clips on the housing and the top is easily removed. Note that charcoal canister for evaporative emission control is safely and sensibly located on the underside of the housing's top. A clean air filter is very important with Mazda's 4-barrel carburetor.

The Mazda Wankel, for example, has an alternator driven by a conventional fan belt, a battery, cables, starter (also on top of the engine), a water pump, radiator and hoses, a pressure cap and ignition system.

The Mazda Wankel ignition system is slightly different, but nothing to really turn anyone off. There are four spark plugs, two for each rotor of the twin-rotor engine. One spark plug at each rotor is called the leading plug, the other the trailing plug, and together they produce a combustion pattern that provides maximum power and driveability. The trailing plugs are shorted out under certain conditions when the engine is warm, to reduce exhaust emissions.

Replacement of the spark plugs is easy. They're on the left side of the engine and there's plenty of working room.

The Mazda Wankel has two distributors, one to fire the leading plugs, the other to fire the trailing plugs. Each distributor has its own breaker points, condenser, vacuum and centrifugal advance mechanisms and each is fed from its own coil. Advance mechanisms and coils are not interchangeable from one distributor to the other.

Each distributor has its own timing mark, so when you check timing with a strobe light, be sure you've got the right mark. Because the trailing plugs' distributor may be shorted out when the engine is warm, you should check timing when the engine is cold. A cold engine is similarly correct for

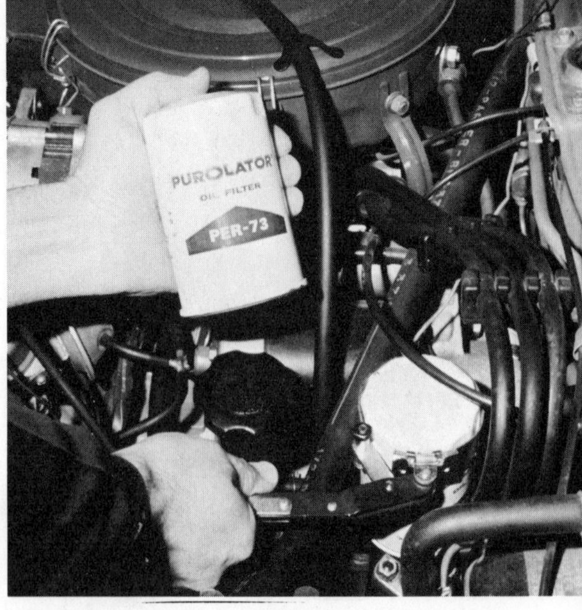

Oil filter is mounted vertically on the highest point on the engine block and there's plenty of room for a wrench, so even a beginner should have no problem changing filters.

On models without air conditioning, the Mazda's four spark plugs are easy to reach although they are pretty far down on the engine block. On air-conditioned cars, the compressor takes up a lot of space alongside the distributors, so you'll probably need a ratchet wrench with a long handle to get at the plugs.

An in-line gasoline filter is located near the gas tank in the Mazda and is reached for replacement through a small panel in the trunk floor. The pleated paper filter element is similar to many used in piston engine cars and any one that fits is an adequate replacement —you don't need an original equipment filter.

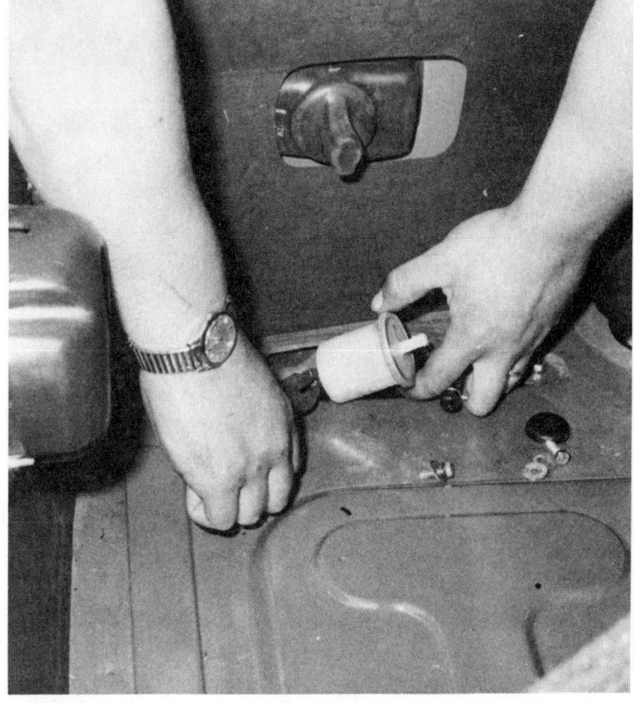

the popular spark test on the trailing plugs' distributor (pulling the thick coil wire from the distributor cap, holding it near a ground, and cranking the engine to see if it is discharging a spark).

Changing of points and condenser, and setting point gap, although it has to be done twice, poses no special problem.

Compression testing a Wankel before installing new plugs and points can be done with a standard compression gauge, although Mazda doesn't recommend it. Here are the pros and cons:

Mazda's viewpoint: A compression gauge inserted into a spark plug hole on a piston engine is measuring only one cylinder. On a Mazda Wankel, the objective is to measure the compression created by each tip seal. Because the piston engine compression gauge has a Shrader valve that holds the dial needle at the highest reading, the result on a Wankel engine is a reading that reflects the best tip seals. If the Shrader valve is removed, the gauge will record compression variations, but the needle flutter will be such that it will not be accurately readable. For accurate readings, therefore, only the special gauge recommended by Mazda for the Wankel should be used.

Pro viewpoint: Actually, two of the three

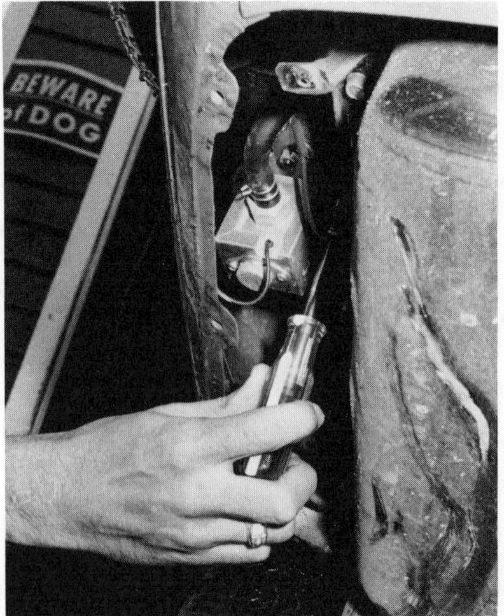

➤The electric fuel pump is mounted near the gas tank inside the left rear fender. Access to the pump, for replacement or testing fuel pressure, is gained by removing a metal plate under the fender.

▼ A triangular rotor twirls around a stationary central gear like a hula hoop around a child's waist (top). The rotor therefore takes an eccentric path through the chamber, compressing the fuel-air mixture down at the spark plug end (fig. 3, top) and then sweeping the exhaust out the exhaust port (fig. 4, top). While this is taking place on one rotor face, the same sequence is taking place—in turn—on the other two rotor faces, giving three "power strokes" for each revolution of the rotor.

HOW THE WANKEL WORKS.

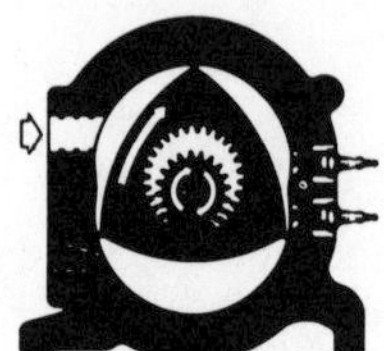	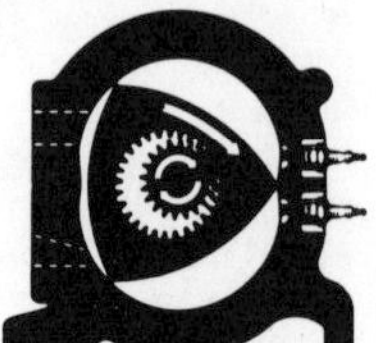	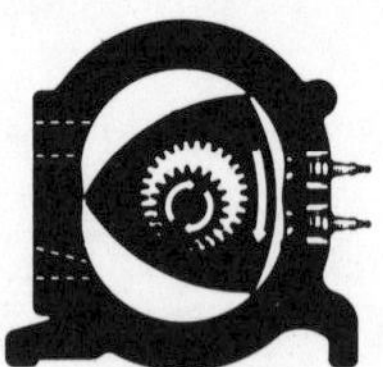	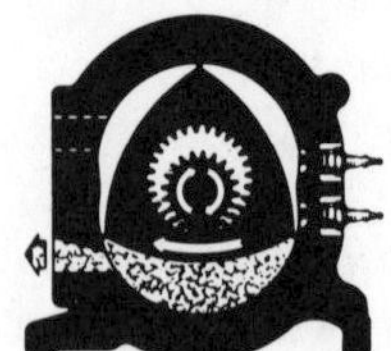
1. Intake. Fuel/air mixture is drawn into combustion chamber by revolving rotor through intake port (upper left). No valves or valve-operating mechanism needed.	**2. Compression.** As rotor continues revolving, it reduces space in chamber containing fuel and air. This compresses mixture.	**3. Ignition.** Fuel/air mixture now fully compressed. Leading sparkplug fires. A split-second later, following plug fires to assure complete combustion.	**4. Exhaust.** Exploding mixture drives rotor, providing power. Rotor then expels gases through exhaust port.

HOW A PISTON ENGINE WORKS.

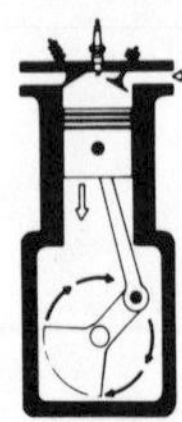	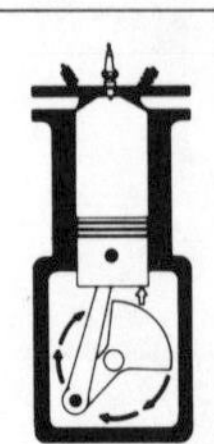	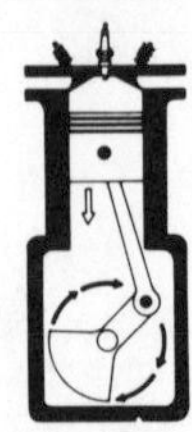	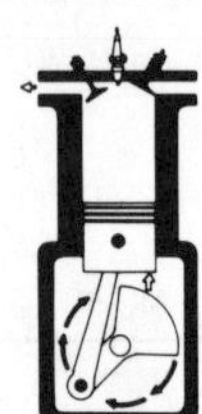
1. Intake.	**2. Compression.**	**3. Ignition.**	**4. Exhaust.**

tip seals are involved in sealing in the compressed air-fuel mixture at any one time. Therefore, the reading with a standard compression gauge is a reasonably reliable indication of tip seal condition. The tip seals all follow the same path in the chamber, so the odds of having one bad seal out of three, without some indication in the form of irregular performance, are low. If the gauge is used merely as an indicator of sound compression in an engine that is showing no weird symptoms, there should be no problem. As for checking compression with the Shrader valve removed, that is an individual matter worth trying before investing in a special tool. If someone can train his eyes to detect excessive needle flutter, he certainly has no need for the Mazda gauge.

The Mazda tune-up should include all the standard items you would check on a piston engine such as air pump belt, fuel pump output and replacement of the in-line gasoline filter.

The Mazda fuel pump is an electric unit mounted near the gas tank, and you can check output and pressure at the pump discharge port. Access to the pump is by removing a bolted-on sheet metal cover at the bottom of the left rear fender. The in-line gasoline filter, a standard pleated-paper element in a plastic canister, is near the pump and is accessible for replacement after removing a cover plate in the trunk compartment. A similar filter made for piston engine cars is a satisfactory replacement—you don't need the original equipment type.

Engine overhaul on the Wankel is beyond the capability of the weekend mechanic at this time, simply because many of the nuances and tricks of the trade are still being determined. For example, fitting of some oil seals must be done very carefully to avoid leaks.

Just as the advanced weekend mechanic learned the ins and outs of piston engine overhaul, however, he will eventually learn the Wankel. Mazda is training professionals in the job in less than a week, and there are lots of amateurs whose only difference from the pro is the lack of speed that is developed in day-to-day work on the engine.

In the meantime, development work is continuing on Wankels with quick-change rotor tip seals. Such a design feature could make the average weekend mechanic more versatile on a Wankel than he is on a piston engine.

Even if Wankel overhaul remains beyond your grasp, you'll find you can do as much of its maintenance as you ever did on a piston engine—with less sweat. P.W.

See also: FILTERS; GASKETS; OIL, ENGINE.

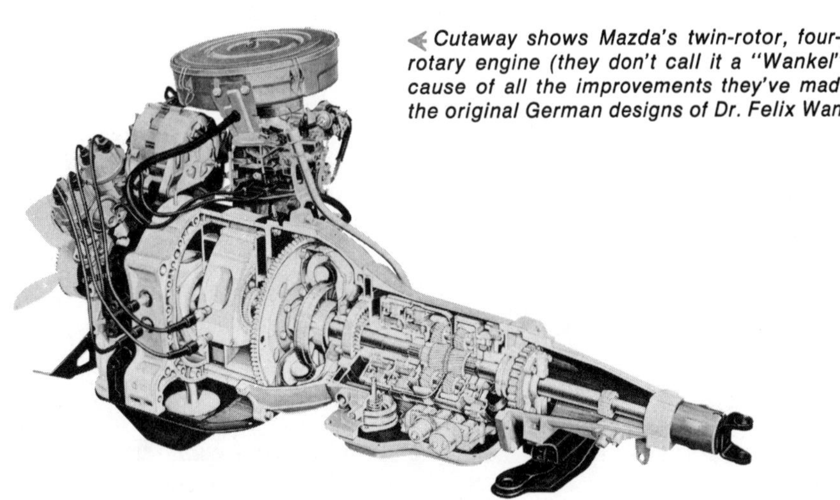

Cutaway shows Mazda's twin-rotor, four-plug rotary engine (they don't call it a "Wankel" because of all the improvements they've made on the original German designs of Dr. Felix Wankel).

Timing an engine. Aim light carefully to avoid parallax error.

Tuning Your Car's Engine

Doing this job properly will take at least four hours of work, but it will pay big dividends in fuel economy, engine performance and driving comfort

A GOOD TUNE-UP CAN DO wonders for a car in the areas of easier starting, smooth idle, better acceleration and higher gas mileage.

Initial checks. To gain performance by tuning, the best place to gain is with a compression test.

If the compression test shows good results, the engine can be tuned. If compression is very high in some cylinder, the cause is probably a carbon accumulation. If compression is uniformly low, there are two possibilities:

1. The condition is normal. Many high-performance engines have camshafts designed for high-speed performance. Compression during cranking will not be particularly high; in fact, it may be as low as 75 psi.
2. There is wear in the engine, either worn rings or valve guides or valves.

The whole point of this initial checking is: Don't expect too much from the best of tuning, unless the cylinders all have close to the same compression.

Inspect the electrical circuits. Clean and

tighten all the battery terminals and fill battery with water. Then follow the ground and starter cables and tighten the other ends to ensure that your ignition is getting all the current it requires for perfect performance. A number of domestic and imported cars have more than one ground strap connecting the engine to the frame or body. It's well worth your time to check these out for tightness and electrical conductivity.

Also check and clean and tighten if necessary, the thin-wire connections at the coil and the external thin-wire connection (if there is one) on the distributor from the coil. On many distributors, the wire goes through a rubber grommet into the distributor itself, and the cap must be removed to check its tightness.

Checking the distributor. First disconnect one spark plug wire at a time from the plugs and, with the engine idling, hold the terminal of the disconnected wire about ¼-inch away from a good ground such as the shell of the plug or a cylinder-head bolt. A good "fat" spark should jump regularly from wire to ground. If the wires have rubber protectors over the ends which cannot be slid back, place a key in the end of the terminal to make contact with the end of the wire and let the spark jump from the key to the ground.

To avoid getting a shock when testing each spark plug wire, have someone start and turn off the engine each time you disconnect a wire, or use pliers with insulated handles to place the key into the rubber socket.

If you get a very weak spark or none at all from one of the wires, it could be due to a wet or dirty distributor cap, a worn or burned rotor or the wire itself, which may have worn spots in the insulation or make poor contact in the cap.

Take off the distributor cap without disconnecting any wires. On most cars the cap is held by two spring clips. On many late-model cars it is held by two spring-loaded locking rods with screw-slot heads.

To undo the locking rod type, press down with the screwdriver and turn to twist the locking rod out of its engagement point in the distributor body.

Wipe the cap clean, both inside and out, with a dry cloth. Carefully inspect the inside of the cap for cracks or carbon deposits along a crack extending from one contact point to another. Carbon deposits, particularly on caps having a smooth inner surface, can conduct electricity and cause engine "miss."

Either replace the cracked cap with a

➤ *Spark check on plug wires with recessed terminals can be made by inserting key into terminals, as shown.*

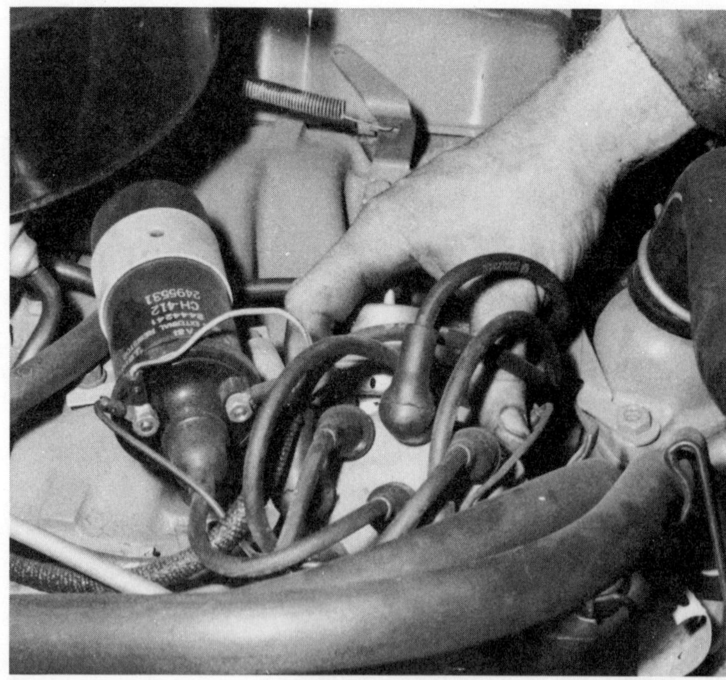

Check thin-wire terminals at coil for tightness.

Distributor cap held by locking rods can be released with screwdriver. Press down on rod and turn to release.

new one or, for an emergency repair, scrape off the carbon along the crack with the point of a knife blade. Seal the scraped-out crack with lacquer or a dab of nail polish to prevent future carbon deposits.

While you have the distributor cap off, remove the rotor, and carefully inspect the tip. If it is burned and pitted so that the edge is irregular, replace it with a new one. Any attempt to file the edge clean would

Carefully inspect interior of distributor cap for cracks.

Removing rotor. On GM cars with V-8 (illustrated), rotor is held by two screws.

increase the gap between roto and cap terminals and interfere with delivery of a good hot spark to the plugs.

Distributor point failure is sometimes due to oil being thrown on the point contact surfaces by the rotating cam. If you notice a black oily smear on the point support plate, called the breaker plate, it is evidence that oil is getting on the points and interfering with engine performance.

If the distributor has not been cleaned in tens of thousands of miles, some oil accumulation is to be expected and can be cleaned off. However, under normal circumstances, the oil is evidence of a worn bushing around the distributor shaft.

The only cure is to have a new bushing installed at a machine shop or to install a rebuilt distributor. (This is the simplest and quickest procedure.)

Installing points. With the rotor off and out of the way, spread apart the points with a screwdriver and inspect the little discs which make and break the ignition circuit to create the high-voltage electricity for the spark plugs.

If they are pitted or burned, they should be replaced. Points normally last 10,000 to 15,000 miles, but in short trip driving, they may burn more quickly. If points fail in very low mileage, such as 4,000 or so, this indicates that something is wrong.

Reasons for burnt points. You'll be wise to do more than merely replace badly burned contact points. Check for the cause among these six common troubles:

1. Coil resistance unit not properly connected into the circuit between ignition switch and the coil positive.
2. Defective condenser.
3. Points do not open wide enough.
4. Oil vapor may seep into the distributor and get on contact points to cause arcing and rapid burning. A smudge line on breaker plate under the points is a clue to this.
5. High-voltage condition may cause excessive flow through points and produce a blue scale on the points.
6. Radio capacitor connected to distributor terminal may cause excessive pitting.

Replacing the points varies slightly according to the make of car. To start, become familiar with the action of the points by watching them as someone cranks the engine.

You will see the points open and close. They will open as a little fiber block on the point assembly comes up against high spots on the distributor shaft. (This section of high spots is called the cam and the high spots themselves are called lobes.) The points will close as the fiber block comes off a high spot.

Actually only one point moves (out and back). The other is stationary.

Each of the lobes is shaped exactly the same (except on Volkswagen and Buick V-6 engines), so the points are separated exactly the same distance each time. That distance is measured with a feeler gauge and should be at factory specifications.

Removing the points is very easy. If there is a wire connected to the points, disconnect it. Then look for a lockscrew holding the points to the distributor breaker plate under them. If there is more than one screw, the larger one is the lockscrew, Remove it and its lockwasher, and you can lift the points up and out.

Install the new points in the same position, but don't tighten the lockscrew except on General Motors V-8 distributors, as explained later.

The points now must be adjusted.

On all but General Motors V-8 distributors, there is a special tool to simplify point adjustment. It consists of a special ring that fits over the distributor cam and a special feeler gauge that is actually thinner than the size stamping says it is.

The point gap is measured in thousandths of an inch when the fiber block is at a high spot of the distributor cam, and this means the highest point. To get the distributor shaft properly lined up requires cranking the engine in very short bursts—a sometimes time-consuming feat.

The ring simulates the condition and the feeler gauge that is provided with the ring is thinner to compensate for the thickness of the ring.

On GM V-8 distributors, the mechanical

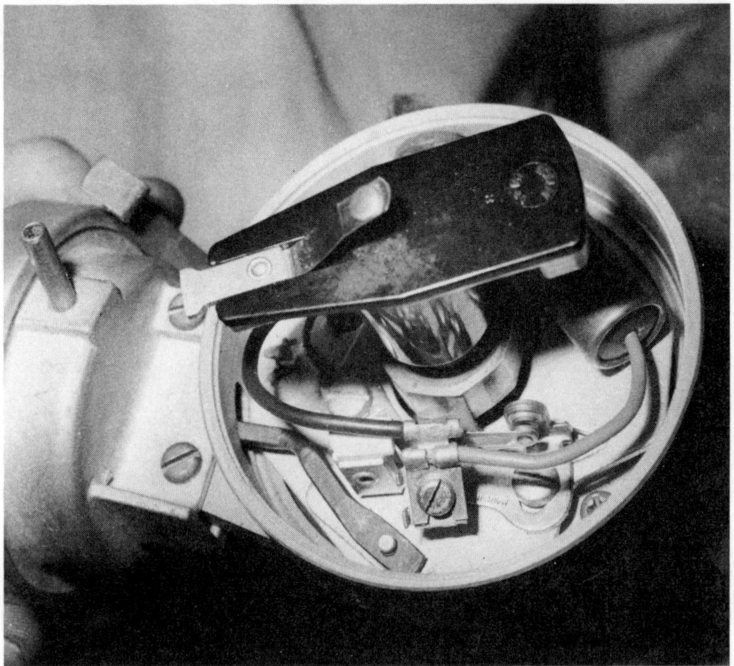

Typical Ford and Chrysler distributor. This type of rotor is just pulled off. Notice adjusting screw just below points, and the elongated hole in the ignition point through which it goes. To adjust points, loosen lockscrew and this adjusting screw, and move fixed point toward or away from distributor cam to adjust points gap. When gap is correct, as measured by feeler gauge, tighten the two screws.

advance mechanism is at the top of the distributor and there is no way to fit a ring over it. You will have to either crank the engine or use the special technique explained later.

To measure a point gap, insert the correct size stamped on the gauge feeler gauge between the points' contact faces. If the gauge can be inserted and withdrawn with light drag on it, the gap is correct. If the gap is too wide or too narrow, it must be changed.

Points can be inspected for burning by spreading them apart with finger.

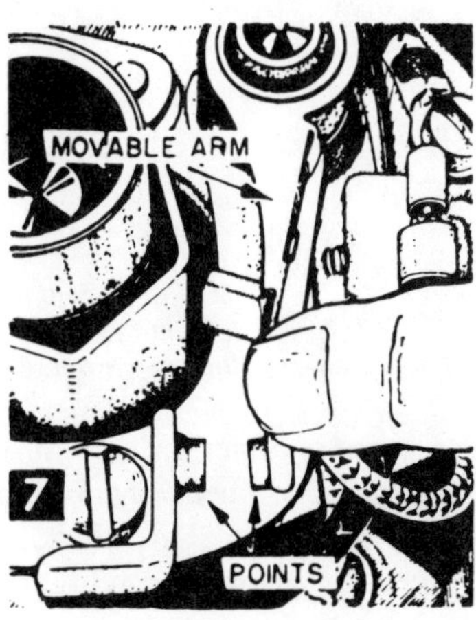

The adjustment is made by moving the stationary point in toward the distributor cam. Sometimes there is an eccentric screw that does this when turned. Other times there is a screwdriver slot in the breaker plate and the stationary point plate and you just twist the screwdriver to increase or decrease the gap.

Once the gap is correct, tighten the lockscrew.

On GM cars with the mechanical advance at the top of the distributor, the following technique will work:

There is an Allen-head adjusting screw at the side of the points and all you have to do is have someone crank the engine while you turn it, until you can see a small gap (about the thickness of a matchbook cover). With this gap, the engine should start, even if it runs poorly.

Refit the rotor and distributor cap, which

Removing points on this typical distributor starts with disconnecting push-on connector with screwdriver, as shown..

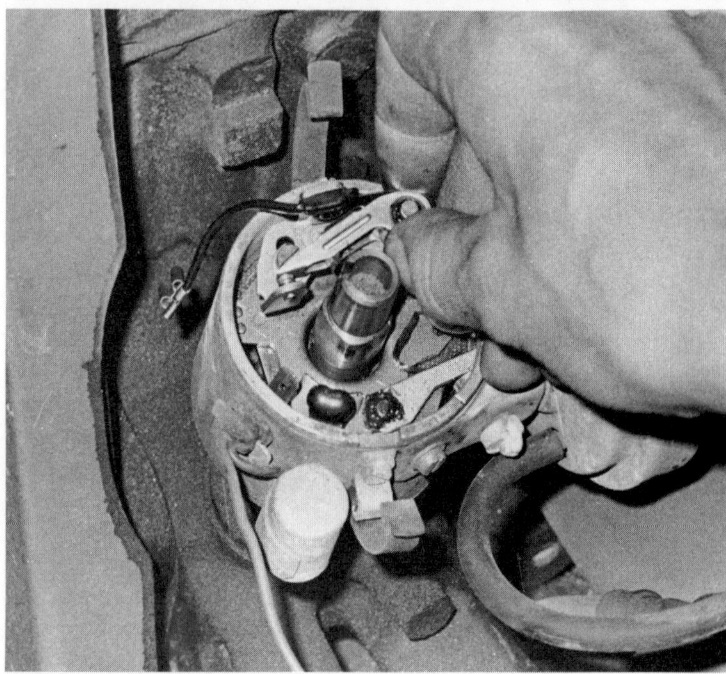

Remove adjusting and lock screws and just pull the points out, as shown.

has a little metal window in its side. This window can be lifted while the engine is running to permit adjustment of the points.

Note: on GM cars with the windshield antenna, there is a metal shield around the points to prevent them from interfering with radio reception. This shield, a two-piece assembly, should be refitted.

On GM V-8's, point gap is set with engine running. Lift up window on distributor cap, as shown, and insert Allen wrench.

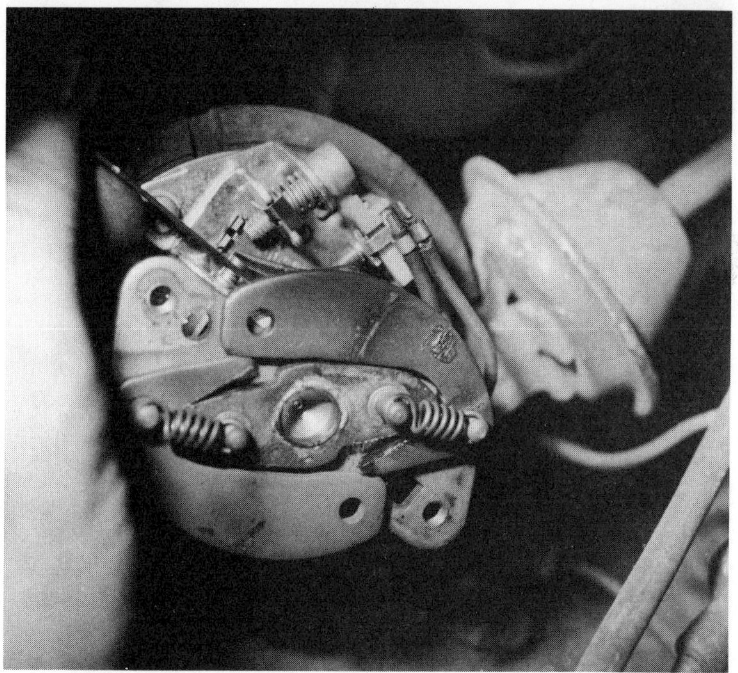

Point gap is adjusted by inserting feeler gauge between points with rubbing block on cam lobe, or special ring inserted.

With the engine running, turn the Allen wrench slowly clockwise until the engine just starts to misfire, then turn it one-half turn counterclockwise to complete the adjustment. (If the engine is running roughly when you first start it, turn the screw first one way, then the other, until it smooths out.)

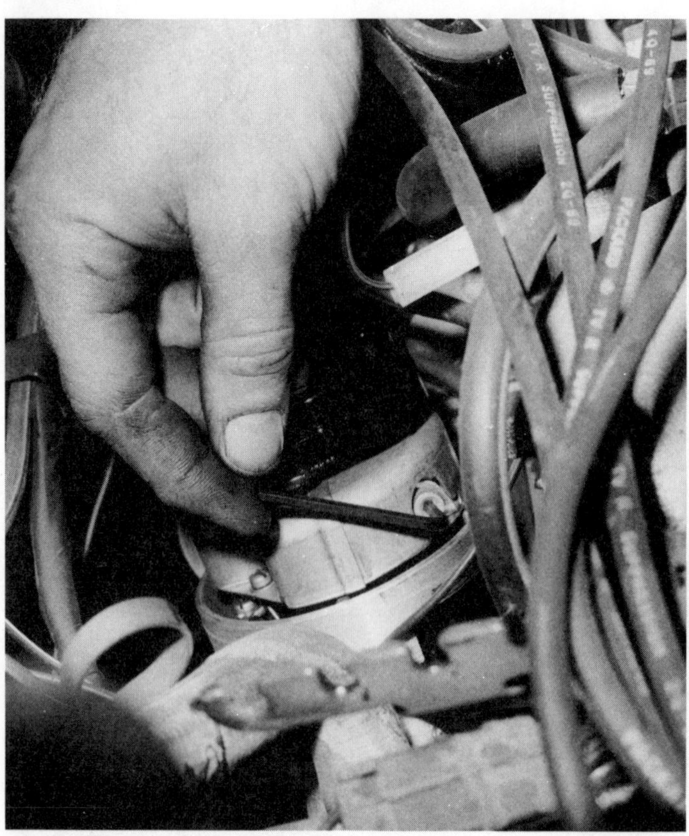

Distributor cap has been removed to show how Allen wrench fits into adjusting screw on GM V-8 distributors. This distributor has radio interference shield.

After the ignition points are adjusted, they should be double-checked with a dwellmeter, which is available in a combination unit with a tachometer.

The dwellmeter measures the number of degrees that the ignition points are closed. It is the opposite of the point gap, but it also is an important measurement.

For it is when the points are closed that the magnetic field builds up in the coil. If the points aren't closed long enough, the magnetic field will not be strong enough, and when it collapses, the spark it produces will be weak. This is particularly true at high engine speed.

If the points are adjusted for the correct gap, the dwell reading should also be within specifications—but not always, hence the desirability of a dwell check.

Car makers provide an acceptable range of both point gap and dwell readings and you may have to modify the point gap to get the dwell that is necessary.

The dwellmeter is easily connected—one wire to the "CB" or minus terminal of the coil, the other to a good ground. Then the engine is started and run.

At the same time you should make a dwell-holding test, that is, see if the dwell reading remains the same as engine speed increases. Slowly increase engine speed from idle to 1500 rpm and then slowly let it drop back to idle. Never exceed 1500 rpm.

If the dwell varies more than three degrees, the distributor is worn and should be removed for service. See the distributor removal section that follows.

A final check of the distributor is made when setting ignition timing. At that time, the mechanical and vacuum advance units are tested with a timing light.

Distributor removal. No matter how well you adjust the points, a distributor may not give good performance if considerably worn or inadequately lubricated. A worn shaft or bushing may cause the points to open unevenly. An overgreased distributor may pick up enough dirt to interfere with operation of advance mechanisms.

With such troubles, the distributor must be removed. This isn't difficult; putting back the distributor is another matter, particularly on Ford products.

If you must remove the distributor, here are recommended precautions.

Remove the distributor cap.

Disconnect the wire from the distributor to the coil at the distributor end.

Crank the engine until the rotor points to a convenient reference point on the engine, or perhaps a time of day on an imaginary clock.

With chalk, mark points on the engine alongside the distributor that align with some portion of the distributor body, such as a cap spring clamp.

Disconnect the vacuum hose or tube.

Slacken the distributor lock. It may be a pinch-clamp or a simple hold-down bolt and bracket.

Twist the distributor body as you pull on it, to break any stickiness.

When you install a new or rebuilt distributor, mark the body as you did on the

POINTS CLOSED (DWELL)

BREAKER POINTS OPEN

BREAKER POINTS OPEN

Dwell Angle

Explaining the meaning of the word "dwell," which is the period of time, in degrees, that points are closed.

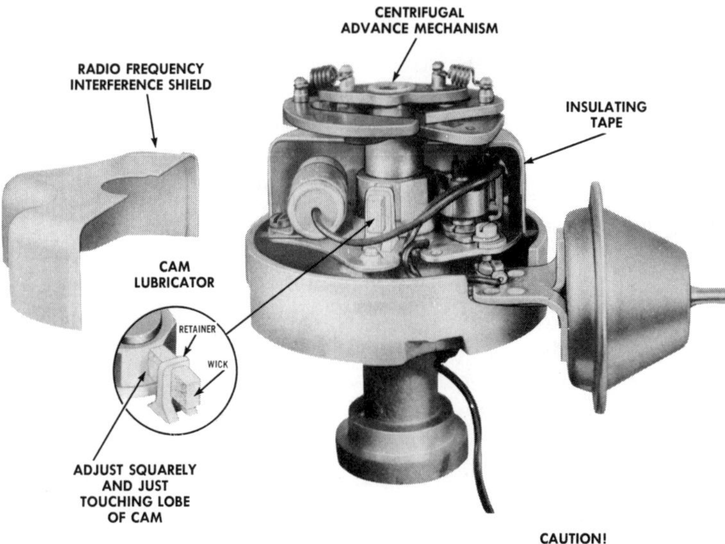

GM cars with windshield antenna have radio interference shield (a two-piece unit) around points. It must be removed to install new points.

◀ *Dwell is checked with special meter, which is normally combined with a tachometer and called a dwell-tachometer. One lead of meter goes to distributor minus (or "CB") thin-wire terminal, other goes to a good ground on engine.*

old distributor, and when you get it in, the engine will start.

Timing may or may not be precise, but adjusting timing is a lot easier when the engine is running.

The condenser. The condenser is an integral part of the ignition system. Without it the points would be pitted, burned, and worn in a few days.

In order to force the electrical current to jump the air gap between the spark plug case and the electrode, the relatively insignificant current from the battery must be built up to 20,000 volts or more. The buildup takes place in the primary and secondary windings of the coil. The low-voltage battery current flows into the primary winding of the coil, setting up a magnetic field in the coil. When the voltage is abruptly stopped, the magnetic field collapses and induces a higher voltage in secondary coil windings.

The low-voltage is stopped by the opening of the distributor contact points. The moment the points separate, the current stops flowing from battery to coil. Collapse of the magnetic field not only keys the needed high-voltage induction in the secondary windings of the coil, but also induces, as a by-product, a higher voltage in the primary circuit, a voltage high enough to jump the point gap. If this were allowed to happen, the contact points would soon become useless, and the arcing would drain needed power from the higher secondary voltage.

The condenser saves voltage and points by acting much like a shock absorber that stores energy that otherwise would keep the springs ocillating. The electrons are crowded into the condenser where they continue to build up. As they work, they set up a reverse direction to their flow pattern. Because the points are still open, the flow is toward the grounded side of the condenser. At a point, the buildup collapses and reverses, building up toward the insulated side of the condenser, then the flow and buildup reverses again and again.

Each time the flow is reversed, the magnetic field it creates collapses, then builds up in the opposite direction continuing from side to side until the electrons are dissipated or stopped by closing of the points. The condenser thus helps retard the flow by impeding or blocking the electrons and keeping them where they can do no damage.

Inside your condenser are four strips, two of metal foil and two of insulating paper. Almost 15 feet long, they are rolled tightly (metal foil sheets are slightly narrower than the insulation to prevent leakage of electrons around the edges) and the roll is placed in a metal case. The case is

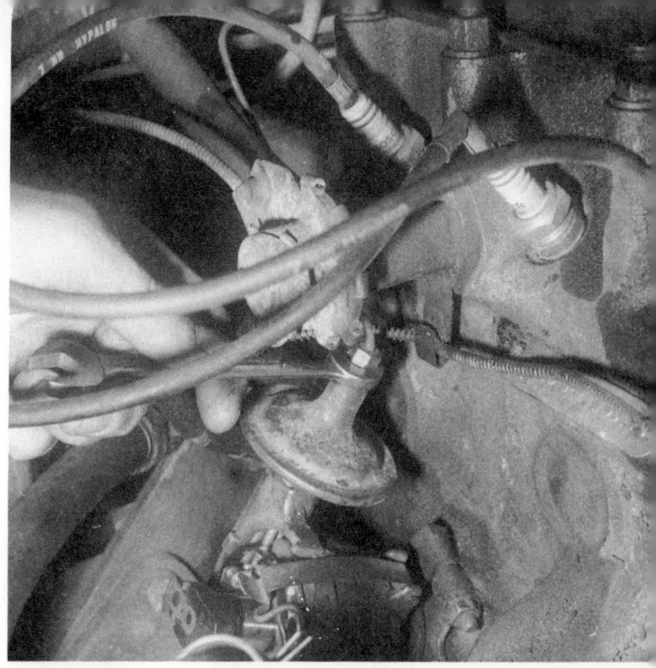

➢ Distributor removal starts with disconnection of vacuum line. On many cars it's a hose that can be pulled off; on this one it's a tube.

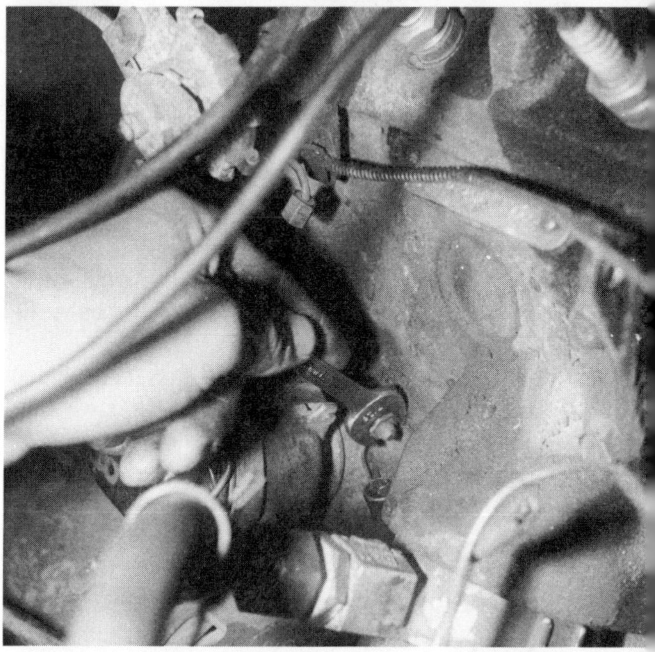

➢ Next, loosen distributor lock. On most cars, it's a bolt and bracket to engine. On this car it's a pinch-bolt.

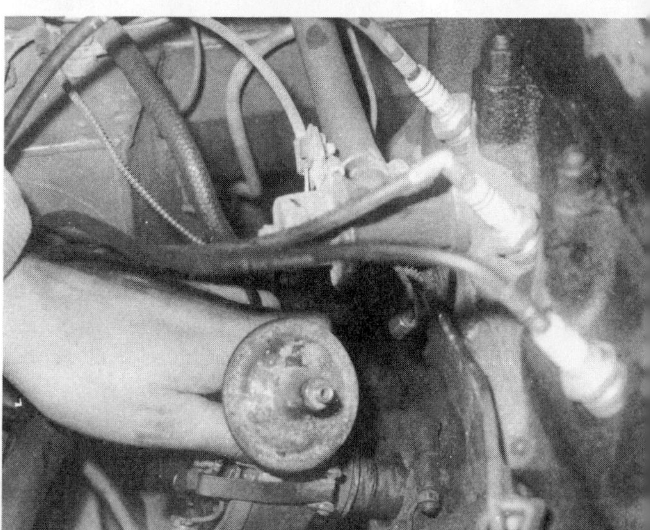

➢ Pull distributor out with twisting motion to break it free.

hermetically sealed to shut out moisture—the enemy of a condenser.

One foil strip is connected to the cap of the condenser and an exterior terminal. The second is connected internally to the condenser case. A pigtail soldered to the outside terminal connects to the primary distributor terminal, placing the condenser in parallel. The case acts as ground so the condenser is wired across the circuit.

Automotive condensers are rated in microfarads. It is important to replace a defective condenser with one of the proper rating for your car.

Although the condenser in your car is a reliable, long-lasting item, trouble could strike when least expected. A weak or leaking condenser usually has absorbed enough moisture to weaken the insulating papers and can no longer hold the buildup charge it was designed to handle. A condenser with poor insulation can drain enough energy from an ignition system to lower the secondary voltage substantially. A weak or intermittent spark at the plugs can be a disastrous result.

Signs of trouble may go unnoticed except when the engine is hot. It is unlikely a leaking condenser would cause misfiring at low or medium speeds, except under conditions which cause it to heat.

Frayed pigtail, broken terminal, or loose insulation can all increase point wear. Under severe conditions, they can render the points useless. If you're experiencing ignition trouble, burned points, hard starting, check the condenser. Remove it from the distributor. Check for broken leads, frayed or loose insulation, corroded terminals, signs of moisture, or poor ground at the mounting.

Some simple tests. Condensers are generally tested on equipment giving three readings: microfarads, leakage, and series resistance. But test equipment costs money and condensers cost but a few pennies. You'll be money ahead if you make these few simple tests; then if the condenser seems faulty or if you're in doubt, replace it and test again.

A condenser can be tested for excessive leakage (short) by charging it from a spark plug as the engine is turned over. Be sure the spark used for the test has a gap no greater than .030. The small gap will limit the voltage involved.

Ground the condenser case to the cylinder head or block, then touch it to the plug terminals. Remove the plug, turn off the engine, and wait one minute. With a *well-insulated* screwdriver, short the condenser terminal to the outer case. One heavy spark should result. If the condenser will not hold such a charge for one minute, it should be replaced.

Caution: Charged in this manner, a condenser can give you a severe shock. A plug gapped to .030-inch and operating in low compression with the engine at idle will develop about 300 volts. This is not enough to injure the condenser insulation, but plenty "hot" if you touch it. Be sure the screwdriver is well insulated before you short the condenser.

A safer test is to check the condenser with the coil. Remove the high tension lead from the coil terminal and fit a 12-inch jumper wire to the terminal. Now make certain you are properly insulated from the jumper wire, then turn on the ignition switch and hold the open end about ¼-inch from the cylinder head as the engine is cranked. If a spark leaps across the gap regularly, coil and condenser are OK. If there is no spark, or if it is weak or irregular, either the coil or condenser are at fault.

Replace the condenser and repeat the test. If there is still no spark, the trouble lies in the coil. If the spark now jumps the gap, the condenser was at fault and the trouble has been fixed.

Another test of a condenser is for internal grounding. Disconnect the condenser wire and connect a test lamp or jumper

➤ *Condenser can be tested for grounding with test lamp. Disconnect condenser lead and attach alligator clip of lamp to it. Turn on ignition and touch prod of test lamp to ignition points terminal. If lamp lights, condenser is internally grounded and should be replaced.*

wire to it. Touch the other end of the test lamp or jumper wire against the battery's starter terminal. If the test lamp should light, or the jumper wire should spark, the condenser is defective and should be replaced.

Setting ignition timing. For this you will need a power timing light. There are inexpensive versions that plug into a household outlet, and for weekend mechanics they are adequate.

Totally inadequate is the neon bulb timing light. It just is not bright enough, and on today's cars you can't get it close enough to the timing marks without risk to your hands.

Timing is set with the engine at idle or another specified speed, and with the vacuum tube or hose on the distributor disconnected and plugged. Factory timing specifications are based on the disconnected vacuum tube or hose, and you should not try to do the job any other way.

Slacken the distributor locknut, lockbolt, pinch-clamp on whatever is used. Connect the timing light and start the engine. The light will start flashing.

Aim the light at the timing marks, which are on the crankshaft pulley or vibration damper and a stationary part of the engine adjacent to it.

If timing is off the mark, turn the distributor body until the marks line up. If you can't see the marks, stop the engine and take a look with a flashlight. You may have to short-burst-crank the engine to find the mark on the pulley.

If the marks are covered with road film (and they shouldn't be if you keep your engine clean), wipe them off. You may find several marks, and you will have to check manufacturer's specifications to find out which are the correct ones for your car. If necessary, mark them with chalk.

Once you have the distributor body positioned so that the marks line up, tighten the locking arrangement (bolt, nut, clamp). Now speed up the engine and the timing should advance. If it does not, the mechanical advance mechanism in the distributor is defective. On General Motors V-8's, the mechanical advance is above the points (just below the rotor) and you can easily see if a spring has come off, or stretched. On other distributors the breaker plate must be removed.

Keep the timing light on the marks and reconnect the vacuum tube or hose. With the engine running at idle speed or slightly above, the timing should advance as soon as the tube or hose is back on. The advance in timing will also cause the engine to speed up a bit. If the timing does not change, the vacuum advance unit is stuck and should be replaced. This can be done on the car in most cases.

Wiring. From the coil to distributor, and from distributor to spark plugs is a mare's-nest of most important wiring. These high tension wires should be firmly soft. If they are hard, cracked, or gooey with oil, replace them all. Cost is low for a new set of high tension wiring, and the results are well worth your trouble. A little cleaning fluid on a clean rag does a good job of wiping off the top of the coil, so electricity can't sneak out of the wires and lose itself to ground.

Check your spark plugs.

Nuts and bolts are next. Use a good set of wrenches to tighten all on the manifold (both intake and exhaust) carburetor attachment, and other odds and ends of hex-headed objects you can find. After thousands of miles of vibration they loosen. Leaking intake manifolds could burn plugs or valves, as well as destroy efficiency of the fuel mixture.

Cylinder head bolts should also be tightened, but this job must be done with a torque wrench.

As you well know, exhaust fumes are both dangerous and unpleasant, which makes a tight exhaust manifold a blessing and a necessity.

Other steps in tuning for power are:

1. Adjusting valves.
2. Servicing the heat riser.
3. Replacing or servicing the air filter.
4. Servicing the hardware installed for smog control.

Road testing the car. This is done in the following sequence: In high, run along a level road at some 10 mph. The engine should pull evenly, without surge or hesitation. Should it not be smooth, work the idle mixture needles until you have as smooth an idle as possible.

Gradual acceleration resulting from a slow even pressure on the throttle is the next check. During this one, you should have even acceleration, without hesitation or leaping forward. Try this several times, paying close attention to evenness of the speed increase. You will then notice that between 40 and 60 mph there will be a sudden surge forward, though you have not moved your foot that much. Action in the engine room comes from the opening of the power valve(s) or secondary throttle blades. All of this is controlled by engine vacuum and position of your foot.

There's more fun to the third checkout. While running 20 to 25 mph, floor the throttle. Here you want a smooth, even increase in speed. Again, lack of flat spots is the most important thing. Should the engine seem to gasp once or twice when you floor the throttle, try moving the accelerator pump lever to another hole. This modifies the amount of fuel pumped into the engine and is an adjustment worth making. Make this test several times so you'll have a good idea how well an engine can run. Then as performance changes when the engine ages, you'll be in a better position to determine when another tuning is needed.

The last test is to hold the throttle in a steady position at 40 to 50 mph on a flat road. Here is where smoothness is the top dog. The engine should keep you rolling at

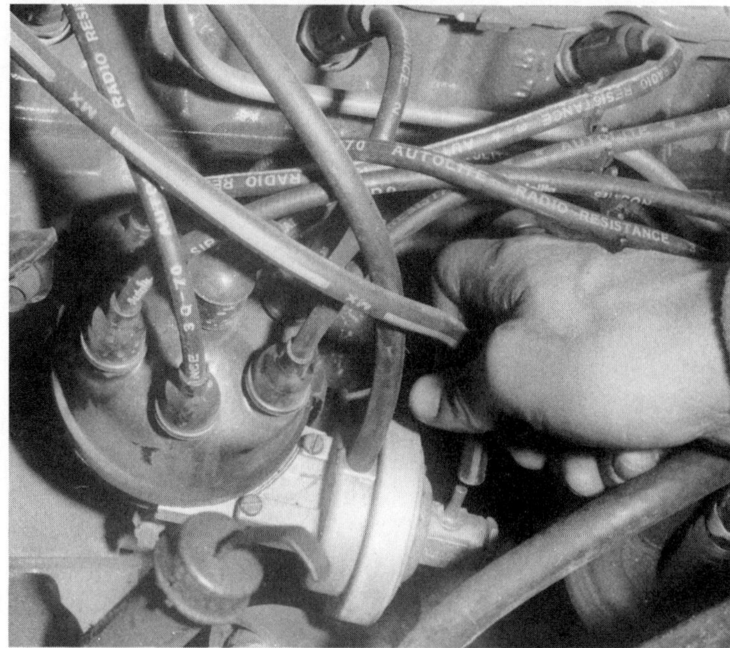

When setting ignition timing, always disconnect vacuum line from distributor and plug the line. (A golf tee makes a suitable plug.)

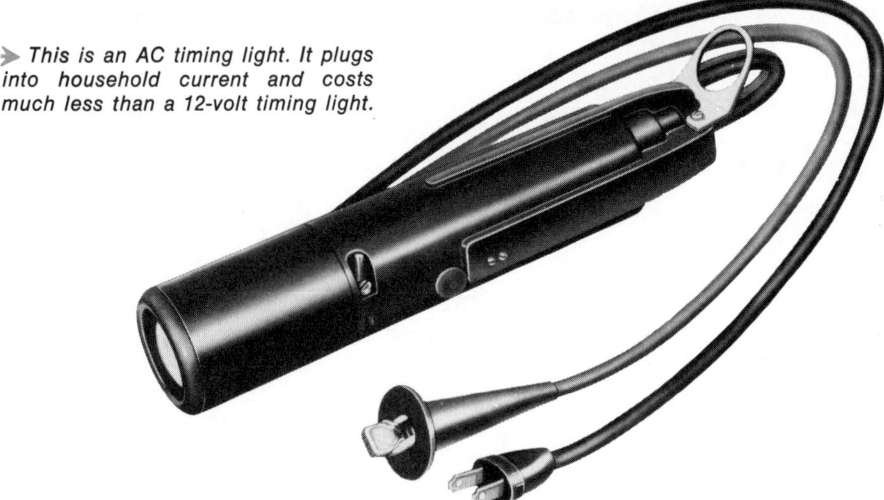

This is an AC timing light. It plugs into household current and costs much less than a 12-volt timing light.

an even pace. If not, the carburetor float level may be off, or the vacuum line to the distributor could be leaking enough to cause spark advance to wander.

One thing is certain—after you've spent the necessary four hours making a thorough tune-up, you will have an engine that outperforms most others of its type. It will also run smoother and be more pleasant to drive, while giving you better fuel mileage than ever before. P.W.

See also: BATTERIES; BEARINGS; CHOKE, AUTOMATIC; COOLING SYSTEMS, AUTO; ELECTRICAL, AUTO; ENGINE; FILTERS; GASKETS; OIL, ENGINE; POWER STEERING, AUTO; SPARK PLUG; STARTER; TRANSMISSION, AUTO; VALVES.

Keep Your Car's Upholstery in Good Condition

Why bother washing and polishing the outside of your car when the interior is a mess? Here's how to keep the inside clean and in good repair

THE BEAUTIFUL OUTSIDE appearance of a carefully washed and waxed automobile is meaningless if the interior does not match.

Fortunately, today's vinyl upholstery is extremely easy to keep clean and, with special products available, also easy to repair and recolor.

Most mild household spray cleaners will do a very nice job on car vinyl upholstery, removing dirt easily, and doing a reasonable job on stains.

If your car's upholstery is beyond quick cleanup, a recoloring is the answer.

There are several brands of recoloring on the market and they work on vinyl, leather and Naugahyde. The recolorings are available both in brush-on or aersol spray form. Generally the brush-on is recommended because it is more economical than the spray, it requires no masking and it can be mixed like paint to the exact shade you want. Each type of recoloring also helps the vinyl resist cracking.

Also available in several brands is a highly effective vinyl upholstery and top repair kit. The material in the kit, a sort of vinyl putty, is available in colors to match original equipment upholstery.

You just trim the ripped area then apply the repair material with a spatula. Smooth over the damaged area with the spatula. Select the proper graining paper. (The kit comes with paper that is embossed to match different car upholstery grains.) Place the graining paper on the damaged area and heat with an iron. Remove the graining paper and you actually will not be able to find the "patch" a week later.

If your car is an older one or an economy model, with broadcloth or flatcloth upholstery, keeping it clean presents some problems.

Broadcloth and flatcloth. Avoid using any solutions containing water on broadcloth no matter how efficiently they remove signs of soiling or stains. Broadcloth finishes are produced by a process employing multiple pressings and other operations which result in the fine finish of this fabric. Water causes the nap to curl and become rough. The result is an unsightly appearance and restoration of the original finish is impossible.

The use of a volatile cleaner is recommended on both flatcloth and broadcloth upholstery. Naphtha or gasoline may be used, but make sure that no coloring or tetraethly lead is contained in the solvent. Since naphtha and gasoline are dangerous as a fire hazard, they should only be used as a last resort when a safer type of cleaner, such as carbon tetrachloride, is not available. Make sure there is plenty of ventilation when using any type of volatile cleaner since the fumes are toxic. Also, remember to wear rubber gloves to protect the skin if it is sensitive to irritation.

After all dust and dirt have been removed from the material, wet a cloth with the volatile cleaner. Spread the cloth open and permit the cleaner to evaporate so that the cloth is just damp. Apply the cloth to the upholstery with a very light pressure and rub over a small area at a time. Change to a clean portion of the cloth every few strokes.

If the material is to be gone over again, give it time to dry thoroughly. This will prevent the solvent from penetrating to the padding underneath. Avoid soaking or heavily wetting the upholstery with any volatile cleaner.

Upholstery on doors is treated in the same way. Remove all seats that can be easily taken out of the car for cleaning or clean them inside the car using the same procedure. For best results, all the upholstery should be dry before using.

Leather. Genuine or imitation leather (such as Volkswagen's), requires the use of neutral soap which is obtainable at almost any drugstore. Never use volatile cleaners, household detergents or soaps, furniture polishes, oils or bleaches. These may mar the finish of the leather permanently.

There is a natural tendency for leather to show signs of wrinkling; it may also bear the marks from the animal's encounters with barbed wire and other scars. Such marks do not impair its durability or quality. However, wrinkles and scars are natural collectors of dirt and dust, and if this condition continues, the dirt becomes a hard

Modern vinyl upholstery is normally cleaned with household spray cleaners.

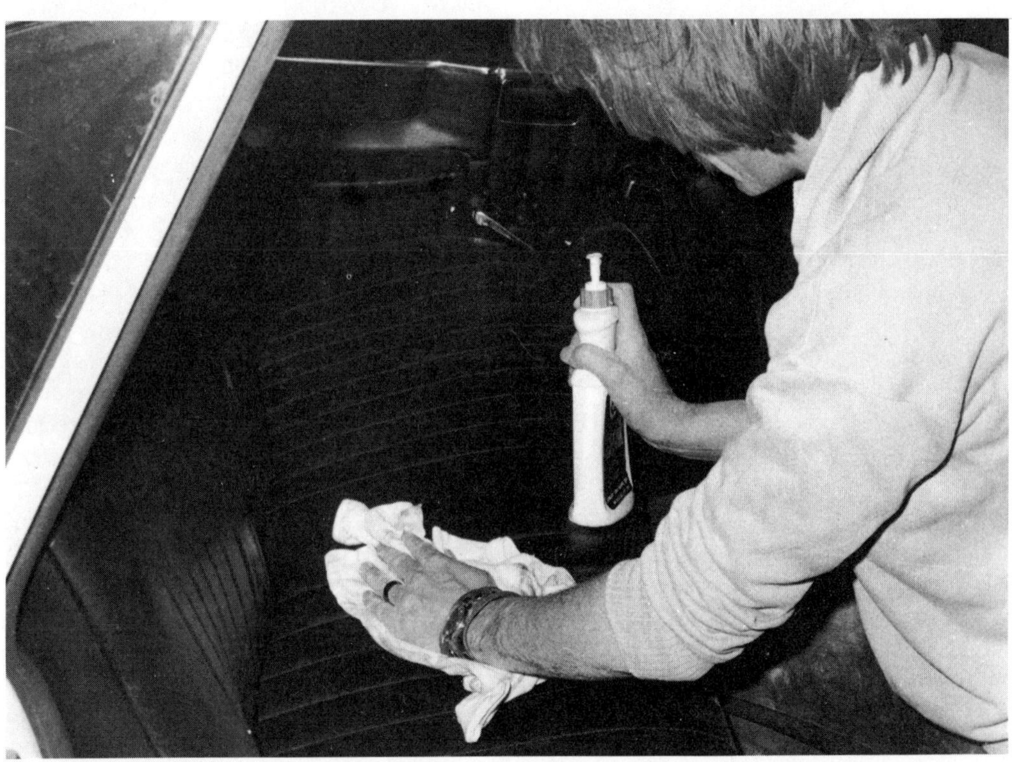

and abrasive grit. Under pressure, this grit will cut into the finish and will be the cause of color bleeding and cracking in pressure areas.

To restore the original bright color, use lukeworm water and a neutral soap. Work up a heavy suds and apply only the suds to the leather. Next, go over the leather again, but this time use only a damp, clean cloth. Then wipe the leather with a soft, dry cloth. This same treatment can be used in the treatment of imitation leathers.

Ceilings and floors. Ceilings should be cleaned in the same way as the rest of the upholstery. Use the cleaning agent recommended to the type of material.

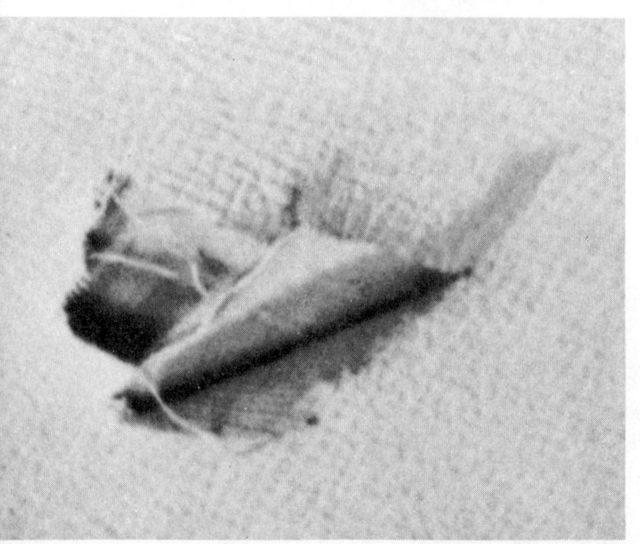

▲ *Vinyl patch kit can make this tear disappear. Start by cutting around tear to eliminate flap.*

Floor carpets are best maintained by frequent and thorough brushing and the use of a vacuum cleaner. If this does not remove the dirt, use a foam-type cleaner to do the job. Do not apply the foam cleaner to more than one square foot of carpet at a time. Use a vacuum cleaner to remove the foam from each processed section. After cleaning, the carpet may be fluffed by working a soft bristle brush gently over the nap. Make sure the carpet is completely dry before using and open the windows to prevent mildew.

If a carpet has been badly stained and must be removed for cleaning, care must be taken to prevent damage. Carpets are cemented or held in place with metal molding, or both. First, remove screws and molding; then turn back a corner of the carpet. Use a wide-blade putty knife to separate the carpet from the cement. Do not pull or jerk the carpet. Avoid getting any of the cement on the face of the carpet. Once removed, use a volatile cleaner to remove oil or grease spots; then clean with foam as outlined earlier.

➤ *Apply paste vinyl to hole and smooth down.*

Stain removal. Different kinds of stains require different treatments and the use of the wrong treatment may cause even worse damage than the stain itself. However, the removal of the most common stains is well within the ability of the average person. It should be remembered that the sooner after occurrence the stain is treated, the better will be the results.

Battery acid. Saturate affected area with common household ammonia. Allow it to remain on the stain about one minute to neutralize the acid. Rub the spot with a clean cloth wet with cold water. Blot with dry cloth and repeat wet rag application. Action must be immediate to limit destructive action of the acid on the fabric.

Blood. Never try to remove blood with hot water or with soap and water. The action may set the stain and make removal almost impossible. With a clean cloth wet with cold water, rub the blood stain to remove as much of it as possible. As the wet cloth absorbs the stain, fold it to present a clean portion to the stain. Failure to do so will work the stain in a diluted form back into the material. If done soon after the stain's occurrence, this procedure should remove all of it. Should the stain be obstinate after this treatment, apply a bit of household ammonia. Let stand a minute or two, then rub the stain with a clean cloth saturated with cold water. Should the water and ammonia treatment fail to have the desired effect, another remedy must be used. Make a thick paste of corn starch and cold water and apply it to the stain. After the paste has dried, remove it to determine if the paste has absorbed the stain. If not, several applications may be necessary.

Candy. Non-chocolate candy stains are best removed by applying a cloth soaked in very hot water to the stain. Rub gently and allow to dry. Should some sign of stain remain, remove by applying a cloth wet with volatile cleaner. For chocolate candy, the same treatment is recommended except that lukewarm water instead of very hot water should be used.

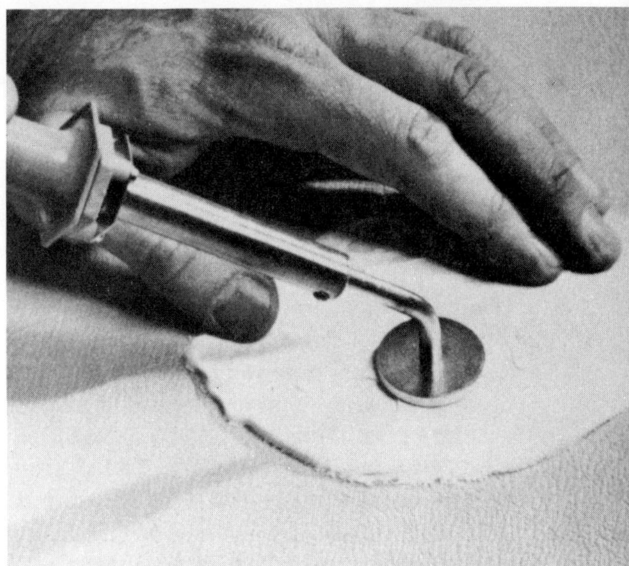

▲ *Place texturing paper over paste and heat with iron to cure paste.*

▼ *Remove texturing paper and the repair is perfect. Texturing paper has matched repaired area to rest of upholstery. Kit has papers with different textures to match all cars.*

Chewing gum. Apply an ice cube to the gum to harden it. Scrape off hardened particles with a dull knife or edge of a spoon.

If all the gum cannot be removed, moisten it with a volatile cleaner. While the gum is moist, remove it by separating it from the material with a dull knife or spoon.

Fruit, liquor or wine. Apply very hot water with a clean rag, and wet thoroughly. Rub briskly with hot water soaked cloth. If the stain persists, scrape with a dull knife or spoon while wet, and allow to dry. If signs of the stain remain, then rub lightly with a cloth dampened with a volatile cleaner. Never use soap and water since such treatment may permanently set the stain. Also, never use heat to dry the treated area.

Enamel, lacquer or paint. Wet a clean cloth in turpentine. Rub over the stain to remove as much as possible. If the stain is stubborn, saturate with a mixture of one part denatured alcohol and one part benzine. Apply dull knife or spoon to stain and scrape away as much as possible. Repeat if necessary. Apply a final saturation of the mixture and follow immediately with a vigorous rubbing with a cloth soaked with lukewarm soapsuds. Rinse by sponging with cold water.

Tar. Moisten the tar slightly with a volatile cleaner. Use a dull knife to scrape away as much as you can. Rub the spot gently with a cloth dampened with a volatile cleaner until it disappears.

Grease or oil. Remove as much of the grease or oil as is possible with a dull knife blade or kitchen spatula. Rub lightly with a cloth wet with a volatile cleaner over the affected area. Rub from the outer edges of the stain toward the center to reduce the possibility of spreading the stain. Keep applying cleaner on fresh cloths as needed. Confine oil or grease to as small an area as possible by pouring a small quantity of the cleaner directly on the stain. Keep doing this until no more grease or oil can be blotted up. This method also aids in the preventing of a ring formation. If repeated treatments with the solvent still leave a dirty stain, rub the area with lukewarm soapsuds. Rinse with cold water applied with a clean cloth. Always rub from the outside to the center of the stain.

Ice cream. Wet the stain with very hot water applied with a clean cloth. Scrape wet area to remove as much of the stain as possible. Rub vigorously with very hot water again. If the stain is stubborn, rub it with a cloth wet with warm neutral soap suds. Rince by rubbing with a cloth wet with cold water, and allow to dry. If faint signs still remain, rub with a cloth dampened with a volatile cleaner.

Mildew. Rub mildew vigorously with warm soap suds and rinse by rubbing with a cloth dipped in cold water. Old mildew stains are harder to remove. The only treatment recommended for treating discolorations caused by old mildew growths is the use of oxalic acid. Wet the mildew with a 10% oxalic acid solution. Let it soak a minute or so. Next use a blotter or absorbent cloth to blot up acid. Rinse with either hot or cold water. Repeat this sequence as often as is necessary.

Shoe polish. White shoe polish should be allowed to dry completely. With a brush, go over the dry stain briskly until it disappears. Should it persist, moisten it with cold water. Allow to dry, then brush vigorously until it vanishes. Wax or paste type shoe polishes need to be rubbed gently with a cloth dampened with a volatile cleaner. Rub from the outside of the stain to the center, changing to a clean portion of the cloth frequently.

Lipstick. Different brands of lipstick are made of varying components which make stains difficult to remove. Use a spoon or dull knife to scrape away as much as possible. Rub lightly with a cloth dampened with a volatile cleaner. Repeat several times. Should some stain remain after repeated treatments, it is recommended that no more be done to it. Other measures might do more harm than good.

See also: SPOT REMOVAL.

How to Repair Your Vacuum Cleaner

You can save on repair bills by repairing this busy appliance yourself

Popular pot style vacuum cleaner is basically of simple construction, easy to open and service. This home and institutional model came with a five year guarantee yet looks and works like new after seven years of hard use.

YOUR VACUUM CLEANER is a multi-functional appliance built to remove loose soil from just about anything in your home, including carpets, floors, walls, draperies, furniture and clothing. It can also be used as a blower to dislodge dust from such hard-to-reach places as behind radiators and piano interiors, to spray moth repellent or paint, and even to fluff and blow out allergenic dust from pillows. But your appliance can do these many necessary jobs only if it is maintained and operated properly.

When your vacuum cleaner fails to start, or stops suddenly while in use, check first to see if it is getting electrical power. The cord plug may have been pulled from the wall outlet, or the wall outlet itself may be dead because of an area power failure or because an overload on the branch circuit in your home has kicked the circuit breaker or blown a fuse. Test the wall outlet with a table lamp. If you have power, flip the on-off switch a few times and jiggle the switch handle while in the "on" position; this simple test will sometimes reveal a switch defect.

If the appliance is alive, but does not clean properly because the suction is not as strong as it should be, see if the hose is clogged by blowing a blast of air through it (out of doors!). Also check the dust bag which may be too full; the bag should be replaced when only about half full. Also make certain that all hose, wand, nozzle and hose-to-tank connections are tight.

If these preliminary tests do not cure the problem, it's time to take a look at the appliance's innards. A pot type vacuum cleaner is shown here, but the same general inspection procedure will apply to almost any style of appliance. First examine the housing carefully to find the bolts that hold the housing sections together. These will be on the bottom of the pot in some cases, or perhaps underneath a mid-level rubber bumper as in the example shown here. After the upper section of the housing has

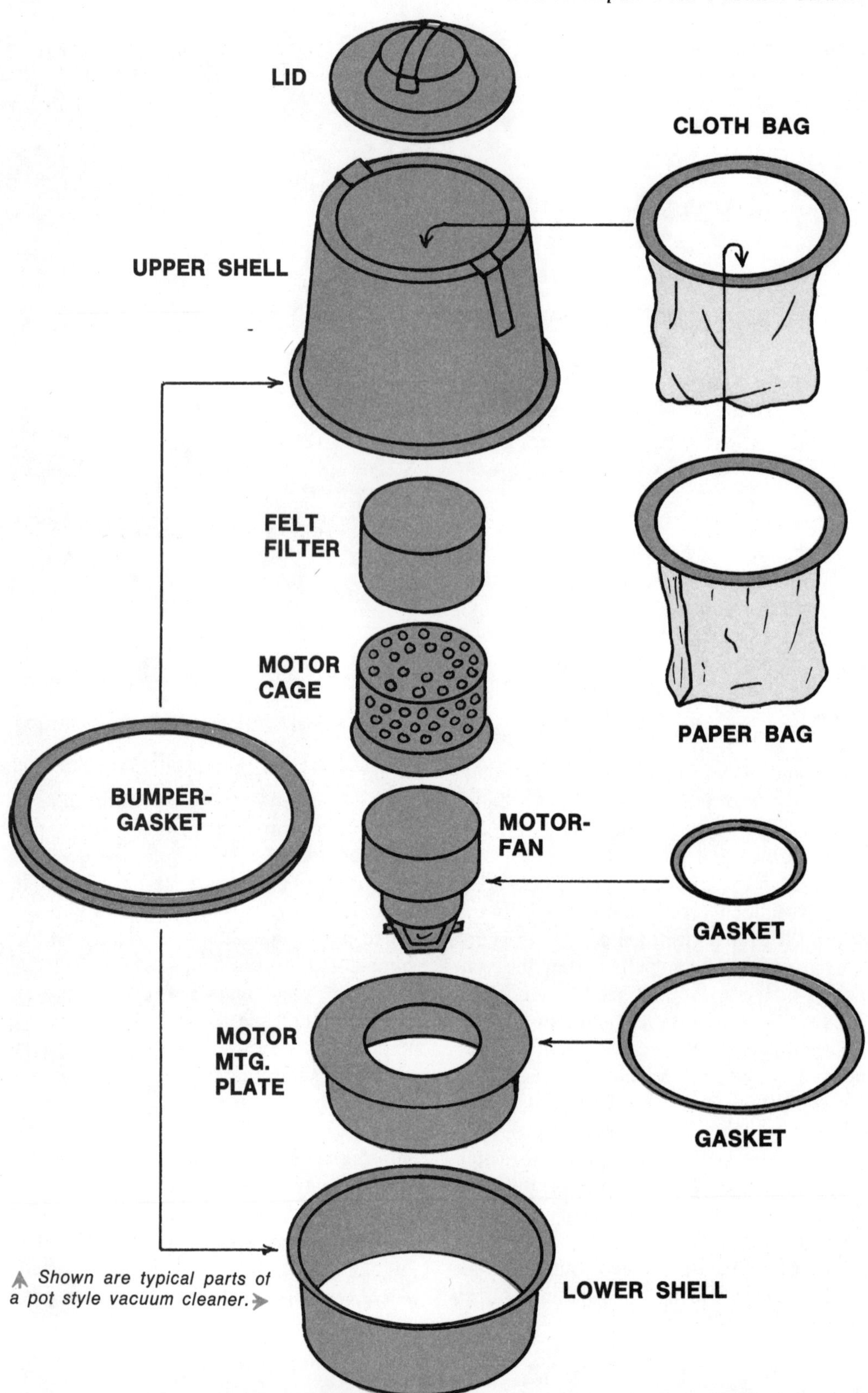

Shown are typical parts of a pot style vacuum cleaner.

been removed, you can probably just lift out the interior section to which the motor and fan unit is mounted. Be careful not to damage the gasket.

If you suspect that the trouble is in the on-off switch, first make sure that the coil spring controlling movement of the foot pad is in good condition, and not jamming the switch action. Next bridge the switch terminals with a short length of insulated wire while the power cord is plugged into a wall socket. If the appliance comes alive, you need a new switch. If the motor remains dead even when the switch is bridged, look for a defective power cord and check all connections between the switch and motor. Maybe a wire nut used to join the wires leading to the motor has vibrated loose and the connection has been broken. Check such connections with the power cord removed from the wall socket. The power cord itself may be defective. The easiest way to check this is by bridging the two conductors of the cord at some convenient points inside the appliance with a test light you can obtain at any hardware store (just a bulb with two short wires having exposed ends); if the bulb fails to light, you prob-

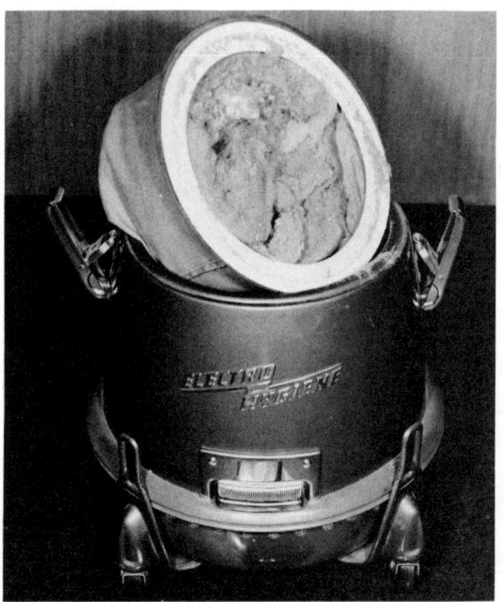

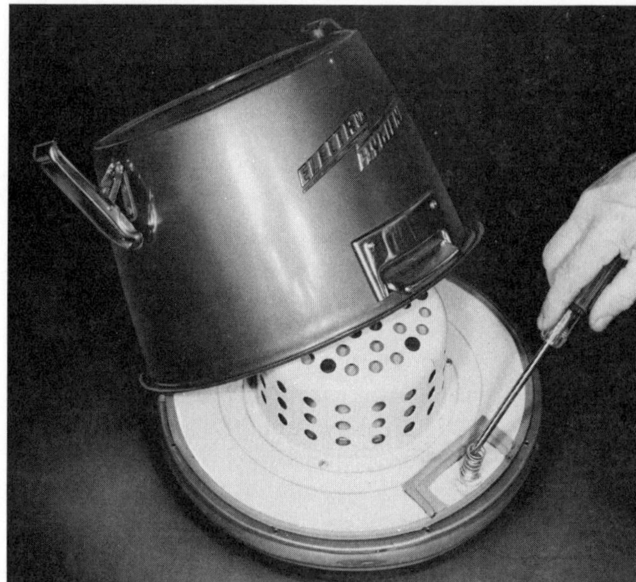

Coil spring around switch button, which controls action of the foot pedal, might be defective and cause poor switching action. Remove the perforated cage around motor/fan assembly only if it needs cleaning. Entire white section lifts out to reveal motor on the underside.

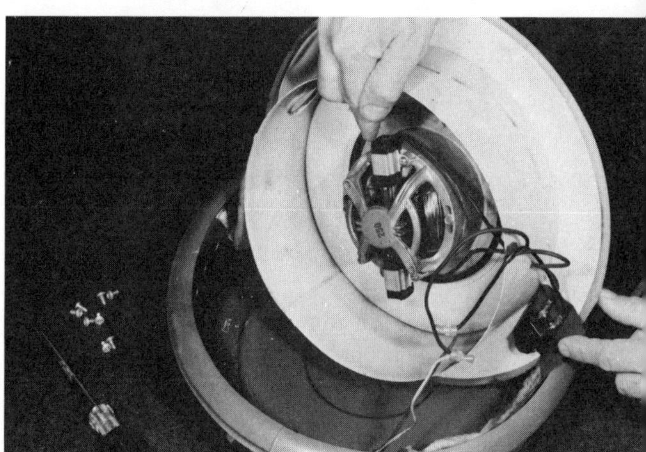

Two common sources of electrical problems are the motor brushes and the on-off switch. Also check wire connections between the switch and motor.

Shown here is a common operational fault. Dust bag should have been emptied or replaced when only half full to ensure proper suction and to provide adequate cooling air flow over the motor.

ably have a bad power cord. Another way is to short the two conductors inside the appliance and bridge the prongs of the power cord plug with a flashlight bulb and dry cell wired in series. Or an ohmmeter could be used in lieu of the bulb and cell; a high resistance reading indicates a broken conductor in the power cord.

If the motor operates, but in erratic fashion, pay special attention to the condition of the motor brushes and commutator. If the commutator is very dirty, polish it very carefully with very fine sandpaper; do *not* use emery cloth or steel wool. If the brushes are worn down so that they do not make firm contact, obtain new brushes of the same size. Sometimes the trouble derives from poor pressure springs, or corrosion on the wire contacts to the brushes, so check these before buying new brushes.

If the motor assembly seems very dirty—perhaps because a torn bag in the dust-collecting compartment lets dirt get through to the motor area—clean it thoroughly and apply lubricant sparingly to all moving shaft and bearing areas. And repair that torn dust bag! Such serious problems as a damaged or loose fan section, frozen bearings or bent armature shaft should be easy enough to spot. Electrical problems within the motor itself, for example a shorted motor coil or a grounded winding, may require professional attention.

When you reassemble the appliance, be sure that all gaskets are in good condition and that you fit them properly in place. Even a small leak here can result in noticeable reduction in cleaning efficiency. **J.H.**

See also: ELECTRICAL, HOME; INDIVIDUAL APPLIANCE LISTINGS.

VACUUM CLEANER TROUBLE-SHOOTING CHART

PROBLEM / POSSIBLE CAUSE	DEFECTIVE CORD OR PLUG	DEFECTIVE SWITCH	MOTOR BURNED OUT	MOTOR BRUSHES AND/OR SPRINGS DEFECTIVE	MOTOR COMMUTATOR DIRTY	MOTOR ARMATURE BEARINGS FROZEN	CLOGGED HOSE AND/OR FULL DUST BAG	HOSE AND/OR NOZZLE IMPROPERLY CONNECTED	TANK GASKET SEALS DEFECTIVE OR LOOSE	MOTOR CAGE CLOGGED	AIR EXHAUST HOLES CLOGGED	SHORTED MOTOR COIL	MOTOR WINDINGS GROUNDED	MOTOR/FAN BEARINGS NEED LUBRICATION	ARMATURE BEARINGS WORN	ARMATURE SHAFT BENT	FAN BLADE BENT OR BROKEN
DOES NOT START	√	√	√	√	√	√											
NO SUCTION						√	√	√	√	√	√						
POOR SUCTION						√	√	√	√	√	√			√			
OVERHEATS				√	√	√	√			√	√	√	√	√	√	√	√
ERRATIC MOTOR ACTION	√	√		√	√							√	√	√	√	√	√
NOISY OPERATION				√										√	√		
SHOCK TO OPERATOR	√												√				

How to Do an Engine Valve and Ring Job

This is a big job, but with some help from a jobber and a machine shop, you can do it yourself

THIS ARTICLE IS LIMITED to overhead valve engines, which represent the overwhelming majority of engines in cars on the American road. There are a few foreign and domestic cars with overhead camshaft engines. Such engines require special handling and/or tools to maintain or restore the relationship between the crankshaft and the camshaft. Clearly, when the cylinder head on an overhead camshaft engine is removed, the camshaft comes with it. Because of the special complexities, do not attempt this work on overhead camshaft engines unless you have a factory shop manual and considerable experience.

If your engine pressure readings indicate trouble, you probably have a valve or piston ring job in the planning stages.

The first step is to isolate the problem. Squirt oil into a cylinder and take a compression reading. The oil will temporarily seal off the piston-to-bore clearance, so if compression readings rise to near normal, the problem is in the valves.

If the readings do not rise significantly, the compression loss is because of worn rings.

In either case, you must remove the cylinder head (the procedure is the one you must follow to replace a cylinder head gasket).

The valves. Before removing the cylinder head, or heads, drain the water, remove the water hose if it is an in-line engine, and remove any other accessories fastened to the head or valve covers.

Next, remove the intake manifold. You'll have to disconnect the fuel line and the carburetor throttle linkage and take off a few hoses.

Normally the exhaust manifold can either be disconnected at the exhaust pipe and pulled with the cylinder head, or disconnected at the cylinder head and pulled away from it, permitting you to lift the head out.

Next, remove the pushrods, and if you wish, also the rocker arm assemblies. If the engine has ball-socket rocker arms, they are simply loosened and turned aside where necessary to reach the head bolts. A ratchet and socket on an extension are used to loosen the head bolts. After all bolts are removed, the head should lift off easily. If it sticks, bump it with a mallet, but do not pry between the head and block with a screwdriver. Lay the head, or heads, aside and clean the piston tops by turning the engine to bring them to the top of the block. Scrape off the carbon and clean off any gasket cement you notice on the block.

Take the complete head assembly or assemblies into a jobber's. He disassembles the head, cleans it, faces the valves, and seats and reassembles the head. A jobber can do the valve job so much quicker than you that his price is well worth it. A big C-shaped spring compressor quickly pops out the valve keepers and the valves are removed, the head or heads are degreased and checked to see that they are true on the gasket face, and, if it is necessary, the face of the head is milled to true it up.

Stems, seals and springs. If you determined that the valve guides were allowing a lot of oil to be wasted, the jobber can now modify the upper ends of the valve guides to permit the installation of premium oil seals to prevent oil leakage past the stem of the valve.

While the heads are in the jobber's shop,

Cylinder head is pulled with pushrods removed and rocker shaft left in place.

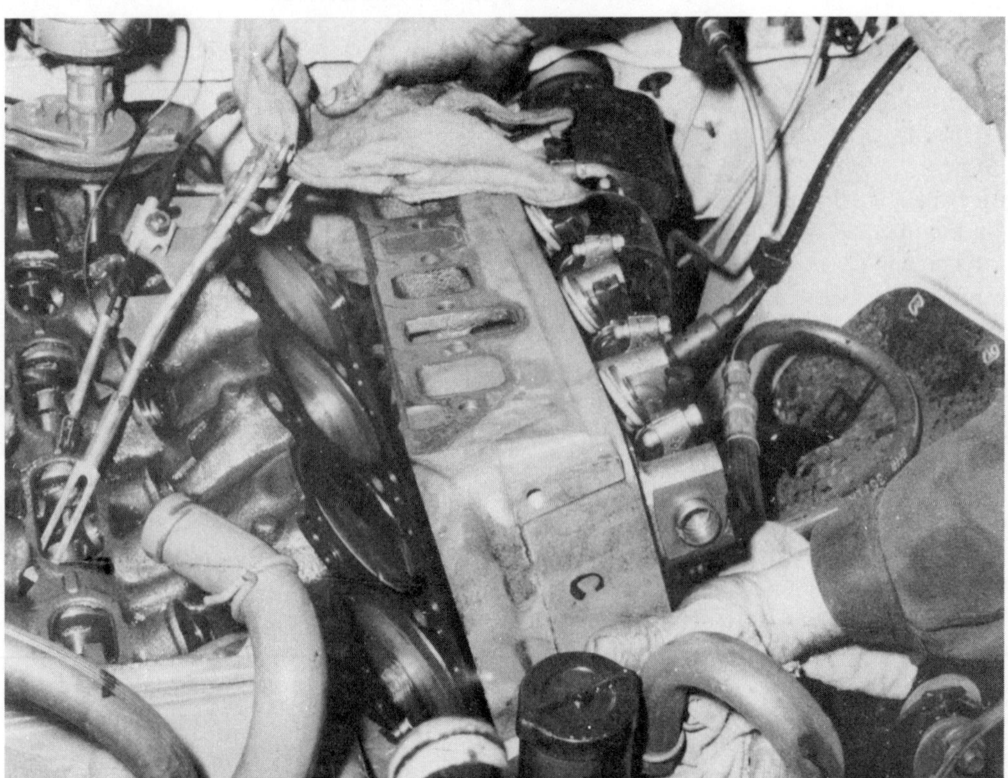

Scrape off carbon from tops of pistons, and gasket residue from block and cylinder head (as shown), using gasket scraper.

Valves are removed from cylinder head with c-shaped compressor.

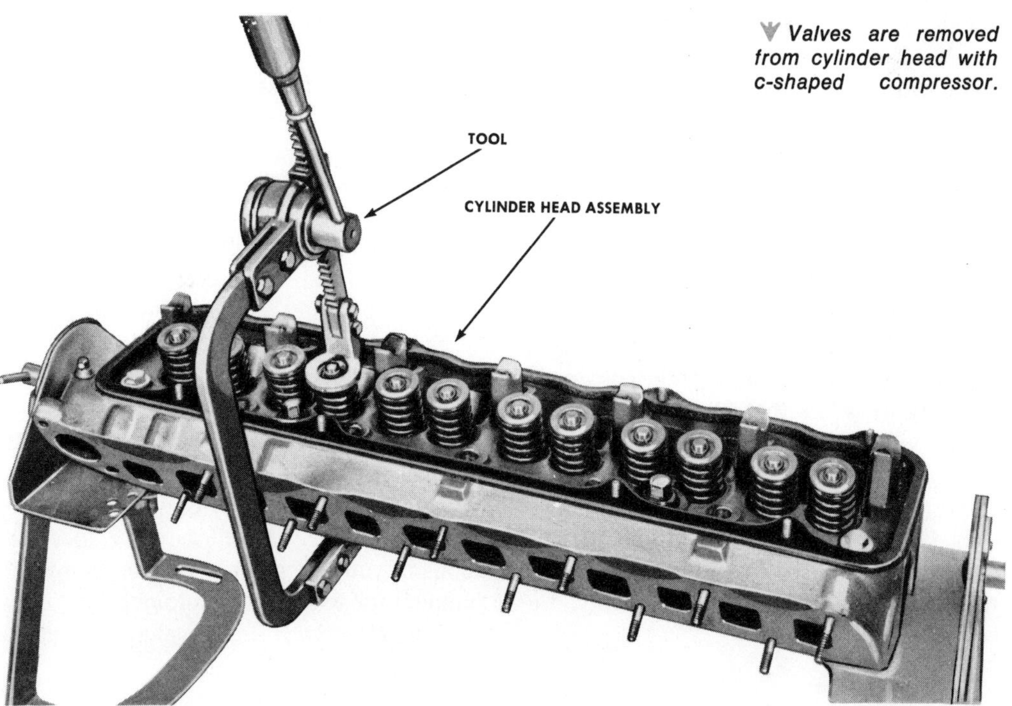

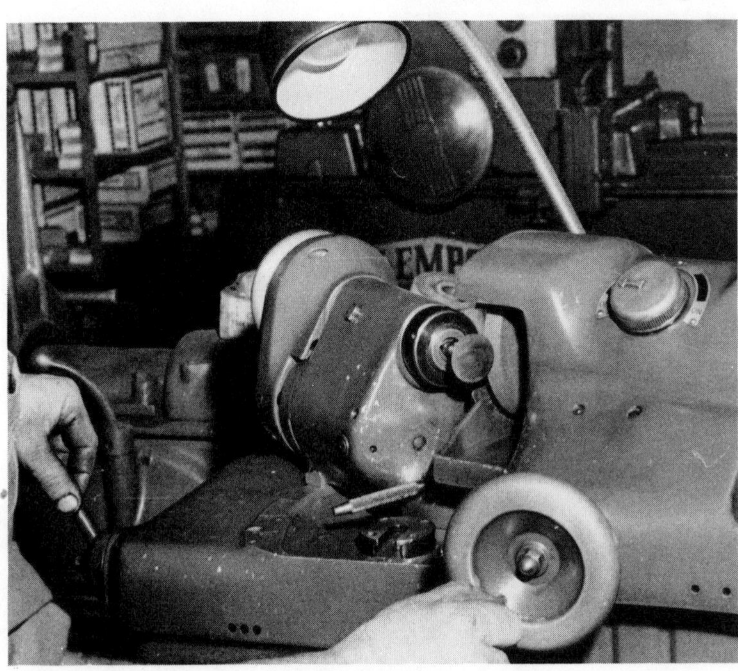

Valves are refaced on special machine. Liquid coolant may be poured over valve during this operation.

the valve springs can be tested to see if they have the correct pressure, and that there is no great variation between the pressures in the set. The jobber slips each spring into a tester that permits it to be compressed a definite amount, to a certain length. A table furnished by the manufacturer gives the specifications that the valve springs from any particular engine should meet. Correct springs are available from the jobber to replace any springs that do not meet specifications.

The valve guides are cleaned with a wire brush spun by a drill. If they are excessively worn, they are pressed out and new ones are installed. The valve seats are recut with a special grinding stone that is positioned precisely by pilots that fit into the guides.

The valves themselves are refaced on a machine that rotates them against a rotating stone, while a liquid coolant is pumped over the valve. Many conscientious jobbers check the valves for fit and hand lap them with grinding compound if necessary, for accurate seating.

The jobber will reassemble your overhead valve head, so all you have to do is reinstall it.

Tightening down the cylinder head does require a torque wrench.

Adjustment. After all the valves have been installed, loosen the rocker arms so each valve is loose and the lifter can be moved slightly up and down when the valve is seated. Using a feeler gauge, set all the exhaust valves .002-inch wider than the hot specifications (if a hot setting is specified) and .001-inch wider for the intake valves. After the head and accessories are reinstalled, start the engine and warm it. Presetting when cold will result in only a few of the tappets requiring a resetting when hot.

The above information is for a solid lifter engine. If your engine has hydraulic tappets, tappet clearance usually is zero spacing. To be sure of this, as well as other specifications in your engine, always use the service manual for your model automobile.

The ring job. Before plunging into a

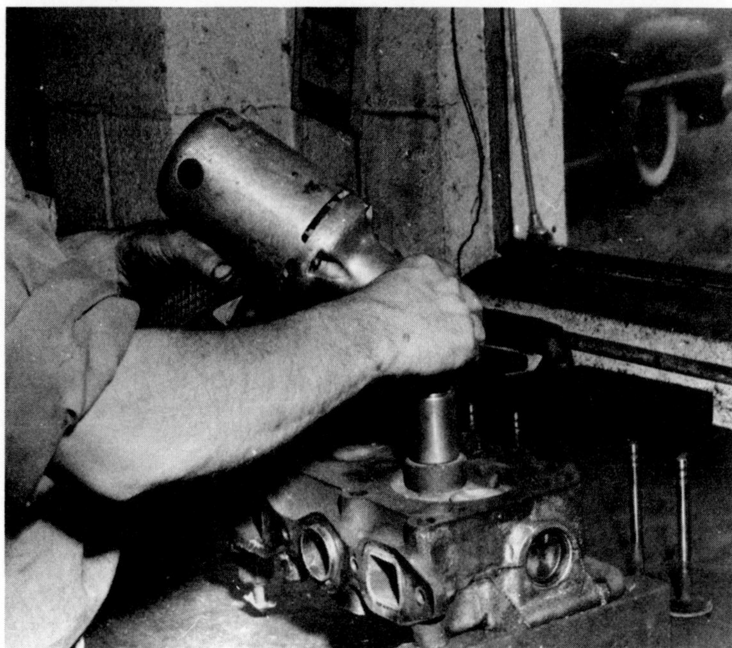

Valve seats are refaced with special grinding stones to precise angles.

ring job, remove the accessory system parts that will interfere with the job. Then, the head, or heads in the case of a V-8, must come off, the oil pan must be removed, connecting rod caps taken off and the pistons slipped out from the top of the cylinder block. In all probability you'll have to remove the "ridge" which occurs at the top of the cylinder bore. The ridge is caused by the wearing action of the upper edge of the top piston ring and is fairly sharp. In many cases you cannot slip the piston out because the ring catches on the ridge and there is danger of breaking the piston or ring lands.

The lands also may be sprung so that you will have trouble installing new rings. Here is where you should get help from a shop man who has a ridge reamer. This tool reams or cuts away the ridge left by the old rings. The job should be done while the pistons are still in the bores, and you probably can rent a reamer from an automotive machine shop, but if you have a shop man come to your garage to do the job for you, he probably can also "mike" the cylinders for taper and out-of-round wear and run a hone in the cylinder bores to break the glaze to make a better seat for the new rings.

Valve spring tension is checked on special rig with torque wrench. Manufacturers supply spring tension specifications.

Start by draining the cooling system, and the engine oil from the crankcase. Then, using a socket wrench with a ratchet remove the cylinder head stud nuts or bolts, and lift the head.

Note the tops of the pistons. There may be an arrow or mark, such as the "dimple" on the piston denoting which way the pistons are installed. If there is no mark, make one with a sharp center punch so you can reinstall them correctly. If you see any strange marks on the heads of the pistons, a valve has been hitting the piston head. This could have been caused by a broken valve spring, or one that is weak, or by someone having the cylinder heads milled to raise the compression ratio, and overdoing it. In some cases there would be a clatter that could be heard when the engine was running.

Connecting rods. To remove the oil pan, jack up the car and put a couple of supports under the front end to give yourself more room to work. Be sure the supports are sturdy.

The actual removal of the oil pan is not necessarily simple. It is true that on some cars all you have to do is remove the screws that hold it and lower away. On other cars, you may have to remove a front crossmember. If the suspension is bolted to this crossmember, leave the work to a professional. In many cases, the engine mounts have to be disconnected and the engine must be jacked up several inches. Again, this is for the professional.

If your car is one of the simple oil pan types, however, go ahead and drop the pan.

When the oil pan is off, you will find some of the connecting rods in a position where you can remove the cotters or other "locks" on the nuts. Remove the caps of these rods and mark them (if they are not already marked), so that you will know from which rod the cap was removed and in what position it was on the rod. On an in-line engine, the rods usually have marks on the rod and cap on the camshaft side of the engine. If you can, have a helper handy to turn the engine crankshaft slowly with the fan belt so the other rods can be brought into position for removal.

➤ Valve guides must be measured for wear. This split ball gauge is often used. Gauge adjusts for width until it is a tight fit in guide, then its diameter is measured. If guide is worn, it must be replaced. If guide is good, it can be cleaned with a reamer.

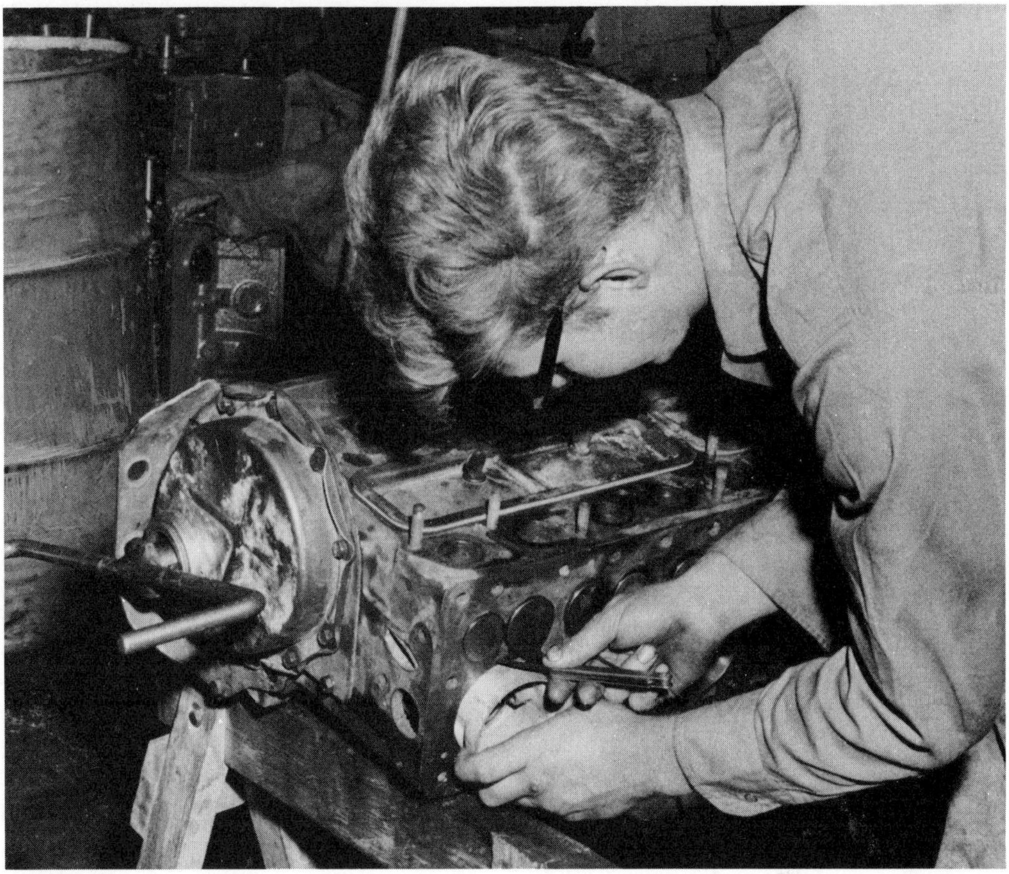

▲ Piston (without rings) also must have adequate clearance in its bore. This is checked by pushing piston with appropriate feeler gauge into bore (piston upside down), as shown.

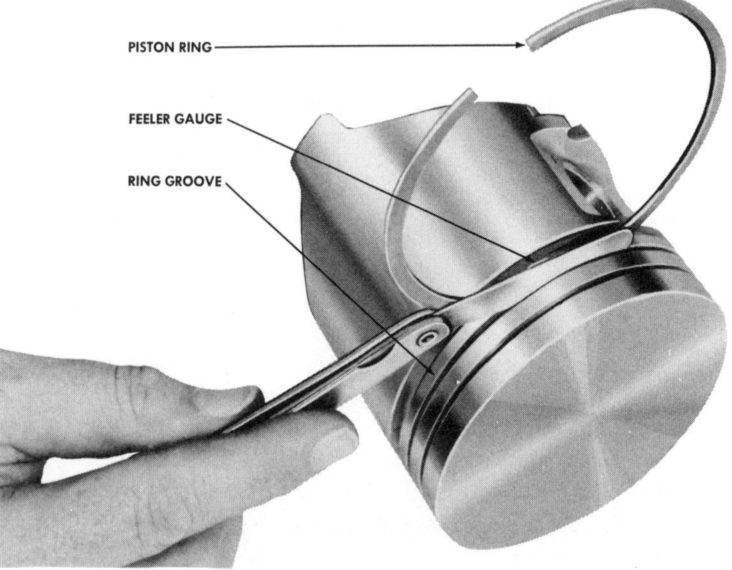

➤ Piston ring clearance in groove must meet specifications. Clearance is measured with feeler gauge, as shown.

Gather up the connecting rod caps and place them in proper sequence on a bench or board. Then rub the tips of your fingers up and down the cylinder bores at the top to determine if you are confronted with a ridge removal job. (Odds are that you will be.)

If you feel a ridge, get the shop man and tell him to bring along a dial gauge, inside micrometer and cylinder hone. After he removes the ridge at the top of the bores, the pistons and rod assemblies can be pushed out of the block. Then the shop man can check each cylinder for taper and out-of-round condition. Many piston ring manufacturers say that where cylinders are not to be rebored, the glaze at least should be removed to let the new rings seat. The shop man will use a spring-loaded hone for this. He may also tell you what rings to use, depending on what his cylinder measurements show.

Variety of rings. The ring makers have done a good job in producing various kinds of rings to meet cylinders with considerable wear. For example, if the taper or out-of-round wear is around .002 to .003-inch, practically any of the standard rings will do a good job. However, if it ranges between .004 and .008-inch, you can get piston rings supported with expanders that will do the work. In any event, you will have the shop man's measurements and any automotive supplier or jobber will recommend the specific rings you should use.

To remove the old rings from the pistons, mechanics use a special tool called a ring spreader, but in its absence you can do it by cutting four strips of thin sheet metal about ⅜ x 3 inches. Slide these strips under the rings and work them around the piston until equally spaced. The rings will then be expanded so they can be pulled off the piston over the strips. Most mechanics simply pull the ring ends apart and break the rings. If you try this, use gloves, since the ring ends can puncture fingers.

The job of cleaning the pistons and their grooves is very important; the measurements for the new rings depend upon it. Also clean out the cylinder bores which have previously been conditioned with the hone.

Inspect the piston for cracks, broken lands or excessive wear of the ring grooves. Here again it will pay you to let the jobber size up the piston-ring groove. He may advise regrooving, a process that also increases the width. Fillers are now obtainable which you slip into the groove over the piston ring to take up the extra space resulting from regrooving.

Finally, while the jobber has the pistons, have him resize the piston skirt. There are various processes used for this, one of which is Nurlizing, which actually makes worn pistons practically as good as new at only a fraction of the cost of replacing them. The process gives a closer fit without scuffing or scoring, prevents piston slap which you might otherwise get even with new rings, and assures adequate piston lubrication.

Fitting the rings. Now comes the actual fitting of the rings to the pistons and cylinder bores. A common practice is to locate two compression rings and two oil rings above the pin. The rings must be fitted into the cylinders so that the rings pass the smallest part of the bore with enough end or gap clearance to prevent binding, but no more than enough.

Place the top compression ring of cylinder No. 1 into the cylinder and push it downward with the top of the piston to the unworn portion of the bore. By pushing it with the piston, it will be square in the bore. If your pistons are not flat, but angle or "pentroof" type, ask your parts house or machine shop to lend you a flathead piston of the correct size to make this test. With a feeler gauge, check the gap for end clearance of the ring according to the ring manufacturers' instructions that come with the rings.

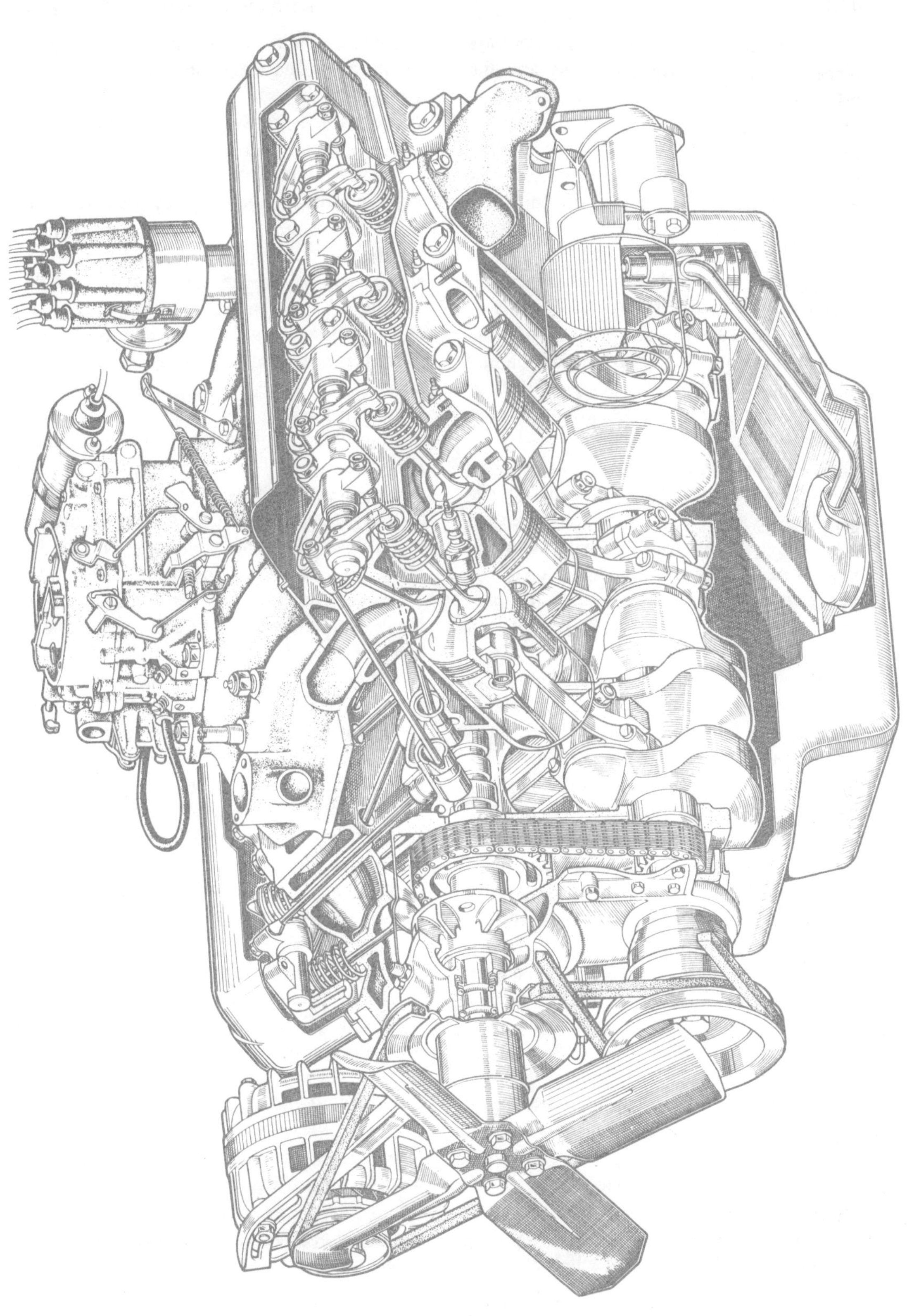

If the specified feeler gauge will not pass through the gap, remove the ring and file it by pushing it back and forth across a flat, smooth-cut file held in a vise. Do this carefully so that the gap is not distorted, but is square top, bottom, front and back. Check the other rings for piston No. 1 in the same way. Now take the top ring of No. 1 piston and roll it around the groove to see that it is free. To make sure that the clearance between the ring and its groove is correct, refer to the instructions packed with the rings or look in your shop service manual for the specifications, and check with a feeler gauge. Then proceed with the other rings for the rest of the pistons.

To slip the new rings into their respective grooves, a tool called a piston-ring applier or expander is used. If you don't want to rent one, you can use the strips of metal which you previously used to slide off the old rings—only this time reverse the procedure.

Replacing pistons. You are now ready to reinstall the piston and rod assemblies in their respective cylinders. Be sure to install them in the same bore and position from which they were removed. Check the mark on top of the pistons. On a three-ring piston, arrange the rings so the gaps are 120° apart; on a four ring piston, 90° apart. Arrange them so that no ring gaps come directly in line with the pin.

Then, grasping the connecting rod of the piston, dunk the piston and rings in heavy oil and spread a film of oil around the bore of the cylinder. Then lower the piston-and-rod assembly into the cylinder, having compressed the rings into the grooves with a ring compressor. This compressor is inexpensive, but like the other tools used, you don't have to buy it; it can be rented or borrowed for the job. With the crankshaft turned so the journal for the cylinder is all the way down, push the piston-and-rod assembly down so the upper rod bearing contacts the journal. Have a helper under the car to guide the lower end of the connecting rod. The rod bolts may project and if they strike against the smooth surface of the journal, a gouge or nick could result that would chew up the bearing insert.

At this point you consider doing some work on the connecting rod bearings. It could very well be that some of the oil consumption was due to worn bearings, in which case the oil throw-off was too much for the oil rings to handle. You may give the new rings a much better chance by installing new bearing inserts in the connecting rods.

It is important, after tightening the connecting rod caps, to secure the nuts with cotters or other "locks." Some connecting rod nuts are "self-locking," having plastic inserts, or they are designed with an inside taper that automatically locks them in place. Especially for this latter type setup, a torque wrench should be used, each nut being tightened according to the manufacturer's specifications. Clean the oil pan thoroughly and reinstall it, using new gaskets and oil seals on the pan ends. Reinstall the cylinder heads and other parts using new gaskets, and refill the cooling system and oil pan to the required level.

After you have the job buttoned up, start the engine and run it at fast idle (1500 to 1800 rpm) for about 15 to 20 minutes or until the engine coolant is warm.

Drive the car easily for 50 to 100 miles, then seat the rings by taking the car out on a highway and doing about a dozen full-throttle accelerations from 35 to 55 mph (cruise at 35, full throttle to 55, drop back to 35 and cruise for a mile, then full throttle to 55, etc.).

Laborious break-in procedures over a thousand or more miles are out of date. Use a good quality multi-grade oil (an additive is unnecessary). P.W.

See also: BEARINGS; COOLING SYSTEMS, AUTO; ENGINE; FILTERS; GASKETS; OIL, ENGINE; TUNE-UP, ENGINE.

How to Repair Waffle Irons and Grills

These devices are extremely simple and there is very little that can go wrong with them beyond a frayed cord and stuck thermostat

ONCE WAFFLE IRON GRIDS have been properly seasoned and well-oiled, your waffle iron should give long care-free service. This is providing the batter has been made with enough shortening. Many successful cooks have found it helpful to use more shortening than a recipe calls for.

Cleaning a grid that has had batter burned on it requires patience and lots of scraping. The dark color of a grid does not matter. It is only the cooked batter that must be removed. After this has been done the grids must be conditioned again before using. This is usually done by coating the grids liberally with cooking oil and letting the waffle iron run for about a half hour without batter. Never wash the grids with detergent. That will remove the oil that has saturated the pores of the metal and the waffle iron will have to be reconditioned.

Some waffle irons have interchangeable grids. The waffle grids can be removed and replaced by smooth grids for toasting sandwiches or, when left open, they provide two flat cooking surfaces on which bacon and eggs can be fried, or pancakes.

Thermostat adjustment will provide controlled temperatures up to 500° F, which is enough to cook any of our foods.

In some models the grids are held in place by a thumbscrew; in others there is a latch. Removing the grids exposes the heating element and thermostat. We strongly recommend that the grids be removed while the unit is cool and disconnected from the power line.

Most waffle irons are designed to operate on a normal 115-volt 15-ampere house circuit. Electrically the two heater elements (1 upper and 1 lower) may be connected either in series or in parallel. The preference seems to be series because there is not much advantage in baking a waffle on only one side.

Some waffle makers have no pilot light but do have a glass lens set in the cover over the heater element so its glow can be seen. This serves as a pilot light.

The temperature is controlled by an adjustable bimetal type of thermostat having an off position. The thermostat is factory adjusted to insure the off position at room temperature and a maximum temperature of about 500° to 525°F. This control should hold even if the waffle iron is left turned on, with cover closed, for many hours. Do not fool around with the thermostat to "improve" its operation unless something has happened to it that prevents it from turning off. This is usually due to the contact points being stuck together. They can be separated and cleaned. If the thermostat will not turn the unit on, the trouble may be in some other part of the electrical circuit.

The analysis included in the electrical test drawing should help you to locate this problem. Always make certain that power is available at the outlet.

The wire used inside a waffle iron to con-

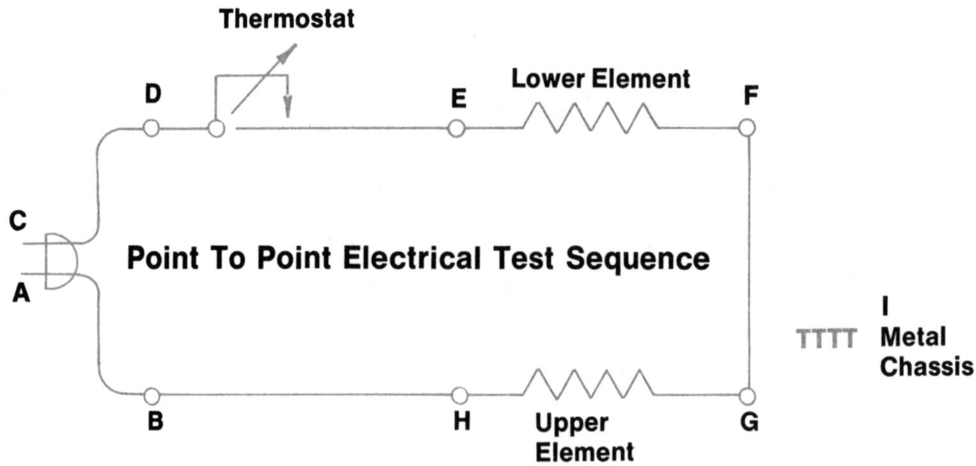

Test Points	Correct Ohmmeter Readings	Possible Cause Of Incorrect Reading
A to B	0 Ohms	∞ = Open Power Cord
C to D	0 Ohms	∞ = Open Power Cord
D to E	0 Ohms	∞ = Defective Thermostat
E to F	5 — 10 Ohms	∞ = Open Heater Coil
F to G	0 Ohms	∞ = Open Hinge Wire
G to H	5 — 10 Ohms	∞ = Open Heater Coil
H to B	0 Ohms	∞ = Open Hinge Wire

Note 1. Thermostat in *ON* Position. Thermostat in *OFF* position will read infinity (∞).

2. Resistance will vary with wattage rating upper element may have a lower resistance than the lower element.

REF. NO.	PART NAME	QTY.
1	Lens	1
2	Handle	1
3	Hinge Assembly, Right	1
4	Hinge Assembly, Left	1
5	Clip, Upper Shell	1
6	Shell, Upper	1
7	Screw, Upper Handle	2
8	Insulator, Element	22
9	Insulator, Element Terminal	4
10	Support, Element	1
11	Cord Set	1
12	Screw	2
13	Element and Terminal Assembly	1
14	Upper Grid	1
15	Retainer, Grid	1
16	Lower Grid	1
17	Retainer, Grid	1
18	Element and Terminal Assembly	1
19	Screw, Element Frame	2
20	Terminal, Element	4
21	Tab, Insulator	10
22	Support, Element	1
23	Thermostat Assembly	1
24	Lead	2
25	Connector	2
26	Conduit Assembly	1
27	Clip, Lower Shell	1
28	Spring, Lower Shell and Stud	1
29	Lower Shell and Stud Assembly	1
30	Knob	1
31	Base	1
32	Strain Relief	1
33	Screw, Strain Relief	2
34	Screw, Leg	4
35	Insulation Sleeve	2
36	Connector	2
37	Connector	2

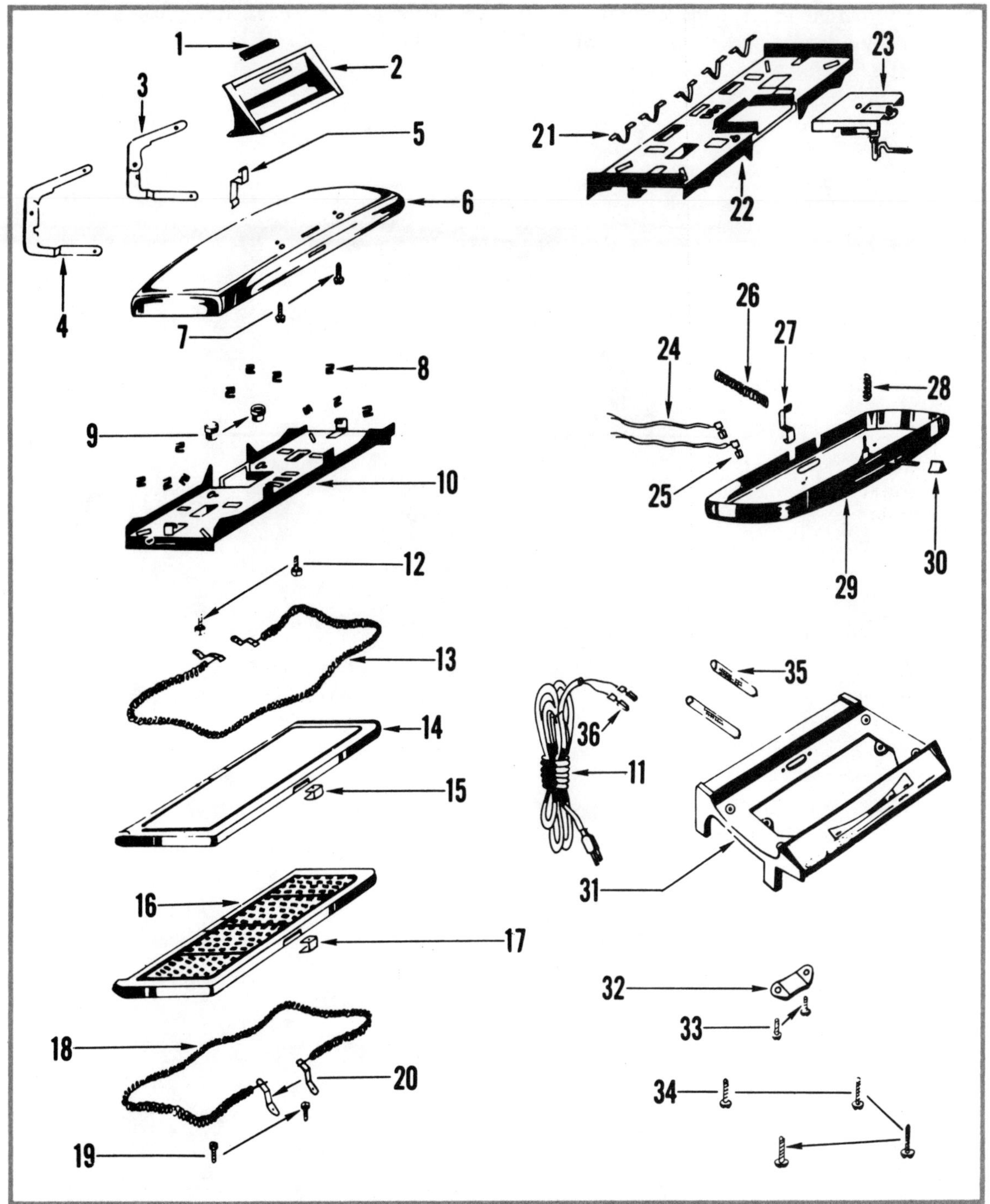

The parts and assemblies of a typical waffle iron. Use the key on opposite page to identify the parts.

nect from the upper to the lower element is usually stranded nickel insulated with asbestos. The other connected wire inside the unit may be solid nickel and will be asbestos insulated. Do not use copper wire with plastic insulation because it will have a very short life.

The heating elements are a nickel chromium alloy designed for their operating temperatures and must not be shortened or

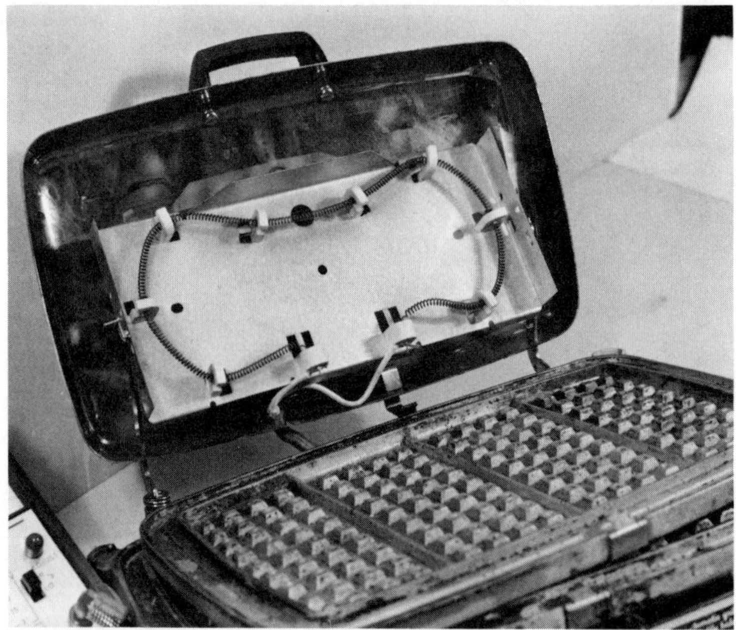

Grid of this waffle iron is held in place with a clip. This makes it easy to remove the grid and replace it with a flat smooth griddle surface for toasting sandwiches and other cooking.

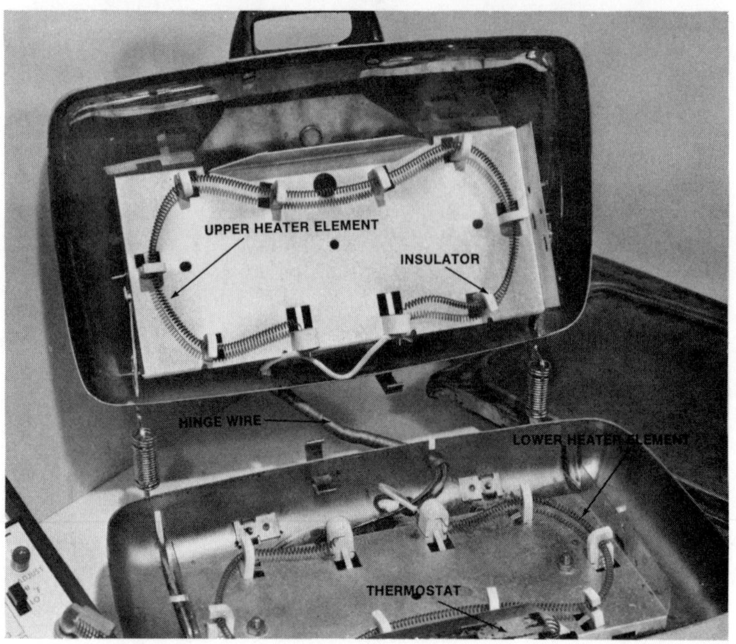

Removing the waffle iron grid surfaces exposes interior wiring and heaters for servicing.

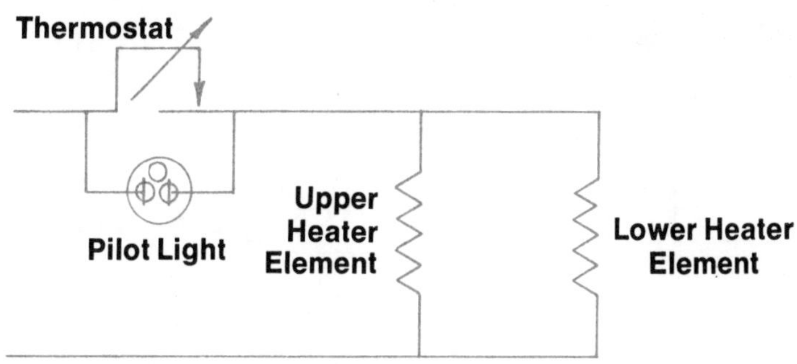

A. Heater Elements Parallel Connected

Pilot light in the waffle iron with parallel heater elements (A) turns ON when the griddle is hot enough to use. Pilot light in the series-wired waffle iron (B) turns OFF when the griddle is hot enough to use. Either pilot light method may be used with either heater-wiring system.

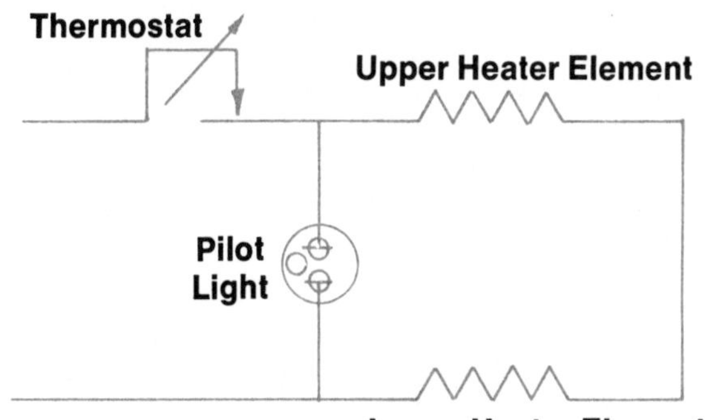

B. Heater Elements Series Connected

patched with some other kind of wire. The insulators are porcelain.

All these special materials are used to provide a long safe life for the appliance.

After working on the appliance make certain all electrical connections are secure and that all bare wires are secure and clear of the metal shell. It would be wise to use your ohmmeter to test from the metal shell to the wire connections at the thermostat. The reading should be ∞ (infinity) or an open circuit. G.M.

See also: ELECTRICAL, HOME; INDIVIDUAL APPLIANCE LISTINGS.

WAFFLE IRON/GRILL
TROUBLE-SHOOTING CHART

PROBLEM / POSSIBLE CAUSE	DEFECTIVE CORD	OPEN HEATER ELEMENT	DEFECTIVE THERMOSTAT	BROKEN HINGE WIRE	SHORTED WIRE	INCORRECT THERMOSTAT SETTING	INSUFFICIENT SHORTENING	GRIDS NOT SEASONED	OPERATOR ERROR
NO HEAT	√	√	√	√					
OVEREATS			√			√			
BLOWS FUSES	√			√	√				
WAFFLES STICK*							√	√	√

*Too much sugar in batter, opening griddle too soon and not waiting long enough for pre-heat will also cause waffles to stick.

How to Install Gypsum Panel Walls

This inexpensive material offers the same smooth, continous surface as a plastered wall, and it can be installed by any home do-it-yourselfer of average skill

ONE OF THE EASIEST AND least expensive ways of covering the bare framing of a new wall is with gypsum paneling.

When properly applied, gypsum paneling provides the same smooth, continuous surface as actual plaster, but requires much less skill and effort to install.

Gypsum paneling is somewhat more difficult to put up than paneling of wood or plastic veneer, but it is more durable, easier to patch when it has been damaged and offers more resistance to noise and fire. In addition, gypsum paneling can be painted and repainted, papered and re-papered over the years, as the decor is changed.

Gypsum paneling, also called wallboard or plasterboard, comes in sheets four feet wide and several thicknesses. It is available in lengths from seven to 14 feet. Each panel is made of plaster laminated all around with a coating of strong, heavy paper. The long edges of each sheet are tapered—some are also rounded—so that the joints can be made invisible once the paneling is nailed in place.

Wallboard can be installed vertically or horizontally. Choose the method which will require the fewest joints. In most modern construction, for example, ceilings are low —from 8 feet to 8 feet 2 inches high. This means that any wall 14 feet long or less can be paneled with two horizontal panels. Any slight gap at floor or ceiling can be concealed with a baseboard or molding.

If you install panels horizontally, make sure any vertical end joints are staggered, like bricks.

The four-foot width of the wallboard panels makes vertical installation suitable for walls built with studs on either 12- or 16-inch centers. The vertical edges of the panels should fall at the studs. Generally, vertical installation is preferred when ceiling height exceeds 8 feet 2 inches.

Gypsum board is easy to cut. Measure and mark the length on each side of a sheet. Line up a straightedge with the marks and score the panel with a knife along the straightedge. Cut through the paper and part way into the plaster. Then, simply snap the panel by bending it away from the score. Complete the cut by slicing through the back paper. Smooth the cut edge with coarse open-grit sandpaper on a block, taking care to keep the edge square. Always score the panel on the face side.

Nailing is the best method for the householder to use to attach the sheets to the wall,

➤*Applying gypsum paneling. Note how the end joints are staggered. Actually, this job would be done better by using longer sheets of paneling that go from floor to ceiling. The fewer the joints, the better the job.*

◄*Completing a cut in a sheet of gypsum paneling by cutting the back paper with a knife. Previously, the opposite side of the cut was scored with the knife and the panel was snapped along the score.*

although adhesives and screws are also used, mostly in large commercial operations.

Be sure to use the nails specified by the manufacturer of the gypsum sheeting. Generally, annular ring nails are used, 1½-inch for ¼-, ⅜-, and ½-inch paneling and 1⅜-inch nails for ⅝-inch paneling. Using the correct nail is important. If nails are too short, they won't hold. If they are too long, the expansion and contraction of the wood is more likely to pop them out through the surface of the wall and mar its appearance.

The way the nails are driven is also important to the quality of the job. Use a special wallboard hammer. Drive each nail slightly below the surface of the panel. When the nail is driven correctly, the head is sunk in a dimple in the surface formed by the head of the hammer, but the paper is unbroken.

Practice this technique on scrap until you are confident you can do it most of the time. When you are installing a panel on the actual wall and you drive a nail in too deeply, drive in another nail correctly about two inches away. When you nail a panel, start at the middle and work outward. Each time you drive a nail, make sure that the panel is firmly seated against the stud or joist behind it.

If you are covering a ceiling as well as a wall, do the ceiling first, and get someone to help you if you can. If there is no help available, build two T-braces. Each is simply a length of 2 x 4 with a 2- or 3-foot length of 1 x 4 nailed across the top like the cross bar of a T. Make the 2 x 4 long enough so that you can wedge the T-brace between the floor and a sheet of paneling on the ceiling. Two of these will hold the panel firmly against the ceiling while you nail it in place.

When paneling a ceiling with plasterboard, always install it across the joists. Drive the nails no more than 7 inches apart on the ceiling, 8 inches on walls.

Wall cutouts for electrical outlets and switches and the like are cut with a keyhole saw. Measure carefully and make the cutouts before the panel is nailed to the wall.

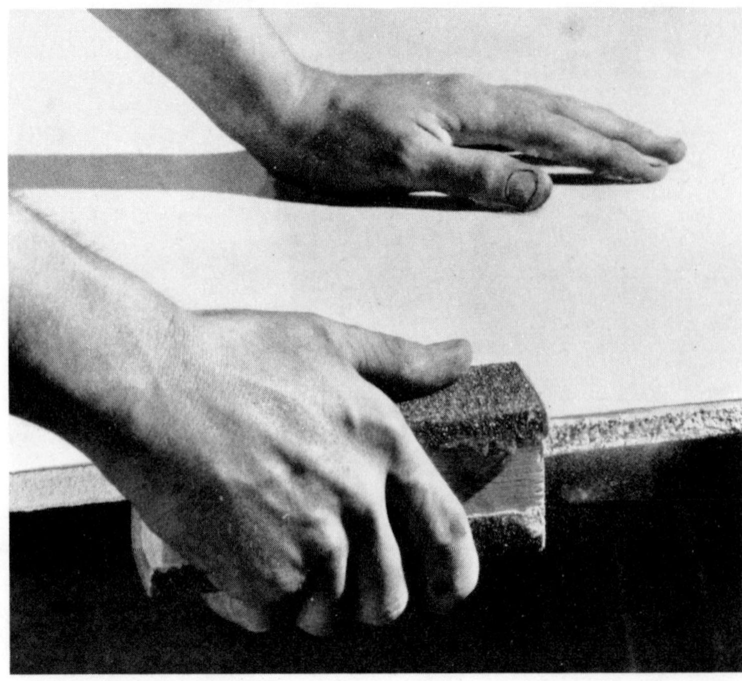

◀ Finishing a cut with coarse open-grained sandpaper on a sanding block. When finishing a cut, take care to keep the edge square.

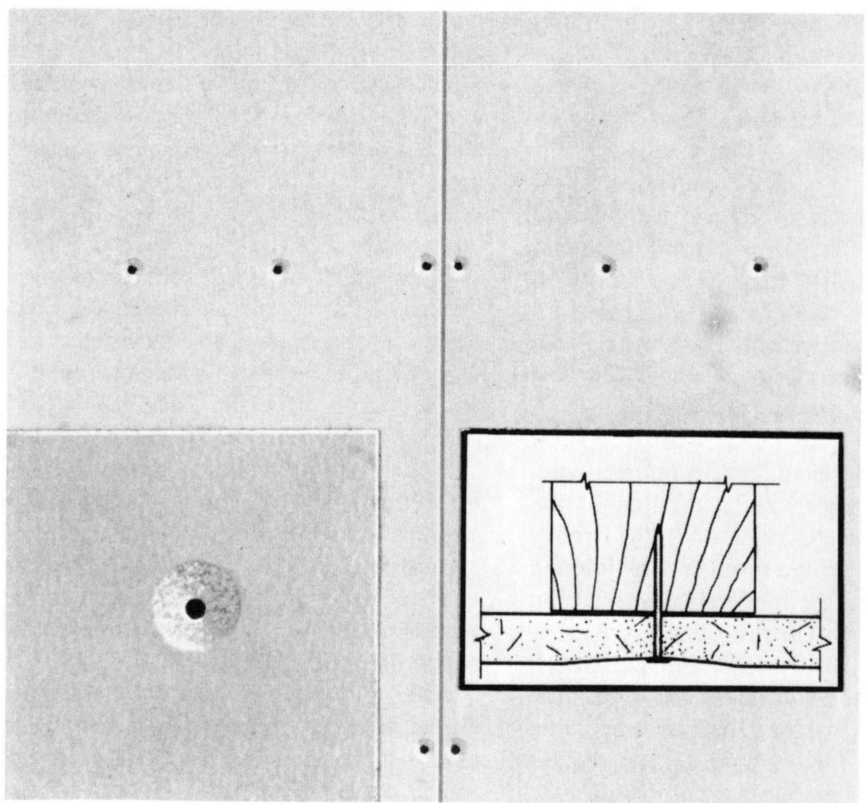

▲ *How gypsum panel should be nailed. Use a wallboard hammer. Drive the nail so the hammer leaves a dimple in the surface, but does not break the paper.*

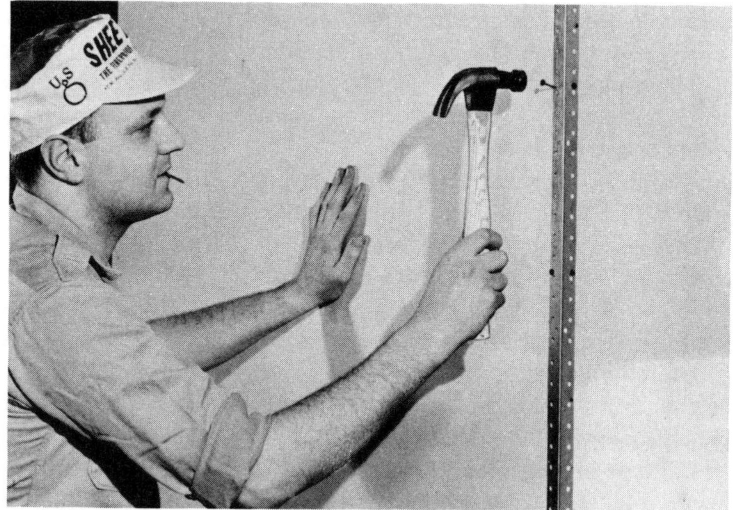

➤ *Nailing on a corner bead. Nail the bead through the paneling to the stud beneath. Space nails nine holes apart.*

Outside corners require a corner bead. The corner bead is cut to length by snipping the flanges with tin shears and bending the bead until it breaks. When the bead is in place, the metal edge running down the length of the apex of the corner will provide a guide for the knife when you finish the corner with jointing compound. When the joint is complete, it will resist the wear and tear that corners ordinarily receive.

When all the panels are nailed in place, check your work. Each nailhead should be sunk in a dimple. If you find any nails driven so deeply that the paper surface of the panel is broken, drive in another nail near it. If a nailhead has popped out, press the paneling against the stud and redrive it. Put in another nail near it.

When you are satisfied with the nailing, it is time to tape the joints and fill the nail holes and any damage to the paneling.

The joints are filled with a special spackle-like compound and reinforced with paper tape. Since the long edges of the panels are tapered, they form a slight valley when they are butted together. The jointing compound and the reinforcing tape fill the valley level with the rest of the surface of the paneling. This is why the joints are invisible after the wallboard has been painted.

On some gypsum panel systems, one jointing compound is used. Others require two different compounds. Consult your supplier about this. Generally, the compound must be protected against freezing temperatures and kept free of contamination. If it is not pre-mixed, mix the compound exactly according to directions. In addition to compound and an ordinary kitchen breadpan to hold it in, you will need a 4-inch jointing knife and a 6- or 10-inch finishing knife.

To tape a joint, apply a large daub of compound across the joint with the 4-inch knife and level it by drawing it along the joint. Leave no bare spots. When the joint is covered all along its length with a stripe of compound wider than the tape, immediately apply the tape along the joint. Center the tape over the depression, pressing it firmly into the wet compound, but leave enough compound under the tape to form a strong bond. Embed the tape by applying a thin layer of compound over it to fill the valley formed by the tapered edges of the panels. Allow the compound to dry. When taping end joints, do not overlap the tape applied at the edge joints.

In some wallboard systems, a special jointing compound is applied to the joints and allowed to dry before tape is applied. Once the special compound has dried, proceed with the taping as you would for any other joints.

When the joints have been taped, coat the nail holes with jointing compound. First, draw a bare jointing knife over the nail depression. If you hear a ringing sound—the sound of the knife blade striking the nailhead—drive the nail slightly deeper.

Be careful to dimple the surface but not break the paper. Fill the depression with a single stroke of the knife and level it with a back stroke. When all joints have been taped and all nail holes and marks in the surface have been filled, allow all compound to dry for 24 hours.

After a 24-hour wait for drying, smooth all the jointing compound with fine, open-grain sandpaper to level the surface. Do not use a power sander at this stage or for any subsequent sanding. Wipe away sanding dust with a damp cloth.

Apply the second jointing coat over the first with the 6- or 10-inch jointing knife. The second coat should be 2 inches wider on each side than the first coat. Feather each edge by pressing the knife as it rides on the panel. End joints should be treated in the same way, but the second coat should be about seven inches wide.

Give each nailhead, or other patch, a second coat of compound and allow the whole job 24 hours drying time.

The third and final coat is applied in the same way as the second coat, but it should be about 2 inches wider on each side. Each nail hole also gets a third coat. When all the compound of the third coat has dried for 24 hours, smooth all imperfections and high spots with fine, open-grained sandpaper on a block.

To tape an inside corner joint, first butter

Selector Guide for Gypsum Panel Nails

Fastening Applications	Fastener Description	Nail Spacing c. to c. (1)	Approx. Lbs. Nails Req'd per MSF SHEETROCK
½″, ⅜″ and ¼″ SHEETROCK Gypsum Panels; ½″ and ⅜″ BAXBORD Gypsum Backing Board to wood frame	1¼″ GWB-54 Annular Ring Nail 12½ ga.; ¼″ dia. head with a slight taper to a small fillet at shank; bright finish; medium diamond point; meets ASTM C380	7″ ceiling 8″ walls	5¼
⅝″ SHEETROCK Gypsum Panels to wood frame	1⅜″ Annular Ring Nail (Same as GWB-54 except for length)	7″ ceiling 8″ walls	5¼
⅝″ SHEETROCK FIRECODE Gypsum Panels face layers to staggered wood studs over ½″ USG Wood Fiber Sound Deadening Board	2¼″ 7d Gypsum Panel Nail Cement Coated, 13 ga., ¼″ dia. head	7″ walls (face layer)	9
⅜″ and ¼″ SHEETROCK Gypsum Panels over existing surface, wood frame	1⅞″ 6d Gypsum Panel Nail Cement Coated, 13 ga., 1¼″ dia. head	7″ ceiling 8″ walls	6¼
⅝″ SHEETROCK FIRECODE Gypsum Panels to wood frame	1⅞″ 6d Gypsum Panel Nail Cement Coated, 13 ga., ¼″ dia. head	6″ ceiling 7″ walls	6¾
½″ SHEETROCK FIRECODE "C" Gypsum Panels to wood frame	1⅝″ 5d Gypsum Panel Nail Cement Coated, 13½ ga., 15/64″ dia. head	6″ ceiling 7″ walls	5¼
⅝″ SHEETROCK FIRECODE Gypsum Panels; ⅝″ BAXBORD FIRECODE Gypsum Backing Board to steel nailing channel	1¼″ Fetter Annular Ring Nail 11 ga., 5/16″ dia. head	6″ ceiling	6
TEXTONE Vinyl Panels (27 finishes) to wood frame	1⅜″ USG Matching Color Nail (Stainless Steel)	8″ walls	2½
	1⅞″ USG Matching Color Nail (Stainless Steel) (Special Order)	8″ walls	4½

NOTES: (1) Spacing shown are for single layer application without adhesive.

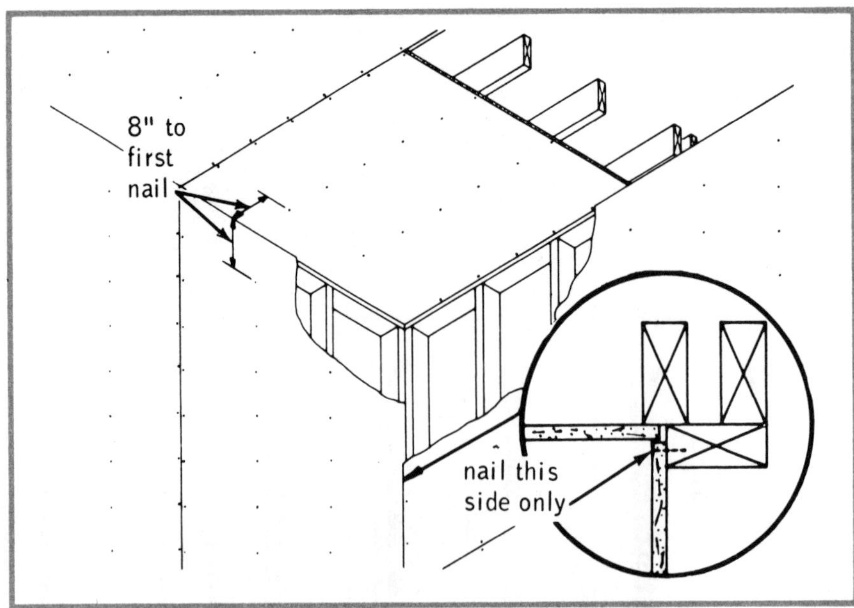

▲ *When paneling both walls and ceiling, this floating joint system will provide improved resistance to cracking caused by expansion and contraction of the framing of the house. The corner between wall and ceiling can be taped, but for greater stress relief, merely conceal the untaped joint with molding.*

▼ *Cross section of taped joint. The v-groove in this paneling formed by the rounded edges is filled with a special jointing compound. Then, the joint is taped in the ordinary way with taping compound.*

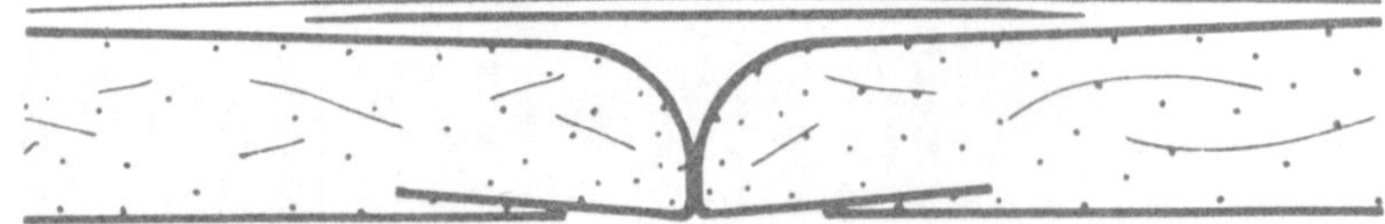

each side of the corner with compound, using the jointing knife. The compound should form a stripe on each side of the corner slightly wider than the tape.

Fold the tape in half along the center, creasing it slightly. You will find that this crease has already been lightly stamped into the tape during manufacture, so it is easy to fold it accurately.

Press the folded tape into the compound with the knife. Press it firmly, but leave enough compound beneath the tape to form a strong bond with the gypsum paneling. Remove excess and let this first coat dry for 24 hours.

Apply the second coat as you would the second coat of a flat joint. Feather the second coat out 2 inches beyond the edge of the first coat. Do one side of the corner and let the compound set. Then do the other

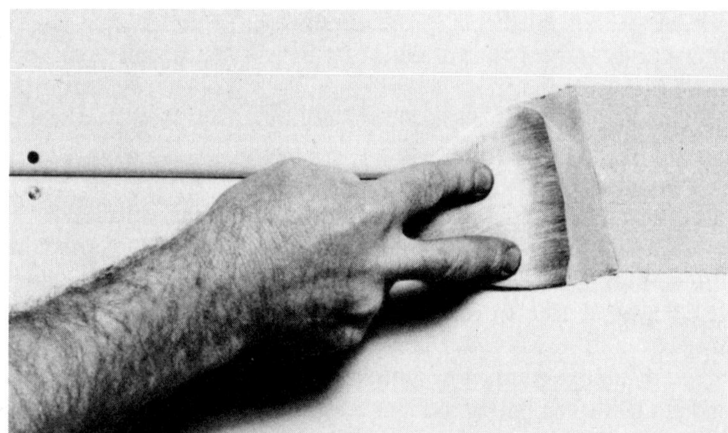

➤ Applying jointing compound to the v-groove formed by the rounded edges of paneling.

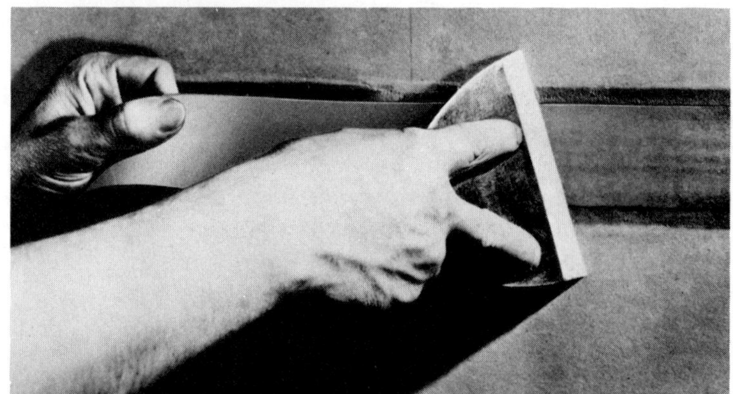

➤ Applying joint tape over a layer of jointing compound.

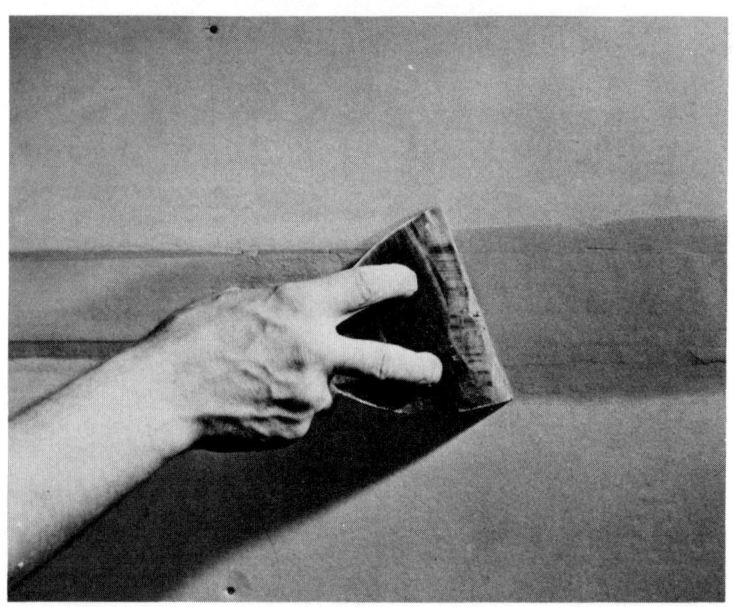

➤ Embedding tape with an additional layer of compound. This operation completes the first coat. After a 24-hour wait to allow the first coat to dry, sand lightly and apply second coat.

side. Apply the third coat in the same way, after the second coat has dried for 24 hours and has been sanded.

Outside corners are easier. Use the jointing knife to apply jointing compound over the flange of the corner bead. Apply enough to cover about two feet of flange at a time. Level the compound by allowing one side of the knife to ride on the bead and the other side to ride on the paneling itself.

Fill the flange completely with compound and allow the compound to feather out onto the face of the paneling to a width of at least 4 inches. Apply the second and third coats in the same way, sanding between each coat and allowing each coat a 24-hour drying period. Remember that each coat is feathered at the edge beyond the edge of the preceding coat by about 2 inches.

Any number of primers and sealers and undercoats are available for wallboard. Consult your supplier about which to use. After the primer coat is applied, treat the wall as you would an ordinary plaster wall.

In addition to new work, wallboard can be applied over existing walls, as long as the surface is flat and the structure is sound. Simply nail through the old wall and into the studs or joists. If it is necessary to use firring strips, use at least 2 x 2-inch stock, unless you can nail through the firring into the existing framing.

Special-purpose plasterboard is available for a variety of applications. For example, you can use special water-resistant board for high-moisture areas such as kitchens, bathrooms or laundries. This wallboard also forms a sturdy, easy-to-apply base for wall tiles. F.C.

See also: ADDITIONS, HOME; HOME IMPROVEMENT; PAINTING, HOUSE; PATCHING.

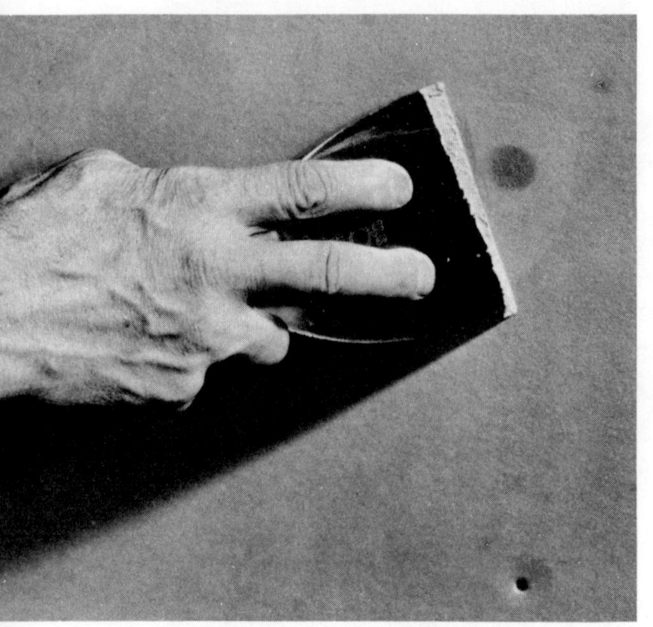

Covering a nail hole with jointing compound.

Applying creased tape to an inside corner.

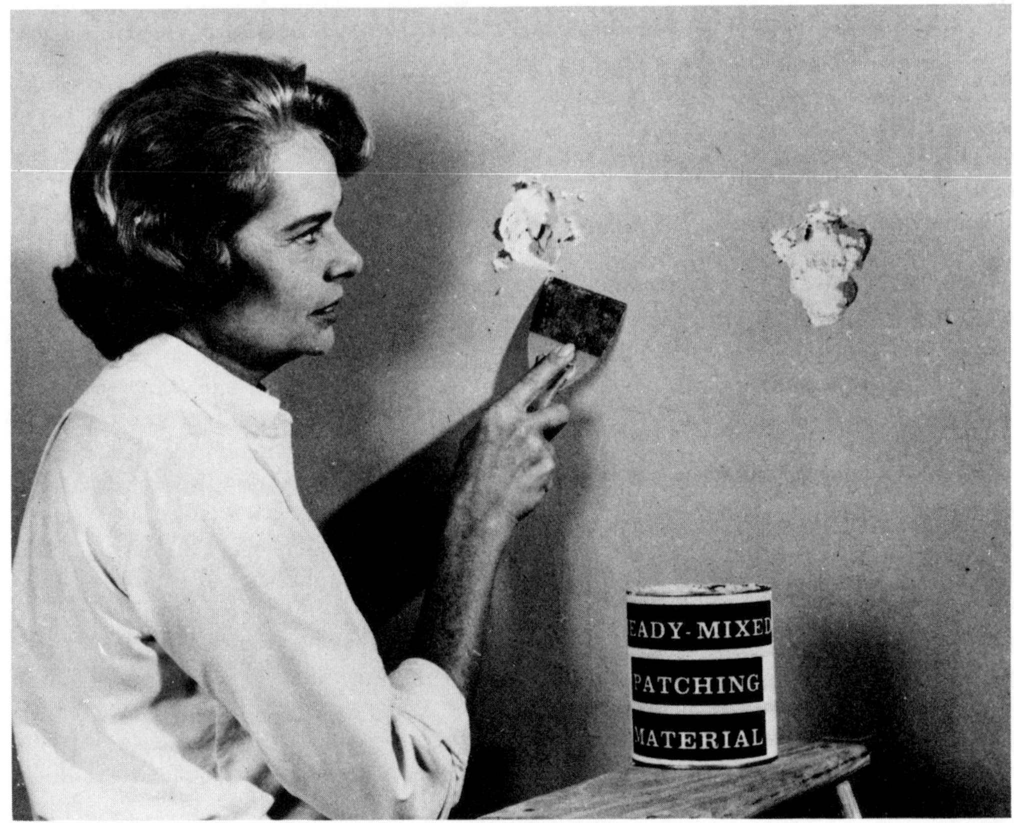

▲ *Filling cracks and holes with patching compound is an essential step in preparing a wall for covering.*

How to Prepare Walls for Papering

If you want a wall covering that is free of cracks, bulges, wrinkles or loose spots, you must hang it on a smooth, clean surface

SURFACE PREPARATION CAN make the difference between a professional-looking job of wallpapering and an amateurish one.

The purpose of preparing the wall is to provide a clean, even surface that the new wall covering can adhere to, without showing any bumps, cracks or depressions.

If the wall you want to paper is already covered with one or more layers of wallpaper, the safest course is to remove the old wall covering and start with a fresh surface. It is possible to hang new paper over old and achieve good results, but if you try it you run the risk of discovering a loose spot while you are in the middle of putting up new paper. Also, a wall covering pasted over an old layer of paper can develop troublesome bubbles.

Never attempt to paper over removable vinyl wall coverings, or over any other slick, water-repellant surface. Fortunately, vinyl wallpaper is easy to remove. You just work a corner or an edge loose and pull it off with our hands.

Removing paper wall covering of the traditional type is more work, but you can save a lot of effort if you rent a steamer. This device is simply an electrically heated boiler that generates steam. The steam travels through a long, flexible tube to a flat applicator.

To use a steamer, simply place it in a convenient location and hold the applicator against the wall. The steam penetrates the old wallpaper and softens the paste underneath. When the paste is soft use either a broad putty knife, or an inexpensive wallpaper scraper specially designed for the job, to peel off the old paper.

When you are finished scraping off the paper, wash the wall with steel wool and a washing compound to remove any traces of paper, glue or wall sizing. Then rinse the wall with clear water and a sponge.

Examine the bare wall and fill any irregularities, such as cracks or holes with spackle. If there is any loose plaster, remove it and spackle the hole.

If the wall is painted, scrape off any loose paint with a putty knife and smooth the edges of the spot with medium-grit sandpaper.

The final step is to apply wall sizing. Use a small brush and a paint roller, just as if you were coating the wall with paint. Sizing is a kind of glue dissolved in water. It fills small cracks and irregularities and can make up for any areas of the wallpaper that might not have sufficient paste, especially at the edges, where some paste is squeezed out when the seam is rolled.

Sizing can also prevent porous or absorbent surfaces, such as old wallpaper, from soaking up paste. When the new paper is hung it will not adhere well, if the surface absorbs too much paste.

Preparing a wall that has been coated with flat paint is relatively easy. All you have to do is spackle it, remove any loose paint, wash it and rinse it. Then apply a coat of wall sizing and the surface is ready to be papered.

Even if the wall looks clean, don't omit the washing. Walls in houses accumulate grease and oil carried in the air from cook-

Before starting on a room, remove fixtures, such as switch plates, wall-mounted lamps, picture hooks and other such items.

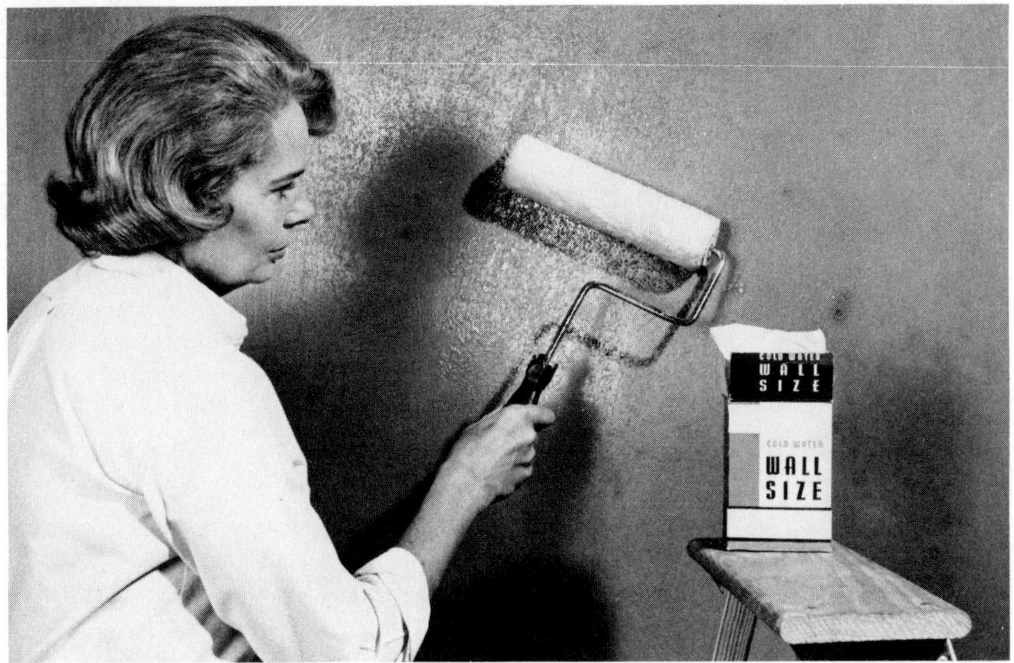

▲ *The last step in preparing a room for papering is to coat the walls with sizing.*

ing, for example, or smog or nearby oil burning furnaces. If the accumulation is great enough, the water soluble paste won't adhere well to the surface and within a short time you could have loose sections of paper drooping from the wall.

Somewhat more work is required for a wall that has been coated with gloss or semi-gloss paint. Sand the wall lightly with medium-grit paper, then wash it with trisodium phosphate or a solution of one part ammonia in six parts water. Rinse it and proceed as you would for any other wall.

To prepare a dry wall for papering, first check the surface for nails that have loosened and popped up above the surface of the board. Drive them back in again so that the last blow of the hammer leaves a depression in the plasterboard and the nailhead is below the surface. Fill each depression and any other irregularities with spackle. Let the spackle dry and re-spackle each patch. After the second application of spackle dries, sand off any high spots. Paint the wall with one coat of an oil-based primer-sealer. Give the primer-sealer time to dry thoroughly before applying wall sizing.

Do not attempt to paper a newly plastered wall until at least 30 days after the plaster was applied. Then fill any irregularities with spackle and paint the wall with one coat of an oil-based primer-sealer. When this is dry, coat the wall with sizing.

Additional tips: remove any fixtures, such as wall-mounted lamps, switch plates, etc., before starting. If you plan to paint the woodwork or other trim, do it before you paper. It's easy to remove spilled paste or sizing from a painted surface. It's extremely difficult, if not impossible, to remove paint from wallpaper.

The actual hanging of the paper can begin once the wall has been sized. F.C.

See also: ADDITIONS, HOME; BASEMENTS; HOME IMPROVEMENT; PAINTING, HOUSE; PATCHING; TILE, CERAMIC; WALLBOARD.

➤ *Care and neatness can overcome a lack of experience in hanging wallpaper. When trimming edges, use a wall scraper to push paper snugly into the angle formed by the casement and the wall and trim with a razor mounted in a holder. Use the wall scraper as a guide while cutting.*

How to Hang Wall Coverings

Modern wallpapers are easy to apply and they can do much to establish the mood and character of a room

WALL COVERINGS OFFER the homeowner one of the quickest ways to establish the mood of a room. Unlike paint, which is usually applied in a single color, wall coverings are available in an almost endless variety of colors, patterns and textures.

Most modern wall coverings are fairly easy to hang and can quickly give a room the look you want to achieve—modern or traditional, bright or subdued, formal or informal—the choice is yours.

Once you have selected a pattern, the next step is to estimate how much wallpaper you need. First, measure the height from the baseboard to the ceiling. If the wall has a picture molding around it near the top, measure the distance from the baseboard to the picture molding. Next measure the distance around the room at the baseboard. Finally, measure height and width of openings, such as doors and windows.

You can take these measurements to your dealer and let him figure out how many rolls you need, or you can use the accompanying chart and estimate the number of rolls yourself. Do it this way:

Step 1: Multiply the height of the area you are going to paper times the distance around the room. For example, 8 feet x 48 feet = 384 square feet. This figure is the total wall area.

Step 2: For each door and window, multiply the height times the width. This gives the area of each opening. Add these areas and you will have the total area of the openings in the wall, 37 square feet for example.

Step 3: Subtract the total area of the openings from the total wall area, 384 square feet — 37 square feet = 347 square feet. The area to be covered is 347 square feet.

Step 4: Divide the area to be covered by 30. 347 ÷ 30 = 11.5. Go to the next highest whole number, which is 12. This is the number of rolls of wallpaper required.

Before going any further, make sure the room has been thoroughly prepared. The surface of the walls must be smooth and covered with wall sizing.

In addition to the wall covering, you will ordinarily need paste, paste bucket and brush, a smoothing brush, a seam roller, a wall scraper or broad-bladed putty knife, razor blades and scissors, a chalk line and weight, a long table and an accurate yardstick with a true edge. If you are hanging pre-pasted wallpaper, you will need a special water tray for soaking the wall covering, rather than a paste bucket. All of these tools are available at the dealer where you buy the wallpaper. The water tray and table can be borrowed or rented.

When you have your equipment and materials assembled, you are ready to start.

First measure the width of the wallpaper and subtract one inch. Measure this distance off from the right edge of the door and make a mark on the wall at the ceiling. Make a plumb line out of the chalked line and a weight—a heavy key will do. Tack the chalked plumb line to the wall at the mark. When the plumb line stops swinging, hold the weight firmly against the baseboard, pull the string away from the wall and let it snap back. This will leave a vertical chalk mark on the wall.

The line will mark the exact position of the first strip of wallpaper once it has been cut and pasted.

Mix the wallpaper paste in cold water

Each end of a pasted sheet of wallpaper is folded toward the middle to make the sheet easier to handle.

Snapping a vertical line. Align the first strip of wallpaper with the chalk line to make sure it is vertical. Subsequent strips will be aligned with the first strip of wallpaper.

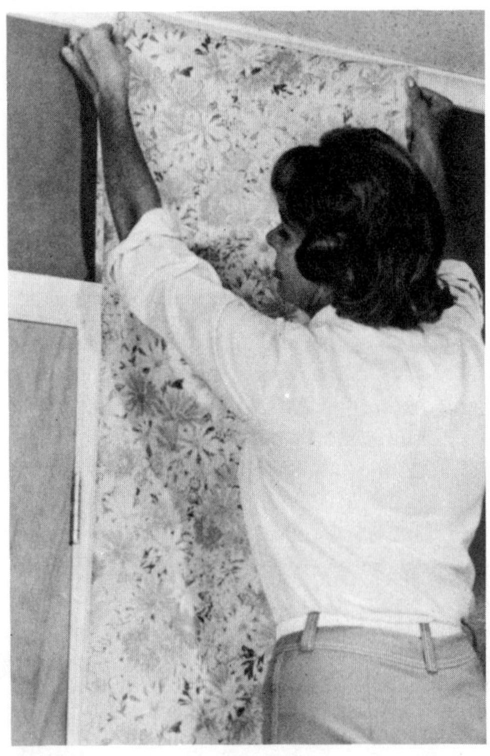

Hanging the first sheet. The ends of the sheet should overlap the ceiling joint and baseboard by a few inches.

Brushing the wallpaper downward with a smoothing brush.

After it is hung, rinse the paper with a well wrung out sponge and wipe any excess paste from woodwork, floor and ceiling.

Trim off excess paper with a razor, using the wall scraper as a guide.

Trimming a corner over a window. Hang the piece first. Then, make a diagonal cut with scissors from the loose edge of the paper toward the corner. Cut across the corner, like a miter joint, and slightly beyond it. This allows the edges at the window to be pushed snugly into the angle between the casement and wall for trimming.

according to the manufacturers directions. It should be free of lumps. If you stick your finger in it, it will adhere like a smooth glove. Tie a string across the top of the paste bucket to hold the brush. This will keep the handle clean.

Unroll a length of wall covering on the table with the pattern side up and cut it six inches longer than the wall height. After it is cut, hold it against the wall to check the length. There should be a few inches overlap at the ceiling and the baseboard.

If the strip is the proper length, put it back on the table, pattern side up and unroll paper for the second strip, matching the pattern on the same side and direction you are working in, and cut the second strip to the same length as the first. Repeat this a few times, but do not cut too many strips in advance. This will prevent mistakes in matching.

Turn the pile of strips pattern side down so that the first strip is on the top. Apply paste with the brush in a figure eight pattern, being sure not to miss any spots. Do the lower half first. Fold the bottom toward the middle with the edges flush, paste-to-paste, and press the two sides of the fold gently together with your hands, but be careful not to crease the fold. Paste and fold the top portion in the same way. This process is called booking.

Wait three to five minutes to allow the booked paper to relax, then carry it to the wall and unfold the top half. Place the paper against the wall so the top edge overlaps the ceiling joint by about two inches and line up the right edge with the vertical chalk line. Do this precisely because subsequent strips will be aligned with this one.

Tap the upper section with the smoothing brush. Then press it with downward strokes of the brush on the center of the strip, working any bubbles or excess paste out to the edges.

Open the lower fold and slide the section against the wall with the palms of your hands, checking its alignment with the vertical chalk line and brush it with the smoothing brush.

The strip of wall covering will overlap the baseboard, ceiling joint and right edge of the door. Trim this excess with a single-edge razor blade, using the straight edge of a wallscraper or broad-bladed putty knife as a guide. Change razor blades frequently to keep from tearing the paper rather than cutting it.

Use a natural sponge to rinse the newly hung strip of wallpaper with clear water. Squeeze the sponge well to keep water from running down the strip. Also, at this stage, rinse off any paste from the woodwork, floor or ceiling. Be sure to do this before the paste dries.

Follow the same procedure for the second strip, butting the left edge to the right edge of the strip already on the wall. Repeat this process until you get to a corner or a window.

When you come to a corner, measure the distance between the right edge of the last strip and the corner at three places, the top, the middle, and the bottom. Add one half inch to the longest of the measurements and subtract this total from the width of the strip. After subtracting, measure the resulting distance from the corner on the new wall near the ceiling and make a mark. Hang the chalked plumb line through this mark and snap the line on the wall. This will give you an exactly vertical line to start papering the new wall with.

Hang a pasted sheet of paper in the corner, butting its left edge against the right edge of the previous strip. Smoothe the sheet well into the corner. When it is in place, cut the piece vertically about one

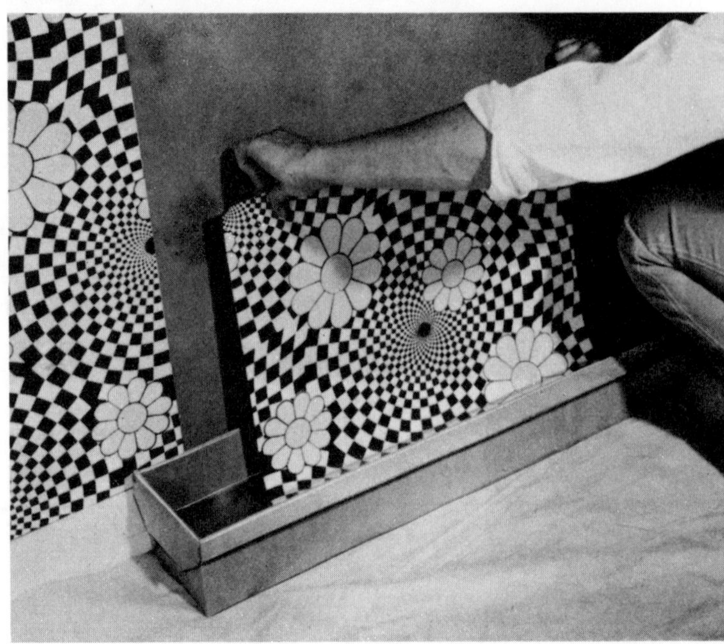

Pre-pasted wallpaper is soaked in a water tray before it is hung on the wall.

half inch from the corner on the new wall. Then slide the remaining section slightly to the left, so its right edge lines up with the vertical chalk line. The left edge slightly overlaps the piece that rounds the corner.

Windows and doors are a little easier than corners. Simply cut a strip as you would any other and hang it in place. It should be butted vertically to the preceding piece and cover part of the door or window. Use scissors to snip the paper diagonally from the inside of the door or window outward so that the cut crosses the corner, like a miter joint. Then the excess paper will be able to bend upward above the door or window and the excess at the side will be able to bend on a vertical line. The next step is to trim away the excess with a razor blade.

Wallpaper seams should be rolled with a seam roller to fix them firmly in place. Wait 15 minutes after the sheet has been hung, then roll the butted edges with the roller, firmly but not too hard. Do not roll the seams of flocked wallpaper. Instead, tap them with a smoothing brush.

Pre-pasted wall coverings are hung in exactly the same way as ordinary wallpaper, with one exception. Instead of mixing paste and brushing it on the wall covering, you dunk the covering in a special water tray that is available from wallpaper dealers.

After cutting a strip to size, re-roll it from bottom to top with the pattern inside and place it in the water tray. Roll it loosely so the water can reach all of the pre-pasted surface.

Use tepid water and soak the wallpaper for the exact length of time specified by the manufacturer. To hang it, simply carry the tray to the wall, grasp the end of the roll. As you lift the end toward the ceiling joint, the strip will unroll. Then proceed as you would for ordinary wallpaper. F.C.

See also: ADDITIONS, HOME; HOME IMPROVEMENT; PAINTING, HOUSE; PATCHING; WALLBOARD.

CHART TO ESTIMATE WALLPAPER NEEDS

Distance Around Room in Feet	Single Rolls for Wall Areas Height of Ceiling			Number Yards for Borders	Single Rolls for Ceilings
	8′	9′	10′		
28	8	8	10	11	2
30	8	8	10	11	2
32	8	10	10	12	2
34	10	10	12	13	4
36	10	10	12	13	4
38	10	12	12	14	4
40	10	12	12	15	4
42	12	12	14	15	4
44	12	12	14	16	4
46	12	14	14	17	6
48	14	14	16	17	6
50	14	14	16	18	6
52	14	14	16	19	6
54	14	16	18	19	6
56	14	16	18	20	8
58	16	16	18	21	8
60	16	18	20	21	8
62	16	18	20	22	8
64	16	18	20	23	8
66	18	20	20	23	10
68	18	20	22	24	10
70	18	20	22	25	10
72	18	20	22	25	12
74	20	22	22	26	12
76	20	22	24	27	12
78	20	22	24	27	14
80	20	22	26	28	14
82	22	24	26	29	14
84	22	24	26	30	16
86	22	24	26	30	16
88	24	26	28	31	16
90	24	26	28	32	18

This chart is based on 30 square feet of coverage per single roll of wall covering. Manufacturers usually ship 36 square feet of material per single roll—the 6 square feet deduction provides for normal cutting and matching while hanging.

To reduce handling and packaging costs most wall coverings now come in double roll bolts.

How to Repair Your Automatic Washing Machine

Except for the gear box, you can repair or replace most of the parts yourself—with a big saving in expensive calls by the repairman

YOUR AUTOMATIC WASHER is designed to wash, rinse and extract water from clothes automatically. It should remove soil from most fabrics quickly and completely. It should retain the maximum whiteness in white clothes and it should not appreciably alter the shades of color in other fabrics. It should destroy bacteria that may be harmful to health when used with a recommended water and cleaning aid. Of course, the machine must be installed correctly and in proper mechanical condition.

Installation. Proper installation will do much to insure correct operation of the washer. Some minimum requirements are:

1. Proper electrical supply. A nominal 120-volt 60-Hz, 15-ampere fused electrical supply at a 3-pronged grounded receptacle is required. It is recommended that this be a separate circuit serving only the washer. Do not use an extension cord!
2. Proper water supply. Threaded faucets on hot and cold water supply lines located within 5 feet of the water inlet on the back of the washer. A minimum pressure of 10 PSI and a maximum of 100 PSI dynamic is recommended. Best washing results are obtained when the hot water temperature is between 140° and 160°F at the washer.
3. Proper drainage facility. The drain hose must empty into a tub or a standpipe at least 34 inches above the floor on which the washer is placed. This height must not exceed 72inches. The tub should have a 20-gallon capacity, and the standpipe should be about 2 inches in diameter.
4. The floor should be solid and the machine set level. Leveling legs are provided on washers for this.
5. All shipping materials must be removed from the machine.
6. The drain hose must be routed to the tub or standpipe in such a manner that it is free of twists or kinks. The end must fit loosely into the drain pipe to provide an air gap.

Failure to provide an air gap will allow the water to siphon from the tub.

7. When connecting the fill hoses, make certain the screen washer is at the faucet end and the flat washer at the machine end. Screw the couplings on straight making them finger tight. Then tighten about ¼- to ⅓-turn with a pair of pliers. Do not over-tighten. Make certain the hot water faucet is connected to the hot water valve on the machine; and the cold water faucet to the cold water valve.
8. After setting the machine in its permanent location, check it for being level. One method is to run water into the washer until it reaches the first row of holes in the basket. It should be level all around. Adjust the leveling legs until it is; then tighten the leg lock-nut.
9. If the electrical outlet is not properly grounded you must connect a grounding wire from the washer to a cold water pipe. This can be fastened under a screw on the back of the machine and to a ground clamp at the pipe. This is an important safety precaution to prevent the user from getting a shock that may be fatal if something happens to the electrical circuit.

Operating principles. The two basic washing actions are:

1. A reciprocating agitator mounted on a vertical shaft swirls water and clothes back and forth in a round tub.
2. A rotating drum mounted horizontally, or at some small angle above horizontal, picks up the clothes and drops them into a pool of water.

Both actions require proper water circu-

A typical washing machine installation. This machine has an optional suds return system. Note that the drain standpipe or tub top must be no higher than 72 inches from the floor and no less than 34 inches.

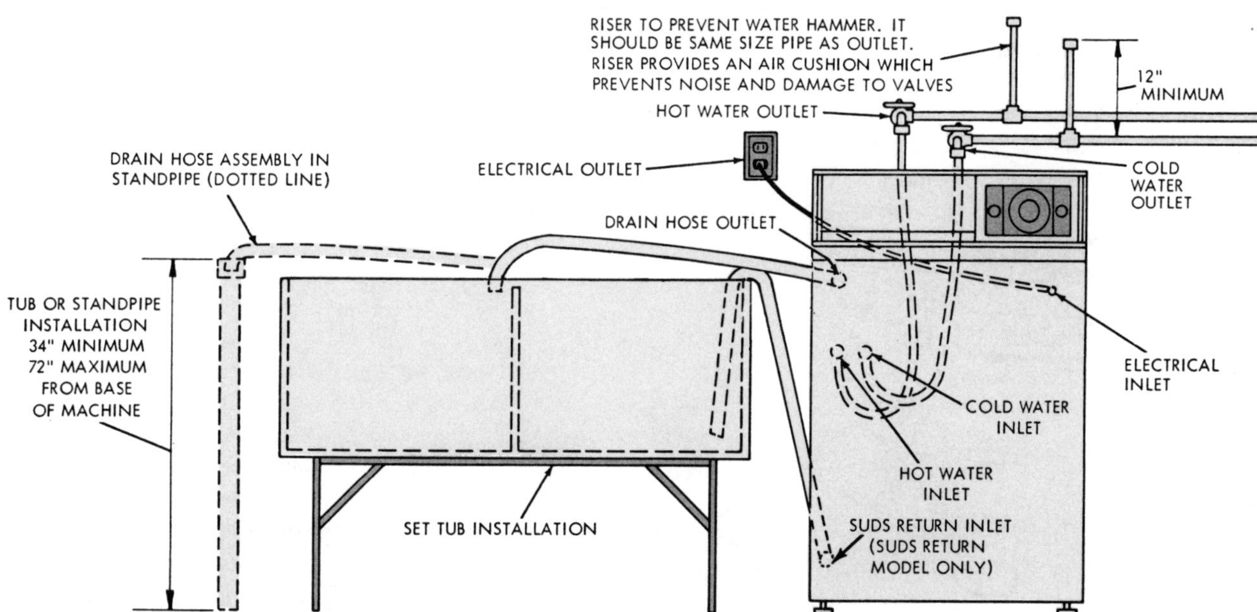

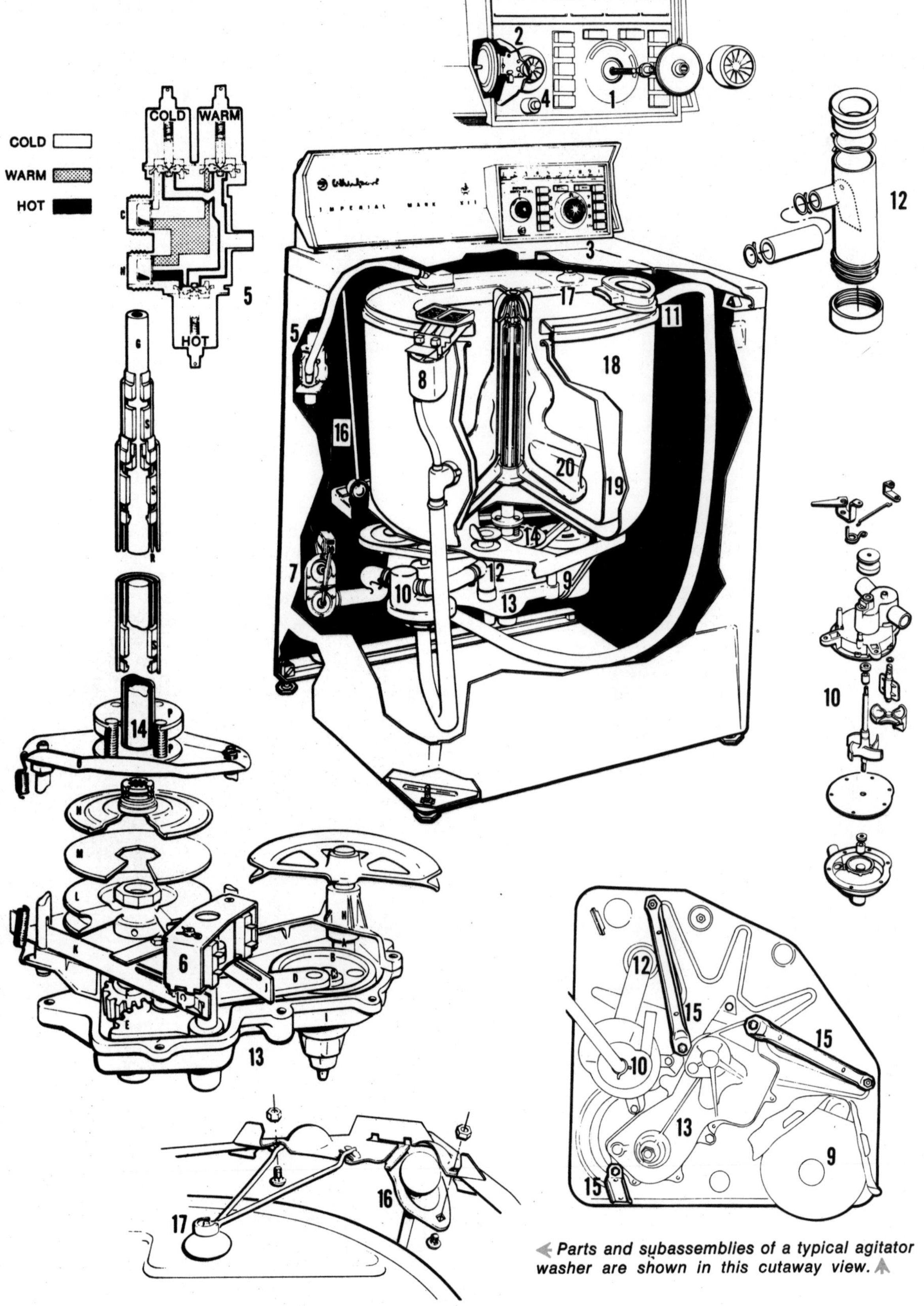

Parts and subassemblies of a typical agitator washer are shown in this cutaway view.

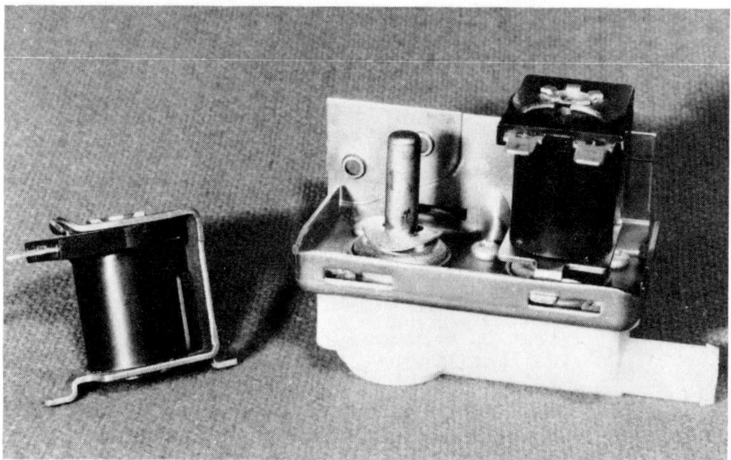

All water fill valves are constructed so that the solenoid coils can be replaced without disturbing the plunger and valve assembly. In this illustration, one solenoid has been removed and the other left in place. Removal of more screws will allow disassembly of the rest of the valve. If the water is very hard or contains iron, the valve may have to be cleaned occasionally. Make certain the valve diaphragm bleed holes are clear of foreign matter.

REF. NO.	PART NAME	QTY.
1	Timer assembly, complete	1
2	Pressure switch	1
3	Spin switch	1
4	Light switch	1
5	Water inlet mixing valve	3
6	Control magnet	1
7	Two-way valve	1
8	Dispenser	2
9	Motor—1/3 hp 2-speed capacitor	1
10	Uni-directional pump	1
11	Filter	1
12	Tub outlet	1
13	Gear case assembly, complete	1
14	Basket drive and brake assembly, complete	1
15	Baseplate braces	3
16	Suspension	1
17	Snubber	1
18	Outer tub	1
19	Basket	1
20	Agitator	1

REF. NO.	INDIVIDUAL PART
13A	Pinion
13B	Main drive
13C	Eccentric
13D	Connect in rod
13E	Sector
13F	Agitation gear and spring
13G	Agitator shaft
13H	Cover
13I	Gearcase
13J	Agitation cam bar
13K	Spin cam bar
14L	Pulley
14M	Clutch lining
14N	Drive disc
14O	Clutch yoke
14P	Brake assembly
14R	Spin tube
14S	Center post bearing and seals

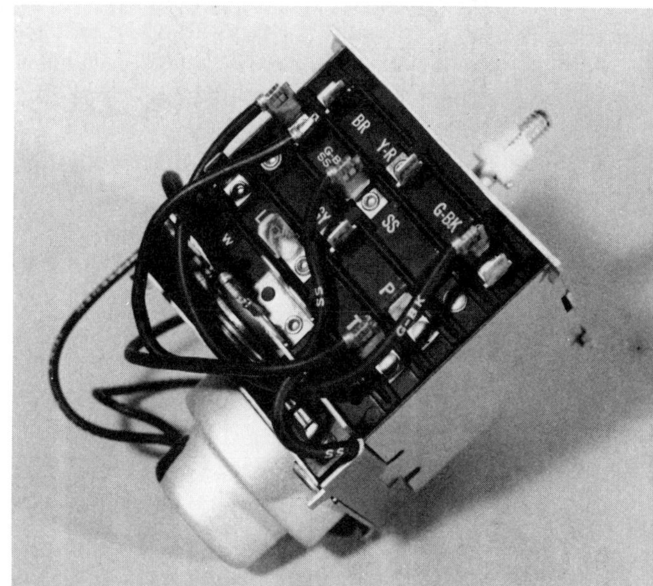

The timer of every washing machine is a series of cam-operated switches turned by a clock motor. Every electrical control circuit is connected to the timer. The terminals are coded to match the wires. G-BK on the timer, for example, means green with a black tracer. BR is brown.

lation, amount and temperature as well as a detergent to free and hold the soil. In each machine the sequence of operations is controlled by a timer.

Controls. The location of controls will

vary from model to model, but the basic function of each part will be the same, regardless of make, model or location.

The timer is the brain of an automatic washer. It consists of a clock-type motor with a special drive mechanism that moves a group of cams in a series of steps or increments. Each timer stop may last 2 minutes. The cams open and close switch contacts controlling the electricity using parts as they are needed during the cycles.

The pressure switch is the water level control used in most washers to turn the fill valves off when the water has reached the proper height. It is usually mounted on the control panel, near the timer, and connected to the bottom of the tub with a plastic tube. As the tub fills, the weight of the water compresses the air in the tube until the pressure moves a diaphragm. This trips the switch to turn off the water valve and restart the timer motor.

Automatic washers that do not use a pressure switch allow a fixed period of time for the fill valves to be turned on during the fill cycle. These fill valves are special in that they include a flow control washer which meters the water flow rate into the machine.

The water temperature control is a switch connected to the fill valves. It determines whether both the hot and cold valves or either one will turn on when the timer connects the fill cycle.

Workers. If you will consider the controls as mechanically operated electrical switches, then you must consider the workers as electrically powered devices used to do a mechanical job.

The fill valve is a pair of solenoid-operated pilot valves. One allows cold water flow and the other hot water flow. The water mixes in the valve body and exists through a common outlet into the tub.

The motor is usually a ½-HP, 120 V, 60 Hz, single-phase, induction type. It operates at about 1750 revolutions per minute. It drives the agitator during the

A washer control panel seen from the rear. This machine has two pressure switches, while most models have one. Some machines have three pre-set water levels. Others have variable levels from 8 to 11 inches of water depth.

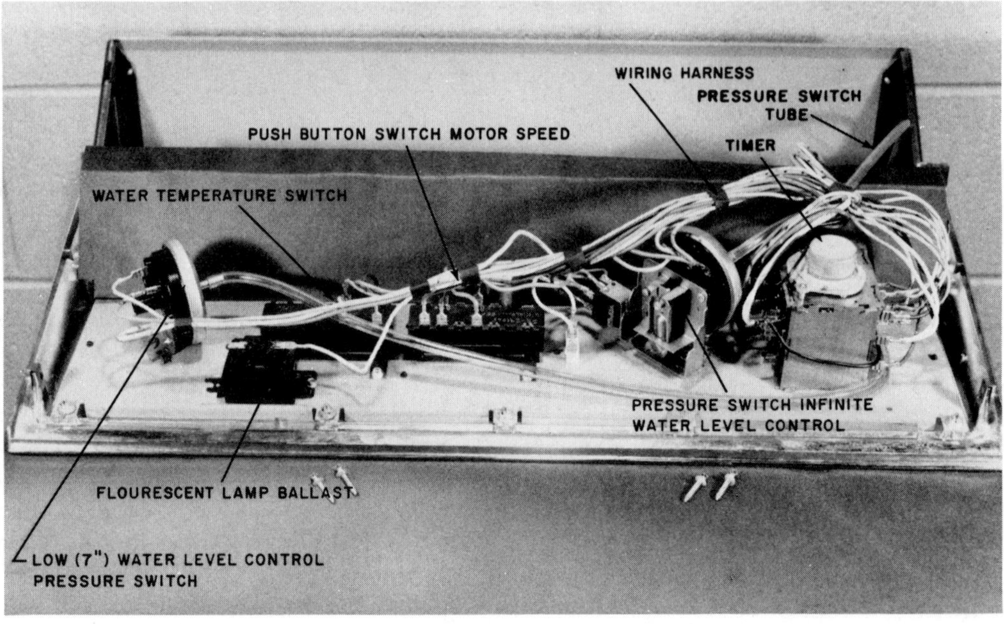

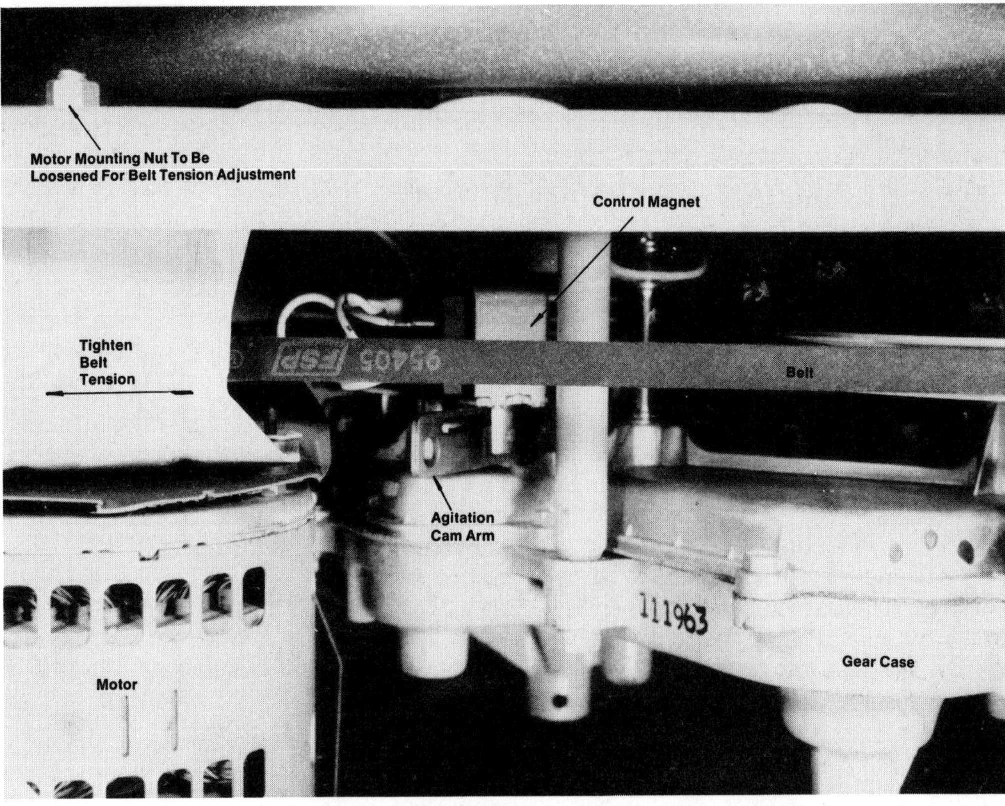

▲ *Washing machine belt tension is usually adjusted by unloosening the motor mount and moving the motor. In this model, access to the motor for belt adjustment is through the rear cover.*

wash cycle, the basket during the spin cycle, the recirculating pump during the wash cycle and the drain pump during the drain and spin cycles.

This much is essentially the same for all washers. Differences will be in the gear case assemblies and the various means used for taking the power from the motor and applying it. The change from one cycle to another is usually made by a solenoid coil which moves a plunger to shift the mechanical action.

A belt, or system of belts, is the most common method of transmitting power from the motor to the three major moving parts: the water pump; the agitator or slow-speed rotating drum; the high-speed spinning basket.

A slipping or loose belt is a common source of trouble. It should be the first thing checked if the motor runs and the machine does not operate properly. Most belt tension adjustments are made by shifting the motor more tightly against the belt and securing its fasteners.

The water system is divided into three sections: the fill system; the recirculating system; the drain system.

The fill system admits hot and cold water from the household plumbing to the tub. It consists of two hoses, two screens, the fill valve, fill hose and a boot with an air gap. The air gap is important because it prevents the suds from getting back into the household plumbing There is no connection between this system and the rest of the water system in a washer.

The recirculating water system consists of a pump and a filter connected to each other and the tub through a set of hoses. Water should always recirculate during the washing cycle.

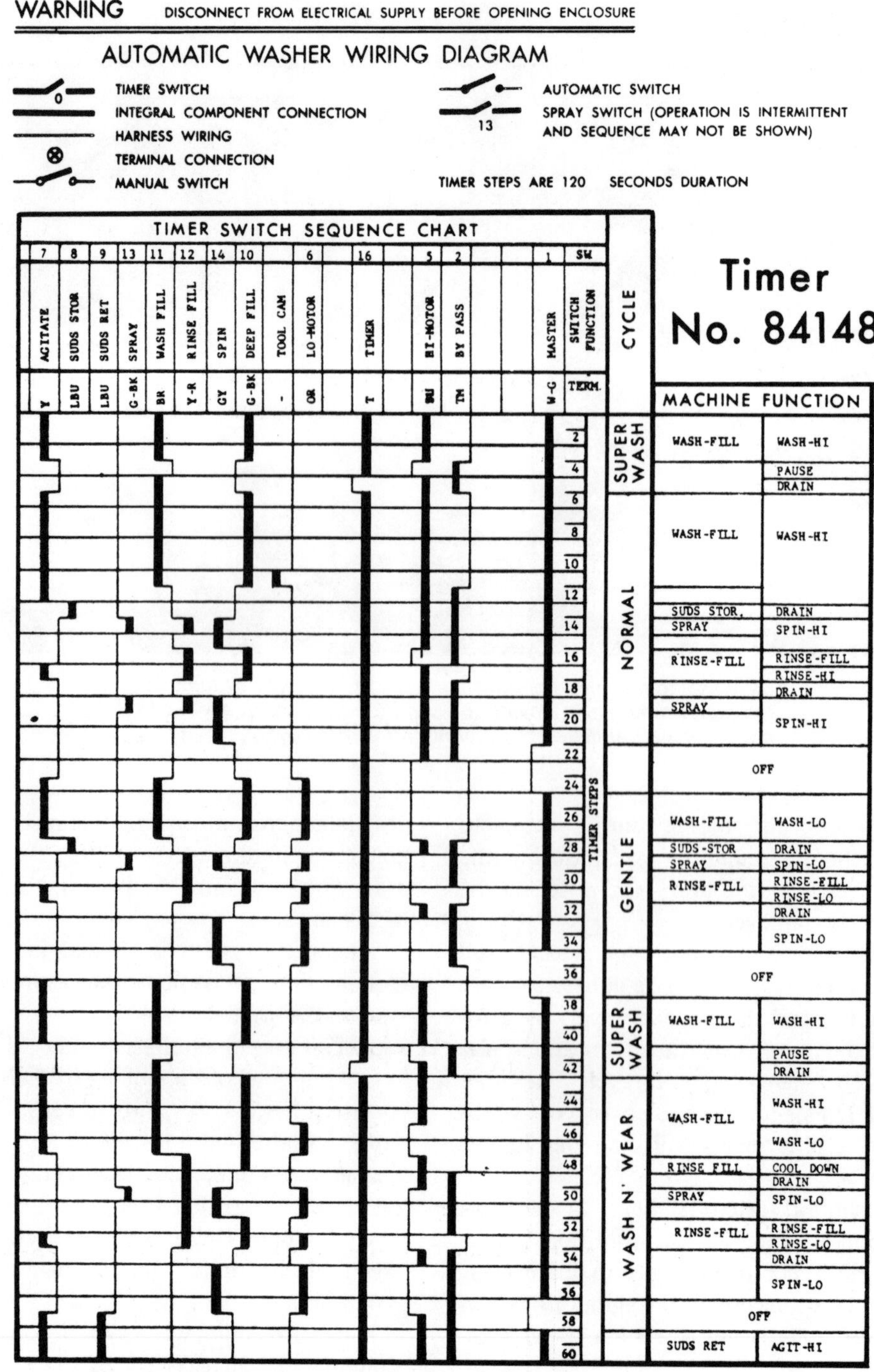

Every washing machine has a schematic diagram, usually on the back. The heavy vertical lines on the timer sequence chart here indicate the circuits that should be in operation at each timer step.

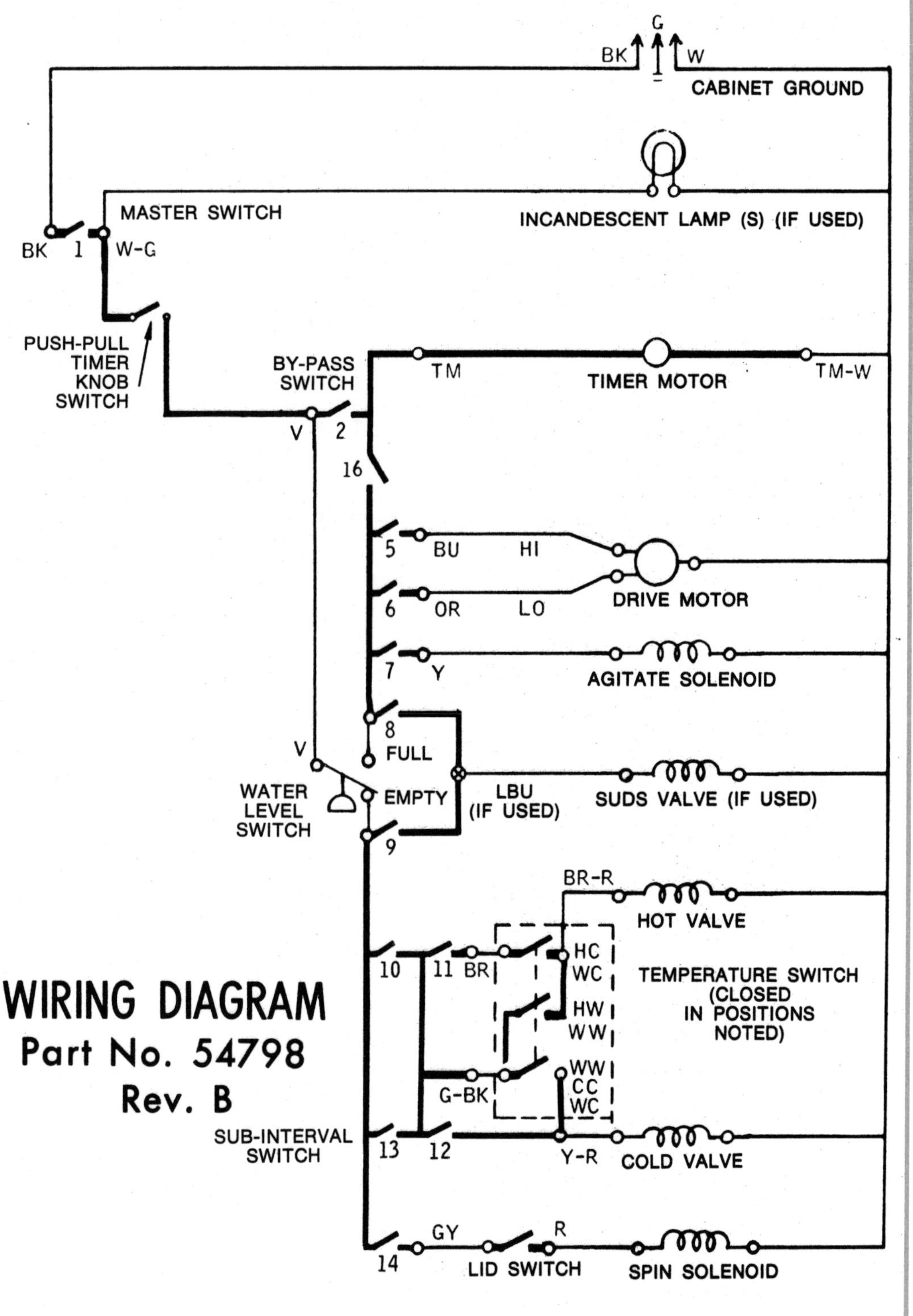
G
BK
W
CABINET GROUND
MASTER SWITCH
INCANDESCENT LAMP (S) (IF USED)
BK 1 W-G
PUSH-PULL TIMER KNOB SWITCH
BY-PASS SWITCH
TM
TIMER MOTOR
TM-W
V 2
16
5 BU HI
6 OR LO
DRIVE MOTOR
7 Y
AGITATE SOLENOID
8
FULL
V
WATER LEVEL SWITCH
EMPTY
LBU (IF USED)
SUDS VALVE (IF USED)
9
BR-R
HOT VALVE
10 11 BR
HC
WC
HW
WW
WW
CC
WC
TEMPERATURE SWITCH (CLOSED IN POSITIONS NOTED)
WIRING DIAGRAM
Part No. 54798
Rev. B
G-BK
SUB-INTERVAL SWITCH
13 12
Y-R
COLD VALVE
14 GY
R
LID SWITCH
SPIN SOLENOID

PRELIMINARY CHECK LIST	
WASHER DOES NOT FILL IN WASH CYCLE	See if electric cord is plugged in correctly. See if the hot and cold water faucets are turned ON. Set timer control knob in FILL portion of wash cycle and push the control knob in. See if house fuse is blown. See that the water inlet hose filter screen is clean. To check: turn off water faucet; remove hoses and check for deposits of foreign material at screens; remove foreign matter present by flushing under running stream of water; replace hose connection over water faucet tightly; turn on water faucet and check for leaks. See that hoses are not kinked.
WASHER DOES NOT SPIN	See if lid is closed. See if electric cord is plugged in correctly. See if house fuse is blown.
WASHER SEEMS TO BE DRAINING DURING WASH AND RINSE CYCLES	Make sure open end of drain hose is higher than the water level in the washer; if hose is lower than the water level in tub, water will siphon out.
WATER WILL NOT DRAIN FROM WASHER	Check to see that drain hoses are not kinked. Make sure drain hose is no higher than 72 inches above base of washer.

The drain system is connected to the recirculating system using the same pump and some of the same hoses. Sometimes the pump has a diverter valve to direct the water flow from recirculate to drain. Other machines will reverse the pump to direct the water out the drain hose. The water must always be drained from the tub before the spin cycle starts. Draining must continue during the spin cycle to remove the water extracted from the clothes.

The electrical system. All automatic washers should have a wiring diagram and a cycle chart pasted on the back of the machine. The accompanying diagram for a typical washer shows how the timer is electrically connected to the other parts. The cycle chart shows which parts should be in use at any particular timer step. Study these carefully because only by knowing what is supposed to happen can you tell if the machine is doing what it should do at any given time. Then when you look for trouble, test those parts that should be activated.

An AC voltmeter or a 25-watt test light connected to the terminals of a working part will indicate whether or not it is getting power. An ohmmeter can be used to determine if a coil is defective.

General. We have not gone into detail on the transmission or gear box because any failure in that area will require special tools for assembly or disassembly. Each manufacturer uses a different approach to gear box design so it is best to leave that part of a service job to a well-equipped professional.

Belts, pumps, hoses, fill valves, timers, pressure switches and other electrical parts are usually available from the local dealer for your machine. None of these parts are readily repairable, except the pump and filter. (These may have jammed with a sock or a collection of lint.) Some of these parts —timers in particular—are available on a rebuilt and exchange basis at a saving in cost.

The accompanying Trouble-shooting Chart should serve as a guide in locating the general area that caused the problem. However, refer to the Check List before you get too involved with the machine itself. G.M.

See also: ELECTRICAL, HOME; INDIVIDUAL APPLIANCE LISTINGS.

WASHING MACHINE TROUBLE-SHOOTING CHART

POSSIBLE CAUSE / PROBLEM	NO WATER FILL	INCORRECT FILL	INCORRECT TEMPERATURE	WATER WILL NOT SHUT OFF	WATER LEAKAGE	WATER WILL NOT DRAIN	MOTOR DOES NOT RUN	NO AGITATION	NO SPIN	SLOW SPIN	EXCESSIVE VIBRATION	MACHINE WILL NOT SHUT OFF	TIMER DOES NOT ADVANCE	DAMAGES CLOTHES	NO WATER RECIRCULATION
NO POWER TO FILL VALVE	✓														
SUPPLY TURNED OFF	✓														
KINKED HOSE	✓					✓									✓
CLOGGED SCREEN	✓														
DEFECTIVE WATER LEVEL CONTROL	✓	✓		✓									✓		
HOSES REVERSED			✓												
INADEQUATE HOT WATER SUPPLY			✓												
DEFECTIVE TEMPERATURE SWITCH			✓												
DEFECTIVE FILL VALVE	✓			✓											
DEFECTIVE TIMER						✓	✓	✓	✓			✓	✓		
DEFECTIVE HOSE					✓										
LOOSE HOSE CONNECTION					✓										
DEFECTIVE GASKET					✓										
DEFECTIVE PUMP					✓	✓									✓
DEFECTIVE VALVE					✓										
MOTOR WILL NOT REVERSE						✓									
LOOSE BELT						✓		✓	✓	✓					✓
FAULTY MOTOR							✓	✓	✓						
LOOSE WIRE OR CONNECTION							✓	✓	✓						
DEFECTIVE TRANSMISSION/CLUTCH								✓	✓	✓					
MACHINE NOT LEVEL											✓				
FLOORING WEAK											✓				
UNBALANCED LOAD											✓				
IMPROPER BLEACH USAGE														✓	
BROKEN AGITATOR														✓	
CLOGGED FILTER															✓
WATER DID NOT DRAIN	✓								✓	✓					

INDEX